Wisdom's Children

Wisdom's Children

Home Education and the
Roots of Restored Biblical Culture

Necessity and Possibility
General Principles and Particulars

by Blair Adams and Joel Stein

TRUTH FORUM
AUSTIN, TEXAS

Library of Congress Catalog Card Number 88-051537
ISBN-0-916387-11-9 Wisdom's Children.

Published by

TRUTH FORUM

P.O. Box 18927, Austin, Texas 78760
Printed in the United States of America

Dedication

To the tens of thousands who, at the risk of their liberty and the sacrifice of their time and energy, have come to know the blessings of Christian home education. And to the memory of Joseph Stein, a child of a man who—through his photography, writing, violin, chickens, ducks, goats, dogs, worm farm, leatherworks, blacksmithing, renovated horse-farming implements, crooked and timid smile, soft-spoken and gentle ways, gangly stride and sweet dark eyes—left more of a mark on the hearts and minds of his fellows than some do by sixty-five. And who, at fifteen, died of having lived and is now one of wisdom's immortal children.

This is what Yahweh says—your Redeemer, the Holy One of Israel: "I am Yahweh your God, who teaches you what is best for you, who directs you in the way you should go." (Isa. 48:17)

Train a child in the way he should go, and when he is old he will not turn from it. (Prov. 22:6)

When they see among them their children, the work of My hands, they will keep My Name holy; they will acknowledge the holiness of the Holy One of Jacob, and will stand in awe of the God of Israel. (Isa. 29:23)

But wisdom is justified by all her children. (Luke 7:35, NKJV)

Contents

CHAPTER SEVEN
General Application of Principles

Part Three
Particulars

CHAPTER EIGHT
Particular Application of Principles

CHAPTER NINE

Preface

Millions today, both individually and collectively, sense a profound upheaval in the world. This upheaval need not, however, prove portentous. It can instead represent the travail that precedes the breaking forth of new life. For God now broods over the earth to conceive and to bring forth a great restoration of His spiritual culture. And just as the All-Powerful chose to expose Himself to the ultimate vulnerability of coming into the world as a babe in a manger two thousand years ago, and then from that child (reared by His parents at home) chose to bring forth the greatest spiritual revolution of world history, so today we will find the roots of this deep spiritual transformation in the simplicity of loving homes where parents educate their children and do so against the pressure, harassment and outright persecution of Statist education systems.

Christian home education surges ahead daily as the most rapidly expanding education movement in America*[2]—even against a nonstop effort to halt its progress. Hundreds of thousands yearly rediscover the contemporary relevance of the oldest of all educational methods. The following study seeks to tap the deepest roots of the vision, purpose and methods that motivate home schoolers.

Yet while we focus on home schools, we also set that focus in a larger spiritual framework. This greater framework will broaden your vision. In turn, you will then more easily penetrate to the essential spiritual meaning of our times. This

---

* "One of the most significant developments in education is taking place far from any classroom. The children involved don't hear the clangor of school bells or join in the bustle of students in school corridors. Their parents, often critical of deteriorating public school systems or driven by religious motives, are educating them at home—a movement that has been exploding across the country in recent years, with no end to its growth in sight . . . .

"Patricia Lines, a policy analyst for the Department of Education, estimates that there were 15,000 home schoolers in the early 1970s; she puts the number today at 120,000 to 260,000. Other estimates range up to a million."[1]

clearing of vision will also help you see why, as in so many other areas, in the rearing and education of children, the oldest movement on earth is becoming brand new.

The testimony of the lives of such home-schooled men as Jesus of Nazareth, His apostles Peter and John, William Penn, George Washington, James Madison and multitudes of others should suffice to silence all critics of home education.*[3] But this study explains why Christian *home* education excels all other ways to "train up a child in the way he should go." In the first part, we broadly outline the contemporary restoration of Biblical culture, with home education taking a central role. To fully and effectively transmit the spiritual knowledge of Israel's God necessitates a radically different educational form than the institutional setting of secular education. Here we sharply distinguish Christian from secular knowledge and show why the home school offers the perfect form to transmit God-centered knowledge. After we demonstrate the necessity of Christian home education, we then show its possibility, as we describe, for example, every parent's God-given capacity to educate his child. In the second part of our study, we see how the distinctive goals of Christian education require distinctive educational principles. We show how to use those principles to achieve our general aim to educate our children. In the third part, we get down to the specifics of teaching particular subjects, but without losing sight of how those subjects connect to our overall goals.

If you find the breadth of the material covered in the first chapters somewhat difficult to relate to your task of teaching children, remember that this material will help give you a full view of the *perspective* most effective in your approach to Christian home education. We can only undertake this task in God's perfect will when we see how the totality, the entire breadth, of our lives and our children's lives forms our worship to God.† How can we reach fulfillment in our own lives or ef-

---

* Can we really say, "Yes, but these were earlier, more primitive times. If God incarnate had come in our day, a home education would have proven insufficient. He would not have been able to cope"? If we say this, we should remember that the things of lasting value are eternal and not temporal and that Scripture says that Jesus came "in the *fullness* of time." Only our conceit allows us to believe that ours is the fullness of time rather than the depletion from the fullness when God chose to come.

† See Truth Forum's *Culture as Spiritual War.*

fectively train up our children in the way they should go unless we apprehend the wisdom that would allow us to teach our children to love God with *all* their heart, soul, mind and strength?

Among all forms of education, *Christian* home education proves unique in producing a wholeness of character both in parents who faithfully administer its life-giving wisdom and in children who become partakers of its fruits. The challenge of this form of education requires the broader perspective and deeper explanations of this study. To meet the challenge of home schooling, we must mine through some difficult, new and unknown terrain to uncover those jewels of God's wisdom, so multifaceted in their reflection of His glory. God requires us to dig through the layers of man's perspectives and philosophies to a bedrock upon which God-centered wisdom can truly "build her house" (Prov. 9:1). This bedrock stood before our childhood days; it existed prior to the colonial American experience; its age exceeds even the ancient Hebrew reflection of its glory. For we seek to build upon nothing less than the *living* Word of the eternal God. This alone forms our bedrock. To fully grasp the radical (which literally means "going to the root") principles of wisdom presented in these pages, we must not only dig through time but into eternity itself, to the vision of the Eternal One, to that very root of Jesse that will bring forth our children as His offspring. The Scriptures speak of this "wisdom" "as the first of His works, before His deeds of old." Wisdom declares: "I was appointed from *eternity*, from the beginning, before the world began" (Prov. 8:22-23). If we desire to hold in our hands the hidden jewels of that "hidden wisdom, which God ordained before the world unto our glory" (1 Cor. 2:7, KJV), we must labor to put on eternity's mind, the mind of Messiah. We feel confident that this book will help all who carefully read it to do that, but only if they read the material prayerfully and diligently in the living, guiding presence of our Messiah, "in whom are hidden all the treasures of wisdom and knowledge" (Col. 2:3). If we do this in full faith, we will discover that truly "He is a rewarder of them that diligently seek Him" (Heb. 11:6, KJV); and in faithfully pursuing this task we will also find the excitement of seeing God's vision come forth in our own hearts and minds. This excitement will grow to a lasting fullness as we see the seed of this vision blossom full orbed in our children's lives.

Finally, we did not write these pages from an ivory tower, but within the day-to-day efforts of over a decade to help educate scores of children who are growing—some of whom have already grown—to become responsible, mature and productive citizens of the kingdom of God. The crucible of the courtroom tested the convictions behind this educational program. There, a self-admittedly hostile judge, after reviewing the program with close scrutiny, reversed himself and exempted those participating in this program from his state's compulsory education laws. If carefully studied and faithfully and prayerfully applied under the guidance of God's Spirit, the perspective and principles related in the following pages will not only bear good fruit in your children's lives—and in the lives of all the children that you love and care about—but they can also work a basic transformation in your own spiritual perspective, helping you to come into a still deeper and closer harmony with the One who fathered us all.

Part One

NECESSITY
AND
POSSIBILITY

When Abram was ninety-nine years old, Yahweh appeared to him and said, "I am God Almighty; walk before Me and be complete. I will confirm My covenant between Me and you and will greatly increase your numbers." (Gen. 17:1-2, NIV, NASV)

Be perfect . . . as your heavenly Father is perfect. (Matt. 5:48)

CHAPTER ONE

Introduction
Education for the Whole Person

Seeking Wholeness

A clear understanding of the practical steps that make up Christian home education can only grow out of a clear vision of what we expect from it. What do we want to see in our child when he emerges from under our educating hand? What vision inspires our thoughts about the kind of person he will become? If we have no such vision, then we should make this our first petition to God as we begin to educate our child. A fuller and more comprehensive vision of what our child should become better enables us to "train" him "up . . . in the way he should go." Throughout the book, our vision of the goal in Christian home education will unfold more clearly as we proceed, but we must *begin* unfolding that vision from the start.

We must ask not only how we picture the person our child will become as a result of his education but also what source will inform and shape this vision: the world or the kingdom? Do we think particularly of the scholarly knowledge that he will acquire? Do his physical capabilities especially concern us? Do we want to see certain particular talents developed, perhaps such as in music? Do we feel that he could become a capable craftsman because he works well with his hands? Do we perhaps envision him working with the land and God's creation? All of these images reflect important *aspects* of our child's education, but they do not reveal the central goal. These descriptions lack the basic essential. And not only do these descriptions omit something central, but also even if we summed up these different images to arrive at a composite picture of our child, the essential would still be absent. Adding together such characteristics as musical talent, skill in woodworking, scholastic knowledge and so on fails to really show our chief aim. Such a fusion of disciplines or areas of interest, knowledge or skills fails to give us an integrated image of a whole person; as it stands, it gives merely a con-fusion.

The Scriptures command that we conform ourselves to the image of Jesus the Messiah (Rom. 8:29). As we educate our children, we must keep His image ever before us as our goal (Heb. 12:2). When we think of His image, we do not centrally fix on any single characteristic referred to above. Rather, when we think of Jesus, we see His perfect character, the unmatched love and compassion that moved and permeated His entire being, His fervent devotion to truth, His clarity of vision, His total commitment to fulfill the will of God. We think of His words, "Seek *first* the kingdom of God and all these things shall be added unto you." We think of man in his wholeness. Jesus was man completely at one with God, for He was God manifest in human flesh, the Almighty revealing Himself to impotent man. God revealed Himself to man as man's Savior, but God intended this Savior as also the *pattern* of our lives (Rom. 8:29, KJV), the "firstborn of many brethren." So we must follow in His footsteps (1 John 2:6); we must strive to perfect our lives according to His example (Matt. 5:48).

We too must seek the oneness with God that the man Jesus of Nazareth fully personified (John 17:11, 21-23). We must seek the living God's love to fill us, to conform us to His image. We must seek His Word to hammer our character and His will to hone our lives. In the education of our children, we aim for a life wholly at one with the God of Israel, consumed with His love, filled with His truth, submitted to His purpose, conformed to His image. As we seek first God's kingdom, His total dominion over our children's lives, we will also give to them all the skills and knowledge that they need. These skills and knowledge will not, however, form the center of our children's education: rather God will stand at the center of all these. They all simply grow out of that center.

Such a fully God-centered life expresses God's command that His people be complete, perfect, integral, whole—that we be people of blameless "integrity" in every facet of our lives (Phil. 2:15; 1 Thess. 5:23). Biblical Hebrew (even contrary to modern Israeli usage) offers a word for this type of person—*tamim*, the Hebrew word in Genesis 17:1 generally translated as "complete," "perfect" or "whole." God-centered education aims for the *whole* person, his *wholeness*, his completeness in Messiah (Col. 2:10). This wholeness in fact constitutes the very meaning of salvation.[1] So Christian education does not merely concern the mind but every aspect of our children's lives—spiritual, physical and intellectual (1 Thess. 5:23). And as we shall see, in contrast, all other forms of education lead not to wholeness and integration but to disintegration and fragmentation.

Education *always* educates the *whole person*. No one can separate one part of a person from another part and exclusively educate that part without fragmenting and distorting the person. Whenever we educate a person, we shape the *whole* person by what we teach him. This doesn't mean that we can't concentrate the educational process upon only one dimension of a person's being, for example, giving him a strictly academic or a strictly physical or a strictly vocational education. But we still educate the *whole* person: we will simply turn out a one-dimensional individual; he will merely be one-sided in his *whole* being. No matter what we do, when we educate our child, we shape the whole person, and therefore we must assume the responsibility to ensure his full development into everything God has ordained for him.

So this book concerns the full development of our children's *whole* lives. As our unfolding study will clarify, we can educate our children from two basic perspectives. One presents Biblical, Judaic or Christian education, centered entirely in the transcendent, personal God of the Scriptures. The other perspective presents what we may call secular, pagan or humanistic knowledge,* knowledge centered entirely in man himself. In this first chapter we will show the radically distinct implications of these two perspectives for the education of children. As we shall see, the Judaic view leads the individual child (as well as the adult) to wholeness, whereas the pagan view leads to the opposite result—fragmentation and disintegration.

---

* See Truth Forum's *Humanism: Chimera of Christian Fanatics or Established Religion of the Public Schools?, Salvation Is of the Jews, The Salvation Seekers* and *Knowledge as Spiritual War*.

True Wholeness

Believers do not stand alone in their claim that education must be of the whole person. The pagan view, however, of what this education of the whole person entails basically counterposes the Judaic one. In the pagan view, the originally defective concept of the *gymnasium**** has further devolved in our day to a mere means for developing the child's body, while the classroom presumably develops his heart or at least hopefully some part of his mind. This education, however, addresses each of the *parts* of man as distinct, specialized entities designated for separate education, as in the Platonic ideal. The child, and then the man, always remain fragmented. The ideal man may be the "Renaissance man," a "well-rounded individual," but only in the sense that each of his "sides" has been "properly" "rounded"—that is, refined or educated. Nothing brings cohesion to *all* the different aspects of the child's whole being taken as one. It cannot be otherwise, since only a center can bring cohesion to something, just as the sun brings cohesion to the planetary system that revolves around it. And man-as-center cannot bring cohesion to his own life any more than a planet can revolve around itself.

Of course, this book does not present this pagan method. Such a method can only rear fragmented human beings, no matter how "rounded" or refined by education the fragments may appear. In these pages, we intend to write about a different kind of education, Judaic-Messianic education, which educates the whole child not into fragmentation but into integration, consistency, at-onement and therefore peace—peace with his God, with his fellowman, with nature and also with himself. Herein lies the meaning of the Hebrew word *tamim*, to be whole, to be a person of integrity—one integrated, at one within himself because he experiences at-onement with his Creator. We can attain this goal if our training of the child coheres around a center that can pull together every

---

* In ancient Greece, the gymnasium was more than a place for training in physical fitness; it was the center of the transmission of Greek culture, which exalted the human body to a place of divinity and was generally based on the worship of man, as scholars as diverse as Goethe, Edith Hamilton, Hannah Arendt and so on (most of them approvingly) have shown.[2] In ancient Israel, at the time of the abomination of Antiochus Epiphanes, the party of the Hellenizers, Jews who supported Antiochus, founded a Greek gymnasium in Jerusalem.[3]

element of his life. Only God can serve as such a center. Our children will learn scholastic knowledge, to play music, to perform skills and crafts and more, but everything they learn will come together into one, complete, whole person, who in turn functions as a part of the integrated, whole community of God's people. And both individual and community will center in the God perfectly consistent with Himself, the God who brings all things together in cohesion around Himself. The single force that will draw God's people into His orbit, hold them together in His vision and in His purpose, is His transforming love.

These two ways of knowledge irreconcilably contrast and even conflict. They remain as incompatible as light and dark.* This incompatibility of light and dark demands separation (2 Cor. 6:14). Integration, as we will see, demands an exclusion of pagan knowledge (our English word *integral* comes from the Latin *in tangere*, which means "untouched"). The integration of every aspect of our being demands separation from that which would fragment: to be wholly integrated, we must also remain wholly "untouched" (2 Cor. 11:2-3). To consistently offer our children godly wisdom we must see the radical contrast between the two mutually exclusive ways of knowing. When we see this contrast, we will come to truly appreciate the value of God's wisdom as a treasure worth possessing even at the price of selling all else (Matt. 13:46).

As defined in numerous art texts, value in a given painting represents the ascending degree of contrast between light and dark, the greater the contrast, the higher the expression of value. Our pursuit of understanding and wisdom in a truly God-centered education, as we become separated more and more from the patterns of pagan education and life, enables us to appreciate in increasing measure the true value of salvation, that is, the oneness with Him who is light and within whom is no "darkness" (1 John 1:5).

Of course, since the child must become whole, he is *not* whole; instead, from his beginning, he is fragmented, divided, atomized within himself (though awareness of this fact only comes with knowledge, and the consequences are not imput-

---

* See Truth Forum's *Salvation Is of the Jews, Justice Is Fallen* and *Humanism* for a full explanation of the incompatibility of these views and the disastrous results of their attempted amalgamation.

ed to the child until this knowledge and awareness come; this unawareness and ignorance of a knowledge actually already present within us many refer to as "innocence").* God did not, however, create man as a fragmented being; this fragmentation of human nature results from the Fall. We can see the restoration of man's wholeness as an "educational" problem because the Fall resulted from the introduction of one type of knowledge (eating of the tree of "the *knowledge* of good and evil") and because Jesus Christ spoke of the solution to the problem as coming through a very different kind of knowledge ("You shall *know* the truth, and the truth shall make you free"; and then, concerning what truth we are to know, He said, "I am the . . . truth").

These two different kinds of knowledge—one inducing the Fall and the other bringing salvation—correspond to the two different perspectives of which we have already spoken: the man-centered or pagan perspective as opposed to the God-centered, Judaic or Messianic perspective. We have already said that only the God-centered perspective can bring the wholeness or coherence that Christian education strives toward; for only a God situated equidistant from all things can serve as the cohesive Center who can bring all things into coherence around Himself. Jesus defined eternal life as "*knowing* . . . the only true God and Jesus Christ," whom God had sent (John 17:3). So we become centered in the one God of Israel by becoming centered in the knowledge centered in Jesus. By its very nature, knowledge rooted in the God who is One (Deut. 6:4) brings wholeness and oneness. In contrast, as we will show, man-centered knowledge brought the Fall and by its very nature brings fragmentation and dissolution. To see how to fully accomplish God's purpose in the education of our children, we must first see the difference between these two forms of knowledge and their results.

---

* See Truth Forum's *Repentance and Faith: The First Foundation Stone.*

CHAPTER TWO

Knowledge
God-centered versus Man-centered

I will bend Judah as I bend my bow and fill it with Ephraim. I will rouse your sons, O Zion, against your sons, O Greece, and make you like a warrior's sword. (Zech. 9:13)

Two Ways of Knowing

We must choose then between two divergent and even opposing paths of knowledge. One way God forbade to man, but the other God held out as the essence of man's salvation. The tree of "the knowledge of good and evil," from which man was forbidden to eat, exemplifies the first. Man chose in the Garden to partake of this forbidden knowledge, the knowledge that he believed would enable him to be "like God," to know, or determine, good and evil *for himself* (Gen. 3:5). In other words, this knowledge *detached and separated* man from the ultimate subject of all knowledge—God—and reduced God and everything else to mere objects of man's detached mind. This knowledge set man *apart* from God, and so also from his fellowman and from all of creation. Fragmentation thus characterizes this knowledge. In contrast, Jesus speaks of "eternal life" as a different kind of knowledge—*relational* knowledge—knowledge that brings man *into relationship* with the living God, and therefore also with his fellowman and with creation (John 17). This knowledge connects us to God rather than separating us from Him; it brings us *together* with God, with God's people and with God's creation. Coherence marks this knowledge.

We can see the differences between these two ways of knowledge in the counterposed ideals of the ancient Greeks and the ancient Hebrews. The Greeks expressed their ideal of knowledge in their mythological gods (separated from men by only a very thin line that allowed some men to easily cross over into godhood and some gods to just as easily assume remarkably human weaknesses).[1] The Greeks distinguished these immortal beings from men in two ways: (1) they viewed the gods as free from death; and (2) they viewed them as *detached spectators* who surveyed human life from their Olympian heights.[2] The gods might involve themselves in the lives of men as a diversion and amusement, but they always remained detached, aloof from the affairs of men.[3] Since the Greeks themselves aspired to the likeness of these gods, they sought out means to look at life in the same way as did the gods. Among these means, they developed their State*-supervised theaters where the audience sat in the place of the Olympian deities,[4] surveying the characters on the stage, vicariously stimulated by the events they watched; but at the same time the audience remained separate and aloof, maintaining the illusion of themselves as godlike spectators who stood above human life's "drama."

The word *theory* derives from the Greek word *theoros*, meaning "spectator," which in turn derives from the Greek word *thea*, meaning "sight." *Theory* also shares a common root with the Greek word for theater; this root word is *theasthai*, which means "to behold, to see."[5] All these meanings intertwine. *Theoros*, "spectator," indicates the "theoretical" approach of a spectator to life. Here we find the root of the philosophical approach that the Greeks developed. The Greeks' "ideal man" was "the man of reason," who, in Plato's words, is a *"spectator* of all time and existence."[6]

> [The] ideal of the philosopher [was] the highest human type—the *theoretical* intellect who from the vantage point of eternity can survey all time and existence . . . .[7]

So, according to the former Director of Social Psychiatry at

---

* In the following pages the word *State*, with a capital *S*, refers to the general institution of civil authority in society. The word *state*, with a lowercase *s*, refers to the political-geographic entities that make up the United States, such as the state of Colorado.

l'Ecole des Hautes Etudes and one of the most respected psychiatrists in twentieth-century France, Henri Baruk, the Roman Cicero (following Plato) describes the ideal man as the philosopher for whom the most important thing is "to look" and in whose "life the contemplation and knowledge of things outweighs all other work":[8] the ideal of the Olympian spectator of Greek mythology[9] became the same ideal for Greek philosophy. For the Greeks and later Romans, *"detachment"* is the ideal for attaining "the path of wisdom."[10]

In this ideal, man knows truth by *detaching* himself from reality and observing things from the vantage point of an "objective," "neutral" observer: that is, reality remains a collection of mere objects to him; he separates himself from all relationship. Detached knowledge forms his ideal. He studies plants, rocks, trees, animals, people, himself and even God as objects to observe, analyze, understand and manipulate from his detached position of the Olympian spectator. He thinks that such a way of looking at things offers the key to truth. Man imagines himself a spectator and not a participant in the experience of what he would know. (No wonder then that the heirs of such a view find their chief pastime in sitting in front of a television for an average of six hours a day as they fulfill the spectator role in life.)

This type of knowledge only "knows" things by tearing them apart and analyzing them (*analyze* comes from the related Greek words *analyein,* meaning "to dissolve," and *lyein,* meaning "to loosen, dissolve" and "to unbind, release," that is, in the sense of "unbinding" or "releasing" from the cohesive force and its covenants that hold all things together).[11] Analytic knowledge does not primarily see the flower as a living part of God's creation, expressing God's glory from its place in a field. Instead, it tears the flower out of the integrated setting in which God placed it, pulls apart its petals, cuts all the parts into minutiae and puts them under a microscope. In other words, this knowledge "knows" things only by destroying them. It is death knowledge. The "life" studied in the "life study" or biology laboratory must first be killed, dissected, and only then can it be "known." In every respect, this man-centered knowledge works *against* cohesion and integration—against life—tending instead toward fragmentation and disintegration, toward, in short, death. In Proverbs, Wisdom says, "They that hate me love death."

This type of knowledge likes to "know" *about* things. Its expertise in swimming comes not by actually swimming but by analyzing swimming from a position detached from the actual experience itself.* This knowledge burdens us with courses *about* "human relations" that objectify and analyze those relationships instead of showing us how to enter into the living reality of such relationships. It makes of certain people "psycho-analysts," analysts (literally, "fragmenters" or "dissolvers") of the soul, who are trained to reduce other human beings to objects for mental or emotional dissection. Similarly, agricultural schools shovel this type of decomposing knowledge onto farmers, explaining the intricacies of computerized cattle breeding; yet those who embrace such knowledge enjoy no experience of the intricate interrelationships between men and creation within the organic harmonies of a godly-patterned farm. All who possess this knowledge know all *about* things, from the outside, from the position of the detached spectator-observer. Yet they do not know the subject of knowledge itself. Consequently, such knowledge nearly always destroys what it would know, even when its claimed intent is to help or even to love.

Even modern scientists and philosophers have come to see this perspective as impossible to consistently maintain.[12] Generally impractical (and often even absurd), it also becomes illusory. Man cannot really separate himself from reality. Like it or not, he remains a participant in, a member of, the real world. His very act of observation has an effect not only upon what he sees around him but also upon how he sees it.[13] So it is that quantum physicists have shown that every scientific experiment distorts the reality it probes, but the experimenter can never say what that reality would be like apart from his probing and the consequent distortion.[14] Philosophers and scientists, such as Michael Polanyi, have pointed out that man cannot separate himself from his own theories about the world.[15] We cannot fully take into account the effects that our theories have upon our observation and

---

* Some may consider this counterposition an oversimplification, saying that one may learn to swim by swimming, but more complex types of learning require an analytical approach. But while some of the complexity and skill level of various activities certainly varies, and while some therefore demand a more rigorous and structured method of instruction, everything can be taught in a relational, experiential context.

our study of the world, at least not in such a way that we can truly say what the world is like apart from those theories.[16] Polanyi compares theories to spectacles (an apt analogy, given the etymological links between the words *theory* and *spectator*) through which we look at the world. Like those wearing spectacles, we cannot look at the world through our theories and examine those theories (the spectacles) at the same time.[17] Man, in other words, cannot step outside of himself and view the world from any position other than his own. His thoughts, his vision, his ideas, will determine the way that he sees things, and man, within himself, has no way to escape his own personal viewpoint with its partiality, bias and distortion. So those who cling to the idea of a detached, unbiased observer cling to an unattainable illusion. Man always sees things from a limited perspective; he always knows "in part." That is, his knowledge is always partial, never impartial (1 Cor. 13:9); and he, in and of himself, must always view reality from a "relative" perspective in time and space. (We do not say, of course, that the relativist perspective gives us truth but only that man can never *within himself* attain to the true knowledge of reality; this knowledge of the whole can only come from the absolute and omniscient God.*)

Yet why would anyone maintain this myth of detached objectivity? They do so only to preserve the illusion offered in the Garden by *ha satan*, the illusion of being "like God." By assuming the detached, superior position of the objective knower, man pretends to himself that he surveys and knows reality from the Olympian heights of deity. The power of this form of knowledge lies in the power of the delusion that one has truly become "like God," the delusion to which God surrenders those who choose to believe the lie and be condemned (2 Thess. 2:11-12). Man seeks to make himself the center around which all things consist, but this center cannot hold. Things fall apart. Chaos is loosed upon the world, ending in disintegration and dissolution—that is, death.

When God warned man against eating from the tree of the knowledge of good and evil, He told him that if he ate of that tree, he would "surely die," death standing as the ultimate manifestation of fragmentation and decomposition. When

---

* See *Justice Is Fallen* for an extensive discussion of this point and refutation of attempted criticisms of it. See also Truth Forum's *Leap Beyond: The Quantum and Human Reason.*

man disobeyed God and partook of the forbidden tree's fruit, his spirit (the element of man's being connecting him with the One who is Spirit) separated from God, from the source of all life. Death means separation from Him who is life. Separated from life's source, man's spirit died within him, and so man lost his center in God, his center in Him who sees all things equidistantly as one. It was as if for man the planet began spinning out of its orbit and slowly breaking to pieces. Man's soul (created from the confluence of spirit and matter)* now came under the dominion not of his spirit, his connection to God, but of his carnal nature, the physical, sensual realm. The physical realm is not of itself evil; it becomes evil only when it assumes dominance in the hierarchy of man's being, moving into the center that God reserved for Himself. God's Spirit then no longer directs man's spirit. And man's spirit no longer directs his soul, the latter of which once looked to a direct relationship with God for its source and spiritual sustenance. Now the soul throws off the covering of God's Spirit. The detached mind of fragmented man separates from the living God and looks below to the merely physical realm for motivation and direction. This is the mind of death (Rom. 8:6). This transformed human nature, wherein the body directs the soul, the Bible calls the carnal or sinful nature, or "the flesh." And so a spiritual warfare was born within the very being of man:

> For those who are according to the flesh set their minds on the things of the flesh, but those who are according to the Spirit, the things of the Spirit. For the mind set on the flesh is death, but the mind set on the Spirit is life and peace, because the mind set on the flesh is hostile toward God; for it does not subject itself to the law of God, for it is not even able to do so; and those who are in the flesh cannot please God. (Rom. 8:5-8, NASV)

Uprooted from his direct connection with the Spirit, with God's own eternal life, man's carnal mind, man's mind moving through only flesh, entered the realm of death. Man's whole being fragmented and atomized: his emotions and his intellect no longer cohered around the Center, the Spirit of God, but now they became divided from and at odds with each other.

---

* Man became "a living soul" when God breathed His Spirit into the earthen, material body that He had formed for man. Just as the body connects us to the physical realm and the spirit connects us to the spiritual realm, so the soul connects us to other souls, to the realm of consciousness.

Detached from his relationship with God, seeking from his position of objective observer to analyze (in effect, "fragment") reality, man became detached, fragmented and atomized within himself as well. He collapsed; he fell.

Against all this detached, objective knowledge, the Hebrews counterposed a completely different kind of knowledge. Hebrew knowledge was *relational* knowledge; it did not rest upon the illusion of man's capacity to survive and live, even when *detached* from God, from his fellowman and from creation; but it rested upon the desire to enter into the fullness of *relationship* with God, humanity and creation, the relationships that God had ordained for man to experience. Through *relational* knowledge, things come together, hold together, cohere, consist. The Hebrews believed that coming into proper relationship with God would bring man back into oneness with that Center in whom all things consist (Col. 1:17). Only then does true coherence and wholeness come forth in our inner being, in our relationship with the whole of God's cosmos.

Relational and experiential knowledge opposes objective *detachment*. Detachment by definition severs relationship, so that nothing connects us with what we know, nothing interferes with our knowing it as an object for our study: as "impartial" judges of reality, we supposedly must disconnect ourselves from all relationship with the reality that we judge. Because this type of knowledge destroys relationship, it destroys oneness, which depends on relationship, whether between the different elements of man's being, between man and his fellowman, between man and nature or between man and God. In this sense, this type of knowledge destroys that oneness, that wholeness that we have described elsewhere as "salvation."* In contrast then to the fragmentation of analytical, detached knowledge, relational knowledge brings wholeness, oneness, coherence.

God wants us to turn away *from* all knowledge that centers us only in ourselves, all knowledge that brings fragmentation and death. Instead, He wants us to turn *toward* that knowledge which places us in the cohesive Center who brings wholeness. He wants us to uproot our children (and ourselves) from this tree of detached knowledge so that He might graft us into the tree of life (John 17:3; Prov. 3:13, 18; Rev. 2:7). He wants to set us free from the delusion of viewing Him, our fellowman and

---

* See *Salvation Is of the Jews.*

creation from the dizzying Olympian heights of theoretical abstractions (heights whence in our *hubris* we must inevitably fall). And He wants to plant us in the middle of life in all of its concrete reality, a spiritual life that we view from the perspective of participants (as we shall see, of a particular sort) and not of abstract observers. He does not want us to have knowledge *about* life but direct, experiential knowledge of life itself, the kind of knowledge that says, "I *know* it because I've *experienced* it. I know life not because of hearsay but because I've *lived* it." (Precisely for this reason God placed the tree of *life* in the midst of the Garden and, unlike His command concerning the tree of knowledge, did not forbid man to partake of it and live forever; and also for this reason God still holds out to man the promise of this tree in the paradise of God, see Revelation 2:7. God still wants man to throw down, to reject, the knowledge of death, the knowledge merely "about," that separates and detaches man both from life and God. Instead, He desires that we partake of the knowledge of life itself, the direct, relational knowledge of God.)

Yet when we speak of "experiential" knowledge in this way, the term *relational* becomes the critical qualifier. We call it "experience" for want of a better word to describe knowledge derived from the direct interplay of *all* the different dimensions of man's being. This *relational* character distinguishes this type of experiential knowledge from other forms characterized as "subjectivism." Strictly speaking, however, such subjectivistic "experiences" or "feelings" are really solipsistic and pagan to the core, since such "subjectiveness" really means the *viewer* stands at the center: the viewer is the "subject" of importance. This type of "subjectivism" also fragments man's being and rests solely on the inturned perceptions of the emotions or the moribund spirit. A relativistic subjectivism that views everything from the perspective of the inturned emotionalism of the fragmented self offers us no alternative to "objective" knowledge, though erroneously labeled its opposite. *Any* form of knowledge centered in man—whether of the emotions or the intellect and whether in an individual or a corporate community—will continue to fragment man and confine him to the realm of death.

Relational knowledge does not disdain the use of the mind but rather limits it to its proper place by demanding its integration in its approach to, its relationship with, the other elements of man's being, creation and God. The knowledge of relational experience does not allow just the mind or just the heart to define what is real (although one proves more foundational than the other).* Instead, it demands the integration and inter-relationship of all the dimensions of man's being in submission to God's order *through His Spirit*. Reality then becomes an integrated whole known through relational experience. We gain through our *whole* being—body, mind, heart and spirit, all working together—a knowledge of reality that transcends any knowledge we gain through any single, isolated, detached part of our being, such as the disembodied mind. Relational, experiential knowledge brings forth true cohesion and whole-ness because through it we relate directly to the transcendent God who alone brings coherence to all things. As we come into proper relationship with this Center of cohesion, He integrates together all the elements of our being into oneness, into wholeness. We then enter into relationship with the world around us with our *whole* being, not merely with fragments of ourselves. This knowledge alone brings wholeness, and we can only impart it through, first, a direct relational experience with God that changes the center of our whole being and, second, through real Christian education (as distinct from those counterfeits which go by that name but merely imitate secular education) that flows from this new relationship with God.

Cambridge's Raymond Williams speaks in this same sense of the knowledge of experience when he defines it as "the *fullest, most open, most active kind of consciousness*," including "feeling as well as thought."[18] This type of knowledge

> involves an appeal to the whole consciousness, the whole being, as against reliance on more specialized or more limited states or faculties . . . . The strength of this appeal to wholeness, against forms of thought which would exclude certain kinds of consciousness as merely "personal," "subjective" or "emotional," is evident.[19]

Williams links experience, used in this sense, to culture, which also refers to the *totality* of human activities.[20]

The knowledge of true experience, then, involves the whole person. When we, by this definition, know experientially, we

---

* See *Justice Is Fallen*.

know through all of our faculties.* Experiential knowledge, understood in the relational sense, calls *all* our faculties into play to work together in proper balance and relationship to each other and to that which we know through them. (We will later give an extended example.) Only an education rooted in relational knowledge brings forth true wholeness, because only knowledge that demands the use of our full being can fully integrate all the elements of that being. Knowledge that relies exclusively on fragmented elements of our being can only bring further fragmentation.

Relational experience that has failed to truly and fully center itself in God may in certain distorted uses prove false, but we can all think of many instances when we know that even such knowledge not *consciously* centered in God (though it may be so without recognizing it, as when it has totally submitted to love) remains very much more accurate or efficacious than autonomous, rationalistic knowledge (but we discuss this type of question in detail elsewhere).† A child learning to walk presents one simple example of such knowledge. No syllogism serves as the basis of the child's *experience* of learning to walk. The child does not read textbooks on walking to *know* how to walk, or even talk, but rather learns through experience—by *doing* it. Again, through this type of knowledge the *total* person participates rather than merely the detached mind alone.

As we mentioned earlier, some might object that this type of learning by experience applies to certain activities, such as learning to walk or to talk, but not to other activities and vocations. After all, can one become a doctor or an engineer by doing rather than through analytical investigation? Should we revert to the practices of Mao's Cultural Revolution, where doctors "learned by doing," where completely untrained men were designated as surgeons and, armed with "Mao Zedong thought," were sent forth to diagnose and treat patients? Obviously not. Nevertheless, how does a trained surgeon get his training? At some point even he must learn by doing, by performing surgery on someone. His unskilled hands guide the

---

* While Williams warns that this wholeness can somehow exclude other "nominated partialities,"[21] this statement contradicts itself, since by definition wholeness is not a partiality at all, but the comprehensive view that brings all parts together into a coherent oneness.

† See *Justice Is Fallen.*

blade into human flesh under the trained eye of a skilled surgeon. He may learn from his mistakes, but the human guinea pig must suffer the consequences. And he will also have "learned by doing" on animals or even human cadavers. In any case, most of his medical school training—Latin, and even much of chemistry and so on—has more to do with creating barriers to protect the exclusivity of the medical priesthood than with learning surgery.[22] When all is said and done, the surgeon does learn what he remembers by doing; he can learn enough to operate in no other way. Of course, some activities require study as well as practical experience. But as we will see later on, we can teach anything essentially from either one of two basic perspectives: the abstract, deductive; or the relational, inductive (although in teaching language in a relational, inductive context, we can teach some things through deductive methods).*

Parents, then, can teach at home even the most complex subjects (surgery aside) so that the child can very quickly start acquiring practical hands-on experience. Then the education can unfold in such a way that the increase in learning accompanies a growing practical experience of the student.

The readers should not confuse this alternative knowledge we speak of with merely sensual experience that offers some momentary gratification or pleasure. True experiential knowledge with God does not produce merely a transient phenomenon, but it transforms us as it integrates us at the very roots of our being. We acquire this knowledge in an intimate, so-called "subjective" way (subjective, that is, in the sense of knowing the *other* as a living, interrelating, participatory *subject* rather than a dead, abstract, detached object—not subjective in the sense of looking at things from a viewpoint centered in the subject; we will use the word *subjectivistic* to describe the latter). We come to this true knowledge as *participants* and not merely as observers. Those who label this knowledge through direct, relational experience "heart" knowledge have not altogether misnamed it, since its basis lies in the intimacy between knower and known, lover and beloved. Such knowledge accepts that affection and love (of what we shall see as a certain degree and type)† serve as the

---

* See "The Inductive Approach" in chapter 7.

† See Truth Forum's *Covenant Love: Its Nature, Commitment and Patterns.*

only legitimate basis of all true knowledge. With certain qualifications, this type of knowledge points us in the direction of the
knowledge of the ancient Hebrews—as Israeli Professor
Israel Efros speaks of it, a "whole-souled union."[23]

Some might warn that such heart knowledge will destroy the
restraints that human reason places upon human action.
Without the restraints of reason, they will argue, all limits upon
man's conduct would cease. "In the Name of God," they fear,
men will perform all sorts of destructive acts, justifying these
acts by claims that some "voice" has told them to do so.
Haven't men in the past, they will say, committed crimes and
claimed that God had instructed them to carry out these mis-
deeds? The only protection we have against such moral anarchy, they insist, lies in the mind of man. But, as we show
extensively elsewhere,* human reason offers little protection
against irrational destruction. Certainly, no one with any
knowledge of the subject would try to refute the claim that all
modern revolutions find their roots in the French Revolution,
which literally slaughtered tens of thousands in the name of its
worship of Reason.[24] One heir of the French Revolution,
Marxism, presents itself as a rationalist movement; in the
name of human reason it has slaughtered tens of millions.[25]
And Hiroshima resulted from the most concerted efforts of
man—both scientifically and politically—to apply human rationality to his problems; but it has left us facing the total annihilation of both man and his world. Many will say, "Yes, but
these weren't true reason; ours is." But believers in God have
recourse to just as "reasonable" a rejoinder: "*He* didn't hear
God's voice; *I* did." No, reason offers little protection against
the excesses of human unrestraint and wanton destruction; on
the contrary, all too often rationalist justifications impel, even
demand, violence and destruction (as in the very "reasonableness" of the man-centered nation-State: what could
be more reasonable than to seek out such a State's protection
from madmen and their collective followers who threaten to
destroy us? Yet, this means that these nation-States must be
predicated upon the use of violence if they are to effectively
protect us. And if those who threaten us escalate in violence,
then our nation-State must also escalate, at least if it would
continue to serve the original purpose for which we pledged

---

* See Truth Forum's *Justice Is Fallen, Holocaust as Spiritual War* and *Salvation Is of the Jews.*

our allegiance—to protect us. This very rational process is precisely what has potentially brought the world to the brink of total destruction.) On the other hand, no historical evidence exists to prove that God-centered belief intrinsically makes people more irrational and violent than those who profess faith in rationality. Again, the evidence, if anything, shows in many cases the contrary.*

In fact, by its very nature man-centered rationalism denotes the elimination of limits and restraints, a striving for more and faster, pushing past all barriers established by nature and that natural order of life that stand in the way of man's "progress," his search to fulfill the goals of godhood he has set for himself. By its very nature, rationalism projects the limited powers of human reason into the realm of unlimited knowledge and absolute power. It makes of limited man an almighty god. Professor of Psychiatry Henri Baruk traced this process back to the "Greco-Roman philosophers." He contends that the liberation from all limitations "by a pure and disembodied intelligence . . . constitutes the greatest danger and gives birth to the most redoubtable monsters."[26] He notes that "for a long time" insanity was

> defined as the loss of reason. However, we now know that excess rationalism and an extremely rigid mind are found at the source of psychoses which are more formidable than passional psychoses. They are more formidable to the exact extent that absolute rationalism can be disengaged from the "laws of humanity" [by which he means the limitations upon humanity], and they result in a dry and cold logic which is even more savage than sentimental excess. When man is detached from his instincts and from all amorous "weaknesses," he is no longer restrained by his feelings; he falls into a deviant logic that is dehumanizing because it is unfeeling.[27]

He sees these frightening implications in "the theory invented by the technocrats," who

> envision a world regulated by an all-powerful, insensitive, cold, and logical bureaucracy, having no other goal than to render all branches of human activity rational and to make this activity function in accordance with a mathematical order. This primacy of reason, this exclusive intellectualism that, in order to carry out its logical ideas, is

---

* See *Justice Is Fallen.*

impervious to human sacrifice, also forms a part of the legacy of the Greco-Roman tradition. However, this legacy has been carried to an absurd point due to pride in the recent attainments of the sciences (at least of the natural sciences).[28]

In contrast to this abstract, man-centered rationalism, as we will show,* God-centered knowledge manifests itself and flows through specific relationships. Relationship by its very nature limits our scale of action. One very simple reason for this is that true relationship requires time and so limits the number of people one can come to know in an abiding and deep relationship; for it requires much more from us than that superficial contact which brings objective knowledge. It takes time and effort to enter into such a relationship; it demands that you truly get to know someone or something. This limits the evil consequences of one's actions both because it limits the scale of one's activity and also because it lends itself toward a personal identification between those involved in the relationship. Each person feels a sympathy and identity with the other. This tends to undermine antagonisms and conflicts and to decrease their scope and consequences when they do break forth.

Furthermore, by definition a relationship speaks of some sort of *pattern*, since no abiding relationship can take place outside of pattern. The established *form*, the pattern, of personal relationship can itself eliminate much caprice in social intercourse. When people relate to one another in a pattern of relationship, this minimizes the anarchy of each person doing his own arbitrary thing. As we'll see shortly, by its very nature, consistent relational knowledge demands covenant; and when we discuss covenant we'll see still more clearly the precise limits that patterns of relationship place upon capricious, willful actions. When people enter into covenant relationship, they obligate themselves to limit themselves, to offer their lives to the checks and balances of others' information, but at the same time without sacrificing their personal responsibility for their own lives and actions. Because of the closeness of relationship that covenant entails, room for erratic, self-centered, even destructive, actions carried out "in the name of God" or reason are minimized. This protects not only those within the bonds of the relational community but also those

---

* See the section "Covenant" below.

outside as well. Certainly, no infallible guarantees will protect us in all circumstances from all violent and irrational outbreaks. Man being what he is, such things will inevitably happen. But particular forms and patterns will help to minimize such outbreaks. From this perspective, relational patterns prove far superior to detached objectivity.

In reality, when all other objections are dispensed with, the outstanding qualification, and certainly the one that compels so many to refuse to attribute any absolute validity to relational knowledge, is that such relational knowledge must be ultimately centered entirely in God Himself. For the Hebrew, the *Shema* expresses the center of this faith: "Hear, O Israel, Yahweh our God, Yahweh is One, and you shall love Yahweh your God with all your heart, soul and strength" (Deut. 6:4-5). Here we find the basic nature of our relationship to God defined—love. And we also find the express command to center our *whole* being in Him through His love. He is one, and so when we center our whole being in Him through love, He brings us into oneness, that is, into salvation. Indeed, we can see the relational character of all Judaic-Messianic knowledge in the central Biblical injunction that we must "confess Jesus as Lord." For our confession of Jesus' Lordship necessitates an ongoing, continual, direct and personal relationship with Him by His Spirit (1 Cor. 12:3; Col. 2:6). Jesus lives with and in His people by His Spirit, and by confessing His Lordship we declare that we seek in all circumstances and at all times to maintain our living, loving relationship with Him by following and submitting to Him. Our confession of Jesus' Lordship defines the *form* that our relationship must take: When we confess Him as Lord, we enter into the *relationship* of total *submission* to His absolute authority over our lives. Through this confession, we enter into true and unbreakable covenant with Him. Then, as we remain completely faithful to this pledge of relationship, God sends forth His knowledge into our hearts and lives, conforming us to the image of His Son.

In John 17, we also see the relational nature of our knowledge of God, for Jesus declares that He has made the Father "known" and *continues* to make Him known "in order that" God's "*love*" "may be in" us. Obviously, love requires a living relationship radically different from objective knowledge. True relational knowledge cannot in any sense result from human effort (though we must actively seek God in order that *He* might *work* within us, moving upon *us* to will and to do *His* will, if we would realize His vision in our lives and in the lives of our children, Phil. 2:13). Only God's Spirit can impart this knowledge to us. This knowledge originates not in man but in God. Only God can regenerate our dead spirits by breathing within us the breath of His own Holy Spirit; and this comes not by the empty words or traditions of men but by a living, powerful experience with God Himself (Acts 2:1-4). Jesus Christ came, died and rose again for the purpose of restoring us unto that living spiritual relationship with God that was lost at the Fall, to make us once again His sons (Rom. 8:5-29). Only when we enter into that personal relationship with, that living knowledge of, God will He make our spirits alive again, integrating the whole of our beings within Himself and activating us toward His purposes.

Our relationship with God is not then an arbitrary one but a familial one with a definite form that defines the relationship. This familial form is sonship. We enter into this relationship with God when His Spirit comes and dwells within us, transforming us into the *sons* of God (Gal. 4:6); for as many as are led by the *Spirit* of God are the *sons* of God (Rom. 8:14). God desires a *spiritual* relationship with us, through which He gives life to our spirits and brings us together with the Father of spirits (Heb. 12:9) as His sons. The spirit within our hearts cries out, "Abba, *Father*" (Gal. 4:6). When we are born of the Spirit, we become His sons, and He becomes our Father, as we come unto the Father through the only begotten Son of His Spirit (Matt. 1:20; John 8:19; 10:1-8; 14:6-10). And as we walk in newness of life with the Spirit, this relationship of sonship characterizes our unfolding relationship with Him, as He conforms us increasingly to the image of His Son (Rom. 8:29). He can only do this as we come into perfect obedience to His will, speaking *His* Word, doing *His* deeds. We must walk on with Him unto the fullness of our inheritance, the complete experiential relationship of our salvation, of complete oneness with God, till at last He shall be all in all (John 6:44-45; 1 Cor. 15:28). By so doing, we become those wise sons who hear their Father's voice (Prov. 13:1), who walk in living, continual relationship with God.

We thus strive through Christian education (literally, education "anointed" by the Spirit) to make our children true sons of God, at-one with their heavenly Father, walking in His Spirit, in perfect obedience to His will. And this familial nature of our relational knowledge of God suggests the means whereby we obtain this knowledge, which includes *all* valid knowledge: the familial, relational knowledge imparted in home education through those whom God gives to us in the most natural of all relationships—parents to children. "If you make your *home* in my word, then you are my disciples indeed. And you shall *know* the truth and the truth shall set you free" (John 8:31-32, JB). This forms the core of all "home" education.

So before parents can establish such a God-centered teaching relationship with their children, they must first themselves bridge the gap that the Fall has created in their own knowledge of God. This leads to the most basic question of the education of every human being: How can either parents or children enter into that relational knowledge that will join them to this Center and that provides the only legitimate basis for true Christian home education? God has ordained a specific form for this relationship, a form of relationship that truly joins us together in oneness with God; and that form of relationship is covenant. We must understand covenant to fully understand the Judaic, relational knowledge that God desires to convey to all His people within the context of that home that becomes the living expression of His Word.

Covenant*

As we have seen, through our relational knowledge with God we reach toward wholeness, which comes through true oneness with God. Yet God does not simply join Himself to man in just any arbitrary relationship. Instead, He joins Himself to man through a specific personal relationship, the terms of which He clearly defines in order to unify man in oneness to God according to God's image and not merely to man's. This can only take place if that joining occurs within the context of God's specific covenant. The covenant tells us how God wants to join each of us to Himself and to the rest of His people and even to creation. It defines the nature of all our relation-

---

* For a fuller treatment of ideas and principles presented here see Truth Forum's *Garden of God: Covenant as the Form That Holds the Content of God's Love, Including a New Testament View of Old Testament Law* and *Covenant Love.*

ships as God would arrange them. And in the process of shaping and defining these relationships, the covenant also shapes and defines us as we submit to the patterns and forms of these relationships. For example, the covenant lays out particular relationships of voluntary authority and submission within the Body of believers: between elders and disciples, between husbands and wives, between parents and children, between employers and employees. The covenant defines our responsibilities and obligations both in relationships where we exercise authority and in those where we submit to authority. For instance, a husband may exercise authority within his family while at the same time he submits to an employer on the job or to an eldership within his spiritual community. These different relationships make different demands upon us, "the demands of" Yahweh's "covenant" (Ps. 25:10). So by our voluntary submission to the covenant definitions of our relationships, God shapes us into the image that He desires for our lives. If given from the heart, then our submission to authority brings forth particular attitudes within us. To submit to, to carry and fulfill the responsibility of, authority also brings forth necessary attitudes within us. As we *all* submit in our places within all of the relationships that the covenant establishes for our lives, God changes us into those new creations that He has redeemed us to be and conforms us to His image.

We can see all relationships as covenants in the sense that they form agreements of one sort or another. So we can say that covenant actually constitutes the form that defines any relationship. In general, the form of anything reveals itself in the pattern that joins together its individual elements, that relates these elements to one another. God has ordained the covenant's form in order to join His people to Him and to one another. As we submit to the form of the covenant, this form (as does any form) excludes particular attitudes, desires, behavior and so forth from our lives while including others. So as we conform our lives to all of the details of the form of the covenant for our lives, the covenant forms our lives into the image God ordained for us. In short, God uses the covenant to shape and mold us into His own image, the image of Jesus.

So the covenant constitutes the form that connects us to God, the channel through which He can truly communicate His relational knowledge to man. As we bend and mold ourselves to meet the demands of the form, excluding and including that which the form demands, God reshapes our lives according to His perfect will. God purposes through His relational knowledge to mold and shape us into His image, and covenant supplies the only channel through which He will transmit this knowledge to us to accomplish His purpose. As His relational knowledge flows to us through the channel of the covenant's form, God molds us into the image of His Son (Rom. 8:29). Covenant constitutes the form and the channel through which God's knowledge can legitimately flow to man, while at the same time it excludes the knowledge that would undermine God's purpose for our lives. Through the covenant form, God informs us while keeping from us the information of the world. In this way, only the reality of God's life may inform, be *form*ed with*in*, us. If this channel breaks, then pollutants seep in, adulterating the godly knowledge that flows to us. Broken channels of covenant introduce the leavened knowledge of man and so fragment our oneness. Only within the confines of the covenant channel can God's pure Word flow to man without admixture of confusion or adulteration.

The covenant relationship provides the only context in which God will transmit His living knowledge unto man. It alone provides the necessary *form* of relationship that allows us to treat the "other" as a subject worthy of respect rather than merely as an object to use, because only the context of covenant offers the possibility of "whole-souled union," upon which true Judaic knowledge depends; the mutual trust that such "whole-souled union" requires can unfold only within the context of the binding commitment and cohering patterns of covenant love. Only in the marriage covenant, for example, can a man and woman come into a relationship of the closest personal intimacy that will truly bring forth complete trust and mutual respect. Such intimacy requires complete openness from both husband and wife, but this openness makes each party tenderly vulnerable to the other. We can only allow such vulnerability in the context of the protective covering of the covenant, the type of lifetime commitment of fidelity and mutual help that this covenant entails. Only this covenant relationship provides room for that mutual love to unfold that brings forth true oneness. Relationships that eschew covenant while mimicking marriage's intimacy between man and woman produce fornication, the use of another person as merely an object for sensual gratification. Only our faithful adherence to the binding vows of covenant allows us to come into true and complete oneness with someone else. Only our faithful adherence to the covenant patterns can realize oneness with God, for only adherence to His patterns can ensure our conformity to *His* image rather than to an image we merely make for ourselves.

Also, this binding together in covenant according to which each unique individual life joins together with each other individual in a way in which collectively they form the image of one man ("Jacob who became Israel") also ensures against each individual doing something wildly different from any others and claiming that God has told him to do so. Each individual has his own unique relationship with God, which determines and confirms for him his unique place in the corporate community, but the corporate community also has a life, will and image of its own that transcends any single individual's will; otherwise, this oneness that man seeks with his fellowman would be impossible. The order through which covenant joins us to this corporate image so that the *corporate* will of God flows through the life of the community (rather than merely any single individual's will) ensures against the anarchy of thousands or millions of individuals running around making conflicting claims in the Name of God. If this latter is happening, then certainly this is not Judaic salvation, since it diametrically opposes Judaic oneness.*

At the same time, true oneness requires a permanent, perpetual relationship. Oneness, like love, cannot be "time's fool." If we are to recognize it as our salvation, as something with the ability to overcome all things, even death, it must prove its power to overcome. Hebraic knowledge means relational knowledge, and this relational knowledge that God desires to share with man serves to bring man and God into oneness. When we bind ourselves in everlasting covenant with God, we commit ourselves to the path that leads to total and perpetual oneness. Temporary unity can obviously never lead us to complete and permanent oneness. The Scriptures explicitly compare our covenant with God to the marriage relationship between man and wife (Eph. 5:31-32; Isa. 62:5). We make the marriage commitment unto death, vowing lifelong fidelity to a

---

* See Truth Forum's *Order of Perfection: Authority and Submission in the Organic Order of the Body of Christ.*

definite pattern of relationship. Through this commitment, two separate beings merge into one. When we enter the living form of the covenant, we commit ourselves to a relationship of everlasting oneness and bind ourselves to the God who has ordained the covenant and to all of those others who enter into it and faithfully abide in submission to its terms.

Judaic knowledge always requires covenant relationship, whether that knowledge pertains to creation, man or God; covenant always defines the relationship through which we receive Judaic, relational knowledge. In contrast, a non-relationship such as prostitution characterizes the detached observer of pagan knowledge. Pagan knowledge treats what is known, whether nature, man or even God, as a mere object of one's momentary need, desire or simple curiosity, only to be discarded again when the fancy has passed. No *binding* relationship occurs. This makes the total sharing that oneness involves impossible. Too much of our old, separate identity remains, and so we do not find total oneness in God's identity. We refuse to lose our lives, and so we cannot find them.

The highest usage in the Hebrew Scriptures of the word *yada*, "to know," illuminates the Hebraic concept of knowledge as subject-to-subject union. This usage shows a definite relationship between the way God and man know each other and the way a man and his wife know each other, the latter in order that they may conceive children. For example, "Adam knew [the root is *yada*] Eve his wife; and she conceived and bore Cain" (Gen. 4:1, KJV). Also in Genesis, God declares of Abraham, "For I know [*yada*] him, so that he will direct his children and his household after him to keep the way of Yahweh by doing what is right and just, so that Yahweh will bring about for Abraham what He has promised him" (Gen. 18:19, NIV, KJV). When God says that He "knows" Abraham, He says something precise about His relationship, or more specifically, about the relationship of His Word, His seed, to Abraham. God conceives His Word within the heart of Abraham, who has entered into covenant relationship with Yahweh, and through that Word's growth and development within the nurturing soil formed by that binding covenant, God's purpose and nature grew within not only Abraham's life but also his children's.

Man's life can only realize God's vision within the context of a binding covenant relationship—a deep, personal, subject-to-subject union—between man and God. God's vision and patterns of life present themselves as more than mere tools, known intellectually and then applied by man independently of God. Rather their use depends upon a continual, living relationship between man and God, which relationship is described by the term *covenant*. Through the covenant, God and man enter into that "whole-souled union" that brings the true knowledge of God and His ways. Only that union brings the oneness between man and God that constitutes man's salvation; for salvation is, as we said above, oneness, at-onement, total oneness with God and with all of His patterns for man's life and being.* Outside of covenant relationship lies adultery, fornication, prostitution and perversion, relationships that merely use the partner as an object for one's own selfish purposes, to be later cast aside in the caprice of changing whims and moods. Only within the covenant do we treat the partner as a subject, loved, respected and cared for, toward whom we assume binding, lasting responsibilities.

Only through covenant relationship, then, can true knowledge of the revelation of God come to man, for this revelation consists not simply of a single event but of an ongoing experience involving one's *whole* life (Rom. 1:17).† Indeed, scholars have called the very word *yada*, "to know," "a covenant term," *yada* meaning to have "a covenanted relationship with" or to behave "in a way consistent with being a covenanted partner."[29] So when God tells Abraham that He "knows" him, He uses the word *yada*, but some translators also render this to mean that God has "chosen" Abraham to enter into covenant relationship with Him.‡ Only in the completion of a life together with God, bound in the covenant relationship of which the marriage covenant presents the prototype, can man receive God's complete revelation and so be completely transformed into the image of God's Son (Rom. 8:29).

Because of the covenant, the fact that God "knows" Abraham means that Abraham will obey Yahweh and train his

---

* See *Salvation Is of the Jews*.

† So the Scriptures say, "You shall love Yahweh your God with *all* your heart and with *all* your soul and with *all* your might . . . when you sit in your house and when you walk by the way and when you lie down and when you rise up." (Deut. 6:5, 7, NASV)

‡ See *Justice Is Fallen* and *The Garden of God* for a discussion of criticisms of this view.

children to serve Yahweh also (Gen. 18:19, KJV); for Yahweh's Word will "go forth and not return void"(Isa. 55:11, KJV). God has sown His seed in Abraham's heart, and it will gestate and come to fruition under the "husbandry" (also a word of covenant relationship) provided by God's covenant with Abraham. Abraham's submission to the form of the covenant defines his heart as good soil,* and so this promise will come to fruition. The covenant between man and God provides the consistent context that enables the knowledge of God to be fully understood by, and His image to be fully made flesh in, His people.

In contrast, "objective" knowledge, in the sense in which we have defined it above, places one outside of, apart from and superior to that which one seeks to know. So, in the pagan view, by intellectual fiat, God becomes a mere "object" of rational analysis and investigation. He becomes the object of study also within theological systems that drain the knowledge of Him of its dynamic, living, personal, relational character (2 Cor. 3:6). People come to know all "about" God, but cease to know Him directly, as He is (1 Sam. 2:12-17; Isa. 29:13; 2 Tim. 3:6-7). It is as if they learned all *about* a language but never learned to speak it so that they might communicate and relate to those who use the language. Ultimately such knowledge can only destroy our experience or consciousness of God, just as it does everything else it would know. Then the hearts of those who originally burned in their love for God grow as bitter and dry as ashes.

Moreover, one's fellowmen, as well as societies in general, also become objects for study and manipulation by the detached "scientific" observer, the self-appointed genetic or eugenic engineers of the perennial pagan master race. Governmentally empowered "experts" bureaucratically dominate society, exercising an anonymous power over their fellowmen, whom the experts view, from the pagan perspective of "objective" knowledge, not as unique, specific individuals but as abstract integers of power—digits that form only statistical data, pieces in the machinery of the corporate juggernaut. These experts, as the noted economist Thomas Sowell has said, "may have a lot of theories and secondhand information at their fingertips," but they lack "the hard, specific

---

* See p. 31.

knowledge" really "needed to make decisions." This knowledge resides not with the experts but "scattered among millions of laymen."[30] Because they know the concrete, specific information about their own situation and suffer the direct consequences of any wrong decision that they make, those whom the experts call "laymen" are the real experts in regard to their "own particular situation" (including home education). The expert may "know more," in an abstract sense, than an individual "layman," but, in Sowell's words, no one man or group of men "knows enough to try to control a whole economy or society of millions of other human beings."[31] In its detachment from reality, "expert" knowledge distorts creation, man and God into mere objects for the expert's own godlike, detached manipulation. Such knowledge remains barren at best, but more commonly becomes oppressive and destructive. In contrast, because of his very attachment to (as contrasted to detachment from) the real circumstances of his life, the "layman" comprehends the concrete situation of his own life more effectively than any expert. Moreover, "since someone else pays the price of his mistakes," the "expert," because of his detachment, busies himself trying "to know too much from too far away" and "has no incentive to admit he is wrong."[32] The "layman," because he must face the consequences of what he decides as right and wrong, true or false, is certainly in a better position than anyone else to make the right assessment, having as he does a direct stake in that assessment. Yet as the power and abstract, theoretical perspectives of the "experts" increasingly dominate society, it invariably plunges into irreversible and cumulative decline, unless men reverse this trend of abstract, anonymous dominance. Reversal, however, begins and ends only with repentance, which in the original Biblical languages means literally "a turning." To reverse the trend we must start with a radical turning.

Education itself offers the clearest example of this distinction between abstract, detached knowledge *about* one's fellowman and direct, relational knowledge. No theories about how children learn can ever replace a parent's specific and concrete *relational* knowledge of his child.[33] No professional concern can ever replace the living, lifelong covenant between parent and child, the parent's commitment to bring his child to maturity and responsibility, the child's commitment to faithfully honor and obey his parents. The covenant provides the one necessary context for the child to mature. When we recognize as our goal the *wholeness* of the child, we will recognize the State education system's total inadequacy, but we will also see that true God-centered education requires the context of the covenant bond. Only those covenant institutions that express God's life-giving Spirit, the family and the spiritual community of believers, can transmit unadulterated relational knowledge to our children.

Covenant supplies the framework in which we can nurture our children and bring them forth to maturity in God. "Objective" detached knowledge cannot bring forth this maturity, since it ultimately views the child as an object of one sort of manipulation or another (no matter how subtly benevolent gestures disguise this manipulation). By their fruit you shall know them, and the tree of this knowledge has borne bad fruit since man first partook of it at the Fall.[34]

This "objective" type of knowledge also makes creation a mere object for exploitation, manipulation, bemusement or control as man exerts his godhood over creation to use it as a backdrop for his own starring cosmic role as the god whose mind rules over all. Man's means of wresting his physical sustenance from nature becomes completely rationalized—that is, detached. He views nature as merely an object for manipulation and exploitation, rather than as an organic reality given by the hand of the Creator for man to enter into a specific kind of relationship with. Ironically, however, man's rationalization of nature reduces man himself to something less than man in the industrialized culture that results. When man destroys his relationship with nature by reducing it to an object of manipulation for mere economic purposes, man reduces himself to a mere object of manipulation in the same economic machinery. As he paves over and rationalizes nature, he crushes his own individual uniqueness, transforming himself into one of the prestamped, standardized gears in the State-run machine.* We rarely think about the implications of this atomized system of economic specialization. We simply take it for granted, but a moment's reflection yields some startling considerations.

Allen Tate once remarked that "until the last generation, only certain women were whores, having been set aside as special

---

* See *Culture as Spiritual War.*

instances of sex amid a social scheme that held the general belief that sex must be part of a whole; now the general belief is that sex must be special." Modern technological society similarly transforms all its members into fragmented "specialists" limited to wasting their "energy piecemeal over separate functions that ought to come under a unity of being."[35] Prostitutes are, of course, women whom others treat, and who treat others, merely as objects, reducing the different aspects of each individual to "specializations" that can be bought or sold as commodities on the open market. In the same way, this "specialization" of economic and social functions reduces all of society's members to this same functional level. Examples span the whole spectrum from assembly line factory work, where a man may spend his whole life continually repeating minutiae, performing the same mechanical operations hundreds of thousands of times, to the Hollywood movie star known for his or her specialty in looks or acting, or the athlete specializing in running exactly 120 yards, jumping over thirty-six-inch hurdles and so on. Or on a more sophisticated level, we find such specializations in the one-dimensional university professor identified entirely with his special discipline. Contemporary culture identifies everyone with a specialized work operation or a single outstanding physical or mental characteristic or talent. While certainly each of us has special gifts and talents, industrialism defines the range of each area of specialization so narrowly as to stultify the full development of our individual inclinations and abilities. It objectifies our very lives and then identifies us with a single dimension of our beings, which in its specialization becomes a saleable commodity on the open market and makes "merchandise of the souls of men." The system turns out professors of history specializing in the labor movement in New York City from 1890-1910; or it turns out eminent authorities on individual viral strains. Most find their identities in these narrow specialities. Men become so specialized that they lose their identity as human beings and become identified only with their specialties, like the woman who is no longer a woman but a whore.

The techno-industrial system moves to crush those human beings who seek to live in the wholeness of relationship with God, their fellowman and creation, engaging in a wide range of fulfilling activities in meeting the needs of others and themselves. They are replaced by detached cogs, commercial objects; such people are regarded as vestigial anachronisms to be removed and replaced by what Mumford calls the "megamachine."[36] Everyone must become a commercial object for sale on the market, each one sold for a particular, specialized purpose. Life becomes prostitution; it forces us to fragment ourselves in carrying out on a detached level particular functions of our being that should have been integrated into the wholeness of our lives and those of our fellowman and creation. Money dictates vocation, which no longer means "calling" but merely employment. Our whole culture becomes one Great Whore, the whore of Babylon spoken of in Revelation and elsewhere (Rev. 17:5; 18:3, 9-13). Money becomes not a medium of exchange but a buying off of our gifts and talents, our bodies and souls.

Of course, people can fulfill special functions within a community, such as that of a skilled craftsman. Such functions become valid if they serve in a larger context that supports a whole-souled vision of life. Then each individual participates in the life of the others with whom he joins in *direct* relationships of reciprocal service and sharing. But in the abstract, detached techno-industrial culture, relationships are severed, and specialization reduces each individual of this culture into an atomized fragment that depends, not directly on other concrete human beings with whom he stands in vital relationship, but simply on the anonymous abstract State upon which he depends as a slave does his master.

God created both man and nature for a purpose. He did not make nature into a prima donna, set on a pedestal for worship. But neither did He make her or us as a prostitute, reduced to a rationalized objectivity that exploits rather than nurtures and husbands in the give and take of covenant relationship. But by prostituting nature, the physical ground of our being, in the end we must also prostitute ourselves.

Contemporary secular education trains us to look at people and things as objects with which we have no *living, organic, vital* connection. We learn to see these things in a detached way (whether they are people, animals, vegetation, earth, mountains or anything else); but we do not let them really touch us and affect us in any sort of deep, personal way. We must not lose our "objectivity," our "rationality," our "detachment," which supposedly provide our sense of meaning and direction while preventing deception. This begs the question, however, whether such purported objectivity is not itself already a type of deception, an illusion, a false view of seeing things.*

We see this attitude of detached objectivity in all areas of secular education and study, such as the study of science and history. Whatever we study remains a detached object outside of ourselves, not a living reality with which we enter into relationship. Knowledge supposedly comes exclusively through objective analysis, that is, by tearing the object of our knowledge to pieces. We learn "biology," "life" science, through the destruction and dissolution of life, for example, in the dissection of carcasses and even cadavers. This knowledge, however, shows us death, not life. But how can life-knowledge come through death-knowledge?† And how much of this knowledge even endures for the average student?

Secular education also detaches us from our historical roots. The past no longer vitally molds and shapes us as the root of our being. "Objective" knowledge teaches us to look upon our ancestors and their ways as though they bore no integral, necessary connection to ourselves; or, at best, it teaches that while a connection may exist, we should sever and break it so that we can see things as they really are. To modern, uprooted man, in the words of Huxley's *Brave New World*, "History is bunk."[38]

Man-centered knowledge does not enable us to enter into living, organic relationship with our fellowman or with God's creation. It opposes the viewpoint, attitude and relational do-

---

* See *Salvation Is of the Jews* and *Justice Is Fallen.*

† For example, does dissecting cadavers really help us to learn to heal? The medical establishment claims, of course, that it does. But voluminous and unchallenged documentation by secular scholars and medical practitioners have recently called the veracity of many of the claims of the medical establishment into question.[37] Obviously a discussion of the failures of the medical establishment and a critique of its methods would take us too far afield here. But even a moment's reflection must raise serious questions concerning the usefulness of dissecting cadavers for studying the effects of surgical interventions in living bodies. Whatever knowledge can be gleaned from cutting open corpses, when the doctor first tries out his techniques on living men and women, these people become the guinea pigs in the surgeon's first experiment on life. What this must do to the doctors themselves can go far in helping us to understand why the medical profession has played so prominent a role in such totalitarian monstrosities as Nazism and Stalinism.

minion that the Bible enjoins us to seek, both for our children and for ourselves, and demands the detached, man-centered domination that has raped the world and left almost every human relationship violated and ravaged.

So pagan knowledge reduces everything to mere objects for analysis, for breaking down and dissolving, for fragmenting—in short, for destroying. The "other" becomes an "it" rather than a "thou," be that "other" the members of one's family, one's friends, one's neighbors, one's fellow workers on the job, even the hills and the valleys, the sheep and the horses—even one's own self—and, ultimately, even God. Man becomes hopelessly fragmented, divided within himself and divided against himself. Any educational system that fails to base itself on God-ordained covenant cannot help but ultimately bring forth such atomized, abstracted life.

In contrast, we must seek for our children and for ourselves knowledge that ends fragmentation and dissolution, knowledge that binds things together, that joins them in *relationship*—living, vital, organic relationship. Creation can only be bound together when bound in covenant relationship with the Creator, for only in the God who is one can all things consist (Col. 1:17); only the living God brings cohesion to all of reality. And He can only bind us together in relationship with Himself if we enter into living relationship with *His Spirit*; for God *is* a Spirit (John 4:24). Therefore, more than the mind *of* the flesh, we must desire to put on the Mind of Messiah (1 Cor. 2:14, 16; Rom. 8:5-6). For God alone sees everything exactly as it is; and Messiah is His expression, His *Logos*, His mind (in contrast to man's mind) in time and space. While we always remain limited creatures, we can put on this mind, through living *relationship* with the Spirit (1 Cor. 2:11-16). This relationship enables us to see the world through the eyes of God, to understand through His understanding. The word *Christian* has come to mean many different—even opposing—things in our world; but originally it meant "anointed" by the Spirit (2 Cor. 1:21; 1 John 2:20, 27). It must come to mean this again in order for the education of which we speak to succeed. Through Christian education we strive to teach our children to truly put on Messiah's mind so that they may enter into *living* relationship with the God of Israel, becoming one with Him, full and complete expressions of His glory and love (2 Cor. 3:3). Again, such relational knowledge can only flow through a relational setting; and no better relational setting to transmit such knowledge exists than that provided by God Himself: the anointed—the *Christian*—family and home.

God has prepared works in advance for each and every one of His children to perform (Eph. 2:10). He has ordained a place in His kingdom for every child of God. We must train up our children so that they can fulfill the purpose God ordained for their lives. Elsewhere we show extensively* that fulfillment requires form, for only a form can be filled full. While men contrive dead and stultifying forms, God ordains a living, organic form through which to express the fullness of His supernatural power and love, the form of the Body of Messiah—the Anointed Body of the Anointed One. We must train our children to fulfill their place within this form.

God's invisible finger points to a path of destiny for each of our children's lives, a foreordained purpose that they must strive to complete. God intends to reveal to our children this unfolding path that He has prepared for them. But we must train them in the way that they should go so that they may find the grace to follow that path, so that they can find that form into which they will pour themselves in order to fill full, to fulfill, their lives. He has ordained a place for them as lively stones within the great corporate Temple of His love, which is His Body (1 Pet. 2:5). Only by finding their places in God's purpose, in fulfilling their destinies, will our children find the true joy, peace and love that God has for them. We must prepare them to find and complete their path to this fulfillment.

As they learn to follow this path, our children will learn to play their parts in the great song that the Scriptures declare that God has made all of creation to sing (Ps. 96:1; 98:4-9; Isa. 55:12), the song of Yahweh (Ps. 137:4); for God holds out the promise to all in His kingdom, and so also to us as parents and to our children as well, to have a part in this song.† He has

---

* See Truth Forum's *Temple*.

† This paragraph and much of the remainder of this chapter greatly condense material that we discuss in detail elsewhere, in books on God's covenant and the great spiritual Temple of His people. Because of this attempted condensation, everything is not spelled out as fully as possible, but we felt that greater detail on this subject right now would take away from the forward movement of our main theme in this study. Yet as you read along, we believe that the central points we are making will be filled in and clarified for you.

melodiously, harmoniously orchestrated all of creation to sing together this song, the song declaring God's great wisdom and love. All the individual parts and pieces of creation blend together in perfect coherence, each part adding its note, its theme, its rhythm, as all combine to bring forth one harmonious symphony. From His Word, God brought forth a world in perfect harmony with His patterns. His patterns guided each element in His creation into perfect harmony with every other element. But when man rebelled against God, he disrupted God's song. Man introduced the grating, jarring noise of disharmony. A cacophony of confusion replaced the symphony of God, and this cacophony will ultimately end in the total disintegration and holocaust of all the earth's elements (2 Pet. 3:10-12). But in the very midst of this disintegrating creation, God brings forth a new creation, a new song (Ps. 98:1). He wants our children to be part of that song. He desires this to the extent that He manifested Himself in human flesh and hung on a rough Roman execution rack so that they could be made new creations (2 Cor. 5:17), playing their parts in His new song. To do this, they must become those perfectly harmonious people whose very beings and lives, whose thoughts, words and deeds, declare the glory of God.

To fulfill our educational responsibilities, we must have this vision of the wholeness that God desires to bring forth in our children's lives. We must train them to be men and women of integrity, people whose lives have become living temples and songs that express God's harmonious love, peace and truth, whole individuals fitted together as members of that corporate temple, that form through which God expresses the fullness of His love.

Unless we all press forward into the form that God has ordained to bring us wholeness, neither we nor our children can find lasting fulfillment, but only momentary satisfaction. For, as we said, without form we have nothing to fill full. Without form, nothing holds together, but all lies squandered and dissipated. Wholeness then becomes impossible, for no form exists to hold us together as one. We see this in the marriage covenant, the form that God ordained to contain the love between a man and a woman. Outside of that form, love dissipates in adultery and fornication, just as water dissipates from a cracked cistern. Then intimate, lasting relationship between a man and a woman becomes impossible. God condemned those who violated their spiritual marriage covenant with Him by describing them as "broken cisterns, that can hold no water" (Jer. 2:13, NASV).

We have seen that the covenant serves as God's form through which flows the relational knowledge that brings oneness and harmony. This covenant binds together His people in the form of the body of a man, the corporate Body of Jesus, of whom His people make up the living members (1 Cor. 12:12). Jesus supremely expressed the living God. "He put flesh on Spirit and turned word into deed. He put God in a trough and made Him bleed." The fleshly tabernacle in which the invisible Spirit of God dwelt, structured in the definite form of a visible human body, became the temple of the living God (John 2:19-21). Just as the individual body of Jesus Christ served as the seed from which has come forth a great corporate Body of His people, so has His life as the individual temple of God served as the cornerstone of a great corporate Temple that includes all His people. God Himself formed this Temple "not made by men's hands" to express the living, concrete reality of His invisible nature (2 Cor. 6:16; Eph. 1:22-23; 2:20-22; 3:19; 4:13).

God desires to express His nature through His corporate Body, His corporate Temple, which includes each one of us and our children. Each of us has a place in the great corporate form that declares His love. He has created us for the purpose of finding and fulfilling our places in this form. True fulfillment comes only when we complete a purpose or meet a necessity that transcends ourselves. We find fulfillment when we con- *form* to the form of the song that lies beyond us, as we stretch and bend our talents, abilities and desires into conformity to the song's given form. When we submit to this, we stretch ourselves to become, both individually and corporately as God's people, something more than what we are—the perfect reflection of the glorious love and liberating truth of Jesus the Messiah (Eph. 4:12-13). So education must bring forth a *form* of knowledge that binds us to God and so in*forms* and con- *forms* us unto His image. Again, this binding to God assumes the form of a certain kind of relationship—covenant. Through Christian home education we bring forth our children to total conformity to the image of God's love. We bring every element of their nature together in the fulfillment of God's purpose, together in that integrated wholeness that fully expresses Him.

God, through the sacrifice and resurrection of Jesus Christ, seeks to restore to man his part in the song of Yahweh. He seeks to restore that direct, personal relationship with man, to breathe His living Spirit into the heart of man. He seeks to renew the life of man's dead spirit, making it resonate once again in perfect harmony with the Spirit of God. Then God's Spirit, through the spirit of man, can once again become the directing power in man's life. Man's whole being then comes into perfect, harmonious relationship with God and in turn with all of creation through the God-ordained patterns for every aspect of human life. Christian home education re-creates human life in God's image. So we must direct our children's entire education toward completing God's purpose for their lives. We must bring every aspect of their beings into a living harmony that fully expresses God's song.

God is joining His people together in increasing measure into the covenant of Messiah's Body, until each man's soul harmonizes in perfect relationship with his brothers and sisters in that Body and works together in the true community of God's holy love under the headship of God's Spirit. We must each find our place in this Body, the place that God ordained for us before the creation of the world. Only by each fulfilling his place, by entering into the proper relationship with his brothers and sisters, will his part in the song of Yahweh resonate in harmony with others, encouraging them to play their proper parts. Our entire education proceeds toward the completion of these purposes of God. Bound in his proper place in the love covenant, first with God and then with God's people and the land, the whole life of each member of God's Body will resonate harmoniously with the song that God sings through all His people. Having uprooted us from Babylon, the land of confusion, the strange soil that prevents us from singing the songs of Zion (Ps. 137:4), God now transplants and roots us in the Jerusalem that is above, the city of peace, the spiritual community that resounds in harmony with God. Once transplanted into this soil we can *sing* our affirmative answer *with conviction* to the song that asks,

> Jerusalem of gold,
> Whose light is the dawn,
> Am I not a violin
> For all your songs?

The Lord is the master Conductor of Jerusalem's song. He

brings the myriad instruments of His Body together to play the harmonious composition that will awaken all those who have ears to hear and overcome the decomposition, the death, of the world.

Limitation and Relational Knowledge

For the harmonious form of this song to come forth, all its elements must come into proper relationship with all the others. To be in proper relationship we must not only fulfill our place, but we must also confine ourselves to the limits that God has set for us: proper relation requires limitation. Coherence around a center requires limitation. To cohere around the sun, the planets must remain within the limits of their own orbits. If they failed to remain within these limits, they would careen off into space, and the planetary system would lose all coherence. When we educate our children, we must teach them to recognize that they, like all of us, are limited creatures (Acts 17:24-28). This recognition opposes humanistic education's encouragement to reject limitations.* Children, however, can only fulfill the image God created for them by recognizing the limits of their finite being, for only within the bounds of our limitations can we bring our tasks and responsibilities within our reach.† Only within our limits can we come into proper relationship with—and therefore relational knowledge of—the portion of creation that God places within our finite hands.

So God defines His limitations upon us not only by our direct covenant with Him and with our brothers and sisters in Christ but also by the way He situates and sustains our finite being in the finitude of a creation that He provides (Acts 17:25-26). Our covenant with God's creation, with the land through which God brings His song down to earth, also defines these limits. Within the limitations God has ordained for him, man's physical being comes forth in wholeness as he joins together in covenant relationship with the land from whose very substance God made him (Gen. 2:7). Within man's covenant with the land, his body works in harmony with the natural culture that God made man's natural being to function within.

---

* See *Humanism*.
† See Truth Forum's *Service of the Temple*.

Yahweh created man in the Garden to nurture the land (Gen. 2:15), and at the Fall, He again commanded man to work the earth, only this time "by the sweat" of his "brow" (Gen. 3:19). God did not arbitrarily dictate this pattern for human life as a mere punishment. Rather He ordained it as the culture, the nurturing habitat, that would minister to the physical, natural body of man, providing the perfect pattern for man's physical sustenance. On the land, man earns daily bread through meaningful, purposeful activity for his body. At the same time, as man works the land, he comes into daily contact with the effects of the curse and so develops a proper sense of what his covenant relationship with the land really means. Man's covenant with the land constitutes a form of relationship that testifies to the body's limits. His labor on the land makes it difficult for carnal man to imagine himself as God, to expand to tyrannical proportions the satanic reach of the human "mind [as] its own place."[39]

As we have seen, pagan education compartmentalizes man, fragmenting and separating the care of his body from that of his mind and his heart. Our modern culture reduces the human body to a kind of superfluity. Some people build it up like a sculpture on a pedestal for display at the gymnasium or health spas and to show it off as the object for their own glorification and worship. Others take it for walks and jogs much as they would a pet, or neglect, purposelessly abuse or simply ignore it. In contrast, in an agri-culture, a land-centered culture, our work brings all of the parts of man's being into relation with each other. Working in direct contact with the land, according to the covenant patterns that God has ordained (with man nurturing the land, which in turn sustains his physical needs), we bring not only our bodies but also our hearts and souls, our emotions and minds, actively into operation. Through our active relationship with nature, with animals, crops, land and the exquisite balances of the creation all around us, God works a change within us, stirring us, bringing forth His song within and through us. Unlike the fragmented, prostituted culture of modern society, an agri-culture integrates our lives. As we work within a self-sufficient agri-culture (as distinct from a mass-mechanized, single-crop agri-business), we must also, on some level at least, become part of a community of people who work the land. We see this clearly when we look, for example, at the community life that bound together the early

Pilgrims or that bound together the westering pioneers in the mutual help that such an agriculture requires.* The practical demands of agriculture help to bring us into God's ordained covenant relation not only with the land but also within the covenant of God's people. We come within the limited reach of real, living relationships with flesh and blood human beings, rather than within the remote and fragmented relationships of an industrial-urban society abstractly connected only through the mass market system and bureaucratic agencies of the State. Our direct covenant relationship with the land provides the most appropriate context or framework for our direct covenant relationship with the community of God's people. Our husbanding of the land necessarily entails a direct interconnection and relationship with others who responsibly work and care for the land. In our life with and labors upon the land, we become interdependent with the members of our families, with friends and neighbors—all in a personal and direct way wholly unknown in urban-industrial culture. The small scale of a land-centered community greatly furthers the close personal relationships of true community life. In such a land-centered culture and community, we no longer work for an abstract marketplace, "serving" unseen millions totally unrelated to us personally. Now we stand in direct, personal relationships of service to others who at the same time serve us on this same level of personal relationship. We truly know those for whom we labor and who labor for us (1 Thess. 5:12). We accept our personal responsibility for one another as our brother's keeper, both because we desire to and because, on this limited scale of relationships, which keeps the extent of our responsibilities for others within our reach, we are able to.*

We fully discuss elsewhere the implications of such an agriculture for God-centered life and the contrasting spiritual results and causes of urban-industrial culture.* But we briefly discuss these questions here because our look at the relational character of an agriculture will help us to understand more clearly the relational knowledge that God desires to impart to His people generally and (insofar as we concern ourselves in this book) to our children in particular. God wants to bring us and our knowledge out of the abstract realm, where the mind operates as its own god, and into the reality of God-

---

* See *Culture as Spiritual War*.

ordered physical, soulical and spiritual relationships through which God's grace operates to make us whole rather than fragmented. God has ordained a *place* for our children (and for ourselves) in His Body, a *place* for our children (and ourselves) on the face of the earth (although, of course, that physical location may change at times during our pilgrimage). By rooting ourselves in this God-ordained place, we come out of the abstract realm of theoretical, spectator knowledge in which, in Milton's rendition of the words of satan, "The mind is its own place . . . ." God empowers us to uproot ourselves from the perspective that believes our own minds should shape and determine reality, that believes, in Berry's words, that "there is no context until [the mind] gets there."[40] God moves us into living relationships that bring us into submission to reality, living relationship with the Spirit of God, soul-sustaining relationship with the community of God's people and physical-sustaining relationship with the substance of the earth.

Even when not in direct connection with the land ourselves, because we remain interdependent members of one another within the Body of Christ and therefore connected to those in direct relationship with the land, we can participate in this land-centered culture (even if we reside in the slums of a great metropolis where we harvest and cultivate the Lord's spiritual field, one that God will transplant into His own pattern for human culture, 1 Cor. 3:6-8). If our larger community participates in this way of life, then our tangible oneness with our brothers and sisters in Christ, our fellow membership with them in a common spiritual culture, makes us sharers together in the benefits of an agricultural life even when our place in His Body limits our direct participation in this form of life. So even in the city, this relational perspective of how man should be joined to the earth dictates the way we study the earth "sciences."*

We must recognize, however, that no mere abstraction can connect us to the larger community of brothers and sisters, but rather real and concrete relationships must actually connect us. We must truly belong to one another, not merely in some "theoretical," "mystical" sense, but by actually participating in one another's lives, sharing in each other's gifts, services, experiences, victories, burdens and activities (1 Cor. 12:26),

---

* See section on "Science" in chapter 9.

being members one of another in the Spirit (Rom. 12:5; 1 Cor. 12). God has different purposes for His people at different times; and if He sends us to live in the city for His purpose (as He has at times done with those who author this book), then only by obeying that call can we truly enjoy the benefits of our relationship with the land, because the central lesson of the land is the lesson of place—that we must remain in our place as ordained by His purpose. Unless we abide where God places us (if we go to the land, when He sends us to the city), we cannot experience the true joy and blessing of being in our place for the simple reason that we are not. But if we will remain in our place *in God*, wherever that place may be at any given time, then we will participate in all the wisdom and blessings of the land-centered culture that God provides for His people: if we surrender all of *our* fields, then we will have the blessing of many fields, not only in the world to come but in this world as well (Mark 10:29-30). Confinement to city life, however, must result from God's call. We should not reside there because we love city life, but because God sends us to work His spiritual field there, as a service to Him and our fellowman, always with a view to calling a people *out* of Egypt to the God-centered culture. This same principle also provides our reason for living in the country.

Wherever we live out our physical lives, God wants to impart His relational knowledge to us in every sphere of our existence, bringing us into the realm of living, concrete relationships. He wants to free us from the illusion of detachment, of abstraction, where we fantasize that in and of ourselves we can do all things, while we actually accomplish nothing. We must realize that only *in Christ* can we do all things (Phil. 4:13), and to be in Christ is to be in our concrete, specific place in the corporate Body of His people, that Body He has prepared to do His will (1 Cor. 12:14-20; Heb. 10:5). He wants us to recognize, to use Berry's simple and cogent words, that for us as isolated individuals "the reach of responsibility is short," and that we must therefore join ourselves together and find our place *in Him*: in relationship to our fellowman, to the earth and most of all, and primarily, to God.[41] Only then can we accomplish God's purpose (Eph. 1:22-23) through the unlimited reach of the fullness of His *whole* corporate Body. For only God's reach is long enough to accomplish all that must be done. And God's reach on earth manifests itself only in that

Body comprised of those who recognize and submit to their individual limits of place. We must decrease to the limitations of what has been given us from heaven (John 3:27-29) in order that He might increase to express the fullness of Himself on earth (John 3:30). He wants to bring us together in true wholeness, relating all the elements of our being together in oneness—body, soul and spirit; and the land-centered culture provides the God-ordained setting for this to come to pass most fully in human life.

In every sphere, we must seek not abstract but relational knowledge, knowledge rooted not in "the mind" as "its *own* place" but in the place God determines. As Berry shows, only abstract knowledge that seeks to recreate the world in its own image makes of "mind . . . its own place." When man seeks this knowledge, he tries to usurp God's place rather than accepting the short reach of his own individual responsibility and submitting himself as a creature under God (Ps. 100:3; Rom. 12:4-5) to his limited place in that Body that in its wholeness can alone accomplish God's will. Such abstract knowledge, as we have seen, detaches us from reality, leading to atomization and fragmentation that can only be "overcome" through confusion, manipulation and coercion. In contrast, Hebraic knowledge brings us into relationship with reality and enables us to fulfill the limited reach of our responsibility in our proper place in the order of God (Ps. 131:1-2). At the foundation of this proper relationship lies our true submission to God and His order, our perfect submission to the limits God has ordained for every aspect of our existence: family, work, personal relationships, our functioning within the Body of believers and so on. Only by staying within our limits can we truly fulfill God's call to take dominion under Him for everything He has placed within our hands.

When well crafted into their proper forms, finely tuned and placed together in the right pattern, instruments bring forth beautiful music. God wants to make us, as individuals and as His corporate people, into such instruments, joining us together in proper relationship within the symphonic orchestra of His Temple so that His purpose can be fulfilled. For His purpose, He imparts His knowledge to us, to make us perfect expressions of Him, of His Spirit and His truth. Here lies the knowledge that we desire that God, through us and through our brothers and sisters in the Lord, would impart to our children. God desires to bring forth our children in integrated wholeness, to make them complete in Him, to bring them to the fulfillment of their whole beings in Him. But to be integrated, to have all the elements of one's being harmoniously acting as a unified whole, we must also keep ourselves *untouched* (which, as we have seen, renders the literal root meaning of *integer*, the root of *integrate*) by everything that God would separate us from. So the impartation of the positive vision and purpose of God must also mean that we exclude that which tears down that vision and purpose. Just as a sculptor brings forth the image of the statue by chipping away from the block of stone, so must we bring forth God's image in our children. Therefore, much as we prefer in this book to concentrate upon the positive vision of God, necessity requires that we for a while turn to that which we must chip away and exclude from our children's education.

CHAPTER THREE

Education
Forming the Child's Image

Information and Exclusion

In the pages above we have shown that true Christian education aspires to bring forth an integrated person, a person whose life fits together harmoniously within the song of Yahweh. The child becomes an individual, living temple, a living stone within the great corporate Temple of Yahweh. But to so tune our child's life that every part resonates harmoniously in an integrated song, we must, as we said, exclude certain things from his life, just as we must exclude discordant notes from the playing of a song. So when we speak of the covenant as the bounds within which God's knowledge flows to His people, we must remember that this covenant excludes things from, as well as includes other things within, its bounds. Marriage loses all meaning unless it excludes adultery: What is the purpose of marrying someone unless we in some way change our relationship with that person and others? Marriage joins us in a particular relationship with our wives or our husbands and precludes relationships of a certain kind with other people. Our covenant with God, through which His knowledge flows to us, proscribes other forms of knowledge, knowledge that would adulterate, pollute and defile the covenant and the image of God that flows through it. Otherwise, this marriage also loses all meaning.

Knowledge comes through information. More than merely some kind of neutral data, information, as its very etymology suggests, *forms* with*in* us the image of the one who informs us. We see this every day in the millions of Americans who, watching television for an average of six to eight hours a day, subconsciously or otherwise conform their lives to the image of those who inform them through television: to the opinions of news programmers and to the dress, habits, behavior and attitudes of characters on other TV programs.[1]

The Edenic covenant predicated God as man's exclusive source of information. God forbade man to eat from the tree of the *knowledge* of good and evil. This excluded knowledge not rooted in God, knowledge derived from a source other than man's Creator. So when man ate the forbidden tree's fruit, he destroyed the covenant's basis. No longer would God alone inform man; a source other than man's Creator would now sow its adulterated seed of alien knowledge in man's heart and mind. So man refused to remain faithful to God's covenant. He received satan's false information and partook of the tree of knowledge of good and evil and so was conformed to the image of his new informing source. Yet in order that every element of our being perfectly come together as one, every element must flow harmoniously from one source. Anything added from a source not in agreement with this Source produces discordance and fragmentation. The Fall introduced just such an incompatible source.

God desires to restore us to the covenant through which He alone informs us so that He can conform us to His image alone. Paul wrote:

> I am jealous for you with a godly jealousy. I promised you to one husband, to Christ, so that I might present you as a pure virgin to Him. But I am afraid that just as Eve was deceived by the serpent's cunning, your minds may somehow be led astray from your sincere and pure devotion to Christ. (2 Cor. 11:2-3)

And in Colossians he writes:

> I want you to know how much I am struggling for you and for those at Laodicea, and for all who have not met me personally. My purpose is that they may be encouraged in heart and united in love, so that they may have the full riches of complete understanding, in order that they may know the mystery of God, namely, *Christ, in whom are hidden all the treasures of wisdom and knowledge. . . . Make sure that no one traps you and deprives you of your* freedom by some *secondhand, empty, rational philosophy* based on *the principles of this world* instead of on Christ. (Col. 2:1-3, NIV; Col. 2:8, JB, emphasis added)

Fidelity to that covenant through which God informs our

children with His pure knowledge necessitates that we exclude the information the world would sow in their hearts. We must resist the world's informing of them with its adulterated seed of knowledge that opposes the relational knowledge of God. James warned the church against receiving such adulterated seed from the world:

> You are like unfaithful wives having illicit love affairs with the world and breaking your marriage vow to God! Do you not know that being the world's friend is being God's enemy? So whosoever chooses to be a friend of the world takes his stand as an enemy of God. Or do you suppose that the Scripture is speaking to no purpose that says, "The Spirit whom He has caused to dwell in us yearns over us—and He yearns for the Spirit to be welcome—with a jealous [that is, exclusive] love?" (James 4:4-5, Ampl.)

To raise our children according to God's perfect patterns, we must transmit all the knowledge necessary to conform our children to God's image, but we must also exclude everything that conforms them to any image other than God's. Again, only when we exclude everything that opposes God can we bring our children's lives to full consistency and wholeness. God promises us that if we will raise our children in accord with His patterns, if we will do His whole will in regard to their lives— teaching them all that He would have them to know and keeping them from everything that He would have us protect them from—*then* our children will remain rooted in His kingdom throughout their lives. They will not only serve Him gladly all their days* but will also become the true expression and manifestation in this world of His love, His very nature.

At the same time, the Bible emphatically warns about what will happen if we fail to fulfill our God-given function in the rearing of our children. Near the beginning of the description of Israel at the time of the judges, the Bible records this tragic statement:

> After that whole generation had been gathered to their fathers, *another generation grew up, who knew neither Yahweh nor what He had done for Israel.* Then the Israelites did evil in the eyes of Yahweh and served the Baals. (Judg. 2:10-11)

Our failure to train our children in the way that they should go,

---

* See Truth Forum's *Community and Family.*

to inform their minds and conform their lives to the living, relational knowledge of God, will deliver them into the hands of their enemy. We cannot wrestle against this enemy and for the minds and hearts of our children by using carnal weapons, as against flesh and blood; but we must pick up the weapons of our spiritual warfare and struggle against spiritual principalities and powers (2 Cor. 10:4; Eph. 6:12). If we renege upon our responsibilities, our children will not be made whole; they will become fragmented people, without integrity, unable to stand against the disintegration of the world—against the world's death.

We have no choice but to obey God in rearing our children. Nor can we raise them with *both* a secular *and* a Christian education. We cannot make them integrated and whole and at the same time also shape them (or willingly allow others to shape them) with information from warring and antagonistic sources. Jesus said that no man can serve two masters (Matt. 6:24). If we impart the positive knowledge of God in our fellowship meetings and in our homes but then send our children off to be adulterated by the seed of secular knowledge in the public schools six hours a day, five days a week, we will fracture, distort and even destroy the image of Christ in their lives. As we have said, if we sow conflicting information in their hearts, we prevent them from becoming integrated, *tamim* people. For this reason the scripture warns us *not* to even learn the way of the pagans, and to beware of being captured by the philosophies of man (Jer. 10:2; Col. 2:8). (Although, as we will see, once we establish our children in the knowledge of God, we can and even must teach them about false paths of knowledge so that they will be able to help free others and keep themselves from deception.)

We follow this pattern not because the knowledge of man proves more powerful than the knowledge of God. But the *natural inclination* of fallen man already tends strongly toward the man-centered way of thinking. That which falls, falls down—not up. Only the supernatural power of God can overcome this natural inclination. Jesus came and died to give us the supernatural power of His Spirit to set us free from our man-centered ways and to conform us to God's. If we ourselves deliberately send our children to be informed by a secular educational system, then what defense will our children have against the man-centered view of the world? No matter how much we might speak against what our children learn in these schools, by voluntarily sending our children to the public schools we give our approval through our deeds to these teachings. Our actions minimize the credibility of our verbal opposition. We then feed our children with fragmented knowledge that wars against the integrated wholeness God wants to bring forth in their lives. Even if absolutely no anti-Biblical teaching took place in the public schools (and certainly anti-Biblical views *are* taught there*), if we allow our children to be taught the lessons of history, the use of language, the tools of math and science, all without any mention of God or His Word, then we allow them, as we shall see more clearly momentarily, to be taught that God is irrelevant to many crucial areas of their lives. So they will come to see their relationship with Jesus Christ as a specialized, peripheral element—in other words, an adulterous affair—rather than both the very center and circumference of their lives.

In fact, to exclude Christian belief from the public schools inoculates children against Christianity more effectively than does open opposition. As Aldous Huxley said in his preface to *Brave New World*:

> The greatest triumphs of propaganda have been accomplished, not by doing something, but by refraining from doing. Great is truth, but still greater, from a practical point of view, is silence about truth. By simply not mentioning certain subjects . . . totalitarian propagandists have influenced opinion much more effectively than they could have done by the most eloquent denunciations, the most compelling of logical rebuttals.[2]

Sir Walter Moberly, former Chairman of the University Grants Committee in England, makes the same point specifically in regard to education:

> The modern university [or, in our case, the public education system] intends to be, and supposes it is, neutral, but it is not. Certainly, it neither inculcates nor expressly repudiates belief in God [although sometimes American public schools do even this†]. But it does what is far more deadly than open rejection; it ignores Him . . . . It is in

---

* See Truth Forum's *Conflict for Control: The Historical and Spiritual Background of the War for Our Children; Brave New Education: The Engineering of a New Society through the Indoctrination of Children* and *Humanism.*

† See *Brave New Education.*

this sense that the university to-day is atheistic . . . . It is a fallacy to suppose that by omitting a subject you teach nothing about it. On the contrary you teach that it is to be omitted, and that it is therefore a matter of secondary importance. And you teach this not openly and explicitly, which would invite criticism; you simply take it for granted and thereby insinuate it silently, insidiously, and all but irresistibly.[3]

C. S. Lewis also showed such subtle methods as even more effective than the open attempt to refute Biblical beliefs. Speaking of the authors (pseudonyms "Gaius and Titius") of a school textbook, Lewis remarks:

The very power of Gaius and Titius depends on the fact that they are dealing with a boy: a boy who thinks he is "doing" his "English prep" and has no notion that ethics, theology, and politics are all at stake. It is not a theory they put into his mind, but an assumption, which ten years hence, its origin forgotten and its presence unconscious, will condition him to take one side in a controversy which he has never recognized as a controversy at all.[4]

Another author, G. Richard Bozarth, writing in the November 1977 *American Atheist*, bluntly described the anti-Christian aims of a purely secular education:

And how does a god die? Quite simply because all his religionists have been converted to another religion, and there is no one left to make children believe they need him [but many are left to make the child feel dependent on the deified State and its priesthood of licensed experts].

Finally, it is irresistible—we must ask how we can kill the god of Christianity. *We need only insure that our schools teach only secular knowledge* . . . . If we could achieve this, god would indeed be shortly due for a funeral service. (emphasis added)[5]

Clearly, then, those who exclude Judeo-Christian values from the public schools make such schools into effective agencies to propagate anti-Christian beliefs.

Of course, those who believe that Christian children should be sent to public schools present many arguments in defense of their position. They claim, for example, (1) that this experience makes children even stronger in their faith, since it forces a child to contend for his faith against competing viewpoints; (2) that going to public school gives children the opportunity to be "witnesses"; and (3) that public school prepares children for the "real world," which, after all, includes the unbelieving millions.

All of these arguments (which we shall directly address later on*) ultimately rest upon one false assumption: the possibility of acquiring a religiously neutral education. Far from being religiously neutral, however, education is *always* religious. Religious suppositions lie at the foundation of all education; education always furthers either one religious faith or another.† In *Who Owns the Children?* we extensively document the religious nature of *all* education, so here we will only summarize some of the main points.

Education as Religion

In the first chapter of this book, we explained that whenever we teach anyone anything, we do more than simply teach him about some particular subject. To some extent, we actively shape that whole person. By its very nature, education molds human life. By teaching something, we proclaim its importance. We declare that we have something worth informing the individual with, some image, or aspect of an image, worth forming within him. And, at the same time, by teaching we also inescapably impart values and attitudes, for example, about neatness, diligence, patience, perseverance and so on. Education, then, by its very nature entails the shaping of values, beliefs, attitudes in, and the image of, the child. This is inescapable. As Stephen Arons has said, writing in an article published in the *Harvard Educational Review*:

> Whatever their values, most parents seem to recognize that a good deal of child rearing will take place at school and a great many basic *values* will be foisted on children there . . . . The effect of the school's molding of children's consciousness is to *alter their concept of reality* and, therefore, *their perception of and reaction to all things.* (emphasis added)[6]

Clearly, education molds and shapes the way children act and think.

In fact, education, even when not explicitly religious, often

---

* See "Christians and the Public Schools" in chapter 4.
† See also *Conflict for Control.*

tells much more about what a person really believes, about what he really values, than do his nominal religious professions of faith. So Philip H. Phenix, writing in a publication of the educational institution widely recognized as having the greatest impact on American public education, Columbia Teachers College, contends that

> a significant test of the governing religious convictions of a person or group is the character of the education promoted by that person or group.[7]

He sees the "field" of "education" as the sphere in which we implement our real (as opposed to professed) "religious commitments." Here we make "faith explicit in concrete act." When we insist that education *must* transmit particular knowledge to our children, we reveal what we really find of "ultimate concern."[8]

Just as the culture in which we nurture a plant—the type of soil, climate and so on—largely determines the plant's growth, so the culture in which we raise our children will largely determine their growth (Isa. 61:11; Mark 4:28). At the basis of every society we find a particular culture (or perhaps a number of different cultures that exist side by side), *culture* being defined by the Nobel-Prizewinning author T. S. Eliot as a "way of life."[9] This culture, or "way of life," will also reflect our values. The way we dress, the way we work, the types of relationships that form our families and so forth: all of these reflect what we value and find important for our lives.

Through our educational system—both its content and its form—we select special aspects of our culture to transmit to our children. Professor Emeritus Gail Inlow of Northwestern University explains that

> a social group first decides what in a *culture* is important and then has formal education transmit it to the young. Most fundamentally, education transmits the *values* that the social order lives by . . . . Simply stated, culture is the composite experiences of a social group. Formal education identifies and transmits the most important of these experiences to each new generation. (emphasis added)[10]

Through his education, then, we place a child in a specially prepared and formed culture to conform him to the values of the greater culture.

So education transmits our values and culture to a child, but both values and culture are inseparable from religion, as Phenix stated above. A number of other writers point to the religious ramifications of all culture. Eliot insisted that "culture and religion" are "different aspects of the same thing"; culture, he explained, is "our *lived* religion."[11] The award-winning secular luminary Ernest Becker similarly contended that "culture *means* that which is supernatural . . . ."[12] The "lived religion" of our culture reflects our true and deepest religious commitments, concerns and values. And just as we define culture in religious terms, so we cannot separate religion from the values of our culture: in his article on religion, in the *Encyclopedia of Philosophy*, Syracuse University professor William Alston quotes humanist A. E. Haydon as saying, "The heart of religion . . . is" man's search "for the *values* of the satisfying life."[13]

When Jesus proclaimed our duty to love God as the first and greatest commandment (declaring the love of one's fellow-man as secondary to this) and when He exhorted His followers to seek *first* the kingdom of God and that all other things would then be added unto them (Matt. 6:33), He gave instructions about a priority of *values*. He told us what we should consider most important, not only in the world to come but in this world as well. Our religious commitments therefore supply the source of our values. *Religion*, rooted in the Latin word *ligare*, means "to bind together." Religion (as numerous scholars, both secular and believing, have shown) does not necessarily entail theistic faith in the transcendent God but simply that which gives our lives meaning, purpose, direction, that highest value which binds men together in a community that pursues common goals and a common destiny. Our real supreme value (in contrast to professed values), the one manifested in our daily lives, identifies our religion. Religions may thus assume either secular or theistic forms. In contemporary America, secular value systems become the religions that, through the compulsory programs of the public schools, "bind" people "together" in an unspoken covenant of common (though always changing) values*—whether economic, po-

---

* The U.S. Supreme Court justified State power to compel education in just such terms:

    A society . . . may in self-protection utilize the educational process for inculcating those almost unconscious feelings which *bind men together* in a comprehending loyalty, whatever may be their lesser differences and difficulties. (emphasis added)[14]

litical, social or philosophical—common values that the people themselves only seldom recognize as the source of their own indoctrination. Indeed, John Dewey, who more greatly influenced American public education than any other twentieth-century humanist philosopher,* went so far as to find supernatural beliefs such as Christianity "encumbrances" to genuine religion.[15] By the latter he meant his own secular humanist philosophy.[16] He hoped that through compulsory public education his belief system would ultimately become the sole "religious faith," "the common faith of mankind"[17] that would "realize the [S]tate as one Commonwealth of truth."[18]

But some authors contend that values do not necessarily tie into any single specific religious system, and certainly different belief systems do hold some values in common. Moreover, people who claim no belief in any spiritual or religious authority beyond man himself do generally hold various values, sometimes very fervently. A plurality of people would probably agree, at least publicly, that people should be honest, should not physically harm others, should keep their word, should allow those with whom they disagree to express their views, should not steal and so on. And a number of other such values come to mind that the vast majority of people might likely ascribe to.

Yet even these statements raise a number of important questions. For example, where do these values come from? Are they traditional or rational? If traditional, then all that we must do to render them impotent as common values that everyone can hold to in spite of differing religious beliefs is to undermine the value or validity of the tradition itself, to merely show that it is arbitrary and not absolute. If we claim that the origins of these values lie in their rationality, we can again ask if the source of this rationality offers absolute or relative standards. Can one *ever* harm others physically, *ever* lie, *ever* steal and so on? Once we raise this question, tremendous disagreements inevitably arise, even over those things that we ostensibly think we agree upon. Many people may permit lying at times, but others never will. How then shall we teach this value in the schools: as absolutely true, or only relatively so? If we say, "Lying is wrong, but some people say you must never

* See *Humanism.*

lie while others say that sometimes you should," then we teach not an absolute value but rather either the relativist view or, ultimately, no permanent values at all. In the latter case, we merely present value choices for the student to arbitrarily make for himself. This at best merely avoids the problem of whether we can teach values in the schools. In fact, as we have shown elsewhere, this approach really teaches the relativist view of humanism and the latter's underlying, unspoken religious values;* for it tells the child that no absolute standard should guide his beliefs but rather that he must simply choose his values for himself.

Ultimately, however, we cannot teach values merely as arbitrary individual, or arbitrary sets of, positive or negative precepts. We cannot simply say that we should not kill, but we must also give some reason for this value. Why shouldn't we kill: because we find killing impolite (but then according to whose etiquette, and are all standards equally valid?); because we wouldn't like someone to kill us (then if we can murder without being caught, is it all right?); because we find it socially unacceptable (whose society, and are all societies equally valid according to their own criteria—for instance, the Nazis?); because we find it "unreasonable" (but then according to whose reasons?); because God has forbidden it (which god, and are all gods created equal)? Without an explanation, we can merely crank out values in arbitrary, mechanical formulas that our children learn to parrot like talking computer cash registers and that they can then choose to reject or accept according to their own relativist whims and standards. Such formulas prove powerless to bring the individual to a place of self-control. Instead, they bring a relativist chaos that finally necessitates the external compulsion of the State. (Such formulas can also, as a "dead" disease injected into a living body, "inoculate" the child *against* receiving the reality of internalized absolute values.) It seems obvious that such value instruction can hold no *internal* compulsion for the individual and loses all power as a standard or value, except insofar as it connects to the *external* compulsion of brute force. Then these foundationless values merely serve, in the crises they consequently produce, as justifications for increasing the powers of the State to totalitarian proportions, as it steps in to

---

* See *Humanism* and *Brave New Education*.

remedy the anarchy of the arbitrary—that very anarchy and chaos that it and its institutions have themselves produced.

When we obscure the relationship between values and their necessary foundations, our value instruction becomes, at best, ineffective. We must present some reason for values if children are to grow to become morally responsible individuals with an *internal* standard of value that will enable them to act rightly even without external compulsion. Yet no one can explain why we live according to certain values without making statements that raise the question of religious authority.

For the humanist, who holds man himself as the ultimate source of authority for all values—the equivalent of a god— this appears as no problem. Values are simply what benefits men and their society. Surely those who hold to Judeo-Christian beliefs, for example, must hold to this same idea of the good, the humanist will assert, whatever "additional" ideas of the good they may ascribe to. Yet leaving aside the fact that people strongly disagree as to what is good for people and their society, and that the Judeo-Christian view sees as essential certain values that the humanist either actively opposes or remains, at best, indifferent to, the Bible believer still holds as central the notion that values must find their roots in the authority of God. To separate values from God, in the Biblical view, destroys their ultimate foundation and serves as the very dynamic of the idolatry of worshiping the thing expressed apart from the One who expresses it. In fact, the humanist also has a root of authority for his value system—man. So we have finally a question of conflict between man's authority or God's. This is not peripheral to religion but the ultimate religious question. It is the question of the third chapter of Genesis.

We cannot separate values from this question of the ultimate source of authority. One will inevitably mention it, even if only to say, "You must do this to be nice to people" or so on. Even statements like the latter presuppose a religious foundation for our morality, namely, the man-centered religion of humanism in the guise of our own concern for our image in the public eye.* From the Biblical view, we undermine values if we teach them without acknowledging their source in God. Without this foundation, they become merely the arbitrary choices of men,

---

* For an extensive discussion of the religious nature of humanism see *Humanism*.

which they accept or reject at their own discretion or whim. The humanist believes we should present values in this way because his religious presupposition gives preeminence to man's decisions while viewing the will of God as a mere illusion. Certainly, the humanist should be free to believe as he wishes and to teach his children what he believes, but we cannot teach values without either embracing or rejecting his viewpoint: neutrality will always elude us, simply because it does not exist. At best, it can only degenerate into a confusion. Every educational system, then, must base itself upon some religious value system and must entail the rejection of rival religious value systems.

In fact, the very nature of an educational institution reflects the religious value system that it seeks to perpetuate. For example, the State's public schools, with their structure of mass socialization, lead to the exaltation of the authority of the peer group,[19] to making the people as God, and so ultimately lead to the exaltation of the corporate embodiment of the deified people—the State—which nurtures and raises the children through its schools.* In contrast, the family setting of the home school leads to the honoring of mother and father and, through them, to the honoring of the child's ultimate origins, the Creator God. By its very nature, the home school rests upon the intimate personal relationships of the family and so provides the natural setting for the impartation of Hebraic, relational knowledge, which brings forth a whole, integrated individual. But the "factory-like"[20] atmosphere of the public schools, with their bell-ringing class changes and assembly-line attendance counts, provides a conducive framework for treating students as the objects of pagan objective knowledge (though not even that type of knowledge is effectively transmitted in these schools anymore†). Such schools can only bring forth fragmented people whose sole coherence lies in the brute compulsion of the State.

Every element of the educational process reflects the spiritual values it transmits. So Professor Gilmer Blackburn in his study on Nazi education explains that modern totalitarian States, modeling their policies after Rousseau's proposals in

---

* See "State School or Home School?" in chapter 4.

† See Truth Forum's *Crime of Compulsory Education: Documenting the Battle Casualties of the Education War and the Case for Untrammeled Private Education.*

his *Considerations on the Government of Poland*, invariably follow "collective, never individual,"[21] educational methods.* In other words, the type of individual, personal instruction involved in home education by its very nature undermines the principles of the totalitarian State. Mass collective educational systems furnish the perfect condition for inculcating Statist conformity, whereas the private environment of the home school discourages such conformity and so always becomes the object of the attacks of tyrants. (Of course, we sometimes do need *voluntary*, community educational activities within the context of a voluntary Christian society, but this differs radically from compulsory collective activities.) In contrast, the educational system of the corporate State must be restricted to those kinds of mass collective activities that breed adherence to the State itself.† Its collective represents the forced fusing together of disparate elements—the Babylon‡ of "confusion"—rather than the cohesive integration that we find among the members of the corporate Body of Christ when they voluntarily conform to God's patterns. Because true Christian education brings forth men and women of wholeness, of integrity, these individuals prove resistant to totalitarian efforts to create conformist masses. In contrast, Statist education produces vulnerable, fragmented men easily fused together in that Babylonian confusion that finds its penultimate expression in totalitarianism.

So the education system, both its content and form, reflects the fundamental values of its culture, of its "lived religion." Through the education system, the culture reproduces its view of "ultimate concern" in the lives of those who shall carry forward the torch of that culture. Through education, the individual undergoes a "genuine religious conversion"[23] (as one leading international secular educator has described what he regards as true education) that conforms the student to the basic world view and beliefs of the culture that nurtures

---

* In his *Emile*, Rousseau presents his educational philosophy through the story of a private tutor teaching one boy. But this simply provides Rousseau with the most effective means for showing how he believed his educational philosophy would transform a human life; it doesn't serve as the model of educational methods he recommends.[22]

† See "Socialization" in chapter 4 for a discussion of the destructive effects of public school socialization.

‡ See *Culture as Spiritual War*.

him. This then religiously "binds" him to others whom education similarly brings together in this value system.

Conflicts about education, then, become essentially conflicts about what the basic world view or religion of a culture, or of the people in a culture, will be. As we have said, the whole culture of a people constitutes its real, as distinct from its merely professed, religion. We can see this in the example of Nazism, which sought to recreate Germany into a "total culture" based around the cult of Hitler worship.[24] As Professor George L. Mosse has said,

> National Socialism was . . . no mere "political" movement but a total way of life; both the natural order and salvation were contained within its world view.[25]

In their efforts to create a new culture based upon this new world view, the Nazis believed it essential "to substitute their world view for Christianity."[26] To do this, "the education of youth was the key . . . ."[27] Because it was a "total culture," seeing itself as the salvation of its citizens (much as those do who profess such concern over the welfare of any children who fail to undergo public education), the Nazis could allow no truly separate and free—truly private—alternative to their educational system.

The Nazis consistently attempted to undermine "Germany's churches and independent schools," which "were considered a major barrier to the total acceptance of Hitlerism and were to be eliminated at the earliest moment so that the 'enlightenment' of the German people about the glories of National Socialism could be complete."[28] The Nazis also sought to replace classes in "religious instruction" in the State schools with classes in "ideological instruction," that is, Nazism.[29] School authorities made a systematic effort throughout the country to force children into these Nazi programs. Hitler, as do many supporters of public education in America today, considered the children of Germany to belong neither to God nor to their parents but to himself and the State as the true embodiment of "the People."[30] So he desired to create an educational system that would conform them completely to the Nazi image, a system free from any vestiges of Christian influence.[31] The struggle to conform children to the Nazi religion took place, above all, through education. Today we see other cultures with equally ostensibly non-religious political programs for the salvation and welfare of man that work far more subtly than Nazism. But their identical words, attitudes and actions in attempting to eradicate private education reveal that the same spiritual dynamic and principles lie behind all such programs.* This same struggle rages in America today.

So we can see the religious character of all education. Since law, as interpreted by the American judiciary, forbids the public schools from reflecting the value system of Judeo-Christianity, this leaves a religious vacuum that must be filled by Judeo-Christianity's spiritual opponents. In America today, as we have shown extensively elsewhere, the humanist faith, a faith that places man at the center of all values (just as the Nazi faith did),* fills this vacuum.†

For Christians to deliberately send their children to such schools makes no more sense than to send them to Buddhist monasteries or Shiite Muslim academies or, more to the point, Nazi schools. Christian children did not become "witnesses" when they donned the brown shirt and joined the Hitler Youth Movement and attended Nazi schools: the Nazis brainwashed and converted them into brutal instruments of the State. Similarly, we today do not make our children "witnesses" by sending them to the seminaries of rival religious creeds, nor do we strengthen their beliefs by indoctrinating them during the most impressionable years of their lives in the values of a religious system antagonistic to Christianity. God spoke to Haggai and said:

> "Ask the priests what the law says: If a person carries consecrated meat in the fold of his garment, and that fold touches some bread or stew, some wine, oil or other food, does it become consecrated?"
> The priests answered, "No."
> Then Haggai said, "If a person defiled by contact with a dead body touches one of these things, does it become defiled?"
> "Yes," the priests replied, "it becomes defiled."
> Then Haggai said, "'So it is with this people and this nation in my sight,' declares Yahweh. 'Whatever they do and whatever they offer there is defiled.'" (Hag. 2:11-14)

When we send our children to public school, they do not con-

---

* See *Holocaust as Spiritual War.*
† See *Humanism.*

secrate the school, but the school defiles our children:

Do not be misled: "Bad company corrupts good character." (1 Cor. 15:33)

We break down the protective wall of covering—the wall of the covenant—around our children; we violate our covenant with them and with God, by sending them to the public schools and inviting the world to form our child's image. When we send our children to these schools, we do not manifest God's light and truth, but we defile our covenant with God. We simply fall into the trap Paul warned of when he said, "I am afraid that just as Eve was deceived by the serpent's cunning, your minds may somehow be led astray from your sincere and pure devotion to Christ" (2 Cor. 11:3); and again when he said, "Make sure that no one traps you and deprives you of your freedom by some secondhand, empty, rational philosophy based on the principles of this world instead of on Christ" (Col. 2:8, JB). Such is the deceit of the rationalistic philosophy of humanism rampant in the public schools.

Indeed, when we send our children to public schools, we transgress the direct commandments of God (Prov. 22:6; Jer. 10:2); and in the trusting eyes of our children, we sanction the authority of those in the public schools who indoctrinate them against God. We send them, in short, through the fires of Moloch (2 Kings 23:10).* When they then depart from the values and religion which we claim to hold so dear, we become bewildered and confused as we search for an explanation. But the only explanation is that we have simply been beguiled by satan's cunning.

Even when we believe that deliberate exposure to a disease offers a valid prevention, we do not send our children to the quarantine ward to combat the disease, but rather we raise them in good health and then expose them to controlled doses of the disease, perhaps via inoculation, so that they can build up their resistance (although recent medical studies have shown that the introduction of even such small doses of disease through inoculation can sometimes prove extremely dangerous, having been found to cause serious brain damage

---

* During times of apostasy, Israel often forced their children to pass through the fires of Moloch. The name in the Hebrew text "carries the article suggesting that the word may have been an appellative for 'the one who rules.'"[32] It was, in other words, a looking to the power of the State as the altar upon which to sacrifice children.

or even death[33]). In the same way, to strengthen our children against false faiths, we cannot send them for the major portion of every day in the most formative years of their lives to be raised in those faiths; rather, we must raise them in the faith of the Messiah and expose them to false faiths in controlled dialectical* doses in a context that enables them to resist the falsehood.

No person dedicated to the secular-humanist view would ever think of sending his child to a Christian school in order to indoctrinate him against Christianity. But largely because of our willingness to accept this deceptive, convoluted and compromising reasoning, which induces Christians to send their children through the fires of secular education, we have seen the decline of Christian influence in society during the past decades. This same mistaken belief has contributed to the tremendous cultural, spiritual and social gap that increasingly separates every new generation from the more traditional values of the former ones. (We call all this "progress," but as Aristotle pointed out, progress must have some goal, and the only goal this seems to have is a kind of backwards running downhill with an eye only on how fast we leave the past behind.) Again, those who hold views against Judeo-Christianity would never send their children to the Christian religious schools to "strengthen" their resistance against that religion. They know only too well that education in a Christian school would inculcate Christian beliefs and would undermine secular beliefs. The same holds true in reverse for the children of believers. By sending their children to secular schools, Christians undermine Christian belief.

When we recognize that Christian education aspires not simply to impart particular skills or facts but rather to bring forth an integrated, an "untouched," whole man or woman, then we must also recognize that our child's education must be *exclusively* Christian, for only in Christ do all things consist (Col. 1:17, KJV). Outside of Him lies fragmentation, dissolution and death. By touching our child with fragmented secular knowledge, we encourage the process of "disintegration" in his life; we touch him with death. We can only bring forth the nurturing, educational culture that will produce *tamim* individuals by bringing *all* elements of our children's education

---

* See pp. 215-19 for the explanation of our use of this term here.

together in Messiah. Only by excluding everything not "in Christ" can we eliminate all those discordant elements that prevent the full harmony of the song of Yahweh from coming forth in our children's lives.

Separation unto God

As we have seen, the covenant through which God joins Himself to His people and His people to one another, through which He informs His people with His relational knowledge, also *excludes* other forms of knowledge. Jesus Christ desires to transform His people into a separate nation (Num. 23:9; 1 Pet. 2:9). Most of us admit that we should not partake of this world ourselves (Exod. 23:32; 34:12; Josh. 23:7; Esther 3:8; Isa. 52:11; Eph. 5:11; 2 Cor. 6:14-18; Rev. 18:4; James 4:4, Ampl.). Since, as we will see, education really amounts to *discipleship*, how much less can we as parents entrust our children's education to nonbelievers? The public school system is designed for the purpose of conforming children to the image of secular culture, not the image of Christ. The ameliorating presence of possible Christian teachers and administrators within this system does nothing to alter this basic purpose. Even if our child's public school teacher or principal is a Christian, the system in which child, teacher and principal all study and work serves—*by law*—the purpose of discipleship in secularism.*

God's Word divides (Heb. 4:12). By its very nature, that Word demands separation: God *speaks*, "Let there be light," and then He "*separates*" the light from the darkness (Gen. 1:3-4). His *Word* brings forth the light and immediately *divides* the light from the darkness. This first recorded utterance of God sets the pattern for all subsequent words that come forth from Him:[34] each Word brings light, and this light demands separation from the darkness. "Sharper than any double-edged sword," God's *Word* "penetrates even to *dividing* soul and spirit, joints and marrow" (Heb. 4:12). Jesus, the Word made flesh (John 1:14), proclaimed that He had come to bring division on the earth (Luke 12:51). Yet this *negative* separation of the godly from the profane (the latter word literally

---

* See *Humanism, Conflict for Control* and *Brave New Education*.

meaning, "in front of the temple" or "outside the temple") serves, in addition, a positive function. For while God's Word separates the profane and ungodly from that truly of God, this division provides the context wherein that which remains, the godly, can come together "in the dispensation of the fullness of times," just as the act of *separating* the waters from the land brought forth the dry land (Gen. 1:9-10). What belongs to God must separate from that not of Him if we would have God "*gather* together in one all things in Christ, both which are in heaven, and which are on earth; even in Him" (Eph. 1:10, KJV). When God *gathers* "together . . . all things in Christ," He will only *gather* those things that are *of* Christ, which means, again, that He must *separate* out all those things that are *not* of Christ (Matt. 13:24-30, 36-43, 47-50). So, a certain type of division forms the very essence of godly unity. Since the patches of darkness that mar the lives of God's people are what create the divisions among us, we can come to true unity only as each of us races as rapidly as possible *into* the light and *away* from these areas of darkness. Only this division, this separating of our lives from all darkness, will allow us to "walk in the light, as He is in the light," so that we may "have fellowship with one another" (1 John 1:7). Only this division will bring unity. Only this fellowship in the light—made possible by our radical separation from the darkness—will bring us all together as that city set on a hill that cannot be hid (Matt. 5:14). Without this negative separation from darkness, the "complete oneness" of God's people that Jesus prayed for in John 17 cannot come forth; for this oneness by definition excludes anything that would pollute our divine *comm-union* (meaning literally, "oneness with"). Again, in this sense, separation provides the key to unity.

Yet God's exclusion of the profane, His separation of everything of God from everything antagonistic to God, presents us with a still more positive purpose. For, as we shall explain, this same process of separation both cuts off that which must be excluded while it also brings forth the conditions necessary for God to pour His abiding life into His people.

Jesus, the Word made flesh, who came to bring division (Luke 12:51), proclaimed Himself to be the light of the world (John 8:12). The Scriptures also speak of the Word of God as a light (Ps. 119:105). When we look at the separation process brought forth through the workings of natural light, we can learn something about how the supernatural light of God's Word separates. As we said above, in the beginning, God created the light and then *"separated"* the light from the darkness (Gen. 1:3-4). Light and darkness mutually exclude each other (2 Cor. 6:14). They can only relate to one another through antipathy, contrast, opposition. In this opposition, darkness never penetrates light; light always penetrates and dispels darkness. When light fully comes forth, darkness ends (Luke 11:36). So greater light makes for less darkness. Yet, as we shall explain, only through this contrast of light and darkness can we perceive value, color and form. Even an elementary textbook on painting teaches us that the secrets of the successful use of the complexities of color lie in the artist's ability to *first* see the varying values of black and white upon which the successful use of color depends (art defines value as the ascending degree of contrast between black and white, between darkness and light).[35] Similarly, for the human eye, the play of light against dark models all forms into discernible shapes. So we can also say that form only emerges through the contrast of light and darkness. (Try a simple experiment with grass: if you look at a yard closely, you will see that what makes the green appear as grass is the texture and what the eye perceives as texture is made up of contrast between light and dark where the minute forms of the individual blades pick up light and cast shadows.) Without the *contrast* between black and white, that is, their mutual exclusion and opposition, we could discern no value and therefore see no variation in color nor any form. If all were light (if such were even possible in our world) or if all were darkness (as very often occurs in the case when clouds shut out even the light of the night's moon and stars), we would have no contrast between dark and light, and so we could never discern any form or, in the case of the darkness, any color at all.

Just as the very shining forth of natural light on anything of substance (like the moon, for instance) automatically creates contrast to and separation from the natural surrounding darkness, so when God's light shines forth through His Word on people of substance, it must bring forth greater spiritual separation from the darkness of the world. As the greater light of the Word shines amid the darkness, the contrast between light and darkness becomes clearer, and through this increasing contrast, the *form* onto which the light pours, the form of the

Body of Christ, also becomes delineated with greater clarity from the surrounding world. As the contrasting "values" increase, the form of the Body of Christ grows more visible to all, as does its detailed diversity—that is, its texture and "color." As we have seen, the form of the covenant is what defines the Body; and the Word—that is, the light—of God comes forth in its fullness only within the context of this covenant form. But as this light, this Word, comes forth more clearly within this covenant form, the form itself must also become more distinct from the contrasting darkness: in its form and character then, the covenant becomes increasingly marked off from the world with ever greater clarity. So we see that the path of increasing light, of increasing truth, must also become a path of increasing separation: through the increasingly precise covenant it evermore excludes the world and consecrates itself unto the Lord. The covenant then delineates our path of separation, and the greater light enables us to see and follow this path more exactly. Finally, as we walk out this path of separation and exclusion, the form of everything included within the Body of Christ—namely, each of our individual lives and the relationships that tie those lives together—must also emerge with greater clarity and consistency.

In the witness of creation, we see this continual theme of the emergence of form through the process of separation. In the beginning, the creation was "formless" and "empty" (Gen. 1:2). The world was "empty" or "void" because without "form" there is nothing to fill full. Then God brought forth the light and separated it from the darkness (Gen. 1:4). Light then emerges into form in its separation from and contrast to the darkness: as in the sun, the moon, the stars. The form of day emerges from the night. The form of the moon and stars came forth only in contrast and opposition to the darkness of the night. God also *separated* the waters above the firmament from the waters below (Gen. 1:6-7), and He *separated* the dry ground from the seas (Gen. 1:9-10). Through this process of separation from formlessness emerged the form of the earth: the form of the lower heavens, the form of the seas, the intricate forms of the land. Within the context of this form, God brought forth the abundant content of life: the fish and sea creatures emerged within the form of the sea; vegetation and land animals emerged within the form of the earth; birds emerged within the form of the atmosphere (Gen. 1:11-12, 20-22, 24-

25). The form of the day fills with the life-giving light of the sun; the form of the night holds the life-guiding lights of the moon and stars for the hours of darkness; all these lights further divide the content of man's journey on earth into the form of seasons, days and years, offering to guide his life into its place in the rhythms of creation, its place in the fullness of the day's light. God's work of separation then brought forth the form that He could fill full with the content of His abundant blessings of life. This positive work of gathering the dry land together, of gathering the light, must mean separation: separation inevitably means gathering, and a gathering together into life-filled form necessarily means separation from the empty void of formlessness and death.

Again, when God gathers that which belongs to Him, He must inevitably separate out all that does not belong to Him. God's Word brought forth separation within His creation to give definition to the formless earth: outlines, contours and boundaries—even in details—emerged. God's Word divided creation, giving order that put everything in its proper place and giving forms into which the content of life could then be poured forth. The form had to be gathered together and separated through the contrast of light and darkness before it could be filled full with the content of life.

Similarly, the exclusivity of the marriage covenant establishes a clear form, a relationship between a man and woman, that God then fills with new life, as children issue forth from and are nurtured and reared within this form.

Life can only be manifest through form: without blood coursing through the veins, the form of the human body becomes a mere corpse, a dead form that holds no meaning, no life; but without the form of a human body neither does the life residing in the blood have a means to relate with, to communicate with, the community of life around it—it has nothing to keep it from splattering in the dust and dissipating upon the ground. Form ties the community of life together through the communication that only form can give. Moreover, form provides the framework for the maintenance of life, which requires a membrane, a skin, a covering. If we violate this covering form or break it, infection and death can overtake life. Again, the covenant supplies the covering form that contains the life of Christ (Isa. 28:18-20, NKJV; Eph. 1:22-23; Col. 2:9, NKJV, NIV). This new covenant provides an inviolate covering that protects God's life from the corruption of man, that gives His life definition, dimension and depth. By its exclusion of everything that can harm the Body, the covenant protects the soundness, health and integrity of the Body.

As we have seen, God's Word and light brought separation in the natural world. This in turn brought forth forms that could then be filled with the content of His life. So in His spiritual creation—His new creation (2 Cor. 5:17)—God's Word separates His people from the world, bringing forth His church, His *ekklesia*, meaning literally the "out-called," those called out of, separated and sanctified from, the world by His Word (John 15:19; 17:6, 16-17; 2 Cor. 6:17; 1 Pet. 2:9). And, again, He separates in order to bring forth a form that can be filled with all the fullness of His riches and mercy: "the church, which is His Body, the fullness of Him who fills everything in every way" (Eph. 1:22-23). So the bringing together, the gathering of God's people within a form, the form of the Body of Christ, must mean their separation from the world.

God has called His people "out of darkness into His wonderful light. Once you were not a people, but now you are the people of God" (1 Pet. 2:9-10). Before God's light shines into our lives, the people of God are a no-people dispersed throughout the world, indistinguishable from the world, *fused with* the world in its darkness, "without form and void," "not a people," mired in the *confusion* from which Babylon derives its name.[36] Then when His Word comes forth into our lives, when His light shines into our darkness, that light increasingly separates us from the world which would bury our godly identity. Through this separation, God brings forth a distinct people bound together within the form of His covenant, a form that can now contain the abundant life that He desires to shed forth within human hearts (John 10:10). God has called out a holy people unto Himself, a people of light *separated* from the darkness of the world within the covering walls of the covenant, brought together within a form that allows us to continually grow with the blessings of increase and fruitfulness (1 Pet. 2:9; John 15:2, 8).

We must follow in the faith of Abraham (Rom. 4:12), whom God brought out from Ur, separated from the world, joined to the form of His covenant so that God could bless him and make of him "a great nation" (Gen. 12:1-2). Because he remained untouched by the world, Abraham could become *tamim*—integral, whole (Gen. 17:1); and we too must be an integral, untouched people. The Scriptures call the church a "holy nation," a "peculiar people," belonging to God (1 Pet. 2:9, KJV), a people called out from this world (John 15:19). God's light has shone forth upon us and works even now to separate us from everything that would tarnish or obscure that light, bringing us forth as a shining city set upon a hill, a beacon to those still in darkness (Matt. 5:14-16; 1 Pet. 2:9). He calls us to walk through the darkness on the path of faith. His Word shines on this path as a lamp unto our feet (Ps. 119:105), illuminating our path in this darkness as step by step we move forward in ever-increasing light (Prov. 4:18), a light that leads to Him, the light of the world. Every time His Word comes to us, it illuminates a little more of the path that we must walk. As His light shines in our pathway and we step into that light, conforming our lives to the pattern that His Word reveals, we at the same time take another step out of the darkness as we leave further behind the patterns and ways of the world. Every step forward in our walk in the light therefore automatically separates us increasingly from the world of darkness. This light shines before us with ever-increasing intensity as we follow that path of the righteous, which, as the first gleam of dawn, grows ever brighter until it becomes the full light of day (Prov. 4:18), until the daystar rises and shines forth fully within our hearts (2 Pet. 1:19). This continuous walking in the light *is* Biblical faith (John 3:20-21). God leads us out of "the valley of the *shadow* of death" toward the One who contains "no variableness or *shadow* of turning" until we completely separate from the darkness and conform to the form of His own image as manifest in the eternal life of His Son (Rom. 8:29).

So, contrary to those who suggest that Christian parents should not "insulate" or separate their children from the world but should rather allow them to be "socialized"* by public schools, the Word of God enjoins us to separate from the world not only our children but also ourselves as well (2 Cor. 6:14-18; James 4:4, Ampl.). Yet we do not separate in order to withdraw in fear. A positive momentum impels our separation, for we withdraw in order that we may draw *unto* the Lord (James 4:8). Our "separation" from the world and its darkness becomes our

---

* See "Socialization" in chapter 4 for further discussion of this point.

"gathering" unto God and His light. We shut out the information of the world that would conform our children to the world's dark image in order that they might conform wholly to Him who will inform them from that treasury in which all the "jewels of wisdom and knowledge are hidden" (Col. 2:3-4, JB). Just so will He bring them to that wholeness and fulfillment that only He can bring forth in human lives. Those who see our withdrawal from the informing power of the world as negative in cause and effect prejudge faith on the basis of unbelief. When they couple this assumption with the compulsory power of the State, they cannot escape violating religious conscience in a way that can only lead to the tyrannizing of all human conscience by the State.

Moreover, anything anyone does for his child can be looked upon in just such a negative light: by feeding our children, we "protect" them from hunger; by housing our children, we "shelter" them from the elements; by loving them, we offer them "refuge" from the world's hate; by teaching them, we "insulate" them from ignorance. Yes, by raising them at home we do—so far as lies in our power—"shelter" and "insulate" and "protect" them from ungodliness. But raising them in godliness (if done in complete consistency) by definition shelters them from ungodliness, just as feeding them well (if done completely consistently) automatically "shelters" them from malnutrition. Those *not* so "sheltered" have become anything but independent, confident, free-thinking individuals. Their insecure, unloved lives have shriveled and withered in overexposure to the world's harshest elements. That a "sheltered" life for children, such as that we speak of here, has become a stigma offers a fitting comment on the increasing barbarism of our age. And it explains the dubious distinction that our generation holds in becoming the first in the history of the world to witness suicide become pandemic among teenagers.[37] Would to God someone had "sheltered" them!

Ultimately, only as we actively seek to *positively* fulfill our places within God's kingdom can He fully answer all our questions about His will for our lives, both the specifics of our own lives and the general principles that must guide a Christian's relationship to (and separation from) the world. God shines His light into our lives both to call us out of the confusion of Babylon and to bring us into the positive fulfillment of our place in His kingdom. His light illuminates a form for our lives that we must fill full. And only as we fill this place in the Body can we as Christians come into our proper God-centered relationship with the world. Unless we walk in ali the light of revelation by which God illuminates our path, all the light leading us to what He has ordained for us, we will be reabsorbed back into the dark confusion of the world (John 12:35-36). By fulfilling the positive revelation that God's light has illuminated to us of what we must become in God, by walking in that revelation, we will also define the negative limits of our relationship to the world, for example, our relationship with the business systems of the world, with the political systems, with the media institutions, with the social systems and so on. If we attempt to define these things negatively first, then we will be merely reacting to the world, as Christians so frequently have in the past; but if we define our relationships to these things from the perspective of fulfilling the positive image of Christ that God brings forth in our lives as we find our place of service within His Body, then we will pursue the positive spiritual road.

Through Christian education we aim, then, primarily not for an attack upon public education but rather toward the positive fulfillment of our God-ordained task to train our children in the "way they should go." Since this "way" entails a whole life in complete oneness and harmony, we must create a special nurturing habitat, which in turn excludes public education. It is the public school system that has launched an offensive to annihilate this Christian education, not the other way around.*

Nevertheless, we must separate from the world so that we may join ourselves unto God (James 4:4, Ampl.), and this so that He may conform us to His image—"ye shall be holy; for I am holy" (Lev. 11:45, KJV). Although a wife enters into other relationships besides that with her husband, a unique level of covenant relationship with her husband nonetheless remains; and if she transgresses this, she becomes an adulteress. The same holds true in our relationship with God (Eph. 5:23-27): we may have a relationship with the world (1 Cor. 5:10), but we must keep that relationship strictly within the limits defined by our covenant with God. As we have seen before, if we transgress those limits, we become spiritual adulterers and adulteresses (James 4:4, Ampl.). Yet public education demands

---

* See Truth Forum's *Who Owns the Children?: Compulsory Education and the Dilemma of Ultimate Authority* and *The Crime of Compulsory Education.*

precisely this adultery. The Scriptures tell us that we should allow our hearts to be sown only with the incorruptible seed of the Word of God (1 Pet. 1:23). And Paul says that he fears lest our "minds may somehow be led astray from . . . sincere and pure devotion to Christ," for we have been "espoused" as a "pure virgin" to Him. Public education sows just such an adulterated seed within the minds of our children, leading them astray from sincere and pure devotion to Christ. Again, when something informs us, it forms its image within us; so whatever informs us conforms us to its image. When God alone "informs" us by His Word, then He alone forms the image within us that our lives will assume. But when unbelievers and the world inform us, they conform us to their image. If we receive such latter information, we violate the limitations set on our relationships by our marriage covenant with Christ: we allow corruptible seed to penetrate our hearts and minds, thus informing us with seed of the world. The world's image is then conceived, formed and finally brought to fruition within us, alongside Christ's. Herein lies precisely the "con-fusion," the adultery, of Babylon.

Some Christian parents claim that passing through the fires of public school strengthens their children's relationship with God (much as the early Israelites no doubt claimed about Moloch, Jer. 32:35). But does an adulterous relationship strengthen a wife's covenant with her husband? Can we play with fire and not get burned (Prov. 6:27)? After all, adulterers and adulteresses have also justified their broken covenants with similar excuses: "trying out" other partners helps them to know how much they "really love" their spouse. Yet speaking of the coming Messiah, Isaiah said, "Behold, the *virgin* shall conceive and bear a Son, and shall call His Name Immanuel. Curds and honey He shall eat, that He may know to refuse the evil and choose the good" (Isa. 7:14-15, NKJV). The child Messiah then, as well as His corporate image in His people now, comes forth from the *virgin* womb, and afterwards he grows on the pure nourishment of "curds and honey." This nourishment in the good things of God—not the imbibing of the evil things of the world—strengthens his ability to discern good from evil. Only a fully consistent Christian education within the covenant context of that virgin church without spot or wrinkle, that church which Paul has espoused to Christ (Eph. 5:27; 2 Cor. 11:2), a church that excludes all ungodliness, can bring forth the child into the fullness of the image of Christ, into the image of a whole man fully in tune with Yahweh's song.

Education and the Call to Dominion

Of this child brought forth from the virgin womb the Scriptures declare:

> For to us a child is born, to us a son is given, and the government will be on His shoulders. And He will be called Wonderful Counselor, Mighty God, Everlasting Father, Prince of Peace.
>
> Of the increase of His government and peace there will be no end. He will reign on David's throne and over His kingdom, establishing and upholding it with justice and righteousness from that time on and forever. The zeal of Yahweh Almighty will accomplish this. (Isa. 9:6-7)

The Messiah has come forth, prepared in the virgin womb, fed on the purity of "curds and honey," to reestablish God's dominion on the face of the earth: and "of the increase of His *government* . . . there shall be no end." His home education, His separation from the world unto the Lord, prepared Him for His task of reestablishing God's sovereign authority, of bringing all things under His dominion.

God is our "only Sovereign" (1 Tim. 6:15, NASV). He alone has dominion over all creation. But God entrusted to man the dominion over planet earth. He made man His viceregent on earth to bring all things under God's authority:

> Be fruitful and increase in number; fill the earth and subdue it. Rule over the fish of the sea and the birds of the air and over every living creature that moves on the ground. (Gen. 1:28)

> Then God blessed Noah and his sons, saying to them, "Be fruitful and increase in number and fill the earth. The fear and dread of you will fall upon all the beasts of the earth and all the birds of the air, upon every creature that moves along the ground, and upon all the fish of the sea; they are given into your hands." (Gen. 9:1-2)

> When I consider Your heavens, the work of Your fingers, the moon and the stars, which You have set in place, what is man that You are mindful of him, the son of man that You care for him? You made him a little lower than the heavenly beings and crowned him with glory and honor.

You made him ruler over the works of Your hands; You put everything under his feet: all flocks and herds, and the beasts of the field, the birds of the air, and the fish of the sea, all that swim the paths of the seas. (Ps. 8:3-8)

But man forgot that the garden belonged to God (not man), because God was the original Gardener: "And Yahweh God planted a garden" (Gen. 2:8, KJV). Since the rebellion in Eden, man has continued his futile attempt to bring the world solely under his own dominion, outside of and against the dominion of God. As we know, the result has been chaos, destruction and death. But God has also continued His offer to bring man back within His kingdom so that man might yet fulfill God's commission to bring all things under His dominion.* God brought forth the Second Adam (1 Cor. 15:45) to fulfill the task that the first Adam so tragically failed to accomplish: to bring all things under the direct dominion of the living God. Through Jesus Christ, God seeks to restore man to relationship with Himself so that He might bring man again into that true submission to His Spirit that would allow us to bring the world under the dominion of God. When we speak of our children taking dominion, we cannot overemphasize the importance of realizing that this dominion must subserve God's—must submit to His Spirit, His patterns, His Word. "Dominion" does not mean rapaciously ravaging the earth and its people for man's selfish ends. It means walking humbly before God, doing His will, bringing glory to His Name, obeying His Spirit. None of this allows for the greedy craving of the carnal nature. As Paul reminded us, using the world does not mean abusing it (1 Cor. 7:31, KJV).

Through education we train our children to follow their Lord and Savior Jesus Christ. We must train them to pursue the task of taking dominion over their world in submission to the Spirit and government of God so that, both in and through their lives, of the increase of *His* government and peace there will be no end. Again, we must impart *relational* knowledge to them, knowledge based above all upon their direct relationship of submission to the living Spirit of God. Education should *not* seek to cram children's minds with unrelated facts and abstract dogmas; rather it should seek to teach them how they can take control of the world around them in order to fulfill *God's* purpose for man, *under God*, in order that they might

* See the chapter "The Eternal Purpose" in *The Order of Perfection*.

have godly dominion *over* the earth. They can only take God-centered dominion if they enter into the living relationship with God, man and nature that God has ordained for them, according to the patterns He has set to govern those relations. Jesus' words clearly show the inseparability of God's call to His followers to take dominion over all things and His command that we teach others, while we ourselves are also taught of and by the Lord:

> Then Jesus came to them and said, *"All authority* in heaven and on earth has been *given to me.* Therefore *you* go and make disciples of all nations, baptizing them in the name of the Father and of the Son and of the Holy Spirit, and *teaching* them to obey everything I have commanded you."(Matt. 28:18-20, KJV, NIV)

Again, God calls us to participate in an unfolding pattern of relationships that reestablishes His harmonious dominion throughout all life and brings to pass the reconciliation of the world (2 Cor. 5:18-20).

All true education must therefore center in Jesus Christ, since He has dominion over all things, and all things hold together only in Him (Matt. 28:18; Col. 1:17). He is the cosmic center who alone can bring coherence to our children's lives as well as to all other life. We can only teach our children to take dominion over the world for His purpose if we center everything they learn in the One who has dominion over all things and who gives all things their purpose and meaning. *Everything* must be centered in "Christ, in whom are hidden *all* the treasures of wisdom and knowledge" (Col. 2:2-3). But though these treasures are "hidden" in Christ, Jesus does not hide them from His people; for to them God has *"made known . . . the mystery* of His will according to His good pleasure, which He purposed in Christ" (Eph. 1:9).

God makes these things known to us by His Spirit (1 Cor. 2:10). His Spirit becomes our ultimate teacher (Neh. 9:20; Luke 12:12; John 14:26; 1 Cor. 2:13; 1 John 2:27). As we come increasingly under God's dominion through prayerful study of His Word and sensitivity to the anointing of His Spirit, God will empower us to teach our children everything they need to know to enable them to come under His dominion as well. As our relationship with the living God unfolds and we grow in Him, our relationship with our child will also unfold, and we will grow in our ability to nurture him in all the ways of God. As

Psalm 119:32 implies, God guides us through our curriculum (*curriculum* coming from the Latin word meaning "a place for running," a "race course"), and He gives us our educational standards. As our children run their curriculum course, God disciples them: so this course must include *every* part of their lives. God tells us what path Christian curriculum leads our children through,

> I run in the path of Your commands, for You have set my heart free. (Ps. 119:32)

As our children run through this path set by God, He conforms them fully to His image and brings them under His dominion so that they can become channels *through* which His dominion can still further spread.

We can only learn to bring all things into submission to the will of God, under God's dominion, if we first come under submission to God's will ourselves. So, foundational to all else, our child must learn the first level of submission—obedience. This begins everyone's relationship with God and remains the unchanging foundation of all other levels.* Before the child can grow to maturity and "make disciples of all nations," he himself must first be discipled. He must come into the proper relationship with God before God can use him to bring others into such relationship. Our relationship of sonship to our heavenly Father necessitates discipline (Heb. 12:4-11)—discipleship—through submission. The child must learn to obey his parents and others in godly authority over him. This lesson serves as the indispensable foundation of his discipleship, of the educational process through which he learns to take dominion over the world only for the purpose of God and not for himself. The educational process constitutes more than merely an important element of the discipleship of our children; we can even interpret it as the very process of discipleship.

Even highly reputed secular sources confirm that education means discipleship. The *Oxford English Dictionary*, the most authoritative dictionary in the English language, defines the word *educate* as "to rear" or "to bring up" children.[38] It also means

> to bring up (young persons) from childhood, so as to form (their) habits, manners, intellectual and physical aptitudes.[39]

---

* See pp. 24-26.

The Latin roots of the word *education* mean "to lead out." So, the Biblical proverb, "Train up a child in the way he should go: and when he is old, he will not depart from it" (Prov. 22:6, KJV) could well be paraphrased as, "Educate a child in the way he should go . . . ." This purpose of education is further borne out by the definition of the word *pupil*, which originally meant an "orphan" or a "ward"—that is, one raised by someone other than his natural parents. And the word *alma mater*, the term applied to the school that one has attended, originally meant "a foster mother."[40] So we can see the "pupil" of public education as an individual who has been brought under the parenthood of the State, which undertakes to disciple him, to train him up in the way it thinks he should go. This becomes the child's fate because his real parents have abdicated their rights and responsibilities and abandoned the task of forming the image of their orphaned child to the State.

The following definitions also associate education with discipleship. A disciple is one who is disciplined, *discipline* meaning "training that corrects, molds, or perfects the mental faculties or moral character."[41] *Webster's* identifies *discipline* as a synonym of the word *educate*;[42] and the authoritative *Random House Dictionary* states that "education, training imply a discipline . . . by means of study and learning."[43] This process of education and discipleship forms the very core of the Christian purpose: "Go . . . and *make disciples*," Jesus declared in the great commission, "*teaching* them to observe all that I commanded you" (Matt. 28:19-20, NASV). Yale Professor Jaroslav Pelikan correctly says:

> The church is always more than a school; not even the age of the Enlightenment managed to restrict or reduce it to its teaching function. But *the church cannot be less than a school.* Its faith, hope, and love all express themselves in *teaching* . . . . (emphasis added)[44]

And Paul in Ephesians 6:4 tells fathers to raise their children "with Christian teaching in Christian discipline."[45] So, again, education forms the very center of the Christian purpose and commission. And by educating their children in the home, parents fulfill a central part of their function in the great commission of Jesus Christ—the very center of His purpose— making disciples of all nations, beginning in the most obvious place, their own children in their own home.

Discipleship can come only through relationship: personal relationship constitutes its Christian basis. Again, the lesson of submission to authority forms the foundation of our children's education or discipleship. They must learn to submit to the will of God as He initially expresses that will to them through people whom *He* has appointed to guide their lives. They will come into proper relationship with God only by coming into proper relationship with the people through whom God has chosen to speak, act and rule. Ultimately, this process of submission toward men will teach the child to hear and obey the voice of the Spirit of God directly for himself, but he will never cease honoring those who served as his origins in God. On the basis of this obedience and submission, children will grow to become responsible, God-controlled individuals who will go forth inspired by the purpose of God, filled with zeal according to the knowledge that they have received of God's Word, God's will and God's world.

Again, we see education as more than an isolated, peripheral part of the child's life. The whole of his life really constitutes his education, forming his whole being into conformity with God's will so that the child can grow to become an instrument of God's loving spiritual dominion. The Greek word often translated as *curriculum, paideia*—in other words, the academic course of instruction that the child was to undergo—actually means "culture,"[46] which, as we have seen, constitutes the whole nurturing habitat in which the child is reared, his "lived religion." According to the outstanding scholar of ancient Greece Werner Jaeger, the Greeks' "culture, their *paideia,* . . . was Greek history itself," that is, the totality of Greek life from its beginnings.[47] The Greeks "believed that education embodied the purpose of all human effort."[48] Education shaped "the living man as the potter moulds clay."[49] While the Greek goals, ideals and methods of education most often antithetically opposed the Biblical view,* they rightly identified the process of education with the process of creating a whole culture that would shape the whole person. But as we have seen, while Greek culture shaped the whole man in the sense of shaping all his being, it could not bring him forth into wholeness, into the integration of the different elements of his being. Only a God-centered culture could do that: thus the fall of

---

* See *Salvation Is of the Jews* and *Knowledge as Spiritual War.*

Graeco-Roman culture and the rise and conquest (not through the compulsory power of the State but through martyrdom, through the "witness" of truth) of Biblical culture. (Only when the pagan doctrine of State compulsion seduced the latter did it begin its decline into the Dark Ages.*)

As we have seen, in contrast to pagan Greek education, Christian education trains the whole man, and so we must bring every element of our children's lives to full development: their hearts, their bodies and their minds. Again, our children can only become the complete expression of God's dominion if they are "complete in Him"(Col. 2:10). This call to dominion under God forces us to come out of the realm of our own fantasy and into the realm of God's reality. And so the educational development of our children must not take place in the realm of abstractions but in the realm of relational knowledge, in the realm in which we see every aspect of their education in its relationship to God's purpose, to their task of bringing all things under the dominion of God's Spirit. As they learn various skills that secular culture usually identifies as strictly intellectual ones—for example, reading, writing, math and so on—they must see these in the concrete relational setting that God would develop them in: as means for communicating with God and man, as means of acquiring skills and knowledge that will enable them to serve God's purpose, to serve their brothers and sisters in the Lord, to serve in their places as a light to the nations and to nurture and care for God's creation. We must seek God's face that He might energize every element of our children's beings toward the fulfillment of these various functions. For example, we must train their minds (and of course we must also inform their emotions and help form their bodies) in areas other than merely the intellectual, for example, in the development of practical skills. The glorification of the intellectual above all else marks the pagan path of life, not the Christian one.† Our children should learn how to build, how to plant, how to grow their own food and how to develop other practical abilities so essential that our lack of them makes us dependent on others for our very sustenance and life. They must learn to bring every area of life under God's dominion, not to dependency on man. As they mature, they should develop one or more skills that they can use to serve the godly community and

---

* See Truth Forum's *Politics as Spiritual War.*

† See *Justice Is Fallen.*

support themselves and their families. They should develop knowledge and skills in a broad variety of areas. Although most people will be able to master completely only a few skills, they should not become stultified "specialists" with lives and perspectives narrowly confined to an imbalanced obsession that distorts their view of and relationship with God, man and creation.

All these things constitute essential parts of training the whole man, a task that modern secular educational systems neglect and often detest, even though they sometimes give it token approval. To create this whole man in Christ, we must bring forth every element of this training from a God-centered perspective, as part of a God-centered culture. As we have said, we must desire to train men and women who will be devoted to and glorify God in their *whole* lives: spiritually, emotionally, physically, intellectually, in every way. Any system of education that does anything less than this has fallen short of fulfilling God's complete patterns. The public schools cannot even get good results in the limited area that they have chosen for themselves—academic education.* Nevertheless, we as Christians will fail if we limit ourselves to success in this one sphere. When we understand the complete definition of Christian education—the rearing and training up of a *whole* man or woman—we shall more clearly understand (when we discuss this later†) the key role of the parent in this process.‡ Only this whole man can come into that complete submission to God that will fully establish God's complete authority and dominion.

Again, through Christian home education we direct our efforts to bring forth whole men and women capable of completely fulfilling their responsibilities within God's kingdom. God ordained the Body of Christ as a whole culture. And that culture becomes the revolving wheel that we seek to use in molding the whole child into full integrity and wholeness; and the Potter who turns the wheel and whose hands form the image of the human life that emerges must be God Himself. So

---

* See *The Crime of Compulsory Education.*

† See pp. 134-45.

‡ Many humanist educators point out that education means more than academic education, but they use this statement merely to excuse their own failures in academic instruction and to justify their usurpation of the function of parents.[50] (See *Humanism* and *Brave New Education.*)

we must seek to conform the whole of our lives and culture to the patterns that God has ordained. The individual must find his proper place in this culture so that God Himself can fine-tune him to play his part in the song of Yahweh.

Education does not merely involve what a child learns to do and to know. Above all, it involves what the child *is*. In this truth resides the most important sense in which God establishes His dominion "in earth, as it is in heaven" and makes us to *be* in His image. As God has designed each facet on a diamond's surface to reflect the brightness of that precious stone, so has He designed every one of us to reflect the purity and goodness of His own nature. Godly character stands as the most prized goal in our children's education. Everything God gives us to do serves ultimately as the means—the refiner's fire, the potter's wheel—through which He does His supreme work of transforming us into His image. While we must teach our children to excel in everything they do, the Bible warns us, as we have seen, of a kind of knowledge that puffs people up (1 Cor. 8:1). True knowledge, godly knowledge, does not puff up (1 Cor. 8:2); knowledge centered in God nurtures humility as we come to comprehend our total and complete dependence on the Giver of all true wisdom. Such an attitude will enable our children to live lives truly guided by God's Spirit, worshiping Him all their days in Spirit and Truth. Our children must acquire, by the grace of God, the character that will enable them to walk humbly before their God, esteeming others more highly than themselves, yet confident in their God-given ability to become the responsible men and women God has made them to be. If we succeed in everything and fail here, then we have failed God and our children. If we succeed in this area, then we shall succeed in every area of child rearing. Then our children will know the joy and glory of resonating as chords in God's great symphonic song, harmonizing with His eternal refrain both now and forever, *wholly* at one with the Creator and King, with the Conductor of the cosmic symphony.

CHAPTER FOUR

Whose Responsibility
Is Christian Education?

Parental Responsibility

Seemingly in our day, even the most obvious must be stated:
our children are born into our families, born into natural
relationship with their parents. So from the very beginning,
parents function as the natural educators of their children, and
that educational process unfolds through relationship. The
parents encourage the child to walk, to talk, to play, to sing, to
do all that growing entails, through *relationship*. The child
learns primarily through relationship with his parents, and perhaps also with older responsible brothers or sisters. The
parental relationship, in other words, provides the natural context for the unfolding impartation of the relational knowledge
of God in all of its ramifications, settings and levels, that
knowledge which brings forth the child into full integrity and
wholeness. God gives the parent above all others the primary
responsibility to see his children grow in proper relationship
with God, with his fellowman and with creation. Only parents
can ensure that their children become responsible human
beings who fulfill the God-given call upon their lives. Parents
alone enjoy the unique position that enables the nurturing of
the *whole* child in body, soul and spirit.

Home education provides the perfect context for transmitting
this relational knowledge, because education occurs within
the framework of the personal, loving relationship between
parents and children. This framework limits responsibility to a
range that it can reach. Because parents feel the responsibility
for their children's education more directly and personally than
anyone else, they can fulfill that responsibility more effectively
than anyone else. They alone occupy that lifelong place of

covenant with their children that compels them, if they will submit to that burden in love, to witness and experience on a daily basis the blessings of success in this educational process. And they alone witness the full extent of the tragedy of failure. Obviously, in order to meaningfully transmit relational knowledge we must abide in a personal relationship of the deepest sort. But parents alone can bring forth, under the direction of God, the fullness of their child's abilities, character, talents—all the elements of his being—into a fully integrated harmony. This relational knowledge that brings true oneness, in this case between the teacher and the student, as well as within the student himself, demands a particular means for attaining its goal; not any means will do. To impart this type of knowledge requires the specific relational setting that God Himself has ordained. The relational nature of godly knowledge, in short, dictates the relational, familial means of transmission. God created that relationship as the means to impart that type of knowledge. This creates the environment that can bring forth the very diverse members that God has ordained for the completion of His Body, rather than the mass-produced alphas and epsilons turned out by Brave New public education.

Parents are the ideal agents, appointed by God, for the task of molding and shaping a child's development so as to equip him to perfectly fulfill his destiny. God has entrusted our children to us (Gen. 33:5; 48:8-9; 1 Sam. 1:20; Ps. 113:9; 127:3-4; Prov. 17:6; Isa. 29:23; 38:19, KJV or Ampl.; Mal. 2:15). They belong to God (Ezek. 18:4), and He has placed them in our care (Job 1:5). Parents must primarily bear the personal responsibility to take direct dominion over the lives of their children for the purposes of God, to raise them as He would have them to. God through His Word entrusted this responsibility not to the State but to the parents (Deut. 4:5-9; 6:1-9; 11:18-21; 32:45-47; Ps. 78:1-11; Prov. 4:20-27; 6:20-23; 13:1; Eph. 6:1-4). We already saw that the most authoritative lexicon in the English language, the *Oxford English Dictionary*, defines *educate* as "to rear" or "to bring up" children. Revealingly, Ephesians 6:4 *explicitly* states in almost every translation and paraphrase that "fathers," not the State, have the responsibility to "bring up" or "rear" their children—in other words, to "educate" their children. Since a man and his wife are "one" (Eph. 5:31), and she serves as the prime minister of his authority within the home and family, the father fulfills this command when the mother functions in this capacity under his supervision.* We cannot in any sense say this about State education. God made the family His basic institution of positive, relational government—not the State.† The State serves primarily in the negative function of "punishment of the evil-doer," not the positive function of cloning the minds and hearts of children in its own image.‡ The State's specific authority and function can under no circumstance serve to bring forth fulfilled, integrated children. When the State steps into the educational process, it can only bring forth fragmented lives, as it has indeed been proving for many decades.** In contrast to the coercive, one-sided State schooling, parental education offers God's pattern for bringing our children under the dominion of God's government, for bringing forth integrated, whole people. As we have said, when we really understand what education means, from a Biblical point of view, the centrality of the parent becomes overwhelmingly obvious, for God equips only the parent to bring forth the full potential of the child into harmonious unity.††

---

* First Timothy 5:14 (KJV) says that the married woman should "guide the house," and Proverbs 31:10, 27, 23, 26 tells us that "a wife of noble character . . . watches over the affairs of her household . . . ." Because she does this diligently, she frees her husband to take "his seat among the elders of the land." Teaching is central to her functions: "She speaks with wisdom, and faithful instruction is on her tongue." God's Word gives the primary authority over and responsibility for education to fathers (Eph. 6:4), but both parents must actively teach their children: "Listen, my son, to your father's instruction and do not forsake your mother's teaching" (Prov. 1:8; see also Prov. 6:20). Clearly, the Scriptures give mothers a central responsibility for the fulfillment of this parental responsibility, as evidenced also by Proverbs 31:2-9, which records the teachings King Lemuel learned from his mother (Prov. 31:1).

† See *Who Owns the Children?* and *Community and Family.*

‡ See *Who Owns the Children?*

** See *The Crime of Compulsory Education, Humanism* and *Brave New Education.*

†† This is why we have written our curriculum the way we have: we have designed it so that the parents function as teachers, not supervisors. Most curriculums offer textbooks and workbooks as teachers for the children. In this case the parents step back to a supervisory role as the books fill the primary teaching position. The parents become dependent on the textbooks and so cannot operate in the Spirit. They are moved along at the book's pace, unable to move as the Spirit would lead. Our curriculum puts the parents into the primary teaching position which Scripture commands. See Part Three and Supplement One for comprehensive discussion of how our curriculum works.

We see this when we realize that God has made parents the natural and spiritual vehicles of His creatorship and authority in the lives of children. The word *authority* derives from the root word *author*. To have authority has always meant that in one sense one authored something. We discover in this the vital connection between sovereignty and origins:* to have sovereignty necessarily implies being the origins or author of that over which one has sovereign authority. As Ingram says, no greater power can exist than to give life to others but to owe one's own being to no one.[1] This explains Paul's description of God as "the Only Sovereign and Potentate," for He alone has being in Himself. He is the Being One, the "I AM THAT I AM" (Exod. 3:14, KJV; John 8:58). He is "worthy . . . to receive glory and honor and power," for He "*created*" all things," and by His "will they were *created* and have their *being*" (Rev. 4:11), and "in Him we live and move and have our *being*" (Acts 17:28). Therefore God alone reigns as Sovereign, having ultimate authority, because He alone is the ultimate Author. The Scriptures make this same point again when they declare of Jesus Christ that

> He is the image of the invisible God; His is the *primacy* over all *created* things. *In Him everything* in heaven and on earth *was created*, not only things visible but also the invisible *orders* of thrones, *sovereignties, authorities, and powers*: the whole universe has been *created* through Him and for Him. And *He exists before everything*, and all things are held together in Him. He is, moreover, the *head* of the Body, the church. He is its *origin*, the first to return from the dead, to be in all things *alone supreme*. (Col. 1:15-18, NEB)

He has "*primacy* over all" things because "in Him everything . . . was *created*." Moreover, all "authority" and "order" was "created" in and for Him. Since He is the "origin" over everything, and particularly of the church, He alone reigns "supreme" in authority over all things, again, particularly over His people. When the State claims absolute sovereignty over every area of life, it puts itself in the place of God, becoming antichrist in the most literal sense of the word.

Nevertheless, God delegated secondary authorship, and therefore secondary authority, to different men and institutions. Among them, parents have *authority* second only to

---

* See *The Garden of God.*

God's over children, because He gave them secondary *authorship* through procreation: they have the closest and deepest natural relationship to their children of any mortal beings. Through them God gives children their very being, and because the fullness of the children's being comes forth through their parents, God equipped parents alone to bring the fullness of that being to harmonious maturity. Among human agencies, not the State but parents have "authored" children, originated them. God has placed His own creatorship of human life under the dominion of fathers and mothers. The root of the word *parent* means "to produce, bring forth, beget." Since God has shared with them the power to bring or not to bring life into existence, parents therefore have the primary *delegated* authority (although limited by God and His law) over that life.

God nevertheless places definite limits on this parental authority. For instance, although the decision to exercise the power to conceive children resides with parents, God does not give parents the right (as was nonetheless exercised under pagan law in Greece and Rome and now in American law) to murder that which they have already conceived (Exod. 21:22-23).

Moreover, we must surely admit that parents have some of the power and authority (at least more so than any other earthly source) of Him who made man in His image, since their children, at least in part, also bear the very image of their parents, according to the Biblical principle that "like seed brings forth after its own kind."

Finally, even the most totalitarian of States has not (at least not yet) sought to take away the parents' power to name their children. The authoritative New Testament word study, Kittel's *Theological Dictionary*, discusses the importance of being the one to give another his name:

> In Israel as among other peoples there was awareness of the significance attached to a name, and of the power which resided in it. The first and later utterance of a name means more than formal endowment with, and use of, a means of naming someone. *By giving someone a name, one establishes a relation of dominion and possession towards him.*
>
> *Thus [according to Genesis] 2:19f. Adam names all the animals. This means that he exercises dominion over creation and relates it to his own sphere . . . .* In times

of distress forsaken and threatened women ensure male protection by requesting the name of a man and *thereby seeking to become his possession* (Isa. 4:1). (emphasis added)[2]

Jacques Ellul remarks:

How important a name was for an Israelite is well known. It is *the sign of dominion* and has a spiritual quality. God gave a name to the first man. Man in turn named all the animals. Thus *a relationship is established in which the one named becomes the [possession] of the one naming.* (emphasis added)[3]

And, in general, man's effort to take dominion cannot be separated from the process of naming. So, as the late University of Chicago professor Richard M. Weaver points out, "natural science" constitutes in large part "a classified catalogue of names" through which man seeks to order and exercise control over the physical world.[4] Weaver quotes Plato's conception of a name as "an instrument of teaching and of distinguishing natures."[5] While Adam's act of naming the animals expressed his dominion over them (Gen. 2:19-20), this process also reflected his ability to find the name that best expressed the nature of each creature. The parents' naming of their children has the same dual significance. The parents' authority to name their children expresses their dominion over them; by naming their child they take the first step in fulfilling their responsibility to discern that child's God-given nature and destiny and then to train the child so that he will become *everything* God intended: The name speaks of the identity of the *whole* person, not just a part of the person. As Freud said, a "name" doesn't "occur arbitrarily to the mind" but rather it is determined by a "powerful ideational complex." In other words, a name denotes essential characteristics of the one named. To name someone is both to recognize the essential character of the one named and also to shape his character, for, to again quote Freud, "a man's name is a principal component of his personality, perhaps even a portion of his soul."[6] In *Mind and Nature*, Gregory Bateson writes that "'things' . . . can only enter the world of communication and meaning by their names . . . ."[7] So when we name something, we give it, in the most elemental sense, its meaning and establish its relationship with the world. What greater authority can exist than this?

To those then who would ask us to show them where the

Scriptures obligate parents to educate their children themselves, we would say that we do not wish to attempt to force our convictions upon others; for this, as in all things of God's Word, comes by revelation of God's Spirit (Matt. 16:17; John 16:12-13; 1 Cor. 2:9-10; Gal. 1:11-12; 1 John 2:27). But in light of what we have said above, and in addition to the scriptures referred to, the very natural process of procreation set in motion by the laws of God (Gen. 1:28; Mal. 2:15), God's own principles of sovereignty and origins, God's divine plan for replenishing the earth and bringing human life into existence, have put this power, authority—and therefore responsibility—. into the hands of the parents. Who but parents enjoys the natural God-given position to nurture the *whole* child according to the patterns of godly upbringing? Upon whom does this burden more naturally fall? The burden of proof rests, then, upon those who would *change* this divinely ordained process and order—an order that has abided with man and nature since the dawn of creation. Those who would abdicate both their authority and responsibility to surrogate parents, namely, to the State in the form of public education or to day-care centers for other child-rearing purposes, must justify going against God's natural order. Those who assume parental responsibility for the direct education of their children do not need to find scriptures to explicitly support this position, although such scriptural evidence does indeed exist, as we have cited above. Rather those who *depart* from the natural order dictated by God's patterns for the family must affirm, foremost to God and themselves, that God has indeed given them permission to depart from His ordered pattern of parental responsibility. The Bible plainly lays out the importance of "*natural* affection" (2 Tim. 3:3), and it also describes the "last days" as "perilous times" in which men shall harden themselves to such feelings. As believers, we must actively strengthen the "natural" God-ordained bonds of love and encourage every possible channel and outlet for their expression, since God has ordained this type of "natural" relationship, as the Scriptures clearly state.

We do not intend, however, to condemn in any way those Christian parents who send their children to the many fine Christian schools. On the contrary, we strongly support their efforts to take their children *out* of the secular public education system. We definitely believe that the church has a place for special educational ministries for children. Yet, so far as we can see, the basic scriptural pattern for the education of children requires that parents not only take responsibility for, but actively serve as the primary agency of, the education of their children. To do otherwise, parents should have a *clear*, scripturally based Word from God.

Our atomized, modern, industrial society makes it very difficult for many people to see clearly the God-ordained character of the family. Even many of us in the Christian community, who today so vitally care about strengthening the family and its godly order, fail to fully recognize God's purpose for the family. For a more accurate picture of the God-ordained purpose of the family, we must think back to the family in Bible times or, at least to some extent, to the founding of America. The family then provided the center of most of the daily activities of its members. The craftsman attached his workshop to his home; most people engaged in subsistence agriculture based upon the *home*stead. Born at home, raised at home, the child came to his first knowledge of praise and worship of the Lord, to prayer, to the study of the Word of God in the home. At home he learned to work with his parents, doing chores around the house and the homestead. Girls would be gradually initiated into all the functions and responsibilities that they would need to run complex households and to someday raise children themselves. Boys would learn their father's trade or be initiated into the multifaceted task of running a self-sufficient farm. Generally, the child would learn reading, writing and ciphering at home, and would study the Bible. The home, within the context of an agri-culture, provided the natural context of God-ordained relationships through which the child learned to fulfill his responsibilities and developed into the man God intended. Sometimes a son would be called to a different profession than that of his father. He might then study under some other man, taking instruction from the priest or rabbi or minister, or entering into the long, arduous process of apprenticeship to learn the necessary skills that marked him as a true artisan of his craft. If he could stay at home and study, then he remained under the direct authority of his father, but if he had to live with the man under whom he studied, the father would then delegate part of his own authority to that man. The father had already, for the most part, fulfilled his God-ordained responsibilities to "bring up" or "educate" the child, and the "child" was now becoming a man. But even these radical measures took place in the context of communities where men knew each other's character well. This radically differs from turning children over to the impersonal, anonymous, ever-changing agents of the State, where an ineffective licensing system[8] that implicitly places all faith in the State supposedly substitutes for the relational knowledge of a man's character.

So we see that the family served as the world into which the child was born and reared. It formed the nurturing habitat, the culture, in which the seedling of the child was brought through *every* stage, from germination to fruition. When we see the life of the child in this context, understand the *relational* character of Judaic knowledge and recognize that we must nurture and educate the *whole* person, we find it hard to see how parents could refuse to serve as the primary agency of their children's instruction in every sense, including the academic. God gives the seed of the child to the parents, who are given the power to conceive. Then God brings the child into existence in the mother's womb, from which he is then born into his parents' home. God ordains that this tender seed, nurtured in his mother's womb, born into his parents' home, be raised in the culture of the same family into which he is born. Those who have been entrusted with that seed must have the primary responsibility in bringing the child to maturity.

Again, only our atomized modern world causes us to think that the child's academic instruction can somehow be divided from everything else. If God gives parents the seed and empowers them to bring the child into existence, then He also gives them the responsibility and the ability to cultivate it in the nurturing habitat of the family home into which He has delivered the child for care. If we believe that we do not have this ability, we believe the brainwashing of the State and those with vested interests in perpetuating such a belief. We then also see God's plan as inadequate and believe that He didn't know what to do or how to do it. As the cultivators of their child's life, parents must take responsibility for every aspect of his nature, and this includes the learning of intellectual skills as well. Even today when the family no longer serves as the economic unit that it did in earlier times (though this can serve as a goal we aspire toward), the family nevertheless can and should provide the nurturing habitat for every aspect of our children's development.

Research also bears out the pattern ordained by God's Word and the natural order that He established.* Raymond S. Moore, a developmental psychologist who has had years of experience in every aspect of the educational process from college president and school superintendent to teacher, and who has served as educational advisor to the White House, the U.S. Congress, to many states and to a number of overseas governments, wrote an outstanding study entitled *School Can Wait*, documenting the importance of home care and schooling for children. His study, following upon ten years of closely documented, comparative research, contends that "we are losing ground academically and behaviorally in the education of our children."[9] He attributes this decline to the fact that

legal and social pressures over the last several generations have taken children ever earlier out of the family and home and have placed them in institutional settings—with attendant transfer of both parental responsibility and authority to the [S]tate or other agencies.[10]

Moore finds the child's attachment to his parents (which he characterizes as the "affectional bond that gives stability in a world full of uncertainties") indispensable in providing the child with "a safe base from which to explore the unknown."[11] In contrast to those who claim that children become free thinking and more "independent" when taken away from parents at an early age, Moore's research has shown that

beyond the first year of life a well-established attachment contributes to a healthy independence. An emotional stability then evolves that builds a desirable independence and makes it possible for a child to persevere in spite of frustrations—to stay with a task or problem until a goal is reached.[12]

Martin Engel, while director of the U.S. National Day-Care Demonstration Center, noted the harmful effects of separating children from parents at an early age:

The motive to rid ourselves of our children, even if it is

---

* Such evidence, however, can never be used to measure the validity of God's Word; rather God's Word measures the validity of scientific evidence. Indeed, as we show elsewhere, scientific knowledge is always shaped by the assumptions upon which it rests. The question then becomes, what are the true bases and assumptions upon which science, and all knowledge, should be based—man's or God's? See *Justice Is Fallen*.

partial, is transmitted more vividly to the child than all our rationalizations about how good it is for that child to have good interpersonal peer group activities, a good learning experience, a good foundation for school life, etc., etc. And even the best, most humane and personalized day-care environment cannot compensate for the feeling of rejection which the young child unconsciously senses.[13]

Socialization

One of the major arguments for public schools concerns their supposed usefulness for the socialization of the child. But does this contention hold any truth? And more basically, what does it even mean? Most people think of socialization as imparting the ability to get along with other people, particularly people of one's own age group. Being exposed to large groups of people every day supposedly facilitates this process.

To see if it does, let us review a typical school day. The child may spend some time with his peers on the way to school, walking, standing in line for the bus or sitting on the bus. He gets to class, his teacher takes attendance and then the day's schoolwork begins. In the junior and high school levels, class changes break up the school day. During these breaks, the student rushes to his next class. Periodic breaks that occur in the day supposedly allow children opportunity to socialize, namely recesses and lunch breaks, and other breaks, such as study periods, when "socializing" generally takes place (even when rules forbid it). Then the student goes home, perhaps spending some time with his peers in much the same way as on the way to school.

Obviously within the class-learning situation little socializing actually takes place, or at least little is supposed to. The classroom really offers no advantages for academic improvement over a private tutorial program such as a home school offers. On the contrary, both evidence and reason show the scholastic superiority of the home tutorial program.[14] The child can learn to express himself verbally in one-on-one discourse with the parent-teacher just as well as in a classroom situation, and often much better. Some group-learning experiences can be rewarding and exciting, but these can and should generally constitute a minor part of the child's learning time, and home-school children can enjoy such experiences within the context of Christian community. Home-schooled children in the Christian community come together under parental supervision for many group-learning experiences, classroom discussions, craft workshops, special projects, field trips and so on, where they learn to work and play with others constructively, fruitfully and joyously.

Indeed, given the *relational* character of Biblical knowledge, life within the context of Christian community greatly assists the full development of the child. The community provides the context of relationship for the family and so provides an important part of the framework in which the child grows. In this context, the child enjoys a wide diversity of relationships with other members of the community, including children outside his own family. He works and plays with them as they grow together in God. These relationships provide vital help for the full development of the child, who thus grows to become a responsible member of a godly community. This kind of community life develops the close bonds and godly affection that constitute true "socialization." The modern world knows nothing of this kind of "socialization."

With the exception of classroom discussions, the socialization argument really centers on nonacademic school time, such as student assemblies, lunch periods, going to and from school, as well as extracurricular activities, such as school clubs, student government and athletic or debating teams and so on. But constructive and positive aspects of these same activities can be found in almost any Christian community life.* Children can come together to work in gardens, farm chores such as milking, small-scale construction jobs like making

---

* Of course, advocates of the advantages of public school socialization vaunt its alleged superiority because it takes place in the context of a heterogenous group of people with many different beliefs. We discuss this view in detail in *The Crime of Compulsory Education* and in *Humanism*. This view of "socialization," however, actually undermines belief in the One God and His absolute Word; for it implicitly asserts the equal validity of all viewpoints, which in effect denies the legitimacy of the exclusive claims of the Bible as God's Word. Such a system of compulsory "socialization" really constitutes only a subtle system of secular indoctrination. (See also pp. 98-102 below.) Certainly, all of us need to learn to live with people of views different from our own, but this view of socialization insists that we can do so only by denying the validity of our own beliefs. Its claims of tolerance therefore mask an uncompromising intolerance against the absolute view of the God who cannot deny Himself (2 Tim. 2:13).

chicken coops, or they can get together with their friends to work on common interests, such as sewing, spinning, weaving, leatherworking, harness-making, cornhusking or shelling, and other similar tasks. They can also come together in recreational activities, such as pitching horseshoes, fishing, archery, horseback riding, hiking, camping and so on. In fact, however, public school rarely brings out the best potential of such social activities. On the contrary, in general, during these periods children compete with one another for popularity, attention and in other ways.

Unfortunately, in large part, the children in these circumstances in the public school setting form a mass of insecure individuals, each vying for prestige, superiority, acclaim or affection from their fellow students. In their interaction at school with their peers, the children learn a form of "socialization" based on dependence upon the approval of one's friends. As Cornell University's Urie Bronfenbrenner has shown, youngsters who spend a great deal of time with their peers "become dependent on their peers."[15] This type of dependency produces what Bronfenbrenner has described as a "social contagion."[16] So public schools serve as breeding centers transmitting the disease of blind conformity to peer pressure, which in modern public education often leads to drug use, violence and sexual immorality. "Socialization" then becomes a popularity contest in which one seeks to favorably impress his peers, sparking "rivalry." This type of socialization basically means learning "to make a good impression outwardly" (Gal. 6:12), how to impress others by demonstrating the characteristics others would like to see. In its ultimate degeneracy, we see it in the atrocities of the mob, even when the mob becomes a whole, supposedly enlightened nation, as in Nazi Germany. As the late educator John Holt has said, "Socialization in public schools is mean, competitive, cruel and status-seeking . . . . I have said this to over 5,000 educators, and not one has publicly contradicted me, even when I challenged them."[17] Psychologist James Dobson concurs, saying:

> I have seen kids dismantle one another, while parents and teachers stood passively by and observed the "socialization" process. I've seen the socialization theory in action, and it doesn't hold much water.[18]

Dr. Moore tells us of children raised in collective, group situations, that they

> grow up more and more dependent upon their peers in all social and emotional respects. Initiative and creativity are stifled. They do not learn the vital art of making independent decisions. By the time they reach adolescence and come face-to-face with the need to do their own thing—without group approval—they often appear virtually helpless, are caught in a traumatic confrontation, and many times cannot make such decisions at all.*[19]

In contrast to the public school, the home-school environment augments the child's security and self-confidence. Writing in the *Teachers College Record*, one of the most highly regarded of American educational publications, Dr. Moore argues:

> Parents and educators usually talk about sociability, but neglect to differentiate the kind of sociability they prefer. The child who feels needed, wanted, and depended on at home, sharing responsibilities and chores, is much more likely to develop a sense of self-worth and a stable value system—which is the basic ingredient for a *positive* sociability. In contrast is the *negative* sociability that develops when a child surrenders to his peers. (emphasis in original)[20]

The home-schooled child's environment does not force him to compete for love and attention, but frees him to grow into what his Maker has made him to be. This child also enjoys ample opportunities for interacting with other people, particularly of his own age; in the context of Christian community, for example, the child's life intertwines with that of his peers in a multitude of activities, crafts, skills, projects, fellowship and recreation. Dr. Moore shows that Christian home-school children surpass the "social skills" of other children, without suffering the impediment of continually seeking the plaudits and approval of their peers.[21] In the context of Christian community life, they learn to work, play, talk, plan, laugh and do all the other things with other children that God has created them

---

* We can explain the extent to which children raised on Israeli kibbutzim do not conform to this description by the extraordinary conditions of the pioneering life of that rising nation, thrust in the midst of a continual conflict for survival. Furthermore, the kibbutz child often enjoys the advantage of living in a land-centered culture. Today, however, we find a growing movement among the kibbutzim away from communal child rearing and back toward family-centered child rearing.

to do. Secure in the knowledge of whom God made them to be, they feel free to make friends without seeking to lose their identity in the crowd. Home school, more than *any* other type of schooling, provides the background most conducive to such development. While they can spend much of the time public school children spend going to and from school, in recesses and so on developing skills in reading and writing, in math, in foreign languages, music, crafts, agricultural activities and other productive functions, they also have time enough for play and peer interaction. The socialization theory of public school breaks down on every count as a viable defense of compulsory public education.

To repeat, researchers confirm that a weak family environment and thrusting children into a daily setting such as that afforded by the public school classroom or day-care centers *stifle* independence and increase pressures on the child toward peer orientation and the desire to conform to the opinions of others. Dr. Moore states that

little if any research evidence supports the belief that young children need more social opportunities than normally come from a combination of parents, relatives, and neighborhood friends. In fact, in urban, suburban, rural, and even remote areas, *most children develop better socially at home than in school.* (emphasis added)[22]

Dr. Moore's research shows that early "socialization," or the socialization of older children, in the school, and particularly the public school environment, undermines the child's personality and character development.[23] A public school environment rampant with drugs, immorality and violence often merely "socializes" the child into this kind of life style. Again, in a public school setting, the child's peers, more than anyone else, raise him. Their opinions and attitudes have the greatest influence upon what he thinks and feels.

Yet at the same time, Professor Bronfenbrenner contends, socialization in such large groups undermines the child's opportunity for *close* ties and contacts.[24] This means that the children experience only very shallow relationships with one another, relationships shaped and formed by the most superficial of social contacts. In such an environment, not the deepest emotions and understanding prevail but the most superficial—the herd instinct. In contrast, in the home setting the child experiences deep personal relationships with his siblings and his parents, and in the case of a Christian community, with other children and adults in the fellowship. His relationships with children outside the home or church also exist on a much more personal basis than the schoolyard or the lunchroom can make possible (after all, classrooms do not supposedly serve primarily as settings for the children's interpersonal communication, and if they do, learning breaks down almost completely).* With his character formed in the home environment, the child grows up with a security and self-confidence that enable him to interact with other people as an integral individual rather than as someone who seeks the meaning, purpose and security of his life in the approval of others.

The home serves as the God-ordained setting in which the child can solve that identity crisis that modern day academics so frequently bemoan. In the context of a loving family, in direct connection to the spiritual and physical roots from which he has sprung, the child really can learn to understand who he is and his purpose in life. This rootedness in the love and purpose of God and family gives a child the secure foundation from which he can relate to other people. The public school cannot provide the cohesive environment that nurtures the whole child as an integrated person, and yet the child's identity can stabilize only as he comes to maturity as a whole, integrated individual. How many children in public schools, even when they excel in academics or sports or in class popularity, nevertheless feel fragmented, without purpose or direction in life? Not the public school, but the home-school environment fosters the full integration of personality, character, talent and ability that constitutes identity.

If by socialization we mean instilling the ability to conform to the opinions of others, to "get along" with the mob by becoming what they demand of us, then, quite purposefully, the home school should fail. In contrast to the home school, the public school inculcates precisely such a conformist mentality, presenting the clearest example of the results of peer pressure. A 1982 survey of over 160,000 teenagers showed that "for most kids, school is a necessary evil that has one major benefit: It's a prime place for socializing" and that "for many kids the actual process of formalized classroom activity is

---

* See *Humanism* and *Brave New Education*.

secondary."[25] As one sixteen-year-old girl said, "My entire life is really school. I don't mean the work, but my friends."[26] But often this socialization in which "friends" come first provides, as we have said, nothing more than the intimidating context that draws innocent children into the world of drugs, immorality and violence.

Dr. Conway Hunter, Jr., director of one of the largest alcohol and drug abuse treatment programs in the country, at Peachford Hospital in Atlanta, contends that

> 90 percent of this country's high school students will use drugs sometime before they graduate.[27]

He says that "drug and alcohol use" have become "the biggest medical problem among girls" of this age group. He characterized the main force responsible for this "epidemic" as "destructive peer group pressure."[28]

This world, in which peer group pressure becomes the highest criterion in one's life, forms a perfect environment, as we suggested above, for the mentality and society so powerfully portrayed in Nobel laureate William Golding's *Lord of the Flies*, the story of a group of plane-wrecked British schoolboys alone on a Pacific island. The society of these young boys, unsupervised on their isolate island, dissolves into a bizarre imitation of pagan savagery replete with murder and torture. The most powerful social force becomes the pressure of the peer group in which children exercise influence in proportion to their brutality, hatred and malice. In the situation in which each one does his "own thing," pressure mounts to do the "thing" of the most savage and brutal, and chaos and mutual destruction ultimately result. In this world ruled by peer pressure, order returns to the children only with the arrival of a British warship. Similarly, in our increasingly humanistic society, some external, coercive power of the total State must act as an arbiter to step in and establish direction and order for this chaotic multitude that the public schools have themselves compulsorily "socialized" into this brute image.

Yet while the public school "socializes" students into a state of mindless conformity, the home school's "socialization" nurtures the child's ability to express his thoughts and feelings clearly, to relate to others as an independent, responsible and caring person while respecting also the integrity of others. Home education provides the most effective of all educational methods for positive socialization.*

The Testimony of History

The history of the Hebrew nation further shows the primacy of home education:

Throughout the entire history of the Hebrews the family was regarded as the fundamental educational institution.[29]

Education in early Bible days took place in the home. The parents served as the teachers, and they generally instructed the child in the duties of daily life.[30] Throughout this period

education within the family consisted chiefly of training and instruction in religion, morals, manners and industrial occupations. The aim of all religious instruction was to develop in the child a consciousness of his personal responsibility to Yahweh.[31]

De Vaux says that one of the father's

most sacred duties was to teach his son the truths of religion (Ex 10:2; 12:26; 13:8; Dt 4:9; 6:7, 20f.; 32:7, 46) and to give him a general education (Pr 1:8; 6:20 . . .).

The father also gave his son a professional education; in practice, trades were usually hereditary, and the crafts were handed down in the family workshop. A Rabbi was to say: "He who does not teach his son a useful trade is bringing him up to be a thief."

This educational role of the father explains why the priests, whose mission was to teach, are called "father" (Jgs 17:10; 18:19). It also explains how Joseph, who became the pharaoh's counsellor, was like a "father" to him (Gn 45:8) . . . . Similarly, the relationship between teacher and pupil was expressed by the words "father" and "son" (2 Kgs 2:12, compared with 2 Kgs 2:3; cf. the frequent use of "my son," "my sons" and "Hear, my son" in the book of Proverbs) . . . . There is, however, no proof of an organized system of schools until a late period.[32]

De Vaux says that the "word 'school' (*beth-midrash*) occurs for the first time in the" third century before Christ, that is, not

---

* See *Humanism, Conflict for Control* and *Brave New Education* for discussions of the conformist character of Statist education.

until after the voice of the prophets had fallen silent and the direct relationship between Israel and God had broken off.

In his study *Educational Ideals in the Ancient World*, William Barclay explains that

> to the Jew the real centre of education is the home . . . .
> In the pre-exilic days of Jewish history there is no trace
> of schools at all. "The home was the only school, and
> parents the only teachers.". . . Certainly in the homes
> of the ordinary people the parents were the only
> teachers.[33]

More specifically, we learn from Proverbs 31:1 that the mother became the representative of the father's authority— the father's prime minister—to teach the children at home.*

Moreover, home-schooled men founded both the Christian church and the American nation. The leaders of the Sanhedrin were "astonished" at Peter and John when they recognized them as "unschooled" men (Acts 4:13), or, as the Amplified Version says, "unlearned *and* untrained in the schools." Of the Author of our salvation, the Lord Jesus Christ, we are told that the amazed people asked of Him, "How did this man get such learning without having studied?" (John 7:15). Obviously, Jesus knew the Word of God, so the studies that they spoke of must have been formal schooling, and, in fact, one translation renders this scripture as, "How does this man know so much when he has never been to school?"[34] Finally, men schooled primarily at home, such as Washington and Madison, laid the foundations of the new American Republic.†

So we see that the Word of God, God's natural order, scientific research and historical evidence all concur that the responsibility for child education best rests with the parents.

State School or Home School?

Moreover, we cannot, without God's express permission, willingly surrender this delegated responsibility to another. God alone possesses unlimited dominion. Jesus told us to

---

* See footnote on p. 90.

† See *Conflict for Control* for a discussion of the home-school character of early American education. For other more contemporary examples of notable men and women educated at home, see p. 108.

render unto Caesar that which belongs to Caesar and render unto God the things that belong to God (Matt. 22:21). Since God delegates parents dominion over the training of their children, parents cannot voluntarily surrender this authority to the State. To do so renders unto Caesar that which belongs to Christ.

As followers of Messiah, we cannot voluntarily submit unto the State the responsibility that God has given to us for the education of our children. The State has no Biblically sanctioned authority to determine the educational standards for our children.* It is not a matter of our individual human rights against the rights of the State. As bondslaves to God's love, we have no rights *per se*, only privileges and obligations that our Lord and Master graciously gives us. But we have a responsibility to obey our Sovereign Messiah in all things and to render unto Him everything due Him. And because God has given the parents responsibility to bring up their children in the way that they should go, we cannot willingly relinquish unto the State the authority to decide what we can and cannot, or must and must not, teach our children. We alone must bear the responsibility before God to decide what they must learn.

When we see the meaning and purpose of Christian education (as we must by now at least to some degree), we can understand why God has entrusted parents with this task, and why the State remains utterly and completely incapable of bringing forth truly educated children—that is, integrated, whole, mature and responsible people able to find the fulfillment of God's purpose for their lives.

Many people, even some Christians, believe that the State holds a legitimate interest to see that all citizens receive a basic education and that therefore we ought to assure the government that we educate our children properly. Of course, God may have Christian parents demonstrate to government officials, as well as to anyone else, that our children can read, write and cipher. But such voluntary demonstrations differ from submission to mandated tests, curriculum standards or certification procedures that assume legitimate State authority and control over our children's education. While God may lead us to provide assurances that our children have mastered learning skills, we cannot submit to compulsory

---

* See *Who Owns the Children?*

educational procedures or State-ordained standards for our children's education. If we submit to such standards, we bring into our home the standards of an anti-God system that we have rejected for our children even outside the home.*

This position does not lead to "anarchism," as some have charged. To those who argue that the State possesses a legitimate concern to know that we properly educate our children, we can ask a number of pertinent questions, such as: What penalty does the State impose upon itself for all the millions of uneducated and often mutilated products of its own compulsory school system?† Since the answer is none whatsoever, how can it legitimately hold parents responsible educationally to the State when the State itself is irresponsible? Does not anarchy rather result from the attempt to apply a law to only one section of society (in this case, parents), a law from which the State declares itself immune? Will the State impose the same penalty upon itself that it would place upon parents? Obviously not, for if it did, the public schools today would be out of business.

And in fact, children educated at home do consistently better than publicly educated children—not only in mental skills proficiency but also in emotional stability and maturity, as Dr. Moore's research, as well as the research of others, has shown:

> For basic learning, the tutorial system has never been excelled by institutions. Students of genius point to the home school as a developer of great leaders, including John Quincy Adams, William Penn, . . . Thomas Edison, Woodrow Wilson, Franklin D. Roosevelt, Konrad Adenauer, George Patton, Douglas MacArthur, Agatha Christie, and Pearl Buck, among others.‡[36]

"A recent national study of home schools confirmed among

---

* For an extensive treatment of this subject see *Who Owns the Children?* The next three paragraphs also appear in that book.

† See *The Crime of Compulsory Education.*

‡ Others educated at home include John Wesley, George Washington, James Madison, Abigail Adams, Mercy Warren, Martha Washington, Benjamin Franklin, Patrick Henry, Thomas Jonathan "Stonewall" Jackson, Robert E. Lee, Phillis Wheatley, Mark Twain, Claude Monet, John Stuart Mill, George Washington Carver, Charles Dickens, Hans Christian Anderson, George Bernard Shaw, Alexander Graham Bell, the Wright Brothers, Pierre Curie, John Burroughs, Andrew Carnegie, Cyrus McCormick, Winston Churchill, A.A. Milne, Brett Harte, Albert Schweitzer, C.S. Lewis, Andrew and Jamie Wyeth, and Sandra Day O'Connor.[35]

its other findings that youngsters educated at home achieve higher than national averages in standardized measures. The Hewitt Research team's clinical experience with several thousand home schools verifies this."[37] Home-schooled children "from New York to California and Hawaii and from Alaska and North Dakota to Nebraska and Louisiana" perform "in the seventy-fifth to ninety-ninth percentiles on Stanford and Iowa Achievement tests."[38] Some of the highest scorers were taught by high-school-educated parents no more than an hour or two a day, "usually utilizing readily available home-school or correspondence curricula."[39]

We may further ask how anyone can define the State's interest in education in such a way as to ensure against tyranny. Would State interest extend merely to the ability of children to read, write and cipher, as the famous U.S. Supreme Court decision *Wisconsin* v. *Yoder* suggests?[40] If so, what level of reading comprehension should the State require? Should the level of functional illiteracy so common in the State schools serve as the standard by which home schools will stand or fall? If not, then we run into the problem of double standards and duplicity. When we ask these questions, we start to realize that most people have simply failed to clearly think through these issues, and the impetuous actions taken on the basis of such muddled thinking extremely endanger everyone's liberty.

For instance, if the State's legitimate interest in education should be to determine that people have a level of reading comprehension sufficient to fulfill the requirements of citizenship, then wouldn't the ability to make clear judgments also form an important part of such knowledge? Should the State then make determination concerning one's ability to judge accurately? Would the ability to hold a job serve as the criterion for a sound education? Should we make the criterion the ability to ascribe to moral standards that will protect the security of society? Once we permit the State to mandate standards, where can we draw the line concerning the State's legitimate interests and the criteria by which the State can determine if these interests are being met? Once we allow any level of State compulsion in regard to educational standards in the name of the State's legitimate interest, we open a Pandora's box of potential tyranny. This reverses a fundamental notion of American civil government, which declares the State the servant of the people, not vice versa. Similarly, in the historically popular American view, the people are supposed to create the State, not the State the people.

For this and even more important reasons, parents cannot surrender to anyone else the responsibility for deciding what their children must learn—parents must bear that responsibility themselves. Believing parents at least must make sure that their children's lives come under the Lord's dominion, that the children reach the full development of the whole persons that God intended them to be. No educational expert or governmental bureaucrat can have the necessary vision, which God gives to parents, to accomplish this. Dr. Moore states:

> In spite of current trends toward ever-earlier schooling or out-of-family care, strong, research-based data suggest that *whenever possible* parents should be their children's only regular "teachers" or care givers . . . . Unnecessary out-of-home or other alternative care may endanger the child socially, emotionally, behaviorally, and even academically. In such cases the psychological and sociological implications for the family and for society may be disastrous as parents relinquish their responsibility—and authority—during their youngster's crucial developmental years. (emphasis in original)[41]

Professor Bronfenbrenner concurs, warning that

> if the institutions of our society continue to remove parents . . . from active participation in the lives of children, and if the resulting vacuum is filled by the . . . peer group, we can anticipate increased alienation, indifference, antagonism and violence on the part of the younger generation in all segments of our society. . . .[42]

Christians and the Public Schools

Defenders of public education present a number of arguments in favor of sending Christian children to government schools. We have, however, already seen that this position stems from the failure to recognize the inherently religious character of all education. Therefore, such people fail to see that all education not completely centered in God will indoctrinate our children in an anti-God faith. Within the context of our understanding of the basic issues involved in this controversy, we will briefly examine some specific arguments presented by those who defend public schools as good educational environments for Christian children. A chief argument rests on financial costs: some parents supposedly cannot afford private education. But the home-school alternative demands very little financial investment, although it does require tremendous amounts of the parents', particularly the mother's, time. But if God tells us to take our children out of the public schools, then we can spare no sacrifice to accomplish that purpose. If God commands us to do this, we have no choice. Moreover, Christian schools have emerged in some of the poorest neighborhoods in America. Everyone can "afford" some form of Christian education if they will make the necessary sacrifice. Sometimes, as in the case of single mothers, the church community must make the financial sacrifice in order for children to be educated at home; but if we as members of the church recognize the importance of home education, then each of us must make the sacrifice for other children as well as our own, at least if we are to fulfill Christ's injunction to love our neighbors as ourselves.

Another argument tells us that many Christian children have in the past attended and presently attend the public schools and have continued to be Christians. In response to this, we may say that even though at times God overlooks our ignorance, He then brings forth a fuller revelation of His will and *commands* us to walk in the greater light that He reveals (Acts 17:30). If in our ignorance God mercifully extends His grace to us, we can no longer expect the same grace when we walk in willful disobedience to the revealed Word of God. We should use neither our past ignorance nor God's abiding mercy to justify disobedience to His commands. If God calls His people out of the public schools *today*, we cannot protest that in the past many have attended the public schools without loss of faith (and, of course, the moral and academic decline of the public schools in recent years has been amply documented*). If God reveals His perfect patterns of Christian education *today*, we cannot now ignore those patterns because we were once ignorant of them: "*Today*, if you hear His voice, harden not your hearts."

Moreover, we must remember that if thousands maintained

---

* See *The Crime of Compulsory Education.*

their faith through the public schools, those schools also corrupted millions, leaving them in the gutters of faithlessness and apostasy. How typical to find scenes such as the following: A father expresses displeasure at the direction his daughter's life has taken. The daughter, approaching the end of her mid-teens, experiences some grief at displeasing her father. A part of her would like to change her life style in order to please him. Yet at the same time, another authority stands over her life, one that she feels even more constrained to please: the authority of peer group pressure, the "social contagion" that first infected her in the public schools and has daily brought her under its increasing control for over a decade. Her god has become the god of popular opinion. But her attitude becomes understandable, almost even inevitable, when we recall that her father abdicated, delegated and released his own authority unto this institution for the purpose of training the mind and attitudes of his daughter. (Object to this assertion as we may, the courts hold it to be the case; for example, they have even ruled in some cases that a parent may not prevent his child from attending sex education classes once the parent has enrolled the child in the public schools.[43]) The authority of the State to which the father has released his own responsibility for and authority over his daughter has utterly undermined and overshadowed any godly authority the father may still represent. No wonder, then, that she bows down in submission to this greater authority! Given their goals, we can understand why secular educators want us to submit our children to this "socialization." But why would Christians want to do this? Why would this father want to ignore today the consequences *he* must weep over tomorrow when his daughter becomes pregnant out of wedlock, addicted to drugs or worse?

Almost every adult has passed through this same system. Why, we ask, do so many adults who at one time seemed to have convictions that would prevent them from giving way to the fashions, the fads, the changing tide of public opinion, end up flowing with the *Zeitgeist* and bowing down to the god of public opinion (just as the Germans did with Nazism before us)? They do so because they were trained in their youth through the very nature of the public schools to bow down to this god; and when they become old, they do not depart from their training. Here we find the explanation as to why many Christian parents, even though apprised of the public schools' condition, continue to insist on sending their children to the public schools: these institutions programmed these parents in their youth, socializing them into a mentality that places priority upon the opinions of their worldly peers, even above the Word of God or the welfare of their children. They have been raised in a school environment in which "sociability" is defined as one's ability to please the majority of one's schoolmates. A person growing up in such a social atmosphere is a person whose religious convictions will ultimately be defined by the opinion of the majority; the general populace will be his god.

Two important sociological studies present a perspective that tell us why public education must unquestionably influence religious convictions destructively because "strong social support is required for the maintenance of a system of religious belief."[44] Such "strong support" obviously does not exist in a system that bans by law the very murmur of God's name in prayer. The peer pressure so prevalent in public education hardly constitutes a "strong social support" for godliness. If we have been unfortunate enough to grow up under such circumstances, but have by God's grace managed to overcome the weight of such negative socialization, why would we want to impose this same disadvantage upon our children? If we truly do overcome this negative socialization, we will not want to impose such disadvantages on our own children. We would only insist that our children be subjected to our same disadvantages because we ourselves still worship the idol of public opinion, and that above and beyond our worship of God.

Of course, the secularist contends that the Christian child's greatest advantage lies in a public education. While he seeks to present this contention in a form convincing to Christians, a brief examination reveals that the supposed advantage that the secularist sees lies in the Christian child's indoctrination in a man-centered perspective antagonistic to Biblical belief. Secular educators often argue that a home-school education deprives a child of his "right to know," confining him to only one particular life style, set of beliefs, viewpoint and so on—that of his parents. While we deal with this question extensively elsewhere,* we should note here this argument's basis in another hidden and false assumption. This argument assumes that the

---

* See *Humanism, The Crime of Compulsory Education* and *Who Owns the Children?*

secularist perspective, which the secular educator insists that *all* children *must* be raised in, provides an all-inclusive, non-exclusionary viewpoint. The secularist believes that his educational system gives a balanced perspective that includes all viewpoints, thus offering the child the opportunity to choose for himself what he will believe. But the secularist view by its very nature rejects the Judeo-Christian view, which, again, it bans by law from the public schools, just because that view rests upon a belief in the *absolute* truth given to man by an omniscient God. Far from being all-inclusive, in its *relativism* the secularist view opposes the very basis of Biblical belief—Biblical *absolutism*. Whereas the Biblical view presents God's Word and His Spirit as the standard of judging truth, the secularist view places man's mind in the center of knowledge and understanding.

These two views mutually exclude one another. Since the advocate of each sees his own viewpoint as true, each believes that the child should be raised in that belief system (although for the consistent Bible believer, in contrast to the secularist, this hope does not include the desire for State compulsion to impose his views on the children of secularists or anyone else*). The secularist's argument for the child's "right to know" merely masks his real aim, the compulsory imposition of his man-centered views upon the children of those who believe differently. While complaining of the narrow-mindedness of Bible believers, the secularists seek to impose their own narrow dogma (so narrow that it excludes their Creator) through the compulsory power of the State—jailing those who refuse to believe in their relativist religion, just like the inquisitors of old. (Ironically, Hitler, too, saw himself as tolerant and open-minded as compared to the Christian dogmatists whom he purposed to eradicate from the earth as soon as he had finished with the Jews.[45]) Statist educators seem incapable of seeing the contradiction between the pluralism they profess and their dogged refusal to allow children to be raised in any viewpoint other than their own relativism. The secularist is blind to this contradiction. He clings so dogmatically to his own man-centered presuppositions that the God-centered alternative becomes simply incomprehensible to him. He is convinced that by keeping children from the truths of God's Word

---

* See *Who Owns the Children?*

he simply delivers them from hopeless superstitions and fantasies and brings them unto the light of scientific truth. The Bible believer cannot allow, however, this secular myopia to blind him to his own obligations.

When the secularist speaks of the child's "right to know," he implies the child's right to know everything; it is "the idea," described by Joyce Maynard, that we should "*not* . . . protect the children" but rather should "'expose' them."*[47] Children should be "dragged through the mud of Relevance and Grim Reality."[48] Raised according to this way of thinking in the sixties, she describes the effects of this "idea" upon her view of life and the view of her generation:

> . . . Now we have a certain tough, I've-been-there attitude. Not that we really know it all, but we often think we do. Few things shock or surprise us, little jolts our stubborn sureness that our way is right or rattles our early formed and often ill-founded, opinionated conclusions.
> . . . We play at vulnerability—honesty, openness, the sensitivity-group concept of trust, but what we're truly closer to is venerability. (emphasis in original)[49]

Ms. Maynard describes going to a circus with a four-year-old girl who, raised according to this same philosophy, remains unimpressed by everything she sees: "The tiger could have bitten the tamer's head off, I think, swallowed him whole and turned into a monkey and she wouldn't have blinked."[50] She describes the girl as suffering from "the kind of unblinking world-weariness that usually comes only to disillusioned middle-aged men and eighty-year-old rocking-chair sitters."[51] Exposed to everything, these children have the sense that they've "seen it all." World-weariness closes their eyes to the possibility of anything new. She describes the reality of the sixties generation, so envied by many of their parents ("Oh, to be young again . . . ," she quotes them as saying), as she experienced it:

What sticks in my head . . . is another image. I hear low,

---

* Ms. Maynard says that "surely there's some sense, at least" in exposing children to things.[46] But who will decide to what, how and when: the State or the parents? Surely someone other than the child will decide. Should the State apply a uniform, mechanical formula to everyone? Or should parents have the liberty to protect their children or to expose them to things according to the parents' individual conscience and convictions? See *Who Owns the Children?* for extensive discussion of these points.

barely audible speech, words breathed out as if by some supreme and nearly superhuman effort, I see limp gestures and sedentary figures. Kids sitting listening to music, sitting rapping, just sitting. Or sleeping—that, most of all. Staying up late, but sleeping in later. We're tired, often more from boredom than exertion, old without being wise, worldly not from seeing the world but from watching it on television.[52]

And what they didn't see or hear about on television, they learned about in the public schools.

What more perfect system could one imagine for undermining the faith that insists that you must "become as a little child" than a system that insists upon exposing children to everything until they no longer care about seeing or experiencing anything? Such a system is designed (whether consciously or not) to engender the world-weariness of an eighty-year-old at the age of ten. No wonder that suicide has become one of the leading killers of children in America.[53] They've seen it all, or so they've been told, and they're convinced that nothing remains to be seen.

From the viewpoint of the secular educator, the State must safeguard children; the State sees children as the victims of parents who would shield them from what they have the "right to know." The State must tear down the walls of privacy that surround the family so that the child can be properly and fully informed according to the principles ordained by the State. Since, as we've seen, to inform means to form the internal image of the person one informs, the assertion of a State-protected "right to know" becomes the assertion of the State's authority to mold and shape the child into the image it desires.

Once the State breaches the family's wall of privacy, nothing stands in its way from entering into the deepest chambers of the child's heart and mind. The State's insistence that the child must be exposed to everything without parental protection means the total exposure of the innermost being of the child. No refuge of privacy remains for him. So the assertion of a State-guaranteed "right to know" becomes the means for tearing down the outer walls of the child's privacy, making even the innermost sanctuary of his life into public property. When we remember that the Scriptures refer to the members of the Body of Christ, including our children, as the temples of the living God (1 Cor. 6:19), what can this desecration of the inner sanctuary of the child's heart and mind be but "the abomination that causes desolation" (Matt. 24:15), the desecration of the holy of holies of God's spiritual Temple? The "abomination" occurs when the "man of lawlessness" opposes and exalts "himself over everything that is called God or is worshiped, so that he sets himself up in God's temple, proclaiming himself to be God" (2 Thess. 2:3-4). The spirit of lawlessness seeks to use the compulsory power of the State to force its way into the seat of God's Temple, the hearts and minds of God's people.

The "right to know" serves merely as a slogan to mask the State's forcible entry into the private depths of the hearts and minds of children. If we recognize that God has made us and our children in His image, that He desires us to present our children "as a pure virgin to him," unspotted by the world, then we must resist the State's insistence to protect our children's "right to know." This resistance cannot entail merely an assertion of *our* rights against the rights ordained by the State.* Someone other than ourselves will dwell in the inner chamber of our hearts. Our choice is only whether we will safeguard this place in our children's hearts for their Creator or allow that place to open to the prince of the kingdoms of this world. If we recognize that God has placed something within us and within our children that no man can legitimately profane, we have no choice but to reject the logic and legitimacy of those who advocate a child's State-compelled "right to know."

Certainly, we cannot shelter ourselves from all worldly influence. Contact with the world is not only unavoidable but, for the sake of the Christian witness, desirable (1 Cor. 5:10). But while the salt of our Christian influence must savor the world, public schools, which form indoctrinating institutions for an anti-Judeo-Christian religion, are not an appropriate place for Christian children to function as salt. They do not salt this institution, retarding its corruption by the savor of their mature, strong influence, but rather this institution removes all savor from the infant salt of these children's lives, making them ineffective in their Christian witness. Moreover, all of us know that people in the world frequent many places that do not serve as appropriate contexts for a Christian witness. Should Christians attempt to "salt" pornographic movie theaters by receiving

---

* See *Who Owns the Children?*

input of information from them, or from witches' covens, sadomasochistic parlors, homosexual parties, satanic churches or from other similar places? Obviously not. Of course, many will immediately object that we cannot compare these extreme examples with the public schools. While people have characterized many of the sex education films shown in the public schools as pornographic,[54] even if the public schools avoided such extreme forms of ungodliness, from a Christian point of view they would still form a destructive educational environment. Even if no one made any *deliberate* effort to undermine Judeo-Christian values (and, of course, in many cases no such deliberate efforts are made), the entire *framework* of our public school system vitiates the Judeo-Christian view. In the public schools, hundreds and thousands of children come together each day in huge conglomerations. The courts legally exclude Biblical values from this environment. So in contrast to a Biblically based Christian school, the entire framework of the public school must exclude godly values from the regulation of social relationships, ethics and all other aspects of the life of the children in the school. That is, by legal definition, godly beliefs can have no acknowledged relevance in an institution that more formatively influences the lives of children in this country than any other, one that through its compulsory attendance laws demands that all acknowledge its supreme power and authority.

Moreover, whereas Bible-believing, Christian education stands upon the assumption that two natures war in every human breast, the carnal and the spiritual, and thus that we must make every attempt to aid the spiritual and restrain the carnal nature in this battle, the public schools exclude such an assumption as ridiculous. The neutralist philosophy, a form of humanist philosophy and the prevailing view within the public schools,* tells us that we have no such battle to fight. This philosophy considers as evil and destructive any attempt to restrain human nature. From the Biblical perspective, if we cannot even wage the battle against man's carnal nature, then that nature must prevail (Rom. 8:7-8). Obstacles confront our climb up the Calvary road that do not obstruct the downward slide of carnal man. In fact, no one need teach anyone how to follow the latter path. We find it as natural as water falling *down*

---

* See *Humanism.*

a precipice instead of rising up. The *natural inclination* of man's fallen nature moves in this direction, and the very object of humanistic education, as we have shown elsewhere, rests in this aim: to teach man to follow his own fallen nature. "Christians" who advocate that parents send their children into the public school environment implicitly accept this neutralist, humanist philosophy that directly contradicts Christian faith. They actively seek to place children in a spiritual environment that corrodes and destroys Biblical faith, and so they bear responsibility for the ensuing undermining of that faith. Ignorant of the spiritual significance of the education process,* through their lack of spiritual knowledge and vision they destroy those who follow their advice.† Truly the blind lead the blind.

Even if some public school teachers, and we know that some do, hold to Judeo-Christian values in their own lives, the law prohibits them from instructing children in their beliefs. And even in the days when prayers were allowed in the schools, the social framework of the public schools rested upon a secular viewpoint that militates against instruction in godly values. As Samuel Blumenfeld has shown, the public schools always viewed themselves primarily as bastions of secular education.[56] By excluding even voluntary prayer and Bible reading from the public schools, the courts have merely forced us to realize the true implications of these schools' secular framework and have torn down the storefront facade of piety behind which the gangster always works. Conversely, restoring school "prayer" would do no more than restore the storefront facade, and if done by constitutional amendment, would enshrine in the Constitution the implicit legitimacy of something never condoned by the Constitution: compulsory public education.

A teacher sitting in his or her geometry, chemistry or English class may have, and many do have, the most sincere desire to teach the student his subject. But the teacher constantly finds himself frustrated in this attempt because the basic purpose of public school education does not lie in the impartation of the subject matter of the courses. Rather we see the central purpose in the "social contagion," as Cornell's

---

* One Christian public school principal sees teaching as a mere technical activity comparable to flying an airplane.[55]

† See *The Crime of Compulsory Education* and *Humanism.*

Bronfenbrenner calls it, of the public schools, the social, peer group pressure placed upon each student to conform to the "spirit of the times" currently reigning in the schools.

As statistical findings show,* we do not reveal a cynical nature when we speak of the power of the "social contagion"; rather we reveal naivety and simple-mindedness when we believe otherwise. If the reader will recall his own school experience, he will find ample memories to substantiate this assertion even on this most personal of levels. As a Christian critic of State education pointed out a century ago:

> Every experienced teacher knows that pupils educate each other more than he educates them. The thousand nameless influences—literary, social, moral—not only of the play-ground but of the school-room, the whispered conversation, the clandestine note, the sly grimace, the sly pinch, the good or bad recitation, mould the plastic character of children far more than the most faithful teacher's hand.[57]

Nothing in this regard has really changed in the last hundred years. Since the basic presuppositions of public education only become more humanistic, the means of inducing conformity only become more sophisticated, devious and effective.

Whose Image?

The Judeo-Christian view *openly* proclaims that the educator, whether parent or classroom teacher, deliberately attempts to exclude certain elements from the child's life in order to nurture and encourage the *positive* values of Judeo-Christianity (though, unlike the narrow view of secular education which must utterly exclude its chief opponent, it introduces the child to all these views on a dialectic level). The believer *clearly* states his desire to exclude the ungodly as part of a positive effort to bring forth the image of God in the child's life. The public schools, however, must by law exclude the *godly*, the Biblical view, from the life of the children. Yet when a sculptor "excludes" pieces and chips from a block of stone, we do not look to the floor to see what he excludes; the *negative* act of "excluding" the chips of stone actually constitutes

---

* See pp. 126-27 below and *The Crime of Compulsory Education.*

the *positive* means whereby the sculptor *creates the image that he desires.* We see the same in the public schools: as the chips of godly principles fall to the ground, a definite image remains in the life of the child—the ungodly, secularized image of man into which public education shapes the child. No one notices the chips lying at the humanist educator's feet, and so the cry goes up, "What do you mean that public education excludes Judeo-Christianity? The purpose of public education does not include teaching the Bible!" But herein lies just the point: what does its purpose include, and what does it exclude? What image does it form through this process of inclusion and exclusion? The results of this process of "exclusion" are summed up in the words of an above-average college student who explains his experience at a secular university:

> You know, when I started college I thought my education would be a liberating experience. I thought I would add new talents, new capabilities, new accomplishments to my life. Instead, it's been just the opposite. Each course I've taken, each good book I've read, each idea I've seriously considered has taken something away from me. I feel like an onion that has had layer after layer peeled away until there is nothing, nothing there at all.[58]

This "neutralist" educational process, if it succeeds in its goal, results in the destruction of traditional values imbued by family and church. It leaves behind the nihilistic image of humanism to which generation after generation of unknowing children have been molded. But while this process has continued for generations, in our own day we see it pursued with deliberateness and zeal, and we find the result in the disastrous decline that we have elsewhere documented.*

When we understand the cumulative effects of this piecemeal exclusion of godly values from education and the piecemeal inclusion of humanistic principles in their place, the misunderstanding expressed in the following words by a high official in the Colorado State Department of Education becomes obvious:

> I personally feel that we have few people in the schools who are actively promoting the tenets of secular humanism as a part of a total philosophy. By this I mean that many teachers and others may be dealing with aspects

---

* See *The Crime of Compulsory Education.*

of secular humanism without connecting these components to a total belief system. I find few people even
aware of the fact that secular humanism has any official
meaning and specific tenets as apparently have been
outlined in various manifestos over the last few years.

. . . I am quite convinced there is no organized conspiracy to promote secular humanism throughout the
schools of Colorado by 99 percent plus of the educators.[59]

Whatever truth lies in these points fails to penetrate to the main
point. Whether or not the individual teachers in the "neutralist"
school system deliberately intend to imbue their students with
the "total belief system" of secular humanism, nevertheless as
students go from class to class and find God excluded
everywhere, they themselves will unconsciously put these
fragments together into a total picture presenting that philosophy. This result requires no deliberate "conspiracy." Court
decisions compel the public schools today to exclude any
alternative to the secular humanist philosophy; so the viewpoints and assumptions that the system does allow, when
added together, amount to nothing other than the secular
humanist philosophy, whatever the intentions of individual
teachers or administrators. In fact, the lack of an overt, explicit
system of indoctrination makes such an inculcation all the
more effective, as C. S. Lewis's earlier-quoted remark about
Gaius and Titius makes clear.*

Many people deny the possibility of imposing a uniform
philosophical outlook on all public schools because

local boards of education often are subjected to outside
pressure, but these pressures do not all emanate from
one political or ideological source.[60]

First, of course, outside pressure does not mean internal
change, especially with a system so entangled with State and
federal moneys, powerful organizations and lobbies, such as
the NEA and so on. Second, various political beliefs and ide-
ologies may influence America's public schools; but since the
courts explicitly and compulsorily exclude Judeo-Christianity
from the public schools, and since an explicitly secular
perspective dominates the universities and colleges that train
teachers and formulate curriculum, on the whole that system
must reflect the secular view to the exclusion of the Judeo-

---

* See p. 56.

Christian. In general, the system's "diversity" amounts to none greater (probably far less) than that between denominations of any single religion, in this case, the religion of secularism; and any apparent bending to "outside pressure" beyond leaning on entrenched "experts" usually amounts to nothing more than tokenism.

By its very nature, a State-compelled, mass educational system must eliminate the relational knowledge of God, basing itself upon the abstract, objectified knowledge of paganism. Its fundamental assumptions, methods and structures reduce the students to rationalized objects who must be inculcated with rationalized, objective knowledge of the world—all of this in a creation from which the Creator has been compulsorily excluded. To the extent that it can impart any knowledge at all, such a system can effectively impart only abstract, objective knowledge that promotes the man-as-god view. By its very nature, this system excludes the relational knowledge of the Biblical view. It thus excludes the manifestation of the image of God in man, which can come forth only through the impartation of this relational knowledge within the context of covenant. Again by their very nature, the public schools corrode godly covenant, since their whole reason for existence lies in the destruction of any kind of exclusive informing of children through the covenant of God.* "Socialization," in their view, means being uprooted from the covenant relations of God and conformed to the man-centered image imparted through the public schools. It is socialization on par with National Socialization—Nazism.

The definition of education given by one of America's leading educational historians, Lawrence Cremin,† confirms that education inevitably concerns itself with creating a definite image in the life of the child. Cremin states that education aims toward "the conscious ideal of perfection."[61] As James Axtell tells us, presenting Cremin's view, "True education implies 'the deliberate, self-conscious pursuit of certain intellectual, ethical, and aesthetic ideals,'" or "the deliberate, systematic and sustained effort to transmit and evoke knowledge, attitudes, values, skills, and sensibilities."[62] Axtell, professor of history at Sarah Lawrence College, states that Cremin recog-

---

* See *Conflict for Control*. See also Blumenfeld's *Is Public Education Necessary?*

† See also *Who Owns the Children?*

nizes that these efforts may be either "non-deliberate" or deliberate, and in his own definition prefers to confine himself to "*the self-conscious pursuit of certain intellectual, social and moral ideals* (which makes it normative)."[63] In any case, all education clearly involves the shaping of children into some "intellectual, social and moral" image. If a given educational system (such as that represented by the Colorado spokesman above) refuses to acknowledge the image into which it shapes its students, it merely shapes them deceptively rather than openly, even if it deceives itself as well as its charges in claiming that it is not doing so. If it attempts to convince itself and them that its educational products will have no image at all but will actually transcend all limitations, viewpoints and beliefs, then it again inculcates nothing other than the man-as-god viewpoint of the humanist religion; for to transcend the human situation means to arrive at godhood.

In addition to the above points, presumably parents do not send their children to school primarily to become witnesses but to receive an education, and given the religious nature of all education, public schools can clearly not serve as places in which to educate Christian children. Professor Arons gives us another confirmation of the religious nature of all education when he says,

> Because value inculcation cannot be eliminated from schooling, the notion of value-neutral education implicit in the legal distinction between religious and secular education is untenable.[64]

Since schools shape the religious and moral values of children, they necessarily influence and ultimately reshape or destroy the immature, partially formed beliefs of children. Many circumstances in life will serve as an opportunity for our children to be witnesses for Christ, but they must first grow in the grace and knowledge of the Lord so that they can serve as His witnesses, and the public schools prevent precisely such healthy, spiritual growth. For the child to resist the secular image that public education would impart to him, he must already stand established in the form of the image of God. But the child lacks just this: a mature form of the image of God. Precisely this immaturity of image defines him as a child, a child vulnerably susceptible in these the most formative years of his life and needing the proper education to shape him into God's image. The educational process trains our children up into the image of the god they will serve, and, again, the educational process of the public schools excludes by law the God of Christianity.

Some object that sheltering our children from evil influences will make them incapable of dealing with those influences when they confront them later in life. They will supposedly become like people who, because they never previously came into contact with a disease, succumb when finally exposed to it. In the first place, saying this acknowledges the infectious, sickening influence of the public schools. Moreover, as we discussed earlier, how does one protect someone against disease? Do we send him in a weakened condition into a diseased environment? No, we strengthen him physically, helping him develop strong resistance. Then we carefully expose him to the sickness we want to protect him from in a very small, controlled dosage so that he can build effective resistance to it. Only then does it become at all safe for him to come into contact with the uncontrolled disease itself. And since no immunization exists against some diseases, such as AIDS, our only protection against them lies in complete avoidance. Most of us also recognize comparable diseases of the soul and mind, such as Nazism. And we have gone to considerable lengths elsewhere* to show that regardless of what we perceive public education to have been in the past, it has now become the carrier of such spiritual, moral and mental diseases. Public schools have, according to Cornell's Bronfenbrenner,

> created and perpetuate the . . . often amoral . . . antisocial, world in which our children live and grow [and are] central among the institutions which . . . have encouraged these socially disruptive developments . . . .[65]

To distinguish evil from good, the child must first become strong in the good. The Christian educational environment affords him the opportunity to do this: to allow him to grow in the knowledge of the right and the true, and then, on the higher levels of his education, to come into contact with controlled dosages of man's false ways. Then the child stands ready to confront the world and overcome it, to truly be a witness and the salt of the earth. (We shall speak more specifically about

---

* See *The Crime of Compulsory Education, Humanism, Conflict for Control* and *Brave New Education.*

how we do all this later on in our discussion of the actual methods of Christian education.*) To fling a six-year-old child (now three or four in some places) into an environment that contains the most insidious and pernicious of evils in order to teach him to confront these things himself is like throwing a babe into stormy, shark-infested seas to teach him to swim. It means simply that we are reneging on our responsibilities as parents. And if we do this, we must search out our real motives. Does our motivation lie in love for our child, or rather our desire for the world's approval, even at the cost of conforming to its ungodly image? Do we seek to avoid that godly separation that elicits the world's opprobrium in order to avoid persecution for the cross of Christ (Gal. 6:12)? Being in the world but not of the world does not mean conforming to the world, but rather being a light, a shining, distinct, *separate* example to the world through our godly culture. By sending our children to public schools we raise them in conformity to the world, making them "of the world"; by rearing them in the nurturing environment of Christian education, we train them to live in the world, while they *refuse* to be of it. Only then can they "overcome the world" and truly fulfill their Christian witness to the world.

So we do not seek to cut our children off from all contact with the world, which is at any rate impossible. We merely seek to limit that contact within godly bounds and to provide a strong, secure and beneficial environment for our children to grow in, and from which they can relate properly to the world. This will provide a culture in which they can grow to maturity in wholeness and spiritual strength. These years prepare the child for adulthood: after coming to maturity, our children can go forth as *tamim* men and women to accomplish God's purpose.

Public school too imposes a controlled environment, a specially created nurturing habitat shaped and formed by educators to turn out a certain type of person. Otherwise, the claims of various courts that they must offer the child an "alternative" to parents' beliefs and values would be meaningless.† The real question centers on who will mold and shape the child's educational environment, the parent or the State? Christians readily admit that they withdraw their children from certain influences in order to shape them into the image that

---

* We also show this concretely in Supplement One, which describes our curriculum.

† See *The Crime of Compulsory Education* and *Who Owns the Children?*

they desire to see them conformed to, the image of Christ. It would help clarify the real issues of the debate if Statist educators would as readily admit what they themselves are doing: namely, seeking to mold and shape children into *their* desired image.* Yet all too often Statist educators repeatedly attempt to dodge clarification, which, according to the words of Jesus, indicates that their intentions are evil (John 3:19-21).

The only scientific findings painstakingly based on the study of *both* sides of the issue again confirm the positive benefits of withdrawal of children from the public school.[66] According to the Hewitt Research Center, separation from peer pressures such as those that the public schools always impose develops the strong convictions in the child that enable him to arrive at an independent evaluation of events free from the pressures of peers and society generally.[67] These positive goals form the basis of our withdrawal of our children from the public schools. In fact, as we have said, any sort of positive ministry to our children can be looked at in a negative light. When we feed our children, we "shelter" them from hunger. When we give them warm and dry homes, we "cloister" them from the wind, rain, cold and other elements. But we also provide them with conditions under which they can grow to be physically healthy and strong individuals, and by sheltering them from a mental and spiritual environment such as that found in the public schools, we provide them with an environment in which they can grow healthy and strong spiritually and intellectually.

Christians cannot "train up their children in the way they should go" (Prov. 22:6) or "bring them up in the training and instruction of the Lord" (Eph. 6:4) if they turn over to nonbelievers the educational process that molds and shapes values. In fact, as we saw, the Bible specifically tells us that our children should *not* learn the ways of the pagan (Jer. 10:2), and Paul warns us lest we be "spoiled" (which means "captured") by the philosophies and teachings of men (Col. 2:8, KJV). He also warns against that which corrupts us from the simplicity of Christ (2 Cor. 11:3). And yet how many times have our children "learned the ways of the pagan" through their association with public school and been "captured" and "corrupted" by public education?

---

* See *Humanism* and *Who Owns the Children?*

As we pointed out before, Jesus said that we cannot serve two masters. The professed Master of those who call themselves believers has given to parents the responsibility to raise their children. He has, as we shall discuss more fully later, also given to parents the *capacity* to raise their children. We earlier suggested that when we send our children to an outside agency for their education, particularly an agency that State authority compels us to send them to, we implicitly acknowledge an incompetency on our part to do the very thing that God has ordained us, and has therefore enabled us, to do. We then posit an outside agency with an authority that God has not given to that agency. This attempt to serve two masters can ultimately end only in the triumph of one or the other. Herein lies the reason the State struggles so ferociously to establish its control over Christian education, whether in the classroom setting or the home. Once we grant the validity of the State's authority in this sphere, the State then pushes forward to gain total dominance over Christian education. Then Caesar absorbs Christ's people into himself, and the church loses its salting influence in the world. We saw this clearly in the state of Nebraska, where the State had established in the courts its authority to compel the licensure of Christian schools and the certification of Christian teachers. It then proceeded to padlock church doors, jail Christian ministers and parents and seize children, church files and records in its bid to establish its total control.*

God entrusted the upbringing of children to parents. Parents, then, must bear the responsibility to pray and seek the mind of God in order to determine His will for their children's lives. Parents must prayerfully study God's Word and diligently seek

---

* We recognize that serious imbalances beset the position of the Christian minister who was most visible in this struggle, imbalances particularly in the attitude he expressed during much of the conflict. But he was not jailed for such imbalances.

In Nebraska, the State has now shifted its focus in its efforts to control Christian education. Rather than compelling the *churches* to report to the State concerning the students in Christian schools, the State now insists that the *parents* of the students report or that a person the parents designate report. While some Christians have seen this as a significant victory for Christian educational liberty, this would hardly be cause for rejoicing for those of us whose convictions dictate home education (see *Who Owns the Children?*). However we would view these concessions, we have now nevertheless seen something of the ferocity of the secular Statist educators' determination to impose their views on Christians.

His Spirit in order to come to their own clear convictions concerning the education of their children. Doubtless, scripturally, the pattern for Christian parents should be a Christian education for their children. But in a day when conflicts with Statist school officials may lead (as it already in many cases has) to the separation of children and parents, or the imprisonment of parents, we must pray past every obscurity, doubt and question in order to establish in each and every one of our hearts exactly what God wants us to do in regard to our children. If we will be faithful to do everything He requires, then He will protect our children under any circumstances, even if the State takes them away from us. But if we surrender to the secular educational system because we fear men more than we fear God, we will answer to Him for the consequences in our children's lives.

We should also remember that in all our dealings with the authorities of State and educational institutions, we must make sure that our spirits remain meek and humble, even when God tells us that we cannot comply with their requirements. (Meek, however, doesn't mean "weak.") We should have a real and living desire in our hearts to obey the ordinances of men in any way possible—without compromising the Word and Spirit of God. We should not seek to rebel against the systems of man, but rather we should desire to submit perfectly to God's will. When these two authorities make conflicting demands on our obedience, we should side with the higher authority and "obey God rather than men" (Acts 5:29).

The church is not a building, nor is it a set of creeds nor even a God-ordained eldership, although beliefs and eldership comprise necessary parts of the church. The church is the Body of believers arranged according to God's divine order and obedient to the Headship of Christ. We believe that we can acknowledge as at least part of the meaning of the church the general definition given in the courts today: "beliefs and believers."[68] The eldership of the church must prayerfully study the Word of God and preach that Word to God's people. But each and every believer must prayerfully receive God's Word and establish in his own heart what his convictions will be. The eldership must guide the saints (Eph. 4:12; Heb. 13:17), but the saints must train their own children. Therefore we do not look upon the training of our children as a separate "school" activity. In fact, the State and the media have transformed the distinction, accepted by many Christians, between church and "school" into a wedge by means of which the State has often inserted itself to undermine Christian education. The Bible teaches that the eldership serves for the "perfecting of the saints" (Eph. 4:12, KJV), and saints serve for the training of their children (Eph. 6:4). All of these functions comprise different elements of the one church of Jesus Christ, because all those involved are part of the kingdom of Christ which *is* the church (Col. 1:13; Acts 2:47, KJV; John 3:5; 1 Cor. 12:13; Rom. 14:17; Luke 17:20-21). Our children cannot be denied their place in His kingdom simply because the kingdom of this world declares that its claims on our children are prior even to God's.

CHAPTER FIVE
The Faith of the Parent-Teacher

The Parents' Capacity

Like any pagan priesthood, public educators have thrown up totems of taboos to intimidate others from entering behind the secret veil of their realm of power over the minds of their charges. This chapter will tear down some of these hollow totems.

As we have seen, the relational knowledge that God would impart to our children in order to bring them forth in wholeness finds its ideal educational setting in the home. God transmits His knowledge in all its spheres through covenant relationship, and for the child, the deepest of these relationships is obviously that out of which the child himself derived his own being: that with his parents. Only the parent can appreciate the total needs of the child's whole growth and education. This unique, God-ordained relationship between parent and child constitutes the central and primary (and unmatchable by anyone else) qualification of parents to serve as the teachers of their children.

Clearly, then, God has given responsibility for Christian education to the parents, and since He entrusts the teaching of children to parents, most instruction will take place in the home. The parents bear responsibility for the rearing of their children. (Indeed, as we have seen, *educate* means "to rear.") But God has not only given parents the responsibility to educate their children; He has also given them the capacity to do so.

Despite the continual propaganda barrage of establishment educators and psychologists, we will see that no one has a greater capacity to train and educate children than those who brought them into the world. We must recognize, first of all, that educators and psychologists have vested interests of power, self-image and money in convincing parents that these very educators and psychologists themselves know best what most benefits children. But the parents, not the professionals, conceive and give birth to the child, nurture him and meet his needs on a daily, even hourly, basis. The parents are most similar to and most familiar with their child. The parents know best his needs and potentialities. The parents have every possible God-given advantage to help them understand and be sensitive to the needs of their child, if they will exercise the "natural affection" that God has given them for their offspring. To again quote Dr. Moore:

> An alarming number of parents appear to have little confidence in their ability to "teach" their children. Research suggests that their ability to *care*, rather than to *teach*, is the criterion of parenthood during the early years, regardless of educational background. Sound care automatically provides sound teaching . . . . (emphasis in original)[1]

Dr. Moore suggests that parents have been intimidated into thinking themselves inadequate to meet their children's educational needs (mostly by those who derive prestige, power, wealth and livelihood by making them think so). In contrast to the educational establishment, however, he speaks of the parents' "astonishing potential as educators."[2] Through evaluation of thousands of home schools, Dr. Moore has discovered no correlation at all between the academic progress of the home-school student and the educational background or teaching credentials of the parent who teaches him.[3] Dr. Moore found that, given a warm and caring environment, children taught by those even lacking a high school diploma achieved as well as those taught by even certified *parent-teachers.*[4] (And certainly home-schooling mothers do consistently better as teachers than State-certified public school teachers.[5])

Dr. Moore's findings agree with those of R. Barker Bausell, a professor at the University of Maryland, who states that educational research shows that

> children taught in a one-to-one setting learn more than children taught in larger groups.[6]

Professor Bausell assures parents:

> . . . You will be amazed at how natural teaching your own child will be for you. No one is more qualified than

you, no one can do a better job, and in the final analysis you won't be able to find anything more rewarding in terms of both the results it achieves and the permanent relationship between you and your child which it helps to solidify.[7]

Likewise Benjamin Bloom, considered a "pioneer" in the movement to begin the institutionalized schooling of children at an early age, is now convinced through his own research that the home serves as the best place for children to learn and that parents serve as the best teachers.[8]

In a report on home schooling for *The Wall Street Journal*, in October 1986, Selwyn Fernstein reported:

> Carl Friedman, who tracks home schoolers for New York state's Department of Education, says they are "passing well above the norm." Parental dedication and the individual attention more than compensate for a lack of credentials, he believes.
>
> Mary Anne Pitman, an associate professor of educational anthropology at the University of Cincinnati, has been studying home schooling, and she concurs. "From what I've seen so far, these children are learning better than their counterparts in school, and they're in no way damaged by the experience," she says. "The more I look at public schools, the more I wonder how much greater harm home schooling could do."[9]

As we have seen, the education of the child's mental skills makes up only one part of his total education, and this part must be integrally related to all the others for true God-centered education to take place. The parents must also responsibly train the child in character, reliability and confidence. They do this through the day-to-day activities in which the child naturally engages when at home, through chores and even through play.

Parents naturally and continuously teach their children. Yet most parents distrust their own ability to teach their children intellectual skills. We too have seen, however, that through the actual practice of home education, genuine parental concern, led and guided by the anointing of God's Holy Spirit, and with help from other members of the Body of Christ, provides the firmest basis for the ability to impart sound training in intellectual skills as well as in other areas. If the parent has a God-centered vision of what his child is to be, and if he consistently and prayerfully nurtures his child in the way that he should go, a natural "teaching" relationship of parent to child develops. Through this unfolding relationship, both the parent's ability to teach and the child's ability to learn move steadily, step by step, to greater maturity. According to an article in the *University of Missouri Law Review*,

> Conscientious and informed parents are the most aware of their children's needs and are best qualified to integrate learning materials with their family's own philosophy and values.[10]

This natural, God-given relationship provides the basis of all sound instruction. The parent must, of course, know enough basic reading, math and so on to get his child going in these areas of his education. But as the child grows, the parents also grow in their knowledge and understanding. The parent does not have to be an expert on a subject to teach it. He simply needs to have the years of experience and knowledge that come with his position as a parent. He then has to be diligent both to stay ahead of his child in the subjects he teaches and also to impart his increasing knowledge to his child. Both parent and child grow together, but the parent must lead so that this growth process can continue. Any deficiencies in the parents' knowledge can find compensation in the Christian community to which they belong. The community should have people available to assist and tutor the parent until he or she can responsibly assume the role of teacher as well as parent.

Neither should parents feel intimidated by the notion that perhaps public school teachers have greater qualifications to instruct children. In the Hebrew Day School of Central Florida, *sixth-grade* students outscored prospective public school teachers on the same examination.[11] No factual evidence exists for believing that public school teachers are more capable than parents to teach.* One former sixth-grade schoolteacher, converted to home education, notes: "Mothers with the least formal education do best as home teachers; they are more creative and natural in their teaching. Everything I did in the classroom I had to unlearn to home teach."[12]

Yet on the other hand, a Christian writer associated with classroom schools contends in a popular Christian newsletter that while mothers may be effective teachers for the first years

---

* If anything, documentation proves the contrary. See *The Crime of Compulsory Education.*

of schooling, "few mothers can match the efficiency of professional teachers once the child reaches the fourth or fifth grade."[13] He offers no evidence or argument in support of this blanket assertion. Nor can he do so, since all evidence points to exactly the contrary conclusion. On standardized tests, for example, home-schooled children outperform classroom-educated children, both in public and Christian schools, far past the fourth and fifth grades.[14] Where do we find evidence of the "professional teachers'" greater "efficiency"? What do they learn in their "professional" education that makes them more competent teachers than parents? When we recognize the perspective from which Christian education should be approached—nurturing the *whole* child—what can professional teachers learn that will enable them to even come close to a parent's ability to educate his child? Obviously, a parent cannot bring his child to a level of knowledge higher than his own. But the parent—because of his or her love and burden for the child, and the natural God-given sensitivity to the child's needs that God places within the parent—can more effectively than anyone else bring the child to the parent's ever-growing level. (This stands in marked contrast to public schools, which, as we show extensively elsewhere, not only fail to teach students to excel above the level of their teachers, but do not even train them up to the teachers' level, which all too often is itself abysmally low.*) The parent also can and does continue to learn as she teaches: if the parent will simply study the subject that she teaches, then she can raise her own level of knowledge on that subject while at the same time imparting this further knowledge to the child. Of course, the point will generally come when the child moves on to learn independently of his parents, but this can happen only as the child becomes mature, after the parent has fully laid the foundation for the child's further development.

This so-called "Christian" writer also tells us that "we must acknowledge the reality of the division of labor," that is, that professionally trained teachers will be the most "efficient" producers of educated children.[15] But we have already seen the fragmenting "prostitute" mentality behind this philosophy. Moreover, our children are not simply another commodity on the marketplace to be more effectively produced by the fac-

---

* See *The Crime of Compulsory Education.*

tory mentality of "division of labor." They are made in the image of God, entrusted by Him to the parents for the purpose of forming their lives; and education is the process of forming a human life. As we have seen, the entire principle of division of labor in an industrial, mass-production economy fragments true God-centered relationship, and this fragmentation and prostituting of relationships can be seen nowhere more poignantly than in close, personal activities such as education itself.

This same writer tells us that "a school is simply an extension of the principle of the tutor" and that "the tutor, in turn, is an extension of the family."[16] Before schools were common institutions, any family that could afford to, he assures us, went out and hired a tutor. Later, he says, some tutors would take students from many different children whose parents could not afford individual tutoring, and so formed schools. This, he tells us, is simply the most efficient way to organize education.[17] But why stop here? Why not extend the principle further, as secular educators—and even some Christian educators—are doing, to television or computer education? Why not simply find the "best teachers" and have them make television tapes, and then all the children can sit in front of the television screens and be taught by the most "efficient" means possible?

The problem with this approach, however, reveals itself in that, as even secular educators like Benjamin Bloom have discovered, the one-on-one relationship, such as in home education, gives very real advantages in education.[18] A living, vital, close personal relationship between teacher and pupil helps the student to learn; the closer and more personal this relationship, the greater its advantages. This means that the individually instructed child has tremendous advantages over students taught through any other educational form. Statistics and research bear this out, while offering little support or conciliation to the above writer, who lauds the benefits of institutional education.[19]

Moreover, we can only believe that the institutionalized, specialist approach to education would be best if we look upon a child as a mere object, a kind of programmable computer. But if we see the child as a subject whom only relational knowledge can make whole, then home education clearly provides the best setting. Jesus told us that the *soil* makes the seed sprout (Mark 4:27-28). Far from being peripheral or incidental, the educational setting constitutes the living soil from which the child's life sprouts forth. Moreover, students are not abstractions with standardized, uniform needs. No single ideal teacher (except the Lord Himself) will be most effective for every student. God has made each individual student different and unique, and He has also specially designed and created a unique instructor, or pair of instructors, to teach that one student: the parents. The above-quoted writer sees education as a mere technique and the child as the product of the technique's factory, but totally fails to see its relational character; if he saw the latter, he would recognize the parent's God-given superiority for fulfilling this function.

We sometimes need private tutors other than the parents, for example, to teach a musical instrument that the parent doesn't know. And sometimes we need a classroom or workshop situation with a special instructor to get us started in knowledge that we do not have or for purposes of group discussion. But these classes will be most beneficial only within the context of individual parental instruction. Outside the classes, the parents must go over what the child has learned, draw out the details and then go beyond. So even if groups of children attend a seminar on history, the knowledge provided by that seminar will only be fully learned when the *parent* actively encourages the growth of that knowledge in the child. The parent must help the child to see this knowledge on a concrete, personal level. Often even when a subject, for example, a foreign language, has to be taught by a teacher other than the parent (and we have found that even here, both child and parent can learn the language together in the home), the child will learn most effectively if the parent learns it also and can thus be the child's private instructor from day to day. Again, all of this (in regard to all forms of advanced training) applies to the *child*. As the child matures, moving to adulthood, he no longer finds himself tied to and dependent on his parents in this way; but this particular type of independence only becomes possible after parents have completed the foundation that must be laid during childhood. During this period, we must always remember that, to repeat, even in those special areas where we need instruction from outside the family, as in various forms of vocational or craft training or in more advanced instruction in particular subjects, the parents must provide the active motivating force to ensure that the knowledge others may impart to the child actually becomes incorporated into his life.

While the writer whose views we have been discussing professes some acknowledgment of parental ability to educate, he actually believes that most parents can't really teach well at all. If a home-school mother teaches well, she is, by this author's definition, *not* "an average mother."[20] Because she rises above average, friends will notice that her child reads well, and other home-school parents will ask her to teach their children. Because they will pay her for this service, like a harlot who cannot resist selling her body for money (after all, she convinces herself, she offers them "love"), she won't be able to resist taking on other students:

> Money talks. Compared to the time it takes to make lesson plans, the extra student can't hurt, and besides, there's money involved.[21]

Since this parent-teacher now instructs children other than her own, she has become a professional educator. This writer has convinced himself that this will be the case with all really good home-school teachers:

> The more successful [the mother] is with her children, the less likely she will be able to resist the financial opportunities placed in front of her to leave home schooling and become a professional.[22]

The dollar's call, then, will transform every competent home-schooling mother into a professional educator. All the rest, presumably incompetent, will send their children to these professional educators, and the private institutional school will prevail.

Again, this logic bears striking resemblance and analogy to that of another professional who cannot understand how love could be a more powerful motive than money—the professional prostitute, who also believes that the professional institute—the brothel—will finally prevail over the home because of convenience, money and expertise. But as logical as this scenario for home education's future may seem to its author, its premises rest in his own fantasies rather than in fact. Possibly this writer has seen home-educating mothers become professional educators in the way he describes; we find it hard to understand that he would make such critical assertions without having any evidence at all. We can only say that in over a decade of home-school experience, with close contact with many hundreds and indirect contact with thousands of home schoolers all across the country, we've never heard of a single instance where this has happened. The trend we have seen is not home-school parent-teachers becoming professionals but rather professional educators becoming home educators, and often trying desperately to unlearn much of their "professionalism" as they do so. They find the "call of the dollar" (apparently so compelling for this author and educator) less appealing than the call of love and fulfillment found in the covenant bonds of Christian home education. The implied assertion that only the children of exceptional home-school parents learn to read well also clashes with the facts. According to Dr. Moore, the Hewitt Research Center's clinical experience with several thousand home schools all over the nation reveals that home-school students often score between the seventy-fifth and ninety-ninth percentiles on Stanford and Iowa achievement tests;[23] often the parent-teachers of these high-scoring students have no more than a high school education. And in the hundreds of home-school families who have contacted the Center for help with legal problems, not one of the students failed to perform well above the national average academically.[24] Our experience matches Dr. Moore's. All the home-school children we know read very well, with higher average skill and comprehension than their institutional school peers. Their knowledge and skills have advanced; blessings, benefits and joy have filled their lives and their parents' lives. These parents are not desperately watching for some competent teacher somewhere to teach their children to read. Surely, some parents need help; some teach better than others, and the better teachers sometimes help the less gifted. But these parents don't offer their assistance because they hear the sound of money talking; they hear and respond to another Voice and receive absolutely nothing for their services except the blessings of giving, which so exceed those of receiving (Acts 20:35).

A few home schools doubtless do fail, but the problem usually lies in the lack of a Christian community to assist and support the parents' efforts. Numerous Christian educators and churches see this need and actively seek to remedy it. In direct contradiction to the view expressed by the author of this scenario, more and more recognize that not home schooling but the Christian classroom-school is the "transitional" form.

Further contradicting this above author's assessment, the Scripture makes very clear the dangers of relying for any sort of responsible care and training upon the "hireling." In order to warn his hearers of the dangers of leaving our spiritual care in the hands of someone who works simply for money, Jesus used the common occurrence in His day of the danger of leaving sheep with a hired hand (John 10). Even if our children do need special instruction and training, to the extent possible this should be *freely* donated by those within the Christian community, those bound together in the covenant of God's love. These brothers and sisters will have a true burden and desire to impart the necessary knowledge to our child.* But, again, this type of instruction will not serve as the rule, but it must be reserved for exceptional subjects, circumstances and needs. It will generally take place when the child has reached a certain level of maturity and has had a good general educational grounding imparted to him by his parents. Whatever the educational experts tell us, God surely chose for His only begotten Son the most effective means of education, and that means was, as the Scriptures themselves testify (John 7:15, NASV), home schooling.

Children may also need special instruction from brothers and sisters outside the home to learn particular crafts. But this instruction should all be directed toward work in the home, moving forward with each child under the guidance of the parents. To the extent possible, particularly with younger children, the parents should be directly involved in any special workshops or classes their children attend, and the parents themselves should serve as the main instructor, learning, if need be, with the child. Those brothers and sisters experienced in certain crafts would then serve as special teachers and advisors giving instruction and advice only as needed. (In chapter 8 we discuss how in our fellowships

---

* If specialized subjects must be taught by someone outside of the covenant, this simply indicates a lack within the Christian community, a lack that will be filled as members of the community go out and themselves acquire the necessary knowledge. But those who go out to learn these special skills will not be children; they will generally be adults who will be able to teach others. Once they learn these skills, no one will need to go outside the community to learn them. Of course, this does not mean that no sharing of knowledge between the Christian community and those outside will occur. The point here focuses on the education of children. And children's education should take place almost entirely within the context of the covenant relationships of the Christian community and primarily within the family.

we have set up such a structure with teachers and advisors to help parents, all based around an annual festival to display the crafts and skills of our community and particularly of our children.) Brothers and sisters with special knowledge in scholastic subjects, such as math, science and English, should also make themselves available to advise and instruct home-schooling parents. But, again, the primary burden for instructing the child must rest directly on the parents. Obviously, from all we said, home schooling entails an intense, comprehensive educational experience for parents as well as children. So parents don't have to think to themselves, "I wish I had the chance to learn that." Home school gives them the blessing of learning the skills and crafts they thought they'd never have the opportunity to learn. Necessity requires that they receive these blessings, because if they want their children to learn these skills most effectively, the parents must learn them, at least to some degree, too.

You must always remember that God has given you the responsibility and the capacity to train your child, that He has placed you in a unique and ideal relationship with your child to meet *all* his needs more effectively than anyone else can. If you remember this, then everything else will take care of itself, with the help and guidance of God's Spirit and of others who follow the same direction in the rearing of children.

In this context, we must make a crucial point concerning Christian home education, a point to which we have already referred in passing. This concerns the ideal situation for teaching children, and indeed for child rearing and Christian living generally. You will find this ideal situation only within the context of the life of a community of believers. Of course, if some rare or unique necessity forces a family into temporary isolation from life within a Christian fellowship, God will make a way to supply all of the children's needs, educational as well as spiritual. In fact, according to Dr. Moore's research, even a bad family provides a better environment for a child than a good institution;[25] how much better, then, should a Christian family be, even an isolated one! But within the context of the Christian community, parents can find added strength, encouragement and reinforcement to do the will of God. As adults fitly joined within the Body of Christ, discipled and taught through a Spirit-anointed eldership, living in the context of the anointed ministry of a thriving Christian fellowship, parents will better disciple and instruct their children.

The context of Christian community becomes vital for the full development of the whole child (as well as the whole adult), whose soul will most fully grow to maturity only in the midst of that concatenation of relationships that thrive in such a community. On one's own, the danger arises that the parents will become susceptible to the weakness of the carnal nature. Then they will ultimately discard in frustration those patterns of God that have proven so rewarding and successful to thousands of other parents and children and that have served the people of God so well over so many centuries. Furthermore, in a community setting, others besides parents can help in the instruction of special subjects and skills—for example, foreign languages, musical instruments, carpentry, farming, ranching and so on—and those in the community with such skills and talents should feel a responsibility to impart them to other children as well as to their own. As we will show when we discuss our Koinonia Curriculum, the community life and particularly this sharing of crafts and skills perform a key function in enabling parents to fully realize their responsibility to train the whole child.* Only in the context of community can children encounter the full range of gifts, knowledge and wisdom that will enable them, under their parents' guidance, to find and wholly fulfill the entire range of gifts and talents that God has ordained for their lives.

If necessity prevents you from becoming part of a Christian community for a time, we do not in any way wish to discourage you from undertaking the education of your own children. We believe that you should do so, but you must be aware of the additional difficulties you face. You should recognize that you and your children are less than ideally situated, and you must prayerfully seek God's will that He would make a way for you to join with a community of home-educating believers so that you and your children may have the blessing of growing together with your brothers and sisters in Christ.

Unless we press on to find our place in the Body, devastating and tragic consequences often follow for both ourselves and our children. The context of the Body, with the pulsating rhythms of its spiritual life, its binding of us together in continuing, day-to-day, personal relationship with our brothers and

---

* See Supplement One, "Koinonia Curriculum."

sisters, forces us to come out of ourselves and to walk in God's light. When we try to walk with Jesus by ourselves, only tangentially related to God's people and without binding relationships, we have a natural propensity to make of ourselves the standard by which we judge our walk with God. When this happens, we will increasingly conform ourselves not to God's image but to our own. The Scriptures warn: "He who separates himself seeks his own desire . . ." (Prov. 18:1, NASV). When we willfully separate ourselves from the Body, in other words, we do so in order to follow our own will rather than conforming our lives to the patterns of God. Left to ourselves, to our own hearts, we will eventually become centered in ourselves rather than in God. Jeremiah makes this danger clear when he describes the heart as "deceitful above all things, and desperately wicked" and reminds us that no man can fully know his own heart (Jer. 17:9). Left to ourselves, our original vision, our "first love," will fade. Our relationship with God will slip away from us imperceptibly as He leaves us to those self-images to which we in our stubborn self-isolation insistently cling.

These above effects of spiritual self-isolation become still more apparent in home-schooled children. Our children do need a sort of peer association, albeit of the positive kind discussed in the previous chapter. If we isolate ourselves and our children from the relationships of a spiritually integrated community, our children too will tend to become their own standard. Unacquainted in real relationship with children of greater gifts and talents in certain spheres than their own, isolated children develop an inflated view of their own abilities. They grow up without living relationships to bring them down to earth. They think of themselves as better than others, rather than esteeming others more highly than themselves (Phil. 2:3), and this often because there simply are no others for them to esteem. Without real humility, they become self-centered and self-assertive. The home school in such situations becomes not God-centered but "child-centered" in the sense advocated by anti-Christian "progressive educators." These humanistic educators, however, advocate "child-centered" education because they *want* to undermine God-centered belief.[26] Christian parents must seek precisely the opposite goal: education that pulls the child out of himself and centers him in God. This is impossible without God-ordained relationships of the Body that express God's Headship, relationships that help each of us to find our place and, with that place, our proper perspective of ourselves and our children. We need penetrating insight from the Spirit to overcome these man-centered tendencies and to direct our child's whole life toward God as the center rather than himself.* But we cannot *consistently* receive such insight in spiritual isolation. How much better we can see when the reflection of the light of God's Word is shining all around us in the faces of our brothers and sisters (2 Cor. 3:18)!

Life in God-centered Christian community cuts these dangers at their very roots. For the community setting conforms the parent to an image that does not originate within himself but with the God who heads the community Body. Since the parent is actually overcoming self-centeredness, he becomes equipped to overcome child-centeredness, to help conform the child to the image of Christ. And why would any Christian persistently resist finding his place in the Body in the first place, except if he desired to protect his self-created image and independence? For such individuals, home schooling, though almost always motivated to at least some degree by godly motives of parental burden and responsibility, becomes leavened by man-centered yeast. The parent prides himself on his special uniqueness and superiority and instills this attitude in the child. The image and demeanor of worldly sophistication and superficial, pedantic affectation begin to leaven the whole loaf of the child's life: leaven inflates things, it puffs them up, and the knowledge we instill in our children in this context becomes the knowledge that puffs up (1 Cor. 8:1). As they grow, we may wonder where the discipline problems in our self-centered children come from, since we taught them at home. But they come from us, from our own refusal to submit to our Father's discipline in the family setting He has provided for His people—the Body of Christ. He has provided the local church for the parents' "home schooling." The human heart carries its own corruption and needs no outside source to poison its offspring. We cannot truly nurture our children in a godly culture unless we ourselves submit to the Husbandman's continual pruning, dunging and weeding (Luke 13:6-8; John 15:1-6). Otherwise the plant placed in the soil will die. Within the con-

---

* We discuss later an example of how such penetrating insight can come through the study of English, particularly of writing skills. See section two in chapter 9.

text of this understanding of the depth of our spiritual need, we see that home-school support groups, while certainly preferable to complete isolation for both home-school parents and children, cannot really meet our need to find the place within that covenant Christian community that constitutes our own home in God. Self-centeredness has become the disease of our age, and God-centeredness is the cure. The home school provides the setting to minister the cure to our child, *if*—as with all of God's promises—we follow on to walk in the light in faith, joined as members to His Body. Our function as parents does not define our whole being, and unless we become the *whole* people that *we* were ordained to be by coming into the fullness of God's relationships for us, we cannot bring our children forth to become the whole people God would have us raise them to become.

While the Christian community provides the essential "home" for the home-school family, the immediate context of home schooling of course remains the home itself. God sets everything up to enable us as parents to teach our children, if only we will follow fully the patterns that He has established. He created in the home, not a "division of labor" of the industrial specialization sort, but the integrated pattern of interworking, functioning members of a Body so that the child can grow up in a perfectly structured order that will meet all of his needs. The Bible clearly specifies that the father should be head of the household (1 Cor. 11:3).* He has the general oversight of the rearing of his children; he functions, so to speak, as the home-school "principal." But the mother functions most directly and actively in the educational process. Although the world today does everything possible to discourage women from fulfilling this high purpose, the mother's primary function in serving her husband remains the discipline and education of her children. She must work to make disciples of her children just as the church must fulfill this function toward its children, the church which is "the mother of us all." The church too serves as the prime minister of her Husband, Jesus Christ (Eph. 5:23), in the discipling of His sons and daughters (Matt. 28:19). Despite the perverse reasoning of modern society, a mother's reward in shaping and molding a human life in love far surpasses any reward garnered from

---

* See *Community and Family*.

pushing buttons on a supermarket cash register (though we are not trying to disparage either those forced into such positions by real necessity or God's special reasons for putting people in such positions) or even functioning as a high-powered executive in a major corporation.

But God has not only given us the capacity, the structure and the natural affection to educate our children. He has also given us His Holy Spirit, which must serve as our main guide in child rearing (John 16:13). By prayerfully seeking His will and being sensitive to His Spirit, you will know what to teach your children and how to teach it (John 16:13; 12:49). (God will also provide you with people to help you in this task—for example: teaching ministries to prepare God-centered curriculum materials; ministries to help disciple you to fulfill your child-rearing functions; other experienced parents to help you through difficulties; brothers and sisters to teach and advise you with the additional knowledge you need to teach in every subject area and craft and so on.) Your goal is not to recreate all the pressures, agonies and problems of the schoolroom setting in your home. You must always remember that through home schooling you take on the total education of your child and that his academic education is only part of this; but at the same time you cannot use the limited importance of academic instruction as an excuse for reneging on your responsibility to impart this instruction. Only God's Spirit can lead you into the proper balance of what and how, when and where, to teach. Although those experienced in home education can recommend a general pattern and curriculum and be helpful in many other ways,* you will always bear primary responsibility for the impartation of the material, for example, when and how to impart it on a daily basis, how fast to proceed and so on. Curriculum helps can greatly simplify this task, but the ultimate burden, responsibility and especially blessing belong to you. You may have to supplement your curriculum materials with other resources and with your own experience and knowledge. Again and again, you must remember that you are training and teaching a total person, not simply an individual ability in that person, and you can only do this by the very impartation of your own life.

For these reasons, under every possible circumstance, a

---

* See Part Three, "Particulars."

parent willing to yield to the natural affection that God has given him for his child makes the best possible teacher. Because of the parent's closeness to the child—the very nature of their relationship—he naturally can best recognize the child's talents, abilities, needs and interests. This fact was once commonly recognized in the United States. As one Illinois court declared in 1887,

> The policy of our law has ever been to recognize
> . . . that the [parent's] natural affections and superior opportunities of knowing the physical and mental capabilities and future prospects of his child, will insure the adoption of that course which will most effectively promote the child's welfare.[27]

Admittedly, as we've said, certain subjects necessitate having help from others, for example, teaching carpentry or a foreign language. But, again, even when we need such outside help, it will be infinitely more productive if reinforced by the parent. And in most areas, the parent himself or herself is always the best possible instructor.

Within our own practical experience, we have never found a parent who really wanted to teach his children who didn't do an excellent job. In fact, we have found that the most difficult children, children who were absolute failures in the public schools, have flowered under home instruction.

For example, children who had serious learning and behavior difficulties in public schools have flourished under home education. And many excellent home-schooling parents were themselves considered problem learners in their public school days. One mother who did not finish high school took her son out of public school in the fourth grade to teach him at home. In the public schools this same boy did academic schoolwork below his grade level, but during his home-school years he was almost two years above his average grade level. Now he carries major responsibility for agriculture and horse farming on a ranch, having also worked as a building carpenter's assistant.

Another girl was also taken out of the public schools in the fourth grade. Her school psychiatrist characterized her as having a severe learning disability and said she had an attention span of only one minute. After working throughout her home-school career well above her grade level, she is now productively employed. In her first job after completing her schooling, her employer continually remarked on the load of responsibility she, still in her teens, was able to bear and the high quality of her work. When she was eighteen, her employer wanted to make her assistant manager of the large fabric store in which she worked, but she left that job to become self-employed as a skilled seamstress.

Nor is such remarkable improvement confined to children with learning problems. Young people who were notorious discipline problems in their public schools have been remarkably and quickly transformed into well-disciplined and truly happy children through home education.

As we have said, you can be sure that God has given you the ability and the capacity to teach your child. In our experience, we have seen that even mothers with an incomplete high school education or those who did very poorly in school can make excellent teachers for their children, given a right heart and a willing and committed spirit. In almost every case, the difficulties that parents had in their own schooling resulted from the very problems in the educational process that a Christ-centered home-education program overcomes. One mother who dropped out of school, bored with her education in her middle teens, has become one of the most enthusiastic and excellent teachers we know. Her oldest daughter, who has received all of her schooling at home, has throughout her ten years of home schooling been consistently above her grade level by about three years! Her mother also now helps to develop curriculum. As we said, as you teach your child, you will grow in confidence, ability and knowledge. God has given you the ability to learn and to teach, and He can bring these abilities to life in you again, despite all of the destructive years that you may have spent in public educational institutions.

Persevering to Life and Victory

So as a parent, you without doubt have the capacity to educate your own children. But this doesn't mean that you won't face obstacles in this task. When you confront those barriers, you'll have to pray, to study and at times to seek help from other brothers and sisters in the Lord to find the power to overcome. But if you persevere, God will certainly bring victory. Through this victorious struggle to overcome, you'll *regularly* ex-

perience His life and love flowing to you and through you to
your children at a depth that you may have experienced only
rarely before.

As we've seen, in addition to the obstacles you must overcome in home schooling that stem directly from your
children's education, you must also overcome the pressures
of a culture that almost universally agrees that your children
need professional educators to instruct them. Beyond this, not
only has our whole society combined to undermine the
parents' confidence that they can educate their children, but
also to most in today's culture it increasingly seems insane
that anyone should fight to *assume any* responsibility,
particularly a responsibility that requires the effort and commitment of home education.

We can recognize the attitude of our society toward assuming responsibility in the words spoken by a German citizen
under Nazi rule. When an American visitor expressed his view
to this German that the people had sacrificed their freedom to
Hitler, he was countered with the remark:

> But you don't understand at all. Before this we had to
> worry . . . . We had *responsibilities*. But now we don't
> have any of that. *Now we're free.* (emphasis added)[28]

Many, if not most, in the urban culture of America today hold
a similar view. To them also it seems increasingly insane that
anyone should fight to *assume* responsibility. Like the Nazis,
they ask why we should struggle to assume such burdens of
life as home education at a time when the State offers the
benefits and the covering of Social Security, Medicare and
certified nursing homes for our elderly, as well as the covering
of licensed medicine, day care and certified teachers for the
birth or rearing and education of our children. But for more and
more parents, overcoming such obstacles as those involved
in raising children becomes a fundamental part of the victory
that comes with fulfilling their lives. Parents who have experienced the excitement of teaching their own children at
home, of meeting the challenges and digging through to overcome the obstacles in educating their own sons and
daughters, have exclaimed that they found it "so rewarding
they would have to chop me off at the shoulders to make me
stop."[29]

To fully understand why parents can, should and must persevere to see their responsibility to educate their children

through to victorious completion, we need to again look at home education in a larger perspective, one that encompasses our entire lives. As we saw at the beginning of this study, we aim through home education to raise *tamim* children, whole children, and we also saw that "education" encompasses our entire way of life. To raise whole children, we must be whole people, *tamim* individuals, ourselves. Yet home education not only demands wholeness from us, it also helps *bring* wholeness to our children and to ourselves as well. In fact, the desire to educate one's own children doesn't generally come to parents as an isolated desire, but rather as part of a whole vision of life, however vaguely perceived this vision may at first be. People who become home schoolers tend to move into a wide variety of related activities, a whole way of life that involves seeking out God-given, natural patterns in every area. Even when they can't understand all the whys and wherefores, they feel a deep desire—a desire so strong it impels them to act—to break away from dependence on the institutions of man (his State, his cities, his giant industries), to get in touch with their roots and bring control of the basic necessities of their lives into their own hands. This includes meeting such challenges as growing one's own food and often delivering one's own babies at home.

But increasingly, the world decries those who seek to meet the types of challenges involved in taking responsibility for and dominion over such basic necessities of life. Instead, our modern society offers many diversions and artificial contests against which parents might pit their "strength." Some attempt to find the "victory" in their lives by becoming a champion softball player or climbing the corporate ladder or entertaining the office as the best jokester or pursuing a multitude of other "directions" modern life has opened before us. In a world that imagines itself freed by the gadgets of technology from its tether to the simple and necessary, people have lost the path to genuine fulfillment in the midst of a bewildering plethora of petty options. Trendy life styles have replaced the abiding essentials of life in a world where technology and the State have supposedly relieved us of all life's burdens. We can't see the old landmarks, which define the path of life, for the clutter of billboards along the way. But to live, you must first discover something worth living for, something worth pouring yourself out for and something capable of holding together what you've poured out, something of intrinsic value, not just the value of the marketplace.

People who pursue the multitude of the world's quixotic quests often arrive at the end of their lives feeling that somehow, even though they may have "gained the whole world," they have lost their own soul. Their senses do not deceive them at that moment of reevaluation, for they have indeed poured out their soul into buckets with holes in them. They could not find the path marked out for them that confronted them with the *real* battles that would give them genuine victories. The culture they participated in just doesn't hold together well enough to contain what they have poured into it. And so their life seems to dissipate before them like spilt water in the sand.

Nonetheless, most people today still chiefly aim to merely gain escape from the labor of pressing against the obstacles standing between them and their full participation in life. It's just too much to ask them to reach for life in its necessary essentials, to press over and past the obstacles, and so to overcome them. Those trapped in this escapist mind-set are simply puzzled: "Why would anyone risk all the legal problems, the demands on time and energy, of home education? Why don't they just send their children to the public schools? Why do they bother trying to teach their own child to read and write? Why study American history with him? Why read all those books? Why pray all those prayers? Why spend hours studying and teaching? Why don't they just send the wife to work, increase their income and let the public school professionals take care of the kids? After all, they pay their taxes whether they use the public schools or not. Why do they teach their sons leathercraft or woodwork? Why not just let them get jobs at McDonald's and then buy their shoes and furniture? Why do they teach their daughters to spin, weave and sew? They can get a job at Burger King and buy their clothing." The questions can go on to cover every area of life: "Why would anyone risk all the legal problems and physical dangers involved in a home birth? Why don't they just go to the hospitals? Why would anyone go to all the trouble of butchering their own meat? Why would they struggle so to grow their own food when they could make twice the money for their efforts if they specialized and sold their labors and just went down to the corner supermarket and bought their meat and vegetables in nice cellophane packages? Why do they try to make life harder than necessary?" Like the prostitute who specializes in an area of life that was to find its place in a unity of being and who cannot understand why a woman would "enslave" herself to the covenant love of marriage rather than simply sell herself for money and buy whatever she wants, our modern Babylon cannot understand why anyone would refuse that specialization of labor whereby people sell certain gifts, talents and functions of their life on the job market and then buy the essentials of life, such as education for their children, foregoing having to actually and directly participate and invest themselves in those essentials.

The obvious answer is that the opposite of life is death, and those who want to truly live determine to forever do battle against that death that they know they must face at the end. To refuse to surrender to death at each step along the way is to strengthen oneself for the last battle at the end of the journey. If they have chosen for life at each step, then perhaps they will be able to make the final step into eternal life as they conquer the last enemy.

Yet to say that we want to live life and fight death is too general, too vague. We can further narrow it down by saying that life is growth and fruitfulness, while death is decay and sterility. Life's growth and fruitfulness speak of a certain power. It is not, however, a political, economic or material power. It is rather the power of life to grow and bear fruit. Only this power can prevail over the impotence of death.

When we, however, refuse to face the tasks that remind us of our limits, that remind us of the death we must overcome (Gen. 3:16-19), and seek instead to escape from the essential responsibilities life entails, we strip ourselves of the opportunity to experience the power of life. Instead, we passively sit under the dominion of death.

People in America today, including many professed Christians, fear to risk their comforts, images and conveniences in order to survive as human beings. They fear the risks of participating in living the most essential elements of life. And what could be more essential to "life" than to give birth to new life, to raise and educate our own children, even to grow our own food in order to sustain that life, and on this basis, in the end to face death with real dignity, with faith in our hearts as the power of our accumulated life triumphs in the final test against the last enemy? Most people, however, fear that they don't have the strength or the knowledge to participate in this level of life. So they feel, as the Nazis did, that they must hand over that responsibility to the State. They fear that the real essentials, responsibilities and decisions of life are "too important" and therefore too burdensome for them to handle. They believe they need, for example, the certified agents of the State to educate their children for them. All these fears of participating directly in the essentials of life, however, only keep them in bondage to the one who has the power of the fear of death (Heb. 2:15). Modern culture promises to relieve them of their burdens, and, foremost, the State promises to cover them from the true risks of life: from sickness via its licensed medicine, from lack of food and clothing by way of its welfare roll, from childbearing by its hospitals, from child rearing by its compulsory education system. In other words, the State promises (or threatens?) to live the real part of life for them, allowing them the *freedom* to play at the empty games of leisure, or merely money-making, life styles. They have lost power over their own lives and so, like a crippled or weakened prey stalked by a predator, they then find themselves defenseless before the Beast of Statism. They have fallen prey to the seductions that promise to liberate them from responsibility, the false promise of deliverance from the fear of death. This is the freedom of the Nazi in his Utopian Reich: "The State will take care of everything if I will only devote myself totally to the State and its political and cultural vision." In our devotion, however, to the State as the savior *from* our responsibilities, the State enslaves us in its vise grip, holding us captive in the dominion of the fear of death (and we must remember that the State has only this negative dominion of death, the power to wield the sword of external compulsion—not the life power of the internal constraints of voluntary love, Rom. 13:3-4). Naturally, this dominion of the fear of death is simply that: death, the refusal to risk living, the absence of any faith to face the unknowns of an open-ended life.

Yet even with an occurrence as simple as when your seven-year-old son, whom your wife has just begun to teach at home, comes to you and says, "Dad, can I read you something? . . . 'G-o-d is l-i-ght,'" and then stands with face beaming and eyes shining under a dark brown shock of ragged bangs, then you understand the answer as to why you face the risks, why you face the death that entwines and constricts around all life in a world under a curse. A feeling arises from deep inside that says, "I helped do that. I participated in this knowledge coming forth in my son: *Because I picked up responsibility for the living of life*, this fruitfulness came forth, at least in part, through me." It's the same sense that we can derive from the birth of our children at home when we as parents assume ultimate responsibility. It's the same sense that we can get even in only doing something as simple as growing our own food.

It's a feeling of power, but, again, not in the sense of political oppression or of the economic or psychological or social manipulating of other peoples' lives so as to conform them to our own desires and images of life, as with the power of the State and its many licensed agents and so-called services. It's not a political power or an economic power of any sort. It's an entirely different kind of power: it is the power of life pressing out into fruitfulness, the sense that life can come forth from and through us, that we actually do have the power to live. It says, "I took the chance and participated in life and not only saw, but also tasted of, its fruitfulness." It's not the warped pride in a "daredevil," unnecessary risk taking; for we speak here of taking only those risks *necessary* to participate fully in the *essentials* of life, not the arbitrary risks taken for peripheral concerns. So it cannot be considered daredevil to demand the right to fully participate in and assume responsibility for what is essential to life. Moreover, the weight of ultimate responsibility in the *essentials* of life crushes any sense of vainglory in our hearts, a vainglory that often arises when we only show our prowess in those peripheral functions and talents that don't serve as direct supports of real life, life lived out in its essence: as in the birth, sustenance, cultivation and harvest of life. Again, the reward is not pride but the immediacy and strength of experienced life itself, that we in our feeble but persistent struggle against death, as we seek to touch life's essentials, have been reduced to our own essential nature, have seen the measure of what we are and have miraculously passed the test—all simply because we had the faith to risk living.

Many people, however, who have never had this rewarding sense of participating fully in such essentials can see no reason to face even the minor risks of home education or home birth. They think that because some of us do not mind-lessly cling to all the technologies and conveniences and State provisions that deprive us of our own direct participation in life's essentials, that we are simply playing a game, a dangerous game. Yet who really plays a game? Is it not those who have mindlessly and irresponsibly abandoned their own participation in those experiences and activities that con-stitute life's essentials, and who do so simply in order to save themselves from the burdens of life and to have more time for leisure activities, unessential activities—in other words, games—such as in the artifice of television? Can we really claim that those who throw off everything that hinders their direct participation in and responsibilities for the realities and necessities of actual life are playing a game?

Still others may say to those who willingly assume the risks and responsibilities in such matters as home education and home birth, "You just want to suffer. You want to be martyrs." But to suffer is not our goal. When we face these risks, these necessary trials to our faith in the power of life, we see the reality of this world for what it is, and it involves some suffering. When humanity first chose the pride of objectively knowing life over the fruit of directly participating in life, they suffered a great separation from life: death has come into the world be-cause of this separation. So no one can now taste life without being brushed by the sword of death. Therefore when we suf-fer, it does not mean that we seek such suffering in itself. On the contrary, it may mean that we are more determined than most to taste the life that lies beyond the flaming sword. By facing the reality of life stripped of its ornamentation and delusions, we confess that we value the exhilaration, the joy, the dominion, the power that comes through truly participating in, tasting, the fruit of life; and we confess that we value this more than we value any possible escape from the necessary suffering, an escape that would only cut us off from the power of such a fully-lived life. We recognize that when we suffer the pressures that come with resisting all that causes death, that is, resisting sin (even though the sin may not be directly our own, it is nevertheless sin that has brought death into the world, Rom. 5:14), we glorify life and the One who is its Source. Again, we do not seek suffering but rather view our lives as seed. We know that in order for real life to come forth we must, like any seed, risk the humus of death if we want to germinate life. The binding ties that relationships, responsibilities, obligations, create—whether to land, creatures, people or to God—are for us simply the ever-turning furrow of events and experiences that covers the seed life within us, dissolving the outer shell of death in which all find themselves encased. These serve to compact around us the soil, the nurturing habitat, that allows the seed to germinate and break through the surface of death and into new life.

Many, even many who call themselves Christian, want to pretend that the real obstacles of life and the enemy of their soul are not there at all. (Captives on their way to Auschwitz in the cattle cars could seriously say, "Maybe they're taking us on a holiday.") But victory comes only through realistically facing the enemy: you cannot have a victory without a battle. We want to face this enemy of death and overcome him so that we can possess the victory of life. When we do that, we know that we must enter into the pressure of ultimate responsibility, the contractions of spiritual labor pain, that will bring forth the fullness of God's victory in our character and, with it, the fruitfulness of life.

As we show extensively in *Who Owns the Children?* the responsibility God wants us to assume for our children extends to every aspect of their lives. It includes not only their education but also the very process by which they are born into this world. As we have seen,* God gives primary authority over children not to the State but to parents. We saw that their authority expresses His authority and that authority finds its roots in authorship, in origins. Obviously, parents serve as the natural origins of children, the means through which the ultimate Author brings His children into the world. Taking responsibility for children begins not with their education but with their very birth. It is for this reason, as we explain in detail in *Who Owns the Children?*, that the State in its effort to gain sovereign control over our lives and our children's lives seeks not only to take control of their education but also of childbirth, the means through which they enter this world—their origins. But if parents have ultimate responsibility for their own children before God, then they cannot cede the responsibility for childbirth to the State any more than they can cede responsibility for educating their children (though this is not to say that

---

* See "Parental Responsibility" in chapter 4.

to give birth to a child in a hospital is to automatically cede responsibility to the State). Once they have ceded the first, they have in principle ceded the second. Parental responsibility for children includes, then, accepting responsibility even for childbirth, for the way in which our children enter into the world. To take responsibility for the preparation for childbirth and then for the birth itself constitutes the first step in our journey of responsibility for raising to maturity Wisdom's Children. (We by no means want to suggest, however, that parents should not begin home schooling unless they feel the conviction to give birth to their own children at home. But even those parents who don't feel ready to take this latter step can see more clearly the impetus behind their own desire to home school through a deeper understanding of the impetus behind and importance of home birth.*)

When, for instance, we face a childbirth without automatically resorting to those interventions and controls of man that often would rob us of our immediate participation in and responsibility for the birth of life, rob us of our right and power to fully live our own lives, even if we come close to death, we nonetheless feel that we've participated in something of irreplaceable worth. Because it is a participation in one of life's essentials, we must pass through the sword to taste it, and so the birth experience also reduces us and allows us to see the naked essence of what we are, the core of our own life. In home education and home birth, many are willing to take any inherent risk in order to assume full responsibility for making their own decisions in a fundamental area of life that God has given to us as essential (and surely the birth of life is one of the essentials of life). Many feel that if they take any risks that involve matters essential to living, then even if they die, they die living, because they've participated in life even as they pass through death—they've assumed full responsibility for the life given into their hands. Under such circumstances we may truly say that they died not of the fear of living but that they died of having lived.

Those, however, who refuse to even consider these God-ordained patterns of life as an option to the State's provision,

---

* We have not attempted to deal exhaustively here with all the questions raised by home birth. For a complete treatment of these questions, see *Journeys Home: Stories of Coming to Home Birth* and also *Who Owns the Children?*, 4th edition.

or to shoulder the essential responsibilities for making such decisions, can only live dying, because they're afraid to even consider taking the risk. They live by fear; they simply have no faith that they can assume responsibilities for and then live out life's essentials. They cannot face the unknowns of an open-ended life and still believe that they have the power to pass through. And so they automatically seek the State and its agents to take total responsibility for this and all other experiences and events that touch the essence of life. For them, the State's provision isn't merely one of many options; it's the one and only path that all must automatically and mindlessly follow. "Don't even consider having your baby at home," they say. "Don't risk teaching him at home." "Don't risk trying to learn to farm." "Let others risk living." "You," they say, "must trust only what the State has certified and sanctioned." In other words, as we've said, the State will automatically live the real part of life for you, assuming all responsibilities, allowing for no alternative but only giving you the "freedom" of play. Following just such thinking, many finally come to believe that life itself is a condition for which they must find a cure. But when they do, their cure only at last solves, or rather dissolves, man himself.

How ironic, in light of all this, that the State claims that it must retain all ultimate authority over and responsibility for "its" children, because, according to the Statist's view, no one can trust parents to be responsible. Especially is this ironic when one considers what makes people parents, what turns a man or a woman into a mother or a father. We, of course, can only become parents when we recognize and take on this ultimate responsibility *ourselves* for the birth, care and upbringing of our children, that ultimate responsibility that comes from being the children's direct origins, both naturally and spiritually. *We become parents when we recognize our own ultimate liability first for each other and then for our children*, when we acknowledge in our hearts that the destiny of our children lies totally and completely in our own hands and that we therefore must assume responsibility for the choices that we make. When we then begin to take the steps necessary to fulfill that destiny, we start out on the road toward fulfilling our parenthood. We become parents when we see clearly that no one else can exercise this ultimate responsibility, that no one else will assure that our children will reach the full potential of the life that God has laid out for them, that no one other than God Himself has the right or the power to possess our children in body, mind and soul. (In childbirth this assuming of responsibility does not correspond to the mere mechanical or principled rejection of the medical alternative, for it is clear that a person can reject those alternatives out of fear or simply out of a fleshly momentum picked up from others but that never approaches becoming responsible before God to faithfully obey Him. For instance, what if God is speaking to someone to have their baby under different circumstances than at home? To assume responsibility, we must face the eternal dimension of the consequences of our decisions and, in that light, faithfully follow the Spirit of God.)

Only when we accept the total responsibility and liability for our children's lives and upbringing and commit to give ourselves completely to meeting this responsibility can we truly parent our children. The nature of the commitment of parenting requires that we give ourselves completely to our children's needs, that we offer our time, our energy, our attention, our material wealth. In short, we must lay down our very lives, giving up anything that interferes with accomplishing our God-given responsibilities of parenthood. So to become mothers or fathers means to give ourselves completely to a love that knows no limits in its efforts to fulfill the burden of serving in the life of another. When we enter the marriage commitment, we vow that we will give ourselves completely to the service of our spouse, to lay down our lives for one another according to God's pattern. To bring forth children is the natural fruit of this commitment. For these reasons, both spouses commit themselves to completely serve, and lay down their lives for, their children.

To proclaim such a love is nothing but a mere pretense of that "love stronger than death," unless we would willingly go to the point of death for our children. Unless we truly stand willing to go that far, we don't experience true love. We must possess that kind of love unto death for our children if we desire to fulfill our responsibility to mold them into the image of God. Only when we possess that love, will our children sense that we serve them for *God's* purpose in their lives and not for ourselves, for then they will see that we do not live merely for ourselves. Our children will then respect us to the degree that will allow us to mold and shape them in God's image and lead them in the way that God has laid out that they should go. When we love our children and bear their burdens in this way, we can then receive the knowledge, understanding and wisdom to know God's will for our children's lives and to direct them in the path that God has ordained for them to walk. Assuming the full liability for this task will alone pull us out of ourselves in the way necessary to fulfill this responsibility. If we accept the fullness of this burden and liability, we can experience the love that is "stronger than death." This love alone can give life meaning. Jesus opened up this pathway of love to us, this channel of relationship to God, when He laid down His life for His brothers. Through His total sacrifice for the sake of love, He opened the door for true at-one-ment, for full relationship, the complete unity that only true love can bring, and set this pattern for all of us to follow.

How, then, do we become such mothers and fathers? We aren't born mothers and fathers; we must *become* parents. How does this happen? Something must transform us from self-centered creatures of pretense into giving beings who will lay down our lives for another. Again, how do we become so transformed? We take the first steps when we willingly lay down our lives for one another as husbands and wives, loving as Christ loves the church and submitting just as the church reveres and submits to God (John 15:12-13; Eph. 5:24-25). The same love that transforms man and woman into husband and wife is the same love that transforms them into father and mother. We must undergo a profound, deeply transforming rite of passage that reveals (to us as much as to anyone) our willingness to lay down our lives for our children in this love "stronger than death." We become parents first by assuming the full liability of giving birth to and rearing (that is, educating) our children. So what is born in our homes is not only a baby but also a father and a mother in a plexus of relationships that forms the family that will live out its integrated life in that very home where *all* these relationships come to birth. And what unfolds in home education is not only a child but also a mother and father.

Of course, the very process of giving birth to the child transforms us from a man and woman into a father and mother. Yet it is not enough to just pass through the physical process of birth or to pay the hospital bills, just as it is not enough to claim parenthood simply because children reside in our home and we feed and clothe them. (We may merely be a day-care attendant keeping children for money for other people who give them away, also often for the sake of money.) Rather, we become parents by accepting the *ultimate responsibility* and *liability* for the birth itself and then for the raising and educating of the children. This birth is the rite of passage that prepares us and transforms us so that we can assume the ultimate responsibility and liability that defines parenthood. In the very process of accepting ultimate liability for the birth and education of our children, and then assuming and fulfilling the responsibilities that these liabilities require, we begin to show ourselves reliable as parents; we begin the process of parenthood. When we take upon ourselves this ultimate liability and then pass through the birth, the birth itself transforms us into the parents of that child and binds us to the child in a love that puts supreme value on the life that came forth, simply because the price that we as parents must pay can come so close to death. Obviously, we become a mother or father at the moment that we give birth to our child. Yet this physical fact goes together with the spiritual process that takes place when we fully assume the responsibilities of parenthood by accepting the responsibilities of the birth itself and then the rearing and education of the child. When we ourselves assume these liabilities, even facing the possibility of death, we begin to experience that "greater love" that "never fails," that love which enables us to pass through every trial of our faith in life, our faith in God. And as we pass through this trial, as we bring this crisis to its resolution, the perseverance that this requires of us brings forth character (Rom. 5:3-5) and carries our essential nature to a place a little closer to the image of God.

Of course, some will argue that parents may risk their own life if they are foolish enough to want to do so but that they do not have the right to jeopardize the child. Certainly the State-certified hospitals and schools are, according to research, far more likely to jeopardize the child's life than a home birth (except perhaps in the most extreme and truly pathological circumstances) or home education.[30] Moreover, our very willingness to give ourselves, even to the point of death or loss of liberties, for our child "certifies" more than any college degree or objective expertise that within this relationship lies the best chance for actually protecting the child's welfare. It demonstrates the absence of the vested interests of selfish power and money that distort judgment. Since children will stand at risk to *any* authority over them, whether the State or parents, and inconsistency of behavior is at least as likely from a social worker as from a parent (the only reliable evidence forthcoming shows that social workers and psychologists do nothing to help children and often positively harm them*), surely we would be wise to assume that superior care will most often come from those who labored and sweat and bled, those who came to the point of death to bring life and love and knowledge to the child, rather than from a trite and transient bureaucratic relationship of brute compulsion built on the clichés of sociological and psychological cookie-sheet standards for all human behavior.

The birth then is a rite of passage for *all those* committed to life, no matter what the cost, because they value life itself above merely preserving their own physical existence. The rite becomes a channel that, as we pass through it, molds and shapes us to assume the characteristics that will mark all the new human relationships that will spring forth from this birth. In birth we make our first and most decisive statement that will determine the course of our familial relationships: whether we will dare to assume full responsibility for one another and so take into our own hands the power of love and life, or whether we will surrender these to the fear of death and so surrender the power and authority of life to a compulsory external power, an external power of compulsion that will exercise itself on our behalf only in an external place (the State hospital and public school) outside the relationships that bind us together as a family—outside the home. (We want to make clear, however, that choosing the hospital as an option under certain extreme circumstances does not yet necessarily mean that we have surrendered the responsibility for the decisions and choices of life to the State.) This external power of the State will then automatically live out and experience this essential event of life for us, and we shall have set a potential pattern for the remainder of our life together. At this birth, we can go far, often without knowing it, in determining which of these powers will bind us together as a family: the love of life or the fear of death; the in-

---

* Studies done in 1939, with a thirty-year follow-up, as well as a study done in 1980, show a direct negative correlation between therapy and/or counseling for juvenile delinquents by social workers, psychologists or psychiatrists and criminal behavior in adult life.[31]

ternal power of God's love or the external force of the compulsory State. (Again, this need not necessarily be the case simply because we choose to go to a doctor, but if this decision is made automatically, or strictly from fear, apart from liability to God, then it likely will produce such results.) In education, we then live out that initial determination.

When, in contrast, we take ultimate responsibility for the birth, we declare, "I take ultimate liability for my life and for this new life that God has placed in my hands, and I accept the liability that goes with this life." This acknowledgment is the antithesis of the macho male who flees the down-to-earth responsibilities of fatherhood in order to merely strut his own superior image, or, the flip side of the same coin, the feminist female who flees motherhood because it offers less than the image of the great white goddess. Neither does it resemble any macho or feminist declarations of self-sufficient strength. Rather it rests upon our acknowledgment of the complete inadequacy *within ourselves alone* to determine our own life or the life of the child; if we had this power of life within ourselves, we could announce, when the scythe swept through to cut us off from the land of the living, that we refuse to go with death. But none of us have this power. Even secular writers, however, speak about the inexplicable *outside* force that enters in the course of birth and gives the mother the strength and ability to bring forth the child.[32] When we stand in our place of liability, we find the grace, the power of life, to give ourselves over to God's life-giving Spirit so that He can bring forth the child and start us on that path of unfolding relationships that will take us all the way to the very core of life, to the tree of life that stands beyond the flaming sword.

So from what we've seen above, the irony in the State's position is that to automatically forbid parents from passing through experiences such as home birth or home education, preventing them from *fully* participating in them, means to prevent them from truly becoming parents. The State forbids them from taking ultimate liability for the child. The State declares to parents, "You cannot, without our approval and control, pass through the rites that transform you into the mother and father of this child, the rites through which you take on ultimate responsibility and liability for this child. We forbid you or the child to confront, apart from us, the agony and risk that it takes to bring new life into the world and then to raise and educate the child to maturity. This responsibility and liability cannot rest in your hands but belongs only to the State." In true circular reasoning, the State justifies preventing parents from confronting the risk of childbirth and home education, because parents can't be trusted. But, of course, parents can't be trusted to be parents if they can never exercise the power of parenting by assuming liability and ultimate responsibility for their children's lives.

"Do what you want with your own life," the State says. "We don't care, but what if something should happen to the child? We have only the best interest, of the child at heart." Yet it is this same State that also gave the mother the right to destroy that child and so concluded that it was in the child's "best interest" to die.* It is this same State that has forced all children into the violence, drugs and illiteracy of the compulsory State schools.† The Statist's claim is too often a sham, the strutting indignation of a self-righteous hypocrite who aggrandizes his power in the name of unassailable causes—"the best interests of the child"—that the State in fact violates itself.

Through such ruses, the State assumes the place of covering in both birth and education. Of course, the State has not actually prevented the deaths of mothers or children in birth or the illiteracy of children who pass through its schools: multitudes of babies and their mothers perish at the hands of the State's licensed agents yearly; and millions of students graduate from high school as functional illiterates. The State's accredited doctors, hospitals and schools are statistically far more dangerous to both mother and child than home births or home education.[33] The State can, however, maintain the *illusion* of its covering. It continues to insist that parents can only truly fulfill their responsibilities to their children when they turn their children over to the State. So in further irony, failure to surrender to the State the responsibility for the child supposedly disqualifies one as a responsible parent. Responsible parenthood, then, comes to mean the willingness to renege upon one's ultimate responsibility for the children and to lay this responsibility down at the feet of the *parens patriae*, the parent of the nation, the State. We thereby supposedly show our love for our children by teaching them to love Big Brother. We must

---

* See *Who Owns the Children?*
† See *Crime of Compuslory Education.*

train them up in the love of the Reich.

Of course, the State's claim to serve as a covering to our children in their education has proven an illusion too, as the massive academic, physical, moral and spiritual casualties of public education testify. And the State's desire to "protect" children and "cover" them in their education also stands revealed as nothing other than the desire to strip parents of their function as parents and to usurp the authority of God in the lives of the children.* As we have seen, the only covering for our children's education lies in our assuming complete responsibility and liability for that education. Many different educational opportunities for children confront parents. Most all of these allow the parents to turn over ultimate responsibility for their children's education in one way or another to someone else—the teacher, the curriculum developers, the experts. But God is now revealing to more and more parents His "more excellent way"—the way of love. We have already seen the nature of a relational knowledge that has the capacity and the power of God's love behind it to accomplish the impossible. He is giving parents the power to overcome by faith every intimidation, every fear, every complex (Rom. 8:15; 2 Tim. 1:7), so that we can assume the full liability for our children's lives,† so that we can overcome every obstacle in pressing forward from death and stagnation to life and victory. Then we ourselves will actively seek to encourage and oversee our children and direct them forward. Even if we do not possess certain skills to pass on to our children and God blesses us with help, advice and consultation from others who do possess those skills, we can still never abdicate our active participation, which allows us to sense precisely our children's needs and place. We as parents can never transfer the liability, the responsibility, to another; others in the community can assist us, but they can never replace us without gross distortion resulting. We must come to a conviction that we as parents must assume the full and ultimate responsibility to impart to our children all the treasures of wisdom and knowledge hidden in Christ Jesus. To uncover this hidden treasure necessitates our actively seeking God's will, not our mere perfunctory

---

* See *Who Owns the Children?*

† This is, of course, with the aid of ministries in the Body that help the parents to fulfill this responsibility. See "Beginning" in Supplement One for a discussion of some of the curriculum materials available to help parents do this.

obedience.

To take full responsibility to train our children in the way that they should go requires that we must have the conviction to assume this responsibility no matter what obstacles we face. As we show in *Who Owns the Children?* only this conviction, a clear word that God speaks personally to us as parents, can empower us to persevere in overcoming every barrier that stands in our path in rearing and educating our children. We can only come to this conviction by taking active initiative in the Spirit. To take such active initiative is to press forward from death into life. We cannot sit back passively and receive a conviction from God, hoping to absorb it secondhand from the people around us. We must instead press forward to receive that conviction by willingly consenting to His Word. This same active initiative that brings us to our place of conviction concerning our children's education must continue to govern and characterize every aspect of our participation in the education of our children. We must hold a conviction that we as parents have the primary, active responsibility to train up our children in the way that they should go. We are not simply passive *reactors*, waiting for some outside agent to show us what we must do with our children. God, through His Word and the spiritual leadership and examples He has provided for us, has shown us the patterns to which we must conform our children. He has anointed and empowered us, given us His grace to bring to pass the things that He has laid out for us to do in our children's lives. Then we must take the active initiative to see these patterns and goals realized in the lives of our children. Only when we allow God to "work in us to will and to do," only when we are "led by the Spirit," are we "the sons of God" (Phil. 2:13; Rom. 8:14), and only if we are willing to have this direct relationship with God through an obedient walk in the Spirit can we in turn train sons and daughters of God. If we sit as slaves awaiting the initiative to move through someone else, then we will in turn train up not heirs but slaves (John 8:31-35; Gal. 4:1-7). We can even attempt to impart the principles of godly living apart from the timing of the Spirit, but we will only see lifeless results. Parents alone have this ultimate responsibility and the capacity to train up children, to see after their needs, to discipline them, to help them to find their positive goals and vocation in their lives. So as parents we must overcome the inertia—the death—that would cause us to idly sit waiting for someone else to take initiative in our children's lives. We must take the initiative and press forward into life. We must stand convicted before God that He holds us liable for the training of our children and that we as parents possess the God-given love to accomplish this task. Nothing else will give rise to the abiding initiative required to accomplish the training and discipleship necessary to raise sons and daughters of God. As we fully accept our liability and responsibility before God for the rearing of our children, we choose life over death. Each day, He empowers us to overcome the obstacles to life that stand in our way. As we overcome these obstacles, we see our children grow to become the children of wisdom—the children of that cohesive power which is life.* And as we impart the overcoming power of life into our children, that power grows within us as well.

Now that we have recognized both our responsibility to educate our own children—indeed the *necessity* that we do so, both for our children and ourselves—and that God has given us the capacity to do so (having already seen what God desires that we educate our children to become) we can now look into the principles by which we can teach our children most effectively to "walk in the way they should go."

---

* See "True Wholeness" in chapter 1.

Part Two

GENERAL PRINCIPLES

CHAPTER SIX
Principles of Christian Learning

The Goals

The goals of Christian education determine the principles of Christian education: what we aim for will dictate the means we use to get there. In ancient Hebrew, the same word, *yarah*, means both "to shoot," as to shoot an arrow, and "to teach." *Yarah* is the root of the word *moreh*, "teacher," and *torah*, meaning literally "direction, instruction, law" (this last is the word by which the five books of Moses are known to the Jewish people). To instruct or teach means to aim for a goal, to move in a foreordained direction toward an established target, just as an arrow does when shot from a bow. Since God is one and oneness is our goal, the end does not justify any means but rather necessitates means perfectly harmonious with the end. So our discussion of the principles of Christian education will begin with a review of the purpose of Christian education. Furthermore, this discussion of Christian educational goals will go into somewhat greater detail in a number of points than did our discussion in our first chapters. At the end of this discussion of goals, we will see exactly *how* the goal of Christian education dictates its principles and what principles it dictates.

As we have repeatedly emphasized, we must direct all our efforts in Christian education toward the education of the whole person, a person brought into perfect relationship with his God, his fellowman and all of creation. Christian education trains the whole person to become fully at one in spirit, soul and body— living, acting, speaking and thinking in perfect harmony with the song of Yahweh, fulfilling his place in the kingdom of God. We also saw that the *tamim* individual takes dominion *under God* in order to expand God's dominion into every area given unto that individual. As we learn to take dominion under God, we are brought forth into His image. This taking of dominion involves every sphere of existence. Every area of life presents an area in which the spiritual conflict between light and darkness rages. In the midst of this conflict, God actively works to restore *His* dominion over all things, but primarily over us.*

It does not follow, however, from this call to dominion in every *sphere* that Christians should occupy every *institution* of life. Rather, for many forms or institutions among men the fulfillment of our call to dominion will not be found in filling the forms of those institutions or by finding places within those institutions. Instead, our call to dominion in these areas will be fulfilled as we bring forth the witness of the reality of God's *alternative* form. We can find no better example of the need to discriminate between those cultural and social forms that dominion calls us to occupy and those that we should act as a radical *alternative to* than our present subject: the institutions of *public* education versus the godly form of *home* education. (See *Politics as Spiritual War* for further discussion of this point.) So we can see the call to dominion as inseparable from God's command that we serve as His witnesses. For if we truly become His witnesses, we will actively expand His dominion when those who receive the witness of our lives and of our living words are brought into His kingdom. These three inseparable goals—to be living expressions of God's glory, to bring all things under His dominion and to *be* His witnesses (as distinct from merely *doing* so-called witnessing)—are what we must work to achieve in Christian education. We must raise up our children as perfect expressions of God's glory in their whole lives, people who live in continual and harmonious relationship with the living God and so live in perfect harmony

---

* Essentially, God has ordained the church as an alternative culture within which God's people will bring all areas of life under God's dominion. This community of believers will comprise a city on a hill, a light that cannot be hid. Given this positive direction of the devotion of God's people to edifying the church, limits must at the same time inhere in the extent of our involvement in the institutions of the world. These limits apply particularly to Christian involvement in directing the institutions marked by coercive, compulsive power, that is, the State and those institutions that depend upon State power for their authority and control, such as public education. The entire basis of Messiah's message and reality lies in a love that can find expression only through voluntary, not coercive, structures. We devote whole volumes to this crucial question. See the next paragraphs in the text, pp. 173-74 below and *Politics as Spiritual War*.

in His patterns of relationship with their fellowman and with creation as well.

As we have explained, we cannot train our child to become a whole person if we raise him as an isolated individual. Again, we must raise him *in relationship with* his God, his family, his community and even with the creation from which he derives the sustenance of his own physical being. He is like a young seedling: just as the Creator has genetically preprogrammed the seedling, so has He already placed the child's essential personality within him when he is conceived and formed in the womb. But then the seedling must be planted somewhere. And the place in which we plant it, the nurture and care we give it— its *relationship* to the world around it—will determine whether it grows into a strong and healthy plant, a plant that serves the function for which it was created, or whether it becomes a sickly plant, destined for nothing but destruction (Heb. 6:7-8).

As we previously explained, the word *culture* refers to the total nurturing habitat within which men live their lives. We saw that for the Greeks the word *paideia*, which we find translated as "curriculum," also means "culture." Since education forms the whole person, the whole culture functions as the fullest educational "institution" in which the child grows. The *whole* culture will influence how the young boy or girl will grow, just as the whole culture of a plant will influence its growth. The plant must have just the right amount of sunlight or shade, of heat or cold, of dryness and rain; just the right kind of soil, be it sand, loam or clay; just the right plants nearby and so on. Weeds must be removed, and the seedling must be planted and harvested at just the right time. Every detail of the plant's culture, of its nurturing habitat, will have a decisive influence upon the plant's growth. Even if every aspect of the plant's culture were perfect except one, that one part could mean severe damage or even death for the plant: for example, too much moisture or too little, too much sun or not enough, too much of one chemical compound or not enough of another, planting or harvesting in the wrong season and so on.

The same sort of considerations apply to the child. Every aspect of the culture in which we raise him has a decisive influence upon the development of the whole man that he will become. The culture, the totality of the way of life in which we bring him up, will educate, mold and shape his life. We saw before that the special educational process the child undergoes has the specific purpose of molding and shaping him to adapt to his culture.

To really understand the whole framework and purpose from which the principles of Christian education arise, we must understand the culture into which we guide our children to take their places. Certainly, they may have to *relate* in certain limited ways to all kinds of cultures in order to bring God's good news to others. But what is a God-centered culture? What type of culture should we seek to root and nurture our children's lives within to help them come forth as God-centered individuals? This, of course, poses a central question in understanding what image we desire to "train them up" to, since culture is, as we've seen, "lived religion."

To understand this question, which we have already discussed to some degree, we must return to our earlier discussion of the song of Yahweh, for the culture in which we raise our children provides the setting for the kind of song their lives will become: the culture will largely determine whether they grow up to live in sympathetic harmony with the song of Yahweh or in discord with that song (Ps. 137:1-4). God has formed His creation through His Word, and that creation is structured and ordered according to definite patterns. When everything in creation flows in perfect harmony with the patterns that God has ordained, a resonance like unto a great symphonic harmony pervades all things. Within this great symphony, God has ordained a place for each of us, and when we find our proper place in God's order, God's Word resonates within our hearts and minds and conforms us to His perfect image. And God has ordained a definite culture which resonates in perfect harmony with Him, which perfectly reflects His patterns for our lives so that we may wholly conform to His image.

This internal sympathetic vibration with the Word that comes from God is in the strictest sense the working of a song. A song can only be created upon our recognition that some sort of given order of melody, harmony and symphony transcends the unique, individual impulse that first gave rise within us to the desire for a song. This is a given, common form to which the impulse, the inspiration, must *conform* to make communicable music. To illustrate this need for form, Wendell Berry points out that if you were to take two identical stringed instruments and place them next to each other, and if you plucked a string on one of the instruments loud enough, you would hear the same string on the other instrument humming and resonating in sympathy with the first.[1] This happens because people have shaped, stretched and manipulated both the strings to conform to a certain form (the form of a note, which also is a form externally given). Therefore a form, the note to which the second instrument is attuned, has been expressed from outside the instrument. So when that same sound comes from beyond the instrument, from another instrument like itself, tuned to itself, the first instrument will resonate sympathetically to that sound. It does so simply because it was created to make music, to share in the order of that communicable form that can make a song, to resonate in harmony with something beyond itself, with a specific range of sound that the maker of the instrument ordained for it.

So to actually become a song, the desire for song must reach beyond the uncommunicated, subjective impulse confined within the self to conform itself to an external order. Once it has conformed itself to this external order of form, it can then resonate in harmony with that which resides outside of the impulse itself. In this way the impulse is transformed from mere sounds into that uncommonly reached form (yet commonly known to all men), the form of music. Only when it attains to that form can the impulse, or the emotion which inspired it, strike the same chord of rapture in another human heart that so resonated within our own. Only then is the gestating seed of the song fully formed and so finally brought to birth into a world beyond its source. All of creation brings forth a song, seeking to resonate in harmony with the voice of Yahweh; all of creation strives to sing this song of Yahweh.

Fallen man, however, has chosen to reject this song; he has sought to sing his own discordant cacophony rather than participate in God's harmonious symphony. Yet when man does submit to God's Word, a harmony arises within his heart and resonates with God's Word as that Word vibrates the notes within man's deepest being. The melody, word and rhythm of the song resonate with the larger rhythms in which the singer is immersed and which fill his life. Just as a string on a violin vibrates sympathetically when the corresponding string is plucked on another violin in close proximity, so the singer of human life, when placed in the proper culture, resounds with "sympathetic vibrations" that join together in a cacophony of chaos or a symphony of cosmos, depending on the word that surrounds and resonates within the singer. Creation forever sings this song: "The mountains and the hills shall break forth before you into singing, and all the trees of the field shall clap their hands" (Isa. 55:12, KJV; see also Ps. 98). This is so because the creative Word that abides ever in and around every part of creation (Ps. 19:1) expresses itself through creation's perfect obedience and perfect harmony with the ultimate creative Word. This makes the cosmos a symphonic uni-verse rather than a cacophonic multi-verse. But man chose not to hear this song, because he had fallen out of harmony with both the source and the expression of the Word. Man has found himself planted in a strange culture, a "strange soil" (Ps. 137:4, KJV, Emph.), a soil dissonant with Creator and creation, and so dissonance reigns within man. Therefore, man's attempt at harmony sounds forth only a dissonant noise of chaos. And as long as man remains rooted in this culture, as long as he resides by the rivers of Babylon, he cannot "sing the song of Yahweh," for he dwells "in a strange land." And Yahweh's song resonates in sympathetic vibration only with the Word of His own creation—not the "strange soil" of man's confused creation. In whatever areas of our lives we do not allow God's Word to recreate us, our individual souls and our corporate cultures will be marked by the "formless and empty" chaos that existed at the very beginning of the creation and that results from man's flight from submission to God's Word.

God has ordained patterns on every level of our existence. As we come into conformity with those patterns, our inner being begins to resonate in harmony with God's great song. We will find that this happens on the level of our personal lives and behavior. It will come to pass also in our relationship with our fellowman. But we will even see it in our relationship to creation; it will affect the nature of our work and select the type of physical environment in which we desire to live. An agri-culture, a land-centered way of life, is the culture God appointed in order for man to live and grow in harmony with God's song.*

God has ordained the form of agriculture, as we have seen, to minister to the physical body of man in such a way as to bring it into relation to the *whole* of man's being. Agriculture

---

* See *Culture as Spiritual War.*

provides not only for the meeting of our needs of physical sustenance through purposeful and healthy physical activity—so offering fulfillment for all of the body's requirements—but it also brings the physical dimension of man's life into relationship with both the heart and the soul of man in a truly God-centered way. Through the covenant with the land, which our bodies directly connect us to, the *whole* of our being comes into relationship with creation, just as our individual spirit's direct relationship to the living Spirit of God relates the whole of our being to God. In the same way, the relationship between our individual souls and the community of souls that constitutes the Body of Christ brings the whole of our being into relationship with God's people. This relationship with the physical creation reminds us that we too are creatures under God, that God has called us to a special relationship to creation (Gen. 2:15) and that, because of our fall from our relationship with God and creation, we have special need of God's grace to rediscover our proper place.

Only through our covenant relationship with God can the whole of our being come into proper relation to the spiritual dimension, and only through God-centered covenant relationship to the Body of Christ can the whole of our being come into proper relation to the realm of human consciousness. In the same way, only through our proper covenant relationship with the land can our *whole* being come into proper relation to the realm of physical existence. We have a definite need within ourselves for relationship to all of these spheres of existence, but only one way, that of relational knowledge through covenant, enables us to enter into that true oneness that constitutes our salvation, oneness with God, and thereby oneness with our fellowman and with creation according to the patterns ordained by God. If we join ourselves to the spiritual realm in any other way than through God's appointed covenant relationship with Himself, or with the realm of human consciousness, of human community, in any other way than through the covenant relationship with God's people, or if we join ourselves with the physical realm in any way other than through the (direct or indirect) covenant relationship with the land, then the song of Yahweh will not resonate perfectly in our hearts, and the image of Christ will not come forth fully or perfectly in our lives.

Agriculture provides the God-ordained pattern to bring man's *physical* being into harmony, and so into wholeness. To repeat, this hardly means that only farmers can find a harmonious life or even that only those living in direct connection with an agricultural community can do so. Because we, as members of the spiritual Body of Christ, are "members" of one another (Rom. 12:5), we experience the blessings of a relationship to the land (nonetheless real even though indirect) because of our direct connection to those brothers and sisters who are joined directly to the land. Not every part of the Body constitutes the member which stands directly on the earth (1 Cor. 12:12-26); but because the feet do so stand, the whole Body stands in this direct relationship to the earth because the whole Body is in direct relationship to the feet. Nonetheless, every member should do everything possible to enter into a direct relationship with the land and provide as much as lies in his reach for the sustenance of his own household.

So it remains true that even though today everyone cannot always live directly on the land, agriculture serves as God's vehicle both to bring man into harmony with creation and also to provide for man's physical sustenance. An agricultural setting nourishes the body, but not to the exclusion of the other parts of our being. On the contrary, as we said, through the living covenant with the land the whole of man's being comes into relationship with the physical creation. A need persists within man's soul (and within man's heart as well) to be related to the land in this way. Through the covenant relationship with the land, all of man's being can sing the song of Yahweh, for all the elements of his being have, or should have, some relationship to his body.

So in the ideal situation, the livelihood of the earthly, physical being of the members of the Body of Christ should be derived from an economy centered in the land. This economy should be as much as possible contained within the Body of Christ to ensure not only independence from the systems of the world (that transform themselves increasingly into the image of the beast) but also for the sake of that fullest measure of oneness with God and His people that a land-centered economy helps promote. Many skills, crafts, arts and services that derive from a vision consistent with a self-sufficient, land-centered economic community can also be a means of bringing us into association with the world in such a way that our livelihood becomes consistent with, and part of, our testimony to the world that a God-centered alternative to the world's growing crisis does indeed exist. Such skills, crafts and services could include carpentry, cabinetmaking, leather crafts, spinning, weaving, the sale of organic produce and land-centered crafts, musical instruments, the making of self-sufficient necessities for a land-centered physical life style, such as wood-burning stoves and so on. As they grow in the context of a self-sufficient, land-centered culture, our children can receive a truly well-rounded education as they have an opportunity to learn and experience on a basic level many of the skills of this richly diverse culture. As they participate in this broad range of activities, their gifts and interests will become manifest as they grow to true mastery in those skills to which they are called.

Since the Lordship of Jesus extends to all aspects of our lives, bringing the earth under God's dominion through our work involves more than working diligently at our jobs or speaking mere words at work about God. God wants the very *nature* of our livelihood, of our vocation, which literally means "calling," to resonate harmoniously with His song of creation, with His patterns for mankind. Through the fulfillment of callings consistent with God's vision for human life, we testify with our *whole* being to the Lordship of Jesus Christ. These types of work all point toward closer relationships, both between those performing the work and those who purchase the goods and services, and also between man and creation. In contrast, if we pursue the types of labor that lead to greater fragmentation between man and his fellowman and between man and nature, then we pour out our energies in a labor that undermines the cohesive work that God carries out in the midst of, and against the stream of, our secular, fragmenting age. The call to a closer relationship with the land and a simpler life style, a call to which even many secular people are becoming increasingly attuned, is a call of God, though many people who feel the call are unaware of the Caller. If Christians fulfill vocations in areas of work that will bring us into contact with such people, we can tell them—not just with our words but with our lives—about the One who has authored the song they feel and hear resounding within them. We know that such people are already predisposed to hear His voice, since they have already responded to that voice on another level, even though they may not yet know the One who is singing to them.

Only in the context and framework of covenant on all its various levels can the complete balance of man's inner being come forth in wholeness (although, again, by being in true covenant with a people who are directly tied in covenant with the land, we may indirectly participate in this covenant). The covenant relationship, through the patterns that it gives to every element of our being, provides the perfect context for all parts of our being to come forth in equally perfect balance. By submitting ourselves wholly to those patterns and finding our specific place within them, we ensure that one element of our being will not grow at the expense of the others or grow perversely or insufficiently, thus making us one-sided, distorted or retarded in some sense or another. For example, when we find our place of submission to God-ordained divine order within the context of the covenant of the Body of Christ, our souls can grow to full potential without becoming self-centered, distorted, suffering either from delusions of grandeur or from inferiority. Similarly, in the context of an agricultural community, which provides for man's physical sustenance, the body can develop to its fully balanced potential without becoming either the self-centered, pampered pet of gymnasium Adonises or a neglected and weak encumbrance. A land-centered culture erects godly obstacles to our propensity to yield our bodies in ways that throw us spiritually out of balance. This culture fosters the harmonious and purposeful integration of the body into its proper place of relationship with all the other elements of man's being. The community of believers serves the same function for the soul that an agriculture serves for the body, offering a God-centered culture, a nurturing habitat, for the soul; and, of course, God Himself directly meets that need for the human spirit, just as He meets the needs of body and soul indirectly through His natural creation and His creation of human community in the Body of Christ. And we must also recognize the necessity of all these areas of man's being working together in harmonious interrelationship if the integrity and wholeness of a God-centered life are to truly come forth: each one of these areas must facilitate and support the others in our reach toward fulfillment and oneness.

As every part of our being comes into balance through covenant relationship, the whole man comes forth in the perfect image that God has ordained for him. Then the child becomes a man in the context of the perfect nurturing habitat that allows Yahweh's song to resonate completely within us, on every level of our being. A land-centered culture can relate all the elements of human life together in such a way that a cohesive culture is formed that can nurture the whole man in a balanced way—physically, mentally, emotionally and spiritually (1 Thess. 5:23). It provides that relational setting, that real place on earth, where man, in planting his feet, recognizes the limits and extents of his abilities and being, that he is not God but a creature under God. Again, we ourselves may not stand in *direct* relationship with a totally land-centered culture, but may still participate in such a covenant by being joined to the members of the Body of Christ who are so joined. Nonetheless we should take every opportunity to tie our own bodies in some direct way to that earth which sustains them.

The family can function most effectively within the context of the Body of Christ (1 Cor. 11:3; Eph. 5:22-24). And home education provides the relational context in which parents can most effectively take responsibility for their children's upbringing. Only the family can effectively provide the type of framework needed for the impartation of relational knowledge to the child (Eph. 6:1-4). In this highly personal, relational setting of family-based education within the Body of Christ, the perfect environment exists to bring forth, not the mass of alphas and epsilons so often tragically stamped out by the public schools of Brave New America, but instead the very diverse members that God has ordained for the completion of His Body. The family "school" emerges within the context of an organic, interrelated whole as an integral unit of the Body of Christ under the Headship of Jesus Christ. The child, as an integral member of the family, is in turn linked up with the whole Body, of which the family forms a part. He is not an isolated individual, like the teacher-student relationship described in the study from which all modern secular education is derived—Rousseau's *Emile*. (And we will find the most fully isolated child not in the natural setting of family education but lost in the crowd of public school—and, as we have seen, Rousseau himself advocated mass, as opposed to individual, educational systems.) Instead, the Christian child lives in vital interconnection with God, the community of His people and the whole of creation.

To the extent that they can participate directly in an agriculture, our children, by learning to submit to the rhythms and harmonies of the seasons of sowing, planting, reaping, of animal husbandry and so on, will learn more perfectly of true submission to the God who has ordained the times and seasons. This will further divorce children from the culture of him who seeks to "change" these "times and seasons" as he makes people dependent on the exigencies of the techno-industrial market system (with its latent threat of the "mark of the beast" as the ultimate economic basis and sanction) rather than upon the God who controls the "times and seasons." By working with God-made creatures rather than merely man-made inventions, our children will acquire a deeper experience of their own creaturehood as well as a greater respect for both creation and the Creator. Certain habits of responsibility, consideration, reliability and so forth can be learned in no other setting as effectively as in agricultural life. Something altogether different inheres in working with creatures that God has made rather than with man-made machines and equipment. When we step behind the horses that have replaced the tractors on our land, when we hear the rhythm of jingling, creaking harnesses and the beat of plodding hooves, this carries more than simple noise to us. We hear "notes" that resonate in sympathetic vibration with God's song, as horses dance across fields that sing for joy and as the trees of these fields clap their hands. This is no mere plodding that lags behind some vague and abstract "progress," a progress that has no discernible goal but merely ever recedes as a desert mirage before thirsty men. This "plodding" of horses becomes a dance to the eternal song.

The earth itself rejoices under the husbanding hand not of creatures in machines made in the fragmented image of fragmented man but of men whose inner life reflects the image of the Creator and whose outer life is made of the substance of the earth itself. Because of their living, direct covenant relationship with God, such men have entered into a living, direct covenant relationship with the land. Instead of merely using and abusing the land as a prostitute, trying to get the most they can from the least amount of real relationship to her, they now husband the earth in covenant. They once again recognize the oneness of their physical substance with the earth, that the dust of the earth comprises part of our very being. And we celebrate that oneness in an abiding covenant with the earth, marrying the labors of our body to the body of that land which sustains us and feeds our physical life.

As Schumacher has remarked, various levels of being exist: purely physical existence, such as that possessed by a rock; life, such as that possessed by a plant; consciousness, such as that possessed by an animal; and, going beyond Schumacher's explanation, we would offer as characteristic of the fourth level of being the spiritual wisdom which sees and subsumes all the interrelationships of all these other levels of being.[2] Among all physical creatures, this ability is potentially possessed only by men. We recognize a difference between these levels because, for example, a dog can be knocked *unconscious* without losing his *life*, a plant can be killed without losing its physical existence and so on. If man lives his whole life surrounded only by objects on the first level of existence, such as machines and concrete, he also becomes one-dimensional, living in a world in which the supernatural reality of his Creator has no meaning, because God's reality as manifest through the natural creation is not even in evidence.* Man needs to dwell together with the higher levels of being in God's creation, with creatures whose life and consciousness reflect a power far beyond man's unaided understanding and which have needs and requirements that are beyond man's control (although man can help to meet those God-ordained needs and requirements by submission to God's patterns). Our relationship to life in the midst of God's creation, His land, His vegetation, His creatures, assists in bringing forth within us the sympathetic vibrations that resonate in harmony with God's universal song and make us more receptive to our part in that song, our place in that ultimate symphonic witness to the total cultural alternative of the corporate Body of Christ.

If man tries to deal with the creatures of God's earth on his own terms rather than the Creator's terms, the result will devastate both man and Creation. As a simple example, man cannot care for domestic farm animals according to the natural schedule of their needs and then arbitrarily change it at his whim. He must rather adhere to the "times and seasons" dictated by his Creator and theirs. If he milks the cows at 6:00 A.M. and 6:00 P.M., then for their own well-being he must with rare exceptions milk them consistently at those times every

---

* See *Culture as Spiritual War.*

day. The farmer cannot change the schedule from day to day, but he must adhere to it consistently. Nor can he often skip days. They should be milked every day, fed every day and so on. And in regard to the planting of the crops, there is a time when they *must* be planted, when they *must* be cultivated and when they *must* be harvested (Eccles. 3:2). The hot weather crops must be in the ground at a certain time and ready to harvest at a certain time or the cool weather will come and retard or kill them before he has reaped their harvest. The farmer must plant the cool weather crops and harvest them early or late in the season, for the middle of the season brings the scorching summer sun that will embitter or destroy them. Animals must be bred at a certain time in the year, and their offspring must come forth at a certain season for their optimum well-being and early growth. What spiritual significance does all this have to man? All of these "times and seasons" are controlled not by man but by God (Acts 1:7). This forces man to real responsibility, responding to the requirements of a Power outside of and beyond himself, and, most of all, to an acknowledgment of and submission to the sovereign authority of God: that God is Sovereign and man bows under God's supreme dominion.

Of course, we recognize that not all children will (or necessarily should) become farmers. But, whatever their individual vocations, people must live in the context of *some* kind of culture. As Andrew Lytle has said,

> Surely . . . it must be taken that a poet, a farmer, a banker, a historian, a schoolteacher, must live in a certain place and time and so exhibit the kind of belief and behavior defined by the manners and mores of that time and place.[3]

One does not need to be a "farmer," he goes on to say, to appreciate the benefits of living in a land-centered culture. But for both spiritual and practical reasons, we want our children, wherever possible, to acquire the practical skills of, and have the experience of participating in, agricultural life. Even though every individual cannot and should not be a farmer, this type of culture will best educate an individual in the three goals of Christian education described above: we have already briefly explained how such a way of life helps to bring forth a God-centered character; it should be obvious to all that such a way of life forces the individual to take dominion over the world around him *and to do so under God*; and such a way of life can itself provide a witness to a techno-industrial world whose ever-greater mechanical and electronic power and achievements seem to send it careening, in ever-greater *hubris*, toward violence and oppression, Hiroshimas and Gulags.

We must remember that Christianity is not merely a religious theology but a way of life. Religion is incarnated Truth. Christianity finds its very foundation and essence in this Truth incarnated—first in Christ, then in His people (John 1:14; 2 Cor. 3:2-3). The center of this way of life that seeks to incarnate Truth lies not in a worldly career but in God. The Word of God constitutes the primary heritage that we must pass on to our children. When we say this, however, we speak of the *living* Word, the Word manifested through our children's lives, lives that become resonating chords, harmonious expressions of God's symphonic Song. God infuses His people more and more each day with the desire to root their whole lives in His Word. The practical skills that we teach our children must be those that serve them best and that enable them to serve their best in living in a God-centered culture and community.* We want our children to excel not in the world but in God. While they certainly must prove capable and proficient in what they do, concern about "careers" and "success" can undermine, rather than further, true godliness. If we seek *first* the kingdom of God, then all these things will be added to our lives as well as to our children's according to God's will (Matt. 6:33).

This contrast between godly values and success can be seen in the following remarks by Professor Jerome Kagan, taken from his study tracing the transformation of educational norms in the twentieth century. By 1920, "pragmatism, moral relativism, and conditioning theory" assumed primary importance in the explanation of "a child's ethical stance."[4] By World War II, Kagan continues, "moral relativism" became supreme:

> *The best child was the one who had been trained to meet the local environmental demands* of achieving educational, vocational, and social *success*, and above all, freedom to actualize his special set of motives and talents. The assumption of *a core set of uniform moral directives* that every child was disposed to practice *had become hopelessly obsolete . . . . (emphasis added)*[5]

---

* See *Culture as Spiritual War* for further discussion of these questions.

". . . Adjustment to local social demands was to replace self-control as the index of maturity: . . . *feeling successful was to take precedence over feeling moral.*"[6] So the standard of worldly success came to replace the importance of moral ideals in the lives of America's children. Much of this resulted, as Kagan and countless others have pointed out, from the industrialization of society.

Of course, everything our children do must be done as unto the Lord to the best of their abilities (Col. 3:23). We want to train them to do their best in all things, in their work and study as in everything else; but we want them to remember in everything to "seek first the kingdom of God" (Matt. 6:33). They should not aim towards a mere career, but to do the best they can in every and any work that God puts into their hands. They will seek then not to rise on the status ladder of the social and business worlds, but to grow in God, to bring glory and honor to His Name. The Bible teaches that faith produces works (James 2:14-18), and a faithful life will reflect itself in works that bring glory to God (Matt. 5:16). But seeking success for its own sake, aspiring to rise in the eyes of men—for example, in the large-scale corporate business structure—contrasts sharply to works produced by faith. The difference between working toward success and working as unto the Lord shows itself most clearly in the attitudes cultivated by each type of work. Striving for success breeds competitiveness, greed, pride and worldly aspirations; working unto the Lord encourages the love and assistance of one's brother and sets one's aspirations in the kingdom of God. The pursuit of success centers us selfishly in our own image. When, however, we are centered in God we seek to do our best, but we do this to His glory rather than our own.

We recognize, as we have said, the necessity of learning the physical and intellectual skills that will enable us to take dominion over the physical world. But as Richard Weaver said, we must "put in their proper modest place those skills needed to manipulate the world."[7] Dominion does not necessitate abuse, but rather we should use this world without abusing it (1 Cor. 7:31).

In addition to imparting the skills that will enable our children to take dominion over the physical world and to earn a living, we also desire that they come forth as witnesses unto the world. Their whole life, if conformed to the patterns of God, will serve as such a witness. And if they live such lives of consistency with God's Spirit, the same God who guides them in their work, in their relationships with family and friends, will also guide them in relationship to their verbal witness to the world. We should not seek to impress people with the intelligence of our verbal answers. One highly educated Hebrew Christian minister explains that when he was an atheist, he asked a young Christian girl how she knew that God lived, and she replied, "I know He does; He lives in me." This witness, which was straight from her heart, had a powerful effect on him. Paul said he came not "with excellency of *speech* . . . but in *demonstration* of the Spirit's power" (1 Cor. 2:1, 4, KJV). Yet the Bible does also instruct us to *be prepared* to give every man an *answer* for the hope that lies within us and to *study* to show ourselves approved (1 Pet. 3:15; 2 Tim. 2:15). This means clearly that preparation is a process which includes, among other things, study. This study should primarily lie in the Word of God (2 Tim. 3:16), but our children need to grow into adults who not only understand the problems of the world (indeed, even more clearly than the world itself does) but who can also present in wisdom and love the good news that overcomes these problems.

The type of education that we want to give our children, that will impart to them such understanding, cannot be defined by the standards of the world. After all, according to the leaders of the Sanhedrin, Peter and John appeared to be "unlearned and ignorant men," meaning literally, men who had not been refined through a systematic course of instruction. Nevertheless, these "unlearned and ignorant men" had a wisdom that could not be gainsaid, a "rhetoric" (a term we shall explain shortly) that included not only the words of wisdom but also the supernatural *acts* of God that could not be denied: ". . . Since they could see the man who had been healed standing there with them, there was nothing they could say" (Acts 4:14). "Unlearned and ignorant," and yet with a wisdom that was unanswerable! Of course, these "unlearned and ignorant" men had spent three and a half years living with the greatest Teacher that the world has ever known. This Teacher instructed them throughout those years by His example as well as by testing, teaching and training. (And that Teacher had Himself never undergone, as we saw, a course of formal schooling, John 7:15, TEV.) Then, when He had completed their instruction, after He was crucified and resurrected, He ascended on high and sent back His Spirit to empower them to be His "witnesses." The Spirit was to now lead and guide them into all truth (John 16:13), and that same Spirit taught and instructed them directly and through each other as it had previously guided them through Jesus of Nazareth in the flesh. This is also the Spirit that must lead and guide us in our curriculum, our pathway, our course of instruction. The world may not approve of our standards, but it disapproves only because our answers differ from its own: despite its professions of pluralistic tolerance, it remains irreconcilably hostile to any genuine alternative to its relativism. Nevertheless, if we fulfill our call in the Spirit, we too shall have a wisdom, and so shall our children, that no tongue can refute; no matter how much the people of the world may disapprove of what we believe, they will *see* its truth and, according to the honesty of their own hearts, either accept or reject it.

We seek through our educational program, then, to develop our children's abilities in every area of their lives. For the purpose of developing their abilities in all these areas, and because we want to teach our children to do their best in everything they do, we must also demand the highest standards of them in any intellectually oriented schoolwork. But right now we will concern ourselves with the basic underlying principles needed to bring forth all these characteristics and skills.

Wisdom

To know these common principles, we must see what all of these characteristics and skills have in common. We will see that what they have in common is precisely what we discussed previously as the feature that distinguishes man from among all the other levels of being in God's physical creation. All these characteristics that we seek to impart to our children involve bringing something forth productively, in the individual person, in the physical world, in producing food, in presenting ideas, in bringing people to Messiah. All involve the bringing of something to completion according to the perfect pattern or will of God. All involve the ability to see all things in the full ramifications of their proper *relationships* and to act in such a way that whatever we do will come forth in perfect concord with everything else to which our action relates, in perfect harmony with all the other notes and chords of the song of Yahweh—in perfect wholeness.

The Scriptures present us with a word that sums up this ability in all these areas, a word that we can take as the summation of the goal of Christian education and that also provides the key to the basic principles of Christian education: *wisdom*. We can summarize the goal of Christian education as the impartation of wisdom.

> When the queen of Sheba heard about the fame of Solomon and his relation to the name of Yahweh, she came to test him with hard questions. Arriving at Jerusalem with a very great caravan—with camels carrying spices, large quantities of gold, and precious stones—she came to Solomon and talked with him about all that she had on her mind. Solomon answered all her questions; nothing was too hard for the king to explain to her. When the queen of Sheba saw all the wisdom of Solomon and the palace he had built, the food on his table, the seating of his officials, the attending servants in their robes, his cupbearers, and the burnt offerings he made at the temple of Yahweh, she was overwhelmed.
> She said to the king, "The report I heard in my own country about your achievements and your wisdom is true. But I did not believe these things until I came and saw with my own eyes. Indeed, not even half was told me; in wisdom and wealth [the latter having the possible meaning of *spiritual* prosperity] you have far exceeded the report I heard. How happy your men must be! How happy your officials, who continually stand before you and hear your wisdom! Praise be to Yahweh your God, who has delighted in you and placed you on the throne of Israel. Because of Yahweh's eternal love for Israel, He has made you king, to maintain justice and righteousness." (1 Kings 10:1-9)

When she beheld the wisdom of Solomon, the queen of Sheba glorified the God of Israel whose reality she saw realized in the life of Israel. Sheba typifies the world coming in search of the spiritual reality of God, the world that has heard vague reports in distant lands of the spiritual wealth, power and wisdom of God's kingdom. Solomon was the head of God's kingdom on earth, the kingdom that typifies the church come to maturity under her Head, "in whom are hidden all the treasures of *wis-*

dom and knowledge," ready and able in the wisdom of God to answer the world's "hard questions." These answers must offer more than mere words; they must incarnate in human lives and relationships what Sheba also saw with her "own eyes."

Here we find the "eternal" purpose for which God has called the church.

> His intent was that *now, through the church, the manifold wisdom of God should be made known* to the rulers and authorities in the heavenly realms, according to His *eternal purpose* which He accomplished in Christ Jesus our Lord. (Eph. 3:10-11)

Through the church, God desires to declare His glory, to express His wisdom, to all the heavens and the earth.

This "manifold wisdom" of God is a comprehensive wisdom that encompasses every area of life. The word translated in Ephesians 3:10 as "manifold" is in the Greek *polupoikilos*, "a strengthened form of *poikilos*, 'most varied.'"[8] *Poikilos* appears many times in the New Testament; we find it in 1 Peter 4:10 where it refers to "the *manifold* [*poikilos*] grace of God (KJV)." God manifests His "manifold grace" through the mutual service His people render to one another; this mutual service brings reality to the Christian witness: "By this love you have for one another, everyone will know that you are my disciples" (John 13:35, JB). By using the form *polupoikilos* in speaking of the "*manifold* wisdom" of God, the Scriptures emphasize that "the wisdom of God . . . has shown itself in Christ to be varied beyond measure and in a way which surpasses all previous knowledge thereof."[9] This wisdom encompasses more, takes on more diverse and various forms, than anyone has ever before imagined. It includes all "things in heaven and things on earth" (Eph. 1:10) that minister life and strength. "*Every* good and perfect gift is from above, coming down from the Father of the heavenly lights . . ." (James 1:17). He meets every need of the spirit, soul and body through the *charismata*, the "gifts," He distributes to and through His people. He has given His people gifts and skills and crafts to meet every practical need as well as every spiritual need. The spiritual gifts of healings, for example, work together with the practical gifts for ministering to the body's health and well-being. God brings forth practical gifts in the context of a way of life and on a scale of activity that allows for relationships that express love while also getting the job done properly. Instead of the huge combine compacting the soil of the field, the horse, guided by its driver, pulls the harrow, the plow, the planter and the rake. Instead of the mass-produced goods of the impersonal, atomized factory system, the leather worker, carpenter, spinner, weaver and seamstress bring forth skillfully crafted products to serve the needs of others. *Every* skill, craft, gift and work of service plays its part in the divinely orchestrated symphony of God's "*manifold* wisdom": A song is what it is.

The Scriptures make clear that God has appointed a specific time to manifest the fullness of the diversity of all the gifts included in His manifold wisdom (Eph. 1:10), a diversity the miraculous character of which becomes evident through the perfect coordination, interworking and integration of every part within one organic whole. That time—"the maturity of the times and the climax of the ages"—now approaches. In this world in which "things fall apart" because "the center cannot hold," at this "climax of the ages" when man's "progress" is reaching the apogee of fragmentation and destruction, God now moves to bring to completion His "eternal purpose." He acts to show forth the extent of His "manifold wisdom" through which "all things hold together" as He makes His people truly "complete in Him" "in whom are hidden all the treasures of wisdom and knowledge" (Col. 1:15-20; 2:2-3, 9-10).

"Wisdom," Proverbs 4:7 tells us, "is supreme; therefore get wisdom."

> Esteem her, and she will exalt you;
> embrace her, and she will honor you.
> She will set a garland of grace on your head
> and present you with a crown of splendor. (Prov. 4:8-9)

If we walk "in the way of wisdom," we shall follow "along straight paths" (Prov. 4:11):

> When you walk, your steps will not be hampered;
> when you run, you will not stumble. (v. 12)

The "man who finds wisdom" is "blessed,"

> for she is more profitable than silver
> and yields better returns than gold.
> She is more precious than rubies;
> nothing you desire can compare with her.
> Long life is in her right hand;

in her left hand are riches and honor.
Her ways are pleasant ways,
and all her paths are peace.
She is a tree of life to those who embrace her;
those who lay hold of her will be blessed.
(Prov. 3:13-18)

So wisdom supplies the key to eternal life: "she is a tree of life." She gives us the key to becoming the *tamim* individuals that God has called us to be.

For whoever finds me [wisdom] finds life
and receives favor from Yahweh.
But whoever fails to find me harms himself;
all who hate me love death. (Prov. 8:35-36)

But wisdom also provides the means through which we can take dominion under God, for "by wisdom" "Yahweh laid the earth's foundations . . ." (Prov. 3:19), and "by wisdom" a "house is built" (Prov. 24:3). By wisdom

kings reign
and rulers make laws that are just;
by me [wisdom] princes govern,
and all nobles who rule on earth.
I love those who love me,
and those who seek me find me.
With me are riches and honor,
enduring wealth and prosperity.
My fruit is better than fine gold;
what I yield surpasses choice silver.
I walk in the way of righteousness,
along the paths of justice,
bestowing wealth on those who love me
and making their treasuries full.
Yahweh possessed me at the beginning of His work,
before His deeds of old;
I was appointed from eternity,
from the beginning, before the world began.
When there were no oceans, I was given birth,
when there were no springs abounding with water;
before the mountains were settled in place,
before the hills, I was given birth,
before He made the earth or its fields
or any of the dust of the world.
I was there when He set the heavens in place,

when He marked out the horizon on
the face of the deep,
when He established the clouds above
and fixed securely the fountains of the deep,
when He gave the sea its boundary
so the waters would not overstep His command,
and when He marked out the foundations of the earth.
Then *I was the craftsman* at His side.
I was filled with delight day after day,
rejoicing always in His presence,
rejoicing in His whole world
and delighting in mankind. (Prov. 8:15-31)

Wisdom, then, serves as "the craftsman" of Yahweh, the means through which the people of God can take dominion for God and under God. The dominion to which God has called His people is not the dominion of the *kratos* of death, but the dominion that comes through the wisdom that leads to life. He has not called us to participate in the power of those "horns," those kingdoms, that assert their strength by butting their heads in brute coercive force, but to participate in the wisdom of the "craftsmen" who overcome by manifesting the creative power of God (Zech. 1:21). In the first chapter of Zechariah God sends "craftsmen" against the powers that have oppressed and scattered Israel. These craftsmen "terrify . . . and throw down" the powers—the "horns"—that exalt themselves against God's people (vv. 18-21), just as in 2 Corinthians 10:4-5 Paul says that we "have divine power to demolish strongholds, . . . arguments and every pretension that sets itself up against the knowledge of God . . . ." These "craftsmen" build up God's kingdom in God's wisdom; and this godly wisdom—not physical violence—defeats God's enemies, just as in Nehemiah not might of arms but the completion of the rebuilding of the walls of Jerusalem defeated the enemies of God's people (Neh. 6:15-16). As we saw, Proverbs 3:19 declares "wisdom" as "the craftsman" that stood by Yahweh's side as He created the heavens and the earth; and wisdom—now manifested in its completeness through all the diverse forms of service performed by God's people—shall serve as the "craftsman" who brings that creation to completion. Creative love will triumph over the coercive and destructive power of death because love is truth, because love is true wisdom, the only creative, productive, life-giving power. For this reason alone will the craftsmen triumph: because they alone have the power to create and to produce positively as opposed to the destructive power of the horns. Love "endures"; destructive power dissipates itself as well as everything it touches.

Since "the heavens declare the glory of God" and "the skies proclaim the work of His hands," because "day after day they pour forth speech" (Ps. 19:1-2), clearly, the works of wisdom *proclaim* the truth of God. "For since the creation of the world God's invisible qualities—His eternal power and divine nature—have been clearly seen, being understood from what has been made, so that men are without excuse." Through the works of wisdom, "what may be known about God is plain . . . , because God has made it plain . . ." (Rom. 1:20, 19). Only the fool, the one who by definition lacks wisdom, says in his heart, "There is no God" (Ps. 14:1). Wisdom, then, becomes the only instrument to effectively express or proclaim God's reality, God's Word. "Wisdom calls aloud in the street" and "raises her voice in the public squares"; she "cries out" "at the head of the noisy streets" and "makes her speech" "in the gateways of the city." Such streets are places of commerce, of men's comings and goings in their daily lives and work. In the "public squares," men gather to discuss and reach conclusions about the important issues of the day. The "gateways" are the places of authority where decisions are reached (Ruth 4:1; Prov. 31:23) and where leaders vie for the loyalty of the people (2 Sam. 15:2). Here at these places of authority and public discussion, here in the concourses of men's everyday lives, we find wisdom proclaiming the message of God (Prov. 1:20-21). "Does not wisdom call out?" (Prov. 8:1):

> On the heights along the way,
>   where the paths meet, she takes her stand;
> beside the gates leading into the city,
>   at the entrances, she cries aloud:
> "To you, O men, I call out;
>   I raise my voice to all mankind." (Prov. 8:2-4)

Through wisdom God presents His case to mankind. Through wisdom, God makes Himself known to men wherever they go, wherever they are: "along the way," "where the paths meet," at "the gates leading into the city," wisdom makes her plea "to all mankind."

All of the goals that God has set for us in Christian education can come to fruition only through the acquisition of godly wisdom, the wisdom manifest in one's "good life, by deeds done in the humility that comes from wisdom." This "wisdom that comes from heaven is first of all pure; then peace-loving, considerate, submissive, full of mercy and good fruit, impartial and sincere. Peacemakers who sow in peace raise a harvest of righteousness" (James 3:13, 17-18). So, as we have said, we can summarize the whole of the goal of Christian education as the acquisition of wisdom.

Wisdom and Meaning

We have earlier defined the goal of Christian education as the nurturing of a whole man who lives in perfectly harmonious relationship with God, with his fellowman and with creation. Yet we will see that these two goals do not really differ, for we will see that only wisdom can bring forth a life of wholeness, and such a life can only then be lived out through wisdom.

But what is wisdom? How exactly can we define its nature and describe its workings? We have already suggested that wisdom is the ability to perceive relationships, not only particular, individual relationships, but the whole interlinked series and patterns of relationships within which any individual person, thing or act exists, which obviously requires a view of reality transcendent to man's. Wisdom enables us to perceive the form, the pattern of relationships, in which any individual act takes place, to recognize the fullness of all the interrelationships between that individual act and the wide diversity of its effects and ramifications. Wisdom, then, gives us the ability to bring something forth in wholeness, completeness, the ability to see the proper form in which something must exist in order to develop into the fullness of what God intended. Again, wisdom provides us with the ability to perceive relationships. Wisdom is, in short, she who builds her house (Prov. 9:1); for what is a house but a series of relationships of various shapes and forms that together can hold the content of life?

This ability to perceive relationships for the accomplishment of purposeful action is also the ability to see the meaning of things, for things receive their meanings through their relationships.* By perceiving relationships, wisdom perceives the meaning of life itself. When we look at any particular object in isolation, simply as a shape, as an isolated *object* for our detached analysis (in the sense that we have earlier seen that pagan, objective knowledge sees things†), it loses all of its meaning. For example, if you had never seen a microphone before, and you simply saw an oblong, funnel-shaped object, rounded at the end and floating disconnected in space, it would have no meaning for you (except to startle you that it could be so *totally* detached, that is, so totally "objective"). Yet we understand its meaning, because we see it in relationship to the people, circumstances and events that surround it. We see someone speaking into it. We hear his voice being amplified through a speaker. So we recognize that somehow this strange-looking "object" magnifies sounds. It *relates* to other things and to other activities familiar to us. Therefore it now means something to us.

Similarly, when we look at a door in a totally objective fashion, what do we see? As Barrett has pointed out, we see simply a rectangular object in space, and perhaps on that rectangular object will protrude a small elliptical object off to one side.[10] From a purely objective viewpoint, that rectangle and that little ellipse have no meaning to us in and of themselves, as mere objects. Yet when we take hold of that elliptical object and turn it and then the rectangular object opens up and we walk through the opening that it has made and step into the light of the outside world, then the meaning of it all comes together for us. So the door only has *meaning* in *relationship* to the world around the door—the room from which the door opens and the outside world into which it offers access—and it only has meaning for us insofar as we have the potential to walk through it: its *meaning* comes through its *relationships* to everything around it and to our own lives. It is wisdom, as we said, that perceives these relationships, that fits things together appropriately and that therefore reveals the meaning of things. As soon as we cease to see reality as a living whole, cease to see it as one, it begins to fall apart and decompose before our eyes. We begin to lose the meaning of life. If we continue in this viewpoint, death finally overtakes us. The insane often see the

---

* See pp. 11-29 for a discussion of the contrast between the Judaic-relational and humanistic views of knowledge.

† See pp. 11-17.

world in this fragmented way and so constitute the walking dead.

Wisdom alone fits things together so that the fullness of their meaning and purpose shows through completely. Wisdom is what enables us to gain the insight necessary to see how all things come together according to God's patterns of life. That wisdom proves necessary to bring true coherence and wholeness can be seen in the scripture that proclaims that those who "hate" wisdom "love death" (Prov. 8:36). We see the meaning of this statement when we recognize the meaning of death: the dissolution of life, life decomposed. Death is the principle of fragmentation, of disintegration, the breaking of things apart, just as wisdom is the fitting of things together. As we earlier saw, the principle of death is the principle of pagan knowledge, the knowledge of analysis, the knowledge that seeks to know things by breaking things apart, by dissolving and destroying them. Whatever we perceive, we must enter into relationship with, if it is to hold meaning for us. But only wisdom enables us to see the proper relationships. Since we inextricably intertwine with and relate to whatever we observe, we can never really "know" anything independently of our particular relation to it. Our relationship to something determines how we will view it. So we cannot determine whether we see correctly without determining the correct relationship. But how can we determine the latter, given that reality consists of a complex of interrelations too vast and complex for the human mind to fully conceive, let alone to fully understand? Man simply cannot autonomously determine whether he stands in proper relationship with reality, nor can he remove himself from relationship with reality. Indeed, when he tries to remove himself from those relationships through detachment in order to "better see" reality from the viewpoint of Plato's detached spectator god, he distorts the meaning of reality. But, again, man has no autonomous way of knowing if any of the views he adopts constitutes a correct view of reality because to know this he would have to know that he stands in correct relationship with reality, and he has no way of knowing what that correct relationship is.

We can see here the basic contrast between relational knowledge and objective knowledge, between the knowledge of the Judaic God, who is One (Deut. 6:4), in whom all things consist (Col. 1:17), and the knowledge of pagan man, who knows things only by fragmenting them and tearing them into objective pieces. While objective knowledge seeks to understand things by tearing them out of relationship, seeing them from the partial human view that abstracts things from their relational and living context, seeing them in a way devoid of all meaning, relational knowledge seeks to fit things together in the light of wisdom. Objective knowledge seeks to *detach* itself from things in order to "know" them, to break off (literally, to "analyze") any relationship with other things. How often the priesthood of secularism has told us that to maintain relationship and forego detachment is to forfeit objectivity. Yet how equally often has this very objectivity only served to fragment man, creation and the human community and cost us the very meaning of life? Relational knowledge on the other hand seeks to join itself to things through the binding relationship of covenant.

Pagan man's knowledge always remains arbitrarily abstract and objective, even when it nominally recognizes the necessity of seeing relationship for the purpose of understanding meaning.

So, writing in the *Humanist* magazine, Drs. Rachel M. Lauer and Mark Hussey of the Pace University Thinking and Learning Center (Dr. Lauer was also formerly the chief psychologist of New York City public schools) recognize that

it is not isolated facts but their interconnections that provide meaning, stimulate questions, and offer insights.[11]

And their article tells us that "understanding the *relationship* between facts should be the true goal of education."[12] As we have seen, these statements stand true in themselves, but they too must be seen *"in relationship"* to the rest of what the authors have to say. And so the question becomes, how exactly should we understand these "relationships" and "interconnections" of which they speak? *How do* all the facts that we perceive interconnect and interrelate with each other? Can the authors' humanist approach provide for seeing the true meaning of the relationships between things in the sense of Judaic wisdom? How can the finite, partial vision of finite man see the infinite interrelationships of all things?

We can see the relationships between facts from a multiplicity of different perspectives and directions, but not all of these perspectives will offer us truth and wisdom. How can we distinguish the valid perspective from the invalid? Relational knowledge must integrate around some sort of center, tie together in some kind of framework, as we earlier saw. Some source of cohesion must exist, binding together the otherwise disparate facts seen from disparate viewpoints. The central questions in regard to relational knowledge all involve the nature of this center, framework or source: What will it be? Remembering that religion means literally a "binding together," we see that this question concerning which center around which the disparity of life's experiences and facts will bind together essentially poses the question as to which religion we will choose. Of course, many different perspectives abound through which we can attempt to relate facts, but the central distinction, the primary difference in the way facts can relate together, is whether we see the center and source of cohesion as lying within finite man and within the created universe or in some infinite source external to and transcendent to man and the created universe.

Lauer and Hussey tell us that

> *our minds* put the infinite mass of what is going on into an order; *we* relate parts to each other and create a whole structure. Thereafter, we use this structure like a template that forever determines what we perceive and how we evaluate, decide, and act upon it. (emphasis added)[13]

But again, how can the *finite* mind "put the *infinite* mass of what is going on into order"? How can the finite encircle and comprehend the infinite? Undoubtedly, people *perceive* order in the universe and the interrelation of facts through their minds. But do our minds serve as either the source of this order or the source of our ability to perceive this order? Does our sense of recognition of the coherence of things begin in our minds? Or has an order already been *given*, and have our minds been created in such a way (Jung's archetypal structures embedded in the mind) that we can perceive this given order (although even this latter perception would, for a Christian, be viewed, as we have seen, as severely impaired by the Fall)?* Is not the very ability of our minds to perceive this order dependent upon a relationship with the source of this order, the Spirit in whom all things consist or relate, albeit even if that relationship is hidden and unacknowledged, or perhaps even denied?

---

* See *Justice Is Fallen* for extensive discussion of this point.

These questions require extensive discussion, which we have given elsewhere,* but here we will concentrate on the most important question in this context, that of the center around which all relations cohere. If the human mind serves as the source of this order, then the center that integrates all of reality is man; all the relationships between various facts and events in the universe will center in him. If a transcendent source external to man is the source of order, then the center for integrating all the relationships between created things lies in this source.

From the perspective of Lauer and Hussey, man's mind is the active force that, as we have seen, puts "the infinite mass of what is going on into an order; *we* relate parts to each other and create a whole structure." So, in this view, the mind of man is the active force in *creating* the patterns of relationship that give meaning to events and things. Man through his mind makes the template, which *Webster's* defines as "a gauge, pattern, or mold (as a thin plate or board) used as a guide to the form of a piece being made,"[14] which our minds then impose upon reality. Given this perspective, it seems that these psychologists must believe that man is the center around which cohere the "interconnections" and "relationship between facts" in the universe.

These authors do not, however, understand the mind merely in an individual sense, for they tell us that man's ability to relate facts to one another derives from two levels: the "inner" level of the human mind and the "outer" level of human culture: "social structures such as language usage, traditions, values, systems, or hierarchical organizations" and so on.[15] Man *in his corporate being* creates "a whole structure" for reality. But, whether in his corporate or individual being, man becomes the center of this relational understanding of reality, the center around which reality coheres.

A problem immediately arises, however, when we recognize man as a mere point within the pattern of relationships between things which we see and that conflicting perspectives arise between various individuals and groups of individuals. This is not a mere academic problem; it lies at the source of all questions of tyranny and oppression. Furthermore, the perspective from which man, even a corporate group of men,

---

* See *Justice Is Fallen.*

views reality is, again, partial and limited. Man as a finite being can never comprehend "the infinite mass" of facts. He can never create a "whole structure" that truly reflects the fullness of reality, simply because he remains a partial, limited being himself. Because he always sees in part, he can never within himself see how *all* the facts interrelate. The fullness of inter-relationship between things necessarily escapes man. Relational knowledge stands upon coherence, but man is in his being both partial and fragmented—death bound—and so he cannot present a source for relational coherence. Facts must relate to be understood, but if they are related only from the perspective of man, from his partial, limited, fragmented view-point, then they will ultimately be improperly interrelated. The consequence of no relationship between facts is a lack of meaning, but the consequence of falsely relating facts is false meaning. Only from the perspective of the transcendent God can facts be related to one another according to their com-plete and true meaning.* Therefore no man "can com-prehend† what goes on under the sun. Despite all his efforts to search it out, man cannot discover its meaning. Even if a wise man claims he knows, he cannot really comprehend it" (Eccles. 8:17). Only "God understands the way to" wisdom, "and He alone knows where it dwells, for He views the ends of the earth and sees everything under the heavens" (Job 28:23-24). Man's finite perspective excludes full compre-hension; only God's transcendent perspective—the perspec-tive of the One who "sees everything under the heavens"— enables him to comprehend the total interrelations and meaning of reality. If no such God exists, then we are doomed to meaninglessness, destruction and death.

By its very nature relational knowledge deals with concrete and specific details, involving real interconnections between particular individuals. But the fullness of these interrelation-

---

* How man can come to this God-centered perspective is discussed in *Justice Is Fallen.*

† Some writers try to make a basic distinction between *comprehension* and *apprehension*, asserting that while the former is closed to man, the latter stands available to him and suffices to guide his judgments in this world. We discuss this question extensively in *Justice Is Fallen*, but here we will point out that the very twofold definition of the word *apprehension* indicates it as insufficient knowledge. It includes both the meaning of "mental grasp" or "understanding" and also the meaning of "anticipate with anxiety; dread." In other words, its grasp of reality is by its very nature insufficient, hence its sense of dread concerning the unknown that lies beyond its grasp.

ships lies beyond the autonomous understanding of man, that is, human understanding centered in man himself.* Man, therefore, when he seeks to center relational knowledge within himself, must arbitrarily abstract from real interrelationships and construct lifeless principles. He then imposes these arbitrary abstractions, as Lauer and Hussey say, as a "template" that forces reality into its mold. The authors therefore propose that educators teach "root concepts" that have been "extracted" (or rather *abstracted*) from reality; these "concepts" supposedly constitute "the various ways of relating, ordering, and structuring." Examples of these "root concepts" are "interdependence, cause and effect, and hierarchies."[16] As an example of how their method works, they tell us that many conquests have occurred in history, for example, the Norman conquest of England in 1066, the United States conquest of Japan in 1945, and that rather than remembering all of these historical facts, the student should be taught "to focus upon the concept 'conquer' and to recognize it as one of several forms of relatedness."[17]

But does this abstract "concept 'conquer'" really express the meaning of the relationship between conqueror and conquered in every circumstance? Is the Israelite conquest of Canaan or the Comanche conquest of the Apache the same as the Nazi conquest of Poland or the Soviet conquest of Afghanistan? Can we really simply impose this category upon reality as a "template" in order to understand things as they really are in their interrelationships, or does this man-made template really serve to distort the true nature of these interrelationships? This abstract principle, derived from the perspective of man, does not bring forth the true meaning of events, but rather it distorts their meanings. We may recognize common patterns and principles, but when we do this on the basis of an incomplete man-centered reason, the principles that come forth do not enable us to see more clearly the relationship between things, but instead they distort and confuse the real dynamic of events and things.

That relational knowledge which enables us to see the true meaning of things and events cannot derive from the perspective of man, nor does it entail the imposition of human abstract principles upon different events and circumstances. Rather it

---

* See *Justice Is Fallen.*

necessitates a perspective centered in the transcendent Source of all true knowledge and meaning, the God of the Hebrews. Obviously, man cannot attain to the fullness of the knowledge of God, but we can enter into a *relationship* with Him—the basis of all true *relational* knowledge—that will enable us to have His perspective of the events and experiences that we do encounter.* Facts related together from the perspective of the mind of man will remain abstract objects still. Merely relating facts to one another does not automatically give them valid meaning; rather they must be related from the perspective and viewpoint that gives them *true* meaning. This is why the Bible contrasts two forms of wisdom: the heavenly wisdom that brings peace and harmony, and the earthly wisdom that leads to "confusion," "disharmony" and "disorder" (James 3:15-17, Ampl., NIV). Indeed, as we said, we may even recognize common principles that apply in many various situations, but these principles too cannot be either drawn out or handled abstractly by man independent of his relationship with God, since God is the source of all cohesion and true relationship. Only through a living relationship with the living God can we come to that true relational knowledge of the world, its meaning and significance. Wisdom does not entail merely the recognition of relationships, but of relationships seen from the perspective of the Source of coherence.

Each of us senses (though many people overcome the sensitivity) that every aspect of our lives somehow connects or should connect to every other aspect and to all life. We sense, even if unconsciously, that to fully understand any part we must somehow be attuned to, even when we can't necessarily comprehend, the whole. This harmony of the total, and not the mere partial workings of the finite human intellect (though it plays its part), determines the true and the false for those still even slightly in tune to the total harmony, the song, of creation. They do not merely ask themselves, "Is this linear, partial, biased, finite, fragmented line of reasoning true?" They ask themselves if each part rings true with the *whole*. Does it resonate in sympathetic vibration with the "truth" of creation and the truth that resides within each human being? In this way we can discern the true or the false as easily as we can discern an instrument or a song in tune or out of tune. Unless we have

---

* See *Justice Is Fallen.*

attuned ourselves to the dissonant and the false, we can hear
the falsehood in an argument or a reason as easily as we hear
a sour note in an otherwise perfect symphony. We do not hear
the sour note of the instrument because we attend only to that
instrument or because we are skilled in playing that particular
instrument or even skilled in the subtle complexities of symphonic orchestration; such skill is seldom necessary: we hear
it because we are listening to the *whole symphony*, and the off-
keyed instrument stands out as false for that very reason. (Of
course, we can attune ourselves to dissonance and so believe
a lie, but in order to do so we must destroy something within
us [Jung's archetypes structured into the mind?] that naturally
resonates in harmony with the external world. We must mark
ourselves as Cains, cursed from creation.) So the ability to
hear truth or falsehood does not hang on the lopsided development of logical analysis (the root of "analysis" meaning "to dissolve") which would know reality objectively, as an object
fragmented from the whole living context of its life and meaning in order to dissect it, as when the flower is known as an object by uprooting it from the ground of its being and tearing it
apart and analyzing each part. Such knowledge only brings
further fragmentation, decomposition—and finally death. The
ability to know truth comes with exactly the opposite: it derives
from a relational knowledge that brings all the parts together
into a living whole and comes, as does the ability to appreciate
a song, with a hearing ear. Moreover, this ability to hear a song
is not the ability to hear one part to the exclusion of the rest,
but to hear the whole, to hear how all the parts are beautifully
and exquisitely and perfectly composed together. When we
hear the whole, we hear then the Composer, He who designed
the whole and who expresses it through its orchestrated parts,
He of whom the whole is a symphonic expression. To know
truth is to hear God.*

Man's mind alone can never autonomously penetrate
through to the fullness, depth and riches of interrelationships.
Even when he sees the relationship between objects from his
own self-centered perspective, they relate only as human
abstractions. A relationship between the door and doorknob
plainly exists, but that relationship may still be seen only
abstractly, as merely that of a rectangle to a circle. Even when

---

* We have gone into this in much greater detail in *Justice Is Fallen*.

he recognizes the importance of interrelationships, pagan man cannot penetrate through to understanding the true nature of those interrelationships and meanings. This hardly denies that pagan man can know that doorknobs may be turned to open doors to give access to rooms; nevertheless, when he "knows" this, he doesn't know it in a strictly objective sense but in a relational sense. When pagan man seeks to objectively understand the true* meaning and significance of things, he runs into the barrier presented by the limits of the autonomous intellect—the human mind centered in itself. At some point, his ability to perceive relationships fails, his mind collapses into meaninglessness and the walls of his room begin to close in around him. So he must then always fall back on relational knowledge.

In one sense, however, our understanding of the door—our ability to perceive its meaningful interrelationship with the world around it—requires that we see it as part of an abstract design. But when we use the word "abstract" here we mean something very different from the sense we gave that word in the previous paragraph. In its negative and rather imprecise sense, the "abstract" refers to the vague, the general, the unexperienced, in contrast to the "concrete," which pulsates with sensate life. It's the difference between, on the one hand, a politician's speech lauding the State as a great "family" that

---

* This point raises many questions that we discuss in *Justice Is Fallen*. Briefly, to explain what we mean, we could say that pagan man cannot ultimately explain *why* anyone should turn the doorknob and enter the next room, yet without such an explanation the true relationship of the door and the room lie hidden from our view. While pagan man may dismiss such assertions, contending that mere practical considerations give sufficient explanation, we can show that ultimately such practical considerations must fail as sufficient explanations of motivation. As Barrett has said, "The will is always haunted by" the "ultimate question, Why? We need only turn to the routines of ordinary life" (such as opening doors?) "and the heavy load we must carry every day. A man in some idle and reflective moment—a normal man, let us say, without the specific afflictions of drink or depression— catches a glimpse of his whole life to come, the limited place that is assigned to his ambitions, the limited satisfactions he will have, and the burdens he must carry for them—all terminated by death. And he begins to wonder. He has at the time some painful choice to make, and for a moment he loses heart. Why go to the trouble? What is the point of it all? But then the questions pass from his mind, habit takes over, and he shoulders his burden once again. . . . We are present here at what, underneath all the formal trappings of philosophy, must remain for most of us its fundamental questions: Why live? Why go on? What meaning does it all have?"[18] Again, in *Justice Is Fallen* we fully explain these issues.

must take care of all our needs, and, on the other hand, a mother hugging her little girl, who has just fallen off her bicycle; the difference between a dissertation on the nutritional requirements of balanced diet written by someone whose cooking tastes like horse feed and makes you want to give up eating, and the smell of fresh-baked corn bread coming out of the oven. But in the positive sense in which we use "abstract" here, it refers to a design or pattern underlying our world of concretes. In this sense of design, the "abstract" is essential to life and meaning, not counterposed to them; it means to abstract, to pull out, the essence from the clutter that obscures it. In its negative sense, to abstract means to make vague and obscure, to cut off light. In its positive sense, to abstract means to bring that penetrating insight that cuts through obscurity and brings the underlying design to light.

As we've explained, the meaning of the door, doorknob and rooms does not lie in the existence of these objects in themselves, but in the way in which they all link together; to focus in upon this abstract pattern of interrelationship, we must in part shift our vision away from the concrete details. So if an artist were to do a drawing of a room with a door ajar, through which one saw into another room, he would (in addition to his small sketches of concrete details) draw "value patterns" of this scene, sketches in which he deliberately *avoids* all concrete details; he usually draws these "value patterns" strictly by shading. In these sketches, he tries to see only the forms of light and dark that constitute the picture planes and how these forms interrelate. (The term "value pattern" refers to the interrelationships of lights and darks.) Through these value patterns, the artist works out the basic pattern, the abstract design, of the composition for his painting.

Design in any art is the pattern that particular, concrete forms make as they reveal the interrelationships that constitute their meaning. The limbs of a tree, though they essentially remain the same in terms of their particular form and components, mean something quite different when attached to a trunk rooted in the earth than they do when cut and stacked as cordwood against a fence. One form of relationship and design between the limbs expresses life; the other speaks of death and burning. When you have destroyed the form or pattern that relates the limbs to one another, you have literally destroyed the tree's life. The limb segments may look exactly the same in themselves—objectively—stacked on the ground as they did arranged in space. But the relationship between them has changed and so reveals a change in meaning—in this case from life to death. Most successful artists therefore *think* or *see* in terms of abstract design and *work* in terms of concrete details. This abstract pattern is a larger, composite form not so readily discernible as the individual, concrete, specific forms that constitute it. It is more abstract because it lies in the *relationships* between concrete forms and not in the concrete forms themselves. And this design includes not only the positive forms but also the negative spaces that surround them (as with the shape and sizes of even the spaces between the limbs).

To return to our example of the artist's sketches, his design largely depends on "value pattern," which, as we've seen, refers to the interrelationships between light and dark. In writing, this would be found in the interrelationships between the author's most simplified view of good and evil (and *every* author who even approaches art has one, no matter how subtle or buried beneath the details) and all the confusions as well as oppositions between the two. This is what creates and sustains the unfolding tension and conflict that hold the reader's attention in any writing. Those who cannot see in terms of black and white, however, can never compose or design anything, or even discern the composition or design of anything. But at the same time, unless the abstract "value pattern" of darks and lights (good and evil) is overlaid with a rich texture of details, those who try to show forth such designs and patterns make them seem unreal, detached from and unrelated to real life. Even such abstractions when valid and true in themselves (as distinct from those formed only by abstracting from reality, or abstract in the sense of being vague and general) hold little interest for most people, because no one can see how they relate to real life. It seems to the average person that those who deal only in abstract design, even when this design is accurate, do not know what they are talking about in the concrete terms in which most people live out their daily existence.

So wisdom requires that we perceive both abstract design and concrete details. We need both; neither gives us the whole picture by itself. In our example of the artist planning his painting, once he settles on a "value pattern" to guide him, he may still significantly alter his overall design once he starts applying the concrete details, for when he puts his details together, the interrelationship of the basic forms may change significantly. For example, if he were drawing a scene of a barn, house and road, his "value pattern" sketch might leave out the windows on the farmhouse and the barn, but when he painted the windows, their placement on the buildings might change the whole balance of the picture. A masterpiece depends upon the perfect integration and balance of abstract design and concrete details. If the abstract design obscures our view of the concretes of life, it brings forth not meaningful relationship but death. We need an abstract design that reveals the essence of relationships, eliminating the clutter that obscures those "perceptible relationships among important facts" that "alone" can give "meaning to the world."[19] Again, this abstract design gives us penetrating insight into reality, in contrast to the vague generalities of abstractions that cast an impenetrable fog that prevents insight and understanding. If we fail to see the concrete details that relate the abstract design to the world in which real people live, instead of more clearly perceiving relationship, we sever relationship. Only the vision of the God of the Hebrews can give us the multileveled vision that sees the design that shows the relationships between the concrete details, which makes those details meaningful, and also shows the concrete details that relate the design to men's lives and so make it meaningful to them.

But while on every level wisdom requires that we know everything relationally (even doors and rooms), the objective knowledge of pagan man (though in everyday life pagan man knows that he cannot be consistent) seeks to "know" the door as a rectangle abstracted *from* the abstract design that gives it meaning. Rather than penetrating through to see the essential relationships that fit the door in its place in a larger design, such pagan knowledge seeks to *analyze* the door, to literally break it into its smallest "knowable" pieces, to atomize it and so to destroy its meaning and purpose. The door then ceases to serve as an opening into another realm, into another place, into the next step in a man's life, and thus an opening into the future. Instead it is now merely an abstract object in space. In such a world, time and space dissolve and fragment (as in the world of Benjy in Faulkner's *The Sound and the Fury*), until at last we are left with a world that has no meaning whatsoever, a world of insanity, where literally even a door can lose its meaning. This is the end result of a totally consistent man-centered knowledge, of the world that is built around man's understanding alone.

We see such a world reflected in much of modern art and literature. William Barrett has spoken of literature as being the portrayal of the history that takes place "behind our backs."[20] Even though it does not present the sort of chronological or explicit explanatory rendition of events that most historians try to give us, very often the literature of an age expresses the real meaning and dynamic of a time. Just as a painting will often capture the experienced reality of a scenario better than a photograph, so too does literature often better reflect the reality of an age than does a history textbook. And in our rationalized, atomized world, in which abstract, theoretical, objective knowledge reigns supreme, we find reflected in such literature the complete atomization of time and space. Barrett has shown how Faulkner's novel, *The Sound and the Fury*, based on Shakespeare's famous description of life as "full of sound and fury, signifying nothing," is, literally, a "tale told by an idiot," who Faulkner in turn portrays as perceiving things as being atomized, fragmented, without real connection or meaning. And this describes precisely the kind of perspective from which uprooted, urban, industrial man, who "knows" things more and more from only this abstract, objective viewpoint, sees the life that spins on around him.[21]

In science too, the most advanced studies have taken us into the sub-microscopic realm of the quantum.* Physicists have analyzed and dissolved matter to its smallest conceivable (actually, inconceivable) components. In the quantum realm, matter has been completely torn apart, until the behavior of these particles cannot be related to the realm in which we normally live. They seem to exist in a dimension where objects seem to move discontinuously through space, passing from one point to another without seeming to move through the places in between, taking the famous "quantum leap." Everything seems to be broken down into total meaninglessness. Through pagan knowledge—through pagan man's science, art, literature and so on—man approaches a threshold that will finally shut him off completely within his fragmented mind,

---

* See *The Leap Beyond*.

where all of reality will lose its coherence and meaning, where past, future, meaning and purpose all terminate, where all relationship totally dissolves and is lost. And what is this place but hell itself, where man's mind has at last truly become the supreme deity of a cosmos that has completely fragmented, in which the elements themselves are eternally "dissolved" (2 Pet. 3:10, Ampl.), where man's mind and being has reached the ultimate place of detachment as it floats meaninglessly through the black void of eternity in the horrific fantasies of its own creation, in "the land . . . of deep shadow and disorder" (Job 10:22).

This is the end result of the objective, analytic knowledge of the pagan mind. But the end of the relational knowledge of the Mind of Christ is the cohesion of things, "that in the dispensation of the fullness of times [God] might *gather together in one* all things in Christ, both which are in heaven, and which are on earth; even in Him" (Eph. 1:10, KJV).

Wisdom builds her house. Wisdom perceives the form into which things must fit together, the form that gives meaning to it all: the form of the Body of Christ, the patterns of an agricultural community, the perfect form for an individual human life, for a family, so that each and all might be properly framed together in the perfect will of God. Wisdom brings forth a man who is truly whole, and through wisdom such a man lives a life in which every component part and act has the fullness of meaning, purpose and benefit that God has ordained for it. It is therefore wisdom that we must seek, both for ourselves and for our children (James 1:5; Prov. 4:7).

Growing in Wisdom

How then do we acquire this wisdom? How can we realize in our lives and help our children to realize in their lives this "wisdom that comes from heaven"? First we must recognize that we do not acquire the full-blown expression of this wisdom all at once. Rather, the Bible teaches that this wisdom comes by stages. The path of acquiring wisdom is an *unfolding* path:

The path of the righteous is like the first gleam of dawn, shining ever brighter till the full light of day. (Prov. 4:18)

One does not step into the full brightness of wisdom's splendor at first encounter, but one's eyes must slowly become adjusted over a period of time. Even Jesus Himself *"grew* in wisdom" (Luke 2:52). The Bible makes clear that believers undergo a growing process through which they grow to maturity and wisdom in Christ:

> It was He who gave some to be apostles, some to be prophets, some to be evangelists, and some to be pastors and teachers, *to prepare God's people* for works of service, so *that the body of Christ may be built up* until we all reach unity in the faith and in the knowledge of the Son of God and *become mature, attaining to the whole measure of the fullness of Christ.*
>
> *Then we will no longer be infants,* tossed back and forth by the waves, and blown here and there by every wind of teaching and by the cunning and craftiness of men in their deceitful scheming. Instead, speaking the truth in love, *we will in all things grow up into Him* who is the Head, that is, Christ. From Him the whole body, joined and held together by every supporting ligament, *grows* and *builds itself up in love,* as each part does its work. (Eph. 4:11-16)

Clearly, then, we must pass through a maturing process to grow into the wisdom that God has for us in order that we may accomplish His purpose and become the people that He has ordained for us to be. And again:

> Although He was a son, He *learned obedience* from what He suffered and, once *made perfect,* He became the source of eternal salvation for all who obey Him and was designated by God to be high priest in the order of Melchizedek.
>
> We have much to say about this, but it is hard to explain because you are *slow to learn.* In fact, though by this time you ought to be teachers, you need someone to teach you the elementary truths of God's word all over again. You need milk, not solid food! Anyone who lives on milk, being still an infant, is not acquainted with the teaching about righteousness. But solid food is for the *mature,* who *by constant use* have trained themselves to distinguish good from evil.
>
> Therefore let us leave the elementary teachings about Christ and *go on to maturity,* not laying again the foundation of repentance from acts that lead to death, and of faith in God, instruction about baptisms, the laying on of hands, the resurrection of the dead, and eternal judgment. And God permitting, we will do so. (Heb. 5:8-6:3)

Here also God speaks about levels of maturity and growth.

He speaks in both of the above passages in terms implicit of levels of growth: "infants," "mature," "the full measure of the stature of Christ, a perfect man." He tells us to "no longer be infants." Similarly, in 1 Corinthians 3, Paul admonishes the people of God to cease being "mere infants," capable of ingesting only the "milk" of God. He urges us to cease being "mere men" who act "worldly," but to instead "grow" to maturity as "spiritual" men, capable of eating the "solid food" of God's Word (1 Cor. 3:1-4). So growth in God clearly comes in levels or stages, and the purpose of that growth, the goal we aim at, finds summary, as we have said, in that one word, "wisdom." Through wisdom alone can we become the clear and full expression of Jesus Christ unto a world that in every literal sense continually dies.

The Stages of Growth

What levels of growth, then, lead to godly wisdom? What must the individual master, or rather, what must master the individual, in order for him to become one of God's "craftsmen," taking dominion over the things that God has placed in his hands and spreading forth the gospel of peace through his life and work, one of God's living epistles, whose life can be read and known of all men as an expression of the glory of God?

An individual must pass through three levels or stages in order to come to the level of wisdom that we have described above. (Of course, he can only pass through these levels of growth once he has been born, and the birth process itself is the culmination of a process of conception, germination and growth. This is true spiritually as well as naturally.*) In Biblical terms, these stages can be called (1) knowledge, (2) understanding and (3) wisdom. In the Greek culture in which these stages of growth came to be applied through Christianity, the respective corresponding terms were (1) grammar, (2) dialectic and (3) rhetoric.† Our relational knowledge grows and

---

* See *The Order of Perfection.*

† You will see that we follow these stages of growth and levels of knowledge in our curriculum. The first four years of formal instruction constitute the grammar stage. The parents receive the complete four-year program at the very start and go through that program step by step, in their own pace and timing, but aiming for completion by the end of the fourth year. The next sec-

develops through these unfolding stages. On each level, we perceive more clearly and widely the ramifications and configuration of relationships of the knowledge that informs us. This unfolding ability to perceive relationships is, at every step along the way, a work of God's Spirit. Only in Him do all things consist, hold together, interrelate. At each step along the way, only the anointing of God's Spirit can show us the interrelationships between events and experiences and phenomena, teaching us knowledge, understanding and wisdom.

The first stage, that of *knowledge* or *grammar*, is the level of *particulars*. Here the individual learns the basic, elementary particulars of life out of which all true knowledge and communication grow, but without yet understanding the way in which those particulars fit into his life and work. To take a simple example from carpentry, the individual at this stage learns *the particular use of particular tools* of the carpenter. For example, he learns how to use a hammer to drive in nails or a level to check the level of a board. (Such skills should be learned as much as possible in a practical context, by making something simple. But on this first level, the learner will have to concentrate more on learning to use his tools than on the task he wants to accomplish.) In regard to mental skill, let us say writing, the child learns how to write an individual sentence, which describes some particular. He thus learns how to use a basic tool of language for an individual operation. In regard to learning about nature, the child learns the name of individual types of trees. Again, he simply learns a particular fact about something. He does not yet clearly see how that information fits into any larger framework, though he may have an innate sense that it does; but he must know the particular before he can go on to try to fit it into any larger framework. As we have said before, this first level is the grammar or knowledge level of development. The child learns a great array of individual particulars, but these particulars are not integrated in his understanding; he does not yet see how these diverse particulars *all relate* together. He learns basic dos and

---

tion of the curriculum comprises the fifth and sixth grades. This is a transitional level between grammar and dialectical. Then the seventh, eighth and ninth grades go fully into the dialectical level. At this time the children will study different viewpoints juxtaposed to each other and learn how to discern the whole truth. The rhetoric level grows forth out of the maturity that comes on the dialectical level.

don'ts, but he doesn't yet see how these individual instructions fit together. He doesn't yet see the deeper sense and meaning of them. In his learning, he sees only the simplest, most basic relationships involved. He learns how to hold the hammer, how to hit the nail with the hammer, how to write the sentence that communicates to someone else an individual statement or fact. This is the first stage of relational knowledge, but the child perceives only one level of relationship in the grammatical stage: the relationship between himself and that which he "knows" and the relationship between himself and his teacher.

On this level the individual acquires a rudimentary knowledge of things. He learns the basic facts, skills and principles. He enters into the elementary lessons of discipline, into the most basic level of godly relationship with those who teach him, mainly his parents. If he can learn the basic lessons of discipline, then he will be able to go on to apply these basic skills and this knowledge. If he learns how to use a hammer, he can someday learn to utilize the hammer in actually making something. If he comes under this basic form of discipline, he can eventually learn to do useful work with his skill.

Likewise, if the individual can learn the elementary lessons of true godly discipline, *then* he can be "trained" to the point at which he can eventually begin to "distinguish good from evil" (Heb. 5:14). How, after all, does the child learn to distinguish good and evil? In the beginning, he totally lacks this ability. But after a prolonged period of relationship in which his parents say "yes" to this and "no" to that, after a period of such training enforced by discipline, the child comes to learn to distinguish for himself between these things. In short, if he learns this basic level of relational knowledge, then he will be ready to go on to perceive, understand and take dominion over the wider and deeper interrelations of things involved in what he learns, and the most readily accessible relationship—that which is easiest to see—is that between opposites. It is easier to see the difference between black and white than between subtle shades of gray. We learned also from the artist that he must first have an understanding of the values ranging from black to white before he can even hope to understand the use of color, which such values underlie. So too with human knowledge in all spheres: we must first have a simple and clear understanding of the range of values between good and evil before we can hope to handle life's "technicolor" diversity.

This brings us to the second step in learning: *understanding* or *dialectic*. This is the level of reason or the *arrangement or composition of particulars* according to their relationship with one another on the basis of a scale of opposition or distinction. In this stage, the child sharpens his mind by observing contrasts (hence, *dialectic*). He understands things by contrasting and comparing them to their opposites and to things from which they differ in general and by understanding them in their *relationship* to other groups of things (relationship here understood with the qualifications we have discussed earlier). The principle holds as true here as in art that value is determined by the contrast between light and dark, and only by that contrast does form unfold to the human eye. The same principle applies to the values of good and evil and the forms of God's creation, including the spiritual form of the Body of Christ. In this stage, the child comes to see more clearly that knowledge must have an arrangement, that facts must relate to each other in some way. He learns that these structures of knowledge will be determined, developed and sharpened by debate with alternative ways of seeing the same set of facts. We must certainly train the child according to the understanding that only one accurate scale exists on which to weigh the facts: the scale of God's truth. But, in the context of God's *absolute* standard of truth, we expose the child on the dialectic level to the falsified scales that men have invented. We do this so that his awareness and sensitivity to truth and falsehood may be sharpened and "exercised," that he may learn to "discern both good and evil" (Heb. 5:14, KJV), truth and falsehood, through his own direct relationship with God, without dependence on other men.* On the dialectic level, we sharpen the sword of Truth.

Williams tells us that beginning in the fourteenth century, *dialectic* was the term used "to describe what we would now call *logic*."[22] We derive the word *dialectic* from the Greek word *dialektike*, which means "the art of discussion and debate, and then, by derivation, the investigation of truth by discussion."[23] This term was also used to mean "the art of defining *ideas* and, related to this, the method of determining the interrelation of ideas in the light of a single principle."[24] From these uses of dialectic there developed the branches of

* See *Humanism* for an explanation and criticism of the contrasting humanistic educational method.

philosophy known as logic and metaphysics. In medieval times, "**dialectic** was the art of formal reasoning," the method of learning "the truth of all things by disputation."[25] This view of dialectic continued beyond the Middle Ages to modern times; in 1656, one author wrote: "Dialectick is the Art of Discourse, whereby we confirm or confute any thing by Questions and Answers of the Disputants." The terms *dialectic, dialectics* and *dialectical* came to refer "to argument in a more general way" from that time on.[26] Williams notes that later in the development of philosophy, with German idealism, notably Kant and then Hegel, "the notion of contradiction in the course of discussion or dispute" was "extended . . . to a notion of contradiction in reality."[27] This view was carried over into Marx's philosophy. In other words, in this later view, truth does not merely emerge through the disputes between opposing sides in a controversy, but—particularly for Hegel—real contradictions inhere in reality itself.

> For Kant, **dialectical** criticism showed the mutually contradictory character of the principles of knowledge when these were extended to metaphysical realities. For Hegel, such contradictions were surpassed, both in thought and in the world-history which was its objective character, in a higher and unified truth: the **dialectical** process was then the continual unification of opposites, in the complex relation of parts to a whole.[28]

The dialectic of which we speak should not be confused with this Hegelian dialectic, which became central to the Marxian philosophy. Our principle of dialectic does not entail the idea of actual contradictions in reality itself, but rather the contrast between contradictory ways of seeing that reality. Truth stands both with greater clarity and stability *in our perception* through this contrast of viewpoints, just as form comes into clearer focus with *our perception* of the contrast between light and dark. The truth that emerges is not a "synthetic" product of the two opposing viewpoints, however, but rather it is the vindication of the clear and unadulterated Word of God, whose light and truth is plainly manifested against the background of human falsehood: ". . . there have to be differences among you to show which of you have God's approval" (1 Cor. 11:19). In the struggle between opposing viewpoints, the truth of God is established with clarity and with power.

On this level, we now begin to see the more complex and multifarious interrelations between things on a deeper and wider level than we did on the simpler grammar level. The Bible also speaks of this level of knowledge as discernment or *insight*. Now we begin to clearly see the so-called "hidden meaning" behind things, "the history behind our back." The mystery that stands behind the world of particulars increasingly reveals itself to us as we learn to recognize the relationship between the concrete details and the abstract design, between the visible and the invisible, between the physical, sensual realm and the spiritual. Proverbs begins by declaring that through that book one will come to *understand* "words of insight." The literal meaning of the original Hebrew phrase indicates the ability to see that which lies behind the obvious. One looks behind appearances to see the reality within, the deeper meaning of things. On this level, we learn to establish truth in its conflict with falsehood (1 Cor. 11:19).

> In Thessalonica (Acts 17:2), Athens (Acts 17:17), Corinth (Acts 18:4), and Ephesus (Acts 19:8), Paul had reasoned with and persuaded (*dialegomenos*) men in Jewish synagogues of the fulfillment of the Scriptures and the reality of the kingdom of God as seen in the life of Jesus, the Christ. *Dialegomenos*, "to argue," was used of Greek logicians and philosophers who practiced dialectic—a give-and-take that attempted to elicit conclusions by discussion.[29]

The dialectic or understanding stage, then, represents the level of conflict between opposing viewpoints and of the arrangement of facts and ideas of a given area of study or knowledge into their proper relationships with one another.

To use our examples from the grammar stage, in carpentry, the carpenter now learns to "bring all the divergent aspects of a particular tool into focus."[30] Each tool may have many purposes: for example, a hammer can hammer in a nail or pry it loose. The carpenter no longer sees each tool only in each of its isolated functions; now he has an understanding of *the total use* of each individual tool. He sees the wider interrelations possible between the tool and its many possible functions by distinguishing the tool and its uses from other tools that differ widely or narrowly in their functions.

In our example of writing, on this level the writer can develop the significance of the particular fact of his individual sentence by writing a paragraph that fits the sentence-fact into the context of *a system* of facts to which it directly relates. The individual fact that he learned to present on the grammar level, he now learns to present in the context of other facts. From this context the meaning of that individual fact now emerges, and the student's writing ability on the dialectic level allows him to bring forth this meaning.

In learning about the trees, he now sees them as they come together into an individual system of relations, a forest. He learns that the forest consists of different types of trees, for example, piñon pines, juniper, blue spruce, Douglas fir, balsam fir. He now learns about these different trees by contrasting and comparing their characteristics: the texture of their barks, the shape and pattern of their leaves or needles, varying qualities for insulation or structural strength in building and so on. By learning the contrasts, the child learns to distinguish the various individual trees and sees how these diverse kinds of trees come *together* in a wide diversity of interrelationships to form a forest.

Because these facts are now seen as they emerge into contrasting systems of interrelationship, they therefore become subject to various interpretations. Therefore this level of understanding is inseparable from the conflicts of different viewpoints and methods of interpretation. Perceiving the systems of relations entailed in the understanding level of Judaic knowledge differs radically from the abstract systematization of facts that characterizes pagan knowledge. In God-centered relational knowledge, the Spirit, God Himself, brings together and reveals the interrelations of things, and this happens only on the basis of our prior relationship with God. In this way of knowing, the mind of man does not pull abstract facts out of their living context and then force them into a rigid, brittle framework. Pagan systematization uproots things *from* relationship, detaches them from the framework in which God has placed them, and transforms them into objects rearranged according to a new order, one arbitrarily formulated through the rationalistic reconstruction of reality. In Judaic knowledge, at this understanding level, the Spirit reveals the true interrelations in which things have actually been placed by God. The very nature of these Spirit-revealed interrelations will frequently contrast sharply with the pagan attempt to arbitrarily classify facts according to man-centered rationalism. Man's interpretation will often contrast with God's revelation, particularly as certain vested interests color that human interpretation: for example, the vested interest that asks, "If I interpret these facts in this way, can I still pretend that man is the ultimate authority?" The individual facts must fit together in broader interrelationship, either from God's perspective or man's; and as we have seen, interrelationships give things their meaning. So the conflict between these different views becomes a conflict about the very meanings of the facts themselves. For instance, a fossil is a fact. But, how did that fossil come to be? This dialectic question, which requires the fitting of the facts together, demands an explanation. Did the fossil result from the Noachian flood or from an evolutionary process? We compare and measure such alternative views in dialectic.

In the third stage, *wisdom* or *rhetoric*, the system is seen to fit together as part of the *whole of reality*. God has brought the individual to the place at which His Spirit is able to reveal the ways in which this particular system of relationship on one level relates with all other such systems. The individual can now go forth and use the knowledge that he has learned, because his eyes have opened to both his dependence upon his relationship with the Spirit and the Spirit's revelation of the wide ramifications of his actions. He does not have this wisdom within himself, but his relationship with God has come to the place at which he hears God's voice and receives His vision. Then He who alone can foresee and comprehend the whole can transmit the revelation of how this person's particular actions will affect the whole. By the Spirit's revelation, this person can see that the individual facts fit together into compositions of relationship and, furthermore, that these individual compositions fit together into interrelated compositions, each composite forming a part of the symphonic whole of the song of Yahweh, which is being orchestrated by Yahweh Himself, who is also the Composer. God has discipled this individual to the place where he walks continually in that abiding relationship with the Spirit—a relationship permeated by God's covenant love. People often stumble into truth on the dialectic level, but *full* wisdom *never* comes without a continual relationship with God. The person who abides in this relationship can see the influence that one fact will have upon another fact, one event on another event, one system upon another system. For example, if I cut down the trees in this forest, what will that mean for the wood supply in coming years; what does it mean for the water table of this area; what does it mean for the future of the soil in this area? Likewise, an individual member of the Body of Christ sees the interconnectedness of his actions and the actions of others, all to one another. He sees that though the members of the Body are many, there is only one Body (1 Cor. 12:12) and thus that his actions will have an effect upon all (1 Cor. 12:26). He sees this because he receives the Spirit's revelation of the wide ramifications and interconnectedness of his actions, because he receives the guidance of the One able to take all these things into consideration. By then allowing his steps to be ordered of the Lord, because he follows in the way of love, he follows the path of wisdom. He acts responsibly because he lives respon*sively*, through the Spirit, to the God who can see all the consequences of each man's actions. Because he consistently puts on the mind of the God who understands what the effects of his actions will be on many different levels (1 Cor. 2:16), the man of wisdom is therefore able *to act* in wisdom.

In this "rhetoric" stage, the individual knows how to apply his knowledge, to take dominion through the knowledge that he has received and to use it constructively. It is the stage at which the disciple can make proclamation in both word and deed, with his total life, in such a way that propels men to action, action that generates deeds and events in keeping with the cosmic purposes of God and therefore "makes known" God's "manifold wisdom." He has come into that level of relationship with His Creator that enables him to see the relationship between his life and actions and the unfolding of the whole of which he forms a part.

He can now actually bring things under dominion, bring them forth unto completion in order to fulfill the purposes of God. Since he has passed through the stages of knowledge and understanding, he stands ready to receive God's revelation from the perspective of the total relationships revealed on the wisdom level. So God can use him to advance His dominion and express His glory on the face of the earth. "The lips of the *wise* spread knowledge . . ." (Prov. 15:7). (We must understand a basic distinction here, which we will discuss more fully shortly, between the *rhetor* and the *orator*, between one who presents Truth that enables men to become free and one who uses his persuasive skills to manipulate others deceptively to do merely his own will rather than God's.)

In regard to our previous examples, on this level a carpenter now knows how *all the tools work together* so that he no longer takes dominion merely over the tool, but he now takes practical dominion over the earth itself through the skills he has developed: "By wisdom a house is built." This truth applies whether the house is a material one or the spiritual house of God. The builder knows the patterns or blueprint of the house, the tools he needs to build the house, the various stages in which the house must be built, the building materials and labor that must go into building the house (1 Cor. 3:10). He can therefore compute the cost and see if realistically the house can be built (Luke 14:28), what the needs are that the house must meet, what kind of house should be built in regard to those needs, the available resources, the geographic location and so on.

In the case of writing, he has now mastered the ability to fit the paragraphs or thematic sections, the individual systems based around particular facts, into an essay that provides the context of the whole through which the facts and systems are presented in their diverse ramifications, consequences and significance. He can present his thoughts and ideas so that the responsible and diligent reader can clearly understand the implications of the facts; the conflict of the dialectic can now be brought to its conclusion, and writer and reader can move together to a resolution of the questions, to the point at which meaningful action can now be taken.

When he uses this ability to move men to action, however, the wise man, the *rhetor*, does not manipulate men's emotions. He does not motivate them by confusing them about the real issues involved and then mislead them with emotional slogans and buzzwords devoid of truth. The *orator* uses such techniques; but the *rhetor* seeks to use his abilities to bring the real issues and choices to light so that men can act in wisdom based on knowledge and understanding.[31] The *rhetor* speaks by the anointing and direction of the Spirit of wisdom, in order that this same Spirit may come to abide within his hearers and so come to internally motivate them. He speaks, not with "eloquence" or "enticing words of *man's* wisdom," "but with a demonstration of the Spirit's power," with "God's secret wisdom," "in words taught by the Spirit, expressing spiritual truths in spiritual words" (1 Cor. 1:17; 2:1, 4, 7, 13, NIV, KJV). Man's "wisdom" fragments and destroys. It uproots people from relationships, first with God, then with their fellow-man, with creation and within themselves. Finally it brings total dependence upon that most abstract, objective and manipulative of all human institutions: the man-centered State.* But God's wisdom brings relationship and wholeness: it leads to dependence on God rather than on man.

The *orator* seeks to manipulate people according to his own vested interests. The purpose of his communication is to bring, by deception and obfuscation, his listeners into a position of servile dependence (first mental, then total) upon himself or the man-centered institution that he represents, at least in those areas that touch upon his vested interests. In contrast, the language of the man of wisdom, the *rhetor*, does not debase its listener to reduce him to a servile, obsequious instrument of the speaker's own desires and self-interests, but it seeks to raise its hearer to the highest level of being. Here we find the communication of God: "speaking the truth in love." His Word engrafts itself in the hearts of His people until it transforms them into instruments of His love through whom He can in turn reach out to and transform others. This rhetoric does not originate from selfish grasping, but from the supreme act of giving as embodied in the sacrifice of Jesus at the cross. Rhetoric culminates the power of the word; and Jesus the Messiah, the Word made flesh, is the supreme rhetor of God. Rhetoric is not merely truth spoken in wisdom. The words of wisdom must be the natural outgrowth of a life that actually embodies wisdom. The words that move men to live in the service of love must spring from lives that have been poured out in such service. In this stage, the facts and systems cease to be mere ideas and are actively shaped into positive truths that can inform and influence the thoughts and actions of other people: ". . . Dialectic . . . can serve only cognition, can tell man only how the terms and propositions he uses are related. Rhetoric, in contrast, serves action. It alone is our means of telling man what to do."[32] And, again, it tells us what to do most effectively when we sense the weight of the example of the one who speaks to us, the living reality in his life of the words he speaks: this is the "authority" with which Jesus spoke and which the hypocritical religious leaders of His time lacked.

---

* See *Justice Is Fallen.*

In our example of learning about the trees and forests, we now no longer study merely the isolated system of the forest; but we see this system as a part of the geography, ecology and economy—the total ecosystem—of the world around it. Only in this context can we decide how exactly the forest relates to the purpose of man *under God.*

On every level, wisdom reveals the fullness of relationship and therefore of meaning to every aspect of our lives. Wisdom shows us how things connect, be they ideas, trees, building materials or human lives. It is wisdom that brings things together in their proper order and relationship, and this kind of wisdom can only come forth from the active working of God Himself.

To sum up these three levels, we may again quote from Proverbs 24:3-4,

By *wisdom* a house is built,
  and through *understanding* it is established;
through *knowledge* its rooms are filled
  with rare and beautiful treasures.

First, through *wisdom* the "house is built": only when through wisdom we see the task in its entirety can we bring it to completion. So Paul, in his apostolic ministry in building the church, refers to himself as a *"wise* master builder" (1 Cor. 3:10). Again, this wisdom must be the direct work of God Himself, for "by wisdom a house is built," but "unless Yahweh builds the house, its builders labor in vain" (Ps. 127:1). Second, through understanding a house is established, that is, made stable so that it can "stand" up "under," understand, the pressure that would cause its collapse. (As Richard Weaver has said, through "dialectic" "we can put our house in order."[33]) Dialectic equips us to face every enemy that would shake our house, aiding us to rout that enemy with truth in order to stabilize or establish our house. And finally, knowledge fills the house's rooms, provides the individual facts, statements and other particulars and concrete details that wisdom and understanding can use to accomplish the purposes of Him who builds the house (Heb. 3:3-4). Knowledge gives the house those finishing details, touches, textures and furnishings that offer us a sense of completeness and of feeling most at home in God's Word (Prov. 24:4). Understanding and knowledge are contained within wisdom: "I, wisdom, . . . possess knowledge and discretion" (the latter of which equals the discernment between contrasts of good and evil and hence of understanding, Prov. 8:12*). As we have said, each of these stages reflects an ever-deepening relationship with God Himself; and as our relationship with God becomes deeper, the depth of our relationship with our fellowman and creation will also deepen. By God's Spirit, we will be able to grasp more fully the meaning of things and so more effectually bring God's purposes to pass.

In the course of the following chapters, we will explore in greater detail both these three stages and also how they specifically apply in various areas of study. But we must make a number of important points before we proceed. First, we must understand that no one can arrive at any of the later stages of this educational development without having previously gone through the earlier stages. No one can grow to maturity without first being born. No one can move to the dialectic or understanding level without first passing through the grammar or knowledge level. If we are unwilling to acquire the knowledge, the basic elemental knowledge that comes by discipline, by obedience, by submission to authority, by serving, then we will never move to the understanding level. Obviously, unless we know the important and relevant facts of a subject, we cannot engage in a meaningful dialectic. Nor can we have wisdom without first having a dialectic understanding. God's Spirit cannot reveal how the multifarious systems fit together unless we first allow Him to show us what the individual systems are. We cannot be the anointed vessels whom God would use to speak and act on the level of rhetoric, the level of comprehensive action, unless we have first understood the conflicting viewpoints presented on the level of dialectic. Unless we bring each level in the learning process under dominion, we cannot effectively fulfill our responsibilities on the next level. Without entering into and perceiving the simpler levels of relationship, we cannot go on to the deeper levels. A man must have successfully learned the lessons of a child in order to later perfectly fulfill his responsibilities as an adult (1 Cor. 13:11). Without bringing each level of the learning process under dominion, we will never reach the full perfection of Christ in our lives. Then our days upon the earth will end in the tragedy of an unfinished life.

---

* See Appendix Two for a further discussion of the use of these terms.

Another essential point to understand is that these three levels continually overlap in our lives. For example, in learning to write, we can look upon the letters of the alphabet as the grammar level, words as the dialectic level and sentences as the rhetoric level. On the next level of study, we can see phrases as the grammar level, sentences as the dialectic level and paragraphs as the rhetoric level. On the next higher level (the level we chose as an example in the above pages), we can see sentences as the grammar level, paragraphs as the dialectic level and essays as the rhetoric level. And, of course, we can go even further, seeing paragraphs as the grammar of chapters which in turn become the dialectic of whole books, which then express the rhetoric level. And finally, highest of all, we can see all accumulated knowledge as the grammar level of a human life that is in turn the dialectic that leads to the full wisdom level of a resurrected life that eternally proclaims the wisdom of God (Eph. 1:8-10, J.B. Phillips). This is when wisdom truly becomes justified of her children (Matt. 11:19). But in every one of these sequences, we must first learn the lessons of the grammar level of whatever stage we are on before we go on to the dialectic level, and we must also learn the lessons of dialectic before we go on to the rhetoric level.

Finally, we must recognize that every one of these levels in every one of these stages requires work, hard work. While these are not *our works* but God's, we must nevertheless *enter into* those of *His works* that He has prepared beforehand for us to do (Eph. 2:10). And to cease from our works to enter His, the Scriptures inform us, requires "labor" (Heb. 4:11, KJV).

> Consider it pure joy, my brothers, whenever you face trials of many kinds, because you know that the testing of your faith develops *perseverance. Perseverance must finish its work so that you may be mature and complete, not lacking anything. If any of you lacks wisdom, he should ask God*, who gives generously to all without finding fault, and it will be given to him. But when he asks, he must believe and not doubt, because he who doubts is like a wave of the sea, blown and tossed by the wind. That man should not think he will receive anything from the Lord; he is a double-minded man, unstable in all he does. (James 1:2-8)

Notice that James calls "perseverance" "work." The Scriptures also declare that the attainment of wisdom requires "a disciplined and prudent life" (Prov. 1:3; Job 28:28). The

Hebrew word translated "prudent" here literally means the ability to see relationships, and the word *discipline*, in the Hebrew, has behind it the idea that it takes hard work, effort and energy to achieve the objective. So we see why the Scriptures specifically compare the seeking of wisdom to the mining of precious metals and gems and the demanding labor that these tasks entail (Prov. 2:4). In the days when these passages were penned, such mining was considered the most arduous, difficult and grueling labor—fit only for the lowest of slaves. (This also reveals why the Bible considers those who "labor in the word" as "the least, the servants of all.") So we can see why we must, like Jesus, humble ourselves and take upon ourselves the form of a servant before we can ever hope that God will exalt us (Phil. 2:5-11).

Even the whole of our lives unfolds as a struggle to attain to the wisdom, the maturity, of Christ. The first stage can be seen as the grammar level, the period of childhood and adolescence, where most of life consists of acquiring knowledge, learning the elementary lessons of living. The next stage, from adolescence to perhaps approximately the age of forty or even later, becomes the dialectic stage. In this stage, everything centers on the conflict to establish doubtful propositions. Life is a battle and a testing to come to stability on every level until at last one can stand secure, spiritually and in other respects as well. Finally, one can then move into the realm of rhetoric, of wisdom. If grace has driven a man to exert himself in this direction, the fruit will be manifested as he enters into that phase of his life where wisdom begins to come. It does not mean that no more battles then occur, but one's own life is not the chief battleground. Rather, one's life becomes a proclamation, a proclamation of the wisdom of God. Of course, many notable exceptions to such a general outline stand out, Jesus Christ being the foremost. Perhaps the Body will in the end become like its Head and mature at a younger age, and perhaps home education will play a decisive role in bringing this to pass. But this above basic outline does give us a feeling for the three levels of life that most men go through, whether early or late, if they ever attain to wisdom.

The level of wisdom or rhetoric is the level that enables us to see the whole. But, as we've asked before, how can the limited contain the whole; how can the finite contain the infinite? It cannot.* In our own day and age, men, in the words of Richard Weaver, generally make a "fatal confusion of factual particulars with wisdom."[34] Many men never even leave the grammar level to go on to comprehend the first principles of dialectic. Many never even learn the particulars. But even at their best, the scientist, the philosopher, the professor, within the limits of their specialized disciplines, can only see a limited aspect, can never step beyond the dialectic stage. So Paul asks, "Where is the wise man? Where is the scholar? Where is the philosopher of this age?" (1 Cor. 1:20). And he answers that their wisdom is mere foolishness that God has brought to nothing (1 Cor. 3:19; Isa. 29:14). As we've seen, the wisdom of man cannot comprehend the whole, nor can it specify the multifarious ramifications of individual actions and events. So the world's solutions continually bring forth more severe problems as its "wise men" act the part of clowns in a tragic farce, a bizarre slapstick in which no one is laughing because everyone has pie in his face.

The whole can only be comprehended from the vantage point of the One who sees the whole, the One who comprehends the whole because He is greater than it: "Therefore, as it is written: 'Let him who boasts boast in the Lord'" (1 Cor. 1:31). Paul rejected the wisdom of man, but he did "speak a message of wisdom among the *mature, but not the wisdom of this age* or of the rulers of this age, who are coming to nothing" (1 Cor. 2:6). Rather, he spoke from "God's secret wisdom," which "God has revealed . . . to us by His Spirit" (1 Cor. 2:7, 10). This wisdom consists of "spiritual truths in spiritual words" that "are spiritually discerned" by those who "have the Mind of Christ" (1 Cor. 2:13-14, 16), "in whom are hidden all the treasures of wisdom and knowledge" (Col. 2:3). Only *that* Mind can give us the wisdom to perceive the whole. Even though we, in and of ourselves, cannot see the whole, we are members of that Body governed by that Head whose Mind does see the whole: for "we have the Mind of Christ." Therefore, because, through our interdependence with God and the members of His Body, we are one with the One who sees the whole, His vision of the whole works its way in all of our lives, through the varying functions and relationships—the dialectic—of His Body.

---

* For a discussion of the implications of this point and objections to it see *Justice Is Fallen.*

But one cannot come to this wisdom of the "mature" without passing through, as we have said, the stages of spiritual growth that lead to this maturity. God does not anoint an empty head, but as we exert effort to learn the elementary principles of the grammar stage and the systems of truth of the dialectic stage, then God's Spirit can take that truth and anoint it for proclamation in love. This is the level of wisdom: when truth is ministered by the Spirit, when God's people have come to maturity as a perfect man, who, not singly, but together as a corporate whole, constitutes the *total* proclamation of the love and truth of Jesus Christ, not only in word but also and especially in deed as well. In our whole lives and beings we will become His image on the earth.

Now we have seen the basic principles and goals of Christian education, but our ultimate goal is to know and understand those constituent goals and principles in such a way that we will be able to apply and realize them—make them real—in every area of our children's education. God's relational knowledge has no meaning unless it becomes real in living relationships, unless it actually comes forth in people's lives. We must move toward the *practical* application of these things. In the next chapters, we will discuss the practical application of the principles of Christian education, first on a general level and then on a specific level.

CHAPTER SEVEN

General Application of Principles

The Importance of Goals

Just as our discussion of the principles of Christian education began with basic goals, so our discussion of the application of those principles must also begin with our goals, now described from a somewhat different perspective. We have seen that our goal is the education of the whole man, to help him grow to the level of wisdom. While we have discussed this goal extensively already, now we must define it more concretely to help us see the practical steps we must take to attain it. In this chapter, we will discuss these concrete goals and methods in a general way, and in Part Three we will discuss the particulars of the impartation of various scholastic skills in the major subject areas.

What specific goals do we aim for in Christian education? What kind of whole person do we hope to see emerge through our Christian educational program? We've said from the beginning that, above all, we desire to bring forth a person who lives in a direct, ongoing, continually growing personal relationship with Jesus Christ, a person responsive to the Spirit of God. We want our child to truly be one of God's sons, led and guided by His Spirit (Rom. 8:14). We look for an individual life based solidly on the *living* Word of God, an individual who becomes a living epistle of that Word, an epistle written, moment by moment, day by day, by the hand of God. We seek to be instruments through whom God can mold and shape a *responsible* individual able to care for his own needs, to meet the needs of others, to take dominion over the things that God has placed in his hands. Such a person must be so open to the grace of God that when it moves through him it makes him hard working (1 Cor. 15:10; 2 Cor. 9:8), causes him to give his best in everything he does and to always work as unto the Lord (Col. 3:23). Such a person works well and cooperatively with others and functions as part of a loving community of Christians, for "by this love you have for one another, everyone will know that you are my disciples" (John 13:35, JB).

While he must learn to work cooperatively with others, a Christian must not be *primarily* dependent upon other people, but his primary dependence must be upon the Spirit of God (though, of course, that Spirit will make him secondarily dependent on the many other members of Christ's Body). So, again, we see the goal of our Christian educational process as a fruitful, mature, responsible, loving individual, able to follow the Spirit of God and to be directed by the Word of God, a person who has real, living relationships with God, with God's people and with God's creation. Such a person perceives and understands the relationships between things—and thus their meaning—in a way that enables him to act in the Spirit to accomplish the purposes of God.

From all that we have said so far, it should be evident by now that a Christian educational curriculum cannot be a mere imitation of a secular program with a word about God thrown in every now and then. Remember, one essential purpose of Christian education is to teach our children to take dominion over God's world in order to fulfill His purpose, to perform those "good works, which God prepared in advance for us to do" (Eph. 2:10). Again, we can only bring God's creation under our dominion if we come under God's dominion ourselves; we can only serve as instruments to bring things into proper relationship with God if we come into proper relationship with Him ourselves. Hence, as we said before, the starting point and basis of Christian education must be to teach our children to submit to the Word of God and to the authorities and functions that God has placed over their lives to serve them.

As Christians we must learn to walk in the Spirit, to follow the leading of God's Spirit and to conform completely to His Word in our day-to-day lives. We must also pass this heritage on to our children. If our children know how to follow the leading of the Holy Spirit based upon knowledge of His Word, if God's Spirit and Truth have become one in their lives, then they will be prepared for every eventuality in life, even if such eventualities should separate them from us.

Just as our first goal must be to rear children who primarily depend on the Spirit and Word of God rather than on men, so the basic purpose of Christian education must be "to teach men how to learn for themselves," that is, how to be taught directly by the Spirit.[1] The book of Acts tells us that the men of Berea were counted as more "noble" because they investigated the truth of Paul's teachings for themselves by searching the Scriptures and so were able to confirm directly from the Scriptures the words he spoke. We want our children to learn to do this in every area of life: to learn how to themselves hear and be taught by the Great Teacher, not merely for the sake of learning as some abstract end in itself, but in order that they may through wisdom take dominion over the earth for the purpose of God. As we explain in detail elsewhere,* the relativistic, humanistic basis of modern secular education makes it impossible for those educated by this system to have any independent criteria through which they can learn without inordinate dependence on other people. Unable to weigh evidence and evaluate data, those trained by this system always remain dependent upon its priesthood of "experts" (usually State authorized) for their knowledge. This dependence on technology, government and their accompanying priesthoods make such people ready, though ignorant, pawns of totalitarianism and tyranny. But if we ground our knowledge and teaching in the absolute standard of the living Word of God, the Word of God administered by the Spirit of God, and impart this standard to our children, then they will have a firm foundation upon which to make God-centered judgments, independent of man's prejudice. They will possess a mastery of principles through which they can learn any subject by applying the standards and methods of the Word of God in submission to the anointing of the Spirit as He teaches them that subject.

As we have already seen, this process of growing to spiritual maturity gradually unfolds through three basic stages: knowledge-grammar, understanding-dialectic and wisdom-rhetoric. Since this growth to maturity develops the *whole* person, each of these three stages must involve the entire life and being of the child as he moves toward maturity. The Scriptures describe this unfolding development of the whole person as discipleship, which, as we have seen, is an educational process: as Jesus said, "Go and make *disciples . . . teach-*

---

* See *Humanism.*

ing them . . . ." As we have shown extensively in another study,* the three levels of learning generally correspond to three levels of discipleship, through which our whole being becomes progressively conformed to God's image for our lives.

The first level of discipleship, corresponding to the *grammar* or *knowledge* level of learning, is expressed by Paul when he tells the Corinthian church, "Be ye followers of me, even as I also am of Christ" (1 Cor. 11:1, KJV). On this level, we are primarily followers or "imitators" of men: like a babe holding an adult's hand when first learning to walk, we take our first steps in learning to walk in the Spirit by using the pattern and helping hands of others' lives to guide and balance us. On this level we learn primarily the basic lessons and facts of living for God—the grammar lessons. The second level of discipleship, corresponding to the *dialectic* or *understanding* level of learning, finds expression in Paul's injunction to the more mature Ephesian church, "Be . . . followers of God . . ." (Eph. 5:1, KJV). On this level, the individual moves to spiritual maturity as he learns to follow the direct leading of the Spirit of God in his life. Our understanding develops as we learn to exercise our spiritual senses in the dialectical conflict between good and evil (Heb. 5:14). The third stage of discipleship, corresponding to the *wisdom* or *rhetoric* stage of learning, is that expressed by Paul to the Thessalonians, "You became *imitators of us and of the Lord* . . . . *You became a model* to all the believers . . ." (1 Thess. 1:6-7, KJV). On this level, the believer has already submitted to the lessons of the first two levels and has now become "a model to all the believers . . . everywhere" (1 Thess. 1:8), because his life is an ongoing epistle, an unfolding proclamation, known and read of all men. Our very lives now directly express the wisdom of God. On all of these levels of discipleship, no matter how great our spiritual maturity, we will always remain in submission to someone on some level within the God-ordained order of the Body of Christ. This brief explanation of the process of discipleship is greatly simplified, ignoring many important questions that arise. But as we've said, we go into much greater detail on this subject elsewhere.*

Discipleship then is the method that God uses to bring people into submission to His kingdom under the rulership of the Lord

---

* See *The Order of Perfection.*

Jesus Christ (Matt. 28:19-20). Through this process we are fed on the Word of God, directed, rebuked, admonished, disciplined, encouraged (2 Tim. 3:16)—all in accordance with the Word of God—until we come to find and are perfected in our place in the kingdom of God, until we become whole men in Christ. Herein lies God's method for "the perfecting of the saints" until we reach "the measure of the stature of the fullness of Christ, . . . a perfect man" (Eph. 4:12-13). Herein also lies the description of how to rear, to educate, our children. And this is what someone else has done or is doing or should be doing for us. At the completion of this process, our need for submission does not end; on the contrary, when God perfectly fits us into our place, our submission will be *perfected*.

This place that God has ordained for us to fit into is our place in His Body. God has ordained a definite form for His Body, a form through which each of us is tied to every other person through each one's place in God. That form entails the submission of the parts to one another according to the pattern of God, just as the parts of the physical body must submit to one another in order for the biological organism of the body as a whole to work effectively. To the extent that the members fail to do this, the body becomes spastic: limbs fly out randomly, helter-skelter and in conflict with one another. Likewise, only when each part of the spiritual Body submits perfectly in its place can this spiritual organism function as the unified, perfectly coordinated expression of the God perfectly at one with Himself.

This process of discipleship, which shapes us for our place in the Body, takes place in time and serves to connect us to both the past and future of God's people. Discipleship comprises the process of spiritual parenthood through which God maintains the continuity of the Body of Christ from generation to generation as it continues to grow to the fullness of His stature (Eph. 4:13). We participate in this process of discipleship when we train up our children in the wholeness of their beings into ever-increasing oneness with God. This training and teaching nurtures and passes on the corporate experience of generations, for we as Christian parents fulfill Jesus' commandment to make disciples as we rear our children to become responsible members of the Body of Christ. The story of this Body, applying Berry's words on a larger spiritual level,

is not the story of *a* life.

It is the story of *lives*, knit together,
overlapping in succession, rising again
from grave after grave. (emphasis added)[2]

The spiritual heritage of this people began with the life, death
and resurrection of one man, Jesus of Nazareth, the son of
Joseph. He fathered twelve men spiritually and then imparted
to them the supernatural power to "make disciples of all nations," giving them the ability to bring forth other spiritual
children in God and to raise them and train them until they fully
conformed to His image. His departure from this world was not
the end but a beginning, for

if a man's life
continue in another man,
then the flesh will rhyme
its part in immortal song.
By absence, he comes again.[3]

His life, imparted by His Spirit, comes alive in each successive
generation, and so the life He lived continues to grow to its full
corporate expression in those who follow after Him. Discipleship offers the key to this unfolding life of Jesus on earth. It ensures that each expression of His life conforms to the original
image of the One who gave this life.

In this work of continuity, we have a responsibility both to submit ourselves to the fatherhood of God through those He would
use to train us in the way we should go and then to also help
father those who come after us—first of all, our own children—
just as we have been spiritually fathered. We must find others
to whom we can entrust that which has been entrusted to us
(2 Tim. 2:2):

What we owe the future is not a new start, for we can only
begin with what has happened. We owe the future the
past, the long knowledge that is the potency of time to
come.[4]

We have the responsibility to plant and nurture in others the
spiritual seed, the unadulterated Word of God, that has been
planted and nurtured in us. ". . . A seed is the memory of the
life of its kind in its place," and "the community of knowing in
common is the seed of our life in this place":[5] "the seed" is
the Word that became flesh in Christ and now becomes so in
us; "this place" is the Body of Christ, and as members of this
Body we participate in a "community of knowing in common,"
for "*we* have the Mind of Christ." But we can only participate

in that common mind, that one mind, if the seed of memory is passed on from generation to generation.

There is not only no better possibility, there is no other, except for chaos and darkness, the terrible ground of the only possible new start.[6]

If we fail to pass on our spiritual heritage, not the mere traditions of men but the heritage of God, and fail to fulfill our responsibilities of spiritual fatherhood, we thrust the next generation into "chaos and darkness." If we fail in this way, we permit

the old ways that have brought us farther than we remember [to] sink out of sight as under the treading of many strangers ignorant of landmarks.[7]

But God has told His people not to "move the ancient landmark set up by [our] forefathers" (Prov. 22:28, NIV, NKJV). Instead, we should nurture the next generation in that spiritual wisdom with which we have been nurtured in order that we might bring souls to birth into God's kingdom and then rear them in the rich heritage of our common Father and God. This is the precious heritage of Christian discipleship, the heritage of which we must partake and which we must minister daily to our children.*

So we see our responsibility to impart to our children the godly wisdom of the generations that have gone before, to nurture and rear them in a spiritual culture that forms them through successive stages into mature men and women who can manifest the wisdom of God. Through this wisdom they can help to build up God's people and bring all things under His dominion. "By wisdom a house is built" (Prov. 24:3), and by wisdom "kings reign." As we come to full maturity, God builds His house, His Temple, through us, and we become expressions of His rulership, His kingdom. Jesus thus reigns as King of Kings, and through our submission to Him, and as "co-heirs" with Him, we also shall reign as "kings and priests" with Him (Rom. 8:17; Rev. 5:10, KJV; Rev. 7). If in the flesh we submit as servants to establish His reign as King over all the earth, then in the Spirit we shall reign as kings and priests with Him. Through wisdom the proclamation of God's truth, both in words and deeds, goes forth to the ends of the earth.

As we have seen in Sheba's encounter with Solomon, God

---

* See *The Order of Perfection.*

desires to manifest through His people a wisdom beyond mere verbal utterances. He desires to express Himself through the wisdom of a whole life, both individually and corporately, as He utters His glory and power through His people. Sheba was impressed not only by Solomon's words but also by the great Temple he had built and, specifically, by the divine order made manifest in the lives of the people of his kingdom: "the way his officials were arranged, the organization of his staff" and so on (1 Kings 10:5, Moffatt, JB). As God fitly frames us together as a perfected corporate Temple for His Name, He shall reveal just such wisdom through us, and He shall be glorified in His people.

When God's glory completely fills our lives, then no room will remain for the flesh (Exod. 40:35); for no flesh shall glory in His presence (1 Cor. 1:29, KJV). But the necessity for this total subordination of the carnal man presents precisely the obstacle that prevents so many from coming into conformity with the perfect patterns of God's wisdom for His Body. To conform to His patterns, to become the full expression of the wisdom of God, we must acknowledge our complete and total dependence on God, our utter creaturehood. We must acknowledge that no good thing lies within us (Rom. 7:18), but that we are merely His creatures who, through being discipled in the Body in our place in God's order, can, *despite* everything that we are in the flesh, become expressions of God's supernatural wisdom.

So, as we have said, the aim of our educational process is to bring forth an individual *primarily* dependent not on man but on God, an individual able to discern and follow the leading of God's Spirit himself in those areas of his life for which God has made him responsible. At the same time this individual will respond in perfect submission to men whom God has given spiritual authority in his life. A person who becomes both responsible and submitted in this way has also become mature and reliable, able to find God's grace for the answer to every need (though often finding this answer through his fellow members in Christ). He can overcome any problem presented to him because he knows how to tune into the voice of the Problem-Solver, even though (or especially when) that voice may be speaking through the voices of his brothers and sisters. He knows and understands the process through which God educates him to take dominion over any situation that confronts him, because that process has been applied to his life as a whole (through the discipleship process that we have detailed elsewhere*). He has thoroughly submitted to the principles whereby dominion can be taken and has overcome various problems already through God's application of those principles in his life. He has passed through internal spiritual battles in the wilderness and gained external victories in the promised land; he has struggled against the flesh, has found the mind of God that enables him to understand and take the steps whereby he might take dominion, and he has seen God overcome what once seemed insurmountable problems. Because he has moved "from faith to faith" and from victory to victory, he can now move on to new faith and new victories.

The person who has moved to the level of wisdom, of rhetoric, lives in that relationship with the Spirit of God that enables him to see God's revelation in its comprehensive wholeness and to understand the ramifications of his actions. He can therefore move into a place of real responsibility, of direct, trustworthy, constitutional reliability in the Spirit. Only when we come to this knowledge of the whole, do we actually take dominion. Yet we shall never hold this knowledge in and of ourselves; it comes only through our ongoing, direct, transparent, dependent relationship—a relationship of covenant love—with Him who alone sees the whole. And He gives this wholeness of vision through the Body and its interdependent members, the members over which He reigns as Head. So we maintain this relationship with Him, through which His vision flows to us, only if we maintain our abiding relationship with that spiritual Body that abides in Him. As we find our place in His Body, taking our place in the context of that spiritual organism, He reveals to us the complete vision we need in order to fulfill our part in His purpose. We can learn all the particulars of truth, but until all of these particulars come together to express themselves in our life, we cannot act responsibly, we cannot take true godly dominion.

To really exercise dominion in a particular area, we must master both the details of all the individual elements within this area and also the interrelationships of these elements. We must learn to think in abstract design and work in concrete details. For example, in building a house, if we are to really build

---

* See *The Order of Perfection.*

it, we must understand not only carpentry and the principles of wood construction, but we must also understand plumbing, electrical work, sanitation systems, ventilation systems, heating systems and so on. We must both be able to see the overall design that properly integrates all these particular systems together and also be able to do the work of installing each of these systems. We must both understand the blueprint and design that reveals how all of these particular elements relate to and affect one another, and we must also gain mastery of each of these individual elements. Only then can we really build a house. (Of course, few individuals can really master all of these things, but the community of God's people can do so as one man under the Headship of God: we will serve as the Body that will put into effect all the details, to incarnate all the concretes, of God's abstract design.)

Similarly, God's spiritual house will not be complete with just separate ministries of evangelism, teaching, pastoring and so on, but only as these separate ministries are integrated according to God's pattern into that living whole that is the Body of Christ. We can never come to this perspective of the whole, the ability to build a house, unless we overcome all of the areas or pockets of ignorance, stubbornness and pride that stand in the way of our complete knowledge; and this complete knowledge only comes when every member of the Body comes into complete relationship with God.

Neither will we ever teach our child all that he needs to know for the remainder of his life, for his whole life in God will be a process of growth and learning. But we can teach him the *principles* that will enable him to seek God and overcome all of the individual pockets of ignorance that stand in his way of taking godly dominion. We can lead him onto the path that will take him, in every situation and circumstance, to God's knowledge of the whole. Because he always knows how to find God's vision, he will always be able to fulfill completely his God-ordained responsibilities.

Means and Ends

We labor then to bring forth a person capable of walking in the Spirit, able to know God's voice, to do His will, to overcome every obstacle as he works to establish God's dominion. And

God has placed something within the child that yearns for these same goals. The child wants to grow to maturity, responsibility, fruitfulness. Of course, he also has a carnal nature that wars against these goals. But if God's vision truly burns in our hearts (and we take the necessary steps of discipline to help the child overcome the flesh), our child too will want to participate in bringing to pass the exciting reality of God's vision. Every child has an urgent desire to do real things that have real effects in the adult world. He wants to take dominion over tangible things: he wants to grow food, to build houses, to work the horses, to craft furniture and other functional things; and she wants to spin, to weave, to fix meals, to make dresses, to care for babies. The child wants to help meet real needs in people's lives: he wants to help people come to God, to see them healed in body and soul, to see them taste of the Lord and His blessings and to assist their growth to spiritual maturity. His excitement in learning does not come from focusing his efforts upon the acquisition of knowledge for its own sake. Rather, he finds excitement in learning when the knowledge he receives helps him to fulfill real goals. So his interest in what he learns will largely depend upon whether he can see the direct relationship between what he learns and these goals. How will this knowledge help him to do real things to fulfill the purpose of God? How will it help him to build and plant? How will it help him to accomplish God's spiritual purpose in his own life, in the lives of the lost and in the other members of his spiritual community? How will it help him assume his place in the adult world of his parents? If he can see how learning skills will enable him to reach these goals, the spark of his interest in what we teach will burst forth into an inextinguishable flame of enthusiasm.

We all remain dependent upon brothers and sisters in Christ, both to meet our own needs and also to help us to fulfill our tasks in the kingdom of God. An electrician can't wire a house unless the carpenter puts up the building structure. Similarly, we all depend on others in fulfilling our spiritual functions as well: God often speaks to us most directly through our brothers and sisters. But God has also placed something particular within each of our hearts—something that He has ordained for us personally to accomplish—and we have an innate desire to fulfill our individual function in God's purpose. We have an individual task, actually many tasks, that we have to fulfill. True education must aim to bring us to that place of spiritual and intellectual maturity where we can receive everything we need from God to accomplish this purpose (whether through our brothers and sisters, through books and other research or directly from the Spirit). We must learn how to work with others and how to submit, but we must also learn to personally acquire the information and the skills we need to bring forth that piece of God's vision that He has entrusted into our hands.

We must direct the knowledge we impart to our children toward enabling them to learn how to acquire everything they need to fulfill their purpose in God. (This doesn't mean simply for natural purposes, such as how to build or plant, for surely the riches of God's Word also extend to the very practical goal of meeting the deepest spiritual needs of the human soul.) Everything we teach our children must be knowledge that edifies, that builds up. It must be knowledge that helps to conform them to God's image and that enables them to fulfill their part in His purpose.

We don't want to cram our children's minds with abstract knowledge for its own sake, knowledge they will not really understand or retain, mere knowledge that "puffs up." A purpose threads its way through all the facts that we teach. Every fact must be tied to that purpose as well as directed toward that purpose. That purpose will not be fully realized merely through the child's mastery of the particular discipline in which we instruct him at any particular time. We will only succeed if, as we teach him that discipline itself, we also teach him to find the fruitful way to work in general, to overcome all problems that he will come up against in his life. If we give our children facts, but do not give them the principles they will need to use these facts, it will be like giving them tools without skills or knowledge, and this poses real dangers. Even if they avoid the dangers, they will always remain helplessly dependent upon those who can use these principles. The public schools create just such a situation in which their students never learn to think independently of human guidance and control. Not only do the victims of this system remain dependent on those who can use the tools of knowledge, but they also become susceptible to manipulation by those who can present a false semblance of truth.

Everything our children learn must point beyond the subject or the facts at hand, back to the Source of all true knowledge and wisdom. Everything they learn must direct them to that personal relationship with the Spirit of God who will faithfully lead and guide them into all truth. Professor Richard Weaver left an incisive refutation of what he calls "the astonishing vogue of factual information," that is, the mere accumulation of facts for their own sake. Since men must have "some knowledge" they trust as reliable and because "relativists" have convinced modern secular men that they "cannot have truth," they must therefore put "facts" in the place of truth as the ground of their knowledge.[8] But wisdom and truth involve the cohesive integration of facts; only this integration makes the facts comprehensible, purposeful, usable. Unless the facts assume a form in meaningful patterns, they remain no more than the disordered pieces of an insoluble puzzle: "The supposition that facts will speak for themselves is [an] abdication of intellect."[9] The facts must be organized according to principles, formed around a center that holds the orbiting circumferences together. But acknowledgment of a center or of principles capable of bringing cohesion "implies" acknowledgement of "the existence of truth," which involves not only "grave duties"[10] but also obligations to an authority beyond us who is the Source of this truth. Therefore, the secularist, in fleeing from his obligation to the transcendent God, must also flee from truth to random facts or to the authority of the State and its license.

Because he eschews the solid ground of truth, modern secular man plods through the swamp of facts, into which he quickly sinks in confusion. The Christian must deliberately avoid the swampy low ground of mere factuality, choosing instead the high ground of truth, which gives him the perspective from which he can judge the relevance of facts and place them in the organic framework that alone makes them comprehensible. "Facts" correspond to the concrete details; truth corresponds to the abstract design that relates those details to one another so that they reveal meaning. And truth, we must remember, is a living Spirit (John 16:13), a Spirit incarnated as a living person (John 14:9-10). We do not come to know truth by abstractly using principles, even true principles, to put facts together; we can only know truth if we come into relationship with the Spirit who is truth (John 14:17) and allow Him to bring the facts together in their own true relationships.

So it can even be harmful to push upon our children abstract knowledge that they cannot understand or relate to, random facts to be known merely for the sake of knowing. This hardly implies that we take refuge in educational slackness. On the contrary, to attain truth rather than mere facts necessitates educational vigor. Clearly, our standards of learning must stand above those in the public schools. The public schools do not teach children how to think, nor can they do so, since by their very nature they cannot transmit relational knowledge. They do the very opposite: they fling at children a great deal of useless material that impresses the children with the "specialized" knowledge of their teacher and so makes them totally dependent upon academic authorities. The public schools have no dialectic. Indeed, as we have said, one half of the dialectic—Judeo-Christianity—has been officially banned from the public schools.

In contrast to the method of the public schools, when you educate your child from a Christian perspective, you teach him to take dominion with his mind, with his body, with his spirit—in fact, with his whole being (1 Thess. 5:23)—dominion over the world that God has entrusted to him: that is, to take dominion in submission to God's Spirit, to God's Word and to godly authorities appointed over the child (yet even those over the child will ultimately derive their authority only from the fact that the child comes into such a relationship with the Spirit so that God can in the end show the child which authority is from God and which is not).

If you teach your child to develop God-centered judgment, when he runs up against the "experts" of academic paganism (for example, evolutionists in biology, geology or anthropology), he will not merely accept what they say on the basis of the intimidation of their priestlike authority. Instead he will be able to take dominion in this area of knowledge and discern if a particular perspective meets the requirements of true scientific knowledge or if it is merely "science falsely so called" (1 Tim. 6:20, KJV). He will be able to understand how science works in a sense that has practical meaning for his life, in the relational sense, rather than merely having his mind crammed full of unrelated and meaningless "scientific" details that have no bearing on his life.

Certainly, the major constellations of facts and theories of genuine science and other areas of knowledge are important and should be known and understood; but without a proper context for understanding and applying these facts and theories, they are, at best, futile. Only within their proper context do facts and theories take on their full significance and importance, both in the practical sphere and in the help they give us in generally understanding the world within which God has placed us. Relational knowledge provides this context. As we said before, the word *theory* derives from the Greek word for *seeing*; everyone has to see things from some perspective or another, but the perspective we seek must be that of Hebraic, relational knowledge, not the arbitrarily abstract, detached perspective of the deified Olympian spectator. Only from the perspective of relational knowledge can facts and theories tie together in such a way as to become relevant to the goals of the God of wisdom. It is only in Him that all things hold together, that the relationships between, and meanings of, facts and theories can be truly seen. Of course, it may be argued as to whether isolated facts are true or not,* but from the perspective of the goals that we have set for ourselves in Christian education, clearly we must seek the truth that makes us whole; and only that knowledge which will bring us into a relationship of oneness with Him who *is* the truth can make us whole. From this perspective, any other type of knowledge becomes at best superfluous.

So everything we teach must tie into our goal of developing a particular type of person, a *tamim* individual, and must tie into developing his ability to take God-centered dominion. Insofar as the various aspects of our curriculum contribute to fulfilling these goals, they find their cohesion. In the context of the goals toward which we press—spiritual maturity and the ability to truly take dominion in the Spirit—the various aspects of our curriculum become important elements of a coordinated symphony rather than disjointed and meaningless notes played in isolation. Math, English, science, history—all subjects become integrated elements in the single composition of an individual life lived in perfect conformity to the will and purpose of God and in the context of all other life as God has composed it. As our children keep before them the goals they press toward, as they see the direct connection between the task at hand and the long-range purpose of that task, their lives swell with an exciting sense of expectancy, meaning and purpose.

---

* See *Justice Is Fallen*.

When they lose sight of the goal, when the meaning of the day-to-day educational activities becomes disconnected from anything beyond themselves, everything degenerates into a boring tedium (Prov. 29:18, KJV).

Yet this link between what the child learns and the goals that we, parent and child together, seek cannot be established only in terms of general and long-term goals. Usually, means and goals must have a more direct, tangible and short-term connection in order to hold the child's interest and to enable him to see the relational character of all the knowledge we impart to him. Insofar as possible, we should orient everything we teach the child toward the achievement of concrete goals and ends that contribute to the design of godly dominion.

We see this principle at work on every level of education. When we teach phonics, we must make clear that the purpose of this extends far beyond linking specific letters and sounds. We must continually stress our goal: to teach the child to read and write. Because he wants to read God's Word, because he wants to be able to study and learn about things that apply to the purpose of God, because he wants to express what he has seen and heard, he will want to learn how to read and write. And this desire transforms the rote, repetitive exercises of phonics into something exciting and even desirable.

Because your child has a desire to read God's Word, his phonics exercises become important and worthwhile to him. The context and the purpose give the rote, repetitive exercises meaning. In his study *The Face of Battle*, John Keegan uses these exact words—"rote" and "repetitive"—to describe the type of learning that all professional soldiers must undergo.[11] By their very nature, exercises cannot be fully relational, because they do not relate directly to reality. (Nevertheless, as in math, exercises sometimes prove necessary, much as a person not doing any physical work must take a periodic walk to keep fit.) While military exercises—or any other type—are boring in themselves, when the soldier considers that his life and the lives of others depend upon learning what the exercises teach him, he readily dedicates himself to mastering them. (But, to repeat, we must always remember that in every way possible we want to eliminate mere exercises and make our children's schoolwork directly meaningful and relevant to their day-to-day lives.)

This comparison has more validity for our children's learning of phonics than might at first appear. The Scriptures clearly describe your child as a spiritual warrior and admonish him to "put on the full armor of God, so that when the day of evil comes, you may be able to stand your ground, and after you have done everything, to stand" (Eph. 6:13). His armor and weapons are not carnal instruments of violence but spiritual. He holds only one offensive weapon, "the sword of the Spirit, which is the word of God" (Eph. 6:17). His desire to read and know God's Word stems from the desire to master this spiritual weapon of power. This power is not the compulsory power to oppress and coerce, but rather the spiritual power to set free both him and others. God's Word will set him free from the intimidating lies of "the cunning and craftiness of men in their deceitful scheming" (Eph. 4:14) and liberate him to enter into direct spiritual relationship with God and to conform to His patterns:

> If you make my word your home you will indeed be my disciples . . . . You will learn the truth and the truth shall make you free. (John 8:31-32, JB)

Because your child desires this freedom, he seeks to make his home in God's Word; because his phonics course helps him to do that, he feels excitement in and dedicates himself to mastering exercises that in themselves might be boring and dull.

We see the same principle at work in music. The child wants to play beautiful songs, but he must develop the necessary skills. To develop these skills, he must repeat the scales. Obviously, no parent would present the musical scales as ends in themselves; to do so would make them hopelessly boring. Every Christian parent knows that only the goal of playing beautiful music makes the scales meaningful. We easily recognize that only insofar as the child can tangibly see how the scales help him to acquire the skill that enables him to play the music will he be interested in practicing. Yet while we all readily see the need to tie means directly to goals in music, we do not always recognize the importance of doing this in the rest of our child's education. But we need to do so as much as possible in *every* circumstance. Every form of educational practice becomes more exciting (and more beneficial) insofar as the child sees how the practice applies to the goals. While no controversy exists about this assertion in the case of playing music, controversy does exist concerning other subjects, such as language education. A brief look at the controversy about how to teach foreign languages will help us to see more clearly the importance of goal-oriented education.

The Inductive Approach

We can use two basic approaches to language education. Really, any successful teacher must employ aspects of both methods, but, in general, one approach or the other will predominate and provide the basic context in which the teaching will go on. These two approaches are called the deductive and inductive methods.

Both the deductive and inductive approaches aim at teaching us how to use a language: how to read and write it, how to speak and understand it. Obviously, both the teacher and the student recognize this goal. But questions arise concerning how best to tie in this goal to the day-to-day learning experience so that the student will move forward in both enthusiasm and achievement. In the deductive approach, we concentrate on learning the rules and principles of grammar, punctuation and syntax, vocabulary words and so on. Our learning efforts focus on these tasks. Because of this focus, it sometimes seems to the child the same as simply learning the scales for their own sake. He sees the exercises as mere rote tasks. In contrast, in the inductive approach, he also receives systematic instruction and drilling in language rules and principles and in vocabulary, but the student learns these rules in response to practical needs he encounters in his efforts to read, write and converse in the language. The student sees directly, on a day-to-day basis, how his scales help him to play songs. The inductive approach is closer to the way we learn our native language. A child obviously doesn't learn the rules of grammar and then apply them. He tries to communicate with people, and in doing this he learns the rights and wrongs of language use.

In writing too, as we will see later on,* the best approach to teaching this skill does not begin by emphasizing grammatical rules. Rather it begins by encouraging the child to express on paper his thoughts and feelings in God; only when he can ex-

---

* See Section Two, "English," in chapter 9 and also "Writing" in Supplement One.

press this in writing should we concentrate on teaching and applying the grammatical rules that facilitate communication with others. (Although we may teach such rules when they apply to our child's writings, even early in his writing experience, we shouldn't make these rules a focus until he becomes somewhat proficient in expressing his thoughts and feelings in writing.)*

In his study *Principles of Language Learning and Teaching*, H. Douglas Brown of San Francisco State University describes the educational theories of David Ausubel as these apply to learning foreign languages. Ausubel stresses that people learn most effectively when they "experience" what they learn as "meaningful" information that is "related to" what they already know and understand.[12] From Ausubel's perspective, "rote learning" (outside of the context of any understanding of the meaning and purpose of that learning), in which the student systematically memorizes seemingly arbitrary rules and information, proves ineffective. In these circumstances, the student feels that he learns "relatively isolated entities" that relate to his understanding "only in an arbitrary and verbatim fashion, not permitting the establishment of [meaningful] relationships."[13] Information learned in this way has no anchor to hold it in the memory, and so we quickly forget it. In contrast, effective learning takes place when information bears a meaningful relationship to what we know and do. Instead of being an arbitrary brick lying haphazardly on the ground, the information becomes incorporated into an unfolding structure in which it has meaning. Brown draws the following implications from Ausubel's research:

> Too much rote activity, at the expense of meaningful communication in language classes, could stifle the learning process . . . .
> . . . In a meaningful process like second language learning, mindless repetition, imitation, and other rotely oriented practices in the language classroom have no place . . . . Rote learning can be effective on a short-term basis, but for any long-term retention it fails because of the tremendous buildup of interference. In those cases in which efficient long-term retention *is* attained in rote-learning situations . . . , it would appear that by sheer dogged determination, the learner has

---

* See Truth Forum's *Right Words: The Grace of Writing*.

somehow subsumed the material meaningfully *in spite of* the method! (emphasis in original)[14]

From this perspective, language instruction proves most effective to the extent that the student sees how what he learns directly helps him in some relevant setting to understand and communicate in the language.

To illustrate the distinction between the inductive and deductive methods, we'll look at how this distinction would affect instruction in New Testament Greek. In the deductive method, the student is systematically taught principles and rules of grammar, syntax, vocabulary and so on; and only after he has a thorough grounding in these, does he then actually try to read a Greek New Testament. In the inductive approach, the student almost immediately approaches the New Testament text, and he learns the language rules and vocabulary in the process of trying to read the text. Here he immediately sees a tangible connection between the goal that led him to study New Testament Greek, which is obviously the desire to read the Greek New Testament, and the tedious task of learning grammatical rules, memorizing vocabulary and so on. In both approaches, the student must systematically learn these rules and words, but in the inductive approach he sees step by step the practical relationship between what he learns and the goal he desires.

In a book on learning to read the Greek New Testament, Dr. Ward Powers presents a number of principles that will help us see how this inductive-type approach to teaching works. These principles all aim toward relating as directly and immediately as possible every aspect of the instructional process to the student's goal of being able to read the original Greek New Testament.

One principle he calls "framework learning," meaning that "the student is introduced in the shortest possible time to the whole framework" of learning that will enable him to practically apply his new knowledge.[15] Rather than thoroughly mastering each individual element of a subject before going on to the next element, the student learns the minimum necessary in each area of the subject for him to begin making practical use of what he has learned. The student then acquires mastery of these individual elements through the learning process that takes place as he tries to apply his knowledge practically and directly to the text problem at hand. Often, texts and teachers naturally apply this principle in teaching basic subjects without even realizing they do. For example, you do not wait until the child writes his *g*'s perfectly before going on to teach him his *o*'s and *d*'s. As soon as he has the basic knowledge he needs in writing a letter, even crudely, you teach him the next one. Then he can practice writing *g*'s and *o*'s and *d*'s by writing, for example, the word *good*. His goal is not to write letters but to be able to communicate with others, and he can more clearly see how writing words rather than merely individual letters enables him to do this. We can use this same approach in teaching practical skills and crafts as well: as soon as possible, give the student all he needs to get him into direct, hands-on work experience.

Another principle Dr. Powers speaks of entails the need to immediately introduce the student to "the target material," that is, the goal toward which he aims.[16] In New Testament Greek, this means that the student is introduced quickly to the Greek New Testament itself. But, again, we can see that this principle has more general application. For example, the main "target material" for reading for the child should be the Bible itself, and as soon as possible, the child's reading ability should be developed to the point where he can begin reading the Sacred Text himself. This does *not* mean that he should not learn the *rules* of reading phonetically, but rather that, as much as possible, he should learn those rules *in the context* of actually attempting to read. Again, we can apply this same principle to every subject of instruction. In arithmetic, for example, the "target material" entails the practical application of the child's arithmetic, putting his knowledge to real, working use in practical examples that seem relevant to his interests. In skills and crafts, "the target material" is making some useful product—a bird house, a wallet, a napkin, a pot and so on. Let the child learn by aiming for the target and firing.

Dr. Powers also speaks of the need to establish a "low threshold of utility," meaning that the student, as soon as possible, must "see how his developing knowledge" of the subject "is already beginning to give him" practical advantages.[17] For example, in teaching phonics you would want to give your children letters that would enable him to start reading many words as soon as possible rather than simply going through the letters of the alphabet in order.

Dr. Powers discusses some other principles that might seem

to apply more specifically to instruction in a foreign language, but we can see that these too can have more general application. For example, he speaks of teaching New Testament Greek, "so far as possible," according to "the procedures followed" in "natural language acquisition," by which he means the procedures "by which the student learnt his own mother tongue." "This means," he explains, "minimal emphasis upon rote learning, and maximum emphasis upon exposure" to the subject being learned, that is, in Dr. Powers's example, the New Testament Greek.[18] We should note here that some rote learning will always be necessary. But we should apply rote learning as soon as possible in a relational context. When he learns to talk, we may practice the *b* sound with our child, but we generally do so in the context of teaching him to say some word, for example, "baby." And this same principle of "natural language acquisition" should be applied as much as possible in the teaching of all subjects: immediately relate what is learned to relevant life situations and practical, relational needs.[19]

In teaching Greek, Dr. Powers concentrates on teaching the student "to recognize recurring patterns in words," and this principle has general application in teaching other subjects too.[20] This also encourages the child to move forward when he sees that the knowledge that he has acquired has practical application in different situations. Again, obvious elementary examples of this sort of recurrent pattern could be found in phonics, where similar letter combinations in different words will give the same sounds, although with different meanings. So, by learning only a few patterns of sounds, the child learns to read many words.

Finally, Dr. Powers speaks about the principle of "progressive presentation followed by systematic revision."[21] This means going over similar material on different levels of study, that is, in the terms that we have used in this book, on the grammar, dialectic and rhetoric levels.* At each step, as we move forward in learning our subject, we make sure that we have also thoroughly assimilated all the information that has gone before. As our study moves forward, we see this old material

---

* These last two principles, recognizing "recurring patterns" and "progressive presentation followed by systematic revision," are not necessarily related to the inductive approach, but they are valuable learning principles that should be used by the teaching parent.

in a new light; we come to recognize more fully the uses, significance and implications of what we learned.

Properly planned review and repetition will greatly increase your child's success in learning. Dr. Paul Pimsleur's principle of "graduated interval recall" reveals the reason for this.[22] Dr. Pimsleur developed an extremely effective method for learning foreign languages. Since learning languages depends largely on memory, Dr. Pimsleur took a deep look at the way the mind remembers things. You remember something when you use it. If you meet someone and learn his name, you will remember it for a short time, but unless you use the name, it will probably slip from you. If a circumstance causes you to call to mind and use the name again before it slips from memory, the name will lodge more deeply in your mind. A greater interval of time will intervene before the name slips from your memory now. But if you recall and use the name again before it slips from your mind during this second interval, then the name will become embedded in your mind still more deeply. Every time you use the name and recall the name, actively summoning up the name from your memory, it becomes more deeply a part of you. Each time, the successive intervals between your use of the name can be longer. Finally, you really possess the name. You no longer have to try to remember it; it belongs to you.

Pimsleur used the graduated interval recall method in his very effective foreign language learning tapes. But you can see how this principle works in any sort of learning. If you wait too long before you call for the information your child has used, he will forget it. So you need some sort of regular system of review that will cause your child to recall and use the knowledge he has acquired before he forgets it. These intervals should be long enough to require that the student work a little to jog his memory, but short enough so that he can still bring the memory back. For example, if you teach addition in math and then go on to subtraction, you will review addition in the course of your instruction in subtraction. When you go on to multiplication, you will review addition and subtraction. When you go on to division, you will want to review all of the earlier learned operations. (In our curriculum, we present reminders to help you use this principle; but you need to know what you're doing to use it effectively. And, of course, you can use this principle with other curriculums as well.)

In his math instruction, John Saxon strongly emphasizes the importance of systematic review. He suggests that you not attempt to drill a concept too thoroughly the first time you teach it. You probably have noticed with your children (and yourself as well) that often they don't fully grasp a concept on the first introduction. But days later, sometimes weeks, you will notice that they have made it a part of themselves seemingly without effort. For example, when we learn new Hebrew songs, the mothers will studiously read their transliterations, studying the singer's mouth, stumbling over the words, getting frustrated, and the smaller children will be just sitting there not even trying. Sometimes they don't seem to be even listening or paying attention. But much sooner than the mother, perhaps a week or two after the song's introduction, the children will suddenly start singing the song perfectly. In the interim since they first heard the song, they have been singing it over and over again to themselves. We're not suggesting that you encourage inattentiveness in your child. We're simply using an example of something you may have noticed in order to point out that many times learning comes through review rather than through the initial lesson.

In math, Saxon stresses that the child may not really grasp a concept at first, but by continually working at it through different examples and exercises he will gain mastery.[23] Like a shoe that may irritate his foot at first but that grows comfortable with wear, he has to keep using new concepts until they become part of him, but this does take an application of effort on the child's part. He must put on the uncomfortable shoe and walk in it until it fits comfortably. In our curriculum, we stress reexamining ideas in different contexts, working with concepts and applying them practically as key means of learning. This contrasts to trying to make the child fully grasp a concept in his head when he first hears it. This type of learning by doing, along with the graduated interval recall method, should be combined for the most effective learning. Saxon uses regular review, calling his instructional method the "incremental" approach.[24] He contends that you must teach each concept on top of the last one—which accords with the Biblical principle of precept upon precept, line upon line (Isa. 28:10)—building toward a higher level on the foundation of the simpler concepts preceding; and he continually reinforces each of the previously learned concepts by review so that they will stay in the child's working memory.

As we pointed out when discussing "graduated interval recall," you remember things most effectively when you actively work at calling up something from your memory. Dr. Pimsleur found that mere repetition alone does not help in learning a language. Such "passive" exercise, through which the student "merely parrots" words and phrases, is worse than useless: ". . . simple, unchallenging repetition has a lulling, dulling effect which, carried to extremes, becomes hypnotic. A word said over and over many times loses all meaning and reverts to a jumble of sound."[25] Instead, Pimsleur contended, exercises should challenge the child to go beyond whatever he can do without exertion.[26] These challenges should not be artificially constructed, but they should relate to real needs and problems that must be overcome. When we educate our children through the relational approach, relating all of his learning to practical and spiritual needs, learning challenges naturally appear relevant and important to the child, because they are. If the child sees the purpose in what he learns, then he sees that the challenge to which he must rise to master the material has real meaning for his life. It's not just an empty exercise, not just getting the dog to jump through the hoop. It has practical importance for his life or the lives of others. He sees that you don't want him to learn to add 963 and 471 just to keep him busy; he sees that this will help him to build that chicken coop or plan the crops for animal feed next year. Given the inherently unrelational nature of exercises, you want to take special care that those you do give your child will encourage his sense of anticipation, build his self-confidence, cause him to stretch beyond the already-attained into the realm that makes education a real adventure.

These principles can be applied on many different levels of instruction: on the most advanced as well as on the most elementary. But all of them help us to see how we can practically apply the *relational* character of true Judaic knowledge to our child's education, even on the most basic levels of instruction. Again, at every point, we should try to show the child the practical, relational importance of what he learns.

Bridging the Gap

These inductive principles of learning apply to every level of education, to the grammar level as well as the dialectic and rhetoric levels. We stress their importance for the grammar stage because on this level we generally find the greatest gap between goals and instruction, details and design. This must be the case since obviously a child first starting out is furthest from being able to apply the knowledge we teach him. The beginning piano student must at least sometimes seem to himself to be hopelessly mired in the swamp of endless scales without any prospect of ever becoming proficient at playing music. Because the child's knowledge is elementary, because he remains on the grammar level of instruction, the relationship between his exercises and his goal will be somewhat vague and tenuous to him, and therefore the meaning of the activity often remains unclear to him. Furthermore, in every learning activity, a breakthrough level must come when the child really develops a feel for what he learns. Before that point, he just plays musical notes, and the exercise of the scale remains largely mechanical. But when the breakthrough comes, he begins to play music, and he directly and tangibly sees how playing the scales contributes to musical proficiency. But in the grammar stage the distance that separates the details of his exercises from the design of his goals often poses a seemingly insurmountable barrier to his shortsighted inspiration.

To see more clearly the problems of elementary instruction, we will take a still more extreme example of the problem than musical scales.

This time our example comes from the animal kingdom. An English pointer is born with the instinct to hunt. He loves to sniff out and chase birds and animals because that instinct has been bred into the structures of his senses over many generations. But much as he has the desire to hunt and enjoys running after animals, so long as he is untrained, his gift remains useless at best, and counterproductive at worst. He can chase after birds for years, but he will never catch one (except maybe the barnyard birds he shouldn't catch). He must be disciplined to learn how to make his gift useful both for his master, the hunter, and rewarding for himself. To do this, his trainer puts the dog through a process that the dog cannot, at least at first, understand at all. He has the instinct to hunt, but that instinct must be brought under the control of the trainer. He cannot just run wildly wherever he wants. He must learn to hunt in the specific area where the hunter directs him. This means that when he hunts on his own, the trainer will discipline him until he learns to hunt where the trainer directs him.

But at first the dog does not understand the purpose of this discipline. He is still on the grammar level and does not yet understand the meaning or purpose of the training because he cannot yet perceive the relationship between the "educational" means and the educational goal, and therefore he cannot see the meaning of these training methods. The dog seems completely baffled at the strange activities his master imposes on him. He cocks his head in bewilderment at his master. Why does his master discipline him? Should he not hunt at all? Yes, he should hunt, but only under the master's direction. So the master must maintain a balance of chastening and encouragement until the dog understands the proper conditions under which he should hunt. He must run and hunt, but always within earshot of the trainer, and then always return immediately at the first command. Then he must be trained on the birds, learn how to hunt by scent, to hold a point without flushing the bird and so on. The dog cannot fully perceive the importance of what his trainer teaches him because the dog does not yet see how all these particulars will work together to enable him to fulfill his larger purpose and function, which is to help put meat on the table while conserving wildlife from unnecessary losses. Nevertheless, step by step the trainer brings the dog through the "grammar" and "dialectic" stages until he becomes an effective hunting dog, able to find the game and hold his point on it while his master comes forth to flush and shoot. Only then, when the dog runs to retrieve the bird, bringing it back to its master, does he receive his reward for submitting to the long and arduous training process: his reward lies in his successful fulfillment of the purpose for which he was created and disciplined. The dog looks to his master for the direction and purpose of his life; his life finds its meaning through this relationship. When he returns with the bird, the dog feels his master's pleasure, and this tells the dog he has successfully completed his task.

While obvious and vast differences exist between training a dog and a person, we can also see important parallels between the animal kingdom and the human one, as James makes clear (James 3:7-8). (A horror to our pride is that Jesus Himself compared the Syro-Phoenician woman to a "dog" and praised her faith when she acknowledged the truth of the comparison, Matt. 15:24-28.) The child has gifts, talents and abilities, too. But he must also undergo a training process (much of which he does not understand at all), so that he may learn that all these gifts and talents are useful only when under the total control of the Master. The child wants to simply give free expression to his gifts, but he must first pass through the character-molding grammar and dialectic stages before he can fruitfully express himself on the rhetoric or wisdom level.

As we said, vast differences separate the human and animal worlds. We cannot speak to the dog so that he can understand what we plan to do with him. But to a certain extent, the child also remains in the dark about the relationship between what he learns and his goal until he can see and experience their tangible relationship himself. The child must at times experience some tedious learning before the knowledge thus acquired can be directly applied. Nevertheless, we can transmit a real sense of excitement to the child, if not in terms of what he can actually do with the knowledge at the very time he learns it, then in terms of what he will be able to do. This is where the first level of discipleship of character—submission to godly authority—pays off for the child: his submitted trust in his parents is what allows him to have the faith imparted to him that will empower him to reach his goals.

Also, one of the great advantages of community life lies in the variety of activities and projects in which each child can participate. In the context of community, he can see a wide diversity of practical tasks, and different people on different levels in those tasks putting to practical use the lessons the child is learning in his schoolwork and offering him the opportunity to use his skills and knowledge. Because he sees and participates in so many different activities and skills, he has the opportunity to discover his place and his calling in the community.

In the context of community, each child shares in the vision and the excitement of participating in God's purpose even when he cannot immediately see the direct relevance of what he learns. On the grammar level, the child sometimes sees only dimly the direct relationship between what he learns and the purpose of this knowledge. And since knowledge of relationship remains so limited, knowledge of the meaning of what he learns also remains limited. This (in addition, of course, to the child's limited reading ability) explains why, on this level, the relationship with the parent-teacher becomes so central to the learning process, demanding the greatest proportion of the mother's time.

Even if we cannot show our child the direct relationship between what he learns and the goal ahead, if he sees the relationship of the goal to his life and is in the proper relationship with his parents, trusting their word that this task and that goal are related, then he will persevere in faith and victory. This faith that what he's learning relates to the goal ahead offers the child the impetus and motivation to push through on the grammar level. The exciting sense of purpose and goal drives the child forward, internally motivating him to press on no matter how much rote learning the mastery of the material may require. If this faith fails, then so will his desire to learn. We must "touch his palate" with the facts that will nurture his desire to grow in the knowledge and wisdom of God. "Rub the palate," that is, to touch the palate, is the literal meaning of the Hebrew that is generally translated as "train" in Proverbs 22:6, KJV, "*Train up* a child in the way he should go: and when he is old, he will not depart from it." This literal meaning refers to an ancient practice in which the mother stimulated the palate of the child with food to induce him to eat new foods during the period before weaning. We must do this with the knowledge of God, stimulating the child's spiritual palate so that he will "taste and see that the Lord is good" (Ps. 34:8), so that he will be induced to eat the spiritual food that he needs for his eternal sustenance. And, at the same time, we must also be careful *not* to touch his palate at this young, impressionable age with those things of the world that we do *not* want him to acquire a taste for. We saw earlier that when the child remains thus untouched, he remains integral, whole.

While we recognize that on the grammar level some gap must separate ends from means, we want to do all we can to minimize this gap. As much as possible, we want to tie the child's education directly and tangibly to realizable goals so that he can experience for himself the practical importance and use of what he learns. We have seen this in such individual subjects as reading, music and foreign language study, but how can we show the practical importance of such subjects as math and science, or history and English, and how can we show practically the importance of all these topics working together for the achievement of tangible goals that the child values?

When we speak of practical in this sense, we include but do not confine ourselves to meeting physical needs such as growing food, making clothing or building houses. By practical, we mean also any knowledge that finds application in practice, that proves useful in any way for our lives. As we've suggested earlier, this includes meeting spiritual needs as well as physical needs. What enables us to see the practical use of the full scope of the knowledge we impart to our children—and enables us to impart this awareness to our children as well—is our spiritual vision. For the spiritual vision will teach our children to value as useful those things that help meet spiritual needs and to see the spiritual significance of all the activities of their daily lives. We must recognize the full scope of God's purpose for our lives in order to understand how we can practically apply the full knowledge God would impart to us. And we can only recognize the purpose of this knowledge through our spiritual vision. The Scriptures declare both that "where there is no vision, the people perish" (Prov. 29:18, KJV) and also that "my people are destroyed for lack of knowledge" (Hos. 4:6, KJV). Spiritual vision enables us to see how we can use our knowledge, how the pieces of knowledge find their place and purpose in our lives. So the child needs the spiritual vision that will show him how the various elements of his curriculum work together to fulfill the integral, practical goal God has for his life. To see how that vision emerges in the child's education, we now turn to what we call "the unit approach" to learning, but which differs markedly from the approach that generally goes under that term.

Introducing the Unit Approach

The relational approach to education aims to interrelate all our children's education in one cohesive whole. When this happens, education becomes most exciting for the child, as he sees all the pieces of his education fitting together in one integrated unit. The word *unit*, derived from the word *unity*, means "one." Through the unit approach to education, your child sees how *all* his diverse subjects fit together as various parts in one coherent body of knowledge, all parts having practical bearing upon his life (in the broad sense in which we have defined "practical" above). Since Christian education strives to bring our child forth as a whole, fully integrated person, the knowledge that we convey to him must also be fully integrated.

The "unit" that ties all education into an integrated unity must ultimately comprehend the child's whole life. Then his life itself must be assimilated and integrated into that unit which integrates all the knowledge he acquires. So to live a fully integrated life, the child must find his place in God's purpose, and he can only do this as his family participates in the forward movement of God's corporate people. The child's immediate unit is his family, but the family's immediate unit is the local expression of the Body of Christ. We've seen that the purpose of home education for the child is to integrate him through relational knowledge. But for all the reasons we want to educate our child at home, so too does God want us, as his children, to come home to His family, His Body.

From the child's place within the family, which has in turn found its place within the corporate community, the child moves forward in the fulfillment of God's purpose for his life and sees practically how all the knowledge he acquires has useful application. From this context of integrated vision and purpose, everything the child learns in regard to scholastic subjects, practical skills, character development and so on, interrelates. Everything the child learns finds its place in meeting needs, answering questions and overcoming problems that relate to an integrated "unit" vision. Because the child's community and family possess an integrated vision and impart this vision to him, the child sees how these various needs, problems and questions affect one another and how each element of knowledge he acquires fits into the unified purpose of God.

The unit approach ties together all the elements of your child's curriculum through the integrated vision and life of Christian community. Only the unity of Christian community establishes the context that makes the unit approach really work. And God's corporate community can only unite as it presses to fulfill the total purpose God has ordained for His people. As we've seen, that purpose centers on manifesting the manifold wisdom of God, the wisdom that meets every physical and spiritual need of man. These needs include both the positive needs of building up God-centered community and, as we shall see, the negative need of tearing down the idols that obstruct the vision of the lost. Within the context of this comprehensive purpose, all the elements of the child's education fit together. Everything combines as an element in bringing forth the complete witness of God to this generation, both in the dialectic through which the church tears down man-centered strongholds and in the rhetoric of building up that spiritual Body which shows forth all the fullness of God's wisdom. This total vision, Body and purpose, as it emerges through the crucible of dialectic with the world, forges the unit that ties together every aspect of our children's education.

As we've seen, wisdom shows the multiplicity of interrelations, how things fit together, how actions in one sphere affect another sphere. Yet we've also seen that children through their education move *toward* wisdom, that they do not begin at this level of knowledge but that they press to attain it. Nevertheless, wisdom can bring forth a unit curriculum that will enable the children to see how the elements of their education interrelate even as they move forward through the various stages of their education toward wisdom.

What, however, is the precise form and content of this unit curriculum? How does it interrelate all the aspects of the child's education? How exactly do we tie in teaching basic scholastic skills (such as reading and arithmetic), practical craft skills, scholastic subjects such as history and science, and Bible study and character curriculum? Obviously, in a general sense we can see that if he sets out to build his chicken coop, the child will soon see that he needs to learn measurements, figure angles, calculate distances and so on; that is, he'll see that his practical craft skills require that he develop math skills. Similarly, he can use reading skills to dig deeper as he learns craft skills and so on. But this offers no help in determining how, concretely, the full range of his educational skills integrate to form a single comprehensive unit. How does the child's knowledge of history, geography, science, the Scriptures and so on, relate to his practical craft skills? How do scholastic subjects and hands-on skills relate to English? How concretely do all these subjects form an integrated whole in your child's vision, so that he will see with wisdom's eyes? As we've said, the vision of a Christian community pressing forward in the purpose of God provides the unit framework that interweaves all the elements of the child's curriculum. But in order to understand how exactly the unit approach integrates all the diverse elements of his education, we must understand more about how the education process prepares the child to fulfill his purpose in God. When we investigate this, we'll find both a deeper vision of that purpose and a more precise vision of how Christian education connects with that purpose. With our vision deepened through this more complete understanding, we'll then be able to see concretely how a unit curriculum can truly emerge. For us at this point, then, the unit approach remains an ideal toward which we press. After we lay further groundwork in the remainder of this chapter, in the next chapter we'll talk concretely about how we can realize that ideal. Then in our description of our Koinonia Curriculum in Supplement One, we'll discuss very specifically how we've attempted to bring forth a unit curriculum to help you educate your children.

Learning to See

First, in pressing toward implementing the unit approach, we must recognize that in order to interrelate the diverse elements of our children's curriculum (such as history, science, English, practical skills and so on), we as parents must see how they interrelate ourselves. We must have the spiritual vision and knowledge that enables us to see the diverse ramifications and implications of the different subjects as well as their interrelationships. How does history tie into science and English? What are the spiritual ramifications and meaning of history? How does it tie into the lives and life style of our children?*

We've shown that only God can give the wisdom and insight to see the interconnections of and therefore the meaning of history and all these other diverse subjects, as well as our relation to them. But how do we receive the *vision* to *see* these interconnections? Jesus spoke of "the eye," the organ through

---

* And, of course, specific ministries within the Body, eldership ministries and particularly teaching ministries, bear responsibility for ministering to the members of the Body so that they *can* see this. Throughout the remainder of this book we refer to materials we've designed for this purpose.

which we see, as "the light of the body." He said that if our "eyes are good," then our "whole body" will be "full of light," but if our "eyes are bad," then our "whole body will be full of darkness" (Matt. 6:22-23, KJV and NIV). Proverbs 20:27 declares that "the spirit of man is the lamp of Yahweh, searching all the innermost parts of his being" (NASV), and Psalms 119:105 tells us that Yahweh's Word "is a lamp to my feet, and a light to my path." How can both the spirit of man and the Word of God be our lamp, that is, our light? Because the Word of God lights our path by igniting our spirit. The Word of God comes to our dead spirits and, through faith, ignites our spirit to become a living flame. Then we must fan that spirit to flame and be as those wise virgins who have a full stock of oil to keep the flame perpetually burning (2 Tim. 1:6; Matt. 25:1-13). Our eye is the vision that illuminates the path before us. This comes to us through our own spirit as it is ignited, quickened, by the Spirit-anointed Word of God. If our spirit burns with the flame set by God's anointed Word, then the eye is good, and it illuminates everything that it gazes upon with the vision and the insight of God. This eye illuminates the whole world, but when the lamp of the eye goes out, as in death, then all the world falls into darkness.

When we truly see with God's vision, then our "whole body," the Body of Christ, will be "full of light." We will see God's vision in every aspect of human life. Nothing will be hidden from our eyes, but everything will be manifest, will be made known. In the days to come, our children will surely need that comprehensive vision to answer the hard questions that the world will ask. We want the light of God's Word to burn in our children so that they can see with this vision that illuminates and dispels all the darkness of the world, so that they can see the meaning of the world and reveal that meaning in order to help lead the lost onto the illuminated path toward home.

Yet how can they acquire such a vision? Of course, to some degree you can always simply hand your child a book that you feel will help him to receive some of the knowledge and understanding he needs. But the impulse that leads you to turn to home education also makes you feel the inadequacy of such a solution. As we've seen, to succeed, home schooling requires a deep and comprehensive relationship through which the parent transmits knowledge to his child. This bond and relationship by its very nature precludes the abstract and objective impartation of knowledge that follows from mechanically handing your child a book and then simply getting out your answer sheet to check off his responses to questions at the end of the chapter. If you follow such a procedure, you short-circuit the purpose of home schooling, for you substitute an objective approach for a relational approach. The home-school relationship requires your personal role in the impartation of knowledge. Yet obviously you can't fulfill this function unless you possess the necessary knowledge. Unless you, the parent, allow God's Word to ignite your own spirit so that you can see with the fullness of God's vision, till your whole body is full of light, then you won't really know if your child is receiving the full vision that he needs. You may talk to him about his historical or spiritual or scientific studies, but your own ignorance about these subjects, the darkness within you, will prevent you from knowing whether you're even seeing, let alone transmitting, the insights that he needs. And so, of course, you won't know if he has the comprehensive vision that he needs.

We've heard many mothers complain of feeling this lack within themselves—that, for example, they have a desire to give their children a deeper understanding of history, but feel too ignorant to do so. One of the advantages about home education, however, is that it forces us as parents to overcome our own ignorance. Perhaps we can make excuses for ourselves and try to just get by, but if we want more than that for our children, we must possess more than that ourselves. Our children can't come into the fullness of their inheritance unless we come into the fullness of ours, because the inheritance is handed down from parent to child, and the parents can only give what they possess (John 3:27).

We've already examined some of the implications of the parents' role as the progenitors of their children, that as those through whom God "authors" His children, parents hold the primary authority over and responsibility for their children. All parents have the responsibility to see that their children conform to the image that God has ordained for each of their individual lives. In a sense, then, we can say that parents become the "authors" through whom the true Author brings forth His children in the perfect expression of Himself. The author of a work is the one who has the overall *vision* to guide and bring forth that work, be it a painting, a book, a building or anything else. For example, the famous Spanish painter Velazquez had many apprentices working under him. Yet even though they were to deftly execute, under his constant tutelage, their particular part of a painting, and by so doing learned the master's own technique, he signed his name to every painting. He did so, because they worked under the direction of his *vision*: his eye directed them. His own spirit illuminated his vision and enabled him to see and to guide them in the particulars that comprised the whole of each painting.

To be the author of your children's lives, in the sense of fulfilling your responsibility to ensure that they conform to the true Author's goals for their lives, your spirit must be fully ignited with your own Author's Word so that you may see with His vision and His insight and execute your part in a masterpiece to which He will not be ashamed to affix His Name. This obligates you, then—if you believe that God has told you to educate your children, to train them up in the way that they should go—to yourself (and for yourself) master the knowledge that *they* will need in order to become everything that God has ordained for them. You must be able to look into history and science, for example, and see those things with the vision of God. Yet many parents have said, concerning history for example, that they can't tell when important facts have been eliminated from a text or have been used to present a distorted vision (as in public school material).

This assessment of their own knowledge, then, becomes something frightening to parents, because they realize their ignorance and don't know where or how to overcome it. As we'll explain, we are in the process of completing the type of teaching material that can help you to acquire the vision and knowledge God would give to parents. Yet whether you feel that this material will meet your needs or not, you must find *some* way to meet that need. You must find some way to overcome the darkness and see, for instance, the political ramifications of ancient Mesopotamian irrigation systems, or the facts that will show you the meaning of the French Revolution, the American Civil War, the Holocaust: every contemporary issue facing us flows out of conflicts and events that originated in the past, even in the remote past. If we as Christians recognize how fundamentally and deeply our lives have been shaped by Adam's sin at the very dawn of history, then we of all people must recognize the immense importance of the past in our lives, particularly the streams that flow into and form our own culture.

Moreover, we as Christians are called to be "the light of the world." The light that God's Word brings forth in us and through us, to illuminate our vision and our children's vision, offers the only light through which the world can see. Yet we can only offer that light to the world if we understand the world; only then can we properly relate to the world. Paul says that "the god of this world has blinded the minds of unbelievers, so that they cannot see the light of the gospel of the glory of Christ, who is the image of God" (2 Cor. 4:4, KJV, NIV). They find themselves ensnared in the "mystery of iniquity" (2 Thess. 2:7, KJV), seduced by "Mystery, Babylon" (Rev. 17:5, KJV).

Mystery means, in the literal Greek from which our English word derives, "to shut the eyes." So the Bible teaches that the lost have been caught by a world system that blinds them. We as the "light of the world" must illuminate this darkness, exposing the nature of this world system. To do this, we must ourselves see it in such a way as to transmit to our children the spiritual meaning of this system, of its history, its science and so on, so that they might answer the world's hard questions.

So understanding these things isn't a superfluity but a necessity, at least if we would fulfill the very dialectical purpose for which God has placed us in this world. We don't study history, science and so on out of some arbitrary or State-compelled principle, but because we need this knowledge and understanding to possess God's comprehensive vision, a vision necessary to fulfill His purpose. When seen correctly, then, what most parents view as secular knowledge taught in Christian education should primarily take shape as dialectic, as insights that will empower us to tear away the delusions that blind the eyes of unbelievers.

Therefore, the first thing needed to make sure your child acquires the comprehensive vision that the unit approach can give him is that you as parents acquire this vision, including the wide array of information that this vision will make meaningful to you.*

---

* We have written a number of books to help supply this vision and information, but it will still take us a while to complete, refine and publish them. (When you plant good seed in a garden, you must still cultivate and weed the garden in order to bring that seed forth to fruition.) We are, however, pressing for-

Our need to acquire this vision and understanding should help us all to see the necessity for a home-schooling family to find its place in the Body of Christ as God would fully constitute it in this day, the place in which whatever ministry God has ordained for us can supply us with the wisdom, insight and knowledge that we need in order to impart the full vision of God to our children.

Just as we can't have successful Christian schooling unless the child is properly connected to his parents, so we can't have successful home education unless the parent is properly connected to those ministries through which the Head ministers His truth into the parents' lives. We as members of His Body can only come into relationship with the Head through our relationship to the other members of the Body, and if our children are to become members of that Body, they too can only find their relationship to the Head through their relationship to the members of the Body. Only when the parent is linked through the proper relations in the Body to the Head can his path be illuminated so that he can lead his child in the way that he should go.

So we can see that the home school needs to be part of the home-school church. The home school should not form a separate compartment in the church but should be an integral part of the church, a key focal point for the fulfillment of the great commission, "teaching" "all nations" "to obey everything" that the Lord has "commanded" (Matt. 28:19-20). The whole church is, according to Jesus' commission, an educational process. It becomes a college, in the original sense: that is, not as an isolated institution where people go to learn fragmented knowledge for a few years. College was originally a Christian concept. In effect, the local church, which was led by a *collegiality* or plurality of elders, was essentially a teaching center in which believers were continually being discipled and instructed by the elders—the "college." This living form was gradually paganized, transformed into a fragmented, secular

---

ward in our effort. We want to present this material to you so that you can see the importance of these questions for your own life, how historical and philosophical currents you may not even be aware of mold and shape aspects of your life and thinking in ways that can even hinder your relationship with God. As you understand these issues and see their relevance for *your* life, you will in turn feel the pressing need and have the insight to impart these truths to your children, using materials such as the unit curriculum we've designed for this purpose.

institution.[27] Yet today God is moving to restore the church itself as a collegiality that encompasses everything in our lives, teaching us everything we need for a life in this world that prepares us for the next. This provides the only *ultimately* effective context in which home schooling can take place.

As we've seen, education *is* discipleship, and discipleship is a relationship of a very specific type, one of fathers and sons (Heb. 12:5-6). In the family, the children must come under the discipline of the father so that God's Word can be imparted to their lives. Unless they come under parental authority, they will not conform to God's Word, and will never become living epistles through whom men can "read" the good news of Jesus Christ. In the church too, only the parents' submission to their God-ordained place in the Body can establish them as sons. Only through this submission can parents experience the *life* of Jesus and pass that life on to their children, for Jesus declared that His Father had given Him authority that He might bring men eternal *life* (John 17:2): we can only receive His life if we submit to His authority. To impart the vision of God to our children, we must incorporate that Word first into our own lives. Only then can both we and our children partake of His life.

Yet to incorporate that life requires more than that we hear the Word through an occasional teaching message. Teaching only informs; training conforms. This relational aspect of discipleship distinguishes home education. Yet parents need to themselves come into that relationship of sonship through which they can be conformed to the Word. Their own lives must conform to God's Word first. They need to come "home" first to God's place for them in His Body. Only by finding their spiritual place in the Body can they make God's Word their "home" and so truly become Jesus' "disciples" (John 8:31, JB). Only then can the parents learn that truth which will set them free (John 8:32) in order to speak with the authority of God to their children, and not merely as the scribes and Pharisees did (Mark 1:22). His Word will then live inside of them.

As we've seen, the relational knowledge that God imparts to us is the knowledge that brings life, in contrast to that objective, detached, analytical knowledge that brings death. This means that God's Word must come to us as relational, not detached or objective, knowledge if it is to impart life to us. If it remains detached and objective to us, then we sit as judges of the Word

(James 4:11). Rather than bringing us life, this Word hardens and deadens our hearts. Yet if we submit to the Word as sons, then the Word can change us into God's image.

Again, this can only happen when we come into binding relationship through which God expresses His fatherhood in our lives (1 Cor. 4:15-16). We must come home to our place in the family of God, under His Fatherhood (Eph. 3:14-15), so that we can receive the relational knowledge that will bring life to us and make us the fathers and mothers who can fulfill all the promise of our home school. In the end, home education can only succeed if the home itself becomes educated, and only the Body of Christ can accomplish this in an approach of relational knowledge that itself stands consistent with the *relational* approach inherent in home education.

This understanding will help us to also recognize that *degrees* and *levels* of teaching exist as we grow toward maturity in the family of God and that, as we've said, the true "unit" of our children's education entails the integration of all aspects of life. When we live together in community, building, farming, planning, growing, worshiping, all aspects of our *lives* become interrelated. So as our children grow within this community life, an education attuned to the harmonies of this community life will naturally move their lives into harmony with the song the community sings. In this context, each skill and discipline plays its notes in the corporate symphony. The children see that they must conquer math in order to build, count, survey; they must master English skills in order to instruct, pass on, communicate, define, convey; they must understand history both to acquire the heritage of the past and to overcome its pitfalls. In the context of community, science has practical application for such purposes as soil management, healing sick animals or finding alternative energy sources (for example, mastering solar heating in order to help cut down on wood fuel consumption). All learning becomes relevant as various needs make themselves known.

Education holds ever before us the goal of taking dominion over the earth in submission to God, the goal of accomplishing God's purpose. We do not merely educate in order to learn a mass of facts. To repeat, the intellectual process comprises only a part of education's larger goal: the shaping of an entire human life. We must direct everything we do toward bringing the child to wisdom, to the place where his whole life reflects the glory of God, to the maturity where he can become a means through whom God restores His dominion over the earth. As soon as possible, and as much as possible, the child should learn to recognize and utilize relationally the things he learns. In the next chapter, we will discuss concretely how the unit approach enables us to do that.

Moving towards Dominion

So we see that everything our child learns must contribute to his spiritual maturity, to his ability to come forth as the offspring of the Spirit, filled with the grace and wisdom of God. Everything must contribute to his ability to take ever-greater dominion over the world around him in the Spirit. All the lessons of his education must contribute to these goals. No room exists for anything superfluous to these. If we keep this vision before us, our child's education assumes a clarity, a freshness, an excitement and a driving sense of purpose that will grow with the passing days and years.

The child will spend most of the grammar years assimilating the essential tools of learning. He will learn to work and do chores with his whole heart, to speak clearly and politely, to dress neatly, to keep himself clean, to develop important character traits, to learn basic practical and scholastic skills, such as reading, writing, arithmetic. He must acquire a basic knowledge of history and science. And above all, he must come to a vital relationship with the Spirit of God based upon a living knowledge of the Word of God. Again, insofar as possible, he should learn all this knowledge relationally, in the context of achieving objectives that arise in the settings of real life.

As we've said, the basic lessons of submission in the kingdom of God will serve as a foundation to all other knowledge. The child must first learn to listen, respect and obey before he can ever learn anything from those who would teach him. The child can never submit to the parent's teaching until he submits to the parent's authority. He must become receptive to knowledge from beyond himself, and to do this he must overcome that sinful nature which clings only to its own "knowledge of good and evil." Submission to God's authority, therefore, stands at the basis of all grammar lessons, and you must repeatedly reinforce it on the grammar level until the child thoroughly learns it. The child must listen and watch in order to learn. He must discipline himself (or be disciplined) to sit quietly, to pay attention, to receive instruction—to open his ears, his eyes, his heart, and to bring his mind into focus on the task at hand rather than letting it roam in uncontrolled daydreaming. If we put this discipline forth in the love of God, we need not fear damaging the child's character. On the contrary, discipline *in love* enables the child to learn the self-discipline essential to developing his character in God. When we *deny* a child this discipline, we do untold damage to his character and personality (Prov. 13:24). We make him a permanent baby. In order to ensure the child's growth and maturity, we must disciple him and teach him how to submit (not merely to obey but to obey with a willing heart, trusting and believing).

To repeat, our child has no need to learn abstract generalities that contribute nothing to the positive formation of his character and abilities. Everything must tie into the press toward spiritual maturity, dialectical insight and practical abilities. Bible lessons should not be mere factual exercises. They should aim concretely at transforming our child's character. (We'll see how to do this when we discuss the *Character Curriculum.**) They should have convicting power to lead him forward on the path to the high calling of God. We must bring the Scriptures to bear upon the real needs and problems of his life. For example, when he falls into the sin of lying, immediately the relevant scriptures on this subject will take on a definite, practical meaning. It then becomes important for him to memorize and understand the scriptures concerning this sin, to hide God's Word in his heart so that he will not sin again. Furthermore, we can explain God's commandment concerning lying within the context of the broader pattern of God's Word and commandments so that the child can understand what exactly God requires of him and why. This will lay the basis of the dialectic stage of learning, when the child will pursue these questions in greater depth as God works more deeply in him.

On the grammar level, scientific facts should also tie into practical needs of the child's life, for example, learning about predicting the weather to help him in his gardening, telling

* See pp. 344-346.

times or seasons or directions by the stars. Problems and difficulties can become opportunities for him to acquire
knowledge to help him overcome. For example, if poison ivy
nails him, it will suddenly become relevant to him to learn about
the various harmful plants and to also learn about other helpful
plants he can use as remedies for the effects of the harmful
ones.*

The child can most successfully learn practical lessons of
dominion when he can work directly with animals and the rest
of God's creation. In the context of a God-centered agriculture, our children can learn important lessons, both spiritual
and practical. When they work with animals and crops, they
learn that God is truly the Master of the times and the seasons.
In the grocery store and the market system, the times and
seasons have been changed, which places corporate, techno-industrial man in charge of setting the times and seasons
but also makes us dependent on certain political systems for
our survival, potential pawns for totalitarian designs. In techno-industrial culture we no longer even have these "times and
seasons" where certain crops and foods are exclusively available. All this has been changed so that we may have a permanent availability, a permanent season of harvest and
consumption, apart from the patterns of the God who reserved
the times and seasons unto His own authority as the chief
means of maintaining His authority over man (Acts 1:7). This
has made us independent of the vicissitudes of nature, and
thereby independent of nature's God who controls such
things. For that dependence on God, we have, however, substituted a dependence on the State-regulated market system,
subject to just as many vicissitudes, fluctuations and controls:
rationing, trucker strikes, grocer strikes, market fluctuations,
oil prices, poisoned packaged food, bureaucratic hindrances,
government manipulations and so on. We have merely substituted dependence on man for dependence on God and in
the process lost many of the invaluable blessings and lessons
that derive from a God-centered agri-culture.

We have also removed ourselves from the dietary rhythms
that God's times and seasons naturally supply for our bodies.
This has resulted in enormous health problems for twentieth-

---

* As you will see in our curriculum description in Supplement One, we structure many of our subjects around practical needs. Much of our math, for example, focuses upon the needs of a working ranch.

century man. This detachment from the rhythms and harmonies of the creation has also brought forth people who do
not know the practical uses of grasses although they know
their Latin names, who do not know the pasture although they
know how to compute its perimeter and who do not know their
God although they know all the major religions of the world.

One sad result of this abstract approach to life came to light
when many of the young mothers in our fellowship wanted to
nurse their babies and *could not* do so without great difficulty.
We realized that something which once had come naturally
and had never caused any problems had suddenly become an
almost insurmountable difficulty. Why? Because these moth-
sers had not learned at their own mothers' knees how it was
done. They had not participated in that learning experience
where without conscious effort, without "formal" teaching, the
learning took place through relationship—through the mother-
daughter bond, through the *living*, participating interaction integral to family life.

As we have said before, in a God-centered agri-culture,
God's dominion over our children's lives has many practical
ramifications that do not exist in any other sort of culture
(though, of course, if it is not God's will for them to live in such
a culture, they can still learn to lead God-centered, Spirit-con-
trolled lives). Yet in such a land- or *agri*-culture, our children
see the reality of God's dominion in such day-to-day activities
as plowing, planting, cultivating and harvesting the fields,
caring for animals and so on. The lessons of a God-centered
agriculture are lessons of submission to the living reality of
God's will, a submission that takes on heightened practical importance for all of us, since man has not yet devised a way to
live without eating. In such an agriculture, to fail to respond to
the God-ordained "times and seasons" is to fail to have food
on one's table and so in one's stomach. Under such circumstances, practical and spiritual lessons work together to teach
our children the importance of responsibility and obedience to
the will of God. If it isn't possible for our children to participate
in such agriculture, we must still do all that we can to relate the
facts of science to what they can observe and experience
themselves, to what they relate to and what relates to them. If,
however, we see the importance for our children to engage in
such work, we will do all that we can to find an opportunity for
them to do so, even if it's merely a garden in our apartment

complex or housing development (which many of the children in fellowships with which we are associated manage themselves).

Again, we must remember that every lesson, every fact, every principle of our child's education, must contribute to our spiritual objectives, both long-term and short-range. Everything must contribute to the forward movement of our child's development in God. Historical understanding forms part of this process too. Through his understanding of history, the child learns to more fully understand and thus take dominion over the forces that shape his own life. And this historical knowledge also helps him to influence others to move in the direction of God-centered purpose.

Even on the grammar level—and then more clearly on the dialectic level—the child can see that history does have a very direct relationship to his life, that just as his life has been shaped by the "history" of his parents' generation, so *each* preceding generation directly shapes the succeeding ones. And so he can see how his life links directly to the history of all the preceding generations. As we have seen, we have a debt to "the future," to our children, to pass on to them "the past, the long knowledge that is the potency of time to come." As members of the Body of Christ, fitly framed together with people of all manner of ethnic, national, racial and religious backgrounds, our children can see how the background and history of all peoples have a direct influence on their own lives and the purposes of God. To recall a previous quote from Berry, they can see how their life in Christ

is not the story of *a* life.
It is the story of *lives*, knit together,
overlapping in succession, rising again
from grave after grave. (emphasis added)

Just as they see how God deals with and shapes them as individuals, so they can see that God has shaped them and the course of human history by continuing to shape the peoples whence they sprang. They can see that God is preparing His corporate Body by shaping "every kindred and tongue" on the face of the earth, from whom He is calling forth all the members of His Bride. Within such a context, our children can see that the facts of history bear a very direct relationship to their lives. For example, a child of Mexican ancestry can see how the history of the Indian peoples in the pre-Conquest era, the coming of the Spanish and the Colonial period and the subsequent history of independent Mexico and then the migration of Mexicans to the United States have all worked together to influence, mold and shape many of the present characteristics of his life; he can see this same sort of historical development as it shapes his brothers and sisters of other ancestries— Jewish, Scottish, Irish, Italian, Black or tenth generation Anglo-American. In Christ, he can see how God takes everything positive in each of these histories, brings them forth and uses them for His purpose as He molds together His multifaceted Body, while at the same time He removes from our lives everything negative in the traditions of our various historical backgrounds.

As we have seen, the *knowledge,* or *grammar,* level lays the foundation for the *understanding,* or *dialectic,* level. The grammar level concentrates more upon basic elements or else, as in phonics, upon seemingly simple facts and unrelated details. On the dialectic level the child comes more fully into the exciting context of conflict between competing systems and, even ultimately, world views. This represents a whole new realm of relationship through which new levels of knowledge open up to the student. Suddenly, on this level, all the facts that he has learned become weapons in the arsenal of truth and clarity in the battle against falsehood and confusion.

Because every fact and principle has now become a spiritual weapon in defense of truth, the dialectical level offers clearer insight into the relational character of learning. Yet facts and principles all have practical purposes on the grammar level too. For one, they contribute to building up our spiritual armory for the dialectical battles ahead. Remember that although the child may be unaware of the nature of the dialectic and rhetoric stages of learning that follow the grammar level, this is not true of the parent. The facts and principles that we teach on the grammar level must not constitute a mere purposeless, random assortment. They must constitute mainly those facts and principles needed to provide the basis for the dialectic level. The grammar and dialectical levels must work together as intertwined, dovetailing elements of the cohesive unit curriculum. (We'll discuss how concretely in the next chapter and in Supplement One.) Again, we don't want to merely saturate the child with as many facts as possible. We should put forth the material that will prepare the way for his understanding when he enters the dialectic stage. We must not simply fill the child with masses of irrelevant, unrelated facts. As much as possible, we must show the relevance—the relationship—to the child's life of the information he learns. If this is impossible, then our own relationship with the child must fill in this gap, allowing him to trust in someone who he knows does possess this relational knowledge.

On the grammar level too, we must provide a spiritual framework to help the child remember and see the relevance of all the facts he learns, to see their relationship to his life. Whether or not the child can fully perceive and understand this God-revealed pattern of relationships, the parent should have this pattern in his mind as he instructs the child. For example, many of the basic Biblical "facts" of God's Word can be understood within the framework of the Ten Commandments, which constitute in their God-centered intention not an arbitrary listing of rules but God's organic framework for the harmonious regulation of human life. Within the context of these few commandments, God has given man basic patterns for proper relationships—for man's relationship with God, with his fellowman, with creation and within himself. Within the context of this basic pattern of relationships, all of God's patterns for human living can be fitted. For example, the many Biblical references to lying fit under the prohibition against perjury (Exod. 20:16; Deut. 5:20), showing honesty as the most basic, essential ingredient to human relationship and therefore to covenant community. As each of the Ten Commandments becomes relevant to the child's life, parents can teach relevant scriptures, particularly from Proverbs, within this context.* When the child sees the details of scriptural truth in the context of this framework, he can begin to see that each of these details will work with all the others to bring him forth into wholeness and maturity in the Spirit. He can appreciate these details as the pieces of a puzzle, pieces that, when put together, will reveal the true image of his life.

In Biblical history, everything can be fitted within the framework of the major historical periods, for example, the time of the Patriarchs, the Exodus and so on, these periods

---

* See chapter 9, Section One, for a discussion of Truth Forum's *Building Christian Character: A Guidebook through the Elements of Christian Character*, which explains how to do this and presents a fuller explanation of why to do it.

marking the major transformations in the lives of God's people, and thus the chief formative developments in history that have brought us to where we stand in our own day. Through the teaching of history, the child can learn basic God-centered principles as those principles apply to historical development: he can learn the consequences, good and bad, of what our forefathers did and of what they were so that he may learn from their failures and their successes, and so find guidance in his future actions.

As we'll see in the next chapter and in Supplement One, the spiritual frameworks of particular subjects can be interrelated to one another through the unit approach. As we've said, the unit that ties all subjects together is the child's life taken as a whole within the context of the vision and purpose of the Christian community of which his family forms an integral part. Because all aspects of this vision, life and purpose interrelate, all subjects and skills tie together. For example, writing skills potentially tie together with any subject, for the child can use this skill to do writings about his experience in any area of life; and as his skills, maturity, interest and knowledge develop, he may also use his writing skills to present to others the information and experience he has acquired. Likewise, as we'll show in the next chapter, his knowledge of history—for example of the change from self-sufficient agriculture to urban industrialism—also relates to his participation in the crafts and skills of a land-based community, from metalworking to farming to leatherwork to spinning to weaving and so on; for these historical studies, as we'll see, tie to the common vision that rejuvenates all these activities, as that vision in turn engages in a dialectic combat with the vision of secular culture. Through his historical studies, then, the child acquires a vision that enables him to see the meaning and purpose of his practical endeavors, thus igniting his enthusiasm, while at the same time equipping him to defend his way of life against secular attacks. The basis for this vision, as we'll see in the next chapter, is laid in the grammar level.

On the *dialectic,* or *understanding,* stage, as we have seen, our knowledge comes into still sharper focus in the myriad living relationships that the Spirit reveals. This living context of God-anointed relationship we now in turn contrast to those man-centered systemizations through which the facts can also be viewed. As we have said, we enter here on the stage of conflict between opposing world views, different ways of seeing the facts of the world and the Word of God. On this level, as we indicated above, the goal and practical purpose of education become still clearer and more readily perceived by the student, who learns the practical relevance of the truth that makes us free in the battle against the lies that enslave us to other men. The facts and truths that have been learned on the grammar stage now come alive in new depth and fullness on this dialectic level, for this is the level of struggle, of exercise, of resistance. Suddenly, all sorts of conflicting interpretations are thrown at us, and we must sift through those interpretations to establish which one is true, which one is consistent with the consistent truth of God's Word and God's Spirit. We "exercise" our senses against the resistance of false teaching, and therefore, just as the body's muscles are strengthened by such activity, we build up and strengthen our spiritual senses in the Lord (Heb. 5:14).

These conflicting interpretations vie with one another in every sphere of knowledge. In the field of science, for example, the central conflict is between God's Biblical revelation of creation and man's evolutionist way of seeing the facts of science. Everything in the world of science can fit into either of these opposing world views. We bear the responsibility to teach our children from a Christ-centered perspective how to discern scientific truth from scientific falsehood.

In the realm of history, we must remember that everything that has taken place in the history of the world can also be understood from one of two perspectives, that of God or that of man. This is not the naivety of simplemindedness or oversimplification but the eloquence of simplicity. Everything that has happened in history finds a place in the unfolding battle of satan to usurp God's place of dominion over the world, and of God's work to finally bring earth back into perfect harmony with His eternal kingdom. The pagan interpretation of history, which predominates in our public schools today, attempts to make all of the facts of history appear incomprehensible and directionless, abstract and relationless. But the Word of God teaches us differently. We know that the law of cause and effect applies to the events of history, just as it applies in every other sphere of human experience ("whatsoever a man soweth, that shall he also reap," Gal. 6:7, KJV). The man-centered view sets us adrift to be helplessly tossed here and there by the currents of history; the God-centered view enables us to exercise our senses to discern good and evil, to find and actively follow God's purpose for our lives. We must be able to discern the cause and effect of historical events within the context of the struggle between God and satan, between God and those in rebellion against His authority.

How can we do this? Pagan history teaches events as isolated occurrences in the mere unfolding "accident" of progressive evolution. No true dialectic can exist in pagan history. All history but the pagan side is simply eliminated and ignored. (Does any public school child ever learn the history of the beginning of creation, of Adam and Eve, of Moses or the patriarchs, of David or the prophets, or even of Jesus and the apostles?) Consequently the events of history have no real meaning or relevance to, no relationship with, the lives of students so instructed. Historical events become mere accidents. For example, much historical writing on the Civil War simply recounts the mass of different crises that led to that war as though it were some isolated and accidental event of history. But we can understand the true causes of the Civil War only when we understand the effects that the Civil War itself had upon the subsequent development of American history. We must see this event, again, in relationship to what came before and after it, and see how its effects continue on to this day, for it is in this sense that we continue to be in relationship with this event and all past events, as well as all future events. Then the American Civil War ceases to be an isolated event, and we can see it as part of the larger historical drama, the unfolding struggle between the forces of God and the forces of those who hopelessly oppose Him for the control of man's destiny. Finally, through this historical insight, we can see the relevance to our own day and our own lives of events such as the Civil War. The same principles apply to the investigation of other major events, such as the Nazi Holocaust: we cannot understand it by seeing it as an isolated happening, by looking at its causes as though it were cut off from the rest of history. We can only understand it when we see it within the context of the broader conflict of history.* As we establish on this

---

* Historians have voluminously debated the questions we discuss in these few sentences. Many contend that history has no broader context, no significance that ranges beyond the events themselves, no direction or purpose and certainly no transcendent meaning. Obviously we cannot enter

dialectic stage the truth on the basis of our examination of the conflicting propositions of two opposing world views, as we see the interrelationship between these events and their effects upon the present, we become ready for the third, *rhetoric* or *wisdom*, stage.

On this third level, the individual now can *put forth* in a constructive way that which he has learned in order to serve the purposes of God. He can now make use of the knowledge that he has acquired in order to take dominion in God's Name and in submission to the direction of His Spirit over that area of life which he has come to know and understand. In short, he incarnates truth both in his own life and in the lives of others as he begins to be used by the Spirit to instruct them. He now directly participates in the process of actually realizing the goal toward which he has been aiming in his previous education: means and goals are now no longer simply related to each other, but they have now become an exciting inseparable unity. He has gone beyond the preliminaries of relational knowledge, learning how and why history and science are relevant and important, and he actively enters into these realms and sees each of them within the context of God's whole purpose and design for man. Now that his understanding has matured, his relationship with God enables him to respond to God's Spirit so that he can act to bring about those consequences that God desires, not only in his own life but also in the lives of others. He does not merely beat the air, but his blows (not blows of flesh against flesh, but of spiritual warfare, "speaking spiritual truths in spiritual words") will land upon and do damage to his supernatural enemies because

---

into these questions in depth here, but we deal with them thoroughly elsewhere (see *Salvation Is of the Jews, Holocaust as Spiritual War* and *Justice Is Fallen*). We can say here, though, that from a man-centered perspective, these claims are understandable, almost inescapable; their consequence, however, is to make all knowledge of history futile, time better spent on crossword puzzles. Santayana's famous dictum, "Those who do not learn from history are condemned to repeat it," becomes meaningless, for those who know it would be condemned to repeat it too.[28] None of us, as individuals or members of communities, could ever escape the ceaseless repetition of the past's mistakes, nor could we hope to deliberately duplicate the past's successes. The only alternative, the perspective that gives history meaning and that makes its study fruitful for us today, lies in the God-centered perspective that flows from the transcendent Source who alone sees the full scope of interrelationships of history across the face of the earth ("under the sun"), past, present and future (Isa. 46:10; 48:3, 5-7).

those blows can be perfectly guided by the Spirit. This is possible because through his education he has been discipled into a vessel fit for the Master's use. He does not merely go about in circles. He directs his activity to take and possess the land and build up the kingdom of God for God's glory and God's Name. He is able, in every realm—physical, intellectual, emotional and spiritual—to take dominion in the Name of Jesus Christ, under His anointing, His spiritual Headship.

As we have said, the individual who has truly mastered the principles of Christian learning by realizing their results in his own life is one fully prepared to take dominion over every area of his life. He is able to overcome every problem presented to him: he has become an overcomer because he has learned to hear the voice and do the will of Him who has overcome every obstacle through His incarnation, death and resurrection.

Overcoming the World

Only by completely overcoming the obstacles of the world through God's wisdom do we truly become His witnesses. And this purpose—to serve as His witnesses—is the task to which God has called us and for which He has placed us in the world. As witnesses, we must engage in a relationship of continual dialectic with the world. This does not mean seeking to appear "relevant" by changing the truths and standards of God to suit the latest trends and fashions, whether in outward appearance or ideas, of the world. Nor does it mean we engage the world in some sort of petty, spiteful hand-to-hand combat. Rather it means providing the God-centered answers to the problems that man has created for himself.

In our children's education, we must work to prepare them to fulfill their part in carrying on this ongoing dialectic with the world. The world as a whole continually changes, though not progressing or merely changing randomly but rather continually sliding *down* what Aldous Huxley called "the inclined plane of modern history."[29] But even in its downward slide, God continually works in the world to bring to pass His upward-moving purpose. He arranges human destiny and events to open men's eyes to the relevance of His good news and watches for those who will open their hearts to receive Him. The church bears the function, indeed the duty, to engage in that dialectic with the world that enables men to perceive God's purpose in bringing to pass the changes that He works in the world. Only when they perceive this can men receive the Word that God has ordained for that particular period of time, the living Word that will enable the honest to see that the Word of God provides the very solution for which they, in their spiritual hunger and thirst, have been seeking.

To take one example of this dialectic, in the 1960's millions of young people, in what was often their depravity and rebellion, nonetheless sought for a spiritual reality and community life that finally found fulfillment for many in the reality of Jesus Christ and His Body. And many lost in the world made it past the murkiness of their sins to the reality of Jesus only because some burdened people in the church, without compromising God's Word or His holiness, saw the hunger and recognized that even in the midst of the rebellion, God was preparing men's hearts to receive His truth. Because some among God's people dared to believe this, they sought God in order to bring forth a Word that would reach the hearts of those honest seekers. Because of this attitude and love, they succeeded. Similarly in every generation, only as we, both as individuals and as a people, fight the good fight of faith, engage in the dialectic, first within ourselves, then with the world, and become overcomers, can we grow to that place of wisdom that will enable us to reach those yet lost in the world's confusion and darkness. As we truly fight this dialectic battle and become overcomers ourselves, we can then truly help others to overcome.

In the midst of the world's decline, God moves through events, through circumstances, through the minds and hearts of men, to prepare people to receive His Word at each stage or level of the world's course. In ancient times, God prepared the Greek-speaking world for the coming of His only begotten Son, who came forth "in the fullness of time" from a virgin's womb. The times and seasons are the Lord's, and before a spiritual harvest can occur, a spiritual plowing, a harrowing, a preparation of the soil, a sowing of the seed, must first take place. If one reads the ancient Greek writers, one will find truths there that helped prepare the way for the coming of the full truth of God, so that Paul could declare, "As some of your own poets have said . . ." (Acts 17:28). This does not mean that these Greek thinkers were divinely inspired or that their works could be used to supplement, interpret or complete the Word of God. If we believed this, we would follow the mistake of those misguided Christian apologists who led the church into the Dark Ages as they leavened the truth of God's Word with the confusion of pagan thinking. Only the Word of God can present us with the whole truth, with the whole perspective that completes the knowledge of those half-truths, that the pagan thinkers have seen. Whatever was true in the pagan thinkers was already contained in the revelation of God, and the "additional" material of the pagan thinkers (with which misguided Christian theologians sought to "supplement" or "complete" God's Word)* was precisely the leaven from which the Greeks had to be set free.

But our main point here is to emphasize the importance of the process of preparation that was taking place in the hearts and minds of the Greeks. They had come to see the worthlessness of their own mythological deities and had become cynical and dubious about their own religious systems; yet the crisis of their era cried out for a deep spiritual solution. Moreover, their comparatively new-found rationalism had left them empty and dissatisfied. Their political and economic institutions were sterile and even crumbling. Into this vacuum and void the Jewish church penetrated the Gentile world, proclaiming the light that God had prepared these people walking in darkness to receive.

Only through its dialectic, its struggle, with the world, could the church come forth into its third stage of growth in the wisdom of Christ, as His manifold wisdom, His *rhetor*, proclaiming His truth unto the salvation of those souls who had been called to eternal life in that age (Acts 19:9-10).

Yet the world has not stood still since then. It has moved on— to ever-deeper levels of sin, cynicism and decadence. Nonetheless, as sin enters into its new levels of sophistication, grace much more abounds; this abounding grace brings the church to the place where she can enter into the struggle with the world at new and deeper levels, which she must do if she is to truly overcome. If we do not find "the victory that overcomes the world, even our faith," then the world shall over-

---

* See *Justice Is Fallen.*

come us and carry us with it in its downward slide to perdition. Yet this faith that overcomes the world is not a stagnant thing but a growing thing: "from faith *to* faith" (Rom. 1:17, KJV). If our faith does not grow in God's ongoing revelation, then we are losing the battle. We cannot grow by hiding from the conflict, but only by engaging in it, both individually and corporately, with every part of our beings—spiritually, emotionally and intellectually—and with all of our strength.

This "overcoming" does not mean despising the world because the world presents to us a spiritual threat. If we do that, we lose the conflict before we even engage in it. One becomes narrowly defensive only against that which is on the offensive and which is threatening in its potential power. One does not feel defensive against that which one has overcome. And only in the spiritual conflict through which God's people overcome the world can God form within His people the current Word, the *rhema*, that will enable us to reach the lost. This conflict is a spiritual battle in which the church travails until she brings forth the living revelation—in Word and deed—that God has ordained in that hour to meet men's needs. God does not change, but throughout history He has revealed Himself to men through a progressively unfolding revelation.* Today, God is revealing the unfolding restoration of His Body, and those who will carry the burden of being His people will give Him and themselves no rest until Jerusalem above, the church of the firstborn, is established in that level of manifestation that God has ordained to reach all those who would come unto Him (Isa. 62:6-7).

So in this conflict, the church overcomes, even to the extent of pulling out still greater numbers from a world that has fallen to these ever-deeper levels of degeneracy. And when the church overcomes on this level, then sin plummets to a still deeper pit, for the world continues on its downward plunge, "progressively" breaking out of all the restraints of God (Ps. 2:1-3), step-by-step stumbling in its headlong rush until it reaches the abyss. As the limits and restraints to sin are removed on one level and a generation arises on this level of sin and degeneracy, that generation, fulfilling the natural propensity of fallen man, will go on to remove still further restraints and limits to sin. And this generation will in turn raise

---

* See *The Temple*.

up a new generation that will be prepared to slide still further down history's "inclined plane" (a slide greatly accelerating with modern, techno-industrial culture's increasing "liberation" of man from his tether to reality in the form of the limits of a land-centered culture and so on). The "inclined plane" of history then rapidly becomes a precipitous cliff. So again and again the church must strive to overcome on still deeper levels of the conflict against sin, overcoming still greater obstacles and thus rising to still greater heights, until finally the world will degenerate into hell itself while the church rises to its final realization of heaven. At each step along the way, the church salvages from the world those who respond to the church's wisdom, its *rhetor* of the hour, that wisdom and rhetoric that have emerged from the church's dialectic with the world. And in this progressively unfolding polarization, the more that the light of God exposes the evil of the world and the more that we cease to be of the world, the more we become "children of light," the more the world will hate us as we walk in the light, because "everyone who does evil hates the light . . ." (John 3:20).

Yet unless we ourselves willingly engage in this conflict, walk in this progressively unfolding light and overcome in this way, then we "hold the truth in unrighteousness," because truth continues to move towards its final revelation and restoration in the coming of Jesus Christ (Acts 3:21, NASV). If we do not move forward with this light, we shall be left behind in the darkness (John 12:35). The light does not change. It remains ever the same, but it *unfolds* in the *corporate* Body of Christ toward that full measure of incarnation that it had in the individual Christ (Eph. 4:12-13). The path to which God calls His people leads "from faith to faith . . ." (Rom. 1:17, KJV). The path takes us forward; we must therefore not stand still or stagnate, but we must continually move toward the path's destination: "The path of the righteous is like the first gleam of dawn, shining ever brighter till the full light of day" (Prov. 4:18). We have merely begun when we receive our first glimpse of light; that light must grow until it becomes a great sunburst reflecting the irradiated brightness of the glory of God, until the daystar arises in our hearts (2 Pet. 1:19).

At the same time that Truth unfolds in its full revelation in the corporate life of God's people, it also flows into the world to the lowest point of need among men, as it seeks to meet the deepest needs of the human heart in any given hour. Unless we are willing to fight the fight of faith (1 Tim. 6:12), to struggle against our flesh and the devil, to enter into dialectic with the world, to overcome the world with love and truth, we cannot be the instruments and expressions of God's love to those to whom He reaches. If we cannot fulfill this function, we shall come out from under the covering of Him who is the Giver of Truth; for, since He continues to move, we will not be covered by Him unless we also continue moving. If we fail to accomplish the purposes of God, then we shall be left behind, and He will seek for other agents to do His will.

And just as we must fight this conflict in this generation, so we must prepare our children to fight it in the next generation. Each generation must overcome, through an ongoing dialectic with the world, the challenges with which its own times present it. Our children will have to overcome the challenges that the world presents to their generation. They will have to meet head-on the conflict that the world brings in their day. For this reason, they must come to that place of spiritual maturity that enables them to establish the truth of God's Word in the context of that coming conflict so that they can proclaim to the world, in the condition that it presently stands in, the message that the world can hear, in terms that it can understand, the message that the honest of the world will receive. (And we must recognize that for this same message of light the dishonest will hate God's people and persecute us. And the more the light of truth shines, the greater will grow this hatred and persecution.) They must find and proclaim the message of truth that God has already prepared for that time. A *rhema* will come forth from God for their own day, a more complete understanding of the Word of truth that God will formulate directly through them; we must train them so that they can receive that Word and meet that challenge when it comes. This is the purpose of their education.

As we said earlier, in Christian education, our knowledge of the secular world—which would include its history, philosophy, art, much of its science (such as information about quantum physics or about evolution versus creation) and so on—finds its place almost entirely in terms of this unfolding dialectic with the world. As we've seen, God is leading His people into a simplified, land-centered life style. We want to come into harmony with creation on a level with which much of modern technology and science generally conflicts. So we're not trying to raise up a new generation of experts in nuclear fission and rocketry. Nor do we seek to train future lawyers, doctors, government bureaucrats, corporate executives, university professors and so on. The purpose of our knowledge of secular history, with its convoluted course of hubris, tragedy, failure, destruction and holocaust, with its crumbling monuments of man's failed achievements in economics, politics, philosophy, art and science, lies elsewhere. We seek this knowledge strictly in the context of our desire and need to address the concerns that confront contemporary secular men and women. We want to expose to them, and we want our children to carry this exposure even further, the failure of the world view and culture that exclude God and seem to make Him irrelevant. Yet, as we've seen, this dialogue with the world does not stand at the incidental periphery of the life of God's people; it is indispensable if we as His Body would pursue the very purpose for which Jesus declared that He had come, "to seek and save that which is lost." Unless we diligently seek the wisdom, understanding and knowledge needed for this task, we ourselves will become lost as we lose our place in His purpose.

This perspective enables us to integrate all of our children's education, all the knowledge that we seek to impart to them, into a relational perspective, and so lays the final necessary groundwork for our discussion of the unit approach in the next chapter. The education we desire for our children is the most truly well-rounded course possible, fulfilling every spiritual, emotional, intellectual and physical need of their lives. But every aspect of it finds its purpose strictly in the context of God's purposes and goals. Again, in regard to the kind of knowledge we mentioned in the previous paragraph, usually associated with secular learning, that purpose and goal lies in the dialectic with the world we've discussed in this section. In this context of God's purpose, we can begin to see more concretely how all of our children's education can form an integrated, cohesive unity. The history and philosophy of man will offer nothing to our children that answers their own questions and meets their own needs, but we can present such subjects in such a way as to enable them to readily see the falsehoods and confusions in which men lie entrapped so that they can help free others from these delusions.

To see through the deceptions and confusions of human philosophy and history and to present the God-centered alternative to this wreckage of human thought and action requires the wisdom and supernatural insight of God. This truth will not come from the mind of man, but it can only come through the wisdom of the mind of Christ. In the days of the first coming of the Lord, God had prepared the world to receive the truth of His Word, but the leavened word of Rabbinical Judaism was impotent to reach the world. Only the full and living expression of the truth of God could set men's hearts aflame with spiritual freedom. And we are today reaching an age when all of our man-centered or man-leavened programs will prove insufficient. God is preparing multitudes to receive His pure and unadulterated Word, and that message, and that message only, will reach them. We must prepare ourselves and our children to bring that Word: to bring the true message of God's wisdom, both for the sake of the world and for our children's sake as well. Even now, we rapidly approach the day when no truth short of the fullness of God incarnate in His people will prove powerful enough to overcome this great pit of tragedy, despair and darkness that the world has become.

So we must train up a generation that will be able to not merely repeat what their parents have said, but, while clinging to every godly pattern and truth they have inherited from their parents, will also be able to speak the *current* Word, the *rhema* that God has ordained for their own time, a word founded solidly in the unchanging Word of the eternal *logos*. If we fail to engage in such a dialectic with the world for our own day, we will either find ourselves isolated by our failure to relate the truths of God to the current situation in the world, or else we will be captivated by the world. We will become captives of the world because we will fail to see that all that unfolds in it has meaning only as an opportunity for the church to address itself to the honest-hearted and to present the true alternative. When we fail to see this, then the world will become our alternative.

To return to our example above, many Christians, failing to come under God's burden for the 1960's, scorned and derided people whose souls cried out for the spiritual sustenance that those Christians could have given them. And tragically, because they would not open their hearts to the burden of the Lord, they often found their own children attracted to the false spiritual experiences and communities of those who desperately sought for what they could only have found in reality in Christ. Unless we train our children so that they may find the fullness of God for their own lives for their own day and thus fulfill their function for their day, we too stand in danger of condemning them to either irrelevance or cooptation. We—and then our children—must penetrate through to see how exactly the trends of the times are preparing men's hearts to receive the light of Christ, and then we must express that light in terms relevant to these times. Otherwise we will either be sterile in our isolation or deceived into going along with the trends of the world.

We must ourselves heed, and then raise a generation that will heed, the words spoken by John Robinson, the pastor of the congregation that traveled from Holland to England and then set sail to America upon the ship called the Mayflower. Because room was not available on that vessel for everyone in the congregation, Robinson stayed behind in Holland.[30] But he spoke the following words to those of his congregation who embarked on the journey that would bring them to rest at Plymouth Rock:

> I charge you, before God and His blessed angels, that you follow me no further than you have seen me follow the Lord Jesus Christ. The Lord has more truth yet to break forth out of His holy word. I cannot sufficiently bewail the condition of the reformed churches, who are come to a period in religion, and will go at present no further than the instruments of their reformation. Luther and Calvin were great and shining lights in their times, yet they penetrated not into the whole counsel of God. I beseech you, remember it,—'tis an article of your church covenant,—that you be ready to receive whatever truth shall be made known to you from the written Word of God.
> . . . But take heed what you receive for truth, and examine, compare, and weigh it well with the Scriptures. It is not possible that the Christian world should so lately come out of such thick anti-Christian darkness, and that full perfection of knowledge should break forth at once.[31]

We still march on the unfolding journey from darkness to light, and we will fail to complete our journey unless we raise up a generation that will continue on this path until the full light of dawn breaks forth, until the daystar arises in the heart of God's corporate people.

We have presented here a basic framework that shows us how the principles of Christian education apply generally in the education of our children. We will now discuss how to apply these principles. We have seen what we want our children to become: individuals who reflect in their whole character, being, lives, works and communities the living reality of the love and wisdom of God. We have seen that they must learn how to follow and rely above all upon the Spirit of God, while working together with their brothers and sisters in productive employment and engaging in the dialectic with the world that can bring the honest-hearted to the realization of the reality of Jesus Christ: we have seen, that is, that they must enter into proper relationship with God, their brothers and sisters in Christ, the people of the world and creation. We shall now discuss specific ways in which we can set up their education to bring about these goals. This discussion will include an examination of different scholastic subjects—such as English, science and history—from the perspective of relational knowledge. We will see how our children's instruction in these subjects will contribute to their spiritual development toward becoming whole adults able to take dominion over creation under God. In the next chapter, we will present the specific contours of the unit approach to teaching. These will become more detailed in our description of our Koinonia Curriculum in Supplement One. So these next chapters and Supplement One will unfold our practical outline for a Christian curriculum.

Part Three

PARTICULARS

CHAPTER EIGHT
Particular Application of Principles

Specific Goals

You should now have a clearer understanding of the goals of Christian education and the general principles that allow you to reach those goals. You've even briefly had a smattering of specific educational methods—the inductive approach and unit approach (which we'll discuss fully in the next section of this chapter)—through which the home schooler can apply these general principles. Now you're ready for the specifics and particulars necessary to impart relational knowledge.

To educate a child, you must remember again that, since education addresses the *whole* person, "scholastic" education can only comprise one part, although an essential one, of any curriculum that purports to completeness. And this part receives meaning only in relationship to all else in the child's total education. Because you must educate the whole child, you cannot merely educate the mind. Seen in this light, chores, duties and responsibilities in home, garden and so on become more than "add-ons" to fill in time and keep our children busy. These activities become vital to the child's life and education, necessary to bring him forth into true wholeness. Just as scholastic work teaches your child to use his mind productively, so these activities teach the child to use his body productively (and this productive use of the body also necessitates mental concentration and discipline and spiritual motivation). Your child must also develop a deep, ongoing spiritual life, a real relationship with God and a living knowledge of His Word: unless this relationship develops, all forms of education become vacuous, dead and meaningless. Again, you must educate the whole child in perfect balance and in the totality of body, soul and spirit so that he may truly become whole, a *tamim* expression of God's love.

Every level of your child's activities becomes a whetstone for honing his character. All his labors—mental work, gardening activities, household chores—represent open doors to new pathways of growth in God. In every area of activity, he must overcome sloppiness, laziness, stubbornness, pride, selfishness—all sin that plagues human life. Our children must work in God's time, at the pace that He desires, rather than the pace of their own choosing (Gal. 5:25). They cannot learn the true sense of responsibility about their work unless definite time limits in which to accomplish their work, limits set by God's Spirit, constrain them.

Cleanliness, discipline, responsibility and hard work motivated by devotion to God not only in scholastic work but also in all other areas must be impressed upon their character.* As they mature (and certainly different children will mature at different paces, but we might say generally at least by their late teen years), we should prayerfully seek the Lord as to their precise calling in life, what sort of functions they will fulfill on this earth, and we should help them prepare to answer this calling. All our sons should learn at least one skill, either at their father's side or in apprenticeship to other brothers in Christ. Our daughters should master the skills of the household (Titus 2:4-5): cooking, cleaning, sewing, homemaking and so on, as well as other special skills if God has called them to serve in a capacity that requires such skills. Many boys can learn skills such as carpentry, mechanics and leatherwork, whether or not they will ever use them professionally; in the same way, we should encourage girls to learn spinning, weaving, sewing, knitting and so on, as well as secretarial skills such as stenography when relevant. Typing and bookkeeping seem generally useful subjects for both boys and girls (at least within certain cultural settings).

Since we aim for total education, toward a fruitful and responsible life, and to have an answer for every man who asks us the reason for the hope that lies within us (1 Pet. 3:15), mental skills absolutely centered in the Spirit have an important place.

---

* Truth Forum has put together a character curriculum program to help us in ensuring our children's development in this most important area of their education. See pp. 344-346.

Our children must learn reading, writing and ciphering to the best of their abilities and callings. All must acquire an excellent knowledge of the Word of God. All should develop a comprehensive knowledge and understanding of history, geography, government and science. Of course, some children should pursue special interests further than the general curriculum carries them. They may want to delve more deeply into particular types of scientific or historical knowledge, and this more specialized knowledge can prove fruitful and rewarding not only for them but also for the instruction of others as well. Some children may even find their vocation (which, as we said, literally means "calling") in these areas. They may, for example, help write Christian textbooks or serve in some other way to inform God's people about the truth of their spiritual and historical heritage. Or, perhaps, those working in construction will require a more advanced knowledge in mathematics or in areas of science that apply to the design of homes and other buildings (for example, for greater energy efficiency) or water systems and other knowledge for agricultural purposes. Agricultural interests might inspire some children to broaden their studies of other branches of science relating to their work: engineering, animal husbandry, biology, parasitology, horticulture, bio-intensive gardening, hydrology, land management and so on.

In order for us to teach the necessary scholastic knowledge, we must, to one degree or another, formally school our children, using textbooks and related materials such as workbooks and flash cards. And we should teach these studies with consistency. As we've said, different callings and capacities in varying areas of study rest upon different children, and we must confine academic education to its appropriate place in the context of the total lives of our children. But we must demand of every child the full measure of his God-given capacity, and he must each day accomplish the full measure of the work that God has ordained for him. In our discussion in the next chapter of each individual subject, we shall discuss what we believe the basic requirement for all children in each area should be.

You should not, however, mechanically administer the textbook material to your child. When you teach, always keep in mind the relational context of the knowledge you want to impart. Remember the principles that we have already discussed, for example, the importance of providing a "low threshold of utility" so that the child can as soon as possible begin to practically use the knowledge he receives. On every level, we want to show the relational character of the teaching material: as it relates to other subjects, to other material taught within the same subject, and, above all, to God's purpose for the child's life.

When your child learns from a textbook, the book necessarily shows him, to a degree, a relationship between any particular piece of knowledge he acquires and other aspects of the subject. This approach builds up the child's knowledge of a particular subject sequentially, step by step, "line upon line" (Isa. 28:10, 13, KJV), on the basis of what he has previously learned in this subject. For example, in arithmetic, he must learn addition first, and then on the basis of addition, he learns subtraction. Similarly, he learns multiplication first, and then, on that basis, he learns division. In every subject, a definite place exists for this type of sequential, "line upon line," learning. History means more to the child when he sees it as a sequential picture of progressive events. He can then see how any particular event relates to what went before and what came after. This in turn facilitates his grasp of how it relates to his own day and his own life as well.

To teach, however, your child only the sequential relationships of historical events falls short of an adequate education. He must also learn how the different subjects that he studies relate to one another, and this type of knowledge will come forth most effectively when tied into the actual use (which includes the spiritual and dialectical use) of his newly acquired knowledge. As much as possible, you should present all of this linear, sequential knowledge within the unit context that we will discuss in the next section: that is, you should present this knowledge as the necessary means to fulfill the unified purpose of God's corporate community, the purpose that encompasses both the positive task of bringing forth the church in all its fullness and the negative task of a dialectical engagement of God-centered truth against the man-centered systems of the world.

We are putting together our own curriculum, to use first with our own children. Our textbooks come forth from our life, which rests upon a God-centered, self-sufficient *agri*culture. (We also use materials written by others, even including traditional textbooks, for example, for teaching aspects of math. But for parents to use such materials, they must see with the vision of God, as we discussed in the previous chapter. Only when they have that vision can they detect imbalances in the material they read and adequately provide an effective dialectic for their children, enabling them to overcome these imbalances; only when they see with the light of God-centered vision can the parents integrate those materials into a truly relational approach to education.)

In our curriculum, we try as much as possible to teach the linear, sequential knowledge within the context of the child's life. The child therefore makes, as much as possible, *immediate* use of it. For example, instead of first learning the different parts of speech in preparation for writing, he writes first and, in the context of his efforts to improve his writing skills so that he can communicate, relate, connect more powerfully or effectively, we teach him rules of grammar, punctuation and style.*

Unit Teaching

As we've repeatedly said, the unit approach offers the context that makes all aspects of our children's education meaningful. At this point in our study, we can now begin to explain in concrete terms this approach, through which all elements of our children's education tie together in one cohesive whole. As we've seen, the integrating unit of Christian education lies in the Body of Christ itself, as the Body moves forward to fulfill its total vision and purpose. Again, this total vision and purpose entails both bringing forth the positive vision of God, of the church as the full expression of the manifold wisdom of God, and the negative dialectic through which the church confronts and overthrows the man-centered view in all its manifestations (2 Cor. 10:4-5). As we've seen, within this context, most of what people generally consider secular knowledge—history, philosophy, much in the sciences and so on—finds its place in Christian education as the church engages in its dialectical conflict with the world. The unit curriculum will, then, bring the child to his place in the cohesive vision of God,

---

* See Supplement One for a full description of our curriculum.

leading him through the successive grammar, dialectic and rhetoric stages to maturity and wholeness. As he passes through his unit curriculum, he emerges fully equipped to fulfill his works of service, "until we all reach unity in the faith and in the knowledge of the Son of God and become mature, attaining to the whole measure of the fullness of Christ" (Eph. 4:12-13).

On the grammar level of his unit curriculum, the child requires reading and study materials that will tie together and interrelate the diverse areas of knowledge and show how these interweave with and flow from the Word of God and a truly God-centered life style (that is, as we've seen, a simple, land-based way of life). In our curriculum, we meet much of this grammar level need through our Bible-based readers, which we describe in detail in Supplement One. These Readers follow the basic scriptural narrative, relating the history of God's people from Genesis through Acts. In the context of the Biblical text, prepared for children on the grammar level, we present related materials on history, geography, culture, science, studies of Biblical truths, Christian character and other topics. These studies all relate the truth of God's Word to the child's life in the context of Christian community, to his deepening relationship with God, his fellowman and creation.

For example, in the context of the story of David shepherding and protecting his flocks, the child learns about the geography and natural history of the Bible peoples, their land, their customs and way of life, and the spiritual lessons of the Scriptures themselves, as all these relate to sheep raising. In addition to being relational in the sense that our land-based community raises sheep, these questions about the life of the Biblical peoples also arise relationally since sheep raising played a vital part in the culture of the Bible times. Geography and natural history also relate to the study since these obviously influenced the Israelites' sheep raising. In this context, the Readers also present scriptures that touch upon the nature and care of sheep, drawing diverse spiritual lessons from this activity. Basic science studies also tie in, explaining the properties of wool, why various wools serve better or worse for different purposes and so on. Studies even explore how the industrial revolution changed wool working, the cultural and spiritual changes that went with this transformation, and why we want to return to the simpler sheep raising and wool working methods. (At the time of this writing, we are still developing and writing these Readers.)

Within the context of a land-based Christian community where the child himself participates in a culture within which sheep raising plays an integral part, these studies all bear a concrete relationship to the child's own life and activities. Even if the child himself doesn't have much opportunity to work with sheep, he knows people who do, and he will probably engage in some form of activity that touches directly on sheep raising. Perhaps he'll do woodworking and make feeders for sheep or spinning wheels. Perhaps a girl will learn weaving, and so work with wool. But no matter how indirect a child's relationship to this particular activity will be, he'll find other activities in the Readers in which he will directly participate, such as black-smithing or leatherwork or spinning or bread making. And all of these activities will also arise in the Readers in a way that brings home their relational meaning, both in the context of the Scriptures and the child's life today.

Given the child's participation in such a God-centered culture, the spiritual lessons of Biblical sheep raising, to return to our example, apply directly to his own life, as do the practical lessons. The historical lessons deepen his sense of continuity with the past, for he sees himself as an active member of the ancient God-centered culture. The lessons about geography help him to see the relationship of his labors and community to the lay of the land. Again, because of the child's practical participation in a God-centered, land-based Christian com-munity—through his craft skills, gardening, animal care and other activities—all the lessons he studies in his Reader relate to his life. The Readers not only describe activities that play a real role in the child's culture, but they also show the spiritual ramifications of these activities as well as presenting the inter-relations of these activities with history, science and other topics. Because he participates in a culture involved in the ac-tivities that the Readers describe, and also because he par-ticipates in many of those activities himself, the Reader lessons come to him with real and deepening meaning for his life. This emphasis on *doing* in learning is important because

> *children learn best by physical, hands-on experimenta-tion. Active* learning is needed to discover and solidify knowledge. It is said that we remember 10 percent of what we hear, 50 percent of what we see, 75 percent of

what we say, and 90 percent of what we do. This is true of everyone, but particularly of young children who actually need physical, hands-on experimentation. (emphasis in original)[1]

For this reason, Jesus not only taught but made teachers of those whom He taught (Matt. 28:20). Teaching or doing what we learn is the best way of making it a permanent part of our own lives. (Older children, therefore, will greatly benefit from teaching younger children some of these subjects.) To return again to our sheep raising example, as the child actually engages in this work, or sees his friends do so, the lesson he's learned in his Readers will take on an immediate relevance for him. He'll see how his scholastic studies fit into his life as he participates in the "unit" that comprises the Christian community.

Numerous lessons in his Readers interconnect a multitude of Biblical practices and methods—agriculture, irrigation, pottery, weaving and so on—both to various elements of Biblical life and culture and to contemporary practices and problems. The child learns lessons about geography, science, history and so on, seeing their practical significance for his life today, including their spiritual implications and meaning. Even though we present the lessons of the Reader under separate subject categories, such as geography, science and so on, the context presented by the Readers themselves—at least when these are read within the framework of a God-centered Christian community as it moves forward in the purpose of God—helps the child to see the unit that weaves together all these diverse elements of study. In this context, he gets a sense of the wholeness, the unit, of his curriculum, the cohesive race course that he runs. Again, through the Readers, he learns about history, geography, science and other subjects—and, above all, the Word of God—in a way that relates directly to his life, or at least that will relate if his parents have the vision of God that enables them to see how these subjects interrelate in their own lives. Also, his family must take its place in a Bible-based culture that makes the Reader lessons meaningful.

So these Readers will help prepare the child to step into the God-centered Christian community. Our fellowship, for example, offers children workshops that teach a wide diversity of skills, from blacksmithing to carpentry to spinning to weaving to pottery and animal care. As children participate in these, the Readers help them see the overall vision within which they work. As he pounds the hot iron and transforms a piece of rough metal into a finely crafted kitchen knife, changes a cow hide into a sandal or a block of wood into a bowl, his studies give him a sense of his work's continuity with an ancient heritage and culture, a sense of the spiritual meaning of what he does, of what has been lost and what he can help to regain. His practical studies, his knowledge of ancient techniques and practices, his readings about how, for example, science ties into those practices, help give him deeper understanding of these practical labors. On a wide variety of fronts, then, his grammar level studies become part of a cohesive unit together with his hands-on activities.

Nor do these Readers and workshops comprise the only elements of the unit curriculum. As the supplement describing our curriculum explains, the child also works with relational nature study materials that show him the interconnection of the diverse elements of creation throughout the changing seasons, particularly as all these elements and changes relate to the seasonal activities of agriculture. Because the child participates in a cohesive culture—a God-centered community of individuals growing in oneness with God, with one another and with creation—all of the relational teaching materials interrelate with the child's whole life and tie together all the diverse elements of his life, studies and labors. (For example, the *Character Curriculum* we describe in the Bible section of chapter 9 also takes its place within the cohesive unit curriculum by showing the child what type of character he displays in performing the diverse activities he engages in each day.)

Writing offers another key curriculum element that begins on the grammar level, although it extends far beyond it. We'll discuss writing further shortly, for it plays a central role in the unit curriculum; as we'll explain, when used properly, writing serves as the key element linking together and undergirding all the diverse elements of the curriculum. In all of the child's school and practical work, literary skills, both reading and writing, play a key role. Obviously, your child will want to read about the growing variety of subjects that interest him, including the crafts and skills he learns. But he'll also write about his experience, particularly as he develops these practical skills. He'll *describe* his activities and his *experiences*—his feelings—as he works in those activities, how these experiences affect and even change his life and so on. By writing about these experiences, he has the opportunity to look at them again (which is the literal meaning of the word "respect"), to feel his way back into an experience and so deepen the experience itself. Sometimes when looking back into an experience, we can see relationships and connections—and so meanings—we did not previously recognize. So our writing about our experience can deepen our participation in that experience; the experience then becomes our possession more fully than it was before, and because we come into a greater possession of it, we have something greater to share with others.

Such free writings, which we explain at length in *Right Words*, become spontaneously written outpourings of the child's thoughts and feelings. We don't contrive them in our minds, but they pour forth from our hearts as we tear down any mental barriers that would block the flow of feeling. (This effort doesn't make us mindless but merely recognizes that, important as the functions of the mind are, they do not serve as the *source* of the mind's inspiration and meaning; to fulfill its function properly, the mind must take a back seat and leave the direction to that which does serve as the true Source.) As our children do such writings (and also as they write notes that will preserve the details that help such writings come to life*), they don't at first stop to think about grammar, spelling and so on, but they simply write as though they were speaking to a familiar friend or relative, someone with whom they feel relaxed and comfortable. (After they've finished the free writing, they can work on it for greater clarity and power, eliminating grammar and spelling errors.) These writings, based on your child's feelings, impressions and experiences—based not only on his practical skills but on any aspect of his daily life or schooling—will help him to see more clearly the work God does in his life, while at the same time teaching him how to open his heart to what he feels and how to communicate his feelings to others.

Once the child has completed our grammar level Readers, he will have begun to develop his writing skills, will have a basic understanding of the interrelations of nature and how his life and chores fit into its seasons and rhythms, as well as a basic

---

* See *Right Words*.

grounding in various crafts, skills and tasks tied to a land-based culture. Because of his studies in the grammar level of his unit curriculum, he will also sense something of the historical roots and spiritual meaning of the activities in which he engages.

Now he's ready to move on to the dialectic level of the unit curriculum, the level at which he can begin an in-depth study of subjects such as history, philosophy and science, those secular subjects that, as we have seen, find their purpose in Christian curriculum in the context of the church's dialectic with the world.

His grammar level studies have helped to prepare him to see the spiritual vision that underlies his participation in the life of a land-based community. But as the child participates more and more in the way of life of the land-based, God-centered community, as he learns the skills of self-sufficiency in workshops and grows to a place of real responsibility in fulfilling tasks such as caring for the land and livestock, the necessity for a deeper understanding of the spiritual vision behind this way of life also comes forth.

Because we live in a society that scorns a simple, self-sufficient, land-based culture, the dialectic between our own way of life and the culture of the world becomes an integral part of the child's unit curriculum. And as we've seen, this dialectic with the world forms a central focus of the very purpose of the church in its mission to set the captives free. Even if the child doesn't yet see the questions concerning the conflict of visions, he will eventually face them, and so his curriculum must show him the relevance of a deepening understanding of this conflict (although, again, the grammar level Readers in our curriculum will already have begun to do this).

In our curriculum, as we explain more fully later, after the child completes the Bible-based readers, we present him with stories that show the pressing importance of the conflict between God-centered and man-centered views. In the first of these stories, for example, the child sees the conflict faced by a family that has recently moved to a land-centered Christian community. In the context of portraying the opposition that this family faces from friends and relatives, the story shows the child the importance of a dialectical understanding of the vision for a land-centered culture. His recognition of this need and of how such a dialectical understanding of culture relates to the practical skills he learns and to the whole Christian community and culture in which he participates, gives him the desire to diligently study the topical materials that relate to this subject. He will see them as integral parts of the unit curriculum that informs every aspect of his life.

Through his dialectical studies, the child will come to understand the spiritual dynamics that stripped our culture of land-based, self-sufficient skills, replacing them with machine-labor. He will see that the contrasting visions of the combating cultures have brought forth real conflicts in history. He will learn the history of why and how these changes occurred and their consequences and so their importance.

This vision, however, doesn't stop with the historical unfolding of human culture. For, as we've already noted in our first chapters, competing visions of culture tie into contrasting paths to knowledge—the relational approach to knowledge, for example, finding expression in a small scale, land-based culture in contrast to the detached analytical approach to knowledge, which finds expression in the fragmented culture of urban industrialism. So a full understanding of alternative cultures necessitates a dialectical understanding of competing world views and philosophies. These contrasting views of knowledge in general also tie into different approaches to scientific knowledge. And we can also readily see that the study of conflicting cultures must also tie into an understanding of the basic institutions of a culture, including government, education and mass media. When we discuss our Koinonia Curriculum in Supplement One, we shall look into the interrelations of these subjects in more detail, but here we mainly want to show that all these subjects cohere in one unit. For through his dialectical studies, the child receives the vision that enables him to see the meaning and purpose of his way of life and that empowers him with the truth to expose and demolish the man-exalting systems of the world. Hence these dialectical studies integrally fit into the child's unit curriculum.*

---

* As we'll explain more fully in Supplement One, we are preparing materials that will enable your children to study these subjects that relate to their dialectic with the world—culture, philosophy, history and so on.

Literary Skills
The Key to Unit Teaching

As we've mentioned before, in our Koinonia Curriculum, literary skills (reading and writing), particularly as presented in *Right Words*, which teaches writing and related skills, link together all other elements of the unit curriculum. They form the backbone that holds together and properly arranges the various ribs, that is, the other subjects, such as history, science and so on. Literary skills stand in this relation to the other subjects because proficiency in reading and writing greatly facilitate clear thought and understanding in every area of study. We discuss this at length below in Section Two of chapter 9. But here we can preview some key points of that discussion, noting, for example, Professor Richard Mitchell's observation that the ability to think predicates the ability to "put strings of sentences together in good order."[2] As Richard Weaver of the University of Chicago, one of the outstanding scholars of rhetoric, has said,

> facility with words bespeaks a capacity to learn relations and grasp concepts; it is a means of access to the complex reality.[3]

Words serve as the medium, the form, of thought, and this form must appear in the proper order to facilitate rather than hinder the fruitful unfolding of its thought-content. We can't run the race while tripping over clumsy grammar and syntax, misused words and so on.

We can see the importance of literary skills by examining the opposition to those skills in modern American education. Samuel Blumenfeld has traced the war against literacy, the most basic of all literary skills, fought by humanist educator John Dewey and his followers. Dewey, a socialist, saw public schools as instrumental in reshaping America's youth so they would desire and become fertile soil for a socialist reconstruction of society.[4] Blumenfeld explains that Dewey wanted to foster "a spirit of social cooperation" (not the voluntary cooperation of uncoerced community but the compulsory "cooperation" of the State) based upon the subordination of each person's "intellectual independence" and "individual judgment."[5] Public schools were to downplay the importance of "literary skills" because "high literacy" promoted these abilities.[6] In his own words, Dewey wanted "language" seen

"not primarily" as "the expression of thought" but rather as
"the means of social communication."[7] Yet while language
must certainly serve for communication, how can we communicate clearly unless our words serve first to express clear
thought? To stress the social function of words at the expense
of individual expression transforms language into a means for
conforming the inchoate multitude into the image of the social
medium, which in practice means the most powerful institution, namely the State.

In their efforts to subordinate literary skills, and particularly
literacy, Dewey and his associates promoted the look-say
method (memorizing words by sight) of reading instruction
rather than phonics (learning to sound out letters and letter-
combinations), even though the superiority of the phonics
method was well known and became even more apparent as
the widely used look-say, "Dick and Jane" method permeated
public school instruction. The author of the most authoritative
textbook promoting the look-say method, Edmund Burke
Huey, excused the known failures of the new method by down-
playing the importance of the child's ability to read what appeared on the page before him. The child, Huey said, could
simply guess at the words he couldn't read.[8] In this view,
"precision of thought and language," as Blumenfeld says,
"belongs to a 'false ideal.'"[9] Huey believed that the reader
should simply substitute "words of his own" when he couldn't
read those on the page, "provided that they express the meaning."[10] But how could the reader tell with assurance that he
had properly expressed "the meaning" of a word he couldn't
read?

The ability to read and write clearly, then, forms indispensable elements of the ability to think and judge clearly. Words
serve as the means of communication, the means through
which one person expresses himself to another. God expressed Himself to man through His Word. The ultimate communication of God to man, Jesus, was "the Word" made flesh,
and His people are the people of the Word, those whose lives
conform perfectly to God's communication of Himself to
mankind. God wants us to serve as "living epistles," His letter
to mankind, "read and known of all men." Our whole lives
should express His Word, but we are also to express His
spiritual truths in spiritual words (1 Cor. 2:13), to be ready to
give an answer to every man concerning the hope that lies

within us (1 Pet. 3:15). So the Christian, within the limits of the gifts and abilities God has given him, must learn to speak and write to express God's truth to his brothers and to the lost. For all these reasons, literary skills, as we've said, should form the backbone of every aspect of Christian curriculum.

Again, most of the children's writings will begin as free writings (or as even less structured notes that the child will keep in a notebook*) through which the children express their feelings, impressions and experiences, describe problems that they've confronted and overcome. In addition to these writings on his experiences, most other writings should meet specific purposes that would generally fall into two categories. The first consists of how-to papers in which the children would describe procedures, crafts, skills, chores and so on relating to the land-centered culture. Our community is developing a book of such patterns to help those just moving into a land-based culture. So children would do this only if the need for such materials or their improvement existed and if the children themselves have developed the desire to do this writing. Even these writings could generally focus on describing these activities so that the reader would sense the feel of the activity as well as how to do it, not merely dryly listing the step-by-step procedure (although such a one, two, three . . . listing of steps could form a supplement to the how-to story). As we'll discuss further later, some children might also feel to pursue research to perfect or develop the best way to perform some practical task, such as irrigating a field, trapping a sheep-killing coyote, extracting methane from waste, developing a water distillation system and so on. If a child is excited to search out those types of projects or perfect systems already in operation, and if it meets a real need in the community, then you should encourage him to do so, assuming of course that he's prepared to take on such a task.†

The other area of writings include those in which the child would present a dialectical defense of the Christian vision, community, way of life and so on, perhaps in a letter to a newspaper editor or in a letter to an inquirer or to a loved one. Such writings could also be published in a church newsletter or magazine, which should become a central part of every net-

---

* See *Right Words*.

† See "Science" in chapter 9.

work of fellowships and their community and life. Such a newsletter can become a focus for the children's writings that show them relationally why they must learn grammar and so on. (And people helping to edit and proofread the newsletter would at the same time serve as home school teacher/advisers helping parents to see specific mistakes and problems that show up in their children's writings.) These writings could include material of all kinds relevant to God's people, such as news and letters from the brothers and sisters, teaching materials to meet spiritual needs in the Body, and reports and comments on relevant questions of the day, how-to studies on practical aspects of land-centered life such as bio-intensive gardening, blacksmithing, sheep for wool, spinning and so on. Children as well as adults could contribute articles and letters, including dialectical responses to events in and statements from the world, such as might appear in newspaper or magazine articles. Again, the child must have a desire to do these writings, and the needs he seeks to meet—whether simple communication that tie brothers and sisters together in diverse places or whatever—must be real, not manufactured. Through these writings, the child may seek to refute secular writers and express the God-centered view as a viable, practical alternative. As he engages in his dialectical studies, he'll face statements and viewpoints filled with deceptions that he'll feel a strong desire to refute. As his love of the truth grows, so will his desire to use the written word to overcome such lies with the truth. So his writings should soon rise above empty exercises. They will arise from questions he *wants* to answer; and as his knowledge, experience and the quantity and quality of his writings grow, together with his vision and understanding, he will feel the need and desire to present in lucid writing answers he wants to communicate to others.

Because of his burden to understand and communicate, questions of English grammar, dialectic and rhetoric will come alive for him with a new urgency. As he does his writings, his mother can use material in *Right Words*, Truth Forum's book on writing, to assess, systematically, point-by-point, whether his work matches the criteria in that book, teaching the child to make changes as he sees new ways to more powerfully express himself. Through this approach, he will see how forms of syntax serve to facilitate clear and effective communication of content.

So through the foregoing two sections we can begin to see concretely how the unit curriculum ties together all the diverse elements of the child's education—his writing, his studies of history, his practical skill development and so on—into one cohesive whole, a cohesive unit that will help to mold him into a whole, *tamim* person, a true son of God. God has anointed you, the parent, to see the total, God-ordained image of the whole person your child should be when you have completely educated him. This understanding and vision will enable you to gauge your goals for your child during each year; God's Spirit will anoint you to see the goal for his life and character, the skills, practical and mental, that you need to help him develop and to what degree you can expect him to develop at any particular time. Only you, therefore, can present all the material that has been put together for your child's individual education at the right pace and according to the proper priorities for his individual upbringing. You must responsibly determine your child's appropriate level of schooling, at what age he should begin, when he is ready to go on to the next level and so on.* Be sure not to start him too soon; you can start teaching the alphabet and numbers in piecemeal fashion to very young children, but it generally seems wise to wait for systematic instruction until the child is seven or eight. Although children can begin to learn academics earlier, they won't derive the greatest benefit from doing so. Too much, too soon, too fast can even hinder the child's desire to learn. You'll generally want to hold off on systematic teaching till your children have developed the self-discipline and level of obedience and maturity that rarely comes before the seventh year. When children start at the right age, having been properly disciplined, trained in chores and developed in character, they move forward in their schoolwork smoothly and confidently, encouraging both parent and child (though, of course, everyone faces rough spots, difficult subjects for them as well as other problems). When children start too soon, they become nervous, proud, discouraged or face some other needless spiritual problem stemming from the parents' impatience to begin. You must make sure that your child does not become bored by work too easy or overwhelmed by work too hard. Again, only you, the parent, can ensure his growth at the pace that God

---

* We provide suggested goals for each grade in our curriculum. See Supplement One.

has ordained for him in every area of his development.

The Need for Curricular Form

Our experience indicates that as the process of home education unfolds throughout the year and over the years, as its demands (and perhaps the size of your family) grow, the parent-teacher must have a clear curricular form, with teaching materials, books, charts and so on, laid out and coordinated in such a way that parents can rely heavily on those materials in the instruction of their children. Again, the parent bears the ultimate responsibility to impart the formal curriculum materials in the Spirit, as God directs, to decide when and how to impart them on a daily basis. The parent—not the textbook—must teach, form and shape the child. Yet to do this, the parent needs a curriculum that expresses the perspective of relational knowledge. Teaching ministries must emerge within the context of the Body of Christ that will actively disciple and educate the parents, as well as bring to birth the necessary curriculum material to enable parents to fulfill their educational responsibilities to their children. What formerly were the positions of principles in Christian schools must now become full-fledged teaching ministries standing among the other members of the five-fold ministries to bring Christian discipleship to every home through home education.* (We hope that our Koinonia Curriculum will equip both church teachers and parents to do this.)

Home school within a home school church provides the only educational form that permits the full development of each child. Only the home school permits the encouragement and growth of the unique combination of gifts, talents and abilities that each child possesses. To fully develop these gifts, we must have a balance between flexibility, which gives the child's gifts a chance to come forth, and form, which molds and shapes the child's natural inclinations. A racecourse, after all, has a very tight, precise form within which the racers must run. Mozart was an example of someone very gifted who appar-

---

* See *The Order of Perfection* for a detailed and in-depth picture of the function of such teachers and their relationship to the remainder of the five-fold ministry.

ently was given the room to bring forth his gift. But it did not bring glory to God because it was not brought forth within the confines of a godly form. He ran well, but he ran on the wrong course. Therefore his life, his ultimate testimony of values, ended wretchedly. Samuel, on the other hand, ran within the confines of God's predetermined course. He was sent to the Temple to minister to Eli as soon as he was weaned! (This was certainly not at nine months of age but was probably not at more than five years.) His gift made room for him in the kingdom of God because his training was within a godly form—the Temple.

As we have said, we recognize each child's uniqueness. Each has a place in the Body that God has prepared for him from the foundation of the world. Each has a purpose in God's kingdom. Each possesses gifts that God wants to use to edify and strengthen the whole Body. God knew each one by name even before he was formed in his mother's womb; God numbered every hair on his head. We want to give our children a flexible enough program to allow their unique gifts to come forth. The parents must work actively with their children, freely pursuing interests and questions that arise in the children's lives. The unit curriculum form we've described in the previous section, and which we'll explain in greater detail in Supplement One, provides the framework of a structured, formal, integrated curriculum that allows the full development of the child's capacity. Yet its effectiveness rests upon the relationship first between the parent and the Body of Christ, then between parents and children, and also on the active participation of both the parent and child not only in each other's life but also in the life of God and His Body; this provides the key to effective growth and education. If this relationship remains centered in the Spirit, the unit curriculum form will serve to bring forth God-centered children who become God-centered adults.

At the end of Hebrews, the writer prays that "the *God* of peace" *may* "strengthen (*complete, perfect*) and make *you* what you ought to be, and *equip you with everything good that you may carry out His will;* [while He Himself] works in you *and* accomplishes that which is pleasing in His sight, through Jesus Christ, the Messiah; to Whom be the glory forever and ever . . . Amen" (Heb. 13:20-21, Ampl.). Our children must be equipped "with everything good" to carry out His will; as parents, we have the primary responsibility to serve as God's agents to "complete" and "perfect" them. This goal defines our task in home education. But what does this complete equipping entail? Paul speaks to Timothy of two things needed to ready us to perform those good works that God has ordained for us before the foundation of the world (Eph. 2:10):

> . . . whoever cleanses himself [from what is ignoble and unclean]—who separates himself from contact with contaminating and corrupting influences—will [then himself] be a vessel set apart and useful for honorable and noble purposes, consecrated and profitable to the Master, fit and ready for any good work. (2 Tim. 2:21, Ampl.)

> Every Scripture is God-breathed—given by His inspiration—and profitable for instruction, for reproof and conviction of sin, for correction of error and discipline in obedience, and for training in righteousness [that is, in holy living, in conformity to God's will in thought, purpose and action], so that the man of God may be *complete* and proficient, well-fitted and *thoroughly equipped* for every good work. (2 Tim. 3:16-17, Ampl.)

So to be prepared to fulfill the works that God has ordained for us to accomplish, we must undergo both a cleansing process that refines our character and also a positive preparation of training in the Word of God. While training in God's Word will unfold through discussions that arise in particular situations as specific questions and needs come up, we also need structured, formal instruction. (We also need structured training to form our character.*) Luke explained the motive behind the writing of his gospel in these terms,

> Therefore, since I myself have carefully investigated everything from the beginning, it seemed good also to me to write *an orderly account* for you, most excellent Theophilus, *so that you may know the certainty of the things you have been taught*. (Luke 1:3-4)

Isaiah speaks of this same principle of instruction:

> Whom shall he teach knowledge? and whom shall he make to understand doctrine? them that are weaned from the milk, and drawn from the breasts.
> For precept must be upon precept, precept upon precept; line upon line, line upon line; here a little, and there a little . . . . (Isa. 28:9-10, KJV)

---

* See the discussion of *Building Christian Character* in "Beginning" in Supplement One.

Knowledge, then, must be taught in some sort of structured, orderly form—"precept upon precept" and "line upon line."

Our children need an orderly account of truth so that they can know it with certainty, so that they can be *fully equipped* for every good work. God wants to give them provision for every circumstance that they will confront in their relationship with Him and His people, with the world and with the creation. We must prepare them to wage full-scale spiritual warfare against principalities and powers and to bring all things (within the limits God has set upon them) under the dominion of Christ: this is what the unit curriculum is designed to do.

To overcome in this conflict, we and our children must grow to maturity in Christ, the *full* measure of His stature (Eph. 4:13). This requires a *complete* curriculum. But we must always remember that the structured, formal curriculum gives us only a *complement* to the other aspects of our children's education; if it ever becomes the complete curriculum, then it will defeat its purpose. It is only the form; if it is not filled with the content of love and relationship and ministered in these, it will absolutely fail. We desire that our children come forth as active participants in God's purpose, not passive recipients and parrots of preprogrammed instructions. To train our children to become active participants, however, we must actively participate in their training, their education. So God-centered education requires a formal curriculum that elicits the active participation of both parents and children. The structure of this curriculum must afford the parents the confidence that they will cover the basic knowledge their children must have. But, as we have said, it must at the same time be flexible enough so that the parents feel free to encourage their children to develop their unique gifts, talents and interests; in fact, it should even allow parents the opportunity to, at times, put the formal curriculum aside to allow their children to concentrate on special interests. But at the same time, the parent and child should aim to meet their grade goals each year. This will give the child the sense of running a race and pressing toward a definite mark (Phil. 3:14). The parents must decide how to pace their children and themselves to meet that goal. So at times your child could focus on pursuing his special interests and spend less time on the more formal curriculum; but at other times he would concentrate on the regular, formal curriculum. For example, your child could take out a couple of

weeks from academic schoolwork in the spring to put in his
garden. (Of course, generally during the school year, you'll
want to do both academic and practical activities at the same
time.) So this curriculum form will enable the parents to feel as-
sured that they cover all the necessary ground to fully equip
their children, but to do it in a way that won't lock them into a
rigid schedule that keeps them from devoting the needed time
to special projects and activities as they arise.

A complete curriculum form must allow parents to teach their
children what they need to know when they need to know it,
but without monopolizing the day, week and year and crowding
out everything else in life. So it will enable the parent to present
comprehensive basic instruction in the Bible, English, history,
geography, science, math, foreign languages and practical
skills—to impart all these as integrated elements of a cohesive
unit—but to impart only what the child needs to learn without
excessive drilling and exercises that merely make work for the
child. And this curriculum should, of course, present all
knowledge from the relational approach, showing the interrelations of the subjects as well as their relationships to the
child's life and to his relationship to God, his fellowman and
creation. So, for example, as we've said, one part of our
curriculum, our Bible-based reader, interweaves scriptures,
science, math, geography, Bible character studies and studies of community and culture.

And after the children complete these readers, that is, at the
end of their first four years of formal schooling, they will later
go on to read, among other curriculum materials, biographi-
cally oriented narratives of history through which they will
receive a deeper knowledge that will begin the dialectic level
of instruction (we explain this fully in Supplement One). These
biographical narratives will also come forth from a relational
perspective, interweaving geography, history, the Scriptures,
art, science and other subjects in cohesive stories focused on
young people. In many secular (and unfortunately Christian)
textbooks, the various subjects become atomized as the
authors separate out the setting of life and call it geography,
the plot of life and call it history and so on. But we want to
present the stories of life-like historical characters, with whom
our children can identify, characters facing and overcoming
real problems that still concern our children today, or rather
that will concern them as they see the complications that

these problems cause in the lives of these characters. They will see a young boy in Abraham's day confronting the State slave society of ancient Ur, a young believer during the time of the Roman Empire confronting State persecution, a young person at the time of the French Revolution confronting that major formative event of history; some stories will include only historical characters, presenting biographies of such men as the first European to travel through the Southwestern United States, Cabeza de Vaca, or the famous scientist, Isaac Newton. Other stories will focus on the lives of fictional characters, but those characters will face the real historical events of that era, and these stories will also include historical characters. (Of course, we'll make clear at the beginning of each book the extent of fact and fiction.)

In the context of these stories of conflict and resolution, we will interweave details of history, geography, customs, religion, art and so on, to make the world of these characters come alive for our children. The children will see how the characters' conflicts with the world relate to the conflicts going on inside the characters themselves, and they'll see how the characters change as they face and overcome their conflicts. So they'll identify with these characters as they live with them through their times, seeing, for example, the bloody cobblestone streets of Paris during the Reign of Terror, the vulture-covered barges loaded with corpses on the river Seine, the mobs screaming through the streets, tearing the steeples off churches, the petulant and babyish but self-righteous and cold face of Robespierre. As the children read these stories, dialectical questions will grip them from a relational, real life context, questions for which they will then desire to find the answers. The stories will lead into more comprehensive, systematic historical studies. Supplementary teaching materials will then guide the children through appropriate questions and some discussion. (We'll describe how all these materials work together in more detail in Supplement One.) So these stories will provide a context for further historical study on the dialectical level. (And other studies as well; for example, an account of the life of Newton may inspire some study of the physical laws he uncovered and of his dialectic with Leibniz and other rationalists whom he opposed.) This approach to history and related subjects (which we discuss further in Supplement One) also coincides with our emphasis on literary skills. This is the case not only because the children must read the books, but also because their reading will stimulate their desire to write, for example, about their sense of the meaning of these historical studies for their own lives.

A form pulls from us the potential that God has planted within us, just as the form of the soil pulls from the seed the potential that lies dormant within it. As Jesus said, the soil "produces crops by itself" (Mark 4:28, NASV), and soil, Berry rightly points out, is a very *formal* thing.[11] As we have seen, form gives us a framework in which we reach outside of ourselves in order to attain to something that seems beyond our reach, but which God has given us the capacity to fulfill. How many times have we seen first and second graders convinced that they would never master the "complexities" of addition and subtraction; but because they were spurred on by their parents, within the setting of a God-given curricular form, they not only mastered these things, but looked back on their earlier trials with amusement. The same principles hold true for more complex subjects as well.

As we've seen, central to a God-centered curriculum form is the unit approach. This approach serves not merely to relate all the different aspects of the child's curriculum to each other but also to integrate the child into the Body of Christ. For, in general, the vision and purpose of the community—*if that community is itself whole*—on every level, will essentially form the integrating unit that brings coherence to the child's entire education. And within the context of that integrated vision, the child can participate in learning skills and working on specific projects that meet practical needs of the community (which, as we've said, could at times include writing on research projects necessary to the land-based community; we will discuss this more under science in the next chapter). The child's participation in these projects will further integrate him into the life of the community of God's people as he helps to meet the needs of the community and to serve God's purpose. As he participates in skill and craft workshops, engages in scholastic studies, learns about history, philosophy and science, learns to express his feelings and insights in writing, everything works together to impress upon him the *entirety* of a God-centered culture—whether he sits down, rises up or walks in the way (Deut. 6:4-7). All these activities work together as integrated elements of the cohesive unit curriculum.

The kind of curriculum form we speak of will not become a substitute for relationship but a means of facilitating relationship. It is not a rigid structure and mechanical pattern that stifles the leading of the Spirit but a flexible, organic pattern that provides a Spirit-directed framework to make teaching even more flexible so that the teacher can respond sensitively in every circumstance to the leading of the Spirit. The curriculum form, in other words, must come forth not from the mind of man but from the Spirit of God, expressing not man's objective rationalism but God's relational love. And such an organic framework cannot be "worked" mechanically; it can only be used by those who consistently seek a living relationship with God, who seek above all things to lead their children into such a relationship and who therefore diligently seek to follow the Spirit in every aspect of the education of their children.

To effectively use the unit curriculum and instruct your child generally you must, as we've seen, find your place in the Body of Christ. Again, this means that you as parents need to come under the tutelage of the ministries God has ordained to minister His Word in His family, the church, ministries that not only speak that Word but disciple God's people into conformity with it, so that they can truly make their home in His Word (John 8:31, JB). Those ministries exist "for the equipping of the saints" (Eph. 4:12, NASV). In regard to home education specifically, this "equipping" must include the functioning of teaching ministries that work under the direction of someone standing as an ordained teacher within the five-fold ministry.* Under his guidance, these ministries should operate workshops and serve as teachers and advisors who can both instruct parents and assist them in teaching their children all subjects, including phonics, reading, writing, arithmetic, math, science, history and so on, as well as craft skills.† Teachers who have mastered the material in these subject areas in a relational (not merely abstract) way should instruct the parents so that they can better teach their children; and advisors

---

* See *The Order of Perfection* for a full discussion of the operation of teaching ministries.

† See above and below in this chapter for our discussion of the operation of craft workshops and teachers and advisors in teaching children craft skills, and see Supplement One, on the Koinonia Curriculum, for our discussion of the instruction of parents to teach their children such subjects as history.

should stand available to help answer parents' questions, either providing the needed information themselves or pointing parents toward those who can provide that information. These teaching ministries will never supplant the parents in their place as primary instructors to their children, but they serve to help equip *parents* so that they can, using the unit curriculum form, fulfill their function of educating and discipling their children.

In your children's daily schoolwork, remember that you will generally, while allowing for variations and flexibility, want to follow a schedule. (Even when you must depart radically from this schedule, you want this form in place to come back to, to help set you on your proper course again.) The curriculum we have developed (or any other you might choose) can serve only as a *help* to you, to *assist* you in your God-ordained function to train your children in the way that they should go. Again, the ultimate responsibility remains yours, and you must know your curriculum materials before you present them to your child. You may, for example, find things in the curriculums you use that you disagree with or would explain differently, and you must stay ahead of your child in order to be fully prepared beforehand for such eventualities.* Before the school year starts, you should examine the materials from which you will teach your child to familiarize yourself with them. Then when you are about to teach a particular area of study—for example, introducing a new math concept or teaching about the use of action verbs in writing or covering a particular period of Bible history such as the Exodus—you can read the whole section relating to the subject you are about to teach, studying it in detail and noting any special points you want to impress upon your child. Then you will be fully prepared to go over the individual lesson with your child at the time that he reads or

---

* You may not always find it best to eliminate these harmful things in the given texts; sometimes you may instead present dialectical questions to help the child focus in on the problem you see. Questions are central to true education. We can only impart relational knowledge if we enter into the proper relationship to the one to whom we seek to impart it. This necessitates entering into dialogue with that person, in this case, our child. We have to ask the questions that bear a concrete relationship to that person's life, thoughts, feelings and so on. The key to transferring relational knowledge lies in asking the right questions. In the gospels, we see Jesus constantly doing this, for example, asking the disciples, "Who do men say that I am?" always asking the question that directly related to the thoughts that ran through their minds, to the trials that they were going through.

studies it. You must understand whatever you teach to your child fully enough to show him its relational meaning. You never want to teach anything to him in an obligatory, mechanical way, which will merely destroy his interest and excitement in learning.

After you have taught the lesson, you will want to review the material to make sure your child has grasped it. In our discussion of our Koinonia Curriculum in Supplement One, when explaining the teaching synopses that prepare our children to engage in dialectic with the world, we talk about various methods of testing and discussion that we use with these materials. You'll find in that section methods that apply to home school teaching in general. There, we explain that a key advantage of home schooling lies in its personal, one-on-one or small group character, which permits the parent-teacher to directly glean from personal discussion how much the child knows. (To the extent possible, fathers should participate in those discussions too. At times, for example, a father may feel a burden to lead a particular discussion and may want his family to schedule this for the evening, when he can be there. Of course, to sensitively follow the Lord's leading in this, the father must be aware on a day-to-day basis of what his children are learning, what topics his wife discusses with them and so on. On the more advanced levels of teaching, working with the dialectic synopsis, the main burden of teaching this material will generally fall on fathers.)

Discussion not only allows us to immediately overcome any confusion or ignorance we uncover, deepening the children's knowledge and understanding of the subject, but it also allows us to more effectively gauge his knowledge than, for example, could a written essay. This is so because the test essay throws up barriers, such as difficulties in writing, that the child is learning to overcome through the writing course but which he may not have yet completed. Moreover, these writing barriers have nothing to do with the extent of the child's actual knowledge of the subject at hand. The public school system must use such an essay approach because it has no means to relate to the individual student personally and discover what he really knows. All the public school teacher can do is ask him to write an essay or take an objective test. The child might know a great deal but has not yet learned all the writing skills necessary to express his knowledge in written form. So this approach kills both the child's interest in the subject and his interest in writing and explains why the majority of the adult population in this country, educated in public schools, is either functionally or marginally illiterate. The home school mother has all the relational advantages to overcome such a situation. Of course, it presupposes that she has been taught and knows the material herself. (See the section on the "Dialectical Synopses" in Supplement One for a full discussion of these points.)

As our children mature, we must strive to teach them to "work as independently as they can" in their studies as well as in their chores and other areas of responsibility.[12]

> The shepherd always knows where his lambs are, and is tender and kind. Yet every child should be trained from his first year to be happy doing things by himself. You do a disservice to your child if you let him feel that he must always be entertained or have someone's attention.[13]

Of course, especially in the early years of schooling, the mother will have to devote much time to teaching the child how to work by himself. If you are a mother with many children, teaching at home, taking care of a household, performing services in a Christian community, how will you be able to find the time to do this? Often, you can't do this all yourself. As your family grows, you will find it necessary to use the older children to help teach the younger ones—the old principle of "each one teach one," each older child being responsible for teaching the younger ones:

> Be a teacher-manager and delegate responsibilities to your children, having them teach one another and alternating your attention between them as needed.[14]

When your older children assume teaching responsibilities, this will bring positive results on every level. It will improve and establish proper and deeper relations between your children, as the older ones take responsibility for the younger ones while the younger ones come into submission to the older ones. And the older ones will themselves exponentially increase their mastery of the subject they teach. No one ever learns a subject so well as when he teaches it. Finally, this will help free the mother to do other things that she must get done. Increasingly, as our families and responsibilities grow, we will find it impossible to fulfill all our responsibilities without using the older children to teach the younger ones. Of course, our children can only fulfill teaching responsibilities if we have discipled them to stand reliably. But when we recognize the necessity of our children fulfilling these types of responsibilities in our homes, then we will seek God for His grace and diligently work with our children until they can reliably accomplish these tasks. So our quantitative growth will help force us to fulfill Jesus' great commission of making disciples—at least if we are responsible.

Above all, the task of making disciples of our children entails the transfer of motivation from an external compulsion to an internal desire within each child. So in all of our children's education, we must strive to instill in them the internal motivation to press forward to reach with all their hearts, souls, minds and strength for the high mark of the calling of Christ Jesus. We want to stimulate them every moment of their day, in everything they do, to "make the most of every opportunity," not to "be vague and thoughtless and foolish," but to understand and firmly grasp "what the will of the Lord is" (Eph. 5:17, Ampl.). We want them to feel a continual, compelling incentive within to strive for perfection in all their work and studies. We can only instill this sense in our children as we enter into deep relationships of love with them, relationships that instill a deep trust in their hearts for us. For such relationships to develop, we must come to know them as their Maker knows them, the One who has entrusted them into our care. We must walk in that continual burden of love that will not rest until our children stand firmly on the path to true fulfillment and eternal life. When we manifest that burden of love to them, then our children will gladly, enthusiastically, desire to press toward the goal Jesus has set for their lives.

We feel that, above and beyond the general patterns and curriculum materials God has given us for our children's education, He has also given us a specific focus to instill a sense of excitement in our children's lives and education and to draw together in a relational context all the aspects of their education. This focus is an annual Children's Fair and Homestead Craft Exposition.

The Annual Koinonia Children's Fair
and Homestead Craft Exposition

The life of the nation of ancient Israel revolved around three central events during the year, great festivals when God's people came together to worship in Jerusalem. To these great festivals were drawn people from among the Gentiles. They came as Sheba came to Solomon, to see whether through the God of Israel she could find the answers to her hard questions. They came as did those Greek men at the Passover festival in Jerusalem who told Philip, "Sir, we would see Jesus." At the Feast of Tabernacles especially, all of the Israelites—men, women and children—would join together in joyous worship unto Yahweh. They would celebrate the annual completion of the harvests and the fullness that God had brought into their lives. Before Yahweh had brought Israel into its promised land, He ordained that His people would come before Him at "the place Yahweh your God will choose as a dwelling for His Name" (Deut. 12:11). To that place the people would "bring everything" He commanded them: their "burnt offerings and sacrifices," their "tithes and special gifts, and all the choice possessions" they had "vowed to Yahweh." There the Israelites would

> rejoice before Yahweh your God, you, your sons and daughters, your menservants and maidservants, and the Levites from your towns . . . . (Deut. 12:11-12)

This time of rejoicing and offering, this time of bringing forth the "special gifts, what you have vowed to give and your freewill offerings, and the firstborn of your herds and flocks" (Deut. 12:6), took place at the great festivals, and especially at the last festival, the Feast of Tabernacles.

These great festivals brought a focus, a goal and a sense of completion to the national life of Israel. This sense of completion produces in turn the sense of entering into rest (Heb. 4:9-10). The feasts served as climactic proclamations of the life God had imparted to His people. God has given us today such a goal and focus to the life of our Koinonia communities, and particularly to our Koinonia Curriculum, to act as a positive incentive to stir us and our children to complete the tasks that He has set before us for the year. This goal—the annual Koinonia Children's Fair and Homestead Craft Exposition in Colorado (which also includes smaller fairs held at different locations during the year)—serves as a complete coordinating focus of the life of our whole fellowship toward an annual goal that presses forward each year the eternal purpose of God. Specifically it serves as the annual coordinating focus and finish line for a great deal of our children's schoolwork and unit projects for the preceding year as well as the larger projects of the adults. Each year we start off all these activities in September or October and aim toward the work of completion for the annual Fair toward the end of the next summer. Both the annual Fair and the smaller local mini-fairs have brought to children and adults alike a powerful sense of victory and accomplishment while extending an equally powerful testimony of God's wisdom to all the Fair visitors who, as with the Greeks who approached Philip, "would see Jesus." The local mini-fairs have drawn people from all over the particular state in which the mini-fairs have been held, and the annual Fair has drawn people from all across the North American Continent and from several foreign countries as well.

Central to the Fair is the life, skills, activities and accomplishments of our children. The Fair also serves as a focus for our children's curriculum. As we know, curriculum means "racecourse," and every racecourse needs a finish line, a goal. Children aren't the only ones who run on a "curriculum"; the Scriptures speak of all believers running a race toward a set goal (1 Cor. 9:24-27; Gal. 2:2; 5:7; Phil. 2:16; Heb. 12:1). As we have seen, our curriculum must offer clear, long-range goals, particularly the goal of a human life shaped in the image of Jesus Christ, a child who becomes an adult whose life expresses the love and wisdom of God; and the finish line for the curriculum we all must run is the point at which we come into total oneness with Jesus Christ, when we can at last be poured out completely as a drink offering unto the Lord (2 Tim. 4:6). In the previous pages, we have also noted very clear and specific intermediate goals that we must set before our children.*

But we also need placed before us—or to place before ourselves—shorter-ranged goals of achievement and attainment as steps towards this longer-ranged goal. God has supplied just such a range in the seasons He has ordained. The annual Fair marks the finish line of completion for the labors of the

---

* See, for example, "Specific Goals" above.

seasons of that year, whether in school, business or daily life. Not only do the goals toward which we stretch in each new year stimulate us to move forward to new levels of accomplishment, but also the fulfillment of the goals already reached acts as a great encouragement and stimulus to us in our *aliyah*—our journey on the path upward—toward perfect maturity in and oneness with God.

Every school curriculum aims toward a finish line. In traditional schools, the administration and teachers give students tests to assess their abilities. But these tests fail in their purpose for a number of reasons. The test is abstracted and detached from any sort of relational life that students will likely ever live and that would incorporate the skills they learn; it bears no relationship to the students' actual lives or purposes or vision. Many researchers explain that, in general, what such tests show is the student's proficiency in test-taking, and even a high test score can indicate a low ability to use in a practical way the skills tested. At the same time that tests fail to accurately assess student skills, researchers show, the tests exercise a tremendous influence upon the entire curriculum. Try as educators will, they cannot get around the fact that any test they give to assess how well the students learn will greatly influence how and what teachers teach: the test unavoidably serves as the finish line toward which students and teachers aim all their efforts. And since the test does not bear any relationship to the child's actual life—to his needs, desires and purposes—since it fails to emphasize the students' practical ability to incorporate subjects into an integrated life style, the teaching in the classroom doesn't emphasize relational knowledge either. Everything taught becomes abstract, atomized and meaningless, like the pencil marks on the standardized test answer sheets themselves.

So a standardized test makes a poor short-range goal, but this Fair provides a perfect short-range, annual goal for our children's curriculum. It provides a relational context for all their activities. (We'll explain specifically how momentarily.) To the Fair, the children—as well as the adults—bring their "special gifts," "choice possessions" and "what [they] have vowed to give" unto the Lord (Deut. 12:6, 11-12). They honor Him through their exercise of the gifts He has entrusted to them. The Fair focuses on relationships of service to God and His people as well as on husbanding relationships with the land and its creatures. It brings the children (and all of us) into relationship with the world as a witness of God's "manifold wisdom." The activities, skills and so on displayed at the Fair encompass all of the life of our community and almost all of the areas of our children's curriculum. Skills and projects displayed at the Fair, varying from a fourteen-year-old boy's thermosiphon, wood burning water heater to the delicately spun and then meticulously woven shawls and dresses by ten- to fourteen-year-old girls, along with the thousands of other crafted pieces of metal casting, furniture, pottery, quilts and displays of skills in animal raising and training, music, poetry, prose and drawing, have made real to everyone the scripture, "Wisdom is justified of her children."

Each year every child—as well as every adult—sets for himself practical goals and projects to complete in time for the annual Fair. If a girl has a talent in sewing, she can bring the quality dresses or blouses, pants or shirts, she has made to the Fair. If a boy has a talent in woodworking, he can bring bookcases, chests, spinning wheels, dishes, kitchen utensils, cabinets, toys or anything else of a high quality that he has skillfully built. If a girl has a talent in spinning, then she can bring quality samples of her skeins of wool or cotton to show at the Fair. If a boy has a talent in working leather, he can bring belts, wallets, sandals, carrying cases, tack or any other quality products he has made to the Fair. A child can bring his writings to the Fair—possibly published in some book form for distribution at the Fair or written out in calligraphy to exhibit on display boards, as we've done in the past.

The Fair gives glory to the Source of every gift and talent in the Body, showing how all work together, showing how the specific acts and relationships through which God's people serve one another make His love tangible, visible and real. It shows for all to see how exactly He is bringing forth a people who through every aspect of their lives and service prove that God is not an abstract concept of men's imaginations but a living power in this world.

At this Fair we show all the things that we have brought to completion in the course of that year. We aim everything not toward some vague "someday," but everything we do moves toward a definite goal and specific time. Every year moves through the seasons of sowing, watering, reaping and the harvest. The Fair, as we said, marks the time of completion, of harvest, and the material, physical sowing also brings forth a spiritual harvest in the lives of others. This bringing to completion, as we said above, also results in a wonderful time of rest.

We have many booths at the Fair; these booths show our crafts and workmanship, particularly those of the children. And the children, as well as the adults, also work at the Fair itself, performing the skills and the crafts that they have learned so that others can see and learn from them: people see them spin and weave, tan hides, work with leather and wood, do calligraphy, pottery, shear sheep, cook on wood stoves and so on. We have had exhibits teaching how to do many of these things: how to spin, how to weave, how to shear sheep, how to cast, how to make soap and candles, how to care for animals and so on. We do exhibits of horse farming, with older children as well as the men working the horses. We want to expand these exhibits to include workshops and literature to teach people how to farm with horses. We have booths selling food. We also have some photographic displays of crafts and skills showing the different steps in the tasks being exhibited, products of workmanship, pictures of children working together, expressing their joy and excitement in their labors (we place these on standing display boards). Some of these photo-essays, drawings and written explanations we plan to incorporate into books we will publish about our life that will also show others how we follow God's patterns. We also want to publish books in conjunction with the Fair, specifically how-to books on self-sufficiency skills and crafts for a land-centered culture. We have published a large-sized album showing the life of our fellowship in words and pictures called *Koinonia Country: Sketches of Home and Community Life*. We encourage our children to help write, take photographs and do drawings for these and other books and displays.

The Fair includes special events, activities and exhibitions, which we plan to expand in forthcoming Fairs. We want to display animals that the children have trained and cared for, including demonstrations in which the boys and young men will drive oxen they have trained, or ride or drive horses that they had trained from foals.

We also have children's music going on at special times throughout the Fair. The Fair may at times present Hebrew hora dancing and singing and Mexican music. At nights, we present music that honors the One who has made our life as a community, the life that the Fair expresses, possible. The music celebrates our joy and thanksgiving and has included gospel singing and songs of worship, but also bluegrass as well as Hebrew music.

So at the end of the year, in the late summer or early fall, the children and all God's people bring forth the first fruits of their year's labor and display it at the Fair. They bring the projects they have completed, the top examples of their schoolwork, their special craftsmanship—everything: examples of their calligraphy, free writings, poems; the products of their leatherwork, woodwork, sewing, spinning and weaving; the animals they have trained and raised. If they have worked on any special projects, such as developing means to use solar energy or wind power; solar stills for distillation of water; models of water wheels, mills, cabins, barns and so on, they can also present these at the Fair. They may present collections of herbs and edible wild plants and animals or Indian artifacts. They may bring quilts, shawls, shirts, dresses, blankets, rugs, saddles, harnesses, headstalls, horseshoes, belts, wallets, Bible covers, pottery, skins, fleeces, vegetables, canned goods, baked goods, handmade bows, tables, chests, benches, bellows, wood-burning hot-water heaters, photos, paintings, drawings, water or solar or whatever projects, hand-cast pewter plates or menorahs or buttons and buckles, carved wooden bowls and spoons, shofars—the possibilities are unlimited.

In preparation for the Fair, and during the Fair itself, where possible and desirable, people can work together in teams and groups to bring their various tasks and projects to completion. For example, one group project, which has already begun, created a model of the Tabernacle of Moses. Boys have cast scale duplicates of the metal furnishings of the Tabernacle; girls have spun and woven the tapestries and so on. Together with their hands-on work, the children also study about the Tabernacle itself. Another group has developed a scale model of the solar system. Others could do displays of varieties of wildflowers and their uses (as in dyeing) or different types of trees and their uses. Obviously a great variety of possibilities exist to present simple, instructive displays and exhibits.

Through the Fair, every element of the curriculum finds its purpose in the outward-directed witness of the Christian community and of the child as an integrated member of that community. Now *all* the work in the curriculum that our children do serves to display God's alternative to this world of chaos and confusion. Our children can now clearly see that whatever work they do will either become incorporated in this display before the world at the Fair, or perhaps through various publications, or will serve to prepare them for the point at which they can bring forth works that display the glory of the Father. The greatest works are the children themselves—and all God's people—sharing, communicating, fellowshiping, with others. All these other works only work *on us* to bring us to this place. So the Fair provides children as well as parents with training and also with the incentive, the goal, to obtain that training.

Whatever work our children do in their curriculum (which includes almost all their activities), they can continue to feel after the Spirit, under their parents' guidance, to see when the Spirit would conceive something in them and bring it forth to witness to the wisdom and power of God. In every moment of their curriculum work (and, again, this "curriculum" increasingly includes every element of their lives, not excluding anything), they can be looking "carefully . . . how" they walk (Eph. 5:15, Ampl.) to make "the most of every opportunity" (Eph. 5:16). Every work in the curriculum becomes an "opportunity" to bring forth those works that will glorify the Father. As the children do their schoolwork, their housework, their yard—and garden—and farm work, they can think in terms of activities and projects they can bring forth to participate in the Fair.

Every area of the child's life and work provides fertile ground for preparing projects to bring to the Fair or writings to publish. For example, perhaps the child's work in some craft or skill or in working the land will evoke a writing that he could display at the Fair, a writing describing his experiences and feelings performing this work. Again, the child will only move forward in excitement about such writings if the parent continually and diligently works with and encourages the child. And even if the child does not bring forth a work of the quality that can be put on public display, he can feel encouraged as he grows, learns and moves toward the point at which his work can be put on public display (appropriate for display at the Fair would also be a comparison of the child's work over the year if it demonstrates great progress in a skill, even if the child has yet to reach a high level of craftsmanship).

In the home-writing workshops in which we feel that all school-age children and home-school mothers and (to the degree possible) fathers should participate,* the same sense of "making the most of every opportunity" can continue. As the child does his free writings, for example, the parents can remind him that this work may turn into something that may end up on public display before, or for public use by, thousands of people. When they do this, however, they must exercise caution not to let the children feel fearful or intimidated or proud. The children must see the privilege and also the joy in the work that they do. They must see that everything lies in God's hands; He has ordained the times and seasons to bring forth those works that glorify Him. Yet each of us can only find those times and seasons if we diligently follow Him and participate with all our being. We must have that sense of expectancy and urgency, and then He will bring forth through us the eternal works He has ordained for us to accomplish.

Every single activity of the curriculum becomes a potential ground to bring forth works to glorify God, works that can appear at the Fair, works that could possibly be published for the Fair (and the displays at the Fair could themselves be photographed to appear in publications that tell about the Fair).

When a child does his calligraphy, he may produce a piece of craftsmanship worthy of public display. As he learns to write in Hebrew, perhaps he could produce a story that could be published (along with its translation). Perhaps he will work on a Bible translation that could be published in some form for the Fair. Perhaps as his Hebrew accent improves, he may be able to do a Hebrew Bible reading or perform a dialogue that could be put on tape. In his nature study, one of his projects may become a display at the Fair or a published article. (Such nature study displays could include not only the materials collected and what we draw or write about them but also handcrafted wooden display cases.) When he practices his music, the child may become so proficient that he would play at the Fair. Perhaps he can work with some of his brothers and sisters to learn a piece of music to play at the Fair. Perhaps they'll write something together that they can play. When a girl cooks in the kitchen, she may perfect or even create some dish that can be served at the Fair.

---

* See Truth Forum's *Right Words* and *Guidelines for Teaching Your Children Writing at Home.*

Everything the children do can be seen in the *relational* context that the Fair provides: parents must urge them to see that their activities will bring them into relationship with their brothers and sisters in the Lord, with the earth and its creatures, with the people of the world as part of the witness of God. (Of course, the Fair is not primarily a goal in itself; above all it serves as a focus to help each of us, and all together, to move forward in the purpose of God as He molds us into His image.) These activities all depend upon and encourage a deeper relationship with God. Everything depends upon the parents' active participation in the lives of their children. The parents must continually remind and urge their children to press forward into the purpose of God. The parents must help their children to recognize when God conceives something in their hearts, something He wants them to bring forth and present as a witness of His wisdom. This means that the parents themselves must press toward the fulfillment of their places of participation in the Body.

The focus of the Fair creates a dynamic that carries over into every area of our and our children's lives. Through this focus we can encourage them to reach out in their labors, to enter into relationship with God and with one another, to find their places of participation in the kingdom. We can encourage them to see the important place that God has made them to hold in His kingdom.

As we've mentioned before, during the course of the year, in our fellowship we present dozens of workshops to teach various skills and crafts to children and to those adults who want to participate in them. We hold workshops on a wide variety of crafts including weaving, spinning, quilting, sewing, pottery, tanning, leatherwork, woodwork, blacksmithing, livestock care, horse farming, gardening, food preserving, photography, musical instruments, calligraphy, drawing and other skills. In the workshops, the brothers and sisters skilled in these crafts instruct the children (and other brothers and sisters). But all of this instruction remains home-centered as much as possible. The instructors offer introductory classes to get the children going in their skill or craft, but then the child works as much as possible at home under his parent's guidance. The children can attend any workshop to see the activity before deciding whether to work in that skill or craft area. After they begin to work in a particular area of skill or craft, the instructor serves mainly as an advisor to help the parents move their children forward in their work. (This pattern of special advisors to help parents teach their children will also carry over to scholastic subjects, such as writing and mathematics, as well.) The instructors hold periodic workshops for special projects, further instruction and giving suggestions to help improve craftsmanship. Some people in the workshops work on group projects, others on individual projects; some projects are suggested by advisors, others by the children themselves. All workshops aim toward hands-on work as soon as possible, geared toward whatever level the student is on. We have had more than sixty different types of workshops operating to teach a wide range of skills and crafts, from blacksmithing to cross-stitching. We've already discussed how both the grammar level Readers and the dialectical studies of culture, science, history, philosophy and so on tie into the vision expressed through our craft and skill workshops, helping to integrate all our children's education into a cohesive unit.

Everyone working for the Fair—adult and child—strives toward the highest standard. And the *standard* we should aim for on all of the various levels is to bring forth the best that has *ever* been done. We won't start here, but we are aiming for the best we can do for the highest we know—for the display of *His* glory. He said, "Be ye perfect as your heavenly Father is perfect, that men will see your *good works* and so glorify your Father." These are the good works that He has prepared in advance for us to perform (Eph. 2:10). In everything, the goal of our workmanship would be not to draw attention to ourselves, but to bring glory to Jesus Christ, to be His witness. So we must strive to perfect our craft until we can bring forth the best saddle blanket that's ever been woven, the best pot that's ever been thrown, the best writing that's ever been written. This must be what we're continually pressing toward, because we want to present to the world the true expression of the nature and reality of Jesus Christ.

Of course, all the children (and adults) will work on different levels. But no matter what level we are on, we must all strive for the highest level of our abilities, "for the display of His splendor" (Isa. 61:3). "Right now," a child might say to himself, "I'm just a beginner. But next year, I'm going to become one of those craftsmen whose workmanship will overthrow the horn that would scatter God's people (Zech. 1:21). Next year, I'll attain to the level of excellence that will qualify my workmanship as an expression of the God who has given me the grace to accomplish His purpose." So the Fair should motivate the children: they will see the examples of fine craftsmanship, and they will want to aspire to, reach and surpass the goals that they saw embodied in that workmanship. This means that every adult has an obligation to participate in the Fair to bring forth workmanship to the best of—and even beyond—his *natural* ability.

Again, the focus of everything is our desire to serve as the witness of God's love, wisdom and truth. All year long, in everything they do, our children see that their *tamim* workmanship will enable them to participate in the witness of God. "If I fold this bed sheet properly, it becomes part of the witness of God." "If I put these clothes away neatly, it becomes part of the witness of God." "If I plant this garden properly, it becomes part of the witness of God." "If I take care of my little brother or sister in love, it becomes part of the witness of God." "Every worksheet written neatly, every page of calculation, every calligraphy exercise, every practice session on the guitar or mandolin or fiddle or trumpet or piano becomes part of the witness of God if I do it to the best of my ability in God. More important than any fairs, it goes towards making *me* a witness, and that witness is on display everywhere I go."

Again, the Fair brings into focus the relational nature of all knowledge: for the Fair itself is a relational context, first in our relationship with God, and then in our relationship with our fellowman (with each other and with those outside the fellowship) and even in our relationship to the land and the animals. As in the great Fairs of ancient Israel, the Fair gives us a context to come together to celebrate the fullness of relationship God has given us with Him, with one another and with His land. And at the same time this Fair presents a context for bringing us into relationship with those who do not yet know Him, but who hunger for the true life that He has given to His people.

So each adult can say to himself at the beginning of the year in October, "This is the goal that I will set for myself this coming year. I will build a cedar chest to display at the Fair" or "I will make a quilt for the Fair." And each parent—working with his child to establish the child's goals—could say at the beginning of the school year, "This will be the goal of my child this year . . . ." Everything the child studies can be geared toward the Fair, fulfilling completely the call to impart relational knowledge through home education. (Of course, different children of different ages and abilities can do different numbers of projects for the Fair. The parent must feel after his child's abilities. Coordinators of various areas of work for the Fair, working with the skill and craft teachers, help parents assess exactly how much their children can really do in the course of a year.) The child can orient his nature study toward making a display of wild "survival" herbs and vegetables to show at the Fair; he can do drawings of garden vegetables for the Fair; he can write a story about the life of our community for the Fair; he can do a story about the Holocaust to present as a display at the Fair. One child will say, "I feel to raise rabbits, skin them and tan the hides so such and such can be made from them." Another might say, "I feel to make gloves or to make belts or to make saddles." We want to show every stage of the whole process, step by step, all the way through the tanning of the hides to the making of the leather items. Every aspect of his curriculum—his nature studies, his calligraphy, his reading and writing, his math and science—all can be oriented toward bringing forth workmanship to show at the Fair. The Fair includes many different projects. Even one child can do many different projects, and of course, all the children taken together engage in a vast number of projects in many different craft and skill areas.

So this annual Children's Fair serves as an exciting focus to channel all our children's energies toward an immediate goal that works together with the long-range goals of God in our children's lives. As each year they press past this finish line for the annual course they run in their schooling, our children feel every aspect of their lives and schooling working together to bring them into greater oneness with God, with God's people and with God's creation. They declare to the world not only a defense of home schooling against secular critics but also the positive witness that declares the superiority of God's alternative in creating exciting, meaningful lives.

Now that we have pointed to both the broad contours and even the specific focuses of the vision of Christian home education, we are ready, in the next chapter, to present a God-centered perspective on the individual subjects of scholastic study. These subjects should *not* be taught in a fragmented, isolated fashion. Your teaching should integrate them all together in the unit curriculum context we've described in this chapter and which we'll describe in detail in Supplement One. But we discuss these subjects separately in the following chapter only to give you a perspective on each area of knowledge that will help you see how it interrelates to the others. As we've said, we are developing and beginning to publish a curriculum that integrates these subjects together in a formally structured course of study that works with Bible-based readers that integrate history, character curriculum, geography and other subjects; guidebooks for teaching writing, arithmetic and other skills, and other materials. To repeat, we describe this unit curriculum in Supplement One, and we refer to it when appropriate in the context of our discussion of the individual subjects. But we discuss those subjects so that anyone using any curriculum will find the subject information of practical benefit.

In learning the different subjects, children will move through the three levels of learning—knowledge (grammar), understanding (dialectic) and wisdom (rhetoric)—repeatedly on different levels. We feel, however, in regard to the course of his *scholastic* education taken as a *whole*, that a home-schooled child generally remains in the grammar stage until the ages of eleven to thirteen, at which time he will enter the dialectic stage, different children moving of course at different paces. (And in a sense we can say that the total of his scholastic education constitutes the grammar level of his life, preparing him to enter into the dialectic of life that comes through actual confrontation with the world and which can alone yield the rhetoric of a mature existence in God.) In our educational course, in general, the first through seventh grades constitute the grammar level wherein the child will acquire a thorough knowledge of the basics, and even some advanced studies, of English, math, science, history and the Bible (in the eighth through the tenth grades, basic knowledge on the grammar level will be reviewed and expanded, but now teaching on the dialectic level begins on a full-blown scale). The fifth through seventh grades constitute a type of bridge between grammar and dialectic. Through the dialectic course, which we describe in Supplement One, children in the eighth through tenth grades will develop a comprehensive knowledge of history, culture,

Some of our visitors at the Fair

Each year, the members of our fellowships all look forward expectantly to the Koinonia Children's Fair and Homestead Craft Exposition held at Rehoboth Ranch in Colorado. This Fair brings focus and practical relevance to all the children's educational activities, including academics, crafts and music. Just as the community life of ancient Israel found focus in their great feasts, our lives and our children's lives find tangible culmination in a yearly event that proclaims the fullness of life God has imparted to us as a people.

Enjoying a hayride at the Fair

Susan Nolen teaching her son

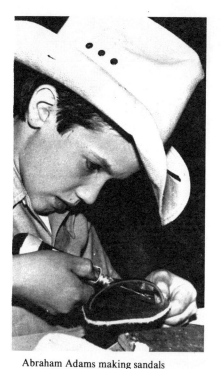

The Fair serves as an annual finish line toward which the children aim their year's schoolwork and craft projects. At the same time it serves to remind both child and parent that true Christian education must flow from a larger life context (a God-centered culture) that can only exist within a community of like-minded believers.

Abraham Adams making sandals

Pewter casting workshop

Frank Strazza making a dovetail cedar chest   Francine Korahais at the potter's wheel

Instruction in hand quilting

Preparation for the Fair begins the preceding fall when families—children and adults—begin formulating their goals for the year. Throughout the year, members of our fellowship conduct dozens of teaching workshops (including those that target scholastic skills) as a part of the teaching and "equipping" ministry to undergird the efforts of our home-schooling families.

Isaac Adams

Pat Chesney and children, Christi and David

Mark Borman practicing the accordion

Ephratah Stein, age 2

Beginning recorder class

"Each one teach one." Home-schooled Sam Hersh teaching Thad Hill

Josiah Wheeler at blacksmithing

Gabrielle Nolen weaving

Martha Quinones setting up a Navajo weaving loom

Brian Salmeri learning to drive a team of horses

Amanda Adams spinning on a Rio Grande spinning wheel

Our 1800 acre ranch: site of Koinonia Children's Craft Fair Exposition

The Ranch: looking west with gardens, orchards and hay meadows

In the late summer, the children (and their parents) bring forth the "first fruits" of the year's labor and display them at the Fair. They bring top examples of their schoolwork, projects and crafts to bring honor to the One who has made Himself manifest in our midst.

Herb booth

Children's crocheting-workshop projects

Leatherwork booth

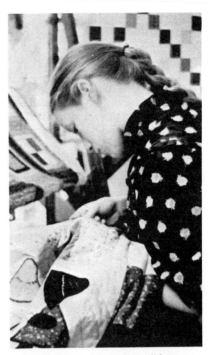

Kelli Reveile demonstrating quilting

Frank Strazza's (age 12) finished dovetail cedar chest

Fair music: a song in sign language for the deaf

Tony Strohmeyer's (age 14) thermosiphon wood-burning water heater

Wooden utensils from boys' woodworking workshop

June, Snipsey, Tina and Rusty and many other horses provide daily horse-farming demonstrations.

The Children's Fair serves as a point of aim and culmination of our home-schooling energies. Each year, as our children press past the finish line for their schooling, they develop a sense that their lives and education work in tandem with the life and purpose of the community of which they form a vital part. They proclaim to the world not only a defense for home schooling (against both the religious and secular critics) but also a living witness that declares the superiority of God's home-based educational pattern in creating exciting, meaningful lives that proclaim, "wisdom is justified by her children."

Open-air tabernacle with fair displays

science, philosophy and related subjects. As we've noted before, the key purpose of such studies lies in enabling the child to engage in a meaningful dialogue with the world, addressing the world in terms that will enable the child to see the relevance of the Word of God. As the child matures, his work in English will also continue to unfold, particularly his writing skills. The child's subsequent schooling will entail deepening dialectical studies in science, history and the Bible, while also continuing to further develop necessary math and English skills and learning research skills to use when he needs them (much of this begins earlier). The continuance of their education will require a "college" level course such as the one we are developing,* speaking of college in the sense defined earlier.†

At each step along the way in instructing your child you must pray and seek the Lord diligently to be clear that what you teach him fits into God's purpose for his life. You must ensure the presence of God's purpose in both the individual subject, such as history or math, and also the particular lesson that you seek to transmit at any given time. The next chapter will help you to do that. *In each lesson you should ask yourself: What main point or points does my child need to understand? How does this fit into what my child is learning specifically in regard to this subject and in his general development and education?* (All this is easier to apprehend in the context of the type of curricular form we discussed before, particularly in the unit approach.) We must be sure every step along the way, day by day, hour by hour, that we have the God-centered perspective in everything we teach our children. Again, this can only be done not by our own works and efforts but by God's grace as we walk in His Spirit.

To repeat, parents must remember that *they* have the responsibility to decide what their children will learn. In the first place, they must decide what their children *should* learn: what subjects, skills and so on. (We do believe, however, that *every* child should learn basic subjects, and in the following sections we will discuss these individually and explain why children should learn them; our curriculum itself, of course, covers those basics we feel necessary.) Then from the materials

---

* For information on this course, see Supplement One.

† See pp. 266-67.

available to help them in teaching their children these subjects, parents must select the materials or curriculum program, whether ours or some other, that they feel best about for their children.* Once they have decided upon a program that they feel confident in, they must still take ultimate responsibility for imparting this material to their children in God's Spirit. If you, the parent, look upon this labor as a drudgery, it will prove impossible. But if you see it as a labor of love, as your opportunity to let God mold and shape your children through you, it will turn into one of the most exciting experiences of your life.

We must always remember the *relational* context of what we teach to our children. If we teach subjects according to the more traditional pattern, such as phonics and grammar, we must remember to use relational principles such as those we discussed earlier,† for example, "framework learning" and "low threshold of utility," so that the children can begin to practically apply the knowledge that they have acquired as soon as possible; they should have the opportunity to perfect and develop their knowledge within the context of that practical use.‡ But these relational *principles* will work for us only if we actually stand in the proper relationship with our children ourselves, that relationship which nurtures them in love, trust and godly discipline. We must always and continually set the goals, both long-range and immediate, before our children, explaining to them how what they learn will enable them to master various skills, accomplish various purposes and so on. For example, the parents can explain that learning the "p" sound will help the child to read the name "Peter," and that learning to read "Peter" will be a step toward reading the Bible on his own. We must also remember to recognize (even if we don't explicitly call our child's attention to) how the knowledge we teach fits into the unit of our child's total education; again, we want to teach our children the things that they need to know in a practical, relational context.

As we have said, Truth Forum is developing curriculum materials to incorporate all of the information that we feel that our children must acquire within the framework and context of this relational approach. But as we have said repeatedly, this material does not constitute a rigid and inflexible pattern: you

---

* See Supplement One for information on *Koinonia Curriculum*.

† See pp. 244-50.

‡ See information on our phonics course in Supplement One.

and your child must always have room to explore the things of particular relevance, importance and interest for you. We simply want to provide a form that will enable you to explore those personal interests while at the same time facilitating your effort to cover all of the educational ground necessary. To further help you in this task, we now survey the major subject areas.

CHAPTER NINE
The Major Subject Areas

We have seen how different subjects interrelate through the unit approach. Now we will examine the individual subject areas themselves. We will discuss our basic requirements for each of the educational levels—grammar (knowledge), dialectic (understanding) and rhetoric (wisdom)—in each of the major scholastic subjects. As we have said before, teaching ministries should present parents with material that will show them exactly what to aim for and how to achieve their aim on every level of education. But to successfully impart this material the parent must learn to see with God's vision and perspective. No matter what level our child is on, this is necessary in order to successfully lead him through his education.

You will find in the remainder of this chapter remarks listed under the subjects themselves—for example, English, arithmetic, history and so on—concerning the teaching of these subjects. As we said, this material will help you relationally impart the knowledge of these particular subjects.

As we've also said, we are developing and publishing right now a curriculum consistent with the vision laid out in this book. All of this material is being developed and interrelated according to the perspective of relational knowledge. After this chapter (and a brief conclusion that follows it), you will find in Supplement One a description of this Koinonia Curriculum. Please write to us for further information on receiving this curriculum as it becomes available.

Section One

Subject: *The Bible*

Hear, O Israel: Yahweh our God, Yahweh is one. Love Yahweh your God with all your heart and with all your soul and with all your strength. These commandments that I give you today are to be upon your hearts. Impress them on your children. Talk about them when you sit at home and when you walk along the road, when you lie down and when you get up. Tie them as symbols on your hands and bind them on your foreheads. Write them on the doorframes of your houses and on your gates. (Deut. 6:4-9)

The Bible does not represent merely a particular area of learning. But, as revealed by God's Spirit, it forms the basis of *all* of man's true knowledge. Therefore it enters into every area of study: history, science, language and so on. In general, the greatest amount of time of any one subject in the child's daily instruction should be devoted to the Bible, to memorization and study of the Word of God.

No Bible study program can replace the prayerful study and reading of God's Word for oneself, which is not to deny the importance of and need for structured Bible study, God-centered and anointed. Parents must carry the responsibility to prayerfully study and teach the Word of God every day to their children, not in a rigid way, but ministered as the living Word of God, spoken and lived by His people, in and through whom it is made flesh. Parents should impart the truths of God's commandments, the heroic tales of the men and women of the Bible and the precious truth of the gospel of Jesus Christ. Many of those topics will, however, also be taught in the normal course of study, since all true Christian curriculum centers on just such Bible stories. For instance, in our curriculum, our main reading materials in the first four grades are based on stories from the Bible, generally using the Bible itself as the story. The truths of God's Word must be imparted in the course of every study area.

No other area of study brings out more clearly than this one that Christian education must seek to impart more than mere intellectual, "head" knowledge. Nothing else shows us more clearly that the education of our child must consistently work to mold and shape a human life in conformity to the pattern of God's Word. The Scriptures serve as the most vital educational tool of what we might call the ultimate "unit" goal of our children's unit curriculum: the bringing forth of a child who is a whole person, a *tamim* individual, flawless in character, full of grace and truth. All instruction in the Word of God must contribute directly to the completion of this "unit" goal. The knowledge of God's Word has meaning only as relational knowledge, in living relationship to our lives. Abstracted from relationships into detached studies (that is, handled by flesh rather than by Spirit), man's knowledge of Scripture becomes the letter that kills all spiritual life (2 Cor. 3:6). All the intellectual knowledge of the Bible means nothing unless God's Word is *realized* in the life of the child. Here we find the true test of his "Bible knowledge," the extent to which the "Word is made flesh and dwells among us" in the child's real life, the extent to which he becomes a *living epistle* "known and read of all men" (2 Cor. 3:2). Again, the knowledge of God's Word must come to bear a living relationship to the child's life. We do not want him to know the Word of God abstractly, but rather for him to himself become a living *expression* of the Word of God. The ancient Hebrew concept of knowledge was, as we have seen, that of knowledge in the experiential, relational sense. "You shall know the truth," and therefore, because it is becoming realized in your life, "the truth shall make you free" (John 8:32, NASV). Many people, though intellectually learned, even in the Scriptures themselves, are yet slaves to their sins, passions and fears. It takes the living Word, truly made flesh, to actually set us free.

As we have said before,* the child's submission and obedience to God-ordained authority in his life form the basis of all of his instruction. The child must first learn to hear and obey his parents' instructions and those of any other God-ordained authority in his life, be it other adults, or even older children who have been given authority over him. Obedience is foundational to everything else the child learns.

In the remainder of this section, we discuss how to apply the three stages of learning to instruction in the Word of God.

1. The *knowledge*, or *grammar*, stage: In this stage, the child

---

* See pp. 82-84 and 269-70.

learns to know the Sword of Truth, which is the Word of God, his basic tool for godly living. As we said above, parents should apply the teachings of the Bible as needs and problems arise in the child's life: again, God's Word can *only* be learned relationally. For instance, lying, false witness, covetousness and so on should be dealt with through the Word of God as these problems come up in the child's life in order to make these Biblical injunctions meaningful in their application to his life. (Of course, you can teach about these things preventively, before problems arise, but such teaching must go forth in the Spirit, or it will otherwise be merely the letter that kills.) The book of Proverbs was considered a child-rearing manual by the ancient Hebrews. It provides in itself a kind of "grammar" book of the Word of God. The child should memorize and understand verses from Proverbs (some have ultimately even memorized the whole book) as they are applicable to his life and as the Holy Spirit leads. (The learning of the Scriptures should not, of course, be limited to Proverbs.) All of this means that the parents themselves must have a good working knowledge of the Scriptures so that they will know which scriptures are relevant. (Our *Koinonia Character Curriculum*, described later in this section and in Supplement One, provides the teaching materials you need in order to perform the tasks we've discussed in this paragraph.)

Parents should teach their young children the basic Bible commandments and their application to their children's lives. Instruction in these commandments should emerge from the crucible of the child's living relationship with God, his fellow-man and the world around him. In our *Koinonia Character Curriculum*, Truth Forum has put together explanations and chain references of such scriptures for different needs at different times in the child's life, for example, teachings and chain references on lying, on hurting others, on stealing and so forth. Parents should also tell their young the wonderful Bible stories.* These all form components of the grammar stage of Bible study.

---

* Much of this instruction will, as we have said, also take place in the Christian curriculum in general, for example, in the basic reading material in our curriculum. In our reading program, for example, grades one through four go through a major part of the Bible. These readers contain the Word of God geared toward the young student level. We also integrate history, geography and other topics into the framework of the Bible narrative.

The child should memorize the verse from Deuteronomy quoted above (Deut. 6:4-9; Mark 12:29-31; the first and greatest commandment and the second commandment), the Ten Commandments, the Sermon on the Mount and the Lord's Prayer. These scriptures provide an excellent framework and foundation for the teachings of the Bible. The parent can relate these scriptures to the child's life as he journeys through different situations, circumstances, problems, trials, questions and so on. Of course, scripture instruction (which could include memorization) and study in godly character will include emphasis on positive character development as well as on the negative things that should be avoided. (These scriptures all present basic principles of Scripture, principles that run throughout the Word of God as cohesive threads through which the Spirit ties together the living Word. We will discuss this in more detail shortly.) In the grammar stage, the child should concentrate on learning the ethical and *moral* laws of God and seeing their relevance for his character and life.

We would do well to remember at this point that true education is a form of discipleship, and discipleship means "training" above and beyond mere "teaching." So the Scriptures admonish us to "*train* up a child." Teaching merely *in*forms the mind, while training *con*forms the life. Training is essentially teaching enforced by discipline. It is discipline that ensures that the teaching of God's Word is incorporated into the very life of the child, making him a disciple (Heb. 12:11).

On this level, the child should start a program that will continue in later years: the memorization of verses, chapters and books of the Bible. David proclaimed God's Word to be hidden *in his heart* that he might not sin against God (Ps. 119:11). At different stages, memorization of different types of scriptures will become more prevalent than others: for example, younger children will focus on scriptures on character building, then focus on scriptures on foundational doctrine as they grow older.

Memorization is very important on the grammar level. To repeat, David declared that he would hide God's Word in his heart, and the grammar years are the easiest to do this in. In addition to the scriptures that we have mentioned above, of course, you might use many others. In our Christian fellowship, we are developing a program of scripture instruction (which for children especially would include memorization) on the basic teachings of the Bible. This will include the following areas: the nature of God, Christian love and character, the foundations of Christianity (Heb. 6:1-2—which include repentance from dead works, faith towards God, baptisms, laying on of hands, resurrection from the dead and eternal judgment), the covenant and the relationships that it governs (relationships with God, church, family, job, world) and so on. These scripture references will be compiled for the grammar and dialectic levels and will work together with a course of instruction on these Biblical subjects. The focus of all this Bible teaching lies not in abstract knowledge but in perfecting the child's character, deepening his relationship with God and God's people and helping him to find and fulfill his place in the Body of Christ. Some scriptures, such as those on Christian character, will be repeated at different learning stages throughout the child's development. But, as we said before, different aspects of particular subjects will be emphasized at different points in the child's development. Generally, the same topics will be covered at each level, but more deeply as the child matures. And as the child begins to enter the dialectic level, he should be taught the use of Bible study helps, for example, concordances, cross-references, topical references, language study helps and so on that will enable him to pursue the study of God's Word himself.

As we have said before, the child in first memorizing scriptures will often not fully recognize their importance (although, again, everything taught to the child should be related to his life as fully as possible), but when he comes to the dialectic level of learning and becomes actively involved in the conflict between competing interpretations of the Scriptures, suddenly he will begin to see the importance of learning what the Bible itself says on controversial subjects (which has come to include just about everything in the Bible). Suddenly, all the verses take on a living, vital and immediate importance and relevance. Again, the parent must, in the grammar stage, prepare his child for the dialectic stage, reminding him of the importance the Scriptures will assume for him later on in his education. But at the same time, as we have already said, scriptures will relate to the child's direct life experience in many vital ways. And on every level, the point of memorization is not simply to fill the child with abstract knowledge but with a *living* Word that relates to his life situation and that, above all, serves to bring him into closer and deeper relationship with the Messiah Jesus. Otherwise the child will merely forget what he learns—the Scriptures must be *applied* to his life, used, repeated, *"impressed"* upon him (Deut. 6:6-7), incorporated into his heart, mind, his very being (Deut. 11:18-19; Prov. 3:1-3).

Character building is absolutely central; for if we fail here, we fail completely. This necessitates teaching and training children on a scriptural basis to be honest, loving, kind, gentle, temperate, faithful, long-suffering, patient, good, generous, dutiful, persevering, responsible, reliable, holy and to conform from their hearts to all the other basic attributes of good character. Though a basic memorization book for much of this will be the book of Proverbs, it would be a great failing to use it exclusively. These different character traits will be related back to our basic framework, particularly the Ten Commandments. (Our book *Building Christian Character* offers comprehensive scripture chain-references with teachings on the key character attributes. We use this book as part of the *Koinonia Character Curriculum.*

We use a form, the *Koinonia Character Curriculum*, which we will describe in the next paragraph, for the specific purpose of teaching and training our children in these basic principles of character so that these principles can truly be "impressed" upon them. Hebrews 1:3 tells us that Jesus Christ is the "express image" or the "exact representation" of God's being. These words are translations of the Greek word *charakter*, from which our word *character* is derived. This same word was used to refer to the stamping of an image on a coin, the transmission of an impression.[1] Character, in other words, is something *impressed* upon us. And we desire to have impressed upon our children, stamped upon them—until their nature is entirely conformed to it—the image of God (Rom. 8:29). Herein, then, lies the intention of the injunction in Deuteronomy 6 that we "impress" the words of God upon our children, that we make their character conform to the nature of God. The injunction that the words of the Law were to be impressed "on your children" meant, in other words, that the Law was to be *internalized*, written or impressed upon their hearts (Jer. 31:33; Heb. 10:16), that their very character was to be conformed to it. This was, of course, the promise of the New Covenant (Heb. 8:8-13; Jer. 32:40); now we have the Spirit to assist in breaking down the stubborn barriers of the flesh so that the law-Word can be impressed on us through the obedience that comes through faith (Rom. 8:4). But, as we have seen on so many different levels, only form can hold the content of what we try to impress upon our children, a form through which God's love can flow. How can our children learn to love the Lord with all of their hearts, souls and strength unless channels exist through which they can express that love? And this is why God gives us a form that can show our children that channels do exist through which at every moment of their lives they can express the love that God gives them. These channels are the daily relationships and responsibilities through which our children serve their parents, their brothers and sisters and other members of the community, giving concrete manifestation to the love and grace of God as it moves through their lives to the lives of others.

The form consists of a character curriculum chart through which each child can keep track of all his regular and special responsibilities and chores (including schoolwork). On this chart, the parents (usually the mother) together with the child can assess his character in the performing of his responsibilities: for example, his attitude in doing his work (for example, whether he must be repeatedly reminded to do it and so on). At the end of each day, the child and mother will assess these areas so that the child can see how he has fulfilled or fallen short of God's image that day, so that he might earnestly seek God for the grace to be more perfectly conformed to His nature. (Of course, it's essential that children not develop a pharisaical, legalist attitude of trying to appear righteous before men. In our character curriculum program, the child learns to see all his positive character attributes as gifts of God's grace and all of his negative traits as works of his flesh that God's grace will overcome in victory and power. He learns to strive for the perfection of grace, to keep his life pure and unspotted.) In the context of the fulfillment of the purpose of God and in the midst of the interrelationships of family and community life, character is developed, hewn, tested and matured. Important as the fulfillment of these responsibilities is in itself, it mainly provides the context and framework of the reality of the Christian witness: the living context wherein our love one for another is made known to all men. While we perform the works ordained for us from the beginning of time, the Master Craftsman is hewing and refining us, perfecting us in

His image. How your child takes out the garbage, does the dishes, cleans his room, does his schoolwork, milks the cow, presents true evidence of his relationship with God and of the depth of his Christian character. Does he do the tedious jobs responsibly or does he have to be continually guided and reminded? Does he truly prefer his brothers and sisters in his daily tasks and chores, as well as in play? Through our digging and pruning with these godly standards in mind, the fruit of the Spirit emerges in your child's life.*

Parents should also instruct children on the grammar level in those basic guidelines of Christian living, the Ten Commandments. The older children on this level can write about each of the commandments, explaining their meaning and importance. (We plan to develop a curriculum form for this instruction.)

The Ten Commandments provide the basic principles† and framework through which our relationship with God deter-

---

* We have put together a character curriculum program based around such a chart of our children's chores and responsibilities. This program works with a book that gives a comprehensive scriptural explanation of the basic elements of Christian character together with detailed scripture lists, *Building Christian Character*. The program includes guidelines for positive instruction in Christian character. Again, write to us for further information.

† One influential Christian writer objects to speaking of Biblical "principles." He identifies all principles with the abstract sort used by the Greeks and rightly objects that

> neither Christ nor the Bible can be reduced to a Greek abstraction or principle: there is never anything abstract about Scripture. Theft, murder, adultery, false witness and more are forbidden, not because of some abstract principle, but because God says so.[2]

But must all principles necessarily be abstract? Can't there be concrete, God-centered principles as opposed to abstract, man-centered ones? (Indeed, the King James Version speaks in Hebrews 6:1 of the "principles of the doctrine of Christ.")

This question obviously requires more extensive discussion than we can give it here. Part of this writer's problem is that he never defines what he means by principles. A principle is a foundation, a source, a point of origin, something upon which something else is based. Are there none of these in Scripture? The writer never defines "principles" nor what it means to reject them. So he leaves the whole problem in the same realm of vague abstraction that he so condemns. Yet when David said that he would sacrifice to Yahweh only that which cost him something (2 Sam. 24:24), was he not expressing a principle? When Jesus speaks of Deuteronomy 6:4-5 and Leviticus 19:18 as the first and second commandments, the former specifically as "the greatest," is He not laying down a principle (Mark 12:29-31)?

This author rightly warns us against abstract principles that originate in the human mind. But we cannot throw out God-centered principles that originate in the Spirit. God ordains these principles as guides to help us walk

mines all the rest of our relationships with our fellowman and creation. Jesus declared that He had not come to abolish this law, but to fulfill it—to fill the form of the law with a righteousness exceeding that of the Pharisees. This fulfillment would result, not from the external imposition of legal strictures but from the internal desire to perform through love the works of a law that has been engraved internally on the human heart (Matt. 22:37; Jer. 31:33). The first and second commandments declare the centrality and primacy of our relationship with God and the subordination of all other relationships and things to this primary relationship:

> I am Yahweh your God, who brought you out of Egypt, out of the land of slavery.
> You shall have no other gods before Me.
> You shall not make for yourself an idol in the form of anything in heaven above or on the earth beneath or in the waters below. You shall not bow down to them or worship them; for I, Yahweh your God, am a jealous God, punishing the children for the sin of the fathers to the third and fourth generation of those who hate Me, but showing lovingkindness [*chesed*] to thousands, to those who love Me and keep My commandments. (Exod. 20:2-6, NIV, NASV)

Nothing is to be elevated to a place of worship alongside God. Indeed, Jesus warns of the necessity of subordinating all of our lives and even the deepest and most intimate of personal relationships to our love and devotion to God (Matt. 10:37-39). It is in this sense that we are to "hate" our mother, father, sisters and brothers and even our own lives (Luke 14:26). To elevate any of these relationships to a place superior to our relationship with God is to commit a form of idolatry that violates the first commandment. This first commandment reminds us of God's work of deliverance in our lives, and of the nature of His covenant faithfulness—*chesed*, "lovingkindness"—toward us if we will abide faithfully in covenant with Him.

The third commandment informs us of the means through which we enter into and maintain this primary relationship—

---

consistently in the way we should go, to conform us to His image. But these principles can only help us when God Himself applies them, when His Spirit and Truth come together as one in our lives. Such living principles must never be ossified to become substitutes for the direct leading and guiding of God's Spirit.[3] (See *Justice Is Fallen* for further discussion of these key points.)

through Yahweh's holy Name,

> You shall not misuse the name of Yahweh your God, for Yahweh will not hold anyone guiltless who misuses His name. (Exod. 20:7)

So in teaching us to pray, Jesus begins, "Our Father who art in Heaven, hallowed be Thy Name." This constitutes the entrance way to our relationship with God; to desire to see God's Name "hallowed" is to desire to see Him exalted, to see His supremacy universally established. Robert Lindsay has compared this prayer to the enthusiastic cheer of fans at a football stadium; we're shouting, "May Your Name be great in the earth, God. May more and more people hallow Your Name. We want to see You victorious, God. We want men to worship and exalt You!" Through this exaltation of the Name, we declare our solidarity with God, our unity with Him and His purposes, our desire to be in a relationship of true oneness with Him, to see His victory in all areas of life and creation. God's Name expresses His authority, and by truly sanctifying and honoring His Name we express our commitment to submit our whole lives to every true expression of His authority, our desire to confess Jesus as Lord.

The fourth commandment gives God's principle for the regulation of work, our use of, and thus our relationship to, nature (notice that the livestock too are to have a Sabbath) and the very state of mind and attitude with which we should approach all of our labors:

> Remember the Sabbath day by keeping it holy. Six days you shall labor and do all your work, but the seventh day is a Sabbath to Yahweh your God. On it you shall not do any work, neither you, nor your son or daughter, nor your manservant or maidservant, nor your animals, nor the alien within your gates. For in six days Yahweh made the heavens and the earth, the sea, and all that is in them, but He rested on the seventh day. Therefore Yahweh blessed the Sabbath day and made it holy. (Exod. 20:8-11)

If we have truly entered into His sabbath rest, we have ceased from our own works and have entered His. This commandment teaches us that all godly activity has a goal: to bring to completion the purpose of God. God did not rest from His works because He was tired but rather because He had *finished* the work, and so likewise are we told to "labor" to enter His rest by making our obedience complete (Heb. 4:11, KJV;

2 Cor. 10:6). This is what we are encouraged to do in the book of Hebrews, to enter into that rest that yet awaits the people of God, the rest from the mere works of human flesh. This rest from the will of man enables the grace of God to be manifest both through us and to us. As has been shown, works are not counterposed to grace, but rather grace is manifested through works (James 2:14-26; 1 Thess. 1:3).* But these works are not the product of man's will, but rather they are predicated on the death of the human will, that the will of God may be fulfilled (John 1:12; Eph. 2:8-10; Phil. 2:13). Only when we die to our own will can we enter that rest of God which enables His supernatural works of grace to be poured forth through our lives.

The rest of the commandments dictate the basic forms of all social relationships: the integrity and centrality of the family and particularly of relationships between parents and children, between husband and wife; the proper bounds of relationships among members of the community in general; the protection of property arrangements and of life; and the necessity of respect for truth in regard to our fellowman, which makes all real community possible:

> Honor your father and your mother, so that you may live long in the land Yahweh your God is giving you.
> You shall not murder.
> You shall not commit adultery.
> You shall not steal.
> You shall not give false testimony against your neighbor.
> You shall not covet your neighbor's house. You shall not covet your neighbor's wife, or his manservant or maidservant, his ox or donkey, or anything that belongs to your neighbor. (Exod. 20:12-17)

This last commandment speaks not only about our external relationships but even about our attitudes; so we see God's Word regulating our very inner thoughts and feelings. (We must turn to the Epistles of the New Testament to find the specific patterns of relationships that God has ordained for His Body: for example, 1 Corinthians 12; 14; 1 Timothy 3; 5-6; Titus 2-3; 1 Peter 2-5.) And, of course, Jesus emphasizes the centrality of this internal, root aspect of our attitude in regard to all of the Law (Matt. 22:37-40).

These few sentences of the Ten Commandments, then, pro-

---

* See *Repentance and Faith.*

vide the basic framework for our relationship with God, our fellowman, creation and even with the inner aspects of our own being. Much of Scripture, as we've seen, fits within their framework. They thus provide organic patterns within which a great deal of the fundamental scriptural revelation fits.

2. The *understanding*, or *dialectic*, stage: In this stage, the child comes to clearly realize that he stands in the middle of a spiritual battle, that an adversary exists who attempts to deceive God's people, to tempt them, to cause them to sin against the Lord our God and who stands against the purposes of God in every area of human existence. And on this level, too, the child begins to see more fully how God is assembling the elements of His Word that the child has acquired on the grammar level, putting them together in the child's heart and mind to build up the spiritual temple of his life. At this stage, the child learns to use the sword of truth, to discern good and evil, to tell what is and what is not of God in his daily life. As he begins to understand how to interpret Bible doctrines, the child learns by the contrasts of these conflicts to distinguish between patterns of right and wrong and so on. Through this conflict emerges the firm, established foundation upon which his life in God will stand, not only in this world but also in the world to come. He learns how to apply what he has learned on the grammar stage to his own life as he now enters into a deeper level of relational knowledge. As the child grows older, entering the dialectic stage, he will be able to "rightly divide the word of truth," to understand the Bible's doctrines. He will see how to differentiate Christ-centered interpretations from man-centered heresies. On this level, the child learns God's truth in a more cohesive framework. This enables him to dig to the secure bedrock of truth. (Truth Forum is developing comprehensive teaching materials to guide parents and children through the dialectic of God's Word, to establish God's people in God's truth so they can withstand "every wind of teaching and . . . the cunning and craftiness of men in their deceitful scheming," as they learn to speak "the truth in love, . . . in all things" growing "up into Him who is the Head, that is, Christ," Eph. 4:14-15.) Upon this bedrock, the grace of God can then lay from God's Word the firm foundation for the child's life. With this foundation established, the child will be able to stand secure and to then go on to perfection in his life in the Body of Christ. The child will learn in every situation of his life to use

the sword of truth to differentiate between the will of God on the one hand and the will of the flesh, the confusion of man and the voice of satanic powers on the other.

On the dialectic level, all the individual truths and scriptures that the child has learned on the grammar level come together to form integrated systems and patterns and to become the exciting weapons of a spiritual conflict in which truth emerges from the struggle between competing viewpoints. The student now finds that all of these individual pieces that have been compiled through the years of the grammar stage have a real purpose and meaning (although, of course, we have done everything we could to show him this in the grammar years too and have not simply thrown pieces of Scripture at him in a higgledy-piggledy, slipshod way). He hears views that conflict with what he has learned that the Bible actually says, and he has the excitement of searching out the Scriptures, of recalling the truths that he has learned, of counterposing various interpretations to one another and prayerfully seeking God until His view comes forth clearly.

This dialectic takes place both between the church and the world and between conflicting interpretations within the church that prevent God's people from coming into the "complete unity" that Jesus prayed for (John 17). In a separate study,* we outline the basic principles of the dialectic of understanding God's Word, God's "laws of consistency." By turning to this study and investigating it prayerfully, you will find the basic guidelines that will enable you to establish the truths of God's Word against the conflicting interpretations offered by men. These principles are not abstractions that we apply mechanically. On the contrary, they, like God's Word itself, are meaningless apart from the Spirit of God.† Unless the Spirit reveals and uses these principles, they remain useless to us; but under the anointing of the Spirit, as expressions of the consistent God, they will help us to ourselves become more consistent expressions of God's Word. (Again, Truth Forum is also preparing materials we will use to instruct our children on the truths of God's Word, as counterposed to various imbalanced interpretations of His Word. These materials will be useful for teaching about basic doctrinal truths about God, salvation and

---

* See Truth Forum's *Laws of Consistency: The Oneness of Spirit and Truth* and, for a shorter version, *Right Words.*

† See *The Laws of Consistency* and *Justice Is Fallen.*

the church, as well as in defending the truths of God's Word against the position presented by the secular world.)

As your child enters this dialectic level, a new world of excitement and spiritual power opens to him, and to you too, and all the years of instruction on the grammar level will quickly bear greater fruit than ever before as your child learns to distinguish the true from the false and to conform his life and understanding to the patterns of God's Word.

3. The *wisdom*, or *rhetoric*, stage: In this stage, the individual is able to use the Word of God to take love's offensive, though never in any manner *but* love's humility and meekness. He no longer merely defends himself with the sword of truth. He can now use it to help others, to "make disciples of all nations teaching them to observe all things whatsoever" Christ has "commanded." The individual can now see the unity of the Word of God in relation to the whole of his life. He can use the Word of God to serve the purposes of God. He is not ignorant but wise concerning that which God desires him to accomplish.

We must remember, as we have seen in our earlier example of instruction in writing, that an interplay always exists between the three main levels of learning. For example, a grammar, dialectic and rhetoric development occurs through which we come to know each of the individual foundation stones of God's Word, such as repentance and faith (Heb. 6:1-2). We must first learn the basic "grammar" of repentance and faith; then we must enter into the dialectic through which we struggle to realize them in our lives until we emerge at the rhetoric stage at which our lives actually become the proclamation of their reality. But the rhetoric of each of these individual teachings then becomes the "grammar" level upon which we learn how these individual parts of the foundation work together with the other parts. And this process by which we see how all of the individual stones fit together as the total foundation of our individual lives and of the corporate Body of Christ also takes place through a sequence of grammar, dialectic and rhetoric. The foundations, in turn, become the basis upon which we are further able to build up the whole temple of God that our lives are to become, and in this process, the foundations as a whole become the "grammar" stage of a new sequence of grammar, dialectic and rhetoric. This process only ends when the temples of our individual lives and of the corporate Body of Christ finally come to be fully conformed to His glorious image. This is the goal that we seek, and when it is accomplished, then the "rhetoric" or wisdom level of God's Word will be *fully* realized in our lives because it will at last be fully realized in the life of the corporate Body of Christ as a whole.

Section Two

Subject: *English*

... What a ... presumption it would be to write less
than greatly on a great subject! How blasphemous to be
willing to do so![4]

Wendell Berry
Standing by Words

The Gospel of John tells us that "in the beginning was the
Word," the *logos*. A word, therefore, was the starting point of
all creation. As Genesis and the Psalms recount, God *spoke*
the world into being: His actual words came to be embodied
in physical reality (Gen. 1:9, 11, 20; Ps. 29:3-9). Finally,
through the *Word* of God becoming flesh, God fully manifested
Himself to mankind through the life of Jesus Christ. And
through God's Word He continues today to reach out to
mankind, to transform human lives into the image of Christ, to
restore His dominion over the earth.

Through His Word, then, God creates and re-creates
mankind, expresses His love, brings all things under His
dominion and enters into relationship with His creation. As
human beings, we are made in the image of God, and our
words too become the central means through which we reach
out to and affect the world around us and enter into relationship
with others. As Christians, the words we speak are to be God's
words (1 Cor. 2:13), God's means to reach out to this world
and bring it under the dominion of His Spirit of love. These
words cannot be thrown together in just any haphazard disorder. The Bible tells us that the heavens declare the glory of
God and that daily all of creation pours forth His speech, His
words (Ps. 19:1-2). This creation expresses God through its
majestic order: the cosmos has form and definition, structure
and design that all express the greatness of the Creator. As
living epistles of God, our words too must express His order
and design; they must be fitly framed together, expressions of
His divine order and dominion. So the Christian must learn to
speak and write well if he is to truly fulfill the function for which
God has created and ordained him, that is, set him in order to
perform. As James says, a perfect man will be perfect in
speech (James 3:2); a life ordered according to God's pat-

terns, empowered by His love, will be manifested in well-ordered words of love. Obviously, not everyone has the same gifts and talents in this area, but everyone should develop his gifts in reading, speaking and writing to the fullness of his abilities.

Language is a creation of God, not of man (Gen. 11:7, 9; Exod. 4:11). God made man with a heart and mind that could understand, with a mouth to speak, with hands to write, and He provided man with language as the medium through which understanding could be transmitted. The purpose of language is communication, to bring the speaker and the one being spoken to into oneness ("comm-uni-cation") with one another, into true relationship. (Raymond Williams points out that *communicate* means to "make *common* to many, impart."*[6]) To serve effectively for communication, language must be able to transmit to the reader (or hearer) precisely what the writer (or speaker) intended. Language, in other words, must be able to communicate specific meanings, be they spiritual, intellectual, emotional, practical or whatever.

So language is the vehicle for the transmission of messages. A message is a communication that contains information. In-form-ation is, as we have said, that which *forms* wit*hin* us a particular image. The information that comes to us defines the image to which we will be conformed. For example, a boy raised on a farm will receive one set of information that will form him into a particular image, whereas a boy raised in city slums will receive a very different set of information that will form him into a different image (provided, of course, that the farm boy is not bombarded six hours a day with TV images from the city).

A communication that contains information is an *ordered* communication, as contrasted to noise or static, which is random or disordered confusion. The order or structure of language—its form—enables it to transmit meaning, and this basic order and structure reflect the nature of the God who made it. Without language's formal quality, no one could

---

* As evangelical scholar Carl F. H. Henry has said, "God's creation of man for interpersonal communion anticipated his condescension and initiative in the use of human language as an instrument of divine disclosure. He is God in whose nature the Word eternally inheres, and the Word, active in the creation of the universe and of man in the divine image, became incarnate and inscripturate in human flesh and language."[5]

successfully transmit information: the one receiving the information could never be sure that he truly understood the one giving the information. The form of language therefore provides the means through which the image desired by the source of the information can be formed within the one receiving the information. And only when the source's image is formed within the one who receives the information does true communication become possible. True communication provides the necessary basis of true community (both words having the same root meaning). Since the Body of Christ is the *community* of those who come under submission to God's *communication* to man—God's living Word—so that they may be conformed to His image, it is critically important that those in this Body have dominion over the proper structures and forms of language. As Richard Weaver has said, ". . . Language is suprapersonal, uniting countless minds which somehow stand in relationship to an overruling divinity . . . ."[7] By learning the proper use of language, we come under greater submission to the One who ordained language. These rules of usage form the underlying foundation of style; no style that would communicate clearly the writer's message can violate them.

God gave language to Adam, and at Babel God created the basic language groups (Gen. 2:19-20; 11:9). Notwithstanding their diversity, all languages basically inter-translate according to similar structural rules. While men have formulated these structural rules, these laws of syntax and grammar inhere within the God-ordained languages themselves (many of which have changed greatly down through the ages, but without losing their basic structures). The structures of language correspond to certain thought patterns of the mind and can thus express and inform the human understanding.* If we disregard these God-ordained structures of language, we disrupt rather than facilitate communication; we replace mes-

---

* And these patterns of thought and language also correspond to the God-ordained patterns of the world in general. As Carl F. H. Henry has said, "In the Genesis creation account Adam is represented as naming the animals according to their nature (Gen. 2:19-20). This passage is striking for its suggestion of an inherent relation between logic and life and language. Not only does it imply a connection between reason and reality, but it also supplies hints of a theistic view of language."[8] In other words, the same God has created language, reality in general and the mind of man according to interrelated principles.

sage with noise. This hardly confirms the truth of all rules of grammar and syntax, but insofar as these rules do correspond to the God-given structure of language, our failure to understand them and use them will lead to confusion, whereas our conformity to them will ensure all the advantages of clarity of thought and communication.

So teaching English is more than a matter of teaching rules of grammar and spelling. By imparting to our children the skills through which they can understand what others say and can learn to express themselves clearly, we provide them with the means through which they can think clearly and can come to understand and influence the course of events. As Professor Richard Mitchell has remarked in regard to teaching correct habits of English usage,

> Those who have the habit of correctness and precision can do things by design; those who don't usually have to depend on luck.[9]

When God expressed the world into being through His Word, He did not "depend on luck." He had a design, a purpose, a plan (Prov. 8:22-31); and so should we when we who were made in His image express ourselves. In explaining the relationship between clear language and clear thought Mitchell says:

> Clear, concise writing is a result of good technique, like an engine that starts and runs.
> Good technique requires the knowledge and control of many conventional forms and devices. They must be conventional because writing is public and enduring, and the path of its thought must be visible to other minds in other times . . . .
> . . . You keep your eye on the subject because it *is* the subject, and not just grammatically. It is the subject of thought, and the sentence is a proposition about it . . . . The rules of the technology of discursive prose are simply aids to thought, and to learn the conventions of writing without learning the habit of thought is impossible. (emphasis in original)[10]

Mitchell further remarks:

> People who cannot put strings of sentences together in good order cannot think. An educational system that does not teach the technology of writing is preventing thought.[11]

Though Mitchell's points are well taken, his talk of language "techniques" and "technology" is misleading. Language serves as a natural tool of relationship, and the rules governing it can only be grasped relationally. The attempt to abstract a linguistic "technology" and then teach it abstractly cannot lead to the impartation of a living, relational grasp of language. Techniques and technologies apply to machines, and to see language in this way is to fail to understand fully its living dynamic.

But despite this confusion, Mitchell rightly recognizes the centrality of the correct rules of English usage for our children's education. If we give our children the tools of grammar, spelling, vocabulary and so on, we give them the means through which they can think clearly (we must never teach these rules abstractly, but always in relationship to our children's effort to communicate their thoughts and feelings or to their efforts to help others do this); only if they can think clearly can they truly take dominion over their world for God's purpose. As Richard Weaver said, generally speaking, "students who display the greatest mastery of words," as shown in their knowledge of vocabulary and general ability to express themselves in writing, are most proficient in any subject that they study. In every field of endeavor, "command of language will prognosticate aptitude."[12] Weaver goes on to say, in a remark we quoted before, that

> facility with words bespeaks a capacity to learn relations and grasp concepts; it is a means of access to the complex reality.[13]

While Mitchell stresses clear "discursive prose" as a medium through which one learns to think with "logic, order, and coherence,"[14] Wendell Berry's discussion of clear writing goes beyond this valid point:

> When we reflect that "sentence" means, literally, "a way of thinking" (Latin: *sententia*) and that it comes from the Latin *sentire*, to feel, we realize that the concepts of sentence and sentence structure are not merely grammatical or merely academic—not negligible in any sense. A sentence is both the opportunity and the limit of thought—what we have to think with, and what we have to think in. It is, moreover, a *feelable* thought, a thought that impresses its sense not just on our understanding, but on our hearing, our sense of rhythm and proportion. It is a pattern of felt sense. (emphasis in original)[15]

So Berry concludes that "a sentence that is completely shapeless is therefore a loss of thought, an act of self-abandonment to incoherence." For Berry, clear writing transmits not only clear thinking but also clear feeling as well.[16] This is important not only for the inner coherence of the individual (that is, his proper integration, balance and wholeness in body, soul and spirit, which naturally seek a medium of clear expression) but also because language is the indispensable requisite of clear communication, a communication that involves not merely thoughts but feelings as well.

So our language does not only express our ideas nor only our emotions; it expresses both of these together, and more. For it expresses our inner being, our character, our nature. When they heard Jesus, they declared, "Never man spoke like this!" (John 7:46, KJV). Our words express the depths of our hearts. Hence Jesus' warning that we would be judged by every idle word, for it is out of the abundance of the heart that the mouth speaks (Matt. 12:34, 36, KJV; Matt. 15:18).

We can observe this same principle at work in writing, which, as we will see, numerous secular scholars and writers have discussed as a true disclosure of our inmost being. This disclosure of our inner self is said to be manifested in our writing *style*. Style is not ornament or decoration but the very way that we say something. It is, as *Webster's New World Dictionary* says, the "manner or mode of expression in language," the "way" we use "words to express thoughts."[17]

Style is our "specific or characteristic manner of expression, execution, construction, or design."[18] Even though we all obey (or should obey) the same grammatical rules, our individual character will find distinct expression in our style of writing. So then to speak of style, E. B. White tells us, does not mean someone's command of the rules of grammar, but

> we mean the sound his words make on paper. Every writer, by the way he uses the language, reveals something of his spirit, his habits, his capacities, his bias . . . . Creative writing is communication through revelation—it is the Self escaping into the open. No writer long remains incognito.[19]

In other words, you can say the same thing in many different ways, many of which will be formally correct. But the words, the phrasing, the sentence structure and so on through which we choose to express ourselves does just that—it tells the reader something about ourselves, about our essential nature and character.

In a famous essay called "Politics and the English Language," George Orwell gave us penetrating insight into what style discloses about character through his contrast between a scripture from Ecclesiastes and a typical modern way of saying the same thing. The original scripture, in the King James Version, reads,

> I returned and saw under the sun, that the race is not to the swift, nor the battle to the strong, neither yet bread to the wise, nor yet riches to men of understanding, nor yet favour to men of skill; but time and chance happeneth to them all.[20]

Orwell then gives it to us as a modern academic might,

> Objective consideration of contemporary phenomena compels the conclusion that success or failure in competitive activities exhibits no tendency to be commensurate with innate capacity, but that a considerable element of the unpredictable must invariably be taken into account.[21]

Orwell claims that "this is a parody, but not a very gross one."[22] He continues:

> The beginning and ending of the sentence follow the original meaning fairly closely, but in the middle the concrete illustrations—race, battle, bread—dissolve into the vague phrase "success or failure in competitive activities." This had to be so, because no modern writer of the kind I am discussing—no one capable of using phrases like "objective consideration of contemporary phenomena"—would ever tabulate his thoughts in that precise and detailed way. The whole tendency of modern prose is away from concreteness.[23]

This modern version, in other words, expresses a particular type of thinking, an attitude, a state of mind. This style reveals a mind dulled by abstractions, cut off from life; it indicates a person whose knowledge is not relational but detached. Every time we speak or write in vague abstractions and programmed stock-phrases, we turn ourselves a little bit more into machines. "The appropriate noises" come out of our "larynx" or appear on the page, but our brains do not operate as they would if we had chosen words for ourselves, words that picture and describe that about which we speak (or write).[24] Abstraction and euphemism are the language through which men seek to defend the indefensible. "The murder of unborn children" becomes "termination of unwanted pregnancy." Political regimes jail their opponents for years without trial, shut them in cold, dark, damp cellars or send them to slave camps on the frozen tundra where they die of starvation or scurvy. This is all labeled the *"elimination of unreliable elements."*[25] Writers use such phrases, Orwell says, when they want "to name things without calling up mental pictures of them." He gives the example of a smug professor in England defending Soviet terror. He could never openly say, "I believe in killing off your opponents when you can get good results by doing so." Instead he must babble,

> While freely conceding that the Soviet regime exhibits certain features which the humanitarian may be inclined to deplore, we must, I think, agree that a certain curtailment of the right to political opposition is an unavoidable concomitant of transitional periods, and that the rigors which the Russian people have been called upon to undergo have been amply justified in the sphere of concrete achievement.[26]

These abstract phrases, Orwell explains, fall "upon the facts like soft snow, blurring the outlines and covering up all the details."[27] When believers write this vague and abstract way, this style indicates that we continue to carry with us the baggage of man-centered thinking. When this happens, we look at things from the perspective of our fragmented minds rather than through the wisdom that flows from God's love.

Again, our style expresses what we are really like inside: "The style is you," Katherine Anne Porter said, repeating what she called "one of those unarguable truths":[28]

> Oh, you can cultivate a style, I suppose, if you like. But I should say it remains a cultivated style. It remains artificial and imposed, and I don't think it deceives anyone. A cultivated style would be like a mask. Everybody knows it's a mask, and sooner or later you must show yourself— or at least, you show yourself as someone who could not afford to show himself, and so created something to hide behind. Style is the man . . . . You do not create a style. You work, and develop yourself; your style is an emanation from your own being.[29]

As Paul Valery said,

> What makes the style is not merely the mind applied to a particular action; it is the whole of a living system extended, imprinted and recognizable in expression.[30]

At the end of his classic study, *The Elements of Style*, White explains that

> style takes its final shape more from attitudes of mind than from principles of composition . . . . Style *is* the writer, and therefore what a man is, rather than what he knows [in the objective sense], will at last determine his style. (emphasis in original)[31]

As Llewelyn Powys says:

> . . . Style is the ultimate expression of the author's unique spiritual consciousness.
> Style is the affirmation of a man's heightened awareness of existence and always grows up from within, from out of the marrow of his bones.[32]

Our style of writing, then, is a revelation of our character, of our inner man.

God has ordained us to be vessels through which He would express His truth in love, and to do this perfectly, we must be free from everything within us that hides the truth. Secular writers, when discussing their craft, often speak of the "moral" nature of writing. Donald Hall summarizes the points made by a number of major twentieth-century authors:

> "If a man writes clearly enough any one can see if he fakes," says Hemingway. Orwell reverses the terms: "The great enemy of clear language is insincerity . . . . When there is a gap between one's real and one's declared aims, one turns as it were instinctively to long words and exhausted idioms, like a cuttlefish squirting out ink . . . ."
> As Robert Graves says, "The writing of good English is thus a moral matter." And the morality is a morality of truth-telling. Herbert Read declares that "the only thing that is indispensable for the possession of a good style is personal sincerity." We can agree, but we must add that personal sincerity is not always an easy matter, nor is it always available to the will.[33]

The obligation of the writer, in other words, is to transmit his message in clarity and without any disguises or hindrances. "What gets my interest," Wendell Berry explains, "is the sense that a writer is speaking honestly and fully of what he knows well."[34] When our message comes from God Himself, we clearly have the duty to express this message without any obstructions whatsoever so that the Word of God can go forth in the fullness of its wisdom and power. When we use stereotyped jargon, outworn clichés, pompous and inflated speech, vague and unclear language, passive sentence structure and so on, we disclose something about ourselves. Passivity in language, for example, generally reflects irresponsibility of character, one of the almost universal spiritual plagues of our age: the passive voice eliminates the responsible, active agent—the subject. "The gate was left open," "The jar was broken"—no one bears any responsibility for the deeds that real people do. (The disclosure of character is not confined to style. It's revealed at every stage in our writing in different ways. For example, disorganization of our material, lack of theme and direction in our writing, indicates confusion and lack of direction in our thought and often in our lives.) Use of clichés and stereotyped speech reveals laziness and unwillingness to make the effort to clear out the mental junkyard of used and abused thoughts so we can truly communicate. This further reveals lack of burden and compassion for our fellowman. Our burden must be to express God's Word with clarity. F. L. Lucas asks and answers the question,

> How is clarity to be achieved? Mainly by taking trouble; and by writing *to serve people* rather than to impress them. (emphasis added)[35]

Our greatest problems in writing stem from trying to appear to be something that we're not. Vagueness in writing is an attempt to disguise our thoughts. Pompous and inflated language discloses falseness or pride of character, the attempt to put on false appearances, to exaggerate our feelings, to "dramatize," and therefore trivialize and corrupt truth.

> The lady who speaks of "luncheon" instead of "lunch" is worried about her social status. She gives herself away. Something has gone wrong, and it has gone wrong inside her mind and her emotions.[36]

The Christian writer and scientist, Pascal, expressed his desire to write free from all such affectation when he said,

> When we see a natural style, we are astonished and delighted; for we expected to see an author, and we find a man.[37]

Peter Elbow throws light on this distinction between "author" and "man" when he talks about "real voice" (which is not to be confused with the technical use of the term *voice* in grammar, that is, the active or passive voice). Just as every outer voice arises from physical differences between individuals—

for example, different size chest cavities and so on—and therefore naturally has a distinct sound, so our inner voice resonates uniquely within the differently formed "cavities" of our separate inner beings and so has a distinct "sound." If we try to put on a voice other than our natural one—whether in singing or speaking (including praying)—it sounds unreal and false. We must speak with real voice to sound out authentically to others.[38] In our infancy we can only imitate other men, but eventually the God of Abraham and the God of Isaac must become uniquely the God of Jacob.

The same thing holds true in real voice must stand behind our writing, a voice that expresses the unique being God made of us. He made each person to declare, even to sing, a part of Himself. He delicately crafted each to play distinct notes in His eternal song: He has given everyone a particular spiritual voice. We do not have to contrive our individuality. On the contrary, our greatest labor is to strip away all contrivances. When we strive to manufacture individuality, we destroy it and turn out plastic factory models conformed to the fashions and fads of the passing times. God has already given individuality to us. We need only remove the artificial hindrances thrown up in its way and let the real voice speak through the grace that God pours through us. The fullness of God's song will only resound in its completeness when each of us finds and expresses his true voice. If we forever try to only imitate someone else, then our voice will not ring true.

So God wants each to play his part, not someone else's part, in the song He ordained for us. Writing only rings true when real voice speaks, when we actually express the experienced truth that God has placed in our hearts in our own voice and in our own way. Writing carries real strength when the words seem "to have been spoken by an individual in the grip of feeling as well as in command of ideas and information."[39] Writing comes to life when the writer has "something to say" that counts for him both when he experiences it and when he writes about it. When we care about what we want to communicate and genuinely feel moved by it, this gets into our "words, which then [take] on rhythms that in turn" move the reader.[40] Our words must "fit" us: they must express our God-created (as opposed to our carnal) being. Readers want to hear a real person, not merely a "writer," that is, someone simply trying to impress them. They will listen only to someone who really has something to say, who transmits important information with a real sense of the need to transmit it accurately, vitally and powerfully. (And we only deceive ourselves if we believe that we don't possess such information. On some level, we as believers must possess it; if not, our relationship with God is dead and void.) As we saw, Wendell Berry suggests that readers look for writers who speak from their hearts about things that they really know.[41] The writer must be present in a tangible immediacy in order for the reader to hear his voice; he must not hide behind false appearances or false experience. You must find words that reveal and cast off words that conceal. You must reach out to find the words that express the vision God has given you. The author of Ecclesiastes tells us that he "searched to find just the right words" or, more literally, "to find delightful words and to write words of truth correctly" (Eccles. 12:9-10, NIV, NASV). In contrast, dull and empty words, shallow words that reveal no search, lack the clear, strong accents that speak with living voice; they therefore fail to gain the reader's trust and confidence. Instead, such words create a spiritual vacuum, tearing down the reader's faith in the writer. And worse, if we purport to express the words of God, we tear down the reader's confidence in Him and leave room for the enemy to move into the vacuum created by our spiritual irresponsibility. So when we put words on paper, we must take responsibility for our words. To consent to expend the energy needed to receive the information that the writer offers him, the reader must hear the clear voice of someone he can respect and trust. One award-winning author has even compared reading a book to entering into a covenant.

Peter Elbow illustrates the enormous effort that reading requires when he describes the different ways in which a musician can read the notes of a piece of music. He can merely look at the music technically to see how the different elements work together, but this does not mean that he will make the effort in his heart and mind to actually *hear* the music that he reads. To put together the notes so that he can *hear* in his mind how the music will sound, he must actually expend energy to participate in and experience the music.[42] He must *spend* time and *pay* attention. But if we do not hear the music in this way, it remains lifeless for us and cannot really move us. To receive a written message, someone must consent not merely to hear the phonics of certain letters combined on the page to form certain words, but he must consent to actually participate in those words, to experience them as expressions of the one who writes them. He must, in short, not merely read the score and analyze the elements, but must also hear the music as he reads. The failure to hear explains why people have read instructions on the use of equipment, have even excelled on written tests on what they read, but then go on to follow "the wrong procedure," break the "equipment," forget "the essential step" and so on. They read the words, but not in a way that enables them to put what was written into practice: they "didn't . . . experience" what they read.[43] They could not understand how the machine worked because they refused to actively participate in the instructions. They weren't reading for the sake of relational, participatory knowledge—knowledge that would enable them to perform a function for a purpose—but only for abstract knowledge that would make them look good on an abstract test. They failed to put the words and their meanings together in their minds so that they could effectually see how the machine operated. They did not consent to the importance for their lives of what they read. They did not consent that the words had relevant meaning and did not even care if they did. This is precisely how some people "read" God's Word. Having "eyes to see and ears to hear," they neither see nor hear, because they refuse to participate in these words, to experience them, to enter into living relationship with the "voice," the Spirit that stands behind them. "Consider carefully how you listen," Jesus said. You can only give entrance to God's Word in your heart by actively apprehending it. The Scriptures speak repeatedly of those who "hear" without understanding—who hear, yet they do not hear (Acts 28:26; Matt. 13:14; Isa. 6:9-10; Jer. 5:21; John 8:43-47). Such people refuse to enter into the experience of God when hearing His Word. They refuse to press into that relationship with God that enables them to see with His eyes, hear with His ears, feel with His heart. They decline the opportunity to feel the depth of love and burden from which His words come forth and so they hear mere words or sounds, but they "are unable to hear" what God actually says (John 8:43):

He who *belongs to God* hears what God says. The reason you do not hear is that you do not belong to God. (John 8:47)

Those who did "not hear" heard the sounds of the words that Jesus spoke, but they could not understand what He said because they did not "belong" to God, *in living covenant relationship*, as a Bride belongs to her husband. He did not possess them. Even though they could technically understand His language, His words had no meaning to them. As we've seen, meaning comes through relationship: we understand the meaning of a message by recognizing how things fit together with one another and with the one from whom the message issues forth. Those who heard but could not understand the meaning of Jesus' words refused to enter into that relationship of oneness with Him that would enable them to experience the depth of feeling from which His words came forth. So the words remained mere meaningless sounds to them. These people were like the two native Chinese men who came upon an American traveling through their land. This American spoke fluent Chinese and asked them directions in their language. Yet they simply stared at him in disbelief and walked away laughing. As they went off, the American heard them asking each other if it didn't sound just as if that American had asked directions in perfect Chinese, even repeating verbatim what he had in fact inquired of them.[44] They heard the sounds he spoke, they even understood that those sounds had meaning, but they refused to consent to the meaning of *his* words. They refused to trust that his words meant exactly what they seemed to mean. They refused to participate in his speech, because they were too arrogant to believe that an American could actually speak their language. So they had no faith that the sounds that came to them had meaning for them.

To actively participate in the way that brings real understanding, you must trust the person whose words you read or hear, even to the point of giving yourself to his words, participating in them until they become part of your own experience. You must actively enter into the works and words of the one whom you seek to know. It is a matter of faith, this covenant between readers and writers. You can stare blankly at a painting—even for a long time—and perhaps vaguely sense that you might have seen some sort of a building, and then look away without ever having experienced what you have seen. Perhaps you are disturbed by important concerns; perhaps you're simply lazy. But whatever keeps you from participating, unless you look with the eyes of the artist and actively seek to reconstruct what he saw and felt and portrayed on the canvas, you can never truly appreciate his painting. You must see more than a building. The building must become what the artist painted—a farmhouse in a field or an office building in a city. You must see the wooden shingles and homespun cotton curtains in the windows or the sheets of glass and steel. If it is a farmhouse, look closer and perhaps you'll see through a window a girl washing dishes. Perhaps off to the side you'll see a lone figure in a straw hat scything in the field. Without active participation, you missed everything, but now the meaning of what you see comes alive as you recognize what the artist reveals through the interplay of the elements of his painting. Before, you simply saw a picture of perhaps a building, an object hung on a wall, suspended in space. Now you see set before you in the details the painter has set on canvas a way of life and a sense of life, a design of color, form, value patterns and so on that convey mood and feeling. You recreate within yourself the painter's experience of that farmhouse, and a whole complex of lives and scene and action comes alive for you. The painting hasn't changed. What's changed is your active participation. The picture has come alive for you now, because you've poured your own life into it. It now has value for you, because you paid the price, you paid attention.

Our experience of anything depends upon just such participation. We can be physically present at an event or place but oblivious to both the event and our surroundings. The more we give ourselves to something, the more we pour ourselves into seeing what someone shows us, hearing what they say to us, doing what they tell us to do, and so the more completely shall we conform ourselves to the image they desire for us. To participate in the words someone speaks to us, we must even trust the reasons why he speaks these words to us. We must believe that his words are relevant as well as true and important, or else what he says will merely constitute sounds bouncing off our eardrums or letters reflecting off our eyes. And then we will not allow the words to penetrate our deepest heart.

So the reader of printed words must expend mental and spiritual energy to hear what the writer has to say in a living way, to hear the "music" of his words. Again, to put forth this effort, the reader must trust the writer; for, as has been said, everyone who opens a book and sticks with it has entered a covenant with its author. As we've seen, the reader must let the writer into his heart and mind, but he won't do so if he suspects the writer of manipulating him in any way—through sentimentality, clichés or some other artificial device. (Of course, there are magicians with words who, through their sleight of hand, "trick" the reader into a "suspension of unbelief.") Such writing destroys, or should destroy, your reader's confidence: for example, through your sentimentality he feels that you feed him false emotions, trying to play on his feelings and elicit responses from him that the content you describe fails to warrant; through your clichés he suspects, perhaps only unconsciously, your shallow concern for your subject, and so refuses to pour himself out in reading your writing. Usually, the reader must feel the integrity of the writer's character expressed in his words. This doesn't mean trying to put "personality" into the words. It means being honest, transparent, true to the message that one transmits. It means, to again quote Peter Elbow, "breathing experience"—*our own* lived experience—into what we write.[45] If we contrive this, we stifle real voice. We must experience what we write about and then honestly express what we see and feel (1 John 1:1-4). We must participate in the reality we try to communicate; otherwise the reader will never feel the power of real voice behind the empty form of words. Again, we must write "honestly and fully . . . of what" we *know* "well"—know in the Judaic sense of experiential relationship. As we've shown, the type of knowledge that has real meaning for the reader's life is not the objective, abstract, intellectual knowledge of the detached mind, but rather the experiential knowledge that comes from a living relationship between the person who writes and what he writes about.* Real voice, then, is the basis of valid *rhetoric*, which is, as we've seen, writing (or speaking) that moves men to action. Effective rhetoric stimulates the reader's desire to participate, to throw himself into the writing. It encourages him to open himself up, to listen and then to agree, to bring himself into oneness with the word that he reads. It culminates in bringing forth that total agreement that leads to action. For all this to happen openly and forthrightly in light and truth (and not through manipulation), real voice must ring from every part of a writing.

---

* See *Right Words* and *Salvation Is of the Jews.*

For the reader to hear "music" in the writer's words, music must be present to be heard. And in order to sing God's song through our writing, we must experience His music. The Elizabethan composer William Byrd explained "that the right *notes* would come without effort to a composer of religious music who succeeded in wholly fastening his mind upon the divine subject."[46] If we will fasten our hearts and minds upon Jesus—upon His experienced love, His experienced reality, His experienced revelation—then words to express His reality will come to us. We must fix our attention upon the subject that we want to communicate rather than upon ourselves or the way we will communicate it. The form will follow and adapt to the nature of the content, but first some content must stand behind the form that reveals it. So we must enter into that living relationship with the Composer of the song, so that He can breathe His spiritual words through us onto the page. After we have placed this inspired word down upon paper, then we can go over what we have written and shape it into that form of grammar, syntax and so on consistent with the content of what we have experienced. This shaping process makes God's message clear to the reader. When we do this, we must learn about various rules of writing. But those rules always remain secondary and important only insofar as they help us to communicate. First and foremost, we must find the "real voice" that God has given us, the voice that enables us to speak the living Word that God has destined to express through us. If we have this, everything else will fall into place. If we don't have it, then all our efforts will prove vain and wasted. As we've said, to find this voice we need not invent anything; on the contrary, we must resurrect from dead inventions (our own or those imposed on us by our peers or by the times in which we live) what God made us to be. To "be ourselves" in this way requires that we allow God's grace to strip us of all contrived exteriors that have shaped us in their twisted images. Then we must open our hearts to the grace that makes us truly transparent. When we become transparent to Him, He breathes forth the notes of His song through us. Our words then flow in the unction of vibrating Spirit. Our voice becomes His voice, expressing some unique facet of His nature through our own lives.

For this reason, when we find our true voice in God, something powerful and real happens, something that the rational mind cannot understand or explain. Others who read such words hear that genuine voice that stands behind them; and because they sense a transparent openness, they open their own hearts to our words. Because our words "fit" us, as God made us to be, they also fit the reader, at least the one tuned in to the score of the same Composer.

Many have spoken of this as "resonance." We too spoke of this earlier when we mentioned the song of Yahweh: we see resonance when we place one violin next to another and pluck a string on one and the corresponding string on the second violin hums in sympathy. When someone finds his real voice in the song of Yahweh, then those chords resonate in the heart of each of those who also seeks (albeit perhaps unknowingly) to play his part in that same song. The voice of God goes forth, vibrating on and in others as they tremble in harmony with His Word.

The style we must aim for, then, is the one that will express our real voice, for style is nothing but the relationship between form and content; to use the right style means to find the appropriate way to express the message we want to share. Cyril Connolly explains "style" as

the relation between what a writer wants to say, his subject—and himself—or the powers which he has: between the form of his subject and the content of his parts.[47]

Our "style" is the way we use language to convey our feelings and ideas. "The perfect use of language," that is, the perfect style, "is that in which every word carries the meaning that it is intended to, no less and no more."[48] This undoubtedly is at least part of what James meant when he said, "If anyone is never at fault in what he says, he is a perfect man, able to keep his whole body in check" (James 3:2).

The form through which we express ourselves should accurately convey the information we want to communicate. If we try to make our "language convey more than" we "mean or more than" we "feel," we become pompous, artificial, even fake.[49] Our yes is not yes nor our no, no. And whatsoever is more than this is evil (Deut. 4:2; Matt. 5:37).

Where the content is less than the form, where the author pretends to emotion which he does not feel, the language will seem flamboyant. The more ignorant a writer feels, the more artificial becomes his style . . . . An author arrives at a good style when his language performs what is required of it without shyness.[50]

Samuel Butler emphasized that the writer should take no "thought for his style," but that it "should be like his dress—it should attract as little attention as possible."[51]

Style is not, in the first place, a matter of technique. It is above all a matter of viewpoint. "You will have a style when you have developed your own point of view."[52] E. B. White said that the "whole problem" in writing "is to establish communication with one's self, and, that being done, everyone else is tuned in. In other words, if a writer succeeds in communicating with a reader, I think it is simply because he has been trying (with some success) to get in touch with himself—to clarify the reception."[53] (Of course, as believers our goal in "getting in touch" with ourselves is to clear away the debris that keeps us from getting in touch with the true source of everything worth knowing and communicating.) Thoreau said that one's style was simply a matter of having something to say: ". . . if one has anything to say, it drops from him simply and directly, as a stone falls to the ground. There are no two ways about it, but down it comes, and he may stick in the points and stops wherever he can get a chance."[54]

Effective style doesn't come because we concentrate on the way we write, but rather because we concentrate on what we want to convey. As scientist-philosopher Michael Polanyi points out, when someone hammers a nail, he doesn't concentrate on how the hammer feels in his hand, but on hitting the nail. If he does concentrate on the feel of the hammer, he will likely miss the nail and hit his thumb.[55] In Polanyi's terms, work requires both a focal and a tacit knowledge: to hit the nail, you must hold the hammer right, but you don't concentrate on this knowledge when you do the work: that's tacit knowledge, not focal knowledge—not the focus of your attention. The focus of your attention should be the job you're trying to get done. When a blind man uses a walking stick, he doesn't concentrate on the feel of the stick in his palm, but on the feel of the stick at its point of contact with the ground. He must handle the stick properly, but this is tacit knowledge. If he concentrates on the feeling of the stick in his palm, he will soon stumble. Again, he must focus his attention on the feel of the stick moving along the ground.

In writing too, we must concentrate on what we want to say, not on the way that we say it. We must have some familiarity with the proper rules of grammar, syntax, vocabulary and so on, but if we concentrate on our word use, we'll hit our thumbs or stumble. If we keep our attention focused on the nail, on what needs to be conveyed to the reader, then everything else will (with practice and work, of course) fall into place. If, as Mitchell says, we keep our eye on the subject we write about—and on the reader's need to receive this knowledge—we will bring forth an accurate match between form and content. Our writing will tend toward conciseness, which brings power: conciseness brings restraint, and restraint compresses energy for the sake of impact. The power of that impact is proportional to the conciseness. If we keep our eyes on ourselves, our language will be dull: our inflated, then punctured, words will flaccidly smother the brain of the dazed and bored reader. The more we free ourselves from self-centeredness, the more we free God to express Himself through us.

When we free our style from falsehood and obscurity, then, we make it more powerful. But how can we find this freedom? Donald Hall echoes the scriptural truth that our falsehoods may be hidden even from ourselves. He then suggests to us that "analysis of one's own style . . . can be a test of one's own feelings. And certainly, many habits of bad style are bad habits of thinking as well as of feeling."[56] Precisely because style *is* an expression of our true character, the examination of our writing can provide a means for recognizing the hidden secrets of the heart and the hidden obscurities of the mind. White urges the writer to "approach style warily, realizing that it is himself he is approaching, no other."[57] Since the style reveals the man, the examination of style can be a vehicle through which the light of God can shine into our inner being, reveal our sin and lead to that repentance that will set us free from our sin.

Donald Hall believes that

> a writer of bad prose, to become a writer of good prose, must alter his character . . . . There must be no gap between expression and meaning, between real and declared aims. For some people, some of the time, this simply means *not* telling deliberate lies. For most people, it means learning when they are lying and when they are not. It means learning the real names of their feelings. It means not saying or thinking, "I didn't *mean* to hurt your feelings," when there really existed a desire to hurt. . . .
> The style is the man, and the man can change himself

by changing his style. Prose style is the way you think and the way you understand what you feel. Frequently, we feel for one another a mixture of strong love and strong hate; if we call it love and disguise the hate to ourselves by sentimentalizing over love, we are thinking and feeling badly. (emphasis in original)[58]

In fact, however, no one can by his own power alter his own character. Nor can we validly assert, if style is the *expression* of the man, that the man can change himself by changing his style: the man must change, and then the style will change. But when we examine problems in our writing style, God can reveal to us our inner problems as well. Then *He* can give us the grace to change, to repent. As He changes us, we become clear and transparent channels through which God expresses His truth: the style is the man, and as God changes the man, the man's style will change. Hall correctly says that it does no good to disguise from ourselves our evil feelings; but honesty does not end when we acknowledge the evil within us. It only begins there. It ends when we have successfully sought the God who will cleanse our hearts and fill us with His love and truth. Many stop at the negative destruction of dishonesty but never find the positive voice of honesty. They're content to expose the dishonest. They become cynical, bitter or at least negative and pessimistic. Their highest virtue is in resignation and stoicism. But they refuse the challenge of that high path that seeks the *positive* voice of the true and the good without the false ring of sentimentality or platitude. In fact, within ourselves we cannot really even be honest. We need God to turn on a greater light that reveals "the real names of" our "feelings," the same God who can transform our inner being to conform to His image. When every word works perfectly to express our God-given thoughts and feelings, our language will be perfect, and, again, James tells us that the one who is faultless in his speech, the same is a perfect man (James 3:2). And Jesus said, "Be ye perfect even as I am perfect."

As we said, this is also the same God who gave us the valid forms and structures of language to begin with, the same God who determines which styles ring with truth and which do not. When we examine our writing in the light of the God-ordained forms and structures of language, God reveals the disparity between our use of words and His ideal for their use. This disparity, as we have explained, in turn reveals weaknesses in our own character. Again, if we step into this penetrating light, God will transform our character and our style of writing as well. Pomposity, clichés and obscurity will give way to simplicity, vividness and clarity in our writing as these same characteristics emerge in our lives. The God who has expressed His nature through His written word can use our written words to lay bare our own natures as He exposes and refines us until our words are transparent vehicles that express His love. Our words express His Word as our lives become His living epistles, written by His hand. Since our writing exposes us and makes us vulnerable, it will at times be a very personal, painful process. But if we continue to step forth in faith, if we seek to find and express our real voice, the rewards will come. A new violin, Peter Elbow points out, is stiff, resonating fully only with a few notes.[59] But the more it is played, the more flexible it becomes and the more notes it will resonate—playing it breaks it in. Like a violin, we too must be "played" or broken in. As we learn, from both our mistakes and successes, we will finally become fully resonant with our part in Yahweh's song. We will find our real voice and fully express the notes of the song He gives us to sing. We will find our place within His eternal symphony.

This brings up a critically important point that derives from the sensitive, self-revealing activity that constitutes writing. We must take care not to destroy our child's desire to write by constantly picking at technical faults and problems, especially in the early years. Instruction in writing primarily serves, as we said, to help our child learn to first find and then write with his real voice—that he be honest and open, that he sincerely seek to express his real identity *in God* and work to fully and truly communicate to others his genuine experience in God. When he learned how to speak, we sincerely and enthusiastically praised his beginning efforts no matter how technically crude—even to the point of unintelligibility in the first stages —they might be. When he said "wark" instead of "rock," we joyfully encouraged him. In the same way, we must wholeheartedly encourage all our child's efforts to genuinely write from his heart, to express his thoughts and feelings in God. At this stage, the sharp critical edge should be brought to bear against insincerity and falseness—against content and not form—in writing. Only when your child has really begun to write consistently with his real voice—and only God's Spirit can show you when he attains to this—should you start to focus in on instruction concerning grammatical faults (although, of course, you will be teaching grammar rules from the beginning). But even on his more advanced levels of writing, our emphasis must continue to be upon helping our child to express the real voice God has given to him.* But form must eventually come, for though when we were children we spoke as children, when we became men we put away childish things (1 Cor. 13:11).

God has given each of us this real voice so that He can speak through us. Nothing false resides in God. If we are false we cannot express His reality. God has made us to be in His image, awakened human forms of dust to express His love. We chose to allow that image to infall within ourselves, turning the light of the real into the darkness of the false. But with His Spirit He has now pulled light out of our darkness. Now our very words must become formal expressions through which God can communicate His love and reality through us to our fellowman. When language loses its "shape," that is, its form, then it loses its meaning, its underlying sense and significance, and it ceases to be an instrument of true communication, becoming instead an instrument of manipulation. As Weaver has said, "Language is a system of forms," forms that, as we have seen, necessarily correlate to meaning and purpose. Words themselves are tied to an underlying sense and significance, or, in Weaver's terms, "inclination or intention."[60] Words are meant to be intertwined with their meanings, with implications and senses that go beyond the "objective" analysis of the individual words themselves. Only within the context of their living origins, their historical roots, associations and relationships to other words (relationships that are governed by forms) does the true meaning of words become known. When the "form" of language dissolves, Weaver points out, "inclination" is also destroyed, leaving room for "a scientific manipulation."[61] In other words, if the underlying sense of words falls away, if the forms that bind a word to its origins and to other words collapse, words come to suspend in a type of bureaucratic soup in which they lose their concrete significance. When the form of language dissolves, meaning also

---

* Because of the special importance of this area of instruction, as part of our total curriculum, we have produced a special writing program based on the principles we've laid out in this book and especially in this section. See *Right Words* and *Guidelines for Teaching Your Children Writing at Home.*

dissolves. Men can then mislead us into thinking that we understand the meaning of their words as we consent to them, when in fact we agree to something quite different from what we suppose. But the problems go beyond even this. Precisely because words themselves do have historical roots that we feel and sense (though often we do not fully understand at a conscious level), they can bind us to others who share a sense of identification with these same roots. But when the words disconnect from their historical roots and receive new, abstract meanings, they instead become means for uprooting us from our origins and from meaningful community relationships. As these new abstract, lifeless words bombard us, we lose our sense of direction and purpose as the landmarks of the concrete collapse into the abstract rubble around us. Separated from where we have been, we have no sense of where we should go, and so we become malleable instruments of manipulation, usually and ultimately by the State.

An excellent example is the word *people*, as in "We the people." "The people" no longer means a concrete or specific community, or even various such communities, each with a particular heritage, tradition, way of life and so on. Instead, it becomes merely an abstract mass of individuals whose only common connection becomes their common subordination to the State's authority. "The people" in the former sense is a counterbalance to State manipulation; in the latter sense it becomes the necessary prerequisite of such manipulation. In this regard, philosopher William Barrett contrasts the views of the French Revolutionary intellectuals of the late eighteenth century to that of the contemporary British conservative Edmund Burke. Burke, Barrett tells us,

> happened to be an uncommonly sharp [observer], and he was in a privileged position to notice the advent of this new breed of mankind—the modern intellectual. These Frenchmen whom he observes were literary intellectuals and they loved large and sweeping abstractions, often without regard to the complex interworking of the very prosaic details that make social life at all possible. They spoke, for example, of something they called The People . . . . How they loved The People! But Burke, as an experienced parliamentarian who had been active on many bills of legislation, knew there was no such thing at all as The People: there was only a multitude of concrete groups, farriers, weavers, farmers, merchants, with

sometimes quite conflicting interests, which had to be balanced and reconciled somehow or other into the actual working of society. As soon as you have replaced this concrete plurality by the abstraction of The People, you have homogenized it into the Mass—a plastic and passive dough to be kneaded at will by the Dictator. You have taken the first step toward Gulag.[62]

This separation of words from their underlying associations, from their relationships and roots, from their "intentional meaning," supposedly serves to remove all grounds for conflict. Obviously, if "the people" means specific groups of individuals with particular traditions and particular heritages, one group of "the people" can counterpose other groups of "the people" who have different traditions and heritages. If we remove from this term these associations, some would argue, we remove the grounds for conflict. But we cannot completely disassociate this word—or any other—from some set of meanings and assumptions. If we pretend to divorce the word from its "intentional meaning," we have merely disguised the conflict, assumed one particular meaning of the term to be the only valid one. Words by their very nature tie themselves to tendencies, that is, to intentional meanings, and we cannot divorce the two except by entering into a self-hypnotic stupor through which we simply acquiesce to whatever mumbo jumbo is brought to bear against us. In the case of our example, the reduction of "the people" to a monolithic mass to be controlled by the State is not the resolution but the provocation of conflict. As Weaver has said:

> Since language expresses tendency, and tendency has direction, those who differ over tendency can remain at harmony only in two ways: (1) by developing a complacency which makes possible the ignoring of contradictions and (2) by referring to first principles, which will finally remove the difference at the expense of one side. If truth exists and is attainable by man, it is not to be expected that there will be unison among those who have different degrees of it . . . . I see no reason to doubt that here is the meaning of the verses in Scripture: "Suppose ye that I am come to give peace on earth? I tell you, Nay; but rather division" and "I bring not peace, but a sword." It was the mission of the prophet to bring a metaphysical sword among men which has been dividing them ever since, with a division that affirms value. But amid this division there can be charity, and charity is more to be

relied on to prevent violence than are the political neofanaticisms of which our age is signally productive.[63]

Any attempt to obscure the true meaning of words, to break down the form of language, to dissolve the relationships that bind together words with their origins and implications, not only destroys communication but also destroys the truth, which alone gives communication its significance.

Berry stresses the following preconditions for clear communication. First, language "must designate its object precisely." Second, "its speaker must stand by it: must believe it, be accountable for it, be willing to act on it." And third, "this relation of speaker, word, and object must be conventional; the community must know what it is."[64] So language must be based upon clear and commonly known rules and definitions. Not only that, but it must be based upon the character of the speaker: "We assume, in short, that language is communal, and that *its purpose is to tell the truth*," the truth being essential to true relationship.[65] While, as Berry says, "these common assumptions are becoming increasingly uncommon,"[66] it is our responsibility to be sure that our children learn and properly use "the structures of language and the meanings of words" that they will need in order to communicate clearly.[67] This is one reason why we cannot submit ourselves to the nonstandards of public education, that increasingly ignore such structures and meanings.* And we must also recognize that the function of language, to communicate *truth*, cannot be separated from the One who declares Himself *to be the Truth*. The importance of speaking correctly in this sense especially is implicit in our previously-referred-to scripture from James, "If anyone is never at fault in what he says, he is a perfect man, able to keep his whole body in check" (James 3:2). Proper discourse proves itself an essential discipline for the *whole* man: our children must master it both for their own sakes and for the sake of the world to which God desires to speak through them.

We cannot communicate the content of truth without the form of truth. For this reason grammar and punctuation take on heightened significance. They constitute the form within which communication becomes possible. We can see the importance of this by returning again to the example of a song.

---

* See *The Crime of Compulsory Education*.

Punctuation and grammar compare to the notes and the rhythms of the song. Even though punctuation marks are very little things, they enable us to recognize the distinctions and divisions that make what we try to communicate intelligible. Imagine if notes are missing from a song, if the notes are run together instead of being played distinctly and so on. All of these things may appear small matters, but it will prove difficult, if not impossible, to discern the song if these problems persist. Rudolf Flesch says:

> . . . Punctuation, to most people, is a set of arbitrary and rather silly rules you find in printers' style books and in the back pages of school grammars. Few people realize that it is the most important single device for making things easier to read.[68]

Carl Markgraf amens this when he says, ". . . Punctuation marks are . . . the signposts we all use in finding our way through the written word to the meaning behind it."[69] So "how you punctuate can make a big difference in whether or not you communicate the meaning you intended."[70]

When we learn punctuation, we do not simply try to memorize rules and apply them mechanically. We write for a purpose: to communicate God's truth in God's Spirit. Out of this burden and desire, we develop an ear for what most easily communicates to people, just as someone develops an ear for music. When we have developed that ear, then the forms and rules of grammar and punctuation will come to us according to their proper usage. If we simply mechanically memorize the rules and attempt to apply them in computerlike fashion, we will find ourselves losing the mental "file" that holds our grammatical information just when we need it.

Through instruction in the English language, then, we seek to impart to our children the ability to clearly communicate, in both writing and speaking, their thoughts and feelings (and ultimately and more importantly, God's thoughts and feelings). Again, as we learn to speak and write clearly, we also learn to think clearly. (And we have seen that we can only develop these abilities as we also undergo spiritual changes in our lives.)

As we explained earlier, in learning to develop any skill or ability—in this case, clarity of written and spoken expression—an overlapping takes place on the grammar, dialectic and rhetoric levels, the rhetoric of one level providing the grammar of the next level and so on.

For example, in speaking, a child must learn how to present a single thought, idea or fact clearly; this could be seen as a grammar level of making himself understood. On the grammar level, the child would learn to explain why George Washington was willing to risk his wealth and status, even his life, in a cause that appeared to many to be a hopeless rebellion. (This subject could come forth in the context of a discussion in which the child confronts the question of resistance to unjust laws in our own day.) On this level the child learns to express clearly a single point, for example, Washington's love of liberty or his belief that Britain had violated her traditional obligations to, or overstepped her rightful authority in, the American colonies.

The next, dialectic, level, could be seen as the process of engaging in a discussion. To carry our example further, the child on this level would be able to express the various questions raised by Washington's actions. For example, what values could be counterposed to liberty, and which of these values (liberty or some other) should rightfully prevail in motivating men to action? Or who had right on their side and to what degree: the British, the Americans, both, neither? Even if the Americans were right, should they, from a Christian perspective, have taken up arms in defense of their cause? If they should not have taken up arms, did the conflict nevertheless conform to God's purpose? If so, how can something that is at least in some ways against God's will conform to His will? On the dialectic level, the child learns to engage in a discussion of such questions as these, considering various points of view and at least understanding what the central questions are.

The third, rhetoric, level, could be seen as the level upon which the student learns to provide a full presentation on a particular subject. In the case of our example, this would involve the ability to present the issues involved in Washington's actions, explaining his motives and views, assessing those motives and views against the central objections, and then arriving at some conclusion as to whether and to what extent Washington's actions were correct. (As we suggested above, the goal of this presentation would be to guide and shape the actions of men who feel themselves today to be in similar circumstances to those of Washington.) And even such a rhetoric-level presentation can be given on various levels of

complexity (the same could also be said of the single statement of the grammar level or the discussion of the dialectic
level in our example concerning Washington), and these too
must develop through a grammar, dialectic and rhetoric level
as they move through deeper levels of complexity and depth.

Within the family, discussion situations can be encouraged;
in the context of a Christian community, special classes can
be held, for example, for such subjects as history and science,
which will present an opportunity for discussions and offer the
opportunity for presentations by the students. Again, however,
the point is not simply to set up some abstract discussion format and "have a discussion," but to seek the Spirit of God, to
flow with the *real* questions and problems that are related to,
have relevance and meaning for, our lives and our children's
lives, and to pursue the study, investigation and discussion of
these subjects in the Spirit. In these times of controversy in
which we live, too many real questions demand real answers,
questions like abortion and so on, to have to spend time looking for things to discuss. Certainly, as we said, historical
questions, such as that in our example given above, have
direct relevance to real questions in our day too and must be
discussed in that relational context. (In our Koinonia Curriculum, the Bible-based readers and the Grammar and
Dialectic Synopses described in Supplement One will serve
as excellent springboards for fruitful discussions.)

The *grammar*, or *knowledge*, level of language instruction
obviously involves first phonics, learning the basics of reading
and also the basics of writing, beginning with the alphabet, and
then going on to grammar, learning the basic rules of language, including such things as punctuation, capitalization,
the parts of speech and so on. This learning on the "grammar"
level also involves various levels of development: first learning
the basic rules and then learning the first steps in how to use
them to express one's thoughts clearly. (See Supplement One
for a description of our phonics/reading/spelling program.)

The *dialectic*, or *understanding*, level involves learning how
to detect false arguments, not falling into the confusion of
presenting false arguments and generally discerning truth
from falsehood through contrasts and distinctions. (Truth
Forum is in the process of developing materials for study on
this level, both in English generally and also in other related
subjects, particularly history, science and, as we have said,

the Bible.) Again, such principles cannot be developed or applied abstractly but only relationally, created and applied by Him who is the living Spirit of Truth. These rules have no meaning as abstractions but only as applied in specific circumstances, and only the Spirit can do that.* On the dialectic level, the student learns to discern the meaning of things, to understand and to detect valid and invalid reasoning. He also learns to detect whether a given subject can even legitimately be considered to lie within the proper province of man's finite reasoning and if so, to what extent. A number of books are available, such as *A Dictionary of Modern English Usage*, by H. W. Fowler, which can be used to a limited extent to find the various fallacies of reasoning simply defined. These include such fallacies as begging the question, *non sequiturs, ad hominem* arguments and so on. (In our book *Right Words*, we define and discuss the key fallacies.) As he comes to understand the correct rules of legitimate reasoning (which, again, cannot be abstracted from the Spirit, who enables us to understand the relationships between things and therefore the meanings and applications of these rules), the student can find when false reasoning is being presented in defense of a particular argument or position. We hope to develop anthologies that will help the student to understand correct, God-centered reasoning and to develop the Spirit-directed skills that will enable him to recognize invalid reasoning.

Some examples will help us to see how to approach this task of detecting false reasoning. We take our examples of confused reasoning from a college textbook that, ironically, purports to give us a guide to clarity in reasoning. The writers tell us that

> rationalizers (as distinct from reasoners) are people who invent reasons for believing what they already believe or what they want to believe.[71]

Presumably, then, the men who wrote these words eschew rationalizing and therefore will not "invent reasons for believing what they . . . want to believe." But what does it mean to "invent reasons"? Do they mean fabricating falsehoods? Or do they mean organizing knowledge according to presuppositions? If they mean the latter, then abundant evidence testifies that everyone always does this; as we have shown, leading

---

* See *Justice Is Fallen*.

philosophers and scientists, secular and Christian, have
demonstrated this conclusively.* If that is so, the attempt to
present others as inventing reasons to "believe . . . what
they want to," in contrast to one's own self-vaunted freedom
from all preconceptions, itself becomes a classic case of
rationalization. At the very least these authors have surely
failed to offer us any "reasons" for believing their initial claim.
No warrant or evidence, which they say is essential to reasoning as distinct from rationalizing, is given. So we must presume
that in their most basic assertion they have failed to meet their
own criterion for "reasoning" and have merely begged the
question. The authors have in fact so completely rationalized
their own presuppositions that they remain totally unaware
that they have done so.

They further reveal their presuppositions as they continue to
instruct us in clear thinking. To see how their presuppositions
break through the surface in compound fractures of their ostensibly valid forms for clear reasoning, we must first peel back
the pretty outer garments of valid reasoning that cover the
fracture. They tell us that valid reasoning entails a three-step
progression: (1) claim, (2) warrant and (3) evidence. "The
claim," they say, "is the proposition to be proved"; "the warrant" links the proposition and the evidence; "the evidence"
provides the reason to accept the claim.[72] In the claim, we
make an assertion, for example, that the earth is round. The
warrant tells us what we would have to prove to show that our
claim is true, for example, that someone setting out from a
point and heading in one direction would return to the point
from which he started from the opposite direction. The
evidence offers proof that this really happened, for example,
that Magellan's ships set sail toward the west and returned to
Europe from the east.

So far, so good. But after giving us this lucid, though limited,
description of the reasoning process, the writers now proceed
to fracture the rules they have just taught us. First, a sample
of their reasoning, and then we will show its fallacies:

> Most of us have a fair working sense of what is good
> evidence and what is not. At a high school rap session a
> student says, "If Paula wants to be an airline stewardess,
> why should she take algebra . . . ?" If we can assume

* See "Two Ways of Knowing" in chapter 2 and also *Justice Is Fallen* for
exhaustive substantiation of this point.

that Paula has found her vocation at sixteen and will have time for nothing but her job and her social life until she dies, the answer is "Why indeed?" But unless we make these silly assumptions, the implied equating of training with education—of a job with a life—is kid stuff [*sic*]. Even in strictly vocational terms the argument is no good: if Paula doesn't make it as a stewardess, she may well find a little algebra handy in some other job. In short, the questioner's "evidence" is mere rhetoric [*sic*].[73]

But where are the writers' "warrant" and "evidence" to support their claims? They more than imply that Paula needs to learn algebra, but why? How does it follow from the obvious fact that her life will not be wholly occupied in "her job and her social life" that she will therefore need algebra? And how does it follow that if she does not work as an airline stewardess, she will therefore find a job that requires algebra? Anyone could use these same assertions to "prove" that Paula should be compelled to learn any subject anyone might choose for her to learn. These points prove nothing; they are "mere rhetoric" (according to these authors' faulty understanding of this term). The authors would also be hard pressed to provide "warrant" or "evidence" that the absence of algebra has voided the validity of a person's education, a "claim" they tacitly make.

For a student on the dialectical level, a series of pointed questions could help him see clearly the mangled brokenness of these writers' arguments. For example, what is the name of the fallacy of which the authors are guilty when speaking of the view they oppose as having "silly assumptions"? (Answer: *ad hominem* argument.) What is an *ad hominem* argument? What does "kid stuff" mean? How is this phrase used by the authors here? Could these authors' "arguments" be characterized as sophomoric? What does this mean? Have they come full circle to "kid stuff"?

The authors next inform us that

there are many other logical fallacies, from equivocation to false analogy, some of which we shall discuss later. But at the heart of all these fallacies is one primary error: the misuse of evidence. Either no evidence at all is advanced, as in the claim that pizza tastes better than hamburgers, or "facts" are set forth, as by Paula's champion, that do not logically support the writer's argument and thus remain mere facts or information, not evidence.[74]

Here the authors specify two possible forms of misuse of

evidence, and we may simply ask the student whether these writers have committed either or both of these misuses in their preceding example. If they have committed any of these errors, in what way have they done so? We could also ask the student whether his personal experience or any statistical evidence bears out the writers' view that most people like Paula find a significant amount of time in between graduation and death to work algebra problems. We might ask the student whether this belief might itself properly be called inane and unrealistic, that is, "kid stuff."

Of course, the authors might want to look for employment in some work that requires algebra if they lost their present jobs, but this gives us neither warrant nor evidence about Paula—in fact, by their own standards, they don't even present an argument. They simply like the idea of girls learning algebra rather than, say, sewing. But their argument then is simply a rationalization for their (presumably feminist) presuppositions.* Given their penchant for rationalization, we do not find it surprising that for these writers, as for so many in our day, the word *rhetoric* becomes a term of abuse. Incapable of skillfully applying rhetoric themselves, they confuse it with sophistry, that is, their own invalid form of argument. (Ironically, these authors, whose book largely centers on questions of rhetoric, don't even define this word in their "Handbook" and seem to use it only as a passing insult thrown at their opponents.) We must train our children to be able to see through such fallacies, particularly fallacies presented in the guise of instruction in the proper means of finding truth.

One other example, also taken from a book that purports to teach us how to think and write, will further clarify the type of discernment and skills our children should learn on the dialectic level. We'll look at the way an influential secular author, Eric Hoffer, presents unsupported and contradictory assertions in an authoritative and conclusive fashion. Our children shouldn't let such facades overwhelm them, but they must

---

* Not, of course, that only feminists believe that girls should ever learn algebra; the feminist element comes in with the implication that *every* girl *must* learn algebra—presumably because boys learn it. This is often the logic of the feminist, who wants to "liberate" women by making them exactly like men. In our curriculum, we encourage students—boys or girls—to learn algebra beyond the elementary level as they acquire skills that necessitate it (if they do acquire skills that need it).

penetrate to the argument's substance to see if it has merit.

Hoffer tells us that "in a society with a high standard of living," people have a "greater readiness to work" than they do in a society "with a low standard." He insists that "we are more ready to strive and work for superfluities than for necessities."[75] His argument goes on, but let's first examine this initial statement. In it we'll find a vast oversimplification that ignores crucial distinctions and treats as monoliths categories that really span wide and diverse spectra.

For example, what kind of "low standard" does he mean? The standard of the pioneers of early America? Or that of the materially impoverished in industrial cultures? The low standards of people dependent upon the Welfare State? Or of the masses in totalitarian societies? Conditions other than material standards affect people's incentives and often show "low standards" to be irrelevant to "a readiness to work." How could you find a much lower standard than among the Scotch-Irish who traversed the Appalachians? But who could deny their obsession with work? Hoffer never even defines what he means by a "low standard." Furthermore, do people who strive for "superfluities" really seek only material luxuries, or do they also want some kind of status through these luxuries? If the latter is the case, then Hoffer's whole theory collapses, since the motive behind people's quest to acquire "superfluities" lies in something beyond those superfluities themselves.

Hoffer goes on to say:

> People who are clear-sighted, undeluded, and sober-minded will not go on working once their reasonable needs are satisfied. A society that refuses to strive for superfluities is likely to end up lacking in necessities. The readiness to work springs from trivial, questionable motives . . . . A vigorous society is a society made up of people who set their hearts on toys, and who work harder for superfluities than for necessities. The self-righteous moralists decry such a society, yet it is well to keep in mind that both children and artists need luxuries more than they need necessities.[76]

Here Hoffer ends by begging the question: he assumes that "superfluities" are really more necessary than "necessities" and so tells us that "children" have a greater need of "luxuries." But wouldn't any starving child have greater need of a piece of bread than a doll? In what sense does the child have a greater "*need*" for the luxury?

Hoffer's last statement is also a *non sequitur*, if not a contradiction in terms. How does it follow from his argument that luxuries are more necessary than necessities? All along he's been telling us that high living standards inspire harder work. But without necessities, we have a low standard, so how can he argue that luxuries are more important than necessities? According to his reasoning, a low standard makes us less prone to work, but how can we strive for superfluities unless we first have necessities? An inmate of Auschwitz or the Gulag certainly knows what it means to strive more for necessities than luxuries, as any reader of survivors' accounts can affirm. Nothing Hoffer says can be construed as establishing his assertions about the superior importance of "toys," "luxuries" and "superfluities."

Hoffer also gives us a *non sequitur* in the first two sentences in the above quote: how does it follow that "clear-sighted, undeluded, and sober-minded people" will allow themselves "to end up lacking in necessities" simply because they will not pursue the production of superfluities? Why will this failure to pursue luxuries distort their ability to foresee their need for necessities? He begs the question because his premises presuppose his conclusion, but he has proven nothing. Here we find an author who likes to hear the sound of his own false voice as he rambles incoherently on in circles about nothing.

Hoffer offers his observations in the form of a purely objective account. He "self-righteously" eschews ethical foundations and offers a purely utilitarian approach. We find no "ought" here; he simply asserts the greater vigor of materialistic societies without questioning whether this type of vigor really is preferable. But even if one could support the assertion that a culture striving for luxuries will be in some sense more "vigorous" than one satisfied with necessities, does this validate the luxury-seeking mentality? Weren't the Nazis "vigorous" in the pursuit of their goals? Of course, a kind of "ethics" underlies Hoffer's perspective, the ethics of materialistic self-assertion. This is the kind of cultural vigor that he *wants*; his *ad hominem* attack against "self-righteous moralists" should not hide from us his self-righteous lauding of the pursuit of luxuries.

We could also muster evidence to show that Hoffer's view conflicts with historical experience: material collapse plagues cultures (such as that of Rome) that pursue luxuries, not those seeking self-sufficiency. This evidence confirms the truth of the Scriptures, which describe the fall of "Babylon the Great." The Bible describes Babylon as an economic, political and religious system:

Fallen! Fallen is Babylon the Great!
 She has become a home for demons
 and a haunt for every evil spirit,
 a haunt for every unclean and detestable bird.
For all the nations have drunk
 the maddening wine of her adulteries.
The kings of the earth committed adultery with her,
 and the merchants of the earth grew rich from
 her *excessive luxuries*. (Rev. 18:2-3)

So both Scripture and historical evidence refute Hoffer's contentions. But our primary concern in this discussion lies in the dialectical skills that can be used to expose the self-contradictions in this author's argument. In this example, we see how these skills can be used to vindicate the truth of God's Word. (In our Koinonia Curriculum, in our discussion of the dialectic level, we mention the use of Dialectic Level Problems; in these Problems, which cover a wide variety of subjects, we guide students through the type of examination of statements that we've undertaken in the preceding pages.)

Once the child has become skilled on the dialectic level, he moves on to the level of rhetoric. The *rhetoric*, or *wisdom*, level involves the ability to clearly present one's position in a way that fully reveals truth. Of course, for the Christian, rhetoric involves not merely being able to present a logically accurate case but also a God-ordained, anointed case. Christian means "anointed one." True rhetoric means God-ordained rhetoric, whether in speech or in writing or in the "declaration" that is one's whole life. But also basic rules help us to present our views clearly, accurately and in a way that others can best understand (although, again, those rules cannot be created, learned or applied apart from the Spirit). For example, a piece of writing must be based upon a coherent theme, with a beginning, development and conclusion.* (While a spoken presentation may also follow such rules, the Scripture specifically declares that at times we are not to prepare exactly what we

---

* See *Right Words*.

are to say, but that we are to take "no thought" of what we are to say, for the Spirit will give us His words, Matt. 10:19-20, KJV. The Spirit does not, however, anoint an empty head. We must "study to show" ourselves "approved," 2 Tim. 2:15, KJV, and then the Lord will use us as anointed vessels for His purpose according to His perfect will.)

Section Three

Subject: *History and Geography*

. . . The forces of the past still live on and exert their influence on us, though we may not be consciously aware of this. It is frightening to realize in full depth what it means to be a human being: that is, to realize that we are all imbedded in the flux of generations, whose legacy of thought and feeling we irrevocably carry along with us.[77]

C. W. Ceram

The Importance of History

Repentance has become obsolete to most people of our day. This makes a turning from our headlong course toward destruction and annihilation less and less likely as we settle into our entrenchments of despair and cynicism. One main obstacle to repentance has been that people no longer see that their lives arise within a historical context. Secular education takes an evolutionary approach to history that cuts people off from their roots. The public schools teach, as we have earlier seen, that people are mere *observers* of history—not *participants* in history. This keeps step with the pagan approach to knowledge, understood from the perspective of the detached, "objective" observer. But no repentance is possible to a mere observer, since only if we recognize that we are *participants*—that our knowledge of history is not detached but relational—can we recognize what we must repent of. If we lose awareness of the historical foundation and perspective that our own thoughts and actions are rooted in and spring forth from, then we will not recognize our complicity in the evil of that perspective. Without confessing the sins of our fathers, our historical roots, we will be caught by that same sin and doomed to repeat it (Neh. 9:2). We can see this clearly in the message spoken by Stephen in the seventh chapter of the book of Acts. In order to bring God's people the message of repentance, Stephen relates to them their history.

Historical knowledge is clearly relational in its very essence: it is *our* history, the history that has shaped each and every one of us as individuals who are members of a specific spiritual community, people with specific ethnic and cultural backgrounds. We cannot escape our relationship with history, since our history molds and shapes us (John 4:20). God would give us a vision of our historical heritage so that we can both honor our fathers (Exod. 20:12) and confess their sins, as we learn to see how historical destiny has molded and shaped us as individuals and as the corporate Body of Christ. Once we catch a glimpse of our direct relationship to our historical past, it becomes one of the most exciting and important of studies.

The whole of the Bible is, of course, mainly a history book (albeit one of an entirely different order than mere secular histories), a book of the history of God's dealings with specific peoples at specific places and times. And the Bible itself continually stresses the importance of history, for good examples as well as for bad. So the eleventh chapter of Hebrews, in which we are taught the great lessons of faith, presents another recounting of the history of the people of God, in this case of their faithfulness. The Bible specifically enjoins us to teach history to our children: "In the future, when your son asks you, 'What is the meaning of the stipulations, decrees and laws Yahweh our God has commanded you?' tell him: 'We were slaves of Pharaoh in Egypt, but Yahweh brought us out of Egypt with a mighty hand'" (Deut. 6:20-21). So, the question about the very meaning of the Law begins with an answer about the history of God's people.

In contrast to the God-centered view, which seeks to show us our historical roots and connections, the man-centered view seeks to sever us from our relationship with the past. The man-centered view wants to throw off the limitations to human existence that the study of history so clearly reveals. The man-centered view wants to cast off such limitations and to see man's world as an open-ended arena for the fulfillment of an infinite human potential, as man strives to recreate the world in his own image. So the man-centered view, expressed for example in contemporary humanism, subordinates history to a world view in which human society is no longer seen as subject to the limitations that history exposes. Man no longer studies the past in order to comprehend the limits of his life and to learn the lessons of history. Man no longer conceives of history as his inescapable origins through the investigation of which he discovers the roots and the limits of present-day society and finds guidelines for the conduct of contemporary life. Instead, in the humanistic understanding, man becomes free to shape his own society according to his own will. Man, in the words of the indefatigable Julian Huxley, now passes "from the psychosocial to the consciously purposive phase of evolution."[78] Given such a view, the past becomes relevant only as a catalog of examples of man's tragicomic subservience to traditions and values that modern man must now outgrow. As Rushdoony has pointed out, history is considered to be merely a "prelude" to the present. History is replaced by the "social sciences," which "nullify the past . . . . There is no norm in the past. The past is only prelude to man playing God" in the present.[79] Modern pagan man conceives of himself as so vastly superior to his forebears that the past has very little useful or positive to teach him. He seeks a new study of man based upon the premise of the unlimited power of humanity, or rather of a human elite, to shape the future according to man's own reason and will. And each one pushes forward, dog eat dog, to try to elbow his way into the elite.

The connection between the destruction of history and a scientifically planned society is clearly drawn in Aldous Huxley's *Brave New World.* Here one of the most important sayings has become that of that high priest of industrial technology, Henry Ford: "History is bunk":

His fordship Mustapha Mond! The eyes of the saluting students almost popped out of their heads. Mustapha Mond! The Resident Controller for Western Europe! One of the Ten World Controllers. One of the Ten . . . and . . . he was going to . . . actually talk to them . . . straight from the horse's mouth. Straight from the mouth of Ford himself . . . .

"You all remember," said the Controller, in his strong deep voice, "you all remember, I suppose, that beautiful and inspired saying of Our Ford's: History is bunk. History," he repeated slowly, "is bunk."

He waved his hand; and it was as though, with an invisible feather whisk, he had brushed away a little dust, and the dust was Harappa, was Ur of the Chaldees; some spider-webs, and they were Thebes and Babylon and Cnossos and Mycenae. Whisk, Whisk—and where was Odysseus, where was Job, where were Jupiter and Gotama and Jesus? Whisk—and those specks of antique dirt called Athens and Rome, Jerusalem and the Middle Kingdom—all were gone. Whisk—the place where Italy had been was empty. Whisk, the cathedrals;

whisk, whisk, King Lear and the Thoughts of Pascal. Whisk, Passion; whisk, Requiem; whisk, Symphony; whisk . . . .[80] In man's "Brave New World," history has been abolished. All that is real are the designs of the social planners of the future liberated from the chains of the past. The past has no meaning or validity. It is an unfortunate blemish best forgotten. The same insight was expressed in Orwell's *1984* where one of the basic principles of the party dictatorship was "the mutability of the past"[81] and the slogan was proclaimed, "Who controls the past controls the future; who controls the present controls the past . . . ."[82] The dictators of these anti-utopias believed with that harbinger of the French Revolution and Reign of Terror, Voltaire, that at best history was made to do tricks.[83] Such an attitude is reflected in one of the most fully planned societies of the Western world, modern Sweden. In his description of Sweden, *The New Totalitarians*, British journalist Roland Huntford, Scandinavian correspondent for one of the most influential newspapers in the world, *The Observer*, points out that

> it is a truism that to change people it is desirable to cut off the past. In the Swedish schools, the study of history has been truncated and the emphasis laid on the development of the Swedish Labour movement. The French Revolution is seen as the beginning of things. Otherwise, the European heritage and the classical background have been dismissed, and an atmosphere created in which only recent decades appear to count. "Nothing matters before 1932" [the year in which the Social Democrats came to power and the Swedish social planning experiment truly began] cries a student of political economy at Lund University. "The young economists," says Professor Gunnar Myrdal, "don't know anything about history, and they don't care." Of course, the antihistorical bias of younger intellectuals is a universal phenomenon, at least in the West.[84]

In the second decade of the twentieth century, the most influential of modern American educators, the humanist philosopher John Dewey, warned against "making the records and remains of the past the main material of education."[85] Dewey's phrase "main material" is ambiguous, but this phrase certainly serves to discourage an emphasis on the importance of the sort of clear and precise knowledge of the past that a study of its "records and remains" would provide. From ambiguity, Dewey proceeds to sheer nonsense when he tells us that such a concern with the past will somehow cut "the vital connection of present and past."[86] How a study of the past will cut the connection between past and present, Dewey never explains. But after impenetrable ambiguity and contradictory nonsense, he finally starts to get to the point when he warns us that too much study of the past can tend to "make it

a rival of the present and the present a more or less futile imitation of the past. Under such circumstances, culture becomes an ornament and solace; a refuge and an asylum.[87]

Now the meaning of Dewey's words begins to come through. To repeat them: to dwell on the past is "to make the past a rival of the present" and the "present an . . . imitation of the past." If our main goal, however, is to *change the present*, to divorce ourselves from the traditions and heritage of the past as we shape a new generation into our own desired image, then we must eliminate the rivalry of the past. This explains why the influential National Education Association (NEA) leaders of Dewey's day "rejected history as trivia—as the games or ornaments of the elite": "For the dictatorship of the past they substituted that of the present . . . ."[88] (We don't suggest that the present should be a mere slavish imitation of the past. We should seek to free ourselves from all that is dead in the past. But from a Biblical view surely the hope for the future lies in a restoration of all that is best in the past, Acts 3:19-21. History too bears out this scriptural truth.*)

But despite the man-centered attempt to create a new world order free from the past, the Bible tells us that nothing is new under the sun. So everything that we see in the world today has its origins in the past (Eccles. 1:9-11). Even if the forms in which the ideas and beliefs of the past exist today have changed, the new forms still grow out of the old ideas and beliefs. The past, in other words, contains the seeds of the present. We can understand this clearly from a simple example illustrated by the food that we eat. Every tomato, peach, plum and so on that we bite into today grew from seeds that go back to the dawn of creation. New strains, hybrids and varieties may develop, but they all spring from the original

* See *Culture as Spiritual War.*

seeds. No food exists that does not derive from the original, ancient seeds. The same principle applies to ideas and beliefs. This is why Jesus could declare that the last generation would reap the harvest of the sins of the world of the past (Luke 11:47-51): each successive generation builds, for good or for ill, upon what has been done before; each moves further along some pathway that starts out from the past. If we continue in the way of past evils, we will reap evil; if we continue in the ways of good, then we will reap the good. We must understand the roots of the past that create the ideas and events of the present and see the origins and consequences that the ideas and beliefs that prevail today had in the past. Otherwise, we will not only fail to make use of the successes of the past, but we will also be doomed to relive the past's failures and to be a part of the process that helps to bring those failures to their final, poisonous fruition.

This is not to say, however, that history merely consists of repeated cycles continually recurring, as many pagan philosophies and religions contend. The history of mankind constitutes a progressive continuum, unfolding toward its final culmination. Patterns repeat, not in cycles, but always linearly on new and deeper levels that reveal more fully the nature of man's rebellion and sin and of God's wisdom and righteousness. Jesus spoke of the process of history in terms of a woman's labor as she gives birth to a child (Matt. 24:6-8; see also 1 Thess. 5:3). The contractions occur with shorter intervals between them, lasting for longer periods of time with greater intensity, until finally the child comes forth. The history of mankind follows this same pattern of development: it had its beginning and moves inexorably toward its end, revealing ever more clearly the human potential for destruction and evil on the one hand and the mercy and love of God on the other hand.

Given the special importance of the study of history, we must stress the particular need for textbooks in this area to be Christ-centered. Unfortunately, even Christian historians have generally not dug deeply enough to write truly God-centered, and therefore accurate, history. Weed seeds that should have been repented of long ago keep cropping up even in Christian textbooks. Most of us have been programmed by the humanist philosophy that permeates all of education, and the roots go very deep. Others write history from the biased perspective of their own theological or denominational vested interests. We are writing curriculum materials that we hope will at least be a step forward in correcting some of these imbalances. (See Supplement One.)

At the *grammar*, or *knowledge*, level, a study of the Bible offers the best introduction to our historical roots, though basic history should not be confined to explicitly Biblical topics. The child should also study basic geography to allow him to more accurately picture the places that he learns about (rivers, mountains, oceans, countries and so on), and should learn about how climate and geography affect the way people live. It would be good to also learn the basic research skills. But most importantly, the rich historical story of our Biblical heritage must go deep into the heart of the child. Our grammar level Readers, which go from the first through the fourth grades, are based on the Bible and incorporate geography, science, community and culture, some math and other topics. (See Supplement One for a more detailed description.)

Although the child may yet be too young to see the total pattern in which the events and stories in the Bible fit together, we can still teach them to him in a framework that will help him to see their relevance. For example, he can see how the events of the history of Israel helped to prepare the way for the coming of Messiah, and how Christ's coming to the world provides the framework for the facts of Old Testament history.* The facts must be directed toward a purpose; they must establish the basis for the understanding of history that the child will acquire on the dialectic level of study. Siegfried Giedion has said, "In themselves or when pinned to isolated facts, [dates] are as meaningless as the numbers on a ticket. But conceived in *interrelation*, that is vertically and horizontally connected within the network of historical objects, they delimit constellations. In such cases dates take on meaning."[89] In such a context, dates become history's "yardstick," which enables us "to measure off historical space" into areas that can be dealt with and be made comprehensible to the human mind. Again, the key is *relationship*, the child's relationship to the facts as he sees how the facts have had a direct bearing on his life, and the facts' relationships to one another. When teaching these

---

* Our Bible Reader includes reading selections that explain and reveal some of God's long-range purposes and connections so that our children can begin to see and understand the overall theme of God's purpose in history as they go through their Readers. See Supplement One.

facts, have the child remember those events most important for the development of history and help him to see how these events tie into other events that come before and after (we are designing our teaching materials to help you do this). Then he will not merely acquire a mass of disconnected facts but will be prepared later to see how all of these events fit together in God's progressive continuum: again, history must be taught relationally.

Some of these key historical events and movements would include: (1) from Biblical history: the creation, the flood, the Tower of Babel, the call of Abraham, the lives of Isaac and Jacob, Joseph and the sojourn in Egypt, Moses and the Exodus, the giving of the Law, Joshua and the conquest of the Promised Land, the period of the Judges, the initiation of the kingship in Israel, the Davidic dynasty, the building of the Temple, the divided kingdom, the Babylonian Exile, the rebuilding of the Temple and the city walls of Jerusalem, the life of Jesus Christ and the birth of the church; (2) from ancient history in general: the rise and fall of the great pagan empires, such as Babylon, Egypt, Persia, Greece and Rome; (3) from post-Biblical world history: the early persecution of the church, the paganization of Christianity, the Constantinian alliance between Rome and the church, the church and culture of the Middle Ages, the Renaissance, the Reformation, the rise of modern science, the Enlightenment and the French Revolution, the Industrial Revolution, the First World War and the Russian Revolution, the Nazi Holocaust; (4) from American history: the founding of the original colonies, the Great Awakening of the 1730's, the American Revolution, the writing and ratification of the U.S. Constitution, the westward movement, the rise of transcendentalism, the Civil War, the triumph of secularism and industrialism, the New Deal. Obviously, some of the above events were positive from a Christian perspective, others were negative, and still others were mixed; some happened over a short space of time, and some were movements that took many years to develop. Of course, many other events were of decisive importance in history, and this list can hardly present any explanation of the ramifications of these events themselves. In our curriculum, the first- through fourth-grade Readers cover points (1) and (2) and the historical studies for the older grades, which will include history stories, a chronologically organized study of world history and a dialectical study of history, cover all four points. (Again, see Supplement One for a description of history in our curriculum.)

On the grammar level, the child can begin to learn the basic history of the world. This history should all be taught with an eye toward our purpose for the dialectic and rhetoric levels, on which the child will grow to understand the God-centered view of the problems faced by man in this age and be able to present the God-centered solution. On the grammar level, the child can begin to see his place in his community, his individual purpose and the purpose of his community in the context of history as God's ordained will for man. The child's understanding of these things will, of course, be limited on the grammar level. He will not fully understand the wide ramifications, meaning and significance of the historical knowledge he learns, but he can still begin to acquire a basic understanding of these things. (In our first- through fourth-grade Readers, we address many key issues about history on a level that relates to children of this age. We also present questions geared to opening up discussion. But the parents must review this material with their child to make sure he understands it and pursue the questions and discussions as they feel the need or desire in their child.)

Even on the grammar level, though, if we teach history *relationally*, it can be very exciting for the child. We can impart to him a basic vision of his heritage and help him to see how his historical past has helped shape him into what he now is and will later become in the kingdom of God. As we impart this knowledge, we also help him to see how the historical backgrounds of his brothers and sisters in the Lord have helped to shape them into what they are and will be. Whatever our ethnic background, whether we are black, white, Occidental, Oriental, Jewish, Gentile, Italian, English, Irish, German, Hispanic and so on, we can see how our historical origins have helped mold and shape us into what we now are.

Only from the relational perspective of God-centered faith can we truly see the purpose in our historical past. From this perspective, if we are, for example, of Scotch-Irish descent, we can see how the religious persecution that our people suffered at the hands of the English in Scotland and then in Northern Ireland prepared them for the central role that they played in opening up the western American frontier from the Appalachians to California and has influenced what we are today

as individuals.[90] The same can be seen whatever our
heritage is: as we said before, if we are Mexican, we can trace
our roots back to both the Indian past and the Spanish conquest; if we are black, we can see the shaping role of our
African past, the ordeal of slavery, Civil War and Reconstruction; if Jewish, the influence of the diaspora, the holocaust and
the rebirth of Israel. All of these historical events have helped
to shape and mold us. God uses all of these heritages to form
for Himself a people who will be able to accomplish His purposes on the face of the earth now at the end of time. When
we look at our brothers and sisters of different backgrounds,
we can see their histories alive in them, as God brings forth
everything positive in their historical heritage, while setting
them free from everything negative, just as He is doing to us.
Even on the grammar level, we can begin imparting such a
vision of their God-given heritage, as members of the Body of
Christ, to our children.

On the *dialectic*, or *understanding*, level especially, the
deeper relationships between these different heritages and
historical facts can be fitted together into the overall pattern of
world history. From a Christian perspective, this underlying
pattern is the epic struggle of those who are in rebellion against
God's eternal kingdom, against those who serve the Lord. In
human history, this has been expressed as the struggle of
paganism versus Judeo-Christianity, of man-centered civilizations against a God-centered people. Remember that all of
history has significance within the context of God's eternal
purpose for man, as opposed to satan's rebellious attempt to
replace God as the head of man. (In our curriculum, we begin
to cover this historical conflict in various biographically-
oriented historical stories and in *Chosen Generation*, read
during the fifth through seventh grades, and then continue to
study it in greater depth in dialectical studies of culture and history, read during the eighth through tenth grades.) As we said
in chapter 7 above, history is not a meaningless jumble. The
law of causality applies to the historical realm as well as to
every other. We must understand the pattern of history within
this framework and see how events either further or undermine
God's purpose for man. We must not look upon events as mere
isolated incidents, but we must rather seek to understand them
in terms of their relationship to God's purpose, either furthering
or undermining it. (Of course, God allows even those events

that oppose His purpose. Ultimately He will use even these things as part of the culminating revelation of the consummation of the ages. Then He will fully expose the depth of depravity of the fallen human heart and the immeasurable depths of His love and mercy through which He overcame that depravity in all men who would allow Him to do so.)

The *rhetoric*, or *wisdom*, stage in history will finally bring us to see the pattern of history as a whole in the framework of God's unfolding salvation for mankind and His eternal purpose. At this stage we will not merely be able to see the spiritual significance of the drama of world history, but we will also be able to spiritually influence that conflict to further the purpose of God and the knowledge of God in the world of men. On this level our understanding of the dynamic forces, underlying principles and the vast panoply of interrelated causes and effects that constitute history has developed to the extent that we, moving in the wisdom of God, can have a positive, practical effect upon history. This means that we not only understand history but we can also act to transform the present in order to further God's purposes. We understand what principles we must further and how to further them. Our relational knowledge of history has come to the point at which we can have a direct relationship to contemporary historical events, a relationship that can serve God's ends in history.

The understanding of American history is central for our children's historical understanding in general. No one can reasonably doubt that God, who ordained from the beginning that He would have a people called out from among every "tongue and kindred," had a purpose in bringing together the people of the United States. No other country consists of so many people from so many diverse backgrounds, and no other modern country was founded to the extent that this one was on the basis of a conscious desire to live in conformity to the Hebraic Scriptures. Neither can anyone reasonably doubt that Biblical principles played an important role in the founding of this nation, that those principles influenced the shaping of the U.S. Constitution and other elements of American law and that this Biblical heritage was instrumental in the shaping of our heritage of liberty that is being undermined today. But unfortunately, from the very beginning of American history serious imbalances inhered in many of the Founders' views, imbalances that were latched onto by others and eventually used to undermine our godly heritage.

From just one example (which clearly underscores the need for "confessing the sins of our fathers") we can see the tremendous mistake involved in an indiscriminate acceptance of the view of the United States as a "Christian nation" or of the view that our government should be the instrument of the Christian's commission to be the salt of the earth. This error, we should note, does not, however, validate the current secularist interpretation of the "separation of church and State," which subordinates the church to the State in the issues of human life in order to exclude any type of political influence by Christians.* Our example of our forefathers' imbalances is very pertinent to home-schooling parents, for it concerns the history of compulsory State education. The first compulsory education laws were passed by New England Puritans who wanted to use the government as an instrument to make sure that all children learned their denominational catechism.[91] They wanted to use the State as a means to ensure that their church doctrine would be taught. Ironically, today secular educators, who insist that public schools be legally *prohibited* from teaching Christian beliefs, use this precedent for their compulsory school system, and they have done so from the very beginnings of compulsory secular schooling in America. Invariably, the attempt by Christians to use the compulsory power of the State to further Christian aims backfires in just this kind of way. This *con-fusion* of State compulsion and Christian aims that has existed in the minds of many American Christians for centuries has had disastrous consequences for God's people. This does not mean that Christians must be restricted from having any kind of influence on government, law and politics, but that the nature of that influence should be limited by the recognition that our primary positive goal, the bringing forth of the Body of Christ on the face of the earth, cannot be *imparted* by law but only by the grace of God (Rom. 3:21-24; Gal. 3:10-14).† From this perspective, our primary "political" goal is to be allowed "to live at peace with all men" and "preach the gospel" (Rom. 12:18, NEB; Mark 16:15, KJV). To avoid these *con-fusions* (such as our example of the fusion of the Christian's commission to "train up the child" with the State as the agency of that commission),

---

* See *Politics as Spiritual War.*
† See *Who Owns the Children?*

we must distinguish between *this country*, this "place in the wilderness" "at the furthermost ends of the earth," and that heavenly country of which the Scriptures speak (Heb. 11:16). God set aside this country not as that holy nation (1 Pet. 2:9), which is the church, but for the purpose of providing (being a "providence") a "place in the wilderness" to bring forth *His church*, His kingdom, within the hearts of men at the end of time. We cannot see *the government and nation* of the United States as God's instruments of restoration, or in any sense identify them with the church itself.*

Obviously, we can only barely begin to discuss these questions here, but we do want to make clear the critical importance of finding a truly balanced, God-centered perspective on American history. As one can readily see, the relational character of this kind of knowledge has very important consequences for what we will do today. We must have a clear understanding of how we are related to our cultural inheritance, the "family tree" of our culture's institutions. We must see how we have been informed by the alien spiritual seed of secular philosophies and institutions. Unless we see the historical roots and the true meaning of the institutions that dominate our life today, we run the risk of moving on the mere basis of preference, simply *reacting* to objectionable *content* within such forms of institutions as public education, rather than *acting* on the force of conviction, seeing that even the *form* itself is alien to God's kingdom. But if we can allow the Spirit "to lead and guide us into all truth," His unveiling of history to us can prevent the tragedy of our being seduced back into adultery with the world. If we let this light of truth illuminate history to us, we will have the opportunity to be members of a faithful Bride who can move forward to purify herself in preparation for the apocalypse, the unveiling of both the Groom, Jesus Christ, and His Bride, the Church.

Here, in the study of American history, we can see concretely how the grammar, dialectic and rhetoric stages all work together to promote the real and practical purpose of God. In the *grammar* stage, our children must first learn the facts of American history and how those facts relate to their lives today. (In our curriculum, we do this in a comprehensive way in the fifth through seventh grades.) Then they must learn the

---

* See *Politics as Spiritual War.*

basic principles that our nation was founded upon, both insofar as these were consistent or inconsistent with (or even antagonistic to) the patterns given in the Word of God. This begins the *dialectic* stage. (In our curriculum, this also begins in the fifth through seventh grades, and really develops in the eighth through tenth grades.) Then they must learn how the conflict between these principles, and also the conflict with other man-centered principles that were introduced in American history, has shaped our historical development (which takes place in our curriculum mainly in the eighth through tenth grades). This takes them fully into the *dialectic* stage. Finally, they must learn how they can influence events themselves, which takes them into the *rhetoric* stage.

God has ordained the institution of civil government, but He has also established definite limits to the power of such government.* As Christians we bear the responsibility to declare these limitations of government and, within the limits that God imposes upon the church, to do what we can to keep government within these limits. (This means not using government to impose Christianity upon others but rather helping to keep government within those God-ordained limitations that would prevent the State from violating the liberty of conscience of any man.) If the Bible instructs us to pray for those in political authority, it would seem that we can exercise what current privileges we still possess to vote for them as well, at least when the Spirit reveals a clear purpose in doing so and shows us that our participation is not merely in a deception or as a profanation of our life.† Our responsibility as citizens of this world must always be subordinate to our citizenship in heaven (Eph. 2:19; Phil. 3:20), but nevertheless we are enjoined to be the salt of the earth. In regard to politics, this means to serve as an influence to retard, to hold back, the corruption of the political system—and the consequent destruction of religious liberties—of our age. To exercise these rights responsibly, we must be informed of the basic issues of our day, particularly insofar as these affect our liberty to serve Christ. These current issues are today's history. And to understand the basic issues of our day we must also understand the spiritual and historical origins of the political system under

---

* See *Who Owns the Children?*

† See *Politics as Spiritual War* for a full discussion of Christianity and politics.

Section Four

Subject: *Mathematics*

Jesus declared the first and greatest commandment to be the revelation that God is One: "Hear, O Israel, the Lord our God, the Lord is One" (Mark 12:29). The oneness and consistency of the God of the Bible is the fundamental truth upon which all scriptural revelation is based. God expresses His oneness and consistency in all of His creation. He created a universe that was at one with Him and with itself, a universe based upon principles of consistency that reflect God's own nature. God is a God of consistency and order, and this consistency and order is also expressed, as it is on every level of being, in the logical and mathematical principles that He created the world in conformity to.

Mathematics expresses the basic consistency and order of the world as God has created it. Secular scientists have spoken of the mathematical orderliness of the world as one of its great mysteries, and so it must be to anyone who does not recognize the God who created the universe. An *accidental* harmony such as that expressed in the mathematical relationships that have been discovered behind the physical creation would be not only a mystery but even an impossibility. The God who does everything in decency and order created a world that is also built in decency and order (although the complexities of that order will always be such that man will never be able to apprehend their full ramifications through his own mind; and, of course, the Fall has fundamentally marred this decency and order).

God's Word is filled with the specification of precise mathematical relationships, with the laying out of precise patterns that God's people are to follow, and with mathematical patterns that God has ordained for His creation to follow. The first book of the Bible begins by telling us what God did on the first, second, third, fourth, fifth, sixth and seventh days: the creation was brought forth in a definite order. When the Tabernacle and the Temple were built in the Old Testament, a clear specification of mathematical relationships was to be precisely followed, and when man obeyed that God-ordained order, the supernatural blessings of God were poured out on God's people in a powerful way. These mathematical relationships underscore the precision of submission that God desires from His people. God reminds us of this precision in scriptures that speak of measuring His people with the plumb line of His Word (Amos 7:7-8).

The basic patterns of living for God necessitate mathematics: most obviously, the tithe, which involves taking definite percentages of all of our earnings. Almost all of man's labor involves the use of mathematics. Jesus Himself, as a carpenter, must have employed mathematics in His work. When the tribes of Israel were settled in the Promised Land, they were apportioned parcels of land, which could only have been divided accurately through the use of mathematics.

God has revealed Himself to be the God of provision: Yahweh-yireh, "God will provide," is the name that Abraham gave to the place where he was about to sacrifice Isaac, when God provided a ram instead to take Isaac's place. Provision requires mathematics, an accurate assessment of what will be needed for the future, as in Joseph's provision for Egypt's seven years of famine. Mathematics, then, is an integral part of our life in, and obedience to, God.

In general, then, we can say that mathematics provides us with an essential expression of the nature of God as He has revealed Himself to man, in His creation and even in His direct instructions to man presented in His Word. Through the precision and the order of mathematics, we learn of a dimension of God's truth and, as we said, of the nature of the precision of submission that He requires. (This connection between mathematical-like precision and submission, which is the central element of discipleship, is seen in the Greek word Jesus uses in Matthew 28:19, which is translated "make disciples." This is the word *matheteuo*, from which the word *mathematics* is also derived.) And through the use of mathematics, we are enabled to take true dominion over the world that God has given into our hands, under His Divine Headship.

Mathematics is basically a study of relationships, of comparisons. The equal sign is the center of mathematics (and much less frequently, the greater than, less than and other related signs). To show the equivalence between different entities is mostly what mathematics is all about. God created the universe with a definite order of relationships, and mathematics expresses, in part, from a very limited perspective, that order. Given this knowledge of the order of relationships, we can use more economically the knowledge that we possess to be able to take practical steps. If we know, for example, that we have ten baskets and that each of them holds eighty apples, we do not have to count out each of the baskets individually, but we can simply multiply.

Mathematics shows us various sorts of constant relationships between things, and it shows us how, given this knowledge of constant relationships, we can apply limited pieces of information to find out greater pieces of information. For example, if we know the diameter of a circle, mathematics tells us of a constant relationship between a true circle's diameter and its circumference and between its diameter and its area. Given this knowledge of this constant relationship, based on the fraction 22/7, known by the Greek letter *pi*, we find that, knowing the diameter, we also can know what the area and the circumference of the circle is. Given the knowledge of this relationship and the information about the diameter of the circle, we do not have to measure out the area of the circle or the length of the circumference, but we can take a much easier step.

The *knowledge* of these relationships comes through practical experience: through trial and error (and the sparks of insight that God lets fall to the human understanding),* people *discovered* this constant relationship between the diameter and circumference of the circle, but man did not *create* this relationship. It was already given, given by the Creator.

We see, then, that mathematics serves as a useful tool for more effectively taking dominion over the world. We can develop and use this tool because of the orderly nature of the world that God has created. Mathematics serves as one of the "grammar" tools for many different disciplines, particularly in the sciences and such practical concerns as carpentry, farming and other related endeavors. And mastering the rules of mathematics, like learning the rules of English usage, also helps us to develop general habits of precision.

You should be aware of the dangers of using any approach to teaching mathematics that stresses the supposed relativity of all knowledge, the view that one plus one equals two because men have made that a useful assumption rather than

---

* See *Justice Is Fallen* for an extensive discussion of how man acquires all forms of knowledge.

because God created the world with a definite order.

Mathematics should, to the extent possible, be learned relationally, for example, through word problems that are based on real-life situations, particularly those that refer to real problems encountered in a land-centered culture, for example, problems of gardening, livestock feeding, irrigation systems, carpentry, sewing and so on. In our curriculum materials, we present arithmetic concepts in the context of their practical use in a culture based on the land. To learn basic arithmetic knowledge, you must, however, also drill. This is unavoidable and generally boring to both children and teachers. Nevertheless, it reaps its rewards when the child puts his math to practical use. When your child gardens and mixes the proper proportions of manure, soil nutrients and soil; when he builds a chicken coop and measures boards so that they fit; when your daughter follows the proportions of a cake recipe that delights everyone who tastes it, then everyone discovers the value of the boring drills. And when the younger children see the practical ways in which the older children apply their mathematical knowledge for purposes of taking dominion on more advanced levels—such as figuring out the flow of water in irrigation or the quantity of sunlight for a solar energy water heater—this will help spur them on to learn their math even more. Even when the younger children don't always have an immediate opportunity to apply the math knowledge they are learning themselves, through the example of the older children they will see that they will be able to apply that knowledge in the future.

At the same time that we must continually point to the practical uses of arithmetic, we can't escape that it is the least relational of all subjects. The drilling inextricably associated with arithmetic instruction underlines its comparatively unrelational character, for, as noted before, rote exercises are by their very nature not relational.* This means that, as we've also pointed out and discuss further in the Koinonia Curriculum supplement, parents can more readily use even secular textbooks, or textbooks provided by various Christian publishers, to teach this subject, provided that parents will scrupulously edit this material and actively seek to make the subject as relational to the children as possible. (Because of

---

* See "The Inductive Approach" in chapter 7.

the comparatively non-relational nature of the subject, the non-relational approach of secular textbooks will not distort arithmetic in the same way that, for example, a non-relational presentation of history would distort that subject.) You can do this by, again, inventing word problems that show the practical relevance of the arithmetic drills the children repeat.

We can try to fill our children's heads with all kinds of abstract mathematical knowledge, but unless they have a real use for that knowledge, it will all disappear, as many of those who took more advanced mathematics in high school and college can testify. In daily life, we need all kinds of basic mathematics for many different types of situations, such as shopping and planning budgets, doing carpentry jobs around the house, figuring out interest rates, sewing and so on. In general, a person will occasionally make use of basic algebra, trigonometry and geometry in his daily life and work, and many people will have a need to learn these mathematical disciplines more thoroughly for their work. Below we have listed a chart that shows the types of mathematical disciplines required for different kinds of work.

Algebra: Electricity and electronics, architecture and woodworking design, water power, wind power, solar power and power systems generally, water systems, sanitation systems, irrigation.

Geometry: Working with solar energy and wind power, architecture and woodwork design, heating and cooling systems, irrigation or gardening (especially bio-intensive gardening).

Trigonometry: Surveying, any kind of work with electricity or electronics, solar power, development of power sources and uses in general.

In our curriculum, we want eventually to develop materials that teach advanced algebra, geometry and trigonometry in the context of teaching the practical skills to which they apply. But we also encourage parents to teach their children with more traditional math textbooks, reminding them to always go over these materials for any imbalances that need correcting. (See Supplement One for a more complete description of mathematics in our curriculum.)

Section Five

Subject: *Science*

Scientific knowledge has become the paradigm of all knowledge for modern man, that is, the paradigm of that kind of objective, analytic, detached knowledge that pagan man has come to believe constitutes the *only* form of knowledge. We have already discussed the disastrous consequences of this kind of knowledge, and we can often see that even the practical "achievements" of this kind of science have destructive consequences, atomic bombs and holocaust gas chambers being only the most obvious sort of examples. But scientific knowledge can also be understood in a relational sense, in a sense that does not detach us as "objective" observers from the creation, but instead brings us into closer and more intimate relation with the creation, the kind of relation that enables us to fulfill our covenant obligations to nurture and care for the earth and the plants and creatures with which God has filled it.

This is the kind of science (the word *science* being based on the Latin word meaning "knowledge") that the Bible speaks about when it discusses the wisdom of Solomon:

> He described plant life, from the cedar of Lebanon to the hyssop that grows out of walls. He also taught about animals and birds, reptiles and fish. Men of all nations came to listen to Solomon's wisdom, sent by all the kings of the world, who had heard of his wisdom. (1 Kings 4:33-34)

Solomon described the purpose of all of these plants and animals in the creation of God from the perspective of "wisdom," the perspective that grasps the wholeness, the totality of things, that reveals their multifarious interrelations. Through wisdom, he perhaps described and explained the things of God's creation within the context of God's written Word: for example, how most of the animals that the Bible spoke of as being unclean to eat also played a vital role in the ecology of creation as scavengers, a role that would not only be undermined if they were eaten by men but, as the "garbage cans" of creation, also made them unfit to be eaten by man. We can see the difference between man-centered knowledge and God-centered wisdom in the contrast between merely knowing an animal's "scientific" name and knowing about the habits, behavior and function of that same animal within its ecosystem. That second type of knowledge, which is God's wisdom, could prove extremely useful for us, while it also helps us to come into real relationship with our natural surroundings. The former type of knowledge may tell us absolutely nothing about the animal, except perhaps for some sort of mythological evolutionary relationship the animal supposedly has to other species.

Solomon perhaps also explained the plants to illuminate their uses, giving glory to God for having made them in all of their diverse beauty and utility. His wisdom was that relational, life-giving knowledge which has become almost completely absent in the world today. This wisdom recognizes the delicate, perfect balance of nature so that we can husband it. (And we should note that the Scriptures tell us that "all the kings of the world" sent men to learn this wisdom from Solomon; this means that much of the true wisdom about nature that has become a part of pagan cultures in the three thousand years since Solomon lived may well have been imparted to them through this revelation of God.) This wisdom recognizes the full ramifications on all different levels of the vital balance of nature that God has provided, for example, in the mountains of New Mexico, where the melting snows disappear just when the seasonal rains begin. This wisdom recognizes how the snowmelts of the Colorado Rockies provide the irrigation and drinking water for hundreds of thousands of square miles around them, all the way to the Pacific Ocean and the Gulf of Mexico. Understanding the harmonious natural processes that God has ordained, we can then *act* in a way that will enable us to also be in harmony with, and take full advantage of, these processes, for example, how to properly store and later utilize the snowmelt, determining the most appropriate times to use these waters and so on. This is the kind of true wisdom that will have vital ramifications for every aspect of our lives, the wisdom that enables us to see our interrelationship with nature and the vital interrelations between all the aspects of the natural world.

The *knowledge*, or *grammar*, stage of science consists mainly of learning practical facts and principles—relational facts and principles—about the world around us. Children should learn to identify plants, wild and domestic, and their uses. They should do the same with rocks, trees, fish and

animals and so on. They should also learn basic facts about
different types of soils and different kinds of bodies of water
and their possible uses, about the skies and determining the
weather, about the stars and moon and the sun "as signs to
mark seasons and days and years, and . . . to give light on
the earth" (Gen. 1:14-15), for example, learning to find direction or tell the time by the stars. All of these areas of study are
spoken of in the Bible and should be related to God's Word. In
this way, our children will learn not only this practical
knowledge about the world, but also that God made everything
for a purpose. (In our Supplement One, describing our
Koinonia Curriculum, we will discuss how we can study all the
various aspects of nature study to show how they all interrelate
to one another and to agricultural pursuits.)

Much instruction in science courses does not increase
children's practical knowledge or their general understanding
of the world. We desire that our children should have a useful,
working scientific knowledge of the world around them, but,
unfortunately, many science textbooks, even Christian ones,
do not seem to present their material in a way most conducive
to accomplishing this purpose: that is, they often present such
knowledge abstractly rather than relationally. We should concentrate on developing a good, practical, working, factual
knowledge that is both relevant to the child's life and that will
also form a good basis upon which to move on to the dialectic
level of knowledge. Nature books, particularly nature guides
about the weather, stars, plants and animals, can be very helpful in teaching your children in these areas. But you must be
cautious to detect the universal bias of evolution in these
books. We are developing a relational approach to nature
study that will incorporate material from various nature hand-
books and study guides, and we are also developing a handbook that shows the practical application of the sciences, for
example, in regard to crafts and agriculture. (We also include
some science in our readers. And we are preparing materials
for science study on the dialectic level. See Supplement One
for a description of science in our curriculum.) We also combine this nature study with nature drawing, encouraging our
children to do sketches of God's creation, animals, plants, sea
shells, scenery and so on.* In our mechanized, atomized, tech-

* We also use a book on nature drawing to help teach this.

nological, urban world, we have forgotten how to see. Nature drawing offers a tool to help us learn to overcome this disability, a tool that God can use to open our blind eyes, which have forgotten how to see into the beauty of the interrelationships of creation to recognize both their intricacy and simplicity. (See "Art" below.)

On the *understanding*, or *dialectic*, level, our children should see more clearly how these various facts of science come to fit together in more complex interrelationships. They should learn that God not only created everything with an individual purpose, but that He also created each thing to be part of a larger order. He regulates His creation with laws and reveals these laws to men so that they can bring the natural order under God-centered dominion as man and creation join in the perfect harmony of God's patterns. The first stage, grammar, is largely the stage of field observation. On the second stage, we more actively work with nature (although we have already begun to do this on the grammar level). At times certain forms of experimentation will be useful, provided that these experiments are conducted from the perspective of relational, rather than detached, abstract knowledge. Here the child can start learning in depth about the laws of nature, about regularity, predictability and so on—principles that inhere in nature, which has been created by the consistent God who expresses His consistency through these principles in creation. We should always teach these principles, however, so that the child sees their practical, relational application.

Our modern secular society makes it important that our teaching of science on the *dialectic* level takes place within the context of the conflict between the two world views of creation and evolution: the creationist view that God created all things according to His purpose, with man to be in submission to God, as opposed to the evolutionary view that the world has evolved from chaos to order by chance, with man as the most highly "evolved" being, the "god" over creation. This two-model approach provides a perfect opportunity for the *dialectic* in the study of science.

In learning about science, you must always remember that this has become one of the great idols of our age. Secular men have faith in science, believing that it will provide the ultimate means through which all of their problems can be solved. They look to medical science for their healing, to technological science for their prosperity and leisure, to what is called "social science" for the answer to the problems of society, to "psychological science" for the answer to the problems of their *soul* (*psyche* being the Greek word for soul). Modern man sees science as the universal panacea, the solution to all of his problems, the means of his salvation.

For the carnal mind to fall into the worship of science is very easy. To look at man's scientific achievements and not wonder, as did John in Revelation, after the beast, that is, the self-exalting product of man's mind, takes a conscious act of resistance that begins with a question: What have all of man's scientific and technological marvels, his scientific knowledge, accomplished? They have created the great weapons of warfare that threaten the destruction of mankind; they have been used to disrupt the God-centered patterns of human life, thrusting men off the land into large cities full of violence, immorality and crime; they have polluted the environment and so on and on.* The positive contributions of science and technology pale against these negative results and are often even delusory.†

Scientific knowledge, understood in a God-centered perspective, has a place in the community of God, but only a limited place. Science, properly understood, can be useful to man and can help him to learn about and come into closer relationship with God's creation. But we must always remember that it remains only a limited tool and that it has a secondary importance. We must also always remember the dangers involved in it, how it has come to play a big part in man's presumptive quest to rely upon himself rather than God.[92] But science will always remain a false god, and its salvation a delusory salvation.

We should also point out that while much talk goes on about a "scientific method," much of this talk is also delusory and confused. First of all, never through our reason can we successfully apply with consistency any kind of objective method that is separated from the Source of all knowledge. All knowledge depends on our relationship with God. No "method" can be pulled out of a hat and applied objectively and abstractly to

---

* For a more extensive examination of these criticisms and their rebuttals, see *Culture as Spiritual War.*
† See chapter 13 in *Who Owns the Children?*

learn about the creation. Truth must always be bound together with Spirit. We can apply, however, certain principles in learning about certain subjects, and when these principles are applied in the Spirit, they can help us to avoid certain problems and so help us to come more directly and easily to the truth that the Spirit would show us. People writing about the "scientific method," however, usually describe an ideal mythology about scientific impartiality, objectivity, willingness to change theories according to supposed changes in facts and observation. All of these have little, if anything, to do with what really goes on in science.* We do not deny that science has a consistent method, but really that "method" comes down to a basic recognition of the nature of God's creation, the limits and proper uses of human understanding and an openness and desire to allow God to show us the truth—on all levels—that He desires to reveal to us. Our contemporary scientific researchers, with their secular, evolutionary assumptions, remain blind to many of the beautiful truths of God and distort truth according to their pagan ideas. By God's grace, we can see the truth through the Spirit, as particular practical needs arise, and gain insight and understanding, while solving problems that need to be solved. This is what "science," which, as we said, is simply the Latin word for knowledge, should be all about. We may find our discoveries and insights coming about in the most surprising way as God reveals His truth to us as He sovereignly wills.

On the *wisdom*, or *rhetoric*, level, all of God's creation comes to be understood in the context of His eternal purpose. We come to see how the various sciences, when understood relationally, work together to enable us to take dominion over the physical world, and furthermore, how true dominion is only possible under God, in submission to His divine will. Only He can see the consequences of all our actions, so only as we submit to Him can we be sure that our labors will bear fruit and bring forth the goals that we seek. Man can properly balance his use of nature only under the rulership of God. Man is a participant in God's creation; he has a God-ordained place in God's "Great Chain of Being." This "chain" is, in Berry's words, a "hierarchical structure," and man's violation of this God-ordained order through "the 'disobedience' or *hubris* of

---

* See *Justice Is Fallen, Knowledge as Spiritual War* and *The Leap Beyond*.

attempting to rise and take power above [his] proper place" causes havoc and destruction.[93] Our children need to see that when man fails to exercise scientific dominion *under God*, devastating consequences follow: ecological crisis, pollution, disease, scientific developments for warfare and so on.* On this level, we come to see the spiritual significance of the creation as the place where God's drama of love is actually experienced, where God's song is sung. Finally, we ourselves come to make practical use of the sciences, again, understood and applied relationally to actually further God's dominion over the earth.

As we have said before, it has been our experience that no setting is as conducive as an agricultural one for developing a genuine, relational scientific knowledge. In the context of a God-centered agriculture, one sees most practically the validity and importance of true scientific knowledge. In such a context, the lessons of dominion and the consequences of failure are brought home as immediate realities rather than vague possibilities. In this context, science ceases to be merely academic and necessarily becomes relational. Our children must learn about how to grow crops, about companion planting, soil composition, animal husbandry, rotation planting, wood lot management, animal and human diet, and the interrelationship of all these different areas of agriculture and land management and so on. When they examine soils and the needs of plants, subjects like chemistry take on a real, relational meaning in their lives. When they study how the chemical composition of what they eat relates to their bodily functions and physical health—their biology—then both of these sciences become directly meaningful. Similarly, when learning practical mechanics, the operation of water systems, irrigation and so on, physics takes on relational meaning. When we really have to think about what our power sources for our water pumps will be, for example, whether we should use wind power, water power, solar power and so on for diverse purposes, engineering sciences must come out of hiding in clouds of abstraction and be made to do real work here on earth. These practical problems force us to weigh the diverse consequences and thus to carefully formulate and coordinate

---

* See *Culture as Spiritual War* for a discussion of the imbalances of both those who claim to defend the natural environment and of those who claim that no environmental crisis exists.

our actions. When things have a practical meaning for children's lives, they learn them especially well. And most important are the great spiritual insights to be gained from the experiences offered in such a culture. Indeed, most of the parables and teachings of the Bible come forth from such an agricultural setting.

As the children in our fellowship mature, some may pursue science research to meet specific agricultural needs of our farm community when such needs arise and if the child feels the desire to do such research. For example, some may research the best types of water systems or irrigation methods to meet particular needs. If their research bears fruit, they will have the inspiring blessing of seeing, and perhaps helping to bring about, the transformation of their paper plans into reality. The various phases of such projects could be incorporated into displays for the annual Fair and how-to booklets.

As we have said in regard to other subjects, in science, too, we want to stress the practical purpose of the knowledge that the children learn. For example, on the grammar level, children studying herbs would investigate their various uses, such as healing or flavoring, while also learning which plants pose a danger and so on; those studying the trees would learn something about how to use different types for various purposes, such as wood for fuel, for building or for cabinet making; those studying the soils would see which are best to grow different types of plants, which would be best to make adobe or pottery clay and so on; those studying the weather would look into how we can predict its changes from different cloud formations and other signs. On the dialectic level, our children would study the interrelationships between these different things, for example, how wood lots help to preserve the soil from erosion and so on. All of these studies build toward seeing how all of these things work together to give us the true perspective of wisdom. We have begun compiling how-to materials, photographs, diagrams, illustrations, descriptions, instructions and so on for writings that would describe in detail what we have learned about not only self-sufficient ranch life but also our whole life as an extended Christian community. Our children will continue to add to these materials (and already are doing so) as they begin to step into their places of maturity and responsibility. These writings can then be guides for others and also jumping-off places for further research and exploration as we endeavor to conform to God's patterns for our lives.

Our knowledge of the land should not be confined to the knowledge of the domesticated use of nature but must also include the wilderness. This would include learning such skills as hunting, fishing and survival skills, while we learn to understand the wilderness in Biblical terms, seeing its Biblical significance and how the wild part of nature is related to the domestic part.

Section Six

Subject: *Foreign Language*

Obviously, foreign languages are by their very nature relational, allowing us to communicate with others and helping to see and understand that we have obligations to the world beyond our own local communities. As we saw in chapter 7, foreign languages should be taught "inductively," but not entirely so.* We should not focus *primarily* on teaching grammar rules and vocabulary, but instead we should focus on the actual use of the language—listening, speaking, reading and writing. But then we should teach rules and vocabulary in the context of the student's practical efforts to use the language.

You should start a foreign language with your child at an early age, while he is in the grammar, memorization stage of development. Biblical Greek and Hebrew seem to be particularly appropriate languages for Christian children to learn, since these will enable them to read the Word of God in the original languages (here, the primary communication is with God—hearing His Word more clearly—but learning these languages will also greatly facilitate learning the modern languages of Greek or Hebrew as well. In our fellowship, we teach contemporary and Biblical Hebrew together. And you can learn Biblical Greek with modern pronunciation, as Zodhiates recommends.[94]) Also modern languages, such as Spanish, which is so widely spoken in the Americas, might also prove desirable and even necessary for some children to learn. Besides the obvious advantage of knowing a foreign language, this discipline provides other benefits as well. For example, we saw earlier in the section on English the importance of precision in language for our children's education, and Professor Weaver notes that "nothing so successfully discourages slovenliness in the use of language as the practice of translation."[95] In Supplement One, we discuss our program for instruction in Hebrew.

---

* See "The Inductive Approach" in chapter 7.

Section Seven

Other Important Subjects

Calligraphy

In our education program, we teach the calligraphic method of handwriting. This is the clearest and most beautiful style we know of and is therefore both useful for entering into communication with others and brings glory to God. If you would like to teach your child this method, you can begin at any age—whether your child is a beginning or an advanced student. See Supplement One under the heading "Penmanship and Calligraphy."

Art

As we mentioned in the "Science" section, we teach nature drawing in our curriculum. As we said, through drawing we can recapture the lost ability to see, in the participatory sense of seeing that we discuss in the section on English earlier in this chapter. In our urban-industrial world, our eyes have closed to the rich details and interrelationships of the elements of God's creation. We no longer look to see, but only to get through and past things so we can get to where we are going (though we're not even sure of where that is or why we're going there). Drawing can teach us to stop and look, to penetrate past the superficial glance so that we might see with the eyes of the Creator, to see the interrelationships that give the elements of creation beauty and meaning. Of course, drawing also serves as an important practical skill, but even if a child never becomes very proficient in this skill, the work of drawing can train his eyes to see.

Music

We also encourage you to have your child learn a musical instrument, which is an excellent discipline and will in later years be a blessing to him and to others as well. If you are not gifted in this area yourself, gifted people in your Christian community will probably be willing to multiply their talents in the lives of others.

Practical Skills

We encourage all children to learn gardening and keep a garden, boys to learn such skills as carpentry and leatherwork and girls to learn such things as spinning, weaving and sewing; we encourage also the learning of other crafts and skills that are useful both to train the young in good work habits and for their practical value. In the context of a self-sufficient, land-centered culture, children have the opportunity to watch, absorb and participate in a wide array of skills and crafts. As the children learn the basics of these skills, they have the opportunity to see where their gifts, talents and interests lead them. In those areas where they feel a calling of God, they can move on to proficiency and then mastery of their craft. As we discussed when we talked about our annual Fair, we hold a great variety of workshops that children can attend to see if they want to learn a particular craft. They can learn any skill or craft they want, and a brother or sister skilled in this discipline will help them to learn and will help their parents to instruct them in it.

Section Eight

Summary

In every area of instruction, we must always remember that no subject is isolated from the others. As we have repeatedly seen, the ultimate importance of each subject can only be understood when we recognize its interrelationship with other subjects of study and the unit context within which all subjects cohere.

While in the previous pages we have discussed the different subjects of our educational program separately, the unit approach provides the framework that ties together all these subjects and gives them their meaning. Through the unit approach, diverse subjects become elements within an integrated whole that gives significance to everything that the child learns.

Our purpose in teaching any particular subject is not to simply impart knowledge to the child, but, as we have so clearly seen, to impart knowledge of a particular kind—*relational* knowledge. As we've said, we do not want to overwhelm our children with abstract knowledge and useless information. All the knowledge imparted to our children must be related to God's purpose for their lives. It must be directed toward the aim that God has set for them, the aim that we are helping them to reach.

We must direct everything we teach toward our ultimate purpose, which is to bring our child forth into the image of God's Son. Every subject of instruction, every topic within every subject of instruction, we must direct toward bringing forth God's wisdom in the life of our child. We desire to transform our child into a *rhetor* of God, an expression of the love, wisdom, mercy and truth of Jesus Christ. Everything that he learns must contribute to this purpose. It must be knowledge that builds him up in God, that enables him to fulfill the purpose for which God has created him, that brings forth the character, abilities and qualities within him that will enable him to find complete fulfillment in God.

So we must continually remember the *relational* character of the knowledge that we teach: its relationship to spiritual and practical needs in the life of our child and its relationship to the purpose of God. Everything that we teach must be seen within this context. Everything we teach must be living knowledge that calls into play all of the aspects of his being: his heart, mind, spirit and soul.

We can never seek to simply teach various subjects, but rather we must transform our child himself into a true subject of God's kingdom, a person subject to the dominion of God's Spirit.

Conclusion

Our conviction is that Christian home education incomparably surpasses every other form of education for children. Your home provides the perfect context, ordained and created by God Himself, for the instruction of your child. God has made a particular pair of teachers especially for your child: his parents. The parent-child relationship is the God-ordained means of bringing forth the child of God into the fullness of the image of God. Whose love and concern for the child can ever match that of his own parents? Who knows a child—his abilities, his potentialities, his faults and his needs—as well as his parents do?

The home school gives us the perfect setting for bringing forth a person who lives in true and living relationship with his God, his fellowman and creation. It forms the perfect environment for the transmission of God's relational knowledge, the knowledge that integrates all of the elements of man's being into true wholeness. It constitutes the perfect setting for the *full* development of our child's life, rather than his partial and one-sided development.

Because we are all coming out of the institutional school setting—a setting that has been generally shaped in our day through secular and particularly public education—we must *un*learn many things as we undertake the God-centered education of our children. All of those involved in Christian home education participate together in an exciting journey, a journey out of the confusion of man-made educational systems, a journey toward the fulfillment of the perfect patterns of God in every aspect of our lives, including the education of our children. As we take the steps along this path, each day new possibilities open up before us. We continually see more clearly how God would have us to train up our children "in the way that they should go" as He sets us free from all the false ways of man. This journey is not a process of trial and error, of blind leaps into the dark, but it is a process directed by the living God Himself, through His Spirit and His truth. And so in each successive stage of our forward movement we see a clearer unfolding of His perfect patterns in the lives of our children, and in our own lives as well.

This path that we walk upon thus takes us through a process of uprooting. We are being uprooted from the goals of the educational systems of the world, from the methods that these educational systems use to reach their goals, from the most fundamental assumptions and orientation of those educational systems. We follow a path that goes against the grain of the world, that challenges the accepted wisdom of contemporary secular man. But the forms and patterns of the world increasingly prove their gross inadequacy in the education of children, and they often bear the bitter fruit of world crisis that comes forth frequently from the most educated of nations. On the other hand, anyone willing to investigate the real and very tangible fruit of Christian home education will see that it, like everything that comes forth from the Creator, is very good.

So everyone engaged in Christian home schooling takes part in an expedition of exploration in the realm of the Spirit. We seek a treasure more precious than the gold for which man "searches the farthest recesses" of the earth (Job 28:3). We seek that precious "wisdom" that God alone "understands the way to"; He "alone knows where it dwells" (Job 28:23). And He desires to lead us into its dwelling place. But to find where He would lead us, we must be willing to "mine" in the Spirit, to diligently search, to cut shafts "in places forgotten by the foot of man" (Job 28:4). And then when we find the vein of treasure, we must be willing to enter the labor that will enable us to recover it. There in your own home, the most exciting and fulfilling of adventures can go on as you recover the ancient treasures of God's wisdom and bring them forth in the living epistles of your children's lives. From your own home, a light can shine to illuminate the world and glorify the living God in the lives of wisdom's children.

Koinonia Curriculum*

Beginning

Anyone beginning to use our curriculum (at whatever level his child begins) must first read *Wisdom's Children* through completely. If you are a part of Koinonia fellowship, you must also read *Who Owns the Children?* and read and fill out the Koinonia "Home-School Conviction" form. This will confirm that you stand upon a conviction from God, so you can then school under the covering of our ministries. Anyone, however, may use our material without doing this if they don't look to us in *any* way as a covering. When you begin schooling, we ask all children to fill out our *Heaven and Earth Catalogue*. This presents a list of the great diversity of practical skills and crafts, spiritual and scholastic study areas and so on that your child can study. As he goes through the *Catalogue*, this will help the child to find his focus for the skills and crafts and other special subjects or projects he wants to study or work on (we are working at preparing how-to manuals and study guides in these various areas as well as selecting materials to recommend). After your child completes this, we ask you to send it to us, keeping a copy for yourself.

We then ask everyone to begin using the *Koinonia Character Curriculum*. This latter requires that the parent read about 250 pages of material before beginning, so it will take you some time to get under way. The *Character Curriculum* course comes with detailed instructions on how you should use it. Read those instructions, and they will tell you what you need to know. You will notice that in the *Instruction Booklet for Using*

---

* The vision for this Koinonia Curriculum was conceived in discussions between Blair and Regina Adams and Jeanne Stein. Jeanne also helped to write this supplement.

the Character Curriculum Chart, we tell you that grades one through four will learn the character traits through their Bible-based reader. But you should begin teaching the character traits in a relational context as soon as you start to work with the *Character Curriculum*. The Reader will then be a *supplement* to your character teaching. When you become familiar with the *Character Curriculum* and start to use it in your home, you'll sometimes find it appropriate to incorporate writing on the character traits into your writing workshop (which we'll explain shortly). See in chapter 15 in *Right Words* the "Complication-Resolution for Your Future" as an example of the kind of *Character Curriculum* work your children can do. As you'll see, younger children couldn't do this exercise, but you could scale it down to the level of a younger child. Take care never to use writing or Bible memorization as a punishment for your children because they've done something bad. Rather, you should emphasize that the writing can help them to see where their problems lie and to overcome those problems.

After you start using the *Character Curriculum*, we recommend that you begin using *Right Words*, together with the *Guidelines for Teaching Your Children Writing at Home*. This means starting a writing workshop with you and your children. (If your child does not yet read, you should do the phonics course before doing the writing book.) Once you begin your writing workshop, you should start to use the rest of the curriculum materials. You'll want to pace yourself so that you can complete on time the work given for the school year.

In *Right Words*, we discuss keeping a notebook and a journal. While keeping this notebook, mothers should use this as a resource to store important material from their teaching experience. Don't laboriously enter each detail of your teaching day, but try to write down highlights, special moments, special insights, useful teaching revelations and so on in the appropriate section of your notebook (*Right Words* will guide you in this). You could write about problems that kept a lesson from going right and how God brought a breakthrough; write down special questions your children asked, how a particular character trait became important to a child, special feelings you had and things the Lord showed you. (Example: You taught a particular math concept and used an original example to make something clearer.) Describe the special times, the victories and so on.

Don't forget that we need feedback from you. Your discoveries and insights will help us improve the curriculum. We also ask parents to let us know of any problems they have with the curriculum, anything that they add to it or any other comments or suggestions that they have.

We suggest that children begin the first grade at the age of seven or eight. Of course, if you feel your child should start earlier, you can do so, but as you'll see, the first-grade reader is really geared toward a child older than six.

When you start working with the Koinonia Curriculum, you will probably find that it differs radically from what you have worked with before. Most curriculums put the parents in a supervisory role, while the textbooks occupied the real teaching place. As the children worked all the workbook pages, read all the lessons and answered all the questions, the books imparted the information and the message. Even highly motivated parents still took a back seat to the real teaching/learning experience. In fact, most parents found themselves relegated to the position of recorder as they dutifully checked their children's answers in the teacher's manuals while the things they had planned to do during their school year were put permanently on hold. Once the old curriculum was under way, it had a dynamic of its own that swept everyone along. But our pagan, man-centered upbringing made us cripples that needed these crutches of workbooks, elaborate teacher's manuals, guidelines and other aids. But now God is healing His people. He is showing us that His power is altogether able to make us walk without such aids from the world. This doesn't mean that we won't have clear curricular forms for teaching our children, but these forms will be flexible, allowing freedom to the parents to follow the Spirit in the education of their children.

This new curriculum will give you the opportunity to actually step into the place of teacher. It is something that more and more parents have not only desired to do, but feel compelled by God to do. Parents are to be the teachers of their own children. They are to impart the information that forms their children into the image of Christ (Deut. 11:19).

But now that you have a curriculum that will enable you to do what you have always felt you were supposed to do, you may feel scared. You may wonder whether you have what you need inside of you. You may ask yourself if you are adequately prepared. So you must pray to a place of conviction, understanding that if God has commanded this of you, He will anoint you to bring it to pass. If you stand in the place of parental *conviction*, you will possess the faith through which God will empower you to fulfill your function as a parent-teacher. (See *Who Owns the Children?*)

If you will move forward in faith, God will soon give you tangible proof that within you lies a great river of wisdom and knowledge just waiting to be released. You only have to overcome the barriers that prevent this river from flowing. Many people who try to write often face such barriers to the flow of words they would put on paper. They call this problem "writer's block." Writers sit before the empty page with things in their hearts that they feel to write, but they cannot release the words from their hearts onto the page. Nothing happens. The flow does not begin. It is frozen or locked up. Years of inhibitions, fears, self-consciousness and self-deprecation act as a dam. In the same way, some parents feel the burden in their hearts to teach and instruct their children, but the same dam of self-doubt and other fears holds back the river that would just flow if they knew how to find and open the head gate that would release it. We could call this "teacher's block" or perhaps even "parent's block." But God has given us our children. And He gives us the grace and the anointing to rear them up in the way they should go.

The first thing we must recognize is that the head gate does exist and that a great body of water stands ready to supply the flow of love and wisdom for our children. This source stems not from ourselves but from our faithful God. He faithfully anoints us to do what He commands us to do. Within us lie those mighty living waters whose Source is the wellspring of life. So we can confidently open the head gate and watch the waters rush forth and give life to our children.

Writers sometimes open the head gate by doing "free writing," which we use in our home writing workshops. Just as an athlete must limber up before running a race to open the flow of strength through his body, so writers sometimes must limber up their hearts and minds to release the flow of words. So writers write for ten or fifteen minutes about anything or everything that comes into their heads without stopping to think or going back to fix a grammatical error or erase a sentence that doesn't "sound good." The point is just to get the head gate open and let the flow begin.

Once he has begun writing through this exercise, the writer can then turn to the project he is working on and write with power and skill. He can give himself to the anointing God would place upon him, allowing God to use him as His instrument.

Start your new school year with a period during which you (the parents) can engage in some "free teaching" to help open the head gates that will release the flow of wisdom through you to your children. Then you will see that a dam holds back a truly powerful river from flowing through you, and that as you start to open the head gates of that dam, you will have as much water as you will ever need. This will take place in your writing workshop. (See *Guidelines for Teaching Your Children Writing at Home* for advice on how to use the writing workshop in this way.) This is why we recommend that you get this workshop going before plunging into the rest of your curriculum. Do this workshop with all your school-age children together in a workshop setting, gearing the material appropriately to and working with each individual child according to his age level, abilities and individual interests and needs. You will probably find that if you have children younger than school age, they too will want to participate. It will be a blessing for all of you if you allow them to sit in and even sometimes participate, if they are disciplined enough to not detract from the workshop lesson.

The First Four Years

In our curriculum, the first period of schooling stretches through four years. You (if you were to use our curriculum) will work with the following material during that four year period:

A phonics course

Bible-based readers (which include studies of community and culture, science, character curriculum, geography, other Bible material)

Arithmetic books

Right Words: The Grace of Writing

Penmanship (which includes calligraphy)

Hebrew

Koinonia Character Curriculum

Skill and Craft projects
At Home in the Universe (nature study)

We give yearly goals to meet during this period, and you should generally keep pace with these annual goals. In general, you should try to keep in step with your work for the given school year. We have arranged the curriculum by grades so that you can have a sense of an average year of schoolwork and so that you and your child can have a definite goal to aim for. As we've said, this will give your child a sense of running a race toward a definite goal, that the times and seasons belong to the Lord and that your child must complete set goals within a set time. So, barring exceptional needs, you should try to pace yourself to finish your grade's schoolwork by the end of the school year. As we pointed out, however, in the course of a school year, you may vary the pace at which you work on academic subjects, and even leave off academic work completely for a couple of weeks at a time to do special projects.

It is up to you how you schedule your school year. You may skip some weeks of school to do a special project in the middle of the spring and spend the additional time on school in the summer. You may also feel to skip a particular course for a time (such as nature study) and work on it later in the year. Or you may want to spend more hours each day on school during the regular school year, so you can end earlier in the year. But in general you will want to stick to the time goals set in the Curriculum.

Remember, this program is designed to be flexible, to meet your child's and your family's needs. We have given you some books and other curriculum materials to work with, materials designed to draw out your and your child's participation, and we've given you a recommended schedule to complete the work for each grade. But you must take the initiative on how to use these materials to suit your schedule and your child's unique needs. The principles outlined in the previous chapters should help guide you in the use of the materials. For example, *the principle of interval recall as described on pp. 251-53 should remind you to maintain the continuity of the course you teach*: you may feel to wait on math until the middle of the school year, or even to concentrate on it alone for a period of time. That would be fine, but what you can't do is spend a day on math and then wait two weeks before going on to the next lesson. You'll have to start all over again every two weeks if you do that.

Another key principle to always keep in mind is: EACH ONE TEACH ONE. You MUST use your older children to teach your younger children *as much as possible*. This will benefit everyone: you and the "assistant teacher" and students. In fact, in the end doing and teaching become the only truly effective and lasting means of learning. And this holds true for everything we can think of.

Phonics

Grade one begins with an intensive phonics course. During the first part of the year, the child will do only this phonics course so that he can acquire the skills he needs to become an independent reader. In this course the child learns all his phonetic sounds (there are forty-three to forty-six sounds depending on which dictionary you use). We supply a how-to-teach manual for the parent. A few days after he starts this course, the child will be able to sound out words such as "God," "at," "it," "cab," "bib," "get" and so on. Very soon thereafter, he will be able to read (decode) and write (encode) sentences such as "God made man." This first period of schoolwork need not be long—in terms of hours—or involved. In fact, it shouldn't be. Otherwise, this may turn the child off to school before he's even started. In this first part of the first grade the child will acquire basic skills that he will obviously use more and more throughout school and the rest of his life.

This phonics course does not consist of pages of workbook exercises as in other curriculums. The materials used are a pencil, a notebook, and a set of flash cards, which the parent will make as she needs them. This puts the responsibility on you, the parent, to learn the information so that you can impart it to your child. This information is provided and easy to learn.

Along with learning how to decode the sounds and words, the first grader will learn how to write with a consistently clear and even hand and how to spell. Reading, writing and spelling are not three separate subjects. They form the essential and inseparable components of literacy. They are the foundations that must be laid in the first year of school. Reading and spelling go hand in hand. Taught together, each reinforces the other. To teach your child how to spell the words as soon as he learns to sound them out will overcome the spelling problems we have encountered with other curriculums, because as the child learns to recognize and use the letters and phonograms in different words he will at the same time learn to spell these words correctly. The spelling rules (such as "an *e* at the end of a one syllable word changes the short vowel sound to a long one") are provided as the children need them in their reading. To try to teach the rules with no context, as many other curriculums do, does not produce good spellers at all! When children learn the rules in the context of reading, however—mastering the different phonograms and words as they come up—they become good spellers as well as good readers.

The child will also learn to identify and write sentences. By the end of the first grade he should write clear, concise paragraphs with appropriate punctuation, capitalization and word usage. (The child starts with printing. You should decide when your child is ready for calligraphy, but we feel you should generally begin sometime in the first months of the second grade.)

So we will start with an intensive phonics course that will include spelling and writing and will make the child an independent reader. Speed will come with practice. In this first part of the first grade the child will acquire a skill he will fully master only as he continues in his schooling. This way of learning to read corresponds to the best way of learning a new language (especially one such as Hebrew, which has another alphabet). If a child tried to learn all the different speech sounds and grammar rules first, before starting to speak, he would become frustrated. But as he learns to use a few words at a time, he gets a taste for the language, which gives him a hunger to learn more. When you have acquired a certain amount of proficiency—even if only very little—it makes you confidently eager for more. You have received a part of the *content*—a taste—which makes you reach out willingly and eagerly for a greater grasp of the larger *form*, into which still more content can then be poured. This principle of learning applies in every level to every subject area. It describes a universal principle of our unfolding relationship with God. God first loves us (1 John 4:19)—we feel the *content* of His love and tender mercy; this draws us to Him and gives us a desire to bind ourselves to Him in a larger *form*—the covenant—through which we can experience a still greater outpouring of His love.* And in our unfolding relationship with God, we experience more and more love leading us into still more clearly defined and binding forms into which God pours still more of His holy love, "until we attain to the full measure of the stature of Christ, a perfect man."

The first part of the first grade, in which your child learns his basic phonics, should take you through December, depending on when you start. We calculated from the first week of October. (Again, this is the average time.) The daily work should take between one and two hours.

Spelling

Spelling is, as we've said, taught in conjunction with the phonics program. Spelling will continue at least through the sixth grade. You can use the method presented in this phonics course for older grades also if desired. If your child is a problem speller, the phonics course will help him to become a good speller.

The Reader

In the second part of the first grade the child will get a Reader. The child should at this point be an independent reader needing only practice and occasional guidance and help from the parent. But he will continue to have writing and spelling practice throughout his school year. The phonics book provides everything that the parent and child will need to decode new sounds and to learn spelling rules. As the child goes through the Readers, the parent can help him to review his spelling and phonics rules when appropriate. For example, when the child comes to a word like "name," he can review the rule about "e" at the end of the word making the "a" sound long. As the child reads, the parent can guide him with the proper phonetic tools. This will provide graduated interval recall of all the preceding phonics lessons.

---

* See *The Garden of God* and *Covenant Love.*

The Reader starts off very simply and becomes progressively harder. First, the child will begin with readings that go with his phonics course. These readings, which you will find at the beginning of the *First Reader*, will include a few lessons about the purposes of God for the child's life, for his family and for the church, and the "song of Yahweh." The child will be able to read these lessons because of his phonics training. Then this Reader will continue with the Bible, Genesis 1. The Readers will go through the book of Acts in the fourth grade. The stopping-off place for the first grade is Abraham's sacrifice of Isaac, which ends the *First Reader*. In the second grade, the end of the story of Ruth marks the stopping-off place. The third grade goes to the end of the Old Testament. The fourth grade begins with a few lessons about the period between the Testaments and then goes on to present the Gospels (based mainly on Luke) and the book of Acts.

Character Curriculum

Interspersed in the lessons of the Reader, as appropriate to the Bible story, are lessons drawn from the *Character Curriculum*. (All the character traits are covered in the first grade in the order in which they are presented in the *Character Curriculum* and where appropriate thereafter.) For example, when the child reads about Adam believing the lie and disobeying his Father, you will discuss honor. "What is honor? How do we honor God?"

When he reads about Cain and Abel, you will discuss obedience and disobedience.

When he reads about Noah, you will discuss active obedience, perseverance, responsibility, good stewardship and taking initiative.

These discussions of character traits are lessons in the Reader for the child to read himself, so they are of necessity simple and short, but the mother can reinforce and supplement them. We want to encourage and elicit parental participation in teaching all subjects. We want the Reader to provide touch points for discussion that can really draw out the children as they grapple with questions on whatever level they are able. As much as possible, we want the parents and children to bring forth something from God. We want to stimulate their interest, excitement and participation as the children grow in the knowledge of the truth. Parents should use questions to encourage their children to really dig out answers. This may involve writings, drawings and other forms of expression in addition to discussion. During the four years of his work with the Readers, your child will read about and discuss many of the character traits over again, but the context will change. In this way, your child should get a deeper and deeper understanding of all the different traits.

Science

We include science in the Reader as it relates to the reading matter. Included are studies of plants, animals, the sun, moon, stars, the solar system, the water cycle, wildlife in contrast to domestic, and other topics. For example, when the child reads about Joshua at the battle of Gibeon (Josh. 10:1-15), we discuss how God kept the sun in the sky, the laws that God has put into motion to govern the universe, and how He is sovereign over all these laws so that if He so chooses He can step in and alter them. This in turn will spark discussion about time and its passing, the days and seasons, the solar system, the functions of sunlight and so on. Science will also be brought in during these years through nature study, which we discuss later on in this supplement.

Below we list the goals that we feel parents should aim for in science for each grade level. The Readers will cover all this goal material in the grade under which we list it.

> *Goals—first grade:* an awareness of the following on a basic level:
>
> —A sense of the cycles and patterns in creation, such as seasons and life cycles in plants and animals
> —Plants and seeds
>   The necessity for water
>   Gardens
> —Animals
>   Their offspring
>   "Instincts" such as migration
>   Necessity of water
>   Distinction between wildlife and livestock

—Light and color
  Uses of light
  The different colors
  Rainbows
—Soil and its "life"
—The moon, sun and other stars
  The inherent order:
  seasons
  direction (the Big Dipper and the North Star)
—The sky and basic weather phenomena
  The rain cycle
  Floods and storms

Goals—second grade:

—Plants of the Bible and their uses
—Seeds
  Sowing, harvesting, storage
—Animals of the Bible and their uses
  Taking dominion over domestic animals
  Wild animals for food
—Diet: God's patterns
—Introduction to microorganisms (yogurt)
—Introduction to gravity
  Dams, irrigation
—Introduction to simple machines
  Wheels, inclined planes
—Introduction to power
  Wind and animal
—Introduction to light
  Illumination and sight
—Transformation of matter
  Condensation, evaporation
  Freezing, melting
—Introduction to the solar system
  General patterns:
  moon phases
  seasons
  day and night
  time and calendars

orbits
—The earth
    Equator and poles
    Longitude and latitude
    Direction
—Introduction to weather
    Seasonal patterns
    Temperature
    Clouds, thunder and lightning, hail
—Introduction to Geology
    Common rocks and minerals: how they influence
      the use of the land
    The earth's crust
    Volcanoes
    Wells and springs

Goals—third grade:

—Identifying the different parts of plants and trees and
    seeing God's wisdom in their function
—Introduction to cells and their specialization
—God's wisdom in creating animals suited to their
    specific living conditions
—Human and animal physiology
    Muscles, bones
    Senses
—Dietary laws
    Hygiene
    Nutrition, digestion
    Disease
—Introduction to sound
    Creation, the Word and the song of Yahweh
    Human voice
    Animal communication
    Natural sounds:
      wind through the trees and so on
    The contrast between natural and man-made
      sounds
    Musical instruments
    Pitch, volume, tone

—Gravity
  Weight
—Simple and complex machines
—Working with nature's forces
  Windmills
  Dams
—Solar system
—Seasons
  Moon phases
  Time keeping and ancient calendars
—The formation of mountains
  The flood and geological time
  Fossils and extinction
—Natural chemistry in contrast to man's technology
  Composting
—The refining of metals
  Common alloys and their properties
—The atmosphere and weather
  Atmospheric pressure
  Clouds, wind, storms

Goals—fourth grade:

—Ecosystems
  Habitats
  Food chains (both land and water)
—Animal cell specialization
  Muscles
  Ligaments
  Bones
—Microorganisms: helpful and harmful
  Yeast, bacteria
—Plant propagation
  Seeds
  Spores
  Pollination
—Human physiology
  Tissues and organs
  Systems (skeletal, muscle, nervous, digestive,
    respiratory, and circulatory)

—The universe
  Beginnings
  Constellations and galaxies
  Signs in the heavens
—Introduction to magnetism
  Compass and cardinal directions
—Introduction to the atom
—Gardens
  Soil types and nutrients
—Global weather patterns and how they affect us
  Atmospheric and ocean currents
—The earth's crust
  Formation of soil
  Rock formations
  Earthquakes
—Bodies of water
  Fresh and salt
  Tides and waves
  Water tables
—Times and seasons
  Seasons
  Moon phases
  Earth's rotation

Community and Culture

Discussions of Community and Culture (which includes "social studies" and history) are also integrated into the Reader. Topics such as the city versus agri-culture, nomadic life and so on are discussed or touched on. Some children will pursue some questions with great interest, and the parent will find herself in a lively discussion or teaching/ministering opportunity. But at times the child may not want to pursue these questions. At such times it may prove best to just let the question lie, unless the parents really feel the need to further pursue it.

In the first grade, for example, we raise such questions as, "What was the difference between Abraham's and Lot's ways of life?" "Why did God 'curse' the land against Adam?" "How did the city of Ur differ from cities we know, or did it?" "Why did God tell Abraham to move out and start a nomadic life?" Again, we want to draw out—to the extent possible on each level—a *real* discussion and active participation by parents and children, really encouraging parents to teach. Remember too that discussions could spark free writings or drawings.

In the second grade, when the child reads about the baby Moses in the river, we ask questions such as, "What do we do when laws go against God?" "Were Moses' parents right to disobey the governmental law and hide their baby in the river?" "Do we or will we ever disobey laws?"

When the child reads about Israel wanting a king, his parent can discuss leaders, governments, our obedience to government and so on, questions raised in the Readers themselves. Who is our king? If Jesus is our king, then what is our relationship to the government? Is it good that our government made a law mandating strapping our babies in car seats? If so, should it also come into our home and tell us to strap our baby into his high chair? Where applicable, we will present these questions in story form, bringing the issue to the child's level of experience. In this way he can begin to see the Biblical questions and issues as they relate to his own life.

In the third grade the children will be better able to get into discussions about more complicated concepts than they can in the first and second grades; the older children can begin to discuss in greater depth questions such as government, urban life versus agri-culture and so on. The Reader itself will include the questions and discussion topics. Generally, you will not pursue an extensive discussion of any one concept, although at times you may. We hope, rather, that through repeated questions and observations about God's interactions in our lives—how He brings His people through the darkness of the world into His light and truth—our children will grow in understanding of His ways, especially of His ways in their lives. It will be up to the parents to pursue these questions and discussions as far as their child is able to understand. Again, we want to elicit active teaching by the parents and real participation and discussion from both parents and children.

In the fourth grade, "Community and Culture" will include historical sketches describing the times in which Jesus lived and the times afterward when the emerging church suffered persecution and victory, as well as the type of questions we had in the earlier grades (only on a more advanced level).

Below we list the subjects we feel parents should aim to cover with their children in regard to community and culture and history on each grade level. The Readers will cover all this goal material under the respective grades.

Goals—first grade:

—Ancient history and culture
    Creation and Fall
-   The flood and Babel
    Noah's descendents
    Abraham called out of Ur:
      The birth of God's Spiritual Nation
    The first empire: Nimrod and Sargon
    The nature of empires
—Community and culture
    The nature of cities
    Contrast of city and rural culture
    The city of Ur

Goals—second grade:

—Ancient history and culture
    Civilizations contemporary with Jacob
    Esau and Edom
    The Exodus:
      the emerging battle between God-centered and man-centered culture
    Exploring the land of Canaan:
      city-states in Canaan
    Jericho
    How God settles people in a specific place (Acts 17:26)
    Conquest of Canaan: not a raid, but to *possess* the land
    The nations around Israel during the time of the Judges, especially Midian, Amalek, Philistines, Moab, Ammon, Hittites, Egypt
    Trade routes, in relation to Ishmaelites selling Joseph into Egypt
    History and culture of Egypt, legal system
—Community and culture
    Trade in the Middle East

Citizenship in ancient and modern times
—Historic parallels (by none of these parallels do we mean to suggest that the ancient and modern events hold identical spiritual significance)
  The Exodus:
    parallels to the pilgrims and others leaving England and settling in America
  Exploring Canaan:
    parallels to Escalante and Dominguez expedition; how the explorer precedes the settler
  Conquest of Canaan:
    parallels to the conquest of Mexico by Cortez
  Canaanites:
    parallels to American Indians
  Gideon and God's deliverance of Israel:
    parallels to American Revolution and Articles of Confederation
  Famine in the time of Ruth:
    parallels to the Irish potato famine
  Ruth's experience as a foreigner in Israel:
    parallels to immigrants coming to America

Goals—third grade:

—Ancient history and culture
  God's repeated deliverance of Israel from pagan captivity and oppression
  Armies and battles, David's victory over Goliath
  Civilizations contemporary with David and Solomon, including Tyre and King Hiram and the Queen of Sheba
  Solomon's Temple
  Solomon's shipping and trade network
  Dates and events of the kings of Judah and Israel compared to each other and to the dates and events of civilizations contemporary to Israel and Judah
  Assyria and the decline and fall of Israel
  Babylon and the decline and fall of Judah
  The captivity, history and culture of Babylon
  Nebuchadnezzar's dream

The Medo-Persian empire and culture

—Community and culture

What happens when man rejects God's rulership: pagan leadership contrasted to God's rulership in history

Different government forms:

theocracy, democracy, monarchy, republic and so on

Buddhism, Confucianism

Mercantilism, commercialism

—Historic parallels

Area near the Dead Sea where David hid from Saul: Dead Sea Scrolls

scrolls and printing press, beginning with the Gutenberg Bible

Issues involved in Israel's choosing of a king: parallel to U.S. Constitution in that Samuel warns them that the king will overstep limits to his authority. How constitution originated as a means of limiting government authority.

Absalom's revolt:

parallels to the French Revolution

Decline of Israel and Judah:

parallels to the paganization of Christianity, Dark Ages

Rebuilding the Temple and the wall:

parallel to the Reformation and the restoration of God's Word

Goals—fourth grade:

—Ancient history and culture

The Greek Empire, Alexander and his successors

Maccabees and Jewish independence

The Roman Empire

Roman rulers of the land of Israel

Structure of government and the Roman army

Herod's Temple

Origins of Hasidim, Pharisees, Sadducees, scribes, teachers of the Law

Jesus and Stephen recount the history of the

Hebrew people: history from a godly perspective
History of Samaritans
Spread of Christianity: Jerusalem, Judea, Samaria
to the ends of the earth
Paul's journeys:
travel during this time
Roman ships
Greek philosophy, Stoics and Epicureans
—Community and culture
Tradition of the "Oral Law":
making laws, legislatures
Origin of synagogue worship
Obeying the State or obeying the higher authority in
history (Acts 4:18-20)
The arms race in history: Sargon's bow to the atomic
bomb

—Historic parallels
The Jewish court, the Sanhedrin:
parallels to the U.S. Supreme Court
Roman centralization:
parallel to centralizing trend in U.S. today, in contrast to original intent of Founding Fathers. In that
context, discuss federal system, state and local
governments.
Paul's Roman citizenship:
parallels to U.S. citizenship; treatment of aliens
versus citizens
Persecution of God's people:
parallels in history
Jewish revolts against Romans:
parallels to the American Civil War and modern
Christian militancy

Geography

The Reader includes maps that the parents can refer to as
the text mentions different places. Other geographical terms
and skills are taught as they arise.

Below we list the goals that we feel parents should aim for in
geography for each grade. The Readers will cover all this
material in the grade under which we list it. (Note that some of

these goals overlap with science and history; the Readers won't needlessly repeat material, but we repeat the listing of them to make you aware what you need to cover in each subject.)

Goals—first grade:

—The earth
    Shape
    Hemispheres
    Finding directions
    Location of oceans and continents
    Mountain ranges
    Peninsulas
—The United States
    Knowledge of location of various states; in our
        curriculum these include location of Colorado,
        New Jersey, Texas, California, Arizona and
        some surrounding states
—Location of Mexico and Canada
—Basic introduction to countries and empires
    Garden of Eden: area of man's first home
    The land of Noah in his time
    The land of Noah today
    The empires of Abraham's time
    The Middle East today
—Maps
    Introduction to maps and their uses
—City versus rural living
—The rain cycle

Goals—second grade:

—The earth
    Review of continents and oceans
    Composition
    Land formations
    Introduction to environment
    Introduction to climate and climate zones
—Geography of ancient Middle East and modern-day

Middle East
—Nile region of Africa
—Historical maps of Israel through the time of the Judges
—United States
  Beginning studies, including the thirteen original colonies
—Water resources
—Plants and animals
  Dominion over domestic
  Wild

Goals—third grade:

—The earth
  Study of the continents and oceans
—Plants and animals of different continents
  Natural resources and formations
  Climate
—Map reading skills
—Special country studies in Europe and Asia
—Geography of the Middle East
  The kingdom of Saul
  Through the exile

—United States
  Introductory study of all fifty states
—Solar system
  Times and seasons
—Community
  Rural versus city life
  Cities, suburbs, towns and villages
  Food and water supply
  Housing
  Communication
  Introduction to various cultures and their relation
    to geography

Goals—fourth grade:

—The earth
    Tides, currents and waves
    Weather
    Climate zones
    Earthquakes
    Elevation
    Islands
—Maps
    More map reading studies
    Using a compass
    Time zones
—Israel
    Overview of land of Israel at the time of Jesus:
      Galilee, Judea, Samaria
    World at the time of Pentecost
    Paul's journeys: the region of the Mediterranean
      then and today
—Greek and Roman empires
—The New World
    North America, South America, Central America,
      Australia
—United States
    Fifty states by region
    Recognition of shapes of states
    Introduction to the concept of state government
—Other North American countries
—Community
    Christian community
    Kibbutzim
    Secular communities

Other Bible Material

Other Bible material will also be included in the Reader, such as repentance, faith, baptism and so on.

Other

Coloring work is provided for the younger grades so they can improve their motor skills and have fun coloring. We also provide tapes of the many songs that are interspersed throughout the Readers.

Arithmetic

We do not suggest starting a systematic arithmetic course in the first grade. The trend in recent years has been to include more and more arithmetic in the lower grades, perhaps in reaction to the low arithmetic scores in the upper grades. But starting children in arithmetic before they are ready for it solves nothing. In fact, in most cases, it does much harm. You will notice that children before and at the first grade level will "pick up" and understand many arithmetic concepts *naturally*, that is, in relation to all the other activities and learning situations they find themselves in. Every young child not forced into a systematic arithmetic program delights in figuring out arithmetic problems. How many preschool children have you heard repeating their numbers from 1-100 over and over (some children can even do it backwards!) or telling you that 6 + 6 = 12 or that if you have 4 apples and somebody eats one, there will be only 3 left? So instead of immediately pressing our children into a daily arithmetic program, we will first help them to stretch their wings and feel confident in their reading. In regular school programs, second-grade teachers find themselves repeating the arithmetic concepts of the first grade anyway because most of the class never learned them when they were taught. As Raymond Moore has pointed out repeatedly, if you wait to start formal teaching until the child is older—you might say *old enough* to really learn—he will learn quickly and efficiently and will easily pass his classmates who started much earlier than he did.[1] We suggest that you wait until your child is reading well independently, is generally spelling correctly and is consistently writing neatly before you start arithmetic. This should be in the second grade, but that will cause no problem. The child will quickly catch on and arithmetic will be a pleasure instead of a hateful duty.

In our arithmetic books, instead of presenting the concepts over and over in each grade, we introduce the concept once through simple stories that relate to the children's lives. We then provide a few examples with steps on how to do them plus

452 | Supplement One

some drill work and problems in workbook format. It is up to the parents to provide more examples from their daily lives, if and when they feel their child needs them. This need *not* take an hour or more a day, five days a week as is almost always the case in conventional schools.

We suggest thirty to forty-five minutes three times a week for arithmetic with the option, of course, of doing it longer or more often as the need arises. (You can see that there will be some days when the parent will introduce a brand new concept, and she may spend more than forty-five minutes explaining, going over, showing, practicing with the child. But, most days, when the child has been introduced to the concept, he will be able to drill and do word problems in a much shorter time.)

We provide workbook exercises that will use the incremental approach, each exercise building on the last ones (arithmetic is "a cognitive structure which builds upon prior learning"[2]), and regular review (graduated interval recall), which will establish long-term retention and understanding instead of only short-term understanding, thereby assuring a strong bedrock in the foundational skills of arithmetic. The word problems will relate to the child's everyday life and to the self-sufficient life on the land that God is bringing us into. As we've noted, you can also use traditional math books to teach arithmetic to your children. If you do so, carefully check through material beforehand for imbalances, and present word problems to help your child see the practical uses of arithmetic.

Goals—first grade: to be met before the child starts our arithmetic workbook:

—Writing numbers
—Counting and associating number symbols with specific quantities 1-100
—Concept of more, less, many, a lot, few, a little, add, subtract
—Days of the week
—Months of the year

Goals—second grade:

—Addition facts 1-9

—Subtraction facts 1-9
—Zero in addition and subtraction
—Place value: ones, tens, hundreds
—Counting to 1000
—Column addition with 3 addends
—Addition to more than 1 place
—Simple fractions: 1/2, 1/3, 1/4
—Introduction to time and calendar
—Skip counting 2's, 5's, 10's
—Introduction to money
—Measurement

1 pt. = 2 cups	1 yd. = 3 feet
1 qt. = 2 pts.	1 yd. = 36 in.
1 gal. = 4 qts.	1 ft. = 12 in.
1 wk. = 7 days	16 oz. = 1 lb.
1 yr. = 12 months	2000 lb. = 1 ton
1 yr. = 52 wks.	12 things = 1 doz.
1 yr. = 365 days	

Goals—third grade:

—Addition with carrying, and terms
—Subtraction with borrowing, and terms
—3-digit subtraction
—Multiplication facts 1-6
—Division facts 1-6
—Addition of fractions
—Subtraction of fractions
—Improper fractions and terms
—Decimals with money, adding and subtracting
—Roman numerals
—Measurement
    1 mile=5280 ft.
    1 mile=1760 yds.

Goals—fourth grade:

—Multiplication facts 7-12
—Division facts 7-12
—Long and short division with and without
    remainders, terms and checking

—Zeros in quotients
—Fractions
  Like and unlike denominators
  Mixed numbers
  Use of the ruler to 1/16"
  Fraction to percent
  Fraction to decimal
—Measurement
  Area
  Perimeter
  Conversions, for example:
    Inches to feet
    Feet to inches

Writing

We do not feel to burden the young child with extensive grammar (and even the older child should learn grammar mainly in the context of his attempts to communicate his thoughts and ideas in writing). We want rather to encourage him to get a feel for the language by reading, hearing, speaking and writing. When you consider how the average seven- or eight-year-old speaks, you can see that he has already acquired quite a command of grammar. In his reading and other school activities, the young child will continually use and be exposed to English. He will already be developing his grammar skills informally, developing a hearing ear for "good" English, learning how to communicate, how to express himself and how to use words. At this stage he becomes familiar with the *content* (the sense and feel of the language) so that when it becomes necessary to learn the *form* (the rules of the language), he will already know them in his heart. Too often we have taught the form first—What is a noun? What is a verb? Where does it go in a diagram? This results in almost completely paralyzing the child when it comes to writing. Yet this information and these skills do prove useful, but we shouldn't emphasize them until the child's writing talents and abilities begin to develop.

We have observed that even when children have an extensive/intensive grammar curriculum and are, in fact, very proficient in answering grammar test questions, they often cannot write proficiently. We would like our children to know how to not only write but write very well. We are reminded of George Orwell's warning, "If people cannot write well, they cannot think well, and if they cannot think well, others will do their thinking for them."[3] We don't want to throw out the grammar rules. As Thomas Middleton wrote, "We are in trouble. When writers don't know the rules, their writing usually turns to mush. When writing turns to mush, thought, which feeds on writing, suffers from malnutrition and is incapable of clear development or expression. When that happens, the perils of this complex world become overwhelming."[4] But we feel that if we concentrate on encouraging writing, expressing, communicating, the grammar rules will easily follow, as the children see their importance in this crucible of really trying to communicate their thoughts and ideas to others. Within the context of his own writings, we can teach the child all the basic English "facts": the eight parts of speech and their interrelationships, punctuation, capitalization, word usage, paragraph form and sentence structure. (We are developing a handbook to help teach these concepts in the home writing workshop context.) But these will come *after* the flow of words has begun to pour forth onto the page in the child's real voice (see "English" section in chapter 9).

Learning is an active, participating occupation. If the child has no avenue for response in any of his subjects, he will soon feel dulled and stultified. We want to therefore provide means for the children to respond to their different subjects, to meditate upon their experiences, to evaluate their activities and feelings. Writing offers some of the most important means wherein the child can partake of what he experiences, that is, take a part in it, becoming increasingly sensitized as he learns to move with and respond to what he feels. In the act of writing, the child begins to *use* the information and knowledge he acquires. If he only passively received the knowledge or information, never responding to it or using it, it could never begin to form him or change him. At best, if he did not immediately forget it, he could parrot other people's knowledge. It would not be his. He would not own it. But in writing he *partakes* of the knowledge. He allows it to come inside his heart and do something to him, impressing him, influencing him, constraining and compelling him. He expresses through his unique voice the memory of what he has learned in a way that only he can do.

One of the main places of active participation will be a

notebook and a journal in which the children will record some of their experiences and their responses to them—including their spiritual experiences, their work activities, their walks in the woods or fields, their fellowships, or anything else they feel to write. (*Guidelines for Teaching Your Children Writing at Home* explains how to teach writing to children on different levels.) Most of the child's writing will take place in the context of a writing workshop involving everyone in the family of school age and above (including the father, to the extent that he has time to participate). We describe the writing workshop extensively and explain how to do it in *Right Words* and in *Guidelines for Teaching Your Children Writing at Home.*

As we discuss in chapter 8 above, in our fellowship this writing workshop motivates the child to aim for the highest standards of workmanship because his writings may be displayed at the annual Fair or could be printed in a fellowship newsletter or other appropriate form of publication, such as a how-to pamphlet or book on and by children.

The core of the writing course, which is contained in a book on how to write called *Right Words*, shows how to stimulate the creative flow of the child's words in his real voice. Within that context, we present key suggestions to help improve the child's style of writing and also basic grammar rules that the first four grades should know. We show how, as the child's writing moves forward, he can improve his grammar and style, always within the context of how these tools can aid communication. We'll show him how to go over his own work to make sure he used rules of punctuation, grammar and so on properly. We also plan to produce a grammar handbook to help him learn parts of speech, sentence diagraming and other basic grammatical concepts and tools. But the goal of this course will primarily lie in encouraging the child to write. Throughout this period, grammar rules and related tools will remain secondary, although they should certainly not be ignored. In our curriculum, the child begins writing and participating in the writing workshop in the second grade (however, it is a very minimal participation compared to that of older children); while you will certainly share relevant grammatical and punctuation terms and concepts with him (sentence, period, comma, question mark, modifiers, nouns, verbs and so on) during his first three years of writing, we encourage you to begin formal instruction with the grammar handbook only in the fourth grade.

It is our desire to encourage our children's ability to communicate with words, in speech and writing. They already have the most important ingredient for writing: if they can talk, they can write. As the Bible says, "My heart is stirred by a noble theme as I recite my verses for the King; *my tongue is the pen of a skillful writer*" (Ps. 45:1). Most of our young children well express the things they have "seen and heard" of God and His great works. Their "voice," speaking from their hearts, rings clear with joy and excitement. We want to bring forth that voice on paper, or help them to bring it back if schooling has stultified it. We hope to bring that voice into active participation with the song of Yahweh so that it can truly sing of His noble themes. The children will therefore begin to write as early as the first grade.

Writing Goals

Goals—second grade:

—Your child should enjoy writing and begin to learn to write from his heart.

Goals—third and fourth grades:

—Your child should feel comfortable and relaxed writing, as though he were speaking.
—He should begin to learn the power words have to express feelings, thoughts and experiences.
—He should learn to show through concrete details, expressing on paper what the senses experience.
—He should learn to write with action verbs and active voice.

Grammar and Punctuation Goals

Below we give the goals for grammar and punctuation. You will undoubtedly have briefly introduced your child to many of these concepts before he reaches fourth grade, but we shall begin more systematic instruction in detail in these areas then. Also, the children will keep reviewing, in each grade, what they have learned in previous grades.

Fourth Grade:

—Introduction to parts of speech
    Nouns
    Pronouns
    Verbs
    Adjectives
    Adverbs
    Prepositions
    Conjunctions
    Interjections
—Capitalization
—Punctuation
    Period
    Possessive apostrophe
    Question mark
    Exclamation point
    Basic comma
    Quotation marks
—Dictionary work, alphabetical order

Penmanship and Calligraphy

We provide a detailed program for teaching neat, consistent handwriting, which begins in the first grade. The child will move from printing to calligraphy sometime early in the second grade. We are developing a book to teach calligraphy and can also recommend other materials you can use to teach your child this skill.

If a child practices a minimum of fifteen to twenty minutes a day, five days a week or at least twenty to thirty minutes a day, three days a week (although at times he may have to work for a full hour), then calligraphy should be no more than a two-year course with continuing practice thereafter.

Goals—second grade:

To print the letters from memory precisely as the book instructs by the end of the third quarter of the school year. During the remainder of the year, practicing and perfecting the letters and word spacing through writing projects. By the end of the year, the child should use calligraphy as his exclusive handwriting.

Goals—third grade:

To write cursive calligraphy from memory precisely as the book instructs by the end of the first half of the school year. During the remainder of the year, practicing both printed calligraphy and cursive calligraphy through writing projects.

Goals—fourth grade:

Using and perfecting calligraphy in their daily writing. Children should do at least one writing per week in calligraphy, focusing specifically on the letter forms, as well as consistent slanting and spacing, in addition to their regular everyday use of calligraphy in writing.

Hebrew

In the second grade, we encourage parents to start teaching their children Hebrew. In our fellowship, they will already have learned the many Hebrew songs we sing and will probably know some Hebrew that they will have picked up from others in the fellowship. Of course, if the family is already studying Hebrew, the second grader might know quite a bit of Hebrew before he even begins formal instruction. In the second grade he will begin to go through Hebrew language tapes that give an excellent basic introduction to modern Hebrew. These are secular tapes designed for adults, but parents can use them with their children if they recognize that the children will sometimes have to go slower than the course calls for. For example, younger children especially may need to take two days or sometimes even more to go over a tape that is designed to be learned in one day. Parents must be sensitive to their child's abilities and needs and help him to move at the optimum pace for him, neither moving too quickly nor too slowly. After the tapes are done, thirty minutes a *day* will probably be enough for this subject.

After learning basic spoken modern Hebrew from the Hebrew language tapes, the children will work with a Hebrew phonics course that teaches them how to read and write Hebrew. Then they will begin to thoroughly study Biblical Hebrew. Their study of Biblical Hebrew will focus, of course, on learning to read the Bible, but because they already have a foundation in spoken modern Hebrew, their study of Biblical Hebrew will also improve their spoken Hebrew. We are preparing this Hebrew phonics course and are preparing and selecting materials for teaching Biblical Hebrew.

Below we break down what we discussed above in more detail, giving goals for each grade level.

Goals—second grade:

The second graders will begin their Hebrew with basic Hebrew tapes. We can recommend some that will serve as an excellent foundation in simple conversational Hebrew. We also provide materials for use with such tapes.

By the end of the year these children should have a good working knowledge of the basic foundation of Hebrew. They will be able to carry on simple conversations in the Hebrew language.

Goals—third grade:

The children who have completed the Hebrew conversation tapes will do them again—completely through. This time they will work with the tapes more intensively, until the children come to mastery of basic Hebrew conversation.

Goals—fourth grade:

The children will begin by learning to read and print the entire Hebrew alphabet with the vowels. At the same time they will begin reading words, including many they learned on their Hebrew conversation tapes. In a very short time they will begin reading scriptures from the Hebrew Bible. After they learn to read and print the entire alphabet, they will go on to strengthen their reading ability by reading out of the Bible. At this time they will also learn how to use Hebrew dictionaries and Biblical Hebrew lexicons to begin translating the Hebrew Bible. Some simple but necessary grammar will accompany this.

Other Languages

We also plan to encourage children, once they have a firm Hebrew foundation, to do basic conversation tapes on Spanish and Greek. After doing the basic Spanish course, students can do further study as their interest takes them deeper into this language. After studying modern Greek, students should at least learn basic Biblical Greek, but they should study this in a modern Greek accent. (We will be working on preparing and selecting materials for teaching Biblical Greek.)

Crafts and Skills

In our fellowship, as we discuss in chapter 8, brothers and sisters offer dozens of skill and craft workshops including leatherwork, woodwork, blacksmithing, metal casting, pottery, animal husbandry, basketmaking, quilting, cross-stitching, spinning, weaving, sewing, baking and many others. These brothers and sisters teach workshops geared toward home learning; they then help the parents and children to move forward in their workmanship at home as the children work on projects they choose. We plan to produce (and in some cases have begun preparing) written materials to help in these different skill and craft areas, including lists of recommended books. These materials will help the child to follow his gifts, talents and interests in a framework that allows parents to teach the various skills and crafts relationally. Even if the parents don't possess great proficiency in these areas, they can learn with their children and so teach their children as they grow.

As we said, all of these craft and skill projects in our fellowship aim toward presentation at our annual Fair. And any of these projects can grow into group projects that teach how to do this work (such as pottery or tanning). As we discuss in chapter 8, these projects might be displayed at the annual Fair or be incorporated into a how-to book to teach the patterns and practices of a land-centered culture.

Nature Study and Nature Drawing

We are developing a nature study course that will stress the interrelations between all the various aspects of God's creation, showing that we truly dwell in a *uni*verse, a cosmos that came forth as one unified Word spoken by the Creator. We want our children to see how everything that God has made fits together for His purpose, how the times and seasons mark the rhythms of Yahweh's song.

God's Word declares that He has placed the "lights in the expanse of the sky to . . . serve as signs to mark seasons and days and years" (Gen. 1:14). The starting point of this course will lie in observing the sky, seeing how the moon, the stars and the planets change night by night over the year. We are preparing charts on which the children can record their observations, can note which constellations and stars dominate the sky at specific times on a particular night, the phases of the moon, the movements of the planets, even the angle of the sun's changing course through the sky during the year and so on.

This information about the sky will also interrelate with information about the changing weather, for example, the kinds of clouds, weather fronts, winds and rains, temperature and so on. As the children learn to closely observe the weather, recognizing its seasonal patterns, they'll also learn something about how to predict it, which, of course, proves critically important for farming and gardening. Agricultural activities will form the focus of the nature study course, as the children record their planting times for different crops, the time when the plants start sprouting, heading and become ready for harvest, as well as relevant seasonal information about domestic animals. The children can also record when different pests or diseases strike in the garden. They will become aware of and sensitive to the diverse interrelations of heaven and earth, how the appearance of a particular constellation in the sky announces the time to plant corn or how the disappearing of a particular constellation might indicate the time to harvest potatoes; how the blooming of a particular wildflower warns of the imminent danger of attacks by tomato worms and so on.

So the children will correlate their nature observations with the shifting patterns of the heavenly bodies in the skies and with other natural changes. When do the bluebonnets bloom? When do the mule deer cast their antlers? When does the sap flow in the box elders or sugar maples? When do the chickens molt? When do the wild geese or sand hill cranes migrate? When do the monarch butterflies emerge from their cocoons and what plants do they like to make their cocoons on? What kind of flowers do the bees make their honey from at different times of the year? The children can record all this information in a coordinated chart, such as the one we are developing, as they learn to closely watch the changing times and seasons, learning the patterns and harmonies of the cosmos, truly recognizing that the times and seasons are Yahweh's and not a product of man's mind or man's will. They will also learn practical information that will help them to take dominion over creation. All of these observations will help them to feel more at home in creation, in all its diversity and fullness, from the celestial macrocosm of the galaxies above to the miniature world of the insect below.

Within the context of this coordinated nature study course, the children can then go on to expand their studies in any area in which they feel an interest, learning more about the wildflowers when they bloom or more about the bees, more about the constellations and so on, pursuing in depth their studies of these various aspects of creation as they become aware of them in the course of their observations. Writing and drawing both play a central part in nature study. Through their writings, the children can relate their experiences and feelings about the natural world as they enter into closer relationship with it through their studies. And through their drawing they can concentrate not only on learning the skill of drawing but, more importantly, on learning the art of seeing, of learning to look into God's creation to see the beauty, wisdom and purpose He manifests there. This will in turn bring them into deeper relationship with creation and so into deeper relationship with the Creator who declares His invisible nature through the visible world (Rom. 1:19-20). To teach nature study, you can do a workshop similar to the writing workshop, only concentrating on drawing, but including writing, discussion, looking at plants, animals and so on, as well as going on walks and doing projects (for example, gathering, drying and noting the uses of wildflowers).

Nature Study

(Some of these goals overlap with science goals covered in the Readers.)

Goals—first grade:

—The sky

The sun, its importance for all life

The earth's daily rotation making night and day

The moon, its different phases

Identifying the Big Dipper, the North Star and the Milky Way

God's purpose in giving us the sun, moon and stars (Gen. 1:14-19)

—Weather

Introduction to clouds, wind, humidity, precipitation, storms, temperature, seasonal changes in the weather

—Gardens and crops

Seeds and growing plants

The need for soil, water and light

How plants flower and produce fruit that we use

—Domestic animals

How they help us

Identifying them and what we call them, for example, "ram, ewe, lamb"

How we take care of domestic animals:

how we feed them and care for them

what kinds of shelters or enclosures we provide for them

Knowing different breeds of animals and why we want different breeds

—Wild animals

Identifying wild animals:

birds, mammals, fish, reptiles, amphibians, insects and so on

Where they live, what they eat, their life cycles
and how they adapt to the different seasons
Safety considerations about wild animals

—Wild plants
Identifying common local wildflowers, shrubs and
trees
Safety considerations about wild plants: poison
ivy, thorns, poisonous plants and so on
Introduction to pollination, seed scattering
Collecting and pressing wildflowers

Goals—second grade:

—The sky
How the earth orbits around the sun
The seasons
The winter and summer solstices
The equinoxes
The moon, its position in relation to the sun and
the earth
The lunar cycle: how the moon "rises" and "sets"
and how it orbits around the earth
Using the Big Dipper and Polaris to help find
some of the brightest stars and key constella-
tions

—Weather
Basics of measuring and recording temperature,
rainfall, pressure, humidity, wind direction and
speed
Different types of clouds, thunder, lightning, rainbows, hail, snow, sleet

—Gardens and crops
Basics of gardening
Preparing the soil
Planting
Caring for the growing plants
Harvesting, storage

—Domestic animals
Taking dominion over animals
Safety around animals
Domestic fowl: chickens, ducks, turkeys, geese

and so on
Incubation and hatching of eggs
Care for the young
Feeding
Growth and changes
Egg laying
Shelters and fencing
Learning about honeybees
Work animals: horses, oxen, mules, donkeys,
    herding and hunting dogs
Animals for food, leather and fibers: cattle, sheep,
    goats and so on
—Wild animals
Distinguishing characteristics of groups: mam-
    mals, insects, fish, amphibians and so on
Usefulness to man:
    meat: wild fowl, deer, elk and so on
    skins: beaver, mink, muskrat and so on
Predators and pests to man
Life cycles of wild animals
How they relate to other wild animals and to wild
    plants, gardens and crops
—Wild plants
Effect on wild plants of different types of soil,
    amount of sunlight, water, temperature, altitude
All the various types of pollination and seed dis-
    persal
How animals use wild plants for food and shelter
How humans use them: medicines, dyes, food,
    tanning, herbs, teas, materials for baskets, furni-
    ture and so on

Goals—third grade:

—The sky
Our solar system
The sun and the other planets
Telling time by the sun
The moon, gravity and tides
Eclipses
Identifying some of the planets in the sky

Learning many constellations and stars
Introduction to telling time by the stars
—Weather
    Frontal systems and weather changes:
        barometric pressure, weather patterns
—Gardens and crops
    Fertilizer, composting, soil structure
    Companion planting, how to lay out a garden
    Watering, mulching, controlling pests
    When to harvest, how to harvest
—Domestic animals
    How to keep animals and their pens, corrals and
        coops clean
    How to feed animals that work and animals for
        meat
    How we get wool from sheep and the hair from
        rabbits and goats
    How to milk cows and goats and take care of the
        milk
—Wild animals
    When wild animals have their young, how they
        provide for them, feed them, train them
    Animals that are active in the daytime, at night
    Animal signs and tracks
    Special relationships between animals in their en-
        vironment
    "Instincts" such as migration
—Wild plants
    Identification of most local wildflowers, shrubs
        and trees
    Identifying the parts of plants and their functions
    Collecting certain local herbs for culinary and
        medicinal use; edible wild plants

Goals—fourth grade:

—The sky
    Our sun and other stars (color, magnitude, size)
    Galaxies
    Comets, meteors, nebulae
    Constellations and telling the seasons by the stars

Making a simple sextant to find latitude, longitude
Telling direction by the stars
—Weather
Making and using simple weather-measuring
devices:
wind gauge, hygrometer, barometer
Worldwide weather patterns and ocean currents
and how they affect us
Hurricanes, tornados, floods
—Gardens and crops
Testing the soil
Greenhouses
Hybrids and plants that reproduce true
Selecting good plants and saving seed
Plant propagation
Combating plant diseases
Weed control
Irrigation, different methods
Estimating food needs and garden yields
Other kinds of plants, orchard, vineyards, field
crops
—Domestic animals
How to combat and control animal predators,
pests and diseases
Training domestic animals
Breeding animals for desired characteristics
Beekeeping: caring for the hives and harvesting
honey
Slaughtering, skinning, cutting meat
—Wild animals
Hunting, fishing and trapping
Cleaning, skinning and preparing game
Proper disposal of blood and offal
Care of meat and hides
Food chains and animal populations:
animal competition
death
Animal diseases that endanger humans and live-
stock
—Wild plants
Learning botanical descriptions and terminology

Growing desirable wild plants in the garden
Bad wild plants for livestock
Controlling noxious weeds
Antidotes for plant poisoning
Beneficial native grasses for livestock

Nature Drawing

Goals—first grade:

—Introduction to basic colors
  Seeing colors in creation
  Relating proper colors to creation (fruits,
    vegetables, flowers, animals and other elements
    of nature)
  Changes in color as related to seasons
—Introduction to basic shapes
  Identifying and making circles, ovals, squares,
    rectangles, triangles and so on with crayon,
    paper and scissor activities
  Creating basic shapes with watercolor brushes,
    pencils and crayons to develop eye-hand coor-
    dination
  Exploring and feeling textures and shapes
    through rubbings of nature objects (such as
    leaves, bark and so on) using crayon, pencil and
    charcoal
—Introduction to field drawing
  Use of pencil for basic gesture, line and contour
    drawings of plants and animals from first-grade
    nature studies

Goals—second grade:

—Field drawing
  Continue line, gesture and contour drawings with
    emphasis on seeing details; paralleling the
    second-grade nature studies
—Colors
  Creating primary, secondary and tertiary colors
  Using water color to explore color blends
  Using watercolor pencils to express realistic color

on plant and animal drawings
—Shapes
Relating basic shapes to masses of natural objects by using outline drawings and tracings (training the hand to communicate what the eye/mind sees)

Goals—third grade:

—Field drawing
Drawing more complex nature objects
Special projects such as weekly drawings that track growth of seed through plant and fruit production
Drawing picture associations (that is, what leaves, flowers or fruit go on different plants, trees, bushes and herbs)
Drawing insects related to the plants they attack to help new gardeners identify pests
Associate pictures of animals with the different kinds of food they eat (draw the grains and so on)
—Introduction to *value* (black, white and shades of grey)
Adding simple concepts of depth perception through use of shade and shadow, texture, placement of items in front of each other and so on

Goals—fourth grade:

—Introduction to keeping a field sketchbook
Emphasize field sketch concepts (focus on identifying varieties of leaf patterns, bark textures, proportion of leaves to limbs or fruit and so on)
Extensive use of charcoal and pencil; introduce use of pen and ink (focus on creating the feel of textures, shades and shadows to create perspective)
—Broaden the study of *value* (black, white and shades of grey)
—Introduce drawing from photos

—Introduce use of camera (with black-and-white film)
—Color
    Combining media (such as watercolor washes
    over pencil or ink drawings)
    Introduce creating shades in watercolor by ad-
    ding opposing colors

Outside Reading

You'll want to share books with your children besides those supplied by our curriculum, particularly stories, which children love to read (unless their desire to do so has been crushed). You'll generally find the best material in historical stories and in stories centered on the land; in contrast, romances, mysteries, science fiction, stories glorifying war and related stories by their very nature will prove harmful to your child, promoting man-centered, man-exalting attitudes and values. Even the historical and land-centered stories, however, will need careful reading (and generally some editing) on your part as you guide your children through them.

As books on writing for children have noted, children read primarily not for entertainment but to learn. So what they read influences them especially greatly because they consciously seek to follow the guidance offered by the writer. This is especially true if you limit their access to other media and restrict their reading matter. If you do this, then you imply your approval of whatever your children read, which gives it even more weight and importance. So you need to read carefully the stories that you share with them and edit those stories diligently when necessary.

As we explain in *Right Words*, a story presents the most powerful form of writing to absorb the reader's attention. The narrative form most compellingly brings the reader into agreement with the author's viewpoint by leading the reader to identify with characters who share the author's point of view. There's nothing wrong in principle with this, for even the Bible does it (in fact, the Bible originated it). But it can prove extremely dangerous when the author's viewpoint rests on man-centered deceptions (and, of course, even those with an ostensibly godly world view can abuse the power of the written word, inserting viewpoints dictated by vested, self-centered interests). And, again, children prove particularly vulnerable to identifying with and absorbing the viewpoints of characters they read about.

All this doesn't mean we should eliminate reading. It does demand reading carefully, watching for subtle nuances. *Right Words* will help you do this (giving examples of ways in which writers try to manipulate their readers through the writers' use of hidden presuppositions and other means), as will the Grammar and Dialectic Synopses we discuss on pp. 474-76 and 494-506 below. These materials will deepen your critical insight so you can identify problem areas in your children's reading and sharpen their critical awareness. You'll want to show your children how the author tries to absorb them into his viewpoint through what's called "the suspension of disbelief." This indicates the means through which the author induces the reader to forget that he's reading about someone and something invented by an author and begins to see the story not only as reality but even as a reality with which the reader sympathizes and identifies. You want to teach your child how to suspend "the suspension of disbelief" so he can discern man-centered views (which often slip into Christian as well as secular stories).

Obviously this ability to see through an author's deceptions grows with maturity and experience, but only if you train your child. As numerous authors have pointed out, every time you read something, you on some level enter a covenant or agreement with the author. Your child is too young and malleable to covenant even on this level with those who oppose God-centered views without becoming conformed to some degree to their image. So you must intervene to prevent this. This intervention won't always mean simply eliminating false material. It may mean presenting written explanations or writing questions in the margin to serve as springboards to discussions. Through these discussions and your general efforts to teach critical reading skills, you will prepare your children to enter into meaningful dialectic with the world. And as the older ones grow, they'll even reach the point at which, under your supervision, they'll be able to edit reading material for your younger children.

Fifth, Sixth and Seventh Grades

Stories and Grammar Synopses on Culture,
  Knowledge, Community and History (for History,
  see following item)
Biographical Narratives and *Chosen Generation*
  (which includes history, community and culture,
  geography, reference and research skills, word
  studies, Bible studies)
Skill and Craft Projects
Right Words
Hebrew
Calligraphy
Arithmetic
Spelling
At Home in the Universe (nature study)
Koinonia Character Curriculum

Stories and Elementary Dialectic Synopses, Biographical Narratives and Chosen Generation

The Bible-based readers will prepare the child to begin this next level of his reading and study of the subjects covered in the Readers. These subjects, as our discussion of the Readers themselves has shown, cover a wide range, including history, culture, community and so on. On this next level, the child will begin a more comprehensive and complete study of the subjects to which the Reader introduced him. As we've discussed in chapters 7 and 8 above, our Koinonia Curriculum finds its meaning and relational context as an integral part within the *unit* of the Body of Christ. The curriculum prepares children to find their places as whole men and women pressing forward to bring forth the church as the complete witness of the manifold wisdom of God. And this positive momentum of the Body in its press toward perfection takes place in the context of the church's dialectic with the world. This dialectic, as we've explained, serves as the framework of Christian curriculum within which fit all the secular academic subjects. To repeat, our Readers lay a grammar level basis for this dialectic, and at the same time they interrelate knowledge for the child to strengthen and deepen his vision of the spiritual purpose of

God-centered, land-based community life, excite him about his participation in that community life and purpose, and give him an understanding to see how his practical activities interrelate with the spiritual vision of the community, with the history of God's people, with the sciences—how all together form integral elements of the unit of the Body of Christ as it presses forward to realize God's vision and purpose. We've already said that, given the child's active participation in the God-centered, land-based culture and the inherent, inexorable conflict between that culture and secular culture, a clear understanding of the spiritual conflict of cultures becomes tangibly important for the child. We must make the child aware of this conflict, opening his eyes to its reality and intensity, and then guide him into and through a comprehensive study of these conflicting cultures.

Both his studies in his Bible-based readers and his participation in the life of his community, including his craft and skill workshops, prepare him to see the importance of, and lay the foundation for, a deeper level of study. These deeper, dialectic studies of the conflict of cultures stand on two levels, the beginning or elementary level of the dialectic and the full-fledged or secondary dialectic level. The elementary level of the dialectic offers a basic introductory view of the God-centered spiritual vision of the topic. It presents this positive vision in the context of the conflict of cultures, but without pursuing that conflict in depth. Then the dialectical level of study offers a comprehensive dialectic with the world. Through this dialectic the child learns the key imbalances and weaknesses of the man-centered view of the subject and the spiritual implications of the man-centered view. All this helps him to see the absolute necessity of the God-centered alternative. We present the elementary level of the dialectic of these studies in the fifth through seventh grades and the secondary dialectic level in the eighth through tenth grades.

Four main areas of study stand out. The child goes through all of them on the elementary level of dialectic before moving on to the secondary dialectic level. These areas include culture, knowledge (including philosophy and science), community (including government, education, mass media, art and literature) and history. Each major area of study begins with a realistic story that shows in a graphic, compelling way the importance of the subject. After he reads the story, the student then studies a first level Synopsis of the subject. This gives him a basic God-centered perspective. For example, as we've mentioned before, the culture course begins with a story that shows the conflict between a God-centered, land-based community and the secular community around it; it focuses on the life of a family that has recently moved into that land-based community. In this context, the child sees the importance of the conflict of cultures. Then the first level Synopsis of Culture presents the basic positive vision of a God-centered, land-based culture and lays a groundwork for understanding how exactly that vision contrasts to the man-centered vision behind urban industrialism. (Before and after reading and studying the first level Synopsis, the child takes a simple true-false, multiple choice test, which we've learned greatly helps children focus their attention on specific areas that they do not know as they read the first level Synopsis.*) Parents teach this elementary-level synopsis in the context of a discussion that becomes the central teaching tool on this level of learning. (See "Secondary Dialectic Synopses" under "The Dialectic Level: Eighth, Ninth and Tenth Grades" for a full presentation of how to conduct this discussion and why it is so important.)

After finishing the first level Synopsis, rather than going to the secondary dialectic study of culture, which will be too difficult for the child at this point, he then proceeds to level one of the next subject, knowledge. Again, he begins with a story that shows the importance of studying the subject. The first level Synopsis follows the story and gives the God-centered vision of knowledge in contrast to the man-centered view. The Synopsis shows the child the nature of relational knowledge and wisdom in contrast to fragmented, man-centered knowledge. It shows how this contrast links to the contrasting visions of culture (as we discussed in the first chapters of *Wisdom's Children*) and how these contrasting views of knowledge shape conflicting visions of philosophy and science.

The child then proceeds to level one of community, which again begins with a story that shows the importance of this subject. Then an elementary Synopsis on community offers the God-centered vision of a voluntary, covenant community based on the family, which transmits God-centered relational knowledge, in contrast to the man-centered Statist vision

---

* See p. 496 below for further discussion of this point.

based on compulsory education and technological mass-media, which transmits the fragmented, detached knowledge of the man-centered view. This first level also covers art and literature. It presents the God-centered view as means for glorifying God, in contrast to the man-centered view, which exalts man above God.

Finally, we proceed to the elementary study of history, which on this level presents the most extensive material and helps to tie together everything that the child has learned so far on the elementary level of the dialectic, and even much that he has learned in his Readers as well. Rather than merely presenting one story here, we will present a number of stories, each of which covers a key period of history. These stories offer a series of biographical narratives that cover the major peaks and periods of history. They will focus on characters, sometimes real, sometimes fictional, the historical conflicts these characters face and the means by which they overcome these conflicts. For example, your child will read a story about characters during the time of Abraham, and during the pagan Roman empire. He will see life in key periods in the history of Israel and in the first centuries of the church. He will read about characters and conflicts in the medieval period, during the Reformation, in the times of Cromwell and Isaac Newton, during the French Revolution, the American Civil War and so on.

These stories will all focus on lifelike characters who face real issues and events. For example, how does a Christian boy relate in real-life situations to the issues raised by the persecution of the church in the Roman Empire or the American Civil War? Within the context of the unfolding story of the main character and the problems he confronts, the stories will interweave accurate descriptions of geography, history, politics, art, culture, customs and so on. So these stories will interrelate material from the subjects he's already studied on the grammar level. Often they will present historical accounts of real characters, such as Cabeza de Vaca or Isaac Newton; other times they will present fictional characters, but characters set in the context of historical people and events.

The stories will present real questions and problems that the characters must overcome, and in this sense they will introduce the student to the dialectic level of study. But they will not themselves present a systematic, dialectical examination of the issues involved: that will take place on the secondary dialectic level. Rather, at this point, the stories will serve as entrees for the children's search for deeper answers to questions they see the stories' characters confront. Because the children will see how the outer conflicts the characters face relate to internal struggles going on within the characters, because they'll see the characters change and grow as they overcome the interrelated conflicts outside and within, the historical questions and problems will take on real meaning and greater urgency for them. Through their insight into these historical conflicts, the children will see the origins of the conflicts people face today and hence the relevance of history for their own lives in the present.

Because the children will see the contemporary relevance of the conflicts and culture of these historical periods, they will want to turn to a deeper study of the issues they find in their narratives, a study that will present a more comprehensive context for learning history. They will find this in *Chosen Generation: A Study of World History*, which presents a first-level dialectic view of history. This book will present a wide-ranging view of the unfolding development of world history (in terms of the daily life, major events, main figures, central trends and so on of each epoch), which will enable the children to see the broader significance and meaning of the events they read about in the narrative. It will present the unfolding story of God's purpose in history, beginning with the Creation and the Fall. On a basic level, it will follow from its beginnings to the present day the historical conflict between paganism and Judaism, between those who seek to center their lives in man and those who seek to center their lives in God and His purposes. It will present a sequential narrative of history in the context of the basic dialectic of historical conflict, interweaving the ongoing development of culture, philosophy, science, art, politics and so on, presenting on a basic level the key historical issues of the day (the issues already touched upon in the biographical narratives).

Through their study of the material in these books, the children will begin to see more clearly both the nature of the man-centered world system that has emerged on the face of the earth today and also God's alternative to that system. Their eyes will open to the golden thread of God's purpose as it works its way through His Body, a purpose that has been woven through the fabric of history. It is the story of this thread that we want to show, as it winds itself through the Middle Ages, the Reformation, the Renaissance, the birth of modern science, the settlement of America, the industrial revolution and on to our own times.

The parts of this book will correspond to the biographical narratives; so after a child reads one of the historical stories, he can then go on to read the parallel section in *Chosen Generation*, which will, however, cover a much wider sweep of history than the corresponding story. These books will encourage more serious thought and discussion about questions of the Christian purpose and relationship to the world than the Readers of the previous grades did. Through their studies of these books, the children can concentrate for weeks at a time on particular subjects, such as the great ancient civilizations or the birth of modern science or the industrial revolution. So, they can study these subjects in some depth to understand their key trends and historical meanings, interrelating studies of science, geography and other subjects when appropriate. These books form the core of the children's academic curriculum in these years.

Following their reading of the biographical narrative and the appropriate section of *Chosen Generation*, the children then go on to work in a study guide that will draw out explicitly the issues raised in the story and in *Chosen Generation*. This study guide will focus on showing the relevance to the children's lives of the issues raised in the stories: for example, the questions raised by the story of the boy at the time of the Roman Empire will raise contemporary questions on the relation between Christians and politics and the use of violence. These articles will explain in greater depth the need to understand these issues in the broader historical context of the conflict of paganism versus Judaism.* The articles will begin to raise the key questions, the "why?" questions. These will inspire the children to seek a deeper dialectical understanding of these issues, to begin to look farther into the questions that excite them. By doing so, it will point them toward the secondary-level Dialectic Synopses they will study beginning in the eighth grade.

We find this sequence of (1) narrative story (as in the

* See "True Wholeness" in chapter 1.

biographical histories) (2) narrative mixed with dialectic (as in
Chosen Generation) and then (3) straight dialectic (as in the
study guide and Dialectic Synopses) in the Bible itself. The Old
Testament begins with the narrative stories of Genesis. This
leads into Exodus, which combines narrative with dialectic:
here we see the continuation of the story of the Israelites, but
we also find elements of the Law, which presents a dialectic
that defines relationships among God's people and their
relationship with the world. Then we have the straight dialectic
of the presentation of the Law in Leviticus. These are followed
by further narratives that show what God's people did with
what they received and then the dialectic of the prophets.

Likewise, in the New Testament, we begin with the narrative
stories of the gospels, move into the combination of narrative
and dialectic in the book of Acts, which parallels Exodus as the
story of the emergence of the church from the world. Then this
in turn moves into the dialectic of the Epistles, which presents
and defines our battle with the world, the flesh and the devil and
defines all the relationships pertaining to God's people.

God begins His testaments with this pattern because the narrative form best evokes our interest, since this writing form
brings us closest to real life, and this in turn stimulates our
desire to search out the deeper questions that the narrative
raises. As author Joan Aiken points out, a story

is a form of authority. If I tell you a story, you are almost
certain to listen. A story is easier to follow, and therefore
to remember, than a chain of disconnected facts, because it has causality, one event leads to another. It is like
swimming with the current—whereas memorising unrelated facts is like swimming upstream.[5]

A story relates facts in a way that makes them most meaningful to the life of the reader. As your child sees Isaac Newton
growing up in the context of Cromwell's England, sees the
spiritual and intellectual conflicts he faces as he seeks to
maintain his Christian faith in an increasingly rationalistic and
secular world, comes to understand the place that his scientific studies played in this conflict, suddenly he'll want to learn
not only about history but also about the science that Newton
developed. The narrative format, by interweaving the elements of life in a lifelike context will open the child's eyes to
the meaning of his studies, which will inspire him to pursue
them rather than kill him with boredom.

We include instruction in reference skills in *Chosen Generation* and in the study guide so that the child can learn to use encyclopedias, atlases, concordances, charts, maps, Biblical language lexicons, topical Bibles and other Bible study helps, dictionaries, synonym books and other helps in research and writing. So the child will learn how to track down and research information from many different sources. He will also begin to learn to really use the Bible to resolve questions.* Much of this can be taught and used in the context of discussions with his parent-teacher.

(We will go on to discuss the second dialectic level of these studies in the next section, on the Eighth, Ninth and Tenth Grades. You'll also find there more information on how you can teach to your children the material that we've described in this section.)

In our fellowships, these studies of secular culture will be taught at the same time as a course on church literature that guides the children by the Spirit through the key truths of God's Word, helping them to mature and grow in their places in the Body. This course is also still in the works at this time.

> *Goals—fifth, sixth and seventh grades (the first three headings describe the elementary-level Dialectic Synopses):*
>
> *—Culture*
> Understanding of the spiritual nature of human culture. The God-centered view of culture versus the man-centered view. The positive purpose behind a God-centered, land-based culture.
>
> *—Knowledge*
> Understanding the two basic kinds of knowledge: contrasting man-centered, detached knowledge to relational knowledge, but focusing on presenting the God-centered view of relational knowledge. Understanding how this relational knowledge ties into wis-

---

* Before beginning *Chosen Generation*, students who begin the Koinonia Curriculum should go through the books of the Reader for the first through fourth grades. Even though these books may be below their grade level, we feel that older children will profit from reading them. (Of course, they'll go through them much more quickly than in four years.)

dom. Basic understanding of why man's efforts to create philosophies, natural sciences, psychologies and social sciences rooted in man-centered knowledge must end in failure and that all truth in these fields of knowledge derives from God's truth.

—*Community*

Understanding the spiritual dynamic behind all human community. How and why pagan man seeks to form communities through the compulsory power of law and the State, in contrast to the God-centered view of community based on voluntary covenants of church and family (with the State limited to the negative role of restraining evildoers). Basic understanding of the role of compulsory education and the mass media in contemporary society. God-centered view of the proper function of the State as a merely negative, restraining force in contrast to the man-centered view, which sees the State as the principle institution for shaping society, for forming the image of corporate man.

Basic knowledge of art and literature as means through which man seeks to find and inform a unified vision for his community. But, again, two contrasting visions are possible—one exalting God, the other exalting man. We shall show, briefly, through paintings and sculpture and then through literature how the man-centered view distorts reality but how the God-centered view shows reality as it truly is. We shall also show the God-centered origins of all that's true in art and literature.

—*History* (this describes the contents of *Chosen Generation: An Outline of World History*)

a. Introduction

The basis of man's life in the present lies in his view of the past, because the past defines the present. Contrast of the Biblical, God-centered view with the man-centered, evolutionary view, wherein man seeks to provide his own origins. Why the man-centered view of history lacks all cohesion and meaning, which can come only through the God-centered view.

b. The ancient civilizations of Babylon and Egypt,

and the birth of the Hebrew people.

c. Ancient Israel from Exodus to Exile.

d. Greek and Roman civilization, from their beginnings to the decline of the Roman Empire; Israel and Judaism during this period; the rise of the church and its paganizing.

e. The Middle Ages: From the fall of the Roman Empire to the Renaissance.

f. Renaissance and Reformation: From the beginning of the Italian Renaissance to the consolidation of Protestant power in Germany, Geneva and England.

g. Exploration, Mercantilism and Empire: From the rise of European exploration and the beginnings of empire to the consolidation of empire by Spain, France and England.

h. Religious Wars, the Rise of Science and the Age of Rationalism: From the religious wars in Europe and England to the beginning of the Enlightenment's triumph.

i. The Enlightenment, French Revolution and Napoleon.

j. British Dominance: From the birth of industrialism to the First World War.

k. America: The Rise of American Power. From the colonization of America to the time of the First World War. (Some of this will have been touched on in earlier parts, in "g" through "j.")

l. The First World War, the Holocaust and Second World War: The rise of Germany, First World War, Russian Revolution, rise of Nazism, the Second World War, and its aftermath, including beginning of nuclear age and world revolution.

m. America and the Twentieth Century: America from the end of the First World War till today, and important changes throughout the contemporary world.

Geography

Most of this material will be taught as part of *Chosen Generation: A Study of World History.*

Goals—fifth, sixth and seventh grades:

—The earth
  Industrialization and its effects on the earth
  Pollution: land, air and water
  Stripping of resources
  Energy consumption
  Greenhouse effect
—Maps
  Latitude and longitude studies
  Locating cities and places on world, country,
    state and city maps
—Countries
  Major countries by continent: Europe, Central
    America, South America, Africa, Asia and
    Oceania
—Israel
  The Middle East today:
  Israel and surrounding countries
—United States
  Review by region:
    learn geographical features, animals, crops and
    so on as they pertain to self-sufficiency
  Learn capitals and major cities
  Territories of the United States
—Community
  Rural life versus city life
  Family farms, neighbors
  Agri-business
  Population migration to cities
  Dependence on the system
  Culture
  The effects of geography on cultures of the world

Crafts and Skills

See "Crafts and Skills" under "The First Four Years."

Nature Study and Nature Drawing

See this heading under "The First Four Years."

Nature Study

Goals—fifth, sixth and seventh grades:

The first four grades have introduced the basic areas of nature study, but much room remains for deeper study and individual projects. Projects, research and study will increasingly focus on the needs of a self-sufficient agricultural community functioning in harmony with God, our fellowmen and God's creation—that is, nature. We can offer a few suggestions for study and projects to show some potential direction, but they are not intended to limit you in any way.

—The sky

Learn to navigate and fix geographical position by the stars

Learn all the constellations visible in your locality and their relationship to the times and seasons

Learn how to use a small telescope to study the stars and planets

Learn how the sun's movements and angle in the sky is a factor in designing solar energy projects

—Weather

Learn how to predict approaching weather by observing animal behavior and plants as well as weather signs in the sky

Photograph cloud formations and other weather phenomena and make a local weather handbook

Learn about the "greenhouse effect," "acid rain," pollution and other problems caused by our industrial culture

Learn how we can depend on God for His provision, rain and good weather in season

—Gardens and crops
  Planting and harvesting seasons
  Protection from pests and diseases, care, saving seeds and so on.
  Husbanding fruit or nut bearing trees, including pest control and grafting
  Growing grapes and berries
  Field crops and how to work the soil with horse drawn equipment, cultivating, harvesting and storing crops
  Growing grass and crops for animals, estimating crop area and yields to meet the needs of various animals
—Domestic animals
  How to care for and use saddle horses and workhorses, and use horse-drawn equipment
  Lambing; other kinds of animal births
  Animal breeding
  Care for sick or injured animals
—Wild animals
  Hunting and trapping animals for food, hides and pest control
  Rifle and bow hunting
  Hunting dogs, blinds and so on
  Fishing for different kinds of fish
  Identifying local mammals, reptiles, amphibians, insects, birds, fish, flowers, shrubs and trees, knowing their habitats, life cycles and how they are affected by the seasons
  Collecting and identifying insects and gathering information on each one to share with the community
—Wild plants
  Tapping tree sap for syrup; knowing the right time; how to tap; how to gather and process the sap into syrup
  Identifying and learning about all the local plants, their benefits and the problems they cause; their life cycles
  Collecting and displaying plants and information about them to help others in the community learn local plants

Nature Drawing

Goals—fifth, sixth and seventh grades:

—Keep a field sketchbook as an in-depth nature study
—Composition
    Thinking through and planning a drawing accord-
    ing to the basic elements of design before you
    actually start
—Introduce more concepts of perspective
—Color
    Introduce more detailed look at relationships of
    colors, to each other, warm and cool, seasons
    and so on and to the items you are representing
    Add pastel chalk to expand experience with
    blending of colors
—Other media samplings: oil painting, block printing, silk
    screening, scratchboard, stenciling, sign making,
    carving, constructing, clay sculpture and so on ac-
    cording to child's interest
—Creating paper from organic sources

Science

In addition to the dialectic discussion of science, we are
working on a practical, relational guide through the sciences—including astronomy, physics, chemistry, geology,
biology and so on. We want to present this material from a
God-centered perspective and in a form that ties it into the
lives and activities of our children, including such things as the
crafts and skills they learn.

Many of the concepts and principles that we study on this
level continue what we began in the first four years. We have
striven to give our children a general framework that includes
most aspects of God's creation. Although the Bible declares
that "there is nothing new under the sun," at each level of instruction, the child's increasing ability to grasp details and
relationships will allow us to build a more comprehensive
house of knowledge within the framework of the previous
years' instruction.

We shall strive to introduce this new information, as has been done in the previous years, so that our children can readily see the relationship between the text and their own lives. As much as possible, we will try to relate this knowledge through specific situations that might be encountered within a family in a community seeking to live according to the patterns of God in self-sufficiency.

Goals—fifth, sixth and seventh grades:

—The limits of science
    Limits of conception
    Limits of perception
    Revelation and the scientific method
—Astronomy
    Order in the universe:
      the earth and the moon
      our solar system
      the galaxies
    Time and distance
    Gravity
    Laws of motion
    Laws of thermodynamics
    Creation versus evolution in astronomy
—Matter/Chemistry
    States of matter
    The elements and molecules
—Physics/Energy
    Solar energy (nuclear):
      electromagnetic spectrum
      light
      heat
    Chemical energy
    Sound
    Electricity and magnetism
    Simple and complex machines:
      force
      work
      friction
    Optics (mirrors and lenses)
    Wave phenomena:
      transmission of energy

observable effects
—Geology
   The earth's structure
   Minerals
   Creation versus evolution in geology
—Biology
   Foundations of life
   Cells
   Metabolism
   Plants:
     photosynthesis
     soil requirements
     tropisms
     fruit and reproduction
   Animals:
     classification
     body parts and their functions
     behavior patterns
     husbandry
   Creation versus evolution in biology
—Health and nutrition
   Nutrition
   Diet
   Hygiene
   Herbs
—Meteorology
   The atmosphere
   Weather:
     temperature, moisture and wind
     systems and storms
   Climate:
     cycles and patterns
     topographical influences
   Prediction:
     clouds
     pressure
     lore
     plant and animal behavior

Writing

The fifth through seventh graders will do more advanced writing than the earlier grades, as described in the *Guidelines for Teaching Your Children Writing at Home*. The fifth, sixth and seventh grader will keep a notebook and journal in which he will record some of his experiences and his responses to them.

Our primary concern still is the development of the child's real voice, his flow of words from his heart onto the paper. But you will now concentrate more on developing style and proficiency in grammar on this level, working with both *Right Words* and the grammar handbook we are developing.

See "Writing" under "The First Four Years."

Writing Goals

Goals—fifth grade:

—Description that shows what we experience through senses
—Comparisons and contrasts
—Describing a character so we can see him
—Simple dialogue
—Describing an event or activity (such as chores or work experience)
—Letter writing

Goals—sixth grade:

—Developing sense of rhythm and sound of words; basics of poetry
—Using metaphors and similes
—Description that shows rather than tells the meaning of what we experience
—Getting inside a character
—Describing a workday
—Writing a scene
—Writing a basic story that shows a conflict and the resolution of the conflict

Goals—seventh grade:

—Effective use of point of view
—Interviewing
—Stories and testimonies that effectively and powerfully
  combine all the key writing elements

Grammar and Punctuation Goals

Goals—fifth grade:

—Sentence structure
   Subject
   Predicate
   Phrases
   Clauses
—Usage
   Direct object
   Predicate nominative
   Modifiers
—Punctuation
   Comma
   Parentheses
   Dash
   Semicolon
   Apostrophe
   Contractions
—Diagraming
   Simple sentences

Goals—sixth grade:

—Types of sentences
   Simple
   Compound
   Complex
   Compound-Complex
—Paragraphs
—Abbreviations
—Usage
   Indirect object

Prepositions
Conjunctions
—Verbals, appositive
—Diagraming
More complex sentences

Goals—seventh grade:

—Case
—Voice
Active and passive
—Mood
—Agreement
—Hyphenation
—Complex diagraming
—Quotations

Hebrew

In these grades the children continue their Hebrew study, pressing on to higher levels of competency in that language: in conversation, reading and writing.

Goals—fifth, sixth and seventh grades:

Developing a basic working knowledge of Biblical Hebrew, including recognizing the different verb forms and understanding sentence structure, for example, the placing of adjectives and adverbs. Begin by reading and translating the book of Ruth.

Calligraphy

The calligraphy course continues from the earlier grades.

Goals—fifth, sixth and seventh grades:

To be able to write Hebrew in calligraphy. (This would

only apply to those children who have begun writing Hebrew in the fourth grade.)

By the end of the seventh grade, in their English calligraphy, children should be proficient in forming and spacing letters, words and sentences correctly and consistently. They will also learn proper composition, layout and execution of a calligraphy quote for framing. Their writing, especially the cursive form, should flow quickly and smoothly.

Additional calligraphy styles and other forms of calligraphic art can be taught in a calligraphy workshop.

Arithmetic

In the fifth and sixth grades, the child will conclude his basic arithmetic skills. In the same way as the earlier grades, line by line, precept by precept, he will work to master certain prescribed goals within a certain time frame. We are developing teaching books that present this subject within the context of life on a self-sufficient ranch. The concepts and problems revolve around real, everyday ranch-farm situations such as measuring flour to make bread, computing cost for chicken feed or measuring angles to make a toolshed. Also, as in the earlier grades, we keep all the earlier concepts fresh in the child's mind by recalling them in exercises and problems throughout the year. (See note in this section under "The First Four Years" about using traditional textbooks to teach arithmetic.)

Goals—fifth grade:

—Larger numbers, all applications and decimals
—Fractions
    Dividing and multiplying
    Equivalent and comparing
    Lowest common denominators
    Reducing
    Operations with fractions and mixed numbers
—Measurement
    Area, volume and perimeter

—Reading problems, finding essentials
—Averages (includes temperature conversion)
    Centigrade to Fahrenheit
    Fahrenheit to Centigrade

Goals—sixth grade:

—Multiplication and division of measures
—Finding percent
    Fraction equivalents, percents over 100%
—Ratio and proportion
—Circles
    Terms
    Finding circumference with diameter and radius
    Finding area

Goals—seventh grade:

—Mastery of all operations using whole numbers, fractions, decimals
—Percent
    Finding percent of increase
    Finding percent of decrease
    Figuring out commission
    Profit and loss
—Measurement
    Compound measures using all operations
—Graphs
    Pictograph
    Bar graph
    Line graph
    Circle graph
    Scale drawings
    Maps
—Introduction to algebra
    Expressions
    Solving equations
    Positive and negative numbers, all operations
—Time zones

Spelling

The child will continue working in our spelling program.

Outside Reading

See this heading under "The First Four Years."

The Dialectic Level
Eighth, Ninth and Tenth Grades

Dialectic Synopses on Culture, Knowledge (including Philosophy, Science, Medicine, Psychology, Social Science), Community (including Law and Politics, Education, Media, Art and Literature) and History.
Right Words
Skill and Craft projects
Math
Calligraphy
Hebrew
Koinonia Character Curriculum
At Home in the Universe (nature study)
Science

Secondary Dialectic Synopses

After your child has completed the elementary studies of the dialectic discussed above (under Fifth, Sixth and Seventh Grades in the section "Stories and Elementary Dialectic Synopses, Biographical Narratives and Chosen Generation"), he's then ready to go on to study the Secondary Dialectic Synopses of all the subjects he's already covered on the grammar level.

As we've discussed before, the principle goal of all these

Dialectic Synopses, particularly on the secondary level, focuses on the church's relationship to the world, in both the defense of God's people, purpose and vision and in the tearing down of idols and spiritual strongholds that hold people captive (2 Cor. 10:4-5). These Synopses present the Biblical perspective and history, as well as the philosophical and spiritual assumptions, of culture, knowledge (including philosophy, science, medicine, psychology, social science), community (including law and politics, education, media, art and literature) and history. The Secondary Dialectic Synopses entail a fuller, more in-depth refutation of the man-centered views of each of these subjects. As noted before, these Synopses will reveal the basic imbalances and flaws in the man-centered view on each of these subjects, will show the implications and ultimate results of that view, and will therefore demonstrate the absolute necessity of the God-centered view, which we've already presented in part in the Elementary Dialectical Synopses.

Our goal in teaching all this lies not in puffing our children up with empty abstractions but solely in enabling them to fulfill God's purpose in this hour. God's Word, not secular studies, provides the answer to all needs. But secular studies, taught from the perspective of God's Word, enable us to relate to the secular world to promote God's purpose. If our children remain anchored to God's purpose, then they'll learn what they need to know without getting the big head. (And as we mentioned earlier, in our fellowship we will teach all this secularly-oriented material together with material directed explicitly toward edifying the Body and deepening the spiritual relationship of our children and ourselves with God and His people. As we indicated, these church materials are also in preparation now.)

Clearly, you can't teach this material in a home-school relational way, however, unless you've first mastered it yourself. No parent can teach these diverse subjects without previously having been taught, either in some sort of classroom or workshop situation or through a correspondence course. We're not only working on preparing these materials but also on developing means to prepare you, the parent-teacher, so that you can teach your children. We want to both impart this material to you and to help you teach this material to your children.

We're developing a program to lead you step by step through the Elementary Dialectic Synopses. Then, after you've completed these, you will begin learning the Secondary Dialectic Synopses. As you complete all the Dialectic Synopses of particular subjects, you'll have the vision, knowledge and understanding to lead your children through the first level Synopses. By the time you complete all the Secondary Dialectic Synopses, you'll be able to start leading your children through these as well.

As you master the Secondary Dialectic Synopses, then, you'll go over the Elementary Synopses with your children, but now as the teacher rather than the pupil (although in our curriculum program we will have teacher/advisers who will work with parents who teach these materials to their children). So part of mastering the dialectic level for the parents must include mastering the teaching materials they would use to instruct their children, beginning with the teaching materials we're developing to help you instruct your children in the Elementary Synopses we described on pp. 474-76.

One key to teaching your children the Elementary Synopses lies in a point we've already mentioned, that is, that each first level Synopsis (and Secondary Dialectic Synopsis too) comes with a test that the children take both before and after studying the Synopses. Because they take this test first before reading the Synopses, they have a keener interest in what they read, trying to confirm or correct the answers they've already given. The test gives them a concrete, immediate goal to aim for in their study. This gives them direction and stimulates their interest. Nor is this merely an arbitrary goal, because in learning the right answers to these questions, they'll acquire the information that will give them the elementary foundation to build a strong dialectical understanding. This in turn enables them to develop the dialectical insight that can engage in meaningful discourse with the world.

The elementary level Questions (and the Secondary Dialectic Questions too) present basic true or false and multiple choice questions. These types of questions, which permit only one simple answer and ask for no discussion, are extremely valuable for the first level of study, for someone who doesn't yet have a dialectical or relational understanding of what he's being taught. Until one has a dialectical understanding of a subject, he can't yet explain that subject meaningfully to others, because he's just learning it himself. But an important part of this first level of learning, on both the elementary level and the beginning of the secondary dialectic level, lies in the unfolding relationship between the student and teacher or the child and parent. On this level, the student doesn't yet have a complete understanding of the dialectic importance of the topic (although the Problem Story—the stories we talked about before, which show the student the relevance of studying a particular topic, such as culture—has started him on the road to seeing its importance). But the primary reason, on this level, why someone studies the topic is that he trusts the person who tells him that it's important to learn and who teaches him. This is a truly relational level of learning, because it can only flimsily stand apart from the teacher-student relationship. It's based essentially on trust, on the relationship of voluntary submission to authority in love.

Even though the student may not be able to explain what he feels, it's important for him to be able to answer these simple questions with conviction, particularly after he's gone through the Synopses. By giving the correct answer, the student declares that even though he can't yet fully explain why he gives this answer, he can recognize the right answer; based on his acceptance of what he's so far been taught, he has a sense of what's right. Because he trusts the relationship that God has ordained between him and his teacher, he can therefore speak the truth with conviction. So these kinds of questions prove very revealing. And they also become an important source of encouragement to the student when the teacher checks over the student's work and gives it back to him, confirming that they see eye to eye on this subject. So the answers show the student's relationship to his teacher and build his confidence as well as making sure that he has the basic knowledge of the subject that he can build upon. Also remember that these tests give the student an immediate tangible goal to aim for and reach. (Of course, we provide you with an answer key—which you would receive only after you've taken the complete Dialectic course yourself.)

To serve as a further teaching help we provide to those parents who complete the whole Dialectic course a teacher's copy of the Elementary Dialectic Synopses. In the left margin of this teacher's copy, you'll find a number of questions. As you read this copy of the Elementary Synopses, preparing to teach your children, you'll go through these questions, underlining material in the parallel text that you think is especially relevant to the answer you expect from your child. (You'll be prepared to assess this because you will have already completed both the Elementary and Secondary Dialectic course on this subject.) These questions will serve you as a guide for your discussion with your children of the material covered in the Elementary Synopsis, helping you to talk about and to teach this material to your children. The questions will take you and your children to the heart of the material presented in this Synopsis and prepare you thoroughly for the Secondary Dialectic. You must completely understand these questions yourself so that you can use them to teach your children. You should never simply mechanically read these questions to your children, but you must put them in the appropriate form for your children (according to age, their years of schooling, how familiar you feel they would be with this material and so on).

The discussion aims at ensuring that your children possess a clear knowledge of the first level Synopses and at preparing them to go on to the next level, to the Secondary Dialectic Synopses. Through this discussion, you'll take advantage of the home-school situation and do in an oral form what most schools would have to attempt to do through a written essay, that is, ascertain the depth of your children's understanding of the material they've read and studied, and also their ability to communicate what they understand. We've already noted how schools must rely on the essay because only a very limited relationship exists between the teacher and students in a classroom situation. Here in your home school, however, because of the one-on-one or small group situation, and because the students are *your* children, you're able to enter into a much more direct relationship with them, deriving from your discussion an immediate idea of what they know, understand and can express.

In fact, this discussion will give you a much more accurate idea of what they really know than an essay ever could. The essay can give only a limited insight into the depth of most people's understanding, because other obstacles besides lack of knowledge stand in the way of their effort to put their thoughts on paper. Due mainly to the nature of public school education, most people haven't been properly trained to write (and even if they're taught well, children must grow to acquire this skill). So the difficulty people have in writing, whether through improper training or immaturity in skill, will at this stage block the flow of their words and even discourage them in both writing and their other subjects.

But lack of writing skill isn't the only problem with asking for essays on the subjects covered in the Synopses at this level of learning. Your children (when they have merely read through only the elementary level Synopsis on a particular subject) also probably won't know enough about the subject to do such writing, and they may not yet feel enough enthusiasm about the subject necessary to write interestingly about it. All this means that you'll generally get a mechanical, boring piece of writing that stifles the child and puts the teacher to sleep. This discussion is geared to overcome this and help realize the natural excitement that inheres in the material once its relevance becomes apparent.

So your discussion will help you overcome all of these problems: it will give your children knowledge, stimulate their genuine interest and excitement and even teach them the skills in communicating their ideas and knowledge that will later help them to write about the subject too. The discussion will deepen the children's knowledge and understanding of the subject, and by the end of the discussion the children should be able to articulate their thoughts and feelings and relate their understanding to others much more fully and readily than they could have done at the beginning. The discussion will develop their understanding, help them to relate to others, and, as we said, even help to develop the skills of expression that will enable them to later write about the topic of discussion. Through this discussion, the child's excitement should grow because the parent imparts his or her own excitement to the child in the course of these discussions. At the same time, the child will be doing other free writings (see *Right Words*) that will help to develop his skill in writing so that at some point down the road—perhaps very soon—he'll be able to take on larger, dialectical writings, should the need arise and should he feel the gift and burden to bring forth such writings (such as letters to editors and so on).

The larger writings for these subjects, if they do come, will, however, come later, when the child has completed the elementary level of all subjects and has moved beyond the introductory dialectic level in a particular subject area. Yet even on the elementary level you can have any possible advantages of essay-type questions but without the problems. On the first level you can have the types of discussions that Jesus had with his twelve disciples as He brought them up from their own elementary stage. In the Gospels, you'll see Him repeatedly posing questions to them that elicit deep discussions. Then through further questions and answers—their efforts to answer His questions and His corrective responses—He led them through discussions that brought them first to a dialectical and then to a rhetoric level of knowledge.

When you ask a question in the discussion, you must have a comprehensive idea in mind of the answer you want (another reason why you as the teacher must complete the secondary dialectic level of a subject before you teach your children the elementary level). Then have your children answer the question as you guide the discussion to bring forth everything you feel that the answer should include. At some point, you may feel that the children aren't seeing the full scope of the answer, and then you'll have to give them the rest of the answer yourself. When you do that, take care to explain what you tell them. The important thing isn't that they memorize some right answer by rote but that they understand. Only then can they relate their knowledge to others. Of course, you don't want to limit the discussion to some preconceived ideas you have in mind, but you want the discussion to unfold freely in the Spirit. The most exciting part of the discussion comes as your children share their own fresh insights.

To repeat, a key advantage of home education lies in your intimate relationship with your children. This allows you, as you teach them, to immediately get feedback from them concerning what they know. You can pose questions to them that will elicit discussions in which they can freely share what they know and understand. So in the home-school context, the parent can see with immediacy how well the child understands the subject. And, to repeat, in the context of the discussion, the skills can develop that will later serve larger writings, if the need for, or inclination to do, these does arise. Above all, you'll find this method of teaching relational, as you develop a deep dialogue with your kids. It's also a lot of fun.

The discussion questions are found on the parents' copy of the Elementary Dialectic Synopsis. It's not in the children's because the children can't grasp this material on their own, but must depend upon the parents. This of course assumes that the parents have not only a greater capacity to understand but also that they themselves have been taught so that they will themselves thoroughly understand the material. Only then can they can explain it and make it interesting and exciting to their children. (You'll obviously have a clearer idea of how to conduct the discussion if you participate in some sort of teacher-student relationship through which someone else has already guided you, together with other brothers and sisters, through such a discussion on this subject.) With that understanding, parents can then use the material already contained in the Elementary Dialectic Synopsis to guide the discussion in the Spirit.

Once your children have completed their elementary dialectical level studies (described under the fifth through seventh grades above), and you have then led them through the Secondary Dialectic Synopsis of a particular subject, for example of culture or science, they can then go on to examine the secondary Dialectic Level Problems we've prepared in each study area. (Again, you will have already gone through and mastered these problems yourself before you teach them to your children.) In these Dialectic Level Problems, the children will confront and seek to refute secular writers who present man-centered perspectives that conflict with God's truth. We also provide you with a thorough teacher's guide to help you lead your children through these problems. Again, you will need guidance through this whole course of study, including the Secondary Dialectic Level Problems (guidance that we plan to offer and provide), before you can guide your children through them.

Goals—eighth, ninth and tenth grades (Each of these italicized headings and subheadings describes various second-level Dialectic Synopses):

—*Culture as Spiritual War*
 A deeper view of the spiritual nature and conflict of human culture. A philosophical, historical and spiritual overview of the origins, development, significance and destiny of the prevalent world culture of urban-industrialism.

—*Knowledge as Spiritual War*
  a. *Introduction*
  How man tries to use his knowledge to overcome
  the fragmentation of his existence, to bring wholeness and oneness to his world, his life and his
  being. The two types of knowledge man can
  choose to base his understanding of the world
  upon; again, these are the man-centered or God-
  centered views, but we now explore these in much
  greater depth than before.
  We then shall proceed to investigate the basic
  forms of knowledge through which man attempts
  to master the world.

  b. *Philosophy*
  The rise of ancient philosophy from mythology,
  showing its basic man-centered presuppositions,
  and the inescapable dilemmas that inevitably follow from these presuppositions. The subsequent
  development of ancient philosophy, its corrupting
  interaction with Judeo-Christianity; then the development of modern philosophy, including positiv-
  ism; its failure to solve the basic philosophical
  problems, which continue, ultimately bringing forth
  nihilism, the view of the meaninglessness of
  human existence.

  c. *Science*
  Rather than solving his philosophical problems,
  man attempts to develop a practical scientific
  knowledge that will enable him, he hopes, to solve
  the crises of his existence, but this too proves futile.
  Here we shall trace the historical and philosophical
  roots of modern science, especially the role of
  Christianity. We will show the subsequent perversion of science in order to further secular and
  rationalistic philosophies. Also we'll investigate the
  philosophical roots of the struggle of evolution versus creationism. We'll discuss the meaning of the
  quantum (man's most advanced knowledge of the
  nature of physical reality) and the limits of scientific
  knowledge.

  d. *Medicine*
  The scientific promise of the modern age centered

on the hope that medicine would enable man to escape sickness and even death, that is, the ultimate fragmentation of his existence: Descartes and the Enlightenment *philosophes* pioneered this illusion, which still prevails today. While medicine has its positive uses, modern man has made of it an idol.

e. *Science of Man*
Men thought that they could develop a science of man (social sciences comparable to the sciences of the physical world). We shall show how this social science arose as a conscious attempt to create an alternative to the Biblical view. In reality, it succeeded mainly in convincing men to see themselves as mere mechanisms to be controlled by social engineers. We shall also show the roots and dynamic behind psychology, how it served essentially as a secular attempt to understand the mechanism of human thought and feeling independently of the spiritual perspective of the Bible. With the Enlightenment, pagan man tried to develop a totally naturalistic man-centered alternative for understanding the human *psyche*, that is, the soul. These efforts culminated in Freud and his successors and in behaviorism, which sees man as a machine for manipulation. We'll also show how social science in general rests on the promise of a perfect rational society, an illusion that brings only totalitarian controls.

—*Shaping Man's Corporate Image*

a. *Introduction*: Here we explore secular man's futile attempts to solve the crisis of his society.

b. *State and Law*
Secular man seeks to solve his social crisis through the compulsory power of the State and law. This attempt transforms the State into the mechanism of man's self-exaltation, his attempt to prove his self-sufficiency from and even supremacy over God. From Ur to the modern world, man has sought to do this, promising the perfect rational society while actually shaping a unified slave system. He seeks to rationalize society, to bring forth

the corporate image of a new, completely man-centered social order. The primary means to shape the corporate image of society lie in the means of shaping the public mind, education and mass media.

c. *Education*
Here we shall show in depth the function of compulsory public education.

d. *Mass Media*
How mass media becomes the central instrument for mass social control.

e. *Art and Literature*
A deeper investigation of the social meaning of the visual arts, literature and music. We examine the role of Romanticism and other artistic and literary movements.

—*History as Spiritual War* (This study, in contrast to the history synopsis on the elementary dialectic level, will go into a deeper study of themes and issues of conflict exploring in-depth themes raised in *Chosen Generation*.)

a. *Introduction to God-centered and critique of man-centered historical method.*

b. *Babylon, Mesopotamia and Egypt* (3000 B.C.-400 B.C.)
These ancient pagan civilizations as means through which man sought to exalt himself above his Creator through his total culture, including political system, mythology, art, economy and so on. We shall examine the ancient origins of modern totalitarianism. The original contrast to, but later paganizing of, ancient Hebrew culture.

c. *Graeco-Roman Civilization* (1000 B.C.-500 A.D.)
The interweaving of classical philosophy, art, literature, politics, economy and so on, and their spiritual significance. The birth of Christianity, as the continuation of ancient Judaism, and the paganizing of the church.

d. *The Middle Ages* (500 A.D.-1400 A.D.)
Developments in culture, economy, philosophy, Church-State conflicts and other areas.

e. *Renaissance and Reformation*
The nature of the Renaissance, the rise of the Reformation, the development of Anabaptism, and how all these related to God's purpose.

f. *Age of Exploration, Religious Wars, Science and Empire*
The urge to explore and to conquer; the birth of mercantilism and empire. How the birth of science was related to and counterposed to the rise of rationalism. The relationship between mercantilism, rationalism, absolutism and the emerging empires of Spain, France and England.

g. *The Enlightenment*
The sources of the Enlightenment. How it affected society, particularly in France and Germany, but also in other countries. The rise of Romanticism and its relationship to Rationalism.

h. *The Settlement and Birth of America*
From the colonies to the Constitution. Is America rooted in the Enlightenment or in Christianity, or both? What were the causes of the Revolution? Was it a Christian movement? What were the origins and nature of the Constitution? Wherein lie the roots of American liberty?

i. *The French Revolution and Napoleon*
The relationship between the Enlightenment and the French Revolution. The French Revolution's hatred of Christianity. Napoleon as the culmination of the Revolution.

j. *The Industrial Revolution and the British Century*
The rise of industrialism and empire. Imperialism and Darwinism. The link between industrialism, Darwinism, Racism, Eugenics, social Darwinism and their subsequent influence.

k. *The Coming and Consequences of the American Civil War*
From Transcendentalism to Progressivism; Industrialism and the American Empire. The shift from an agricultural to an industrial nation. The causes and consequences of the American Civil War. The closing of the frontier.

l. *The Rise of Prussia*
Frederick the Great's rationalization of politics; the
role of public education; Bismarck's anti-Christian
policy. Industrialization of Germany and the search
for empire.

m. *World War I and the Russian Revolution*
The causes of the World War. The causes of the
Bolshevik Revolution. Russia, industrialism and
world power.

n. *Depression, New Deal and Universal Ascendence of Statism*
The victory of Statism, focusing on America. Industrialism and State-dependence in America and
other countries.

o. *The Rise of Nazism and the Second World War*
The causes of the rise of Nazism.

p. *The Atomic Era, China and the Era of World Revolution*
The rise of nuclear weapons. The global struggle
to industrialize and the worldwide growth of political revolution.

q. *Apostasy and Apocalypse*
The issues of our era: equalism, feminism, abortion, Statism, technology, ecology and so on.

Geography

This material will be taught in conjunction with the secondary
dialectic history synopses.

Goals—eighth, ninth and tenth grades:

—World political geography in detail:
God's direction for the lives of men and their nations
through history, following the development of
countries historically, adding and reviewing physical geographical concepts as they are relevant.

Writing

As we said before, writing will provide a chief means or vehicle whereby the child can participate in his learning experience. As before, the child will continue to concentrate on stimulating the flow of his words from his heart onto the paper, but he will also strengthen his knowledge of English grammar. He will deepen his knowledge and understanding of the skills necessary for writing effectually, forcefully and clearly. As we've said, *Right Words* also includes material to help improve style and grammar skills, but all in the context of primarily stimulating the child's writing in his real voice. This writing book will also teach skills of God-centered reasoning and research. The child will continue to keep his notebook and journal.

Part of the writing course will consist of the child's writings about his skill and craft projects. We already noted that some children will write how-to studies for publications and for materials to display at the Fair. Part of this material will be written by the adults who function in these various skill and craft areas in our community. And part of it will be written by children as they move into their places of responsibility and service. These publications and displays will also include drawings, photographs, maps and charts, when appropriate. Some children will also engage in dialectical writings, such as letters to the editor or correspondence with loved ones, to present the vision of God-centered community and culture in contrast to the secular culture that opposes it.

At this point, the child should have completed the grammar and punctuation goals given for grades four to seven, which will give him a complete knowledge of the basics of this subject. If he hasn't completed these, see the earlier grades under this subject for these goals.

Writing Goals—eighth, ninth and tenth grades:

—Dialectical writings that expose falsehood and convey truth (optional, except on basic level needed for the Secondary Dialectic Level Problems)
—Growing maturity in story writing and conveying experience
—Ability to convey information, research and so on

concerning practical subjects, as the need arises, and as the child feels the gift and burden to do this writing

Math

At this point, children should know the basic arithmetic skills and should be able to use them as they become necessary in the child's experiences. Each child should be confident enough in these skills to be able to learn more complicated operations as the need arises. For example, if he needs to figure out measurements for a structure that would employ elementary geometry, even though he will not have had extensive practice in geometry, he should be able to learn it as this need arises, having a strong foundation in elementary arithmetic. (We do, however, present some further goals that we feel children should master in basic mathematics for the eighth grade, including some geometry, algebra and trigonometry.) We've discussed before how parents can guide their children through a number of different traditional math teaching materials, being careful to glean out imbalances and helping the children to see the relational purpose of the material they study. Again, math invariably involves rote drilling and memorization, reinforcing the fact that this is the least relational of all subjects. We need to bear this in mind as we encourage our children to submit themselves to the discipline required to learn it, while at every opportunity pointing to its practical uses.

If a parent or a child sees a need for extensive mathematics,* the child can pursue this knowledge with the help of textbooks and brothers and sisters knowledgeable in math skills. We will have special advisers to help parents and students in math work as needed.

In other words, not all children will learn extensive algebra or

---

* We make the differentiation between arithmetic (the science or art of computing by positive, real numbers, specifically by adding, subtracting, multiplying and dividing) and mathematics (the group of sciences—including arithmetic, geometry, algebra, calculus and so on—dealing with quantities, magnitudes and forms, and their relationships, attributes and so on, by the use of numbers and symbols); we teach the former in the first through sixth grades, while the latter is a separate subject to be learned by those who need it, although everyone should have a basic foundation in geometry, algebra and trigonometry.

geometry, as some will never need these skills, beyond the basics, for their lives. These children will learn and master arithmetic skills that will enable them to function in their normal circumstances and situations. These children will also have enough foundational knowledge to be able to step off from their knowledge into other more complicated areas of arithmetic and basic mathematics with ease and dexterity. But some children will require more extensive mathematics in order to pursue areas they feel called to fill, such as working in solar heating and building. These children will learn the required mathematics (more advanced algebra, geometry and so on) so that they can have the necessary skills or tools to meet the need. As we've said, if the parent is unable to teach these more complicated subjects by himself, he'll receive help from advisers knowledgeable in this subject.

After completing our arithmetic books, we would like to develop a math book with chapters on different topics that require math. The parents and their child would then decide which chapters he would study. For example, we would offer a chapter on travel that includes the metric system, conversion formulas, time changes and distance calculations. We would offer a chapter on running a general store. This would include credit, debit, percent of increase and decrease, profit, overhead, sales computation, checkbooks and so on. We want to offer a chapter on "home" math that would include recipe conversion formulas, how to compute gas and electric bills, how to measure area in the home and so on. Another chapter would discuss buying land, including surveying skills, area, perimeter and so on. The child would work through those chapters that he and his parents feel would pertain to his life.

The math skills taught within the different chapters would sometimes overlap, but this problem would be offset by the advantage to the student of being able to find all the math information he needs for his topic of interest in a single chapter.

This math book would grow as we find more areas to take dominion of. We would include chapters on solar energy, building dams, making musical instruments, and other subjects.

Goals—eighth grade:

—Accurate work in all basic math skills
—Algebra

Exponents
Square roots
Multiplication and division of powers
Word problems using algebra
—Geometry
Symbols and definitions
Geometric plane shapes
Perimeter and area
Angles:
  constructing angles
  bisecting angles
Geometric solid shapes
Surface Area
Volume
—Metric system
Measures
Conversions
—Trigonometry
Pythagorean rule
Finding the tangent
Finding the sine
Finding the cosine
Using tables to find tangent, sine, cosine

Nature Study and Nature Drawing

See this heading under "The First Four Years."

Nature Study
Goals—eighth, ninth and tenth grades:

Major areas of interest in nature study should start coming into focus for children at this age. They will move into areas where God wants to open to them in more direct ways the treasures of His wisdom and knowledge (Col. 2:2-3). Knowledge and understanding will grow into wisdom as God unfolds his truth to an open heart. For example, a young man interested in horse farming will see the importance of good breeding; of matching the type of horse to the job at hand; of knowing about insects, pests and diseases that affect horses; of knowing proper care and sanitation for horses; of knowing about nutritious plants for horses and how to grow, harvest and store such plants; of knowing harmful wild plants and what to do if a horse eats them; of knowing about harness and tack and how to care for and repair them; of knowing how horse farming fits into God's vision and purpose for living in community on the land and so on. Most importantly, the young man or woman must have a living and obedient relationship with God so that they can take their proper place of dominion over God's creation, under God's authority and as a part of His body.

Nature Drawing
Goals—eighth, ninth and tenth grades:

Students, on this level particularly, must pray about direction to really apply themselves in perfecting their art techniques in light of the purpose their drawings have in community. Drawings should increasingly come from the internal impetus of the Spirit as He moves through and illuminates the vision of each unique person (not merely what they see with their physical eyes). Students give themselves to refined and narrowed projects to experience deeper growth in one style or technique as opposed to broad samplings.
—Drawings become more complex combinations of the various techniques they have already learned.
—Shade and shadow as pertaining to architectural-type drawings in order to communicate designs, solar concepts and so on.
—Creating dyes, inks and papers and use of other media.

Science
See this heading under the "Fifth, Sixth and Seventh Grades."

Goals—eighth, ninth and tenth grades:

On this level, our science course works together with

our Secondary Dialectic Synopsis described previously in this section. With this science material, the students will further learn to overcome secular perspectives that directly oppose the Word of God and the patterns of His people.

The theory of evolution is perhaps the most prevalent example that our children will encounter of secular thinking in the sciences. This theory, though with little true scientific basis, underlies much of the thinking behind modern science today.

In an effort to equip our children to discern truth from falsehood in their encounter with secular sources, we shall look at a variety of areas within the field of science that clearly show the contrast between the "wisdom" of man and the truths of God.

In some areas we shall be able to offer suggested texts from which to choose in order to build your own reference library.

The main areas of science we will discuss in light of the conflict between Christian and secular thought include:

—Astronomy
    Genesis
    The Big Bang
    Stars
    Black holes
—Chemistry
    Natural reactions
    Man's technology:
      Synthetics
      Toxic waste
—Physics
    Kinetic and potential energy:
      Energy conversions
      Entropy
    Nuclear reactions:
      Nuclear waste
      Radiation hazards
    Sound:
      Natural sounds

Man-made sounds
Electricity and magnetic fields
High-tension power lines:
  their effect on plants and animals
Microwave emissions:
  effect on plants and animals
—Biology
  Heredity
  Genetics:
    dominance
    genetic engineering
    mutations
  Missing links:
    no evidence, past or present
    spontaneous generation
  Plants
  Reproduction:
    open pollination
    hybrids
  No new species
  Man and animals:
    Natural immune systems
    Vaccines
  Ecology
  Pollution
  Man's bad stewardship:
    extinct plants and animals
    upsetting natural balances
—Meteorology: man's effect on climate
  Regional:
    Dams
    Cities: concrete and asphalt concentrations
    Temperature inversions: smog
    Upsetting the water cycle
  Global:
    Ozone layer depletion
    Greenhouse effect
—Geology
  The earth's structure:
    Erosion-Uniformitarianism
    Submarine canyons

Evidence of sea life at high elevations
Sedimentary rock
Fossils
Fossil fuels: how were they formed?
Methods of dating

Spelling

We hope that at this grade level, the child, if he has followed the spelling program used in the previous years, will know the rules so that he can spell words correctly. But if the child has not had the opportunity to learn the spelling rules, we suggest he follow the same procedure as the younger grades. It will, of course, take the older child a much shorter time. Even if your older child is a good speller, learning the spelling rules and phonograms given in the phonics course will help him to improve; he'll especially need to do this if you have younger children whom he can help instruct.

Vocabulary

In order to enrich the child's vocabulary, we suggest that he compile his own vocabulary list from the words he will encounter in his reading and studying. He should look up these words, checking for roots, origins, derivations and so on. Then he should use the words in original sentences to solidify the meaning in his own experience. This should never be an activity solely for puffing up his mind. Words should be studied in order to help the child to communicate more precisely.

Calligraphy

At this level we feel the child can go on his own if he has finished our suggested course. If he hasn't, he can continue his work in the regular course.

Goals—eighth, ninth and tenth grades:

See section "Fifth, Sixth and Seventh Grades."

Hebrew

For those who want to advance beyond the level prescribed under Hebrew in the previous sections, we can recommend various books and study materials to use.

Crafts and Skills and Special Projects

See this heading under the previous sections.

Remember too, as we discussed under "Science" in chapter 9, that some children may feel the desire to work on practical research projects, when such projects prove necessary or desirable to the child. Sometimes a group of children could work together with a teacher on a project to meet an important community need, such as solar heating. There are areas in which we have taken some steps but which still need more work to be completely brought under dominion. In these areas the child would have the help of brothers and sisters who have gone before him. But there are other areas where no one has yet broken ground. It may be that one of our children will be the first to step in and break that ground and meet the need. Some children have already done this. One example is in the area of tanning. Many brothers through the years had felt the need to learn how to do it, but they never pursued it or brought it to completion or dominion. But one young brother recently saw the need, pursued it, researched it, experimented, worked very hard, failed, tried again and successfully tanned a hide practically all by himself. Now a number of brothers, adults and older children are working in a workshop in this area. Again, in our fellowships all such projects will be directed toward presentation at the annual Fair.

As these areas are brought under dominion, the children can add their writings about their work to the how-to publications and Fair displays we plan to produce.

Outside Reading

See this heading under "The First Four Years."

The Advanced Dialectic
The Eleventh and Twelfth Grades

At this level, the principal schoolwork will consist of a course based upon Truth Forum's multivolumed study, *Justice Is Fallen* and on *Holocaust as Spiritual War*. As this material is published, it will provide the "textbook" for the course. We will hold discussions based upon the questions that these books raise. Adults could also take part in this course.

Goals—eleventh and twelfth grades:

—Justice Is Fallen

Justice Is Fallen presents a complete demolition of the man-centered view, based on all the dialectical studies that have gone before. First, this book shows the results of building the central institutions of modern society on a secular standard: how the insoluble crisis of modern society inevitably follows from this man-centered standard. Then it traces the roots of modern secularism in the crisis of religion, the failure of the Judeo-Christian heritage to arrive at a consistent spiritual perspective. It explores this crisis in terms of the repeated attempt by leaders of Christianity and Judaism to base knowledge of God and His ways on the mind of man rather than on the anointed Word of God. This exploration takes us to a detailed uncovering of the limits of human reason, logic, science and all knowledge based on the natural senses. After showing the total failure of all efforts to find a man-centered knowledge of truth, the book concludes with a thorough demonstration of the validity of the God-centered view, which bases reason, logic and all understanding on a relational knowledge of God and His Word. A student completing this course will not only stand on solid ground against all man-centered attacks on God's truth, but he'll also stand ready to advance the kingdom of God in the hearts and minds of all those honest and willing enough to acknowledge their need of love's truth.

After finishing *Justice Is Fallen*, the students would read, study and reply to *The Spectre of the Absurd*.

This book claims that Biblical belief, by raising man's hopes that he can know a transcendent, all-powerful, loving God (who according to this secular author's presupposition does not exist), creates nihilism, the view that life has no hope or meaning. This course would come with a complete critical teacher's guide that will thoroughly refute all this author's arguments and show the Biblical view as the only alternative to nihilism.

—*Holocaust as Spiritual War*

This book shows the roots of the Nazi holocaust and the forces at work in our world culture today that once again move in that same direction. It marshals together philosophical, historical, cultural and spiritual material to bring a comprehensive understanding of the central crisis facing modern man. Again, not only will this understanding open the student's eyes, but it will also equip him to help others see "how to interpret this present time" (Luke 12:56).

To receive information on how to obtain the Koinonia Curriculum, send your name and address to:

Truth Forum
P.O. Box 18927
Austin, Texas 78760

Teaching Guidelines*

The following is a list of godly attributes in a teacher. We include these not as a mechanical checklist, but as an encouragement to all parents to seek the very best that they can offer their children through and by the grace of God.

1. Teach your child to follow the Spirit, the path of love, in all things. To teach him this, you must do it yourself.

2. Help your children to see relationally. Wisdom is seeing relationships and how to move in them. Grow in that wisdom yourself and impart it to your children. Help them to see in terms of contexts so that what they learn is always alive because it has meaning for their lives. Help them to see the purpose in everything they do.

3. Be an example for your children. Be enthusiastic about the curriculum (the racecourse) and about the work that you are doing together. Be thankful for the fact that God has given you this time to be with your children. And give them your whole heart. This will be especially important in your writing workshop. Let your children hear real voice from you; then they will be able to find theirs. "Does not the ear test words . . ." (Job 12:11)?

4. Help them to fall in love with the truth. Help them to develop an ear for it so they can discern it and not accept any counterfeit.

5. Expect the best from your children. Jesus said, "Be ye therefore perfect, even as your heavenly Father is perfect" (Matt. 5:48, KJV, NIV). Set godly standards for your children. Expect them and encourage them to aspire towards the highest standard in everything they do.

---

* These guidelines were written by Jeanne Stein, based in part upon material compiled from other sources.

6. Always allow the love that God gave you for your children to motivate your teaching. Do not ever be mechanical with them or unreal or fearful. Make sure you are always connecting—heart to heart.

7. Let discussions, questions, dialogues, happen often. Look for the questions in what you do and pursue them to a godly resolution. Answer your children's questions.

8. Help your children to see tests in a positive light. "Test me, O Yahweh, and prove me . . ." (Ps. 26:2, NIV, KJV). If the goals are realistic and desirable, testing should be seen as just another means to achieve the goal, a necessary prod, a refiner's fire. Give tests in the same light. Never give tests because of the fear of man. Grade in the same light. Tests and grades should always be a helpful tool; they should never be an executioner's weapon. (Remember that your gauging of your child's knowledge will generally come forth in the context of discussions, although sometimes you will give different types of written tests. See discussion of testing in Supplement One, under "Secondary Dialectic Synopses.")

9. Encourage your children to move from faith to faith and glory to glory, but allow them occasional failures. If we acknowledge our failures as failures they turn into victories.

10. Help your children to grow into responsibility by encouraging them to make choices. Don't "tell" them everything. Guide them to the correct answer or the acceptable way. Let them participate in finding the solution. Develop the art of asking the right questions that bring light into the darkness.

11. Don't lose your patience. Don't make learning a frightening experience.

12. Help your children to bring all things to quality completion. Don't let your children leave a trail of unfinished projects behind them. Bring everything to resolution.

13. Help your children to participate in their learning so that what you teach them becomes their own.

14. Help and encourage your children to respond to God. Help them to trust their godly emotions and to give expression to them. Don't allow them to become hard or sophisticated or cynical. Help them to laugh when appropriate and to cry when necessary.

15. Teach James 2:14-26. Show your faith and your love by your deeds.

16. Look at your children's work with real love. Do not praise what is not praiseworthy (but also realize that what is not praiseworthy for an eleven-year-old may be for a five-year-old). Help your children to recognize for themselves when their work needs refining. Help them to *want* to bring it to quality completion. Help them to *not* be satisfied with less than God's perfect will (but don't discourage them with a standard of perfection that seems forever out of reach—praise them when they reach levels that they have aimed for; even if it is still not perfect, it may be "perfect" for that level).

17. Give your children a desire to reach the world outside with all that God has given them. Help them to see themselves as part of the city on a hill.

18. Help your children to do unto others as they would have done unto them (Matt. 7:12) so that they can constructively advise or minister to others without judging and to help them receive help from others with grateful hearts.

19. Save your children's works of excellence and share them with the community to bless and inspire others (Prov. 20:11). (Of course, the annual Fair encourages children in our fellowship to do this.)

20. Teach your children Colossians 3:23-24, "Whatever you do, work at it with all your heart, as working for the Lord, not for men, since you know that you will receive an inheritance from the Lord as a reward. It is the Lord Christ you are serving." Help them to develop good work habits that will stay with them for the rest of their lives.

21. Schedule your life so that teaching and learning can happen at the optimum times. Don't allow yourself to be so scattered and unordered that school is relegated to those odd moments when you "can get it together." Let the God in whom all things hold together put order into your life so that everything is "done decently and in order" (1 Cor. 14:40, NKJV).

22. Learn to see what God sees in your children. Learn to see past their cuteness, their imperfections, their childishness and look toward their calling and their gifts. Seek His vision for their lives.

23. A time will come when your children will surpass you in knowledge, and where He will even use them to speak *His* wisdom to you. Pray for the grace to recognize that time and be thankful for it.

24. Pray also for the grace to take a break when everything becomes overwhelming. Don't push yourself beyond what God is calling you to do because you will hurt yourself and your children. Allow yourself to rest so that you can come back renewed and refreshed. But remember that resting is the respite, not the norm for our days.

25. Finally, in your teaching show integrity (Titus 2:7).

APPENDIX ONE

Testing*

We arrived at our present position on testing slowly. For many years, we administered several standardized tests: Stanford, California Achievement, Iowa, Science Research Associates (SRA). Our children have always done well. All of our school-age children have scored above their grade level, and most scored high above. A number of students scored *many* years above their grade levels. We began to find, however, that much of the test material conflicts with our beliefs and convictions. In fact, the material is obviously written by the same educators, psychiatrists, guidance counselors and social workers who write the textbooks in our public schools. The tests are, of course, virtually always presented from the perspective of pagan rather than Biblical knowledge.

As has been pointed out, tests can be made to prove whatever the testers want to prove. The following statement refers to intelligence tests, but could be applied to any other type of testing as well:

> [The formulators of the Stanford-Binet Test] determined ahead of time through their selection of questions how people would do on their IQ test. They said men and women are of equal intelligence and we will adjust the test until the results conform to this principle . . . . But if the choice of questions used predetermines the results for groups of people taking the test, just how fair, scientific, and objective can these tests be? Could not the test writers sit down and decide how well Chicanos or Asian-Americans or whites from Scarsdale or Appalachia or Texans or Alaskans or any other recognizable group will do? Could they not sit down and either eliminate or create score discrepancies among various groups, merely by

---

* Much of this material was written by Howard Wheeler and by Jeanne Stein.

changing the questions asked? The fact is they could. No one is suggesting that the testers consciously do this sort of thing at present as part of some conspiracy to fix the tests. But the selection of the questions to be asked is such a powerful factor in determining how you do on the test that if subconscious class or cultural inclinations of the testers play a part in question selection, then test results can be seriously misleading. If you can fiddle with test questions in such a way as to control the outcome for test takers, at the very least this means to me that I'd want to write the questions for a standardized test I had to take, and if that weren't possible, I'd want the test to be written by people as much like me as possible.[1]

Whoever makes a test must have some standard by which he intends to grade those who take the test. If secular academics make the test, then obviously the standard will be that of secular thought, not of Christianity. If we accept the standards of contemporary secular testing, which are already largely anti-Christian, what will we do on the day when the testing standard becomes completely and explicitly anti-Christian? After all, tests can be designed to automatically define as an idiot anyone who believes the Bible to be the Word of God. Examples abound of questions on standardized tests that will call forth different answers from Christian and secular students. One question on a nationally standardized test asked students what "superstitious people" believed were the causes of such "calamities" as crop failures and epidemics. The test gave the correct answer as "supernatural forces."[2] Christians, then, must define their own beliefs as "superstition." Other choices on the test would have offered a more appropriate answer from a Christian perspective, but these were ruled wrong by the testers. Another question asked "how the earliest men" spent their time. While the Bible specifically tells us that these men grew crops and raised livestock, the choice "growing crops" is marked wrong on this test.[3]

Despite such evidence, and further evidence we will present later in this appendix, questions may nevertheless exist about the usefulness and validity of standardized testing for voluntary use by home educators. But we believe that without question State-compelled standardized testing, which has found support even among some leaders of the home-education movement, undermines the Biblical basis of home education that we have presented in this book, in *Who Owns the*

Children? and elsewhere. Such compulsory standardized testing assumes that children ultimately belong to the State, that in the final analysis, the State, not the parent, should decide and set the standard of what is valid and necessary for our children to learn.

Whose Standard: The State's or God's?

What does the acceptance of the standardized test as a standard of exemption from compulsory education laws require that we acknowledge in our hearts? To understand fully the subtle implications of standardized testing, we must recognize that more than merely the *content* of the questions and answers can reflect an anti-Christian bias. The *format* of the test itself, the very notion of an "objective" academic test as an instrument for evaluating educational progress is, as we've seen, rooted in the pagan notion of the exalted human mind and its "objective," fragmented knowledge. Whatever one acknowledges as the basis of accountability to the compulsory power of the State implicitly attains the status of being "most important." For Christians to use the testing of "objective" academic achievement as the *basis* of accountability puts inappropriate emphasis on mental achievement apart from the spiritual growth of the child. As we have seen, such a fragmentation of academic studies apart from spiritual growth directly conflicts with the principles of a Christian education. Again, Christian education transcends mere academics—it trains up the *whole* man, not by bits and pieces but as an *integrated* whole; for a child cannot finish his "course" of faith in obedience unless he can love the Lord with *all* his heart, soul, mind and strength. This wholeness is the very meaning of Biblical salvation.[4] For the Christian, the mind represents only a part of man's being, and not a part that remains apart but which must fit consistently into the whole through subservience to the love and worship of God. To give credence to standardized tests as a *basis* of accountability simply gives credence to the pagan notion of the mind as the means of salvation. Indeed, the original sin tempted man to *know* good and evil apart from God (Gen. 3:5). It separated the function of the mind from its living relationship with God, and so "secularized" the mind's operation. Any believer who knows that God is One should clearly understand that the charge of training up our child to conform to the image of God does not allow us to quantify and fragment such a process. Paul clearly shows that our standard of spiritual success lies not in fragmentation but wholeness; he expresses this principle in 1 Thessalonians 5:23,

> And may the God of peace Himself sanctify you through and through—that is, separate you from profane things, make you pure and wholly consecrated to God—and may your spirit and soul and body be preserved sound *and* complete ["whole," KJV] [and be found] blameless at the coming of our Lord Jesus Christ, the Messiah. (1 Thess. 5:23, Ampl.)

When the world imposes its standards, such as the standards of secular standardized tests, as a measurement of our children, what does this imply? First, Paul says that those "measuring themselves by themselves, and comparing themselves among themselves, are not wise" (2 Cor. 10:12). Indeed, humanism proposes to build upon the foundation that "man is the measure of all things."[5] To support legislation that would submit our children to such a State-imposed standard of evaluation supports then the anti-Biblical premise of humanism.

Yet the implications of our willing submission to such a standard extend even further. For a standard not only measures but also, as with a "standard" raised before a marching army to serve as a rallying point, a standard becomes an instrument to *in-spire* (literally, "to breathe the spirit into") allegiance. Whatever lifts itself up as the measure to strive toward becomes the standard that will command our allegiance; the spirit of that standard, whether that of Christ or of the world, will pour into us. If we lift up the full measure of the stature of Christ as the standard, then we will devote ourselves in allegiance to Him and become at one with Him as He transforms us from glory to glory into the image of the Lord (2 Cor. 3:18). If, however, we lift up the standard of this world before our children, then they will conform themselves to the image of the world and become enslaved, marching in lock-step allegiance to the beat of its drummer, the god of this world.

We cannot serve two masters; we will either love one and hate the other or hate one and be devoted to the other (Matt. 6:24). We can see both how this process of polarization can take place and also the wisdom in God's prohibition against serving other gods: if we have lifted up the standard of these tests as the basis of exemption from attendance at public schools, our allegiance would soon shift as the pressure to prepare to meet the demands of the standard would super sede the vision God would give us for our children. As we said in chapter 8, the test becomes the finish line for the race-course (the curriculum), and you cannot help but direct your race toward the finish line. We would feel constant pressure to adapt and modify curriculum to meet that standard, even as that standard becomes increasingly godless.[6] Education Professor W. James Popham, an advocate of standardized testing, admits

> few educators would dispute the claim that these sorts of high-stakes tests markedly influence the nature of in-structional programs. Whether they are concerned about their own self-esteem or their students' well-being, teachers clearly want students to perform well on such tests. Accordingly, teachers tend to focus a significant portion of their instructional activities on the knowledge and skills assessed by such tests. A high-stakes test of educational achievement, then, serves as a powerful *curricular magnet*. Those who deny the instructional in-fluence of high-stakes tests have not spent much time in public school classrooms recently.[7]

And the impact of the content of the test material upon the children while in the pressurized, heightened state of con-centrated test taking (made even greater by the fact that failure could jeopardize their very relationship to their parents) cannot help but have an especially deleterious impact on their malleable minds, hastening their conformity to the standards of this age that we as parents have irresponsibly lifted up before them as a goal to strive toward.*

In his book *Keywords: A Vocabulary of Culture and Society*, Cambridge University's Raymond Williams confirms this. He explains that from the original meaning of *standard* as the flag

---

* The effects of these "high-stakes" tests apparently bring pressure upon even the ethical judgment of some public school officials and testing com-panies as demonstrated by the now widely publicized and startling dis-closure that all fifty states reported their students "above average" on a standardized achievement test, a statistical improbability to say the least. As Gerald Bracey, a director of testing in a large Colorado school district, ad-mits, "The pressure to get test scores high is just extraordinary."[8]

or emblem extended before the authority's subjects (indeed, *standard* derives from the Latin *extendere*, from which we get our word *extend*) comes the modern meaning of *standard* as "a source of authority."[9] So what presents itself to us as a standard presents itself as an "authority," which in this case clearly extends the State's claim to have authority over the training of our children. The standard as the source of educational authority then "authors" its image within the child, and even the most cursory glance at the social quagmire of public education clearly shows that this image has indeed been effectively inscribed on the hearts of this nation's children.*

Williams goes on to distinguish between what he calls the "ordinary plural" usage and the "plural singular" usage of the word *standards*. He explains that following the rise of modern educational institutions, the ordinary plural *standards* (referring to many differing standards) was joined with a quite different use. This new use of *standards*, though plural in form, gains assent to what in fact asserts a singular standard, that of the speaker, for example, "We all know what real standards are," or "Anyone who is concerned with standards will agree." Williams laments that "it is often impossible, in [this 'plural singular' use,] to disagree with some assertion of standards without appearing to disagree with the very idea of quality; this is where the plural singular most powerfully operates."[10] This insight helps us penetrate through the facade of the State's claim to want to uphold educational "standards." For the State has no interest in a true plurality of standards. Instead, it cares only about establishing *its* singular standard, the establishment of itself as the "source of authority" over and against God. And, just as Williams described, this Orwellian use of language has made those who disagree with the State's mock standards appear opposed to the very idea of quality when in fact only private schools have given us any consistent standard of quality.

Williams continues, "The power of the plural singular always depends on its not being spotted as a singular. If it is not spotted, it can be used *to override necessary arguments* or *to appropriate the very process of valuation and definition* to its own particular conclusions."[11] We can readily see then why Christians, because they follow, not a lower, but a radically *dif-*

---

* See *The Crime of Compulsory Education*.

ferent standard, automatically find themselves on the defensive against the charge that they oppose "quality" in education when they oppose State-imposed "standards," even though the State's mythical standards have produced anything but quality in modern education.* Arguments against the State's imposition of its standard are overridden in the muddled thinking of most, including that of many Christians themselves, as the intimidation of the "plural singular" does its work on the undiscerning mind, and this in spite of the indisputable fact that the actual quality of Christian education far exceeds that of State education.[12] The Statist mantra, "The State must uphold standards in education," conceals with serpentine subtlety the real question: "Whose standards?" Once this statement's "reasonableness" stands exposed as a mere presumptive assertion of the State's own singular standard, we can begin our exodus from the grasp of its presumptuous authority.

To penetrate through the pretensions of the State, Christians must face the choice between two irreconcilable standards, the measure of Christ and the measure of the world; they must recognize that no "common" ground exists. The "common standards" in education are mythical and only serve to veil the encroachment of the State into every human mind to conform all its citizens to its image. For the Christian, it inserts a "source of authority" other than God into Christian families.[13] Joseph Goebbels's methodical entrapment of the Jews through his slanderous propaganda does not exceed in diabolical brilliance this snare now laid for Christians in the appropriation by the State of the "very process of valuation and definition to its own particular conclusions," that is, as it seeks to invalidate in the public mind all educational standards other than its own.[14] And surely if we hear no clear sound of a warning trumpet, then both the manipulators and their gullible victims in this war for our children will eventually become equally as vulnerable as were the propagandists and propagandized in the Third Reich in falling for some "final solution" to this "stubborn" Christian refusal to give their children a "quality" education. Christian complicity in the continuance of this Statist confusion is not only wrong but also suicidal.

Furthermore, the acceptance of the "innocuous" stand-

* See *The Crime of Compulsory Education.*

530 / Appendix One

ardized test as a valid criterion for whether the child can
remain at home with his mother and father reduces the authority of the parents from that authorized (or authored) by God
to merely the arbitrary authority or whim of a bureaucrat. The
Philistines wanted to postpone killing Samson so that they
might mock him and ridicule his God. Just so, the enemy of our
souls desires to emasculate the authority of parents in the
eyes of their children so that the child's final allegiance will be
total in its shift from the parents and God to the "higher" authority of the State. In offering this compromise to the State of
compulsory standardized tests, parents would confess that
they no longer parent at the command of God, but at the threat
or sufferance of the State. Of course, submission to the compulsory attendance laws alone accomplishes this devastation
of parental authority, but the extension of the State's usurped
authority that inheres in those laws tangibly expresses itself in
the form of the "innocuous" compromise, the standardized
test. Tragically, in some cases those initiating the compromise
are so-called Christian leaders. Many of them are novices to
home schooling; and though they little understand the issues,
they nonetheless ignorantly strive to impress the powers that
be that Christians are righteous, patriotic, "law-abiding"
citizens—all according to the standards not of the Bible but of
an increasingly anti-Christian State. In so doing they become
in fact lawbreakers in the eyes of God.

Besides the more subtle cultural bias that lies hidden in the
nature and format of a standardized test, a still more obvious
cultural bias against Christians fills the content of the test
materials themselves. The claim of "objectivity" for standardized tests largely comes simply from "objective" grading
techniques—that is, from allowing only one correct answer as
opposed to an essay-type test that requires so-called "subjective" grading. Yet this multiple choice approach in no way
precludes subjectivity in the standardized test; it merely shifts
the subjectivity from the grading end of the testing process to
the preparation end. Those preparing the test must make subjective decisions on format, material covered, sampling variety and so on, as well as on which answer they will accept as
correct. For example, this "subjectivity" shows through abun-
dantly in all the documentation that we've seen substantiating
many tests and norms designed and manipulated purposely to
achieve certain desired results. Questions mysteriously ap-

pear and disappear until the desired norms are obtained. The history of I.Q. tests and their sordid connection with the eugenics movement of the 1920's and 1930's offers a revealing glimpse into the manipulation possible in "objective" testing.[15]

As we have shown extensively in *Who Owns the Children?*, even if the tests were not biased against Christians, we still could not willingly submit to State-compelled standardized testing, for to do so would be to posit an inordinate authority to the State. We would be worshiping a false god by bending down in obeisance in an area of authority that has not been truly delegated to the State by God. But many Christians have already recognized that the standards in the public schools are not only foreign to, but even in direct opposition to, their own values. This is why they removed their children from those schools in the first place. Hence, if we submit to the standardized test, we ultimately submit to a standard we have already rejected as illegitimate.

But, in any case, the viewpoint of the standardized tests is unmistakable: the tests present the perspective of this world's culture. In standardized tests, the subjectivity prejudices everything toward the perspective of certain particular gimmicks and fads of world culture, as the tests measure children against a background of television, competitive sports, street jargon and, soon, even computer literacy. The issue is not whether we or anyone else agrees or disagrees over the relative value of these activities and topics. Rather, the issue lies in whether the State should have the right to *compel everyone* to study or know these activities—such as watching TV. Do these things constitute cultural values of such "compelling interest" that the State can forcibly take a child from his parents because the child lacks knowledge of them? This would mean that, in effect, TV, as just one example, would become a State-mandated activity!

As we show in *Who Owns the Children?*, however, prosecutors in Christian education cases use as one tactic probing into the consistency of the parents' separation of the child from what the parents consider worldly. Cases have been won and lost over such issues as the presence of a television in the defendant's home. The court reasoned that if the parents claim a religious conviction about separating their children from humanistic influences in the public schools but expose them to those same values via the television in their home, then the parents must not have a sincerely held religious conviction and therefore fail to satisfy requirements for protection under First Amendment rights.[16] Yet the standardized tests that the State would require Christians to take contain material that involves just such an exposure to worldly values and culture (even to the point of kindergarten children identifying TV apparatuses).[17] Though it may seem farfetched, it would nevertheless be a logically consistent extension of legal precedent for the State to argue that you have no real conviction concerning separation from the world because you allow your children to read the State's standardized test!

Indeed, many Christians would feel their convictions compromised if they allowed the State to expose their children, particularly at the very stressful and vulnerable time of test taking, to such worldly nonsense as the following "reading comprehension" story from the popular California Achievement Test:

As they drew near, they saw that the pyramid's sides were washed in a violet glow. The violet glow seemed to dissolve the stone directly in front of them, opening a passageway to the interior of the pyramid.

Entering the pyramid, they stood in a dimly lit chamber before two doors of polished bronze. Their eyes grew wide as the doors opened. Each door revealed a road stretching toward a far horizon. Through the door on the right was a road covered with sparkling green and blue gems. It wound toward shadowy mountains crowned with silver mist. The earth seemed to ripple, and the wind whistled an enchanting melody. The door on the left revealed a road that was like every road Hassim and Shasa had ever traveled. It was the road of things as they are now and always will be.

A soft wind from the mystery road whistled sweetly. Hassim grew pale and trembled. Feeling that the mystery road would snare him with invisible hands, he bolted through the door on the left and ran down the road. Shasa paused, letting the whistling wind gently touch her face and hair. She entered the door on the right and walked down the road toward the silver-misted peaks.[18]

Obviously from the above example, and hundreds of others such as the one given below, you cannot test a child's ability to read and comprehend without having him read and comprehend something, and that "something" will stand upon some religious value system or another, whether occult paganism, secular humanism or Christianity. Another test offers the child this poem:

To me, this old concrete pipe
is the secret brain center of the world,
the biggest spaceship, the deepest cave,
the longest tunnel, a haunted house,
a submarine, the home of the queen.
Like a lizard that changes colors,
I can live in different worlds.
Like treasures in a pirate chest, my secrets
are hidden in
this old concrete pipe.[19]

Do not we, as Christians or Jews, have the right to question whether we want our children at an impressionable age and under very intense testing pressure to have their minds seduced into hiding away in such fantasy? Do we not have the right to raise them to put their trust in God instead? And once again, even if we do not personally disapprove of such material, is it of such importance that it should be forced on someone else's children? How would the secularists respond if Christians came to power and couched all test questions in similar garb, but with Christian terminology and thought? If the Christian testers contemptuously shrugged off complaints with the response that "all that's tested is reading comprehension," would this satisfy secularists in comparable situations?

Another sample of anti-Christian bias finds the Iowa Achievement Test giving a discourse on the evolutionary theory of petrified trees, presenting the methods used to substantiate this theory as accurate and factual.[20] Remember, the issue does not ride on whether our children should be so sheltered under the parents' covering as to have no contact at all with the false theories and values of a pagan world. On the contrary, as we've shown in this book, at a certain point in our children's education they must grapple with these theories and learn to overcome them. Yet to submit to standardized testing means that we establish these false theories and values as the *standard* for our children's development, not that we sharpen their spiritual senses by exercise in the conflict against them!

Even standardized testing on such supposedly value-free areas as *punctuation* subjects the child to such reversals of godly values as, "The thing that impresses me most about America is the way parents obey their children," and "Jupiter was the supreme ruler over both heaven and earth."[21] This comes from a public school system that purports to separation of church and State and zealously enforces it against the slightest nuance of Christianity! The State claims to test the child's ability to punctuate, but our children would find of much more critical importance the distortion of truth contained in these questions and hundreds of others. Television also pervasively influences these tests. Questions involve "TV serials," and television is presented as little Marie's "old friend." The tests tells the children that everybody ("our whole town") watches television.[22] Again, whether you agree or disagree with the value of TV and other similar features of our culture, should they be *compelled by the State as a standard for all families*? It is not Christians but the State that has made an issue of such things through compulsion. If they are really so trivial and unimportant, why does the State put its full weight of power behind them until failure to comply can mean loss of liberty or even children? Standardized testing also presents competitive sports as "fun" and important to their participants. Again, whether we ourselves accept athletic competition as healthy or not, have we arrived at a place in this country where such values have become a "compelling interest" of the State that overshadows freedom of conscience? The tests also reverse role models for men and women with feminists getting out "the vote," women skydiving, Aunt Thelma "shooting the rapids," women carpenters and so on.[23] To accept such nationally standardized tests as a criterion for our ability "to train up the child in the way he should go" is to accept the world as the standard-bearer to lead the child in the way he should go.

Can we believe, given the standardized testing industry's dependence upon the public schools' business, that the tests will ever reflect any values other than those from which most home schoolers have deliberately separated their children by taking them out of those same public schools? Of course, as we have seen, even if the cultural content of the standard against which we would measure our child has not been so corrupted as to make the test unfair, we still could not offer as a compromise its imposition as a criterion for approval: by offering it we would posit an inordinate authority to the State, worshiping a false god by bending down in obeisance in an area of authority that God has not truly delegated to the State. Even on such a seemingly limited level as mandated standardized tests, the State has no legitimate authority based on Biblical principle to interfere in the family-centered process of child rearing. If we ourselves support legislation to mandate State-imposed standardized testing, then surely we acknowledge the State's claims of authority and sovereignty over the molding and shaping of our children; and along with it, we legitimize its claim as being the god into whose image our children must be formed.

But, as we have suggested, our experience with standardized tests raised basic questions about using them even when they were not State-mandated. As we've already said, since the test situation is one of high energy, the children are keyed up and in a very vulnerable frame of mind. Much of what they read on the tests, therefore, makes a special impression on them. Some of this was definitely harmful, as in many of the examples we looked at above; others were simply trivial, but nevertheless, because of the high pressure test situation, important. We wondered, for instance, what valid area of our children's competency was measured by idiomatic expressions such as these from one test: "pulling my leg, turning over a new leaf, tooting her own horn, putting my foot in my mouth, buttering up the star player, pulling strings" and so on.[24] While some of these expressions may not seem objectionable in themselves, and we may even use some of them ourselves in daily conversation, we questioned why our children should be tested on a knowledge of them.

By the time we had taken our fifth test (none of which were taken under State compulsion), we realized that we had to change so much that it almost completely invalidated the test. There is no "neutral" point of view, and the point of view of the test writers was contrary to what we believe is God's. Also, we began to feel that much of our curriculum and teaching time was beginning to reflect the standards of the tests. We found ourselves "getting ready" for the tests, including things in our teaching that we would not have necessarily included if we were not taking them. (Again, the finish line must affect the running of the race.) For instance, we were using an arithmetic book put out by Rod and Staff, which uses a down-to-earth, old-fashioned approach to teaching arithmetic to the lower grades. We added, however, another arithmetic book with a more modern approach even though we were not that satisfied with this new book. We also added some social studies textbooks that we were not altogether pleased with because they included material that was "on the test." Of course, we want our children fully informed in every valid, necessary area, but sometimes the test required unnecessary information while leaving out much that was necessary. Given the importance of the testing situation, this could lead you to give your children a false sense of priorities.*

We began to remember that we were called to step out of the world, not to bring the world in. We felt that much of what we were adding, in order to meet the standards of these tests, was exactly what we had felt repulsed by in the first place. We felt that we were touching the palates of our children with worldly things, giving them a taste of man's knowledge, man's intellect, man's opinions and points of view.

Lastly, we felt that the tests did not adequately test our children anyway. We believe that what Walter Lippmann said of intelligence tests holds true for testing in general:

> . . . Because the results are expressed in numbers, it is easy to make the mistake of thinking that the intelligence test is a measure like a foot rule or a pair of scales . . . . But "intelligence" is not an abstraction like length and weight; it is an exceedingly complicated notion which nobody has as yet succeeded in defining . . . . If the impression takes root that these tests really measure intelligence, that they constitute a sort of last judgment on the child's capacity, that they reveal "scientifically" his predestined ability, then it would be a thousand times better if all the intelligence testers and all their questionnaires were sunk without warning in the Sargasso Sea.[25]

And as two educators have stated:

> We have placed our faith in these "objective" tests because we did not trust the "subjective" parents and teachers who know our children best. We forgot that the nameless "theys" out there can also be subjective, biased, or plain stupid too. Only their subjectivity masks itself in "science" and is even harder to combat.[26]

We believe, however, that we must trust the "subjective"

---

* For further discussion of the problems of standardized testing, see the fourth edition of *Who Owns the Children?*

parents (who are the teachers) because they do in fact "know" their children best. If God gave us the responsibility to teach them, then if we follow His Spirit and seek His guidance, He will show us what we need to know about our children and for our children. And because we are responsible to God, our "subjectivity" can be transcended. We can conform our teaching, and when needed, our testing, not to our ideas or opinions, but to the Word and Spirit of God. Therefore, we believe that the preparation of any tests we might use must be closely correlated with the needs perceived by the teachers, that is, the parents, themselves. So we want to work closely with parents in developing tests for them to use with their children.

As we've already said, the annual "finish line" for our fellowship curriculum lies in the Children's Fair. To this Fair we shall bring our children's craft products, projects, photographs, writings and so on. The works they produce fit for display at the Fair will present the main test of their workmanship and schoolwork. But in the course of our children's education, at times we will also present other tests to check their proficiency. As we've noted, in the home-school situation, most of the gauging of our children's knowledge should take place in discussions. But sometimes written tests perform useful purposes. (See discussion of testing in Supplement One, under "Dialectic Synopses.") But any such tests that we will administer will reflect the needs, interests and experiences of our children instead of the "contemporary student" who has been fed on television and public school propaganda all his life: in other words, they will reflect a God-centered culture rather than a secular culture. They will relate directly to the curriculum that we are developing and using; we will test children concerning what God has shown us they must know and leave out questions about things that they have no need to know. We have striven to educate our children within the guidelines that God has shown us, to bring them up in the way they should go according to the revealed holy Word of God. Our tests, therefore, will reflect this curriculum. In the end, the only real test is life itself, and we want all the tests we give our children throughout the course of their curriculum to help prepare them relationally to emerge victoriously through life's trials.

Written tests can help us to discern our children's mastery of their basic scholastic skills such as reading, writing and arithmetic. We want to see, above all, whether they have a *working,* relational knowledge of these skills. These basic skills could include spelling, capitalization and punctuation, vocabulary, reading comprehension, word usage and penmanship. In regard to mathematical skills, tests might sometimes help to show our children's proficiency in the skills they have learned, to test whether they can think through problems that call for the use of such skills. We would like our children to learn their mathematical skills so that they can cope with even unfamiliar problems by thinking them through in the Spirit. Again, any test questions we use will reflect the perspective of relational knowledge.

We also use tests on other subjects as well, such as history and science, as we explain in our discussion of the Dialectic Synopses in Supplement One. Tests can serve as a guide to show us where exactly our children need more work in any given area, as well as fulfilling other functions we describe in Supplement One. But, again, in home schooling most assessing of student knowledge takes place through discussions.

Finally, to repeat, the ultimate test will be life itself, and the key annual test is our Children's Fair. Yet occasional tests may help us to gauge our children's knowledge to help them move forward in areas where they need extra help. These tests will be written by the same people who are writing our school curriculum, mainly the fathers and mothers of home-schooled children in our fellowships.

The Three Levels of Knowledge

The Mesorah Publications book, *Succos—Its Significance, Laws, and Prayers*, tells us that there are three stages of knowledge. The first stage it calls חָכְמָה [*chochmah*], which is said to be "the spark of an idea." The second stage is בִּינָה [*b'inah*], when "the idea is developed and applied, its ramifications and implications are compared with known facts and other hypotheses." The third stage is "when the newly acquired knowledge is perfected and has become fully assimilated by the student[;] it is called דַּעַת [*da'at*]."[1] The authors correctly point out that the second level of knowledge, בִּינָה/*b'inah*, is "usually translated understanding," but for some reason they tell us that דַּעַת/*da'at* means wisdom, but do not tell us that this word is generally translated as knowledge, while חָכְמָה/*chochmah* is usually translated as wisdom.[2] Furthermore, it seems clear from a perusal of Scripture that *chochmah* generally corresponds to "the final stage of wisdom."[3] Thus, it seems that the terms used by the authors of *Succos* for the first and third stages of knowledge should be reversed, with *da'at*, or knowledge, being the first stage and *chochmah*, or wisdom, being the final or third stage.

It is not surprising, however, that the authors of the study of *Succos* should reverse these two terms, or at least should have seen *da'at* or knowledge as representing "the final stage of wisdom." This is because *da'at* is used not only to describe the first stage of knowledge, but also the process of knowing, including knowledge, understanding and wisdom, as a whole. As we have seen, "to know" in Hebrew denotes entrance into a covenant relationship that brings oneness, and so the same word, *yada* (the root of the word *da'at*), denotes not only marital union (Gen. 4:1) but also the knowing of man by God (Deut. 34:10) and of God by man (Deut. 9:24). *Yada*, "to know," thus expresses the initial conception stage of knowing, but the seed that is conceived contains the germ of the whole ongoing relationship that issues forth in the completed knowledge of wisdom. As Jesus said, His kingdom is like a seed that is planted and that springs forth, "first the stalk, then the head, then the full kernel in the head" (Mark 4:26-29), this full kernel being a multiplication of the original seed that was planted. So the full kernel of wisdom was already contained in the original seed of knowledge. Nevertheless, as we have said, while knowledge can be seen as the all-inclusive term for this process of development as a whole, when speaking of the three stages of the development of knowledge, it seems most appropriate to regard knowledge, *da'at*, as the initial stage, *b'inah*, or understanding, as the second, and *chochmah*, or wisdom, as the third or final stage.

Notes

Preface

1. Selwyn Feinstein, "Domestic Lessons: Shunning the Schools, More Parents Teach Their Kids at Home," *Wall Street Journal*, 6 October 1986.

2. Raymond and Dorothy Moore, *Home-Spun Schools: Teaching Children at Home—What Parents Are Doing and How They Are Doing It* (Waco, Tex.: Word Books, 1982), p. 9; William H. Wilbur, *The Making of George Washington* (N.p., 1976), p. 104.

3. John 7:15, TEV; Acts 4:13, Ampl.; Raymond S. Moore, "Research and Common Sense: Therapies for Our Homes and Schools," *Teachers College Record*, vol. 84, no. 2 (Winter 1982), p. 372; John W. Whitehead and Wendell Bird, *Home Education and Constitutional Liberties: The Historical and Constitutional Arguments in Support of Home Instruction*, Rutherford Institute Report, vol. 2 (Westchester, Ill.: Crossway Books, 1984), p. 23.

CHAPTER ONE
Introduction: *Education for the Whole Person*

1. The Scriptures repeatedly speak of the redemptive work of God in terms of at-one-ment and the integration of all the aspects of man's whole being in the worship and love of God (Rom. 5:11, KJV; Deut. 6:4-5; Mark 12:29-30; 1 Thess. 5:23). See Carl G. Vaught, *The Quest for Wholeness* (Albany, N.Y.: State University of New York Press, 1982), p. xi. See also Truth Forum's *Salvation Is of the Jews*.

2. Walter F. Otto, *The Homeric Gods: The Spiritual Significance of Greek Religion* (Great Britain: Thames and Hudson, 1955; New York: Random House, Pantheon Books, 1979), p. 236; Edith Hamilton, *The Greek Way* (New York: W.W. Norton and Co., 1930), pp. 56-57; Hannah Arendt, *The Life of the Mind*, part one, *Thinking* (New York: Harcourt Brace Jovanovich, A Harvest/HBJ Book, 1978), p. 130; Rousas John Rushdoony, *The Philosophy of the Christian Curriculum* (Vallecito, Calif.: Ross House Books, 1981), p. 5.

3. Will Durant, *The Life of Greece*, part 2 of *The Story of Civilization* (New York: Simon and Schuster, 1939), p. 582.

CHAPTER TWO
Knowledge: *God-Centered versus Man-Centered*

1. Walter F. Otto, *The Homeric Gods: The Spiritual Significance of Greek Religion* (London: Thames and Hudson, 1955; New York: Random House, Pantheon Books, 1979), pp. 128-129, 131.

2. Hannah Arendt, *The Life of the Mind*, part one, *Thinking* (New York: Harcourt Brace Jovanovich, A Harvest/HBJ Book, 1978), p. 130.

3. Ibid.

4. Werner Jaeger, *Paideia: The Ideals of Greek Culture*, vol. 1, *Archaic Greece, The Mind of Athens*, trans. Gilbert Highet, 2d ed. (New York: Oxford University Press Paperback, 1979), p. 247.

5. Raymond Williams, *Keywords: A Vocabulary of Culture and Society*, rev. ed. (New York: Oxford University Press, 1985), p. 316; C.T. Onions, *The Oxford Dictionary of English Etymology* (1983), s.v. "theory" and "theatre"; William Barrett, *Irrational Man: A Study in Existential Philosophy* (Garden City, N.Y.: Doubleday Anchor Books, 1962), p. 77.

6. B. Jowett, trans., *The Republic of Plato*, 3d ed. (Oxford: Clarendon Press, 1888), p. 182.

7. Barrett, *Irrational Man*, p. 76.

8. Henri Baruk, *Tsedek: Where Modern Science Is Examined and Where It Is Attempted to Save Man from Physical and Spiritual Enslavement* (Binghamton, N.Y.: Swan House Publishing, 1972), p. 170.

9. J. W. Roberts, *City of Sokrates: An Introduction to Classical Athens* (1984; reprint, London and New York: Routledge and Kegan Paul, 1987), p. 112.

10. Barrett, *Irrational Man*, p. 77.

11. *Webster's Third New International Dictionary*, s.v. "analysis" and "lose."

12. Heinz R. Pagels, *The Cosmic Code: Quantum Physics as the Language of Nature* (New York: Simon and Schuster, 1982), pp. 64-65.

13. Ibid., p. 65.

14. Ibid.

15. Michael Polanyi, *Personal Knowledge: Towards a Post-Critical Philosophy* (Chicago: University of Chicago Press, 1962), p. 3.

16. Ibid.

17. Michael Polanyi and Harry Prosch, *Meaning* (Chicago: University of Chicago Press, 1975), p. 37.

18. Williams, *Keywords*, p. 127 (emphasis added).

19. Ibid.

20. H. Richard Niebuhr, *Christ and Culture* (New York: Harper Torchbooks, 1951), p. 32.

21. Williams, *Keywords*, p. 128.

22. Nien Cheng, *Life and Death in Shanghai* (New York: Grove Press, 1986), p. 190; Milton Friedman, *Capitalism and Freedom* (Chicago: University of Chicago Press, 1962), p. 148.

23. Israel I. Efros, *Ancient Jewish Philosophy: A Study in Metaphysics and Ethics* (Detroit: Wayne State University Press, 1964), p. 86.

24. See Christopher Hibbert, *The Days of the French Revolution* (New York: William Morrow and Co., 1980).

25. See Iosif G. Dyadkin, *Unnatural Deaths in the USSR, 1928-1954*, trans. Tania Derugine (New Brunswick, N.J.: Transaction Books, 1983).

26. Baruk, *Tsedek*, p. 173.

27. Ibid., pp. 173-174.

28. Ibid., pp. 174-175.

29. Mont W. Smith, *What the Bible Says about Covenant* (Joplin, Mo.: College Press Publishing Co., 1981), p. 6.

30. Thomas Sowell, *Pink and Brown People and Other Controversial Essays* (Stanford, Calif.: Hoover Institution Press, 1981), p. 36.

31. Ibid.

32. Ibid.

33. Raymond and Dorothy Moore, *Home Grown Kids: A Practical Handbook for Teaching Your Children at Home* (Waco, Tex.: Word Books, 1981), pp. 32-33.

34. "A Nation of Illiterates?" *U.S. News and World Report*, 17 May 1982, p. 53; Roger Sipher, "Compulsory Education: An Idea Whose Time Has Past," *USA Today* (September 1978), p. 18; Rudolf Flesch, *Why Johnny Still Can't Read: A New Look at the Scandal of Our*

Schools (New York: Harper and Row, 1981), pp. 60, 62; Connie Bruck, "Are Teachers Failing Our Children?" *McCall's* (May 1979), p. 174; Edward B. Fiske, "Reading Analysis Is Called Lacking: Study Finds Students Failing to Go beyond a Superficial Assessment of Content," *New York Times*, 12 November 1981; Sally Reed, ". . . But Many Students Continue to be Hobbled by Illiteracy," *New York Times*, 6 January 1986; *A Nation at Risk: The Imperative for Educational Reform*, Department of Education, National Commission on Excellence in Education (April 1983), p. 9.

35. Allen Tate, "Narcissus as Narcissus," in *The Literature of the United States: An Anthology and History from the Civil War to the Present*, ed. Walter Blair et al., vol. 2, 3d ed. (Glenview, Ill.: Scott, Foresman and Co., 1970), p. 1132.

36. See Lewis Mumford, *The Myth of the Machine: Technics and Human Development* (New York: Harcourt Brace Jovanovich, 1967).

37. See Robert S. Mendelsohn, M.D., *Confessions of a Medical Heretic* (Chicago: Contemporary Books, 1979).

38. Aldous Huxley, *Brave New World and Brave New World Revisited* (New York: Harper and Row, Harper Colophon Books, 1965), p. 24.

39. John Milton, "Paradise Lost," in *The Poems of John Milton*, ed. Helen Darbishire (London: Oxford University Press, 1961), p. 187.

40. Wendell Berry, *Standing by Words* (San Francisco: North Point Press, 1983), p. 115.

41. Ibid., p. 201.

CHAPTER THREE
Education: *Forming the Child's Image*

1. Jerry Mander, *Four Arguments for the Elimination of Television* (New York: William Morrow and Co., 1978), pp. 258-260; "Weekly TV Viewing by Age," *Information Please Almanac: Atlas and Yearbook 1987*, ed. Otto Johnson (Boston: Houghton Mifflin Co., 1987), p. 727.

2. Aldous Huxley, *Brave New World* (1946; reprint, New York: Time Reading Program, 1963), p. xviii.

3. Sir Walter Moberly, *The Crisis in the University* (London: SCM Press, 1949), pp. 55-56.

4. C. S. Lewis, *The Abolition of Man: or Reflections on Education with Special Reference to the Teaching of English in the Upper*

Forms of Schools (New York: Macmillan, 1947), pp. 16-17.

5. G. Richard Bozarth, "On Keeping God Alive," *American Atheist* (November 1977), p. 8.

6. Stephen Arons, "The Separation of School and State: *Pierce* Reconsidered," *Harvard Educational Review*, vol. 46, no. 1 (February 1976), p. 98.

7. Philip H. Phenix, *Religious Concerns in Contemporary Education* (New York: Bureau of Publications, Teachers College, Columbia University, 1959), p. 19, quoted in Rousas John Rushdoony, *The Philosophy of the Christian Curriculum* (Vallecito, Calif.: Ross House Books, 1981), pp. 3-4.

8. Ibid.

9. T. S. Eliot, *Notes towards the Definition of Culture* (New York: Harcourt, Brace and Co., 1949), p. 29.

10. Gail M. Inlow, *Education: Mirror and Agent of Change: A Foundations Text* (New York: Holt, Rinehart and Winston, 1970), pp. 35-36.

11. Eliot, *Definition of Culture*, pp. 28, 30 (emphasis in original).

12. Ernest Becker, *Escape from Evil* (New York: Macmillan, Free Press, 1976), p. 64.

13. A. E. Haydon quoted by William P. Alston, "Religion," in *The Encyclopedia of Philosophy*, ed. Paul Edwards, vol. 7 (1967; reprint, New York: Macmillan and Free Press, 1972), p. 141.

14. Minersville School District v. Walter Gobitis, 310 U.S. 586, 600.

15. John Dewey, *A Common Faith* (New Haven, Conn.: Yale University Press, 1980), p. 2.

16. John F. Gardner, *The Experience of Knowledge: Essays on American Education* (Garden City, N.Y.: Adelphi University, Waldorf Press, 1975), pp. 213-214.

17. Dewey, *A Common Faith*, p. 87.

18. Robert M. Crunden, *Ministers of Reform: The Progressives' Achievement in American Civilization, 1889-1920* (New York: Basic Books, 1982), p. 58.

19. Raymond S. Moore et al., *School Can Wait* (Provo, Utah: Brigham Young University Press, 1979), pp. 60-61.

20. Joel H. Spring, *Education and the Rise of the Corporate State* (Boston: Beacon Press, 1972), p. 45.

21. Gilmer W. Blackburn, *Education in the Third Reich: A Study of Race and History in Nazi Textbooks* (Albany, N.Y.: State University of New York Press, 1985), p. 3.

22. See Jean-Jacques Rousseau, *Emile or On Education*, trans. Allan Bloom (New York: Basic Books, 1979).

23. Frederick Mayer, *Education for a New Society* (Bloomington, Ind.: Phi Delta Kappa Educational Foundation, 1973), p. 7.

24. George L. Mosse, *Nazi Culture: Intellectual, Cultural and Social Life in the Third Reich*, trans., Salvator Attanasio (New York: Grosset and Dunlap, Universal Library, 1968), p. 133.

25. Ibid., p. 240.

26. Ibid., p. 235.

27. Ibid., p. 238.

28. Theodore M. Black, *Straight Talk about American Education* (New York: Harcourt Brace Jovanovich, 1982), p. 40.

29. Mosse, *Nazi Culture*, p. 238.

30. William L. Shirer, *The Rise and Fall of the Third Reich: A History of Nazi Germany* (New York: Simon and Schuster, 1960), p. 249; Robert G. L. Waite, *The Psychopathic God: Adolf Hitler* (New York: Basic Books, 1977), p. 91.

31. Norman Cameron and R. H. Stevens, trans., *Hitler's Secret Conversations: 1941-1944* (New York: Farrar, Straus and Young, 1953), pp. 51-52.

32. J. D. Douglas et al., *New Bible Dictionary*, 2d ed. (Leicester, Eng.: Inter-Varsity Press, 1982), p. 789.

33. Robert S. Mendelsohn, M.D., *The People's Doctor: A Medical Newsletter for Consumers,* vol. 8, no. 12. Evanston, Ill., p. 3. Polio, measles and smallpox vaccines themselves have often become the primary cause of the sickness that they supposedly prevent. Vaccines against relatively harmless childhood diseases also cause more serious diseases like SSPE which causes hardening of the brain and is invariably fatal. Ataxia (inability to coordinate muscle movement), mental retardation, aseptic meningitis, seizure disorders and hemiparesis (paralysis affecting one side of the body)—all are associated with the measles vaccine. Secondary complications associated with vaccinations may be even more frightening, and include multiple sclerosis, blood clotting disorders, juvenile onset diabetes and even Hodgkin's disease and cancer. A growing number of studies and reports link both the transfer and possibly the origins of AIDS to mass vaccinations. Researchers have linked the DPT vaccine and Sudden Infant Death Syndrome (SIDS) which results in the death of eight to ten thousand infants a year in the United States.

34. This is a widely recognized principle of Scripture interpretation,

known among other things as the principle of "the first mention."
According to Conner and Malmin, this "is that principle by which the
interpretation of any verse is aided by considering the first time its
subject appears in Scripture." They tell us that "in general, the first
time a thing is mentioned in Scripture it carries with it a meaning
which will be consistent throughout the entire Bible."

The first mention is:
-*A key* which unlocks the door into the full
 truth
-*A gateway* into the path of truth
-*A guide* to discovering the truth in its
 progressive unfolding
-*The first link* in a long chain of revelation
-*A seed* which has within it the full truth that
 is to be developed in all subsequent mentions
The Bible describes God's Word as seed (Luke 8:11), and then in
Genesis it says like seed produces after its own kind (Gen. 1:12). So
when we see the seed of a thought expressed in God's Word, that
seed will produce according to the principles contained in its first
expression. So we can see why, according to these authors, God
"was able to formulate in the first mention of a thing that which
characterizes it in its progressive unfolding" (Gen. 1:11, 21, 24)
(Kevin Conner and Ken Malmin, *Interpreting the Scriptures* [Port-
land, Oreg.: Center Press, 1976], p. 91). Genesis, as the etymology
of the word suggests, provides the genetic base of all the rest of
Scripture. If this universally held principle is correct, Genesis 1:3-4
establishes the general character of God's Word as an instrument
of division and separation.

35. Wendon Blake, *Color in Water Color* (New York: Watson-Guptill
Publications, 1982), p. 4.

36. James Strong, *The Exhaustive Concordance of the Bible: Show-
ing Every Word of the Text of the Common English Version of the
Canonical Books, and Every Occurrence of Each Word in Regular
Order; Together with a Comparative Concordance of the Authorized
and Revised Versions, Including the American Variations; Also Brief
Dictionaries of the Hebrew and Greek Words* (Nashville: Abingdon
Press, 1980), p. 18 of the *Hebrew and Chaldee Dictionary*.

37. Fern Marja Eckman, "Teen Suicide," *McCall's* (October 1987),
pp. 71-74.

38. *Oxford English Dictionary,* compact ed., s.v. "educate."

39. Ibid.

40. *Webster's Third New International Dictionary*, s.v. "alma mater."

41. *Webster's New Collegiate Dictionary*, 8th ed., s.v. "discipline."

42. Ibid., s.v. "teach."

43. *The Random House Dictionary of the English Language*, unabridged ed., s.v. "education."

44. Jaroslav Pelikan, *The Emergence of the Catholic Tradition (100-600)*, vol. 1 of *The Christian Tradition: A History of the Development of Doctrine* (Chicago: University of Chicago Press, 1971), p. 1.

45. J. B. Phillips, *Letters to Young Churches: A Translation of the New Testament Epistles* (New York: Macmillan, 1957), p. 408.

46. Werner Jaeger, *Paideia: The Ideals of Greek Culture*, vol. 1, *Archaic Greece: The Mind of Athens* trans. Gilbert Highet, 2d ed. (New York: Oxford University Press paperback, 1979), p. xvi.

47. Ibid.

48 Ibid., p. xvii.

49. Ibid., p. xxii.

50. Elizabeth Léonie Simpson, *Humanistic Education: An Interpretation*, A Report to the Ford Foundation (Cambridge, Mass.: Ballinger Publishing Co., 1976), pp. 6-7.

CHAPTER FOUR
Whose Responsibility Is Christian Education?

1. T. Robert Ingram, *The World under God's Law: Criminal Aspects of the Welfare State* (Houston: St. Thomas Press, 1962), p. 24.

2. Gerhard Friedrich, ed., *Theological Dictionary of the New Testament*, Geoffrey W. Bromiley, trans. and ed., vol. 5 (Grand Rapids, Mich.: Wm. B. Eerdmans Publishing Co., 1967), p. 253.

3. Jacques Ellul, *The Meaning of the City*, trans. Dennis Pardee (Grand Rapids, Mich.: Wm. B. Eerdmans Publishing Co., 1970), p. 15.

4. Richard M. Weaver, *Ideas Have Consequences* (Chicago: University of Chicago Press, Midway Reprint, 1976), p. 149.

5. Ibid., p. 168.

6. Paul C. Vitz, *Sigmund Freud's Christian Unconscious* (New York: Guilford Press, 1988), p. 43.

7. Gregory Bateson, *Mind and Nature: A Necessary Unity* (Toronto: Bantam Books, 1980), p. 68.

8. See S. David Young, *The Rule of Experts: Occupational Licensing*

in America (Washington, D.C.: Cato Institute, 1987), esp. chapters 6 and 7.

9. Raymond S. Moore et al., *School Can Wait* (Provo, Utah: Brigham Young University Press, 1979), p. 1.

10. Ibid.

11. Ibid., p. 31.

12. Ibid.

13. Martin Engel, "Rapunzel, Rapunzel, Let Down Your Golden Hair: Some Thoughts on Early Childhood Education," unpublished manuscript, National Demonstration Center in Early Childhood Education, U.S. Office of Education, Washington D.C.

14. Gene V. Glass and Mary Lee Smith, *Meta-Analysis of Research on the Relationship of Class-Size and Achievement* (September 1978), Laboratory of Educational Research, University of Colorado, p. v.

15. Raymond S. Moore, "Research and Common Sense: Therapies for Our Homes and Schools," *Teachers College Record*, vol. 84, no. 2 (Winter 1982), p. 366; see also Urie Bronfenbrenner, *Two Worlds of Childhood: U.S. and U.S.S.R.* (New York: Russell Sage Foundation, 1970), p. 101.

16. Moore, *School Can Wait*, p. 55.

17. Jerry Richmond, "Parents Find Education Option in 'How to Teach Your Own,'" *Denver Post*, 29 November 1981.

18. Sue Welch, Ginny Wells, and Eric E. Wiggin, "Counting the Cost," *Moody* (March 1984), p. 28.

19. Moore, *School Can Wait*, p. 32.

20. Moore, "Research and Common Sense," p. 366.

21. Moore, *School Can Wait*, pp. 60-61.

22. Ibid., p. 227.

23. Ibid., chapter 3.

24. Urie Bronfenbrenner, *Two Worlds of Childhood*, pp. 116-117.

25. Jane Norman and Myron Harris, "Teen-agers Finding School Irrelevant, Boring," *Denver Post*, 17 February 1982.

26. Ibid.

27. Verbal communication between Kevin Durkin, Truth Forum, and Darcy Edwards, secretary to Dr. Conway Hunter in June 1983. In response to our request for documentation of this statistic, Dr. Hunter responded to Darcy Edwards that it "was derived from a primary study which Dr. Hunter conducted in the Atlanta area public

schools in 1978 and has since been confirmed by Dr. Hunter's numerous contacts across the country."

28. Ibid.

29. F. H. Swift, *Education in Ancient Israel from Earliest Times to 70 A.D.* (Chicago: Open Court Publishing Co., 1919), p. 50.

30. Isaac Landman, ed., *The Universal Jewish Encyclopedia*, vol. 3 (Universal Jewish Encyclopedia, New York, 1941), p. 629.

31. Swift, *Education in Ancient Israel*, p. 49.

32. Roland de Vaux, *Ancient Israel*, vol. 1, *Social Institutions* (1961; reprint, New York: McGraw-Hill Paperbacks, 1965), pp. 49-50.

33. William Barclay, *Educational Ideals in the Ancient World* (1959; reprint, Grand Rapids, Mich.: Baker Book House, 1974), pp. 14-15.

34. John 7:15, TEV.

35. *Getting Started in Texas*, Texas Association for Home Education (Richardson, Tex., July 1984), p. 14; John W. Whitehead and Wendell R. Bird, *Home Education and Constitutional Liberties: The Historical and Constitutional Arguments in Support of Home Instruction*, Rutherford Institute Report, vol. 2 (Westchester, Ill.: Crossway Books, 1984), pp. 23-24.

36. Moore, "Research and Common Sense," p. 372.

37. Ibid.

38. Ibid.

39. Ibid.

40. Wisconsin v. Yoder, 406 U.S. 205, 32 L Ed 2d 15, 92 S Ct 1526, 238.

41. Moore, *School Can Wait*, p. 2.

42. Moore, "Research and Common Sense," p. 365.

43. Charles E. Rice, "Conscientious Objection to Public Education: The Grievance and the Remedies," *Brigham Young University Law Review*, no. 4 (1978), pp. 862-864.

44. L. B. Brown, "A Study of Religious Belief," *British Journal of Psychology*, vol. 53 (August 1962), p. 268; S. E. Asch, "Effects of Group Pressure upon the Modification and Distortion of Judgments," in *Group Dynamics: Research and Theory*, ed. Dorwin Cartwright and Alvin Zander, 2d ed. (Evanston, Ill.: Row, Peterson and Co., 1960), pp. 189, 191, 193-194.

45. Hermann Rauschning, *Men of Chaos* (New York: G. P. Putnam's Sons, 1942), pp. 98-99.

"The glorification of the weak and morbid is Judaism, is Christianity.

That is why we hate both. We talk of the Jew, but we mean the Christian as well. Jew and Christian are one and the same thing, don't forget that. The time is coming when we shall destroy the Christians, just as today we are persecuting the Jews. Christianity is the mortal sin against the healthy life." Gauleiter Forster, Nazi leader in Danzig. (Hermann Rauschning, an ex-Nazi who worked closely with Hitler before fleeing from Germany, said of the above comment by Forster, "In such utterances Forster was the primitive mouthpiece of Hitler. It is worth while to take these trivial utterances seriously, for they express what Hitler was planning.")

46. Joyce Maynard, *Looking Back: A Chronicle of Growing up Old in the Sixties* (Garden City, N.Y.: Doubleday and Co., 1973), p. 5 (emphasis in original).

47. Ibid.

48. Ibid.

49. Ibid.

50. Ibid., p. 3.

51. Ibid., p. 4.

52. Ibid., pp. 5-6.

53. Fern Marja Eckman, "Teen Suicide," *McCall's* (October 1987), p. 71.

54. Claire Chambers, *The SIECUS Circle: A Humanist Revolution* (Belmont, Mass.: Western Islands, 1977), p. 182.

55. Barbara R. Thompson, "The Debate over Public Schools: The View from the Principal's Office," *Christianity Today*, 7 September 1984, p. 23.

56. Samuel L. Blumenfeld, *Is Public Education Necessary?* (Old Greenwich, Conn.: Devin-Adair Co., 1981), pp. 30, 192-193, 101-102.

57. Robert L. Dabney, *Discussions*, vol. 4, *Secular*, ed., C. R. Vaughan (Vallecito, Calif.: Ross House Books, 1979), p. 208.

58. James Karman, "I Feel Like an Onion," *HIS* (October 1981), p. 1.

59. Letter from Calvin Frazier to Lowell Anderson, 13 October 1981, Colorado Department of Education, Denver, Colo.

60. Guenter Lewy, *False Consciousness: An Essay on Mystification* (New Brunswick, N.J.: Transaction Books, 1982), p. 78.

61. James Axtell, *The School upon a Hill: Education and Society in Colonial New England* (New York: W.W. Norton and Co., 1976), p. xi.

62. Ibid.

63. Ibid. (emphasis in original).

64. Stephen Arons, "The Separation of School and State: *Pierce* Reconsidered," *Harvard Educational Review*, vol. 46, no. 1 (February 1976), p. 78.

65. Bronfenbrenner, *Two Worlds of Childhood*, pp. 152-153.

66. Moore, "Research and Common Sense," p. 373.

67. Moore, *School Can Wait*, p. 58.

68. David C. Gibbs, Jr., *Conviction versus Preference* (A CLA Minutebook), Christian Law Association, Cleveland, Ohio, p. 3.

CHAPTER FIVE
The Faith of the Parent-Teacher

1. Raymond S. Moore et al., *School Can Wait* (Provo, Utah: Brigham Young University Press, 1979), p. 229.

2. Raymond and Dorothy Moore, *Home Grown Kids: A Practical Handbook for Teaching Your Children at Home* (Waco, Tex.: Word Books, 1981), p. 14.

3. Raymond S. Moore, "Research and Common Sense: Therapies for Our Homes and Schools," *Teachers College Record*, vol. 84, no. 2 (Winter 1982), p. 372.

4. Raymond S. Moore, quoted by John Eidsmoe, in *The Christian Legal Advisor* (Milford, Mich.: Mott Media, 1984), p. 320.

5. Moore, "Research and Common Sense," p. 372.

6. Verbal communication between Mary Salmeri, Truth Forum, and Professor R. Barker Bausell of the University of Maryland, March 21, 1988.

7. Ibid.

8. Moore, "Research and Common Sense," p. 370; Benjamin S. Bloom, "Helping All Children Learn Well in Elementary School and Beyond," *Principal* (March 1988).

9. Selwyn Feinstein, "Domestic Lessons: More Parents Teach Their Kids at Home," *Wall Street Journal*, 6 October 1986.

10. "Home Education in America: Parental Rights Reasserted," *University of Missouri Law Review* (1981), p. 193.

11. "Sixth-graders in Orlando Outdo Teachers on Test," *Daily Sentinel*, Grand Junction (Colo.), 8 June 1983.

12. Sue Welch, Ginny Wells, and Eric E. Wiggin, "Counting the Cost," *Moody* (March 1984), p. 27.

13. Gary North, *Dominion Strategies*, vol. 11, no. 2, Tyler, Tex.: Institute for Christian Economics (February 1986).

14. Moore, "Research and Common Sense," pp. 372-373.

15. North, *Dominion Strategies* (February 1986).

16. Ibid.

17. Ibid.

18. Moore, "Research and Common Sense," p. 370.

19. Moore, *Home Grown Kids*, pp. 32-33.

20. Gary North, *Dominion Strategies*, vol. 11, no. 4 (April 1986).

21. Ibid.

22. Ibid.

23. Moore, "Research and Common Sense," p. 372.

24. Moore, *Home Grown Kids*, p. 24.

25. Moore, *School Can Wait*, p. 36.

26. John Dewey, *A Common Faith* (New Haven, Conn.: Yale University Press, 1934), p. 2.

27. Trustees of Schools v. People, 87 Ill. 303, 308.

28. Ernst Cassirer, *The Myth of the State* (New Haven, Conn.: Yale University Press, 1975), p. 288.

29. "Citing 'Illiterate Society' Dad Teaches Own Kids," *Daily News* (New York), May 1979.

30. Sally Inch, *Birthrights: What Every Parent Should Know about Childbirth in Hospitals* (New York: Pantheon Books, 1984), pp. 3-4; Robert S. Mendelsohn, M.D., *Confessions of a Medical Heretic* (Chicago: Warner Books, 1979), pp. 121-129, 135, 152-153, 202-209, 217-222; Shelly Romalis, ed., *Childbirth: Alternatives to Medical Control* (Austin: University of Texas Press, 1981), pp. 20, 27, 171; Raymond G. DeVries, *Regulating Birth: Midwives, Medicine and the Law* (Philadelphia: Temple University Press, 1985), pp. 26-27, 52; Gena Corea, *The Hidden Malpractice: How American Medicine Treats Women as Patients and Professionals* (New York: Jove Publications, Jove/HBJ Books, 1978), pp. 211-212, 259; Judith Randal, "Where Should Your Child Be Born?" *Parents* (March 1979), p. 76; Suzanne Arms, *Immaculate Deception: A New Look at Women and Childbirth in America* (New York: Bantam Books, 1977), p. 274; Ezra Bowen, "Getting Tough," *Time*, 1 February 1988, pp. 54-55; "Now It's Suburbs Where School Violence Flares," *U.S. News and World*

Report, 21 May 1979, pp. 63-64.

31. Robert S. Mendelsohn, M.D., *How to Raise a Healthy Child . . . in Spite of Your Doctor* (Chicago, Ill.: Contemporary Books, 1984), p. 207.

32. Alice Jordan, "Twice a Cesarean: The Birth of Onna Chunaha," in *The Vaginal Birth after Cesarean Experience: Birth Stories by Parents and Professionals*, ed. Lynn Baptisti Richards (South Hadley, Mass.: Bergin and Garvey Publishers, 1987), pp. 107-108.

33. Inch, *Birthrights*, pp. 3-4; Mendelsohn, *Confessions of a Medical Heretic*, pp. 121-129, 135, 152-153, 202-209, 217-222; Romalis, *Childbirth*, p. 171; DeVries, *Regulating Birth*, pp. 26-27, 52; Corea, *The Hidden Malpractice*, pp. 211-212; Randal, "Where Should Your Child Be Born?" p. 76; Arms, *Immaculate Deception*, p. 274; Bowen, "Getting Tough," pp. 54-55.

CHAPTER SIX
Principles of Christian Learning

1. Wendell Berry, *Standing by Words* (San Francisco, Calif.: North Point Press, 1983), p. 76.

2. E. F. Schumacher, *A Guide for the Perplexed* (New York: Harper and Row, 1977), pp. 15-17.

3. Andrew Lytle, "Reflections of a Ghost: An Agrarian View after Fifty Years," *Southern Partisan*, vol. 4, no. 4 (Fall 1984), p. 24.

4. Jerome Kagan, "The Moral Function of the School," *Daedalus* (Summer 1981), p. 153.

5. Ibid., p. 154.

6. Ibid., p. 151.

7. Richard M. Weaver, *Ideas Have Consequences* (Chicago: University of Chicago Press, Midway Reprint, 1976), p. 73.

8. Gerhard Friedrich, ed. *Theological Dictionary of the New Testament*, trans. and ed., Geoffrey Bromiley, vol. 6 (Grand Rapids, Mich.: Wm. B. Eerdmans Publishing, 1978), pp. 484-485.

9. Ibid., p. 485.

10. William Barrett, *Time of Need: Forms of Imagination in the Twentieth Century* (New York: Harper and Row Torchbooks, 1973; Middletown, Conn.: Wesleyan University Press, Wesleyan Paperbacks, 1984), p. 109.

11. R. M. Lauer and M. Hussey, "A New Way to Become Educated,"

Humanist (January/February 1986), p. 6.

12. Ibid., p. 5 (emphasis in original).

13. Ibid.

14. *Webster's New Collegiate Dictionary* (1981), s.v. "template."

15. Lauer and Hussey, "A New Way to Become Educated," p. 5.

16. Ibid., p. 5.

17. Ibid., p. 6.

18. William Barrett, *The Illusion of Technique: A Search for Meaning in a Technological Civilization* (Garden City, N.Y.: Anchor Books, 1979), pp. 293-294.

19. William H. McNeill, *Mythistory and Other Essays* (Chicago: University of Chicago Press, 1986), pp. 5-6.

20. William Barrett, *Time of Need*, p. 5.

21. William Barrett, *Irrational Man: A Study in Existential Philosophy* (Garden City, N.Y.: Doubleday Anchor Books, 1962), pp. 51-54.

22. Raymond Williams, *Keywords: A Vocabulary of Culture and Society* (New York: Oxford University Press, 1983), p. 106.

23. Ibid.

24. Ibid. (emphasis in original).

25. Ibid., p. 107.

26. Ibid.

27. Ibid.

28. Ibid.

29. Ronald B. Mayers, *Both/And: A Balanced Apologetic* (Chicago: Moody Press, 1984), p. 2.

30. William N. Blake, "A Christian Philosophy of Method in Education," *Journal of Christian Reconstruction*, vol. 4, no. 1 (Summer 1977), p. 32.

31. Richard M. Weaver, *The Ethics of Rhetoric* (South Bend, Ind: Regenery/Gateway, 1953), pp. 9-12.

32. Richard M. Weaver, *A Rhetoric and Handbook*, rev. ed. (New York: Holt, Rinehart and Winston, 1967), p. v.

33. Weaver, *Ideas Have Consequences*, p. 168.

34. Ibid., p. 58.

CHAPTER SEVEN
General Application of Principles

1. Dorothy L. Sayers, "The Lost Tools of Learning," *Journal of Christian Reconstruction*, vol. 4, no. 1 (Summer 1977), p. 25.

2. Wendell Berry, *Collected Poems* (San Francisco: North Point Press, 1985), p. 243.

3. Ibid., p. 244.

4. Ibid., p. 159.

5. Ibid.

6. Ibid.

7. Ibid., p. 158.

8. Richard M. Weaver, *Ideas Have Consequences* (Chicago: University of Chicago Press, Midway Reprint, 1976), p. 58.

9. Ibid.

10. Ibid., p. 59.

11. John Keegan, *The Face of Battle: A Study of Agincourt, Waterloo and the Somme* (New York: Viking Press, 1976; Penguin Books, 1984), p. 19.

12. H. Douglas Brown, *Principles of Language Learning and Teaching*, 2d ed. (Englewood Cliffs, N.J.: Prentice Hall, 1987), p. 65.

13. Ibid. (brackets in original).

14. Ibid., pp. 69-70.

15. Ward Powers, *Learn To Read the Greek New Testament* (Sydney, NSW, Australia: Anzea Publishers, 1983), p. 5.

16. Ibid.

17. Ibid., p. 6.

18. Ibid., p. 5.

19. Ibid.

20. Ibid., p. 6.

21. Ibid.

22. *The Pimsleur Tapes: The Sure and Easy Way to Learn Another Language* (Concord, Mass.: Heinle and Heinle Enterprises, n.d).

23. John H. Saxon, Jr., *Algebra I: An Incremental Development* (Norman, Okla.: Grassdale Publishers, 1982), p. vi.

24. Ibid., front cover.

25. *Pimsleur Tapes*.

26. Ibid.

27. Lawrence A. Cremin, *American Education: The Colonial Experience, 1607-1783* (New York: Harper and Row, 1970), p. 211; Edwin S. Gaustad, ed., *A Documentary History of Religion in America to the Civil War* (Grand Rapids, Mich.: William B. Eerdmans Publishing Co., 1982), p. 201; R. Freeman Butts and Lawrence A. Cremin, *A History of Education in American Culture* (New York: Holt, Rinehart and Winston, 1953), p. 81; Lawrence Stone, ed., *Schooling and Society: Studies in the History of Education* (Baltimore, Md.: Johns Hopkins University Press, 1976), p. xiii; *Oxford English Dictionary*, compact ed., s.v. "college."

28. Robert C. Solomon, *History and Human Nature: A Philosophical Review of European Philosophy and Culture, 1750-1850* (New York: Harcourt Brace Jovanovich, 1979), p. xii.

29. Aldous Huxley, *Brave New World and Brave New World Revisited* (New York: Harper and Row, Harper Colophon Books, 1965), p. xv.

30. "John Robinson: Spiritual Advice to Pilgrim Planters," in *1493-1754, Discovering a New World*, vol. 1 of *The Annals of America* (Chicago: Encyclopaedia Britannica, 1968), p. 61.

31. Jerry Combee, Laurel Hicks, and Mike Lowman, *The Modern Age: The History of the World in Christian Perspective*, vol. 2 (Pensacola, Fla.: A Beka Book Publications), pp. 229-230.

CHAPTER EIGHT
Particular Application of Principles

1. Raymond and Dorothy Moore et al., *Home Style Teaching: A Handbook for Parents and Teachers* (Waco, Tex.: Word Books, 1984), pp. 63-64.

2. Richard Mitchell, *Less Than Words Can Say* (Boston: Little, Brown and Co., 1979), p. 46.

3. Richard M. Weaver, *Ideas Have Consequences* (Chicago: University of Chicago Press, 1948; Midway Reprints, 1976), p. 162.

4. Samuel L. Blumenfeld, "Looking Backward 100 Years Later," *Chalcedon Report*, no. 278 (September 1988), p. 2.

5. Samuel L. Blumenfeld, *NEA: Trojan Horse in American Education* (Boise, Idaho: Paradigm Co., 1984), pp. 98, 105; Blumenfeld, "Looking Backward," p. 2.

6. Blumenfeld, "Looking Backward," p. 2.

7. Blumenfeld, *NEA*, p. 104.

8. Ibid., p. 100.

9. Ibid.

10. Ibid.

11. Wendell Berry, *Standing by Words* (San Francisco: North Point Press, 1983), p. 205.

12. Moore, *Home Style Teaching*, p. 50.

13. Ibid.

14. Ibid.

CHAPTER NINE
The Major Subject Areas

1. W. E. Vine, *An Expository Dictionary of New Testament Words: With Their Precise Meanings for English Readers* (Old Tappan, N.J.: Fleming H. Revell Co., 1940), s.v. "charakter."

2. Rousas John Rushdoony, "Elitism," *Chalcedon Position Paper*, no. 67 (Vallecito, Calif.).

3. Ibid.

4. Wendell Berry, *Standing by Words* (San Francisco: North Point Press, 1983), p. 99.

5. Carl F. H. Henry, *God, Revelation and Authority*, vol. 2, *God Who Speaks and Shows: Fifteen Theses,* part one (Waco, Tex.: Word Books, 1976), pp. 176-177.

6. Raymond Williams, *Keywords: A Vocabulary of Culture and Society* (New York: Oxford University Press, 1983), p. 72.

7. Richard M. Weaver, *Ideas Have Consequences* (Chicago: University of Chicago Press, Midway Reprint, 1976), p. 150.

8. Henry, *God, Revelation and Authority*, p. 174.

9. Richard Mitchell, *Less Than Words Can Say* (Boston: Little, Brown and Co., 1979), p. 67.

10. Ibid., p. 44.

11. Ibid., p. 46.

12. Weaver, *Ideas Have Consequences*, pp. 161-162.

13. Ibid., p. 162.

14. Mitchell, *Less Than Words Can Say*, p. 43.

15. Berry, *Standing by Words*, p. 53.

16. Ibid., pp. 53-54.

17. *Webster's New World Dictionary*, 2d college ed., s.v. "style."

18. Ibid.

19. William Strunk, Jr., and E. B. White, *The Elements of Style*, 3d ed. (New York: Macmillan, 1979), pp. 66-67.

20. Donald Hall, *Writing Well* (Boston: Little, Brown and Co., 1973), p. 126.

21. Ibid.

22. George Orwell, "Politics and the English Language," in *The Modern Stylists: Writers on the Art of Writing*, ed. Donald Hall (New York: Free Press, 1968), p. 20.

23. Ibid.

24. Ibid., p. 23.

25. Ibid., p. 24 (emphasis in original).

26. Ibid.

27. Ibid.

28. "Katherine Anne Porter," in *The Modern Stylists: Writers on the Art of Writing*, ed. Donald Hall (New York: Free Press, 1968), p. 121.

29. Ibid.

30. Hall, *Writing Well*, pp. 5-6.

31. Strunk and White, *The Elements of Style*, p. 84.

32. Llewelyn Powys, "Letter to Warner Taylor," in *The Creative Process*, ed. Brewster Ghiselin (New York: New American Library, A Mentor Book, 1952), pp. 176-177.

33. Hall, *The Modern Stylists*, p. 2.

34. Wendell Berry, "Some Thoughts I Have in Mind When I Teach," in *Writers as Teachers, Teachers as Writers*, ed. Jonathan Baumbach (New York: Holt, Rinehart and Winston, 1970), p. 23.

35. John R. Trimble, *Writing with Style: Conversations on the Art of Writing* (Englewood Cliffs, N.J.: Prentice-Hall, 1975), p. 13.

36. Hall, *The Modern Stylists*, p. 5.

37. W. F. Trotter, trans. *Pascal's Pensées* (London: J. M. Dent and Sons, 1931), p. 8.

38. Peter Elbow, *Writing with Power: Techniques for Mastering the Writing Process* (New York: Oxford University Press, 1981), pp. 291-295.

39. Ken Macrorie, *Writing to Be Read*, rev. 3d ed. (Upper Montclair, N.J.: Boynton/Cook Publishers, 1984), p. 1.

40. Ibid., p. 2.

41. Berry, "Some Thoughts I Have in Mind When I Teach," p. 23.

42. Elbow, *Writing with Power*, p. 317.

43. Ibid.

44. Barbara W. Tuchman, *Stilwell and the American Experience in China, 1911-45* (New York: Macmillan, 1971), p. 67.

45. Elbow, *Writing with Power*, p. 322.

46. Ibid., p. 325 (emphasis in original).

47. Cyril Connolly, *Enemies of Promise*, rev. ed. (New York: Macmillan, 1948), p. 10.

48. Ibid., pp. 10-11.

49. Ibid., p. 13.

50. Ibid., p. 17.

51. Ibid., pp. 21, 25.

52. Roger Garrison, *How a Writer Works*, rev. ed. (New York: Harper and Row, 1985), p. 5.

53. E. B. White to Alison Marks, 20 April 1956, *Letters of E. B. White*, ed. Dorothy Lobrano Guth (New York: Harper and Row, 1976), p. 417.

54. Garrison, *How a Writer Works*, p. 31.

55. Michael Polanyi and Harry Prosch, *Meaning* (Chicago: University of Chicago Press, 1975), p. 33.

56. Hall, *The Modern Stylists*, p. 2.

57. Strunk and White, *The Elements of Style*, p. 69.

58. Hall, *The Modern Stylists*, p. 6.

59. Elbow, *Writing with Power*, p. 281.

60. Weaver, *Ideas Have Consequences*, p. 153.

61. Ibid.

62. William Barrett, *The Truants: Adventures among the Intellectuals* (Garden City, N.Y.: Anchor Press/Doubleday, 1982), pp. 13-14.

63. Weaver, *Ideas Have Consequences*, p. 154.

64. Berry, *Standing by Words*, p. 25.

65. Ibid., p. 26 (emphasis added).

66. Ibid.

67. Ibid., pp. 25-26.

68. Rudolph Flesch, *The Art of Plain Talk* (New York: Harper and Brothers, 1946), p. 92.

69. Carl Markgraf, *Punctuation* (New York: John Wiley and Sons,

1979), p. vii.

70. Ibid., p. ix.

71. Wilfred Stone and J. G. Bell, *Prose Style: A Handbook for Writers*, 3d ed. (New York: McGraw-Hill Book Co., 1977), p. 22.

72. Ibid., pp. 23-24.

73. Ibid., p. 24.

74. Ibid.

75. Jacques Barzun, *Simple and Direct: A Rhetoric for Writers*, rev. ed. (New York: Harper and Row, 1985), p. 43.

76. Ibid.

77. C.W. Ceram, *Gods, Graves, and Scholars: The Story of Archaeology*, trans. E. B. Garside (New York: Alfred A. Knopf, 1951), p. 298.

78. Julian Huxley, ed. *The Humanist Frame* (New York: Harper and Brothers Publishers, 1961), p. 7.

79. Rousas J. Rushdoony, "Providence of God in History" (Middleburg Heights, Ohio: Christian Schools of Ohio, 1976), "sound cassette."

80. Aldous Huxley, *Brave New World* (New York: Harper and Row, 1946), pp. 38-39.

81. George Orwell, *1984* (New York: New American Library, A Signet Classic, 1961), p. 25.

82. Ibid., p. 204.

83. Carl L. Becker, *The Heavenly City of the Eighteenth-Century Philosophers* (New Haven, Conn.: Yale University Press, 1932), p. 88.

84. Roland Huntford, *The New Totalitarians* (New York: Stein and Day, 1972), p. 211.

85. John Dewey, *Democracy and Education: An Introduction to the Philosophy of Education* (New York: Free Press, 1944), p. 75.

86. Ibid.

87. Ibid.

88. Frances FitzGerald, *America Revised: History Schoolbooks in the Twentieth Century* (New York: Random House, Vintage Books, 1980), p. 174.

89. Siegfried Giedion, *Mechanization Takes Command: A Contribution to Anonymous History* (New York: W.W. Norton and Co., 1969), p. 11 (emphasis added).

90. Robert Kelley, *The Shaping of the American Past*, 2d ed., vol. 1 (Englewood Cliffs, N.J.: Prentice-Hall, 1978), pp. 72-73.

91. Samuel L. Blumenfeld, *Is Public Education Necessary?* (Old Greenwich, Conn.: Devin-Adair Co., 1981), pp. 16-17.

92. Alexandre Koyré, *From the Closed World to the Infinite Universe* (New York: Harper and Row, Harper Torchbooks, 1958), p. 276.

93. Berry, *Standing by Words*, p. 47.

94. Spiros Zodhiates, Preface to *Learn or Review New Testament Greek: Vocabulary and Answers to the Exercises in New Testament Greek for Beginners*, by J. Gresham Machen, comp. Spiros Zodhiates (Chattanooga, Tenn.: AMG Publishers, 1976).

95. Weaver, *Ideas Have Consequences*, p. 167.

SUPPLEMENT ONE
Koinonia Curriculum

1. Raymond S. Moore et al., *School Can Wait* (Provo, Utah: Brigham Young University Press, 1979), pp. 85-86.

2. Stephen Hake and John Saxon, *Math 76: An Incremental Development* (Norman, Okla.: Grassdale Publishers, 1985), p. xiii.

3. George Orwell, quoted in Kathryn Diehl and G. K. Hodenfield, *Johnny Still Can't Read—But You Can Teach Him at Home* (Bloomington, Ind.: Johnny, 1977), p. 4.

4. Thomas Middleton, "Light Refractions," *Saturday Review*, 24 November 1979, p. 10.

5. Joan Aiken, *The Way to Write for Children* (New York: St. Martin's Press, 1982), p. 40.

APPENDIX ONE
Testing

1. Andrew J. Strenio, Jr., *The Testing Trap* (New York: Rawson, Wade Publishers, 1981), pp. 9-10.

2. *Stanford Achievement Test*, Intermediate Level II, Complete Battery, Form A (New York: Harcourt Brace Jovanovich, 1972), p. 25.

3. Ibid.

4. The Scriptures repeatedly speak of the redemptive work of God in terms of at-one-ment and the integration of all the aspects of

man's whole being in the worship and love of God (Rom. 5:11, KJV; Deut. 6:4-5; Mark 12:29-30; 1 Thess. 5:23). See Carl G. Vaught, *The Quest for Wholeness* (Albany, N.Y.: State University of New York Press, 1982), p. xi. See also Truth Forum's *Salvation Is of the Jews*.

5. *Encyclopaedia Britannica Macropaedia*, 15th ed., s.v. "Humanistic Scholarship, History of."

6. The experience of the public schools proves that it is undeniable that setting up test scores as a standard will drastically alter curriculum. Ben M. Harris, Professor of Education Administration at the University of Texas, states that because of making standardized tests the standard of acceptability "teachers will teach the tests and students will study to pass them; test scores will rise and students will remember less and care less." According to the state testing director of Virginia, "teachers are under tremendous political pressure" to meet the standard of the tests and are ordering curriculum accordingly. Parents who have objected to a currriculum that is molded to standardized tests are told by one associate superintendent of public shcools that "if you do well on the tests, everybody believes you are successful, so why not teach the tests?" (Dennis A. Williams et al., "Go to the Head of the Class," *Newsweek*, 4 October 1982, p. 64; "Va. Official Doubts Validity of Tests' Favorable Results," *Washington Times*, 24 June 1983; "Education 'Reform' Effort Failing," *Austin American Statesman*, 11 January 1986).

7. W. James Popham, "The Merits of Measurement-Driven Instruction," *Phi Delta Kappan* (May 1987), p. 680.

8. Amanda Covarrubias, "Standardized School Tests Face Increasing Attacks on Accuracy," *Rocky Mountain News* (Colo.), 27 March 1988.

9. Raymond Williams, *Keywords: A Vocabulary of Culture and Society* (New York: Oxford University Press, 1983), p. 296.

10. Ibid., p. 297.

11. Ibid., p. 298 (emphasis added).

12. Raymond S. Moore, "Research and Common Sense: Therapies for Our Homes and School," *Teachers College Record*, vol. 84, no. 2 (Winter 1982), p. 372.

13. Johnson v. Charles City Community Schools Board of Education, 368 N.W. 2d 74 (Iowa 1985).

14. Williams, *Keywords*, p. 298.

15. Strenio, *The Testing Trap*, pp. 9-10.

16. David C. Gibbs, Jr., *Conviction versus Preference* (A CLA Minutebook), Christian Law Association, Cleveland, Ohio, pp. 17-19.

17. *Iowa Tests of Basic Skills*, Level 5, Early Primary Battery, Form 7 (Iowa City, Iowa: Houghton Mifflin Co.).

18. *California Achievement Tests*, Book 17C (Monterrey, Calif.: McGraw-Hill, 1957), p. R6.

19. Ibid., Book 16C, p. R12.

20. *Iowa Tests of Basic Skills*, Multi-Level Booklet for Levels 9-14, Form 7.

21. Ibid.

22. *California Achievement Tests*, Book 17C; *California Achievement Tests*, Book 12C; *Iowa Tests of Basic Skills*, Form 7.

23. *Iowa Tests of Basic Skills*, Form 7; *California Achievement Tests*, Book 15C; *Iowa Tests of Basic Skills*, Form 7; *California Achievement Tests*, Book 11C.

24. *SRA Achievement Series*, Level E, Form 2 (Chicago: Science Research Associates, 1978); *SRA Achievement Series*, Level F, Form 2.

25. Walter Lippmann, quoted by Paul L. Houts, ed., *The Myth of Measurability* (New York: Hart Publishing Co., 1977), pp. 14-15.

26. Ann Cook and Deborah Meier, "New York Students Show Spectacular Rise in Reading/New York City Students' Scores Indicate Steady Decline in Reading," unpublished paper distributed at the Fall 1979 NCT Conference, quoted by Andrew J. Strenio, Jr., *The Testing Trap*, p. 110.

APPENDIX TWO
The Three Levels of Knowledge

1. Nosson Scherman and Meir Zlotowicz, eds., *Succos—Its Significance, Laws, and Prayers: A Presentation Anthologized from Talmudic and Traditional Sources* (Brooklyn, N.Y.: Mesorah Publications, 1982), p. 26.

2. Ibid.

3. Ibid.

Bibliography

Books

Aiken, Joan. *The Way to Write for Children*. New York: St. Martin's Press, 1982.

Arendt, Hannah. *The Life of the Mind*. Part 1, *Thinking*. New York: Harcourt Brace Jovanovich, A Harvest/HBJ Book, 1978.

Anthony, Katherine. *First Lady of the Revolution: The Life of Mercy Otis Warren*. Garden City, N.Y.: Doubleday and Co., 1958.

Arms, Suzanne. *Immaculate Deception: A New Look at Women and Childbirth in America*. 1975. Reprint. New York: Bantam Books, 1977.

Artz, Frederick B. *The Mind of the Middle Ages, A.D. 200-1500: An Historical Survey*. 3d ed. rev. Chicago: University of Chicago Press, 1942.

Axtell, James. *The School upon a Hill: Education and Society in Colonial New England*. New York: W. W. Norton and Co., 1974.

Barclay, William. *Educational Ideals in the Ancient World*. 1959. Reprint. Grand Rapids, Mich.: Baker Book House, 1974.

Barraclough, Geoffrey. *The Times Atlas of World History*. London: Times Books, 1978; Maplewood, N.J.: Hammond, 1979.

Barrett, William. *The Illusion of Technique: A Search for Meaning in a Technological Civilization*. Garden City, N.Y.: Anchor Books, 1979.

―――. *Irrational Man: A Study in Existential Philosophy*. Garden City, N.Y.: Doubleday Anchor Books, Doubleday and Co., 1962.

―――. Time of Need: Forms of Imagination in the Twentieth Century. New York: Harper and Row Torchbooks, 1973; Middletown, Conn.: Wesleyan University Press, Wesleyan Paperbacks, 1984.

―――. *The Truants: Adventures among the Intellectuals*. Garden City, N.Y.: Anchor Press/Doubleday, 1982.

Baruk, Henri. *Tsedek: Where Modern Science Is Examined and Where It Is Attempted to Save Man from Physical and Spiritual*

Enslavement. Binghamton, N.Y.: Swan House Publishing Co., 1972.

Barzun, Jacques. *Simple and Direct: A Rhetoric for Writers*. Rev. ed. New York: Harper and Row, 1985.

Bateson, Gregory, *Mind and Nature: A Necessary Unity*. Toronto: Bantam Books, 1980.

Baumbach, Jonathan, ed. *Writers as Teachers, Teachers as Writers*. New York: Holt, Rinehart and Winston, 1970.

Becker, Carl. *The Heavenly City of the Eighteenth-Century Philosophers*. New Haven, Conn.: Yale University Press, 1948.

Becker, Ernest. *Escape from Evil*. New York: Macmillan, Free Press, 1976.

Bergan, John R., and James A. Dunn. *Psychology and Education: A Science for Instruction*. New York: John Wiley and Sons, 1976.

Berry, Wendell. *Collected Poems, 1957-1982*. San Francisco: North Point Press, 1985.

———. *Standing by Words*. San Francisco: North Point Press, 1983.

Black, Theodore M. *Straight Talk about American Education*. New York: Harcourt Brace Jovanovich, 1982.

Blackburn, Gilmer W. *Education in the Third Reich: A Study of Race and History in Nazi Textbooks*. Albany, N.Y.: State University of New York Press, 1985.

Blake, Wendon. *Color in Water Color*. New York: Watson-Guptill Publication, 1982.

Blumenfeld, Samuel L. *Is Public Education Necessary?* Old Greenwich, Conn.: Devin-Adair Co., 1981.

———. *NEA: Trojan Horse in American Education*. Boise, Idaho: Paradigm Co., 1984.

Bronfenbrenner, Urie. *Two Worlds of Childhood: U.S. and U.S.S.R.* New York: Russell Sage Foundation, 1970.

Brown, H. Douglas. *Principles of Language Learning and Teaching*. 2d ed. Englewood Cliffs, N.J.: Prentice Hall, 1987.

Butts, R. Freeman, and Lawrence A. Cremin. *A History of Education in American Culture*. New York: Holt, Rinehart and Winston, 1953.

Cassirer, Ernst. *The Myth of the State*. New Haven, Conn.: Yale University Press, 1975.

Ceram, C.W. *Gods, Graves, and Scholars: The Story of Archaeology*. Translated by E. B. Garside. New York: Alfred A. Knopf, 1966.

Chambers, Claire. *The Siecus Circle: A Humanist Revolution*. Belmont, Mass.: Western Islands, 1977.

Cheng, Nien. *Life and Death in Shanghai.* New York: Grove Press, 1986.

Combee, Jerry, Laurel Hicks, and Mike Louman. *The Modern Age: The History of the World in Christian Perspective.* Vol. 2. Pensacola, Fla.: A Beka Book Publications, 1981.

Conner, Kevin, and Ken Malmin. *Interpreting the Scriptures.* Portland, Oreg.: Center Press, 1976.

Connolly, Cyril. *Enemies of Promise.* Rev. ed. New York: Macmillan, 1948.

Corea, Gena. *The Hidden Malpractice: How American Medicine Treats Women as Patients and Professionals.* New York: Jove Publication, Jove/HBJ Books, 1985.

Cremin, Lawrence A. *American Education: The Colonial Experience, 1607-1783.* New York: Harper and Row, 1970.

Crunden, Robert M. *Ministers of Reform: The Progressives' Achievement in American Civilization, 1889-1920.* New York: Basic Books, 1982.

Dabney, Robert L. *Discussions.* Vol. 4, *Secular.* Edited by C. R. Vaughan. Vallecito, Calif.: Ross House Books, 1979.

de Vaux, Roland. *Ancient Israel.* Vol. 1, *Social Institutions.* 1961. Reprint. New York: McGraw-Hill Paperbacks, 1965.

DeVries, Raymond G. *Regulating Birth: Midwives, Medicine and the Law.* Philadelphia: Temple University Press, 1985.

Dewey, John. *A Common Faith.* New Haven, Conn.: Yale University Press, 1980.

―――. *Democracy and Education: An Introduction to the Philosophy of Education.* New York: Free Press, 1944.

Diehl, Kathryn, and G. K. Hodenfield. *Johnny Still Can't Read—but You Can Teach Him at Home.* Bloomington, Ind.: Johnny, 1977.

Dobson, James. *Dare to Discipline.* Wheaton, Ill.: Tyndale House, 1970.

Douglas, J. D. et al., eds. *The New Bible Dictionary.* 2d ed. Leicester, England: Inter-Varsity Press; Wheaton, Ill.: Tyndale House Publishers, 1982.

Durant, Will. *The Life of Greece.* Part 2 of *The Story of Civilization.* New York: Simon and Schuster, 1939.

Dyadkin, Iosif G. *Unnatural Deaths in the USSR, 1928-1954.* Translated by Tania Derugine. New Brunswick, N.J.: Transaction

Books, 1983.

Efros, Israel I. *Ancient Jewish Philosophy: A Study in Metaphysics and Ethics.* Detroit: Wayne State University Press, 1964.

Eidsmoe, John. *The Christian Legal Advisor.* Milford, Mich.: Mott Media, 1984.

Elbow, Peter. *Writing with Power: Techniques for Mastering the Writing Process.* New York: Oxford University Press, 1981.

Eliot, T. S. *Notes towards the Definition of Cultures.* New York: Harcourt, Brace and Co., 1949.

Ellul, Jacques. *The Meaning of the City.* Translated by Dennis Pardue. Grand Rapids, Mich.: William B. Eerdmans Publishing Co., 1970.

FitzGerald, Francis. *America Revised: History Schoolbooks in the Twentieth Century.* New York: Vintage Books, 1980.

Flesch, Rudolph. *The Art of Plain Talk.* New York: Harper and Brothers, 1946.

————. *Why Johnny Still Can't Read: A New Look at the Scandal of Our Schools.* New York: Harper and Row, 1981.

Friedman, Milton. *Capitalism and Freedom.* Chicago: University of Chicago Press, 1962.

Fromm, Erich. *The Anatomy of Human Destructiveness.* New York: Holt, Rinehart and Winston, 1973.

————. *Psychoanalysis and Religion.* New Haven, Conn.: Yale University Press, Bantam Books, 1967.

Gardner, John F. *The Experience of Knowledge: Essays on American Education.* Garden City, N.Y.: Adelphi University, Waldorf Press, 1975.

Garrison, Roger. *How a Writer Works.* New York: Harper and Row, 1985.

Gaustad, Edwin S. *A Documentary History of Religion in America to the Civil War.* Grand Rapids, Mich.: William B. Eerdmans Publishing Co., 1982.

Giedion, Siegfried. *Mechanization Takes Command: A Contribution to Anonymous History.* New York: W.W. Norton and Co., 1969.

Hake, Stephen, and John Saxon. *Math 76: An Incremental Development.* Norman, Okla.: Grassdale Publishers, 1986.

Hall, Donald, ed. *The Modern Stylists: Writers on the Art of Writing.* New York: Free Press, 1968.

————. *Writing Well.* Boston: Little, Brown and Co., 1973.

Hamilton, Edith. *The Greek Way*. New York: W. W. Norton and Co., 1930.

Henry, Carl F. H. *God, Revelation and Authority*. Vol. 2, *God Who Speaks and Shows: Fifteen Theses Part One*. Waco, Tex.: Word Books, 1976.

Hibbert, Christopher. *The Days of the French Revolution*. New York: William Morrow and Co., 1980.

Hitler's Secret Conversations, 1941-1944. Translated by Norman Cameron and R. H. Stevens. New York: Farrar, Straus and Young, 1953.

Houts, Paul L., ed. *The Myth of Measurability*. New York: Hart Publishing Co., 1977.

Huntford, Roland. *The New Totalitarians*. New York: Stein and Day, 1972.

Huxley, Aldous. *Brave New World*. New York: Time Reading Program, 1946.

————. *Brave New World and Brave New World Revisited*. 1958. Reprint. New York: Harper and Row, Harper Colophon Books, 1965.

Huxley, Julian, ed. *The Humanist Frame*. New York: Harper and Brothers, 1961.

————. *Religion without Revelation*. New York: New American Library, Mentor Books, 1957.

Inch, Sally. *Birthrights: What Every Parent Should Know about Childbirth in Hospitals*. New York: Pantheon Books, 1984.

Ingram, T. Robert. *The World under God's Law: Criminal Aspects of the Welfare State*. Houston, Tex.: St. Thomas Press, 1962.

Inlow, Gail M. *Education: Mirror and Agent of Change: A Foundations Text*. New York: Holt, Rinehart and Winston, 1970.

Jaeger, Werner, ed. *Paideia: The Ideals of Greek Culture*. Vol. 1, *Archaic Greece, the Mind of Athens*. 2d. ed. Translated by Gilbert Highet. New York: Oxford University Press, 1979.

Jowett, B., trans. *The Republic of Plato*. 3d. ed. Oxford, England: Clarendon Press, 1888.

Keegan, John. *The Face of Battle: A Study of Agincourt, Waterloo and the Somme*. New York: Viking Press, 1976; Penguin Books, 1984.

Kelley, Robert. *The Shaping of the American Past*. Vol. 1, 2d. ed., Englewood Cliffs, N.J.: Prentice-Hall, 1978.

Katz, Arthur, and Jamie Buckingham. *Ben Israel: The Odyssey of a Modern Jew*. Plainfield, N.J.: Logos International, 1970.

Kaufmann, Walter. *Critique of Religion and Philosophy*. 1958. Reprint. New York: Harper and Row, Harper Torchbooks, 1972.

Kohlberg, Lawrence. *The Philosophy of Moral Development: Moral Stages and the Idea of Justice*. Vol. 1, *Essays on Moral Development*. San Francisco: Harper and Row, 1981.

Koyre, Alexandre. *From the Closed World to the Infinite Universe*. New York: Harper and Row, Harper Torchbooks, 1958.

Lamont, Corliss. *The Philosophy of Humanism*. 5th ed. New York: Fredrick Ungar Publishing Co., 1965.

Landman, Isaac, ed. *The Universal Jewish Encyclopedia*. Vol. 3. New York: Universal Jewish Encyclopedia, 1941.

Lewis, C. S. *The Abolition of Man* or *Reflections on Education with Special Reference to the Teaching of English in the Upper Forms of Schools*. New York: Macmillan, 1947.

Lewy, Guenter. *False Consciousness: An Essay on Mystification*. New Brunswick, N.J.: Transaction Books, 1982.

Macrorie, Ken. *Writing to Be Read*. Rev. 3d ed. Upper Montclair, N.J.: Boynton/Cook Publishers, 1984.

Mander, Jerry. *Four Arguments for the Elimination of Television*. New York: William Morrow and Co., 1978.

Markgraf, Carl. *Punctuation*. New York: John Wiley and Sons, 1979.

Mayers, Ronald B. *Both/And: A Balanced Apologetic*. Chicago: Moody Press, 1984.

Maynard, Joyce. *Looking Back: A Chronicle of Growing up Old in the Sixties*. Garden City, N.Y.: Doubleday and Co., 1973.

McNeill, William. *Mythistory and Other Essays*. Chicago: University of Chicago Press, 1986.

Mendelsohn, Robert. *Confessions of a Medical Heretic*. Chicago: Contemporary Books, 1979.

———. *How to Raise a Healthy Child in Spite of Your Doctor*. Chicago, Ill.: Contemporary Books, 1984.

Mitchell, Richard. *Less Than Words Can Say*. Boston: Little, Brown and Co., 1979.

Moberly, Sir Walter. *The Crisis in the University*. London: SCM Press, 1949.

Moore, Raymond and Dorothy. *Home Grown Kids: A Practical Handbook for Teaching Your Children at Home*. Waco, Tex.: Word

Books, 1981.

————. *Home Spun Schools: Teaching Children at Home: What Parents Are Doing and How They Are Doing It.* Waco, Tex.: Word Books, 1982.

————. *Home Style Teaching: A Handbook for Parents and Teachers.* Waco, Tex.: Word Books, 1984.

————. *School Can Wait.* Provo, Utah: Brigham Young University Press, 1979.

Morris, Barbara M. *Change Agents in the Schools.* Ellicott City, Md.: Barbara M. Morris Report, 1979.

Mosse, George L. *Nazi Culture: Intellectual, Cultural and Social Life in the Third Reich.* Translated by Salvator Attanasio and others. New York: Grosset and Dunlap, Universal Library, 1968.

Niebuhr, Richard H. *Christ and Culture.* New York: Harper and Row, Harper Torchbooks, 1975.

Orwell, George. *1984.* New York: New American Library, A Signet Classic, 1961.

Otto, Walter F. *The Homeric Gods: The Spiritual Significance of Greek Religion.* 1954. Reprint. New York: Random House Pantheon Books, 1979.

Pagels, Heinz R. *The Cosmic Code: Quantum Physics as the Language of Nature.* New York: Simon and Schuster, 1982.

Pelikan, Jaroslav. *The Emergence of the Catholic Tradition (100-600).* Vol. 1 of *The Christian Tradition: A History of the Development of Doctrine.* Chicago: University of Chicago Press, 1971.

Phenix, Philip H. *Religious Concerns in Contemporary Education.* New York: Bureau of Publications, Teachers College, Columbia University, 1959.

Phillips, J.B. *Letters to Young Churches: A Translation of the New Testament Epistles.* New York: Macmillan, 1957.

Polanyi, Michael. *Personal Knowledge towards a Post-Critical Philosophy.* Chicago: University of Chicago Press, 1975.

Polanyi, Michael, and Harry Prosch. *Meaning.* Chicago: University of Chicago Press, 1975.

Powers, Ward. *Learn to Read the Greek New Testament.* Sydney, NSW, Australia: Anzea Publishers, 1983.

Rauschning, Hermann. *Men of Chaos.* New York: G.P. Putnam's Sons, 1942.

Roberts, J. W. *City of Sokrates: An Introduction to Classical Athens.*

London: Routledge and Kegan Paul, 1984.

Romalis, Shelly, ed. *Childbirth: Alternatives to Medical Control.* Austin, Tex.: University of Texas Press, 1981.

Rousseau, Jean-Jacques. *Emile; or, On Education.* Translated by Allan Bloom. New York: Basic Books, 1979.

Rushdoony, Rousas John. *The Institutes of Biblical Law.* N.p.: Presbyterian and Reformed Publishing Co., 1973.

————. *The Philosophy of the Christian Curriculum.* Vallectio, Calif.: Ross House Books, 1981.

Russell, Bertrand. *What I Believe.* New York: E. P. Dutton and Co., 1925.

Saxon, John H. *Algebra I: An Incremental Development.* Norman, Okla.: Grassdale Publishers, 1982.

Scherman, Nosson, and Meir Zlotowicz, eds. *Succos—Its Significance, Laws and Prayers: A Presentation Anthologized from Talmudic and Traditional Sources.* Art Scroll Mesorah Series: Exposition on Jewish Liturgy and Thought. Brooklyn, N.Y.: Mesorah Publications, 1982.

Schumacher, E. F. *A Guide for the Perplexed.* New York: Harper and Row, 1977.

Shirer, William L. *The Rise and Fall of the Third Reich: A History of Nazi Germany.* New York: Simon and Schuster, 1960.

Simpson, Elizabeth Léonie. *Humanistic Education: An Interpretation.* A Report to the Ford Foundation. Cambridge, Mass.: Ballinger Publishing Co., 1976.

Smith, Mont W. *What the Bible Says about Covenant.* Joplin, Mo.: College Press Publishing Co., 1981.

Solomon, Robert. *History and Human Nature: A Philosophical Review of European Philosophy and Culture, 1750-1850.* New York: Harcourt Brace Jovanovich, 1979.

Sowell, Thomas. *Pink and Brown People and Other Controversial Essays.* Stanford, Calif.: Hoover Institution Press, 1981.

Spring, Joel H. *Education and the Rise of the Corporate State.* Boston: Beacon Press, 1972.

Stone, Lawrence, ed. *Schooling and Society: Studies in the History of Education.* Baltimore, Md.: Johns Hopkins University Press, 1976.

Stone, Wilfred, and J. G. Bell. *Prose Style: A Handbook for Writers.* 3d. ed. New York: McGraw-Hill Book Co., 1977.

Strenio, Andrew J., Jr. *The Testing Trap*. New York: Rawson, Wade Publishers, 1981.

Strunk, William, Jr., and E. B. White. *The Elements of Style*. 3d. ed. New York: Macmillan, 1979.

Swift, F. H. *Education in Ancient Israel from Earliest Times to 70 A.D.* Chicago: Open Court Publishing Co., 1919.

Theological Dictionary of the New Testament. Edited by Gerhard Kittel. Vol. 5. Edited by Gerhard Friedrich. Translated and edited by Geoffrey Bromiley. Grand Rapids, Mich.: Wm. B. Eerdmans Publishing Co., 1978.

Trimble, John R. *Writing with Style: Conversations on the Art of Writing*. Englewood Cliffs, N.J.: Prentice-Hall, 1975.

Trotter, W. F., trans. *Pascal's Pensées*. London: J. M. Dent and Sons, 1931.

Tuchman, Barbara W. *Stilwell and the American Experience in China, 1911-45*. New York: Macmillan, 1971.

Vaught, Carl G. *The Quest for Wholeness*. Albany, N.Y.: State University of New York Press, 1982.

Vine, W. E. *An Expository Dictionary of New Testament Words: With Their Precise Meanings for English Readers*. Old Tappan, N.J.: Fleming H. Revell Co., 1966.

Vitz, Paul G. *Sigmund Freud's Christian Unconscious*. New York: Guilford Press, 1988.

Waite, Robert G. L. *The Psychopathic God: Adolf Hitler*. New York: Basic Books, 1977.

Ware, Caroline F., K. M. Panikkar, and J. M. Romein. *The Twentieth Century*. Vol. 6, *History of Mankind: Culture and Scientific Development*. New York: Harper and Row, 1966.

Weaver, Richard M. *A Rhetoric and Handbook*. Rev. ed. New York: Holt, Rinehart and Winston, 1967.

———. *The Ethics of Rhetoric*. South Bend, Ind.: Regenery/Gateway, 1953.

———. *Ideas Have Consequences*. Chicago: University of Chicago Press, 1948.

Weller, Richard H., ed. *Humanistic Education: Visions and Realities*. A Phi Delta Kappa Publication; distributed by McCutchan Publishing, Berkeley, Calif., 1977.

White, E. B. to Alison Marks, 20 April 1956. *Letters of E. B. White*. Edited by Dorothy Lobrano Guth. New York: Harper and Row, 1976.

Williams, Raymond. *Keywords: A Vocabulary of Culture and Society.* New York: Oxford University Press, 1983.

Wittfogel, Karl A. *Oriental Despotism: A Comparative Study of Total Power.* New Haven, Conn.: Yale University Press, 1957.

Young, David S. *The Rule of Experts: Occupational Licensing in America.* Washington, D.C.: Cato Institute, 1987.

Zodhiates, Spiros. Preface to *Learn or Review New Testament Greek: Vocabulary and Answers to the Exercises in New Testament Greek for Beginners* by J. Gresham Machen. Compiled by Spiros Zodhiates. Chattanooga, Tenn.: AMG Publishers, 1976.

Pamphlets

The Pimsleur Tapes: The Sure and Easy Way to Learn Another Language. Concord, Mass.: Heinle and Heinle Enterprises, n.d.

Getting Started in Texas. Richardson, Tex.: Texas Association for Home Education (July 1979).

Gibbs, David C., Jr. *Conviction versus Preference.* Cleveland, Ohio: Christian Law Association, n.d.

Glass, Gene V., and Mary Lee Smith. *Meta-analysis of Research on the Relationship of Class-Size and Achievement.* Laboratory of Educational Research, University of Colorado, September 1978.

Mayer, Frederick. *Education for a New Society.* Bloomington, Ind.: Phi Delta Kappa Educational Foundation, 1973.

Whitehead, John W., and Wendell Bird. *Home Education and Constitutional Liberties: The Historical and Constitutional Arguments in Support of Home Instruction.* Rutherford Institute Report, vol. 2. Westchester, Ill.: Crossway Books, 1984.

Articles

"A Nation of Illiterates." *U.S. News and World Report*, 17 May 1982.

"Does David Gibbs Practice Law As Well As He Preaches Church-State Separation?" *Christianity Today*, 10 April 1981.

"Home Education in America: Parental Rights Reasserted." *University of Missouri Law Review* (1981).

"John Robinson: Spiritual Advice to Pilgrim Planters." In *The Annals of America.* Vol. 1, *1493-1754: Discovering a New World.* Encyclopaedia Britannica, 1968.

"Now It's Suburbs Where School Violence Flares." *U.S. News and World Report*, 21 May 1979.

Alston, William P. "Religion." In *The Encyclopedia of Philosophy*. Edited by Paul Edwards. Vol. 7. 1967. Reprint. New York: Macmillan and Free Press, 1972.

Arons, Stephen. "The Separation of School and State: *Pierce* Reconsidered." *Harvard Educational Review*, vol. 46, no. 1 (February 1976).

Asch, S. E. "Effects of Group Pressure upon the Modification and Distorion of Judgments." In *Group Dynamics: Research and Theory*, edited by Dorwin Cartwright and Alvin Zander. 2d ed. Evanston, Ill.: Row, Peterson and Co., 1960.

Ball, William B. "What Is Religion?" *Christian Lawyer*, vol. 8, no. 1 (Spring 1979).

Berry, Wendell. "Some Thoughts I Have in Mind When I Teach." In *Writers as Teachers, Teachers as Writers*. Edited by Jonathan Baumbach. New York: Holt, Rinehart and Winston, 1970.

Blake, William N. "A Christian Philosophy of Method in Education." *Journal of Christian Reconstruction*, vol. 4, no. 1 (Summer 1977).

Bloom, Benjamin S. "Helping All Children Learn Well in Elementary School—and Beyond." *Principal* (March 1988).

Blumenfeld, Samuel L. "Looking Backward 100 Years Later." *Chalcedon Report*, no. 278 (September 1988).

Bowen, Ezra. "Getting Tough." *Time*, 1 February 1988.

Bozarth, G. Richard. "On Keeping God Alive." *American Atheist* (November 1977).

Brown, L. B. "A Study of Religious Belief." *British Journal of Psychology*, vol. 53, part 3 (August 1962).

Bruck, Connie. "Are Teachers Failing Our Children?" *McCall's* (May 1979).

Combee, Jerry, Laurel Hicks, and Mike Lowman. "A Christian Philosophy of Method in Education." *Journal of Christian Reconstruction*, vol. 4, no. 1 (Summer 1977).

Combs, Arthur W. "An Educational Imperative: The Human Dimension." In *To Nurture Humaneness: Commitment for the 70's*, edited by Mary-Margaret Scoby and Grace Graham. Washington, D.C.: Association for Supervision and Curriculum Development, NEA, 1970.

———. "Humanistic Education: Too Tender for a Tough World?" *Phi Delta Kappan* (February 1981).

Cook, Ann, and Deborah Meier. "New York Students Show Spectacular Rise in Reading: New York City Students' Scores Indicate Steady Decline in Reading." Unpublished paper distributed at the NCT Conference (Fall 1979).

Dunphy, John J. "A Religion for a New Age." *Humanist*, vol. 43, no. 1 (January/February 1983).

Ebel, Robert L. "Declining Scores: A Conservative Education." *Phi Delta Kappan* (December 1976).

Eckman, Fern Marja. "Teen Suicide." *McCall's* (Oct. 1987).

Engel, Martin. "Rapunzel, Rapunzel Let Down Your Golden Hair: Some Thoughts on Early Childhood Education." Unpublished manuscript, National Demonstration Center in Early Childhood Education, U.S. Office of Education, D.C.

Jordan, Alice. "Twice a Cesarean: The Birth of Onna Chunaha." In *The Vaginal Birth after Cesarean Experience: Birth Stories by Parents and Professionals*, edited by Lynn Baptisti Richards. South Hadley, Mass.: Bergin and Garvey Publishers, 1987.

Kagan, Jerome. "The Moral Function of the School." *Daedalus: Journal of the American Academy of Arts and Sciences*, vol. 110, no. 3 (Summer 1981).

Karman, James. "I Feel Like an Onion." *His* (October 1981).

Lauer, R. M., and M. Hussey. "A New Way to Become Educated." *Humanist* (January/February 1986).

Lytle, Andrew. "Reflections of a Ghost: An Agrarian View after Fifty Years." *Southern Partisan*, vol. 4 (Summer 1981).

Mendelsohn, Robert S., M.D. *People's Doctor: A Medical Newsletter for Consumers*, vol. 9, no. 2. Evanston, Ill.

Middleton, Thomas H. "Light Refractions." Review of *Less Than Words Can Say* by Richard Mitchell. *Saturday Review*. 24 November 1979.

Moore, Raymond S. "Research and Common Sense: Therapies for Our Homes and Schools." *Teachers College Record*, vol. 84, no. 2 (Winter 1982).

North, Gary. *Dominion Strategies*. Tyler, Tex.: Institute for Christian Economics, (February 1986).

Orwell, George. "Politics and the English Language." In *The Modern Stylists: Writers on the Art of Writing*, edited by Donald Hall. New York: Free Press, 1968.

Popham, W. James. "The Merits of Measurement-Driven Instruction." *Phi Delta Kappan* (May 1987).

Powys, Llewelyn. "Letter to Warner Taylor." In *The Creative Process: A Symposium*, edited by Brewster Ghiselin. New York: New American Library, A Mentor Book, 1955.

Porter, Katherine Anne. In *The Modern Stylists: Writers on the Art of Writing*, edited by Donald Hall. New York: Free Press, 1968.

Randal, Judith. "Where Should Your Child Be Born?" *Parents* (March 1979).

Randall, John Herman, Jr. "What Is the Temper of Humanism?" In *The Humanist Alternative: Some Definitions of Humanism*, edited by Paul Kurtz. Buffalo, N.Y.: Prometheus Books, 1973.

Rice, Charles E. "Conscientious Objection to Public Education: The Grievance and the Remedies." *Brigham Young University Law Review*, no. 4 (1978).

Rushdoony, Rousas John. "The State as an Establishment of Religion." *Freedom and Education: Pierce v. Society of Sisters Resconsidered*, edited by Donald P. Kommers and Michael J. Wahoske (Notre Dame, Ind.: University of Notre Dame Law School, 1978).

―――. "Elitism." *Chalcedon Position Paper*, no. 67. Vallecito, Calif.

Russell, Dwane. "Goals for American Education: The Individual Focus." *Educational Leadership* (March 1971).

Sayers, Dorothy L. "The Lost Tools of Learning." *The Journal of Christian Reconstruction*, vol. 4, no. 1 (Summer 1977).

Sipher, Roger. "Compulsory Education: An Idea Whose Time Has Past." *USA Today* (September 1978).

Tate, Allen. "Narcissus as Narcissus." In *The Literature of the United States: An Anthology and History from the Civil War to the Present*, edited by Walter Blair et al. Vol. 2, 3d ed. Glenview, Ill.: Scott Foresman and Co., 1970.

Thompson, Barbara. "The Debate Over Public Schools: The View From the Principal's Office." *Christianity Today*, 7 September 1984.

U.S. Department of Education. "A Nation At Risk: The Imperative for Educational Reform." *The National Commission on Excellence in Education* (April 1983).

Welch, Sue, Ginny Wells, and Eric E. Wiggin. "Counting the Cost," *Moody* (March 1984).

Whitehead, John W., and John Conlan. "The Establishment of the Religion of Secular Humanism and Its First Amendment Implications." *Texas Tech Law Review*, vol. 10, no. 1 (1978).

Sound Recordings

Rushdoony, Rousas John. "Providence of God in History." Middleburg Heights, Ohio: Christian Schools of Ohio, 1976.

Poems

Milton, John. "Paradise Lost." In *The Poems of John Milton*. Edited by Helen Darbishire. London: Oxford University Press, 1961.

Acknowledgments

The indispensable assistance of the following people, without whom this book could never have been written and produced, deserves special recognition:

Denny Allensworth helped coordinate research and various stages of production. Jay Cummings coordinated scripture references and compiled the indexes. Rafael Quinones oversaw layout and production, including the cover, camera work, platemaking, printing, folding and binding.

Typesetting: Gail Gardner, coordinator; Cindy Douglass; Lisa French; Rivka Jacobson; Helen Kenihan; Carolyn Moberg; Roxie Ray; Judy Richardson; Roberta Weitze.

Checking: Camille Risucci, coordinator; Regina Allensworth; Lisa Bradford; Wanda Breault; Frances Bull; Donna Rose Iannacone; Krissy Lev-Cochav; Maria Mosquera; Nola Mostyn; Rebecca Pelto; Bonnie Simpkin; Diana Turner.

Proofreading: John Haldenstein, coordinator; Christine Annunziato; Arnold Arce; Marcia Bench; Adi Jacobson; Kerry Matthews.

Research, references: Mary Salmeri, coordinator; Deanne Ballerino; Theresa Dela Cruz; Bette Hinol; Robert Kobasic; Shirley Moore; Martha Nolte; Elsie Quinones.

Pasteup, camera and platemaking: Denise Bautz; Doyle Borman; Maria Hofmann; Kathy Klingensmith; Melissa Morton; Bill Nolen.

Printing, folding, collating and binding: Grace Arnold; Steve Breault; Bill Carter; Steve Douglass; Jean Fritzlan; Lynn Fritzlan; Bill Hand; William Haynes; Jim Holliday; Sholom Jacobson; Bill Klingensmith; Robert Matthews; Marty Mostyn; Joe Quinones; Raymond Reveile; Jim Utter; Hector Valdez; Lonnie Wilson.

And a special thanks to all those who helped make this book possible through their labor of love by organizing and preparing meals, babysitting, running errands, answering the telephone, clean-up, encouragement and prayers.

Index

Geology, 242

Geometry, 411, 508, 509

Germany, education under Nazis, 65; industrialization of, 506; and Nazi culture, 65

Giedion, Siegfried, 397

Goebbels, Joseph, 529

Golding, William, *Lord of the Flies*, 104

Graduated interval recall, 251, 253

Grammar, 356; English, 246, 308, 336, 379, 455-457, 490; level of language instruction, 382; level of learning, 212-213, 217, 224, 226, 231-232, 250, 254, 256-257, 273-275, 298, 303, 334, 338, 352, 381

Graves, Robert, 362

Great Awakening, 398

Greek, language, 461; mythology, 13; New Testament, 248, 250

Greeks, 12; and education, 84; principles used by, 346n

Gulag, 378

Gymnasium, 8, 8n

Hall, Donald, 362, 373, 374

Harte, Brett, 108n

Harvard Educational Review, 57

Haydon, A. E., 59

Hebrew Day School of Central Florida, students outscore prospective State teachers, 134

Hebrew, 329, 459, 515; ancient, 171; Biblical, 6; goals for teaching, 460, 491

Hebrews, 12, 17, 22, 203, 208; and the family, 105

Hegel, Georg W. F., 216

Hell, and the mind of man, 210

Hemingway, Ernest, 362

Henry, Carl F. H., 355-356n

Henry, Patrick, 108n

Herbs, 327, 333

Hewitt Research Center, 109, 127; data on standardized tests, 139

History, 55, 268, 273, 276, 277, 296, 391, 392, 405, 473, 478, 481, 504; American, 278, 401, 403; and biographical narratives, 314, 476; dialectic level, 400, 404; goals for teaching, 444, 446; grammar level, 399, 400, 403; ignored, 279n; Pagan, 278; as progressive continuum, 396, 398; and public schools, 391; rejection of, 393, 394, 395; and relationship, 398, 399; rhetoric level, 401

Hitler Youth Movement, 66

Hitler, Adolf, worship of, 65, 114, 149

Hitlerism, 65

Hoffer, Eric, 386-389

Holocaust, 264, 278, 333, 398, 400, 412, 517

Holt, John, 100

Home birth, 151, 160, 164

Home education, 27, 86, 88, 147, 148, 151, 226, 310, 426, 427; academic superiority of, 98, 108, 133, 139; in ancient Israel, 106; educational advantages, 136; godly nature of, 63; growth of, xv; of Jesus, 140; public school teachers convert to, 134, 138; and socialization, 104; and social skills, 101; undermines totalitarianism, 64

Honesty, 275

Horse farming, 147, 326, 330

Horticulture, 295

Hospitals, hazardous to childbirth, 161, 164

Huey, Edmund Burke, 306

Humanism, 121-122, 392, 526, 533; and man-centered values, 62; relgious values of, 61

Scripture Index